MW01195351

797,885 Books

are available to read at

www.ForgottenBooks.com

Forgotten Books' App
Available for mobile, tablet & eReader

ISBN 978-1-333-27615-7
PIBN 10482603

This book is a reproduction of an important historical work. Forgotten Books uses
state-of-the-art technology to digitally reconstruct the work, preserving the original format
whilst repairing imperfections present in the aged copy. In rare cases, an imperfection in
the original, such as a blemish or missing page, may be replicated in our edition. We do,
however, repair the vast majority of imperfections successfully; any imperfections that
remain are intentionally left to preserve the state of such historical works.

Forgotten Books is a registered trademark of FB &c Ltd.
Copyright © 2015 FB &c Ltd.
FB &c Ltd, Dalton House, 60 Windsor Avenue, London, SW19 2RR.
Company number 08720141. Registered in England and Wales.

For support please visit www.forgottenbooks.com

1 MONTH OF
FREE
READING

at

www.ForgottenBooks.com

By purchasing this book you are eligible for one month membership to ForgottenBooks.com, giving you unlimited access to our entire collection of over 700,000 titles via our web site and mobile apps.

To claim your free month visit:
www.forgottenbooks.com/free482603

* Offer is valid for 45 days from date of purchase. Terms and conditions apply.

English
Français
Deutsche
Italiano
Español
Português

www.forgottenbooks.com

Mythology Photography **Fiction**
Fishing Christianity **Art** Cooking
Essays Buddhism Freemasonry
Medicine **Biology** Music **Ancient
Egypt** Evolution Carpentry Physics
Dance Geology **Mathematics** Fitness
Shakespeare **Folklore** Yoga Marketing
Confidence Immortality Biographies
Poetry **Psychology** Witchcraft
Electronics Chemistry History **Law**
Accounting **Philosophy** Anthropology
Alchemy Drama Quantum Mechanics
Atheism Sexual Health **Ancient History**
Entrepreneurship Languages Sport
Paleontology Needlework Islam
Metaphysics Investment Archaeology
Parenting Statistics Criminology
Motivational

GENEALOGY

OF THE

LYMAN FAMILY,

IN

Great Britain and America;

THE

ANCESTORS AND DESCENDANTS OF RICHARD LYMAN,
FROM HIGH ONGAR IN ENGLAND, 1631.

BY

LYMAN COLEMAN, D.D.,

PROFESSOR IN LAFAYETTE COLLEGE, EASTON, PENNSYLVANIA.

Nil me poeniteat sanum patris hujus.

ALBANY, N. Y.:
J. MUNSELL, STATE STREET.
1872.

THE LIBRARY
BRIGHAM YOUNG UNIVERSITY
PROVO, UTAH

TO

THE MEMORY

OF

Miss Julia E. Lyman,

THE FAITHFUL AND DILIGENT GENEALOGIST

OF THE LYMAN FAMILY,

TO WHOSE LABORS THEY ARE INDEBTED FOR

THIS WORK,

IT IS AFFECTIONATELY, SORROWFULLY,

DEDICATED

BY THEIR UNANIMOUS VOTE AT THEIR
LATE REUNION ON MOUNT TOM,

NORTHAMPTON,

Aug. 29, 1871.

PREFACE.

The authorship of this genealogy of the Lyman family is to be ascribed to our deceased friend Miss Julia E. Lyman. It was the labor of her life, the completion of which she was not permitted to see. But by her tireless researches through life, she had collected materials from .every quarter, and reduced them to such order in her admirable chart, that it was just practicable to take up the labors of her hands when they were palsied in death. This chart was the last labor of her life. The memory of it is saddened by the reflection that her assiduities. in extreme debility from the advanced stages of disease may have hastened prematurely the fatal issue.

Had the pen dropped from her hand but a little earlier, before the completion of the chart, the labors of her life would have remained incomplete. The continuance of this work, begun only in reliance on the aid of the deceased, would have been dropped; and the work remained unpublished. But in an evil hour the undersigned, quite unconscious of the task he was assuming, resolved to carry on, according to his ability, the work suspended by the untimely decease of the principal agent and author. Under innumerable discouragements, embarrassments and difficulties resulting from the indifference and neglect of very many, the record of whose families was repeatedly sought in vain, and in the midst of accumulated domestic afflictions, the toilsome task has been pursued. New lineages of families totally unknown have been developed, often making up a record of several hundred names. The utmost diligence and care have been held in requisition to make the book a reliable and accurate record of the families whose register it may contain. But mistakes and errors without number may mar the record; for these we must bespeak a charitable indulgence. Notices of all errors and mistakes are particularly requested, that they may be entered in their proper place in an interleaved copy to be kept for that purpose for further reference.

Due acknowledgments have been made in another place for the invaluable contribution of the ancestral lineage of the Leman, Lyman family in Great Britain by H. A. Lyman, Esq., of London, who has traced this back to the Norman conquest, and connected it with the Malcolms, kings of Scotland, A.D. 1000–1057. Grateful acknowledgments are also due for valuable and important contributions from the Rev. J. T. Dickinson, Middlefield, Conn.; Rev. P. W. Lyman, Belchertown, Mass.; Rev. H. Lyman, Marathon, N. Y.; G. H. Lyman, M.D., Boston; Geo. T. Lyman, Esq., Bellport, L. I.; A. S. Lyman, Esq., N. Y. City; Prof. C. S. Lyman, Yale College; Dea. Samuel Lyman, Southampton, Mass.; Dea. N. B. Lyman, Andover, Conn.; and Dea. C. W. Lyman, Columbia, Conn. Without these collateral aids, the work could never been brought to its present degree of fullness and completeness, and probably would never have been published.

Thankful for all encouragement and aid, weary and worn by these protracted and fameless labors, too much depressed for exhilaration at the conclusion of them, the author quietly commits the book to the indulgent consideration of that great family, singularly unique and peculiar as being of one blood, offspring of one common ancestor, to whom this work is but their own family register. Scattered broadcast over all the land, may it be to them a bond of union to bind them together in firmer bonds of a common brotherhood. May it be an incentive to present and future generations to emulate the noble and sterling virtues of their venerable ancestors. May it invite them back, occasionally at least, to their New England homes around the dear old hearthstones, to study the outgrowth of their several families, to kindle anew that spirit of civil and religious liberty, which there, they or their forefathers first caught; and to carry back to their distant homes, those principles of intellectual and moral greatness from which our country's grandeur springs; "that makes her loved at home, revered abroad "

Long after we of the present, like former generations, shall have passed through life to our silent graves, some few may rise up, age after age, to bless the hearts and hands that formed and executed the purpose to collect the perishable materials, just passing into irrecoverable oblivion, of which the work of the genealogist is composed. The future historian may gather thence some shreds for the web he may then be weaving, and the historical painter may catch some lingering lineaments of the stern old Puritans for his group, on the canvas of other days, of those representative men who have left the grand, effaceless imprint of their character on succeeding generations. Whatever may be the result, the consciousness remains of having labored long and faithfully to perpetuate the memory of the worthy ancestry of a great, far-spreading family who have achieved an honorable position among many other families descended from Puritan ancestors in New England. Reposing in this quiet consciousness this work is commended to the attention of all of this family who would learn something of their ancestral history or cherish the memory of their honored ancestors.

LAFAYETTE COLLEGE,
  EASTON, PENN, *May* 1, 1872.

SYNOPSIS OF THE GENERATIONS OF LYMANS.

The number of the several generations of this family, so far as the count has been carried, is found to be, as follows :

First Generation,	1
Second Generation,	9
Third Generation,	27
Fourth Generation,	64
Fifth Generation,	191
Sixth Generation,	381
Seventh Generation,	947
Eighth Generation,	1982
Ninth Generation,	2020
Tenth Generation,	511
Eleventh Generation,	33
	6166

The Eighth Generation,	1982
The Ninth Generation,	2020
The Tenth Generation,	511
The Eleventh Generation,	33
Numbered among the living are	4546
Of these generations the deceased are	486
Still living	4060
To these add of Seventh Gen. still living, say	40
The number of Lymans now living,	4100

Of the 5th and 6th generations 572, 26 were in the Revolutionary war; allowing $\frac{1}{5} = 114$ to be able to bear arms, $\frac{26}{114}$ or more than $\frac{1}{4}$ of the able bodied men were in the army battling for our independence.

Bearing the name of Lyman 100 were in the war of the late rebellion. The 8th and 9th generations equal 4002; $\frac{1}{5}$ fighting men equal 800, of whom 100 or $\frac{1}{8}$ were in the war of the rebellion. Of these many died in the rebel states of disease or on the field of battle, some by the slow torture of starvation in Andersonville or the Libby prison, but, of all these no accurate count has been made.

From 10 colleges 93 Lymans have graduated, but the number graduating from all the colleges in the country has not been ascertained. Our intention was to ascertain the entire number of Lymans and descendants from Lyman mothers, together with the number in each of the learned professions, but having neither leisure nor health for the further prosecution of these inquiries we remit them to the inquisitive reader who has the data at hand in the book for these and similar researches. A large proportion have filled the office of the ministry, and a much larger number have held office in the church as deacons and elders.

The descendants of the six grandsons of Richard[1], severally are as follows according to the record:

1. Descendants of Richard[3], son of Richard[2],...... 2735
2. Descendants of Thomas[3], son of Richard[2], say,.. 400
3. Descendants of John[3], son of Richard[2],......... 519
4. Descendants of John[3], son of John[2],............. 1370
5. Descendants of Moses[3], son of John[2],........... 1200
6. Descendants of Benjamin[3], son of John[2], ... 1030

    Total,   7254
Add Third Generation, ... 27
Second Generation, ... 9
Addenda,... 25

    Total of descendants of Richard, ... 7315

ADDENDA.

Page 12, No. 313.

MARGARET CREGO, wife of Enoch Lyman, d. at Ava, Oneida Co., N. Y., Jan. 19, 1872, aged 67 years, 2½ months.

Page 129, No. 20.

JOSEPH LYMAN, m. March 27, 1817, Lavinda Woodworth in Williamsfield, Ashtabula Co., Ohio, removed Feb., 1838, to Meigs Co., in Oct., 1836, to Seagles Co., Ill., and d. Dec. 26, 1862.

Children, Eighth Generation.

1. Carrel Coles, b. Oct. 12, 1818.
2. Alvin, b. May 24, 1820.
3. Frederic, b. Feb. 24, 1822.
4. Luther, b. Aug. 10, 1825; d. in Athens Co., O., 1840.
5. Gaylord, b. Dec. 15, 1827.
6. Maria, b. March 15, 1832.
7. Abigail, Feb. 27, 1835; d. in Meigs Co., Sept. 18, 1846.
8. Emily, b. July 20, 1838.
9. Irvin, b. Jan. 20, 1842.

1. CARREL C., m. June, 1838, Mrs. Huldah Conant in Orange, Meigs Co., removed 1852 to Lucas Co., Iowa, d. there in 1860.

Children, Ninth Generation.

1. Dryden.
2. Charles Newton. Dryden d. young. Charles resides in Clarinda, Page Co., Iowa; Newton, in Chariton, Lucas Co., Iowa.

2. ALVIN, m. Sept. 12, 1845; Margaret Magee, removed 1836 from Meigs Co. to Seagles Co., Ill., d. leaving a dau., who m. J. H. Deane of Independence, Ill.

3. FREDERIC, m. Oct. 12, 1843, Elizabeth Nelson, Salem, Meigs Co.

Children, Ninth Generation.

1. Rush R., b. July 16, 1844.
2. James M., b. Sept. 28, 1846.
3. Charles H., b. Feb. 28, 1851.
4. Ella, b. July 28, 1856.
5. Lizzie, b. Sept. 25, 1860.

5. GAYLORD, m. Marinda Conant, Chariton, Iowa, d. July 2, 1870. Shot by a horse thief, whom he, as sheriff of this county, was endeavoring to arrest. Six children, names unknown.
6. MARIA, m. Sept. 10, 1849, L. E. Humphrey, of Pomeroy, O., killed at the storming of Petersburg, April, 1865.

Children, Ninth Gen.: Lavinda, Elmore, Emma.
(1) RUSH R., son of Frederic, m. Nov. 28, 1867, Flora Davis, of Salem, Meigs
    Co. 2 children, Pomeroy, O.
    He enlisted in the 18th Ohio Reg., April, 1861, remained in service
    until the surrender of Richmond.
(2) JAMES M. was a volunteer for some time in the army, and one named
    Irving after having been a prisoner of war 21 months in Richmond and
    Andersonville, was killed in 1864, by the blowing up of the steamer
    Sultana.

Page 273, No. 697.

KEZIA M. HUBBARD, d. at Sunderland, Mass., April 19, 1872.

Page 275, No. 787.

The materials for a suitable obituary notice of Dr. Lyman came to hand
too late for insertion in its appropriate place. The following extracts from
his last sermon on the "Hidden Life of the Christian," are given as a beautiful illustration of his own Christian life and character:

Ye are dead and your life is hid with Christ in God. When Christ, who
is our life, shall appear, then shall ye also appear with him in glory. COL.
III : 3.

Our physical life, mysterious and subtle though it be, is exposed to the
malice of its enemies, and liable at any moment to be destroyed. It is
hidden in ourselves, and held by a feeble tenure. Disease may poison it,
accident may crush it, the assassin may stab it, and it dies. It is ever in
the road of death. Not so our spiritual life. It is hidden away in God,
where disease cannot reach it, where the poison of the world cannot infect
it, and where no enemy can assail it. God is its fountain. It has its
spring in Him, and the strong arms of the Almighty protect it, and eyes
that never sleep keep ceaseless guard over it. No foe which is not stronger
than God can ever storm its citadel or penetrate its hidden home. So not
only is its fountain protected, but all its channels are covered and guarded.
Human wisdom, and not even Satanic cunning, can explore them or seek
out their hiding place. As the stream which has its head on some bald,
ice-bound, inaccessible mountain top, and whose channel is buried and
concealed in its rocky bosom, until it bursts forth from the earth at your
feet, so is the Christian's life, in its fountain and all its channels, protected,
and hidden in the bosom of God. Here and there you see a Christian life,
on the earth and among men, and yet so manifestly not of the earth or of
the spirit of men, that it seems like some rare and beautiful exotic. By
any earth born theory it cannot be accounted for. You see it in its peace
and beauty, in its daily outgivings of blessing, and it fills you with wonder
and admiration. You call it a miracle and so it is—one of Christ's silent
miracles—the miracle of a Christly life.

But there is yet another sense in which, to-day, this life in Christ is to
us a hidden life. It is the eternal life, the Christian life only in its early
beginnings, dimmed and obscured by the weaknesses and frailties of the
flesh, and darkened and overshadowed by its mortal and carnal surround-
ings. Its *glory* doth not yet appear. It is hidden in the rubbish of the
earthly and the sensual. "Eye hath not seen, ear hath not heard, neither
have entered into the heart of man the things that God hath prepared for
them that love him." But this is not always so to be. "It doth not yet
appear what we shall be; but we know that when he shall appear we
shall be like him," "for we shall see him as he is." Great honor is yet to

be rendered to the Son of God, before all the universe, for the Christly work of human redemption. Peerless is to be the glory of man's Redeemer. Now, he, who is our life, is hidden from mortal vision. Though present, he is yet concealed. But in the fullness of time he is to be made manifest. He shall come in the glory of the Father and with him all the holy angels. Not a part simply of the heavenly host, but all the mighty army of the skies shall form his retinue. Beyond all human conception of glory, shall be the greatness and the splendor of that day. He comes to meet, and recognize, and gather home his redeemed children on earth, and every eye shall see him. And then, in that glorious hour, "when he who is our life, shall appear, shall we also appear with him in glory," if we are his children. And then, in the presence of the intelligent universe, shall Christ welcome his elected bride, his blood bought Church to her home in the mansions of the Father, and with her sit down to the marriage supper of the Lamb. Who can conceive the glory of that hour?

Other eloquent sentences, belonging to this discourse, fell from the lips of the lamented author, but the opportunity of recalling them is gone forever. It escaped with the breath that gave them utterance. He was wonderfully gifted in the power of extemporaneous speech, and many of his written sermons were doubly effective by reason of these interjected, or closing sentences, inspired by the occasion. The members of the Second Presbyterian Church will never forget the foregoing sermon, preached on the day of their communion Sabbath, January 14, 1872, only five days before he fell asleep in Jesus.

We cannot better close our allusion to the pastor of the Euclid Avenue Presbyterian Church, than by reprinting these lines of Bonar, so frequently quoted by Dr. Lyman, and so beautifully characteristic of his short but blessed ministry:

> "My name, and my place, and my tomb all forgotten,
>   The brief race of time well and patiently run.
> So let me pass away, peacefully, silently,
>   Only remembered by what I have done.
> Gladly away from this toil would I hasten,
>   Up to the crown that for me has been won;
> Unthought of by man in rewards or in praises,
>   Only remembered by what I have done."

Page 395, No. 84.

Mr. B. S. Lyman of Philadelphia, who was lately in the service of the British government in India as a mining engineer, boring for rock oil in the Punjab, has published two brief but valuable memoirs on the Punjab oil region (lying in the corner between Cashmere and Cabul, between latitudes $32° 31'$ and $33° 47'$), which is also a region of historical interest, being near the supposed cradle of the Aryan or Indo-European races. It is within a few miles of Attok, where Alexander the Great crossed the Indus, and of Taxila, where he was hospitably entertained by King Taxiles; the "fabulous Hydaspes," now the Jhelum river, flows across one corner of this oil region, and near by is the traditional site of one of the compassionate miracles of Buddha, who once traversed this nook of the world. The first of Mr. Lyman's memoirs was his "General Report of the Punjab Oil Lands," printed by Lord Mayo's government at Lahore in 1870, an official folio of 50 pages with a set of maps attached; but this is not generally accessible. The second is a briefer paper on the *Topography of the Punjab Oil Region* read before the American Philosophical Society of Philadelphia, last January, and printed in Vol. xv of its *Transactions*. It is also published separately by the author, making 14 large quarto pages, and with a geological and topographical sketch-map of the region added. It is an interesting paper, speaking briefly of the main features of the region described, its geological character and mineral products, and communicating much information that is at once new and valuable. Although several English geologists have spoken of this tract in the Punjab, none have studied it so minutely as Mr. Lyman, who was also the first American geologist to visit it.

Page 429, No. 343.

HORACE S. LYMAN, m. Nov. 30, 1871, Nettie M. Graves, dau. of Harrison Graves of Easthampton, Mass.

CONTENTS.

LYMAN GENEALOGY.

PART I.

The Lymans in Great Britain

I. THE LYMAN NAME.

The origin and significancy of modern English names, involved in inexplicable mystery, opens a boundless range for theories and fanciful speculations quite foreign to our taste and purpose. In Anglo-Saxon, *Leoman,* (*lion-man ?*) appears as the name of an Anglo-Saxon land holder prior to the Norman conquest. Léoman, rolling swiftly from the tongue in familiar conversation, might easily become Leman. Whether this is the true origin and meaning of the name — *deus aliqui viderit* — some theorist of keener insight may determime. In authentic history the original name was LEMAN.

Like most of the English surnames, this has passed through many changes in settling down to the present orthography. It has been written Lehman, Leyman, Lyeman, Lemman, Lemon, Leman and de Le Man. The French, supposing the name to be derived from *l'aiman*, have written it L'aiman. In America the name has taken the form, Liman, Limen, Limon, Limmon, Lemon, Leamond and Lemond. In the records both of the town and of the church in Northampton, for the first fifty years or more, the name is generally written Liman; early in the last century it took the fixed and settled form of the present appropriate orthography, LYMAN.

The pedigree of the Lymans in England, the orthography of the name and identity of the Lymans and the Lemans have been the subject of a protracted and exhaustive investigation by H. A. Lyman, Esq., of London, to whom we are indebted for the following summary of the pedigree of the family in England. Every English record likely to

2

throw light upon the subject has been searched, particularly the De Banco, Coram Rege, Subsidy and Quo War-
ranto Rolls, extending from the 5th Richard I Rolls. From
all these the conclusion is irresistible that the names Leman
and Lyman are one and the same. That they were recog-
nized as the same appears from the fact that Sir John *Leman*,
lord mayor of London, 1616, had a correspondence with
the widow of Henry *Lyman*, brother of Richard, respecting
her return to England ; and that the father of Sir John held
part and parcel of the same estate which came into the
possession of the Lymans by the marriage of Thomas
Lyman, of Navistoke, with Elizabeth Lambert. The name
Lyman, in this orthography, appears in the parish records of
High Ongar as far back as 1521.

The change of the vowels *e* and *i* to *y* is in entire accord-
ance with the analogies of our language in its primitive
forms; "*i* exchanges with *y* in writing and sometimes with
ea, miht, myht, meaht, might, *y* is *i-umlaut* of *u* and *ea*.
It was a favorite letter with the penmen, and is often found
for *i* and sometimes for *e, ae :* cyning, king, *eald, yldest,*
old, oldest, *lyden, leden.* Latin." *March's Anglo-Saxon,
Grammar* p. 12, § 23.

The following illustrations are also given by the *same* author : " Latin, in the Anglo-Saxon, *Leden,* is often written
Lyden. In the preface to the Heptateuch of Ælfric, the
fourth line, has *of Ledene,* from Latin; line 20, *Lyden un-
derstandan,* to understand Latin; the ending *nes,* Gothic
is very often *nys,* § 228. Thus in Math., 5 : 6, *righteousness* is *rightwisnesse* in one manuscript; *nysse* in another,
and so other words in *ness;* nêten is often written *nyten,* neat
cattle; Ps., 135 : 8, *hel,* hell, is written *hyl,* Cadman, p. 307,
line 27 and elsewhere *hlehhan, hlahian,* laugh is found
hlyhhan, in Ædelstan, 47, Judith, 23, and examples without number might be enumerated."

The substitution of *y* for *i* is too frequent and familiar to
require illustration. *Flynt, Lynd, Lyndsay, Van Syckle,
etc.* The German pronunciation of *Lyman,* is precisely
the same as ours of *Leman.* The two forms of orthography are only different methods of representing by symbols the same sound, and the names *Leman, Liman* and *Lyman* are doubtless one and the same.

The careless and variable orthography of this family
name in ancient records is apparent in the follow
ing references : In the Subsidy Rolls for Kent, 1st Ed.,
iii, the name is written *Lycman,* and in the subsequent

rolls for the same place *Lemman* and *Leman*. In a pedigree of the family, John, the grandfather of Sir John, Lord Mayor, is called " John de Le Mans, " but Sir John's name is uniformly Leman. In a pedigree from " The Visitation of London, 1663-4," the father and brothers of Sir John are written " *Lemman*," while Sir John is entered " *Lemon*." The eldest son of Sir John's brother is entered " *Lemon*," and his youngest son " *Leman*."

Savage, in his *Genealogical Dictionary*, has the names Lemon, Leamond, Lemond, Leman and Lyman. Through all these intermediate changes the conclusion is easy, natural and irresistible, that the ancient *Leman* has changed to the modern Lyman — both one and the same.

II. THE FRONTISPIECE AND ARMS OF THE FAMILY.

The Lyman family have, at different times, borne five separate armorial bearings or emblems, of which two only are worthy of particular notice. The arms that form the frontispiece seem to have been adopted long before any official grant of arms was made. They are the oldest and apparently the original family bearings. They appear in an old manuscript roll of arms, under the name of Lyman. They are now recorded as used by " Lemon, Lemmon, Leeman and Leman." The same arms are found in *Burke's Armory* where they are entered as the arms of "Lyman or Leman."

We are indebted to Mr. H. A. Lyman, of London, for the following extracts from the best authorities relating to English heraldry, which give, in a concise form, the substance of many hundreds of books which, from time to time, have been printed on this subject:

" In the beginning of the 16th century, owing to the multiplicity of abuses and irregularities which had crept into all matters appertaining to the descent of arms, commissions were issued under the great seal empowering the heralds to visit their different provinces or districts, as often as they deemed it necessary, and to convene before them all those who bore or assumed to bear arms, and to cause them to produce and to show by what authority and right they challenged the said use of arms. These circuits were called visitations. The earliest of these visitations was held in 1528–1529. These were regularly made every twenty-five or thirty years, until the close of the 17th century. The records or register book of these visitations are of the highest importance. Unfortunately, many of the books are now lost, and those that remain are scattered among the private and public libraries of the kingdom."

" Nothing is absolutely known concerning it beyond the fact that the middle of the 12th century is the earliest period to which the bearing of heraldic devices properly so-called can be traced ; and the commencement of the 13th, the time about which they became hereditary.

"The earliest roll of arms of which we have any notice is of the reign of Henry III (1216), and the reign of Edward I presents us with the earliest heraldic document extant.

"The oldest writer on heraldry was Nicholas Upton, whose treatise was composed in the reign of Henry V, (1413). His definitions and explanations can only be looked upon as assertions made nearly three hundred years after the origin of the practice, and, consequently, to be believed, or not, according to the discretion of the reader.

"College of Arms was founded reign of Richard III, (1483)."

In the frontispiece the central figure, within and under the crest of the helmet and the rampant bull, is divided into four parts representing *three coats of arms.* The first and fourth is that of the Lymans repeated in the fourth division to make up the quarterly. In the Lyman arms the significant figure is the *annulet* or *ring* within the triangle. This very ancient and frequent emblem in heraldry is differently interpreted. It is said to be an emblem of eternity, having neither beginning nor end. In *Webster's Dictionary* it is described as " formerly reputed to be a mark of nobility and jurisdiction. It is also a mark of distinctive form by the fifth brother of a family in his coat of arms."

The second figure in the quarterly is the arms of Elizabeth Lambert, the heiress, who by her marriage about 1488, with Thomas Lyman, of Navistoke, near High Ongar, brought large estates into the family.

The third is the arms of Sarah Osborne, the wife of Richard[1], the original immigrant to America, the ancestor of all the Lymans, recorded in this book.

The coat of arms most frequently adopted by the Lymans, in which dolphins play a conspicuous part, is that of Sir John Lyman lord mayor of London, a few years before the first immigration to this country. Sir John was largely interested in the Fishmongers Company, and the dolphins, it is suggested, may have some reference to this interest. The crest is surmounted by a pelican in her nest feeding her young. The significancy of these emblems and the origin of these armorial bearings is given by Burke: In the 12th year of the reign of King James the first, Jan. 25, 1615, a coat of arms was granted to Sir John Leman, viz: " Azure, a chevron embowed, three dolphins Naiant, Argent." These dolphins are said to be " symbols of social love." The crest has a pelican with a bloody crest feeding her young — also an emblem of love.

III. PEDIGREE OF THE LYMANS IN GREAT BRITAIN.

The old records of England throw but little light upon the origin, or early history of this ancient Saxon family; and although inheritors of estates at the time of the conquest of England, often derived their surnames from the place of their abode, our investigations do not enable us to determine what the connection of home or inheritance was, if any ever existed, between the Leman family, and the little ancient place called Lymen, that was once a hamlet in the county of Kent. Our first knowledge of this family name is obtained from the register or survey of the lands of England, framed by the order of King William the Conqueror, and known as *Doomsday Book*. The translation from this record of eight hundred years ago (vol. I, p. 38a), is as follows:

" HAMPSHIRE. The King's land. Bosmere Hundred. The King himself holds $2\frac{1}{2}$ hides[1] in Hayling Island.

LEMAN held them in parcenary[2] of King Edward, Harold deprived him of them when he usurped the kingdom, and converted them into a royal manor, and they so remain. They were then assessed at $2\frac{1}{2}$ hides, now at nothing. There are $1\frac{1}{2}$ ploughland,[3] one in demesne,[4] with one villein,[5] and eight cottagers,[6] with half a ploughland. There

NOTE.—[1] Saxon measure, about 100 acres, probably varied with the value of the land. [2] Holding in equal portions, both in property and as to right, &c. [3] Norman measure, about 100 acres. [4] As lord of the manor. [5] Belonging or annexed to a manor whereof the Lord was owner, and were usually sold with the farm to which they respectively belonged. This word often occurs in Doomsday, and some think they were boors, or husbandmen, with a small parcel of land allowed to them on condition that they should supply the lord of the manor with poultry, eggs, and other small provision for his board and entertainment.

is also 1½ acres of meadow. In the time of King Edward
it was worth forty shillings, afterwards twenty shillings,
now seventy shillings."

"MEONSTOKE Hundred. The King holds SOBERTON.
LEMAN held it of Earl Godwin. Harold, when he reigned,
took it from him, and made it a royal manor, and it so remains. Leman himself could not remove where he wished.
It is said that he held lands in Finchdean Hundred, in
parcenary. It was then assessed at 4 hides, now at nothing.
It contains 2 ploughlands, half a ploughland in demesne.
There are six villeins and three cottagers, with two ploughlands, and two mills, which pay fifteen shillings, and one
acre of meadow. Its value was and is, three pounds."

There can be little doubt but that this Saxon Leman continued the tenancy of the lands described, until his death,
and that he was succeeded in the tenancy by his son Os-
BERT described as "OSBERT FIL LEMAN," and who in the
time of Henry I, was a witness to a charter touching the
grant of certain lands to the Abbot of Battle. This Osbert
was succeeded by his two sons, JOHN and RICHARD, both
paying taxes upon their lands during the reign of King
Stephen, and Henry II, the former holding in the island
of Hayling, and the latter in the counties Southampton,
Norfolk, and Kent. This first Richard Leman, had issue,
JOHN, who held lands in the county Southampton, time
Henry II, and Richard I, and from the receipts for the
Exchequer we find he was one of the contractors for the
supply of timber for the repairing and enlarging of the
fortifications of the castle of Rochester, Kent. He was
succeeded by his eldest son ELDRED, who continued in the
possession of the lands in county Southampton, and also
held lands in Luthyngland, county Suffolk, conjointly with
his brother ROBERT, which said lands they held of the king
in capeti, time of King John. This Robert, the brother of
Eldred, married and had issue. Eldred had issue: two
sons, ALAN and ROBERT, the latter settled in St. Edigie,
county Cambridge.

ALAN held lands at Staue and Wilburham, county Cambridge, of
the Knights Templar, time of Henry III.

I. THOMAS Lyman, alias Leman, held divers land
county Wiltes, during his father's lifetime, reign of
Henry III. In 3d Edward I, A. D. 1275, he was fined
twenty pence by Walter de Sterteslegh, sheriff of Wiltes,
for default in attending a certain inquisition to which he

had been summoned. He also held land of the abbot of St. Edward, of Oxford.

H. RICHARD Leman held lands of the Knights Templar, County Bedford, time Edward I.

WILLIAM Leman, tenant to Sir John de Grey, county Bedford, 10th Edward I, A. D. 1282.

III. ALISALON Lyeman purchased lands in the Hundred of Beawisberg, now called Beaksbourne, county Kent, time of Edward I. Had possession of these lands during the reign of Edward II, A. D. 1307 to 1327, and was living 1st Edward III, at the collection of the 20th, being the tax then levied, as appears by the Subsidy Roll for that year, for the said Hundred.

JOHN Leyman of Colchester, county Essex, taxation of his effects from 24th Edward I, to 2d Edward II, A. D. 1309.

IV. ESPILON Lyman, alias Lemman, succeeded his father in the possession of the estate at Beawisberg, county Kent, upon which he was taxed until the 2d Ed. III, A. D. 1349.

JOHN Leman and NICHOLAS Leman held during the life time of their father under Thos. de Sugterton, returned Knight of the shire Norfolk, I Ed. II, A. D. 1307.

V. SALOMAN Lyman, eldest son and heir, became possessed of the estate at Beawisberg upon the death of his father and was succeeded by his son.

WILLIAM, about the 13th Richard II, A. D. 1380, who from the Subsidy and De Banco Rolls must have held this estate for a period of 22 years. This Salomon mentioned had also issue JOHN and ROBERT, and it is believed, one Richard, defendant in a plea of debt, time Henry IV, about A. D. 1405.
ROBERT of Norfolk.

VI. ROBERT Lyman of Beawisberg, defendant in a plea of debt, 5th Henry V, A. D. 1418, and 8th Henry VI, A. D. 1430.

JOHN Leman, alias Lyman, citizen and merchant of London, A. D. 1414 to 1422. time Henry V, afterwards purchased lands at Navistoke, Wethersfield, and Norton Munderville, county Essex. In the 10th Henry VI, A. D. 1432, he was bound in the Kings Chancery in the sum of one hundred pounds, to answer for one Master Thomas Mireton, a Scotchman, who, coming into England with letters from the king of Scotland to the council at Westminster, was taken prisoner by Sir William Iver, Kut., married

Johanna, daughter and heiress of Roger Trethewy of Southampton.

VII. Thomas Lyman, of Navistoke, county of Essex, gentleman, succeeded his father in the possession of the estate at Navistoke and Wethersfield. In the 3d Henry VII, A. D. 1488, this Thomas Lyman and Elizabeth his wife, lately called " Elizabeth Lambert, Gentlewoman," brought suit in the Court of Kings Bench against one Cecilie Barantyn, executrix to a will, for unjustly detaining a sum of money, m. Elizabeth, daughter and heiress of Henry Lambert of High Ongar, county Essex.

Robert Lyman, possessed of divers lands at Southwelde, Brentwood, county Essex, defendant in a plea of trespass, brought by Sir Thos. Ferrers, Knt., 38th Henry VI, A.D. 1460.

Robert Lyman, of Southwelde, eldest son and heir, also held lands at Noke Hill, county Essex, 3d Henry VII, A. D. 1488.

Robert Lyman, of Noke Hill, county Essex, living 14th Henry VIII, A.D. 1523.

John Lyman, of Ingestre, county Essex, living 15th Henry VII, A.D. 1500.

John Lyman, of Noke Hill.

Julian Lyman of Noke Hill, living 37th Henry VIII, A.D. 1546.

Robert Lyman, of Noke Hill, living 37th Henry VIII, A.D. 1548.

Robert Lyman, of Borham, county Essex, ob. Nov., 1605.

John Lyman, second son.

John Lyman, county Essex, heir of Robert.

Simon Lyman, of High Ongar.

Robert Lyman, of Noke Hill, deprived his brother John of his lands.

Robert Lyman took proceedings in chancery against Robert, his uncle, 18 June, 1630, to recover estates in Essex, of which his father had been deprived.

VIII. Henry Lyman, of Navistoke and High Ongar, county Essex, " gentleman," had possession of the estates at Navistoke and Wethersfield, 2d Henry VII, A.D. 1487, living 8th Henry VIII, A.D. 1517, m. Alicia, daughter of Simon Hyde, of Wethersfield, county Essex.

Thomas Lyman removed to, and purchased lands at Heyton and Alscombe, county Devon, 20th Henry VIII, A.D. 1529.

IX. John Lyman of Navistoke and High Ongar, county Essex, "gentleman," eldest son and heir, also possessed lands at Ovyngton, Asshe, and Beauchamp St. Paul, county Essex, and at Clare and Chylton, county Suffolk, which he sold, 14th Henry VIII, A.D. 1523, living 37th Henry VIII,

A.D. 1546, having possession at that time of the Navistoke and Ongar estates. He was a contributor towards the carrying on of the war; m. MARGARET, daughter and heiress of William Gerard, of Beauchamp, county Essex.

X. ROBERT Leman, *alias* Lyman, second son, m. MARY, daughter of John Green of High Ongar, first wife, ob. without issue, 1570 m. HENRY Lyman, *alias* Leman, succeeded his father in the possession of the estates at Navistoke and High Ongar, Essex county, living at High Ongar in the year 1598, died about 1609, m. PHILLIS, daughter of John Scot of Navistoke, county Essex, living, a widow, 1629. Second wife, m. Ralph Green, of High Ongar, second husband, ob. before 1st Charles I, before 1625.

JOHN Leman of High Ongar, Essex, and Gillingham, county Norfolk, living 37th Elizabeth, A.D. 1595, m. MARY, daughter of John Alston, of Farenham, Bedfordshire.

XI. HENRY Lyman, of Navistoke, county Essex (baptized 7 June, 1591), and Elizabeth, his wife, and Phillis Green, widow, in the year 1629, sold to Anna Heywood, widow, one messuage, four cottages and divers lands arable; also a meadow and pasture, all at Navistoke. The Phillis Green mentioned was the mother of Richard and Henry, and had dower in said lands. This sale being effected, Henry with his wife, emigrated to New England with his brother Richard, in the year 1631, and died soon after his arrival in that country, without issue.

ELIZABETH emigrated to America with her husband, 1631, and upon his death, in the same year held a correspondence with her cousin, Sir John Leman, Knt., concerning her return to England. It is supposed she remained in America, and died soon after her husband.

JUDITH, bapt. 2 Nov., 1578.

RUTH, bapt. 20 Oct., 1579.

DIONISIA, bapt. 28 Nov., 1585.

MARY, bapt. 18 Jan., 1587.

SIR JOHN LEMAN, KNT., son of John Leman, of High Ongar, citizen and alderman of London, sheriff of London, 1606; lord mayor of London, 1616; also president of Christ's Church Hospital. He was born at Saxlingham, in the year 1544; was possessed of the manors of Rampton, Cambridgeshire, Wardeboys, Huntingdonshire, and of Barnes in St. Bottolph's, White Chapel, and Stepney, London. Entailed his lands by deeds dated 7 April, 1629, and will dated 8 July, 1631. He died 16 March, 1632, and was buried in the parish church at Hackney, near London,

where he had a beautiful monument.   At Fishmongers Hall.
London, is an original drawing of a portion of the pageant ex-
hibited by the Fishmongers Company, 29th Oct. 1616, on the occasion of Sir John, who was a member of this ancient guild, entering upon the office of lord mayor of the city of London.   A
lithograph drawing of Sir John's house at Hackney is at the present time (1868) in possession of Mr. H. A. Lyman, of Upper
Norwood, Eng.   Sir John assumed a new coat of arms in his connection with the Fishmongers' Company, viz. : " Azure, three Dolphins, Naiant, Argent."   He died *sine prole*.   For disposition of
estates see " The Leman Family Estates."   The children of Sir
John Leman were :

THOMAS Leman.

PHILIP Leman, ob. without issue.

ANN m. BARBER.

WILLIAM Leman, citizen of London, had estate at Beecles.   Died
in the lifetime of his brother, m. ALICE, daughter of Mr. Bourne,
of Norwich.

PHILIP, obiit without issue.

Priscella, Margaret and Anne, daughters of John Leman, of the X
generation.

XII. SIR WILLIAM Leman, 1st baronet, and heir to Sir
John Leman, his uncle, created a baronet by patent dating
3 March, 1665, purchased and added to his vast estates the
manor of Northaw, in the county of Hertford.   He was
buried in the chapel at Northaw, 3 Sept., 1667.   Will
dated 1667.   He was the son of William Leman of the XI
generation (for disposition of estates, see " The Leman
Family English Estates,") m. REBECCA, daughter of E.
Prescott, Esq., of London and of Thurby Hall, Essex.
Buried at Northaw, 22d January, 1674-5.

JOHN Leman, m. MARY, daughter of Jno. Sherson.

ROBERT Leman, of Ipswich, Nettleton, and Brightwell Hall, Suffolk; died 1637;   buried at Ipswich;   m. MARY, daughter of
William Coke, of Broom Hall, Norfolk.

MARY m. Richard Bennett, had issue Mary, who m. Sir Henry Capel, K. B., created Baron Capel of Tewksbury. Ob. without issue.

ALICE, dau. of Robert Leman, m. 1st, Thos. Barker, of Suffolk ; 2d
to Chas. Greug, 2d Bart., of Norwich.   Ob. without issue.

REBECCA, and Martha, daughters of Robert Leman.

ROBERT Leman, bapt. 1632 or 1633, physician.   Will dated 1697.

BARNABAS[1], son of Robert Leman, m. SARAH.   JOHN, SARAH,
JOSHUA, SAMUEL, BENJAMIN, ELIZABETH, SARAH, ANN, HAN-
NAH, MILDISTABE, children of Robert Leman.

BARNABAS[2], m. MARTHA, dau. of Mr. Howard.

WILLIAM, son of Barnabas[1], m. ANN, dau. of Mr. Collins.

ABRAHAM[1], m. JAMESON, dau. of Thos. Potter.

ANN, MARY, children of Barnabas[1].

BARNABAS[3], d. s. p., 1799. MARY, SARAH, MARTHA, children of Barnabas[2].

RORERT, son of William, m. ANN, had 4 daughters.

ABRAHAM, BARNABAS, ROBERT, TIMOTHY, JOUPT, MARY, JAMESON, ANN, children of Abraham[2].

JOHN, ob. s. p., ROBERT, children of Abraham[1].

XIII. SIR WILLIAM Leman, 2d baronet, eldest son and heir to the title and estates of his father, Sir William Leman, 1st Bart. Married in the year 1655. Represented the county of Hertford in Parliament in 1690. Will dated 17 November, 1692, proved 8 September, 1701. He was buried in the chapel at Northaw, 28 July, 1701 (for disposition of estates, see "The Leman family English Estates") m. MARY, daughter of Sir Lewis Mansel, Knt., and granddaughter of Henry, Earl of Manchester.

JOHN Leman, of Northaw, son of Sir William Leman, 1st Bart., buried at Northaw, 22 April, 1729, aged 91; m. ANN, dau. of Healy, Esq., of Edgware, Middlesex.

JOHN, ELIZABETH, ANN, children of John Leman, of Northaw.

THOMAS Leman, bapt. 17 Sept. 1640, ob. 1682, m. MARY, dau. of Thos. Hickford, of London.

LOYD. HICKFORD, ob. 1732. ROBERT, ob. 1719. REBECCA, children of Thomas Leman.

EDWARD Leman, of London, son of Sir William Leman, 1st Bart., born 1641, buried 17 Oct., 1700, m. MARY, dau. of Sir Thos. Holt.

ROBERT, d. s. p., EDWARD, d. s. p., EDWARD, d. s. p., children of Edward Leman, of London.

JAMES Leman, died unmarried.

TANFIELD Leman, of London, barrister of the Inner Temple, died unmarried 16 January, 1704. Will dated 1704. Buried in the Chapel, at Northaw.

REV. PHILIP Leman, rector of Wardeboys, Hunts. Born 1650. Died 1694. Will dated 1693. He m. CATHERINE, daughter of Richard Carker, of Colne.

XIV. MANSEL Leman, eldest son of Sir William Leman, 2d Bart., m. in 1683, but died 13 March, 1687, in the lifetime of his father, m. Lucy, dau. of Richard Alie, Esq., ob. Sept., 1745.

ROBERT Leman, ob. inft.

REBECCA, ob. 1695. LUCY, ob. inft. MARY, daughters of Sir William Leman.

WILLIAM Leman, born 1680, ob. inft.

ELIZABETH, bapt. 19 Jan., 1661, m. Henry Alie, son of Richard Alie, Esq., who was an alderman of London.

RICHARD Alie, of Mincing Lane, London, who, by the will of his cousin, Sir Wm. Leman, 3d Bart., became possessed of the manors of Northaw, Wardeboys, and Rampton, and thereupon took the surname and arms of Leman. He died without issue, and was buried in the chapel at Northaw, 17 July, 1749. By his will, dated 6 Nov., 1745, he gave the estates to his sister, Lucy Alie, although by the will of Sir Wm. Leman, 3d Bart., it was pro-vided that in the event of default of heirs (male), by this Richd. Alie, the estates should go "to the person who shall have in him the right of succession to the Leman family."

LUCY Alie, to whom her brother Richard gave the manors of Nor-thaw, Wardeboys, and Rampton. Buried in the Chapel at Nor-thaw, 8 Oct., 1753. She gave the estates to one John Grainger, who took the arms and surname of Leman, and died without issue, at Bath, 29 Sept., 1781. For further disposition of estates see "The Leman Family English Estates."

THEODOCIA, m. Lewis Newnham, of London. Elizabeth Newn-ham, dau. of Theodocia.

SARAH, m. George Hutchinson, of Gray's Inn, London.

These are the 9 children of Sir William Leman, 2d Bart.

REV. WILLIAM Leman, son of REV. PHILIP Leman, rector of Wardeboys, bapt. 7 April, 1681, ob. 1731, without issue, m. Jane Mappletoft, dau. of a clergyman.

PHILIP Leman, chemist, of Snow Hill, London, bapt. 29 Aug., 1686, died, 1732, m. FRANCES. Will dated 1734.

JOHN Leman, bapt. at Northaw, 28 July, 1689, m. 20 Jan., 1718. Buried at Nottingham, 1759, m. SARAH Godfrey.

CATHERINE, bapt. 2 Aug., 1683, ob. unmarried, Sept., 1744.

FRANCES, bapt. 29 March, 1685. Buried 12 April, 1744, m. Wm. Battersby, of Huntingdonshire.

MARY, born July, 1689. She was a twin sister of her brother John. These are the 6 children of Rev. Philip Leman.

XV. SIR WILLIAM Leman, 3d baronet, eldest son and only of Mansel Leman, grandson and heir of Sir William Leman, 2d baronet. Will dated 1 Nov., 1712. Died 22 Dec., 1741. Buried in the chapel at Northaw, 2 Jan., 1742. No issue. For disposition of estates, see "The Leman Family English Estates," m. ANNA MARGARETTA, dau. of Col. Brett, by the Countess of Macclesfield. She was the only English mistress of King George I. She was to have been rewarded for her degradation with the coronet of a countess, but the king died suddenly, and her reign and influence immediately ceased. Ten years after the death of the king she married Sir Wm. Leman.

Wharton says of her, that "she was dark, and her flashing black eyes resembled those of a Spanish beauty."

LUCY, buried at Northaw, 3 Oct., 1745.

SARAH Leman, a legatee in her aunt Catherine's will.

CATHERINE, a legatee in her aunt Catherine's will.

SIR TANFIELD Leman, 4th baronet. Bapt. at St. Margaret's, Lothbury, London, 13 April, 1714. He was a physician in London, and assumed the title of baronet upon the death of Sir William, 3d baronet, in 1741. Plaintiff in a suit in Chancery 1748, 1753 and then described "of St George's, Southwark, county Surrey, Bart." He died without issue, in 1762. Will dated the same year. m. CATHERINE.

These were the three children of Philip Leman, chemist, of Snow-Hill, London.

JOHN Leman, of Nottingham, bapt. at Nottingham, 6 Oct., 1724. Married 25 May, 1745. Died May, 1792; m. MARY Smithham.

GODFREY Leman, bapt. 14 Sept., 1753; m. 16 Feb., 1777. Buried 4 March, 1827; m. ANN Whitaker.

EDWARD Leman, bapt. 11 Dec., 1759. Died unmarried, 1833.

Godfrey Leman and Edward, were sons of John Leman, of Nottingham.

RICHARD Leman, born 15 Oct. 1730; married Alice. No issue.

EDWARD Leman, of Nottingham, bapt. at Nottingham (as son of John Lemmon and Sarah), 5 June, 1733. Married at Nottingham as Edward Lemon, 8 Oct., 1765. Said to have died abroad; m. ELIZABETH Bates, 1765.

EDWARD GODFREY Leman, of Nottingham. Bapt. at Nottingham, 28 April, 1766; m. 1 April, 1793. Died 11 July, 1847. Claimant to the 6th baronetcy and estates; m. MARY Burton.

EDWARD Leman, of Nottingham, son of Edward Godfrey Leman, born 25 Dec., 1804. Received from his father power of attorney, under date of 22d January, 1840, to prosecute his claim to the title and estates of the Leman family. The claim not being brought to a successful issue, the estates remained in Chancery, waiting the rightful heirs.

SARAH, REBECCA, HARRIET, SOPHIA, HELINA, daughters of EDWARD Leman.

The children of Godfrey Leman were William, John, Sarah and Sir John Leman, 5th Bart. WILLIAM Leman, bapt. 14 Feb., 1778. Buried 5th Oct., 1787.

JOHN Leman, bapt. 28 June, 1779. Buried 16 Nov., 1780.

SARAH.

SIR JOHN Leman, 5th baronet in succession from Sir William Leman, Bart., of Northaw. Bapt. 28 Aug. 1781; m. 28 April, 1800. Died, without issue, 5 June, 1839. The following obituary is from the *Nottingham Journal* and *Morning Herald*, of July 1st, 1839: "The deceased was not long since an humble frame work knitter in Nottingham. He had succeeded in making good his claim to the title, but had not obtained possession of the estate. His indefatigable labor of mind and body in a just cause has shortened his days. He has for the last six months been sinking under the great anxiety of mind which his case naturally produced ; and though he was attended by three eminent physicians from Wakefield and Leeds, he gradually sank and died at the very time when his labors were being crowned with success, his case having passed through the House of Lords, the Herald's College, and received the signature and seal of the queen, and he had only to go to London to ' suffer recovery,' but which his failing strength would not permit. His next heir, Edward Godfrey Leman, will have comparatively nothing to do in order to obtain possession of this immense property. Sir John's dying request was, that every person who had lent him money should be speedily paid, which request his executors will see punctually complied with as soon as possible. He was interred on Monday last, in a manner suitable to his rank, at Sandall, near Wakefield."

The Leman Family English Estates.

Sir John Leman, knight, citizen, sheriff and alderman, lord mayor of London, 1616, member of the Fishmongers' Company, was born 1544, died 1632, left by his will dated 8 July, 1631, the manor of Barnes (*alias* Goodman's Fields), in St. Bottolph's, White Chapel and Stepney, London, To the use of his nephews Robert, Thomas, Philip and William Leman, and their heirs male, in succession, and in default to his niece, Ann Barber, and her heirs male and in default to his own right heirs for ever. Likewise the manors of Wardeboys, in Huntingdonshire, and Rampton, in Cambridgeshire, did he will to his youngest nephew William.

William Leman, nephew and heir of Sir John Leman, and son of William Leman, of London, came into possession of the said estates and to the possession of the manor of Northow, county Hertford, by purchase, as follows : Upon the death of the Countess of Wanouk, William Lord Russell came into possession of the estate at Northaw, and after having granted part of the common, amounting to 268 acres, 3 rods, 17 perches, by two grants, in the years 1618, and 1622, to the king, James I, for the enlargement of his park (Theobald's), sold this manor, estate, and rectory to William Leman, Esq., in the year 1632.

This William Leman was created a baronet under a patent granted by King Charles 1st, and bearing date 3 March, 1665.

He was treasurer of war, and represented the county of Hertford in parliament. Upon his death in the year 1667, his eldest son William was his successor in title and estates, holding the same under indenture by his father Sir William Leman, bearing date 14th and 15th June, 1655. To trustees in trust to the heirs male of his body, the eldest always to take before the youngest, and in failure of issue male, the estates were to go to his own right heirs. This Sir William, 2d Bart., was sheriff of Hertfordshire, 1676, and was elected to represent the borough of Hertford in parliament in the 2d year of the reign of King William and Mary. He died possessed of the estates, 18 July, 1701, and was buried in the chapel at Northaw, 28 July, 1701. Mansel Leman, eldest son of Sir William, 2d Bart., having died in the lifetime of his father, his son William, and grandson of Sir William, 2d Bart., was the successor in title and estates. Under the will of Sir William Leman, 2d Bart., dated 17 November, 1692, he apppointed his brothers, John Leman, Edward Leman, and Tanfield Leman, trustees to his estates, in trust for this grandson William, and they were to receive the rents of the manor of Barnes (alias Goodman's Fields) in order to pay his daughters' portions and other legacies. This trust he directed should be performed for one hundred years, and in failure of male issue of his grandson William, the estates in Huntingdonshire, Cambridgeshire, Hertfordshire, Middlesex, and London, were to go to his own right heirs for ever. Edward Leman, one of the trustees, died in 1700, and Tanfield Leman died in 1704, leaving John Leman the only trustee, who died in 1729. This John Leman had a son John, who was absent at the death of his father. Sir William Leman, 3d Bart., died possessed of the estates, but without issue, on 22 December, 1741, and was buried in the chapel at Northaw, 2 January, 1742. To fully show the manner and disposition of his estates, the following is a true copy of his will, dated 1 November, 1712, as extracted from the registry of the prerogative court of Canterbury:

"In the name of God, amen. I, Sir William Leman, Baronet, of Northaw, in the county of Hertford, having my sound and perfect reason (praised be God), do make this my last will and testament. First, unto thy hands, O Lord, I commit my soul, trusting in the goodness of Thy mercy for the pardon of all my sins, and in the merits of my blessed Saviour and Redeemer, Jesus Christ, and waiting for a joyful resurrection at the last day. My body I leave to the earth, and desire it may be interred in the vault of my family in Northaw Church. I desire that 10 pounds may be distributed to the poor of Northaw, on the day of my burial. I desire that all my debts and funeral charges be paid and discharged by my executrix; I mean those only of my own contracting, and not those heavier debts of my family which are charged upon the Manor of Goodman's Fields. Whereas, upon the death of my grandmother, Dame Mary Leman, the Manor of Northaw, in Hertfordshire, with all its rights, members, and appurtenances, is to devolve upon my mother Lucy Leman, and the Manor of Wardboys, in Huntingdonshire (at present in possession of my said mother), with all its rights, members, and appurtenances is to devolve upon me and my heirs; I therefore give and bequeath (viz., after the decease of my aforesaid grandmother), the said Manor of Wardboys, in Huntingdonshire, with all its rights, members, and appurtenances, to my dear mother Lucy Leman, for her to have, hold and enjoy the same for and during her natural life, subject to the condition of paying the annuities I shall charge upon the said estates. Item—I give and bequeath to my dear mother, Lucy Leman, all that my Manor of Rampton, in Cambridgeshire, with all the Lands, Tenements, Heredits thereunto belonging, both freehold and copyhold, as also every part and parcel thereof or appertaining to it whither situate, lying and being in the Parish of Rampton, aforesaid, or in the Parishes of Co. Henham or Willingham adjoining thereunto, to have and to hold and enjoy the Manor of Rampton, aforesaid, with all rights, members, and appurtenances for and during her natural life. Item — I give and bequeath to my cousin, Richard Alie, of Mincing Lane, London, all those my Manors of Northaw, in Hertfordshire, of Wardboys, in Huntingdonshire, and of Rampton in Cambridgeshire (viz., after the decease of my dear mother, Lucy Leman), with all rights, members, and appurtenances. To have and to hold and enjoy the aforesaid manors of Northaw, in Hertfordshire, of Wardboys in Huntingdonshire, and Rampton in Cambridgeshire, to him and his Heirs Male lawfully begotten; but upon default of such heirs male of the said Richard Alie's body lawfully begotten, after the said Richard Alie's decease, I give and bequeath the said Manors of Northaw, in Hertfordshire, of Wardboys, in Huntingdonshire, and of Rampton in Cambridgeshire, with all their rights, members, and appurtenances, to the person who shall have in him the right of succession to the Leman Family. Whenever all or any of my aforesaid estates, shall come into the possession of my said cousin, Richard Alie, I charge the said estates or estate with £3000 to be immediately paid by the said Richard Alie, to his sister Lucy Alie, spinster, for her fortune. I will and desire the said Richard Alie, immediately upon the possession of any or all of my estates, to take upon him the surname of Leman. I give and bequeath an annuity of £100 per ann., to my cousin Hickford Leman, during the term of his natural life. I give and bequeath an annuity of £40 per ann., to his brother, Robert Leman, for his natural life. Item — (orig¹ 50). The aforesaid annuities to be paid out of the Manor of Wardboys in Huntingdonshire immediately upon the first person possⁿ of the said Manor of Wardboys in my right. I give and bequeath to Brian Fairfax, Esq., of Westminster, £100, and desire he would buy a ring with it in remembrance of me. Item—That whoever is in possession of Wardboys when the living becomes vacant, to give the said living, gratis, to my cousin Robert Leman, but when in possession of the said living the annuity shall cease and become void. I give and bequeath to Richard Lockwood, Esq., £20 to buy a mourning ring. All my personal estate, goods, and chattels whatsoever, I give and bequeath to my dear mother, Lucy Leman, desiring she would pay all my just debts very exactly. And I hereby declare my said mother Lucy Leman, my full and sole executrix of this my will and testament; and I hereby revoke and make void all former wills by me heretofore made.

" In witness whereof, I have to this my will, containing one side, and this part set my hand to the first side, and my hand and seal to this my part, this first day of November, in the year of our Lord 1712.   WM. LEMAN.
" Witnesses.
" Signed and sealed in the presence of
          IRWIN ARTHUR INGRAM,
          GILBERT WALMSLEY,
          ARTHUR INGRAM."

" The 2d day of April, 1742, appᵈ personally Richard Alie, of Northaw, in the county of Hertfordshire, Esquire, and made oath that he the depont, some short time after the death of Sir William Leman, late of Northaw, in the county of Herts., in searching in the Deceᵈ'ˢ Bureau, found the last will and testament in the Deceased hand writing annexed, which at the time of finding thereof, was obliterated in the manner it now appears.
                              " RICHARD ALIE.
                                        the 2d April, 1742."

" The said Richard Alie, was sworn to the truth hereof before me.
          ROBERT CHAPMAN, Surrogate,
                    on the 2d April, 1742."

" A power was granted to the said Richard Alie, the cousin of Sir William Leman, of Northaw, in the county of Hertfordshire, baronet, deceased, to administer the Goods and Chattels and Credits of the said deceased, according to the tenor of said Will, for that Lucy Leman, widow, the Mother, sole Executrix, and revˢ Legatee, renounced the Exorship, of the said Will, and also the admsn. with the said will annexed, being sworn duly to administer. Dame Anna Margaretta Leman, widow, the relict of the said deceased, also renouncing the letters of admon. with the said Will annexed.
          Signed,   CHARLES DYNELY,
                                        JOHN INGRAM,
                                        CHARLES BROPIN.═
                                        Dep. Rig."

By the death of Lucy Leman, sister of Sir William, 3d Bart., in the year 1745, all the issue of Mansel Leman, son of the 2d Sir William and father of the last Sir William, became extinct, and the estates passed into the possession of Richard Alie, who thereupon took the surname and arms of Leman. He died in 1749, without issue, and by his will, bearing date 6 November, 1745, and proved 19 July, 1749, he gave the estates to his sister Lucy Alie. She died, and was buried in the chapel at Northaw, 8 October, 1753, leaving the estates to one John Grainger, who thereupon took the surname and arms of Leman. This John Leman, *alias* Grainger, died without issue, at Bath, 29 September, 1781, and was buried at Wardboys, in Huntingdonshire, on the 11th October, 1781. He left the estates to his wife, with a reversionary interest to William Strode, Esquire. The widow, Dame Leman, *alias* Grainger, afterwards married this William Strode, and died without issue at Bath, 15 December, 1790, and was buried with her first husband, at Wardboys, on the 29th day of the same month, and William Strode, esquire, died on the 21st July, 1809. The estate of Northaw was, pursuant to a decree of the Court of Chancery, bearing date 17 August, 1810, sold by auction on the 24th and 25th days of October in that year, and was purchased, together with the living or donative of Northaw, by Patrick Thompson, Esquire, of Turnham Green, in the county of Middlesex, who was the possessor in 1821. The value of these immense estates, now in Chancery, and including the manor of Northaw, with the properties in the funds, that are awaiting the rightful heirs, is estimated at four million pounds sterling (twenty millions dollars).

In consideration of this famous marriage of Thomas Lyman of Navistoke, county of Essex, time, Henry VI, with Elizabeth, daughter and heiress of Henry Lambert of High Ongar, and of the large estates which thus came into the family, the pedigree of this Elizabeth Lambert is subjoined with that of Johanna Umfreville, wife of Sir William Lambert.

Pedigree of Elizabeth Lambert, wife of Thomas Lyman, Esq., of Ongar, County of Essex, England.

I. Sir Radulphus Lambert, Knight, grandson of Lambert, Count of Loraine and Mons, came into England, with his kinsman William the Conqueror, and was present at the battle of Hastings. He had a grant of divers lands and manors in the county of York, his chief seat being at Skipton, in Cravin, county of York. He m. Alidnora dau. of Sir Ralph de Toney, a Norman nobleman, who came into England with William the Conqueror, and was one of his chief generals at the battle of Hastings, Oct. 14, A.D. 1066.

II. Sir Hugh Fitz Lambert, s. of the preceding knight, Lord of Skipton, in Cravin, county of York, time Henry I; m. Maud, dau. of Peter Ross, Lord of Ross, county York.

John Lambert, 2d s. of Sir Hugh Fitz Lambert.

III. Sir Henry Lambert, Knight, Lord of Skipton in Cravin county of York, time, King Stephen; heir of Sir Hugh Fitz.

William, 2d son.

IV. Sir John Lambert, Knight, Lord of Skipton in Cravin, county York; time, Henry II.

V. Sir Edward Lambert, Knight. Sir Edward Lambert, Knight; time, Richard I.

Thomas Lambert, s. of Wm., and sheriff of London. Henry II.

VI. Sir John Lambert, Knight, etc., living in A.D. 1187.

Edmund Lambert, 2d son.

VII. Sir Thomas Lambert, Knight, etc., time, Henry III.

Edmund Lambert[2], eldest son of Edmund; time, Henry, III.

VIII. Sir William Lambert, Knight, etc., time, Edward I, m. Jane, daughter and heir of Sir Thomas Cresey, Knight.

John Lambert, s. and heir to Edmund[2], time Ed. I; m. Elizabeth, dau. and heir of Sir Gilbert de Pijkeryng, Knight, county York.

IX. Sir Henry Lambert, Knight, etc., of Owlton, county of Durham, time, Edward II; m. Isabella Lambert, sole daughter and heir.

X. Sir Nicholas Lambert, Knight, Lord of Skipton, etc., and of Owlton, county Durham; time, Edward III, and Richard II.

XI. Alan Lambert, Esq., of Owlton; time, Richard II, and Henry IV.

Thomas, 2d son of Sir Nicholas.
John, 3d son of Sir Nicholas.

XII. Sir William Lambert, s. of Alan and Knight of Owlton, 9th Henry V; m. Johanna, sister and co-heir of Gilbert De Umfreville, Earl of Kyme, a famous soldier in the French wars in the time of Henry IV and V; slain with Thomas, Duke of Clarence and others, A.D. 1421.

XIII. Robert Lambert, Esq., of Owlton.

XIV. Henry Lambert, Esq., of Ongar, county of Essex, living 25th Henry VI.

XV. Elizabeth Lambert, dau. of Henry, m. Thomas Lyman, Esq., of Navistoke, county of Essex—time Henry VII—ancestor of Richard, the patriarch of all the families of Lyman in the United States and British provinces in America.

Pedigree of Johanna Umfreville, wife of Sir William Lambert XII.

I. Sir Robert Umfreville, knight, Lord of Tours and Vian in Normandy, commonly called "Robert with a beard," kinsman to William the Conqueror, with whom he came into England, and who in the 10th year of his reign gave him the forest of Riddesdale with all the castles, manors, lands and woods, pastures, waters and pools which were formerly possessed by Mildred the son of Akman, lord of Riddesdale, and which came to the king upon his conquest of England, to hold the same by the service of defending that part of the country from thieves and wolves with the sword which king William had by his side when he entered Northumberland.

By that grant he had also authority for hearing, determining, and judging all pleas of the crown as well as others happening within the precincts of Riddesdale by any proper officer for the time being according to the laws and customs of the realms.

II. Gilbert de Umfreville who, in the time of Henry I, gave a rent-charge of twenty-two solidos per annum unto the monks of Tewksbury for the soul of his wife.

III. Sir Robert de Umfreville, knight, Lord Baron of Prudhoe, and Lord of Riddesdale, county Northumberland, living 31st Henry I, 5th Stephen and 1st Henry II.

IV. Sir Odowell de Umfreville, knight, who on the collection of the scutage, 8th, and 18th Henry II, paid 40 solidos upon the assignment of the scutage on those who sent not in their certificates of the fees they held of this Odowell, a monk of Tynemouth, grievously complained about that time for his exactions upon his neighbors to repair the roof of his castle Prudhoe, which he presumed to do because he was the chief person in that county and partly through the interest he had at court by a great man having married his daughter. In the 20th Henry II, his castle of Harbotell was taken by the Scots, and his castle of Prudhoe besieged, but Robert de Stuteville, then sheriff of York, with the help of some northern barons timely relieved it.

In 23d Henry II, he was one of the witnesses to the king's arbitration between the king of Castile and Sancho, king of Navarre.

V. Robert de Umfreville, only son and heir, died in the lifetime of his father 29th Henry II.

VI. Sir Richard de Umfreville, knight, who in the 6th Richard I, gave £100 to the king for remitting that fine which he had made with the bishop of Durham, when the county of Northumberland was on the bishop's hands and that he might enjoy the king's favor though he did not go into Ireland in that expedition then made thither. In 7th Richard I, he stood indebted to Aaron, the Jew, in the sum of £23 6 8 for which his land in Turnay was engaged. In 5th John he had a grant of divers lands in Riddesdale. In the 14th John, the times being then turbulent, he delivered up his four sons in hostage with his castle of Prudhoe to secure his fidelity, so that in case he should thenceforth transgress, all to be forfeited, and his body to be disposed of as a traitor's, nevertheless so little did he regard this his great obligation, he joined the barons in arms, 17th John, for which his lands were seized and given to Hugh de Balliol; but soon after Henry III began to reign, and the times becoming more calm and quiet, he had restoration of his castle of Prudhoe notwithstanding the king had no confidence in him or regard. He, the king, discovered that he forfeited his castle of Prudhoe, and thereupon, in the 6th of his reign directed his precept to the sheriff of Northumberland to impanel a jury of twelve knights of that county to view, and having done so to destroy whatever had been added thereto in point of fortification since the war. He held the baronetcy of Prudhoe of the king by his service of two knights' fees and a half, as all his ancestors had done from the time of Henry I. Ob. 2d Henry III.

He m. Matilda de Torrington, cousin and co-heir to Mathew Lord, of Torrington.

VII. *Gilbert de Umfreville.* Lord Umfreville, of Prudhoe, doing his homage, and £100 for his relief, and livings of his lands 2d Henry III, and in 13th Henry III, he was one of the northern barons appointed by the king to be at Berwick-upon-Tweed, on Sunday, before mid-lent, thence to attend Alexander, king of Scotland, to York, where King Henry met him. In 17th Henry III, doing his homage, also had livery of the lands of his cousin, Matthew de Torrington, who died without issue. In 24th Henry III, he gives a fine of 100 marks over and above his scutage to be freed from attending the king in Gascoigne. Died in Passion week. 29th Henry III, he gives a fee. He was called the famous baron, the flower and keeper of the northern parts of England.

VIII. Gilbert de Umfreville[2], Earl of Angus, Lord Umfreville, baron of Prudhoe, lord of Riddesdale, being an infant at the death of his father, 29th Henry III, his wardship was committed to Simon de Montford, earl of Leicester, he paying 10,000 marks to the king for the same. In 43d Henry III, being then of age, upon the collection of the scutage of Wales, he paid £11 12 0 for five knights' fees, and a half and a fourth and the twentieth part of the fees of Matthew de Torrington. He held the manor of Prudhoe, likewise Riddesdale by the royal power. In the 49th Henry III, being then in arms with the barons, for awhile he did no mischief, but in 3d Ed. I, Walter de Swethorpe came to the king and made a sad complaint against him, setting forth that after the end of the troubles, and peace being proclaimed and published by the king, Henry III, this Earl Gilbert did seize upon him and keep him in prison in the castle of Harbottel, until he had given him 100 marks. The king, therefore, directed his precept to two persons to hear and determine this injury. He was constituted governor of the castles of Dundee and Forfar, and of the whole territory of Angus, in Scotland. In 23d Ed. I, he was summoned to parliament as lord Umfreville, and 25th Ed. I, he was summoned as earl of Angus. Died 1st Ed. II, 1307.

The wife of this Gilbert[2] was Matilda, Countess of Angus, a lineal descendant from Malcolm III, king of Scotland, slain at Alnwick castle, co. Northumberland, A. D. 1093.

Three of his sons succeeded to the throne. I. Edward, d. 1097, s. p. (i. e., without issue). II. Alexander, d. 1124, s. p. III. David, d. 1153, m. Maud, dau. of the earl of Northumberland. His son Henry, m. Adama, dau. of William Earle, of Warren, d. 1152.

Children:

1. William the Lion, king of Scotland, d. 1214. II. David, earl of Huntingdon. III. Ada m. Gilchrist, 3d earl of Angus, who performed many glorious exploits in king William's wars: Issue: Duncan, 4th earl of Angus.

2. Issue: Malcolm, 5th earl of Angus, m. Mary, dau. and heir of Sir Humphrey Berkeley, knight, living 1225.

3. Issue: Matilda, countess of Angus in her own right, who m. Gilbert de Umfreville.

IX. Gilbert de Umfreville[3], died in the lifetime of his father, 31st Edward I.

Robert, Lord Umfreville, 2d son of Gilbert[3], 2d earl of Angus, had livery of his lands. 1st Ed. II, in which year he was one of the king's lieutenants of Scotland, and one of the governors of Scotland, and of the Scottish marshes. He was summoned to parliament from the 2d year of Ed. II, until the 18th Ed. II, when he died.

Gilbert de Umfreville[4], son of Robert, 3d earl of Angus, lord de Umfreville, in 5th Ed. III, favoring the title of Edward Baliol to the crown of Scotland, and having afterwards accompanied him into Scotland, obtained a great victory over David de Brus, king of Scotland. In 9th Ed. III, he was again in the wars of Scotland. In the 19th Ed. III, he was in the French wars, and in 20th Ed. III, he was commander-in-chief of the English army at the battle of Durham. He was summoned to parliament, from the 6th Ed. III, to 4 Richard II, when he died, Jan. 7, 4th Richard.

X. Sir Thomas de Umfreville[1], son of Gilbert, heir to his brother Sir Robert, who d., s. p., in the lifetime of his father, had living of the castle of Harbottel. He m. Joan, dau. of Lord Rodam, county of Northumberland.

4

XI. Sir Thomas de Umfreville[2], knight, Lord de Rid-desdale and Lord Kyme, 2d son and heir to his brother Sir Robert, living, time King Henry IV.

Children :

1. Gilbert de Umfreville[5], Earl of Kyme, a famous soldier in the French wars, in the time of Henry IV, and V, slain with Thomas Duke of Clarence and others, 1421, s. p.
2. Johanna, sister and co-heir of Gilbert[5], earl of Kyme. She m. Sir William Lambert, knight of Owlton. 9th Henry V — XII in the pedigree of Elizabeth Lambert, wife of Thomas Lyman.

Thus the ancient and honorable lines of Lambert and Umfreville unite in the marriage of Sir William Lambert and Johanna de Umfreville, and they become the ancestors of the Lyman family, by the marriage of their great-grand-daughter with Thomas Lyman, Esq., of Navistoke, county of Essex in England, in the time of Henry VII, who died A. D. 1509.

This Thomas Lyman becomes the great-grandfather of Richard, the original immigrant to America, the succession being Thomas, Henry, John, Henry, Richard.

Henry, son of John of High Ongar, m. Elizabeth ———, name and date unknown, buried April 15, 1587, at Navis-toke, leaving

Children :

1. Judith, bapt. at High Ongar, Nov. 2; buried Nov. 24, 1578.
2. Jane, bapt. at H. O., Oct. 20, 1579; buried the 21st.
3. RICHARD, bapt. at H. O., Oct. 30, 1580.
4. Henry, bapt. at H. O., Nov. 19, 1581; buried at Navistoke, March 13, 1589.
5. Agnes, bapt. at H. O., Nov. 28, 1585.
6. Sarah, bapt. at H. O., Jan. 18, 1587.

Henry m. 2d wife, Phillis, dau. of Richard Stane of H. O., who, after the death of Henry, May 4, 1605, m. April, 1608, William Green of Luton.

Children of Henry and Phillis :

7. Henry, bapt. at H. O., June 6, 1591.
8. William, bapt. at Navistoke, March 2, 1594·
9. Phillis, bapt. at N., May 12, 1597.

According to another record the second wife of Henry was Phillis Scott, who had issue as follows

Children of Henry and Phillis Scott :

1. RICHARD, bapt. 1580, paid taxes 1610, 1627, 1629. In this year he sold all his land and in 1631, sailed for America.

2. Henry, m. Elizabeth, went to America, and d. there childless.
3. Simon, m. Kenbruga.

Children of Simon and Kenbruga :

  1 Richard, bapt. April 22, 1616.
  2 Elizabeth, bapt. Sept. 14, 1620.

4. Judith, 1575;   5. Ruth, 1579;   6. Dionisia, 1585;   7. Mary, 1586, or '87.

Both records agree in the essential facts relating to Richard our ancestor, and the reader is left to his own conclusions.

Richard Lyman, the patriarch of all the Lymans recorded in this volume, and all of English descent in America, born in High Ongar, Essex Co., in England, about 25 miles east by south from London, was baptized, Oct. 30, 1580. The date of his birth is not given. He married, date unknown, Sarah Osborne, daughter of Roger Osborne, of Halstead, in Kent. She went to America with her husband Richard and all their children, in 1631, and died in Hartford, Conn., about the year 1640, soon after the death of her husband.

Children, Second Generation

2   1 William, buried at High Ongar, Aug. 28, 1615.
3   2 *Phillis, bapt. Sept. 12, 1611 ; came to N. E., with his father; m. Wm. Hills, of Hartford, became deaf.
4   3 Richard, bapt. July 18, 1613, died young.
5   4 William, bapt. Sept. 8, and died in Nov., 1616.
6   5 *Richard, bapt. Feb. 24, 1617.
7   6 *Sarah, bapt. Feb. 8, 1620.
8   7 Anne, bapt. April 12, 1621, died young.
9   8 * John, bapt. 1623, according to his fathers will.
10   9 * Robert, b. Sept., 1629, as appears from his father's will; m. in Northampton, 15 Nov., 1662, Hepzibah Bascom.

Five of the children denoted by an asterisk*, came to New England with their parents, and all born and bapt. at High Ongar.

PART II.

Richard and his Family in America.

At what time Richard began to institute measures for his removal to America does not appear; but in the 5th Charles I, A.D. 1629, he sold to one John Gower two messuages, a garden, orchard and divers lands arable; also a meadow and pasture, all at Norton Mandeville, in the parish of Ongar, county of Essex, and about the middle of August, 1631, embarked with his wife and children in the ship Lion, William Pierce, master, for New England, taking their departure from the port of Bristol. We are informed, that there went in the same ship, Martha Winthrop, the third wife of John Winthrop, at that time governor of New England, the governor's eldest son and his wife and their children; also Eliot, the celebrated apostle of the Massachusetts Indians; and that the ship's passengers consisted of about sixty persons all told, and, after being ten weeks at sea, arrived at Natascot, having lost none of their company but two children; and that as the wind was contrary, the ship stayed at Long Island, but the governor's son went on shore, and that night the governor went on board the ship, and remained on board over night. The next morning, November 2d, the wind being fair, the ship made anchor before Boston, and on the 4th of November all the passengers landed, the ship giving them a a salute from six or seven cannon.

> What sought they thus afar?
>   Bright jewels of the mine?
> The wealth of seas? the spoils of war?
>   They sought a faith's pure shrine.
>
> Aye, call it holy ground,
>   The soil where first they trod;
> They have left unstained what there they found
>   Freedom to worship God.

On landing, the captain, with his companion in arms, entertained them with a guard, and gave them welcome by the salute of many guns; and the greater portion of the people of the near plantations went to receive them and brought or sent for many days a great store of provisions, such as fat hogs, kids, venison, poultry, geese, partridges, etc. ; and we are further told that such joy and manifestations of love had never before been seen in New England; and it was a great marvel that so many people and such an abundance of provisions could be gathered together in so few hours notice.   On the 11th day of November, a day of thanksgiving was held in Boston in commemoration of the event.

Richard Lyman first became a settler in Charlestown, Mass., and with his wife united with the church in what is now called Roxbury, under the pastoral care of Eliot, the apostle to the Indians; he became a freeman at the General court, 11th June, 1635, and on the 15th of October, 1635, he took his departure with his family from Charlestown, joining a party of about one hundred persons, who went through the wilderness from Massachusetts into Connecticut, the object being to form settlements at Windsor, Hartford and Wethersfield.   He was one of the first settlers at Hartford.   " The journey from Massachusetts was made in about fourteen days time, the distance being more than one hundred miles and through a trackless wilderness. They had no guide but their compass, and made their way over mountains, through swamps, thickets and rivers, which were not passable but with the greatest difficulty.   They had no cover but the heavens, nor any lodgings but those which simple nature afforded them. They drove with them one hundred and sixty head of cattle, and, by the way, subsisted in a great measure on the milk of their cows.   Mrs. Hooker was borne through the wilderness on the shoulders of the men.   The people carried their packs, arms, and some utensils.   They were nearly a fortnight on their journey. This adventure was the more remarkable, as many of this company were persons of figure, who had lived in England in honor, affluence and delicacy, and were entire strangers to fatigue and danger.— *Trumbull's Colonial Records.*

The party first struck the *Connectiquot,* the *Quinnitukut, the long river* in East Windsor near the Scantic river, and began their first settlement, on the west bank of the Connecticut in Windsor called by the Indians, Manutineang.

Richard Lyman, on this journey, suffered greatly in the loss of cattle.   He was one of the original proprietors of Hartford, and there is little doubt that he and his wife

Sarah formed a connection with the first church in Hartford, of which the Rev. Thomas Hooker was pastor. His will of 22d of April, 1640, is the first in the valuable collection of Trumbull, and stands, *Record*, I, 442 and 443, and followed by an inventory of his estate. All the children are named in his will, and his daughter Phillis is called the wife of William Hills. He died in August, 1640, and his name is inscribed on a stone column in the rear of the Centre Church of Hartford, erected in memory of the first settlers of the city. His widow, Sarah, died soon afterwards.

Richard is reported to have begun life in the New World as a man of "considerable estate, keeping two servants." In an account in the *Massachusetts Historical Collections*, of the moneys paid out of the common treasury of the colony, is found the following item: "Paid to Goodman Lyman for a fat hog for to victual the pinnace sent for the taking of David Bull £3 10s. 0. Goodman was the common title of the age for gentleman or Mister. This was doubtless Richard Lyman who victualed thus the pinnace.

The following extract is copied from the record of Eliot, the apostle, in his own hand writing: "Richard Lyman — he came to New England in the 9th month, 1631. He brought children, Phillis, Richard, Sarah, John. He was an ancient Christian, but weake, yet, after some time of tryal and quickening he joyned the church; w—n the great removal was made to Connecticot, he also went, and underwent much affliction; for, going toward winter, his cattle were lost in driving, and never were found again; and, the winter being cold and he ill-provided, he was sick and mellancholly; yet after, he had some reviving through God's mercy, and dyed in the year 1640."

Richard Lyman's name is on the list of the original proprietors of Hartford in 1636. His relative portion of the land obtained from the Indians was a fair average of that of the other proprietors. Of the purchase, he received thirty parts, one or two on the list receiving two hundred parts. The land of the seproprietors extended westward to Farmington. The house lot on which Richard, settled as appears on the ancient chart of Hartford for 1640, was on the south side of what is now Buckingham street, between Main and Washington streets, the fifth lot from Main street west of the South Church and bounded apparently on Wadsworth street either on the east or the west.

The following extract is taken from the public records of the Colony of Connecticut by J. H. Trumbull: "At a meeting of the General Court Sept. 5, 1639, Richard Lyman complayneth against Sequassen for burning upp his hedge which, before Mr. Governor, formerly he promised to satisfy for, but yett hath not done it. Saquassen appeared and promised to pay within four days, or else an attachment to be granted."

The will of Richard Lyman, the first on record at Hartford, is dated 22 April, 1640. The inventory of his personal property was made 6 of Sept., 1640. In the interval between these dates, he must have d. at the age of 60 years. Sarah, his wife d. before the presenting of the will at court, Jan., 1642.

His will and the inventory are as follows ·

[From *Colonial Records* vol. I.]

HARTFORD, CONN.

The last Will and Testament of RICHARD LYMAN, being in p'fect memory, I giue unto my wife all my houseing & lands dureing her life, and one-third p'te of my lands to dispose at her death amongst my children as shee pleaseth, and I giue to her all my moueable goods, as Cattell and houshold stuffe, and all other impliments or mouables. And the other two p'ts of my land I give to my elder sonne Richard, and to his heires forever, and if he dy without an heir, then I giue yt to my sonne Robert, and to his beires forever. For my son Richard my mynd is that the Cattell I have formerly giuen him that he shall enjoy. To my daughter Sarah, besids the Cattell I formerly haue giuen her, my will is that my wife shall pay her twenty pounds to yeres after my death. To my sonne John Lyman I giue him thirty pownds, to be paid him by my wife, att two & twenty yeres of age, and the hoggs that I formerly haue giuen him, I giue unto my wife, and if he contends w'th her and will not be content my wife should enjoy the hoggs, then yt is my will that shee should not pay him the thirty pownds. To my sonne Robert, I giue twenty fower pownds, to be paid him at twenty-two yeres of age; and to my daughter Fillis, the wife of Willia Hills, I giue tenne shillings; and I make my wife sole executrix to this my will.

Dated the 22d of Aprill, 1640.

The two p'ts of my land and howse I giue to Richard Lyman my sonne; the reson of writeing this is because the word howse was not formerly expressed.   RICHARD LYMAN.

Read, sealed and del'd
  in the p'sents of us,
    Tho. Bull, John Moodie,
    Andrew Bacon.   July 24th.

The wydow Lymans myud is that her sonne Richard Lyman should performe her husbands will, and that her sonne Robert should liue wth him till he be twenty two yeres of age, and then shee giues Robert Lyman the third p^{rte} of the howsen & grounds, & for p^{rfor}mance of her husbands will shee giues Richard all her moueable goods both wthout the howse and w^{t..}in, only her wearing cloathes, and some of her lining shee will dispose of.

JOHN MOODY,
ANDREW BACON.

A Inuentory of the goods of Richard Lyman, deceased, made the VIth of Septeber, 1641.

Imp^{ra}. A Cow & a Cow calfe..........................	£8. 10. 00
Item, a heifer of a yere & half old....	4. 00. 00
It: a bull, 4*l*. 10*s*.; It: a goate & 2 kids, 1*l*. 13*s*..,..............	[6. 03. 00
It: 8 hoggs and halfe a sowe, & the pewtre,.................	10. 00. 00
It: one acre of mislin (a mixture of wheat and rye),	3. 10. 00
It: an acre of summer wheat, 2^l, 10^s.; an acre of oats, 2^l,......	4. 10. 00
It: 3 roods of pease and barly,.............................	1. 10. 00
It: 5 acres of Indian Corne,..............................	8. 15. 00
It: for squared tymber, planke & board,..................	1. 05. 00
It: a cart & plow & tacklin belonging to them,..............	1. 08. 06
It: a Tabell, forms & chaires, 8^s; It: a Cubbard, 15^s	[1. 03. 00
It: 4 chests, a trunke, a old one,.......................	0 18. 06
It: 2 beare vessells, 5*s*.; It: 4 old firkins, 3^s, ...	[0. 08. 00
It: 1 payle & a wooden platter, 2*s*.; an old byble, 2^s, 6^d.......	[0. 04. 06
It: 3 kettells, 2 skillitts, and old brasse pot,...............	2. 04. 00
It: 2 brass pans and a baking pan,........................	0. 12. 00
It: a pestell, a mortar and old kettell,...................	0. 06. 06
It: 4 platters, 2 cansticks, drinking pott wth some other smale pieces of pewter,................................	1. 02. 00
It: a warming pann, a chaffin dish & pewtre botell,.	0. 09. 00
It: 2 frying pans, 3 Iron potts,..........................	1. 00. 00
It: a cob iron, a gridiron, a trammel, a fire pan, doggs & some other old iron,.......	0. 11. 00
It: 2 fier locke pieces, a sowrd and belt,..................	2. 03. 00
It: a sacke and wool,....................................	0. 08. 00
It: 2 bedds and bowlsters & pillowes,...	6 00. 00
It: 3 Couerlids, 4 blankets, 3 straw bedds, ...	4. 08. 00
It: 8 Curtens, 1*l*.; 3 bedsteds, 6*s*.; Tewed¹ skins, 8*s*.,..........	[1. 14. 00
It: 2 Wheels, 9 p^{re} sheets & one odd one,.................	3. 13. 08
It: 4 table cloathes and a dossen and halfe napkins,..........	1. 09. 00
It: 7 pillobers and 2 other smale peeces of linnen,......	0. 13. 06
It: a coate, Jergen, 2 dubletts, & a pre of breeches,...........	1. 10. 00
It: 2 sythes wth their tacklin, 2 ladders,...................	0. 12. 00
It: a churne & meat in y^t., 4 howes,......................	0. 16. 00
It: 2 wedges, 2 betel rings, 2 sawes,......................	0. 16. 00
It: a broad axe, 2 narrow axes, wimbell and chisells,........	0. 11. 00
It: a powdering trofe,...................................	0. 01. 00

Some is 83^l. 16^s. 2^d

JOHN MOODIE.
ANDREW BACON.
JOHN BARNARD.

¹*Tewed* or *tawed*, l. e., dressed white.

" Probate Court this 27th of Jan. 1642.

" The will and inventory of Richard Lyman deceased, is brought into court.   John Moody makes oath that it is the last will of said Richard ; and also the noate then brought in is the noate of the widow Lyman deceased.   The several parties present at the presenting of said will agree that John Lyman if he live, will be 22 years in Sept. 16, 1645; Robert Lyman 22 in Sept., 1651."

From the death of their father until their settlement in Northampton, little is known respecting the sons of Richard[1], Richard[2], John and Robert. They were taxed A.D. 1655, in Hartford, in a rate assessed to build a mill.   They probably removed the same year to Northampton, where, in December of this year, Richard was chosen one of the selectmen.   He sold his father's household at Hartford in 1660. He and his brother, John, were m. before their removal to Northampton.

Richard[2] m. Hepzibah, daughter of Thomas Ford of Windsor. She was sister of the wife of Elder John Strong of Dorchester, Windsor and Northampton, the patriarch of the Strongs, whose genealogy has recently been published in two large volumes.   Her 2d husband was John Marsh of Hadley, Mass.   Richard resided some time in Windsor, owned land there, and occupied some of the land of his father Ford " in East Windsor near the Hartford line."   He appears to have been a man of decided character and influence.   Immediately on his removal to Northampton he was appointed one of the first selectmen chosen in that place, and through his short life was engaged in public business.   He died June 3d, 1662.

Children of Richard and Hepzibah Lyman, Third Generation .

11   1 Hepzibah, b. at Windsor; m. 6 Nov., 1662, Joseph Dewey.
12   2 Sarah, m. 1666, John Marsh, Jr.
13   3 Richard, removed to Lebanon, Ct., from Northampton; b. in Windsor, Ct.
14   4 Thomas, removed to Durham, Ct.
15   5 Eliza, m. 20 Aug., 1672, Joshua Pomeroy.
⁓16   6 John, settled in Hockanum, Hadley.
17   7 Joanna, b. at Northampton, 1658.
18   8 Hannah, b. 1660; m. 20 June, 1677, Job Pomeroy.

⁓ John[2], known as Lieut. Lyman, b. in High Ongar, Sept., 1623, came to New England with his father, m. Dorcas, dau. of John Plumb, of Branford, Conn. 1654, settled in Northampton, Mass., where he resided until his death,

20 Aug., 1690, at the age of 67. Lieut. John Lyman was in command of the Northampton soldiers, in the famous Falls fight above Deerfield, May 18, 1676. The American House, which was burnt a few years since in Northampton, stood in front of his house lot. His epitaph in Northampton, the *fifth* in the collection of Hopkins, Bridgman & Co., is given as an example of the rude simplicity of the times ·

LIVtENAN
iOHN LIMAN
AGED 66 yER
DyED AVGst
the 20th 1690

Children, Third Generation:

19 1 Elizabeth, b. at Branford, Nov. 6, 1655.
20 2 Sarah, b. at Northampton, Nov. 11, 1658; m. Samuel Wright.
21 3 John, Lieut., b. at......Aug. 1, 1660; lived at South Farms; died Nov. 8, 1740, aged 80 years.
22 4 Moses, b. Feb. 20, 1663; died Feb. 25, 1701.
23 5 Dorothy, b. June 8, 1665; m. Jabez Bracket, Wallingford, Ct.
24 6 Mary, b. Jan. 2, 1668; m. Samuel Dwight, Northampton.
25 7 Experience, b. Jan. 8, 1670, died in infancy.
26 8 Joseph, b. Feb. 17, 1671; died 1692.
27 9 Benjamin, b. Aug., 1674; m. 1698, Thankful, dau. of Medad Pomeroy, died Oct. 14, 1723.
28 10 Caleb, b. Sept. 2, 1678; d. at Weston, Mass., Nov. 17, 1742, leaving no children.

28. Dea. Caleb Lyman[5], Esq., son of John, and grandson of Richard,[1] was born at Northampton, Sept. 2d, or 3d, 1678, and resided in Boston. He was one of thirteen from the Old North Church who organized the New North Church of that city and was one of the first deacons of the New Church. This enterprise was begun in 1712. Its original families were " substantial mechanics " who built a church of small dimensions as the record is " without the assistance of the more wealthy part of the community, excepting what they derived from their prayers and their good wishes." The church was dedicated May 5, 1714. It was a custom of the churches of New England then publicly to ordain both ruling elders and deacons. The New England version of the Psalms was continued in use in this church until 1755. It was then changed for Tate and Brady's version; not long after this the practice of reading and singing the psalms line by line, alternately, was abolished or discontinued. These facts, given in *Drake's History of Boston*, are presented

as a part of the record of those scenes in which our venerable ancestor was a prominent actor.

Deacon Lyman died at Weston, Mass., Nov. 17, 1742, in the 65th year of his age after an illness of twelve weeks. A sermon was preached on the occasion by the Rev. William Williams of that place, a distinguished preacher, whose praise was in all the churches in the eastern part of the state. Of this sermon a copy is still extant from which the following extracts are taken. After characterizing him as " a kind, tender and most loving husband, of a sweet, pleasant and cheerful temper, and an amiable pattern of the virtues of the married state — good and useful in all the relations which he sustained both in church and state," the preacher proceeds :

" Having used the *Office of a Deacon* well, he was, many Years since with other pious and worthy Brethren, chosen to assist the *Pastors* of that Church in their watching over and *regulating the Flock*, in which Service I am well informed he was greatly assisting, by his prudent Care, *Inspection and Vigilance*, his kind *visiting* the sick and afflicted, warning and rebuking *the unruly and disorderly*. He was a very *ministerial* Man, honoring and befriending upon all Occasions, his *spiritual* Guides, who greatly loved him and heartily bewailed the Breach, made upon them.

" In his military Capacity he was a Man of firm Courage and Resolution, of which he gave early Proofs ; of *steady* Loyalty, a Lover of good Order and military Accomplishments.

" As a Justice of the Peace, he was concerned and studious to suppress Vice and Profaneness, and to promote Order, Righteousness and Peace.

" He was a kind, courteous and loving Neighbor, a faithful and obliging Friend, a prudent Peace-Maker, a Hater of Strife and Division.

" As through his Industry, Frugality and honest Dealing he had acquired a considerable outward Estate, so he was ready to improve it for the Good of others, *willing to distribute, ready to communicate,* very courteous and hospitable in his House where many, especially Ministers of Christ, have been often entertained and refreshed."

" In his lingering Illness his usual Reply to Inquiries of his Health was ' Waiting upon God ;' ' As God wills.' A short time before his Death, when his Wife wished him a good Night, he replied, I wish you a comfortable Repose, and when you wake may your Thoughts be of God and

Christ and Heaven, may your Heart be filled with the Love of God, and the Joys of refreshing Rest, and may God bring you to his heavenly Kingdom. Amen." He died childless and his lineage became extinct at his decease.

He left a legacy of 500 pounds for the use of the pastors of the church and their widows.

Robert, Lyman youngest son of Richard[1], is reputed to have been a sportsman, devoting much time to fishing, hunting, trapping, etc. Roberts' Hill and Roberts' Meadow in Northampton are said to have taken their names from him as being his favorite place of resort. From public records it appears that he discovered the lead mines of West-hampton.

He was one of the original purchasers and proprietors of the tract of land now occupied by the city of Newark, N. J., as is indicated by the following extracts from the early records of that place, kindly furnished by S. H. Congar, Esq., a distinguished antiquary of Newark.

On June 24, 1667, forty-one of the then present inhabitants, among whom was Robert Lyman, subscribed "with their own hand unto the two fundamental agreements, together with twenty-three of the party from Branford. On the principles of these agreements, our town on Pesayak river was to be governed." The settlers of 1666, 1667, thus uniting, proceeded to make "a sure list" of every man's estate. Robert Lyman was set down at £285, or with a deduction of one-third made to every man £190. May 7, 1668, the common fence was proportioned to every man's estate and lands within the same. Robert Limon has 44 rods.—Jan. 1, 1669, '70, Robert Limon in the division of salt meadow lot, drew No. 26.—Feb. 21, 1670–1, at a second division of salt meadow he drew No. 29.—May 26, 1673, "after due preparation and solemnization for it," the town agreed to draw their lots in a second division of upland, Robert Limon had lot 31. Feb. 6, 1677–8, another proportioning of the fence was made and one rod of fence was required for two acres, one rood, and twenty poles of land. Robert Limen of this fence had 3 rods and 3 feet. In Oct., 1681, another division of the fence was made, but in this his name does not appear. In 1684, from a deed on record in the office of the secretary of state at Trenton, it appears that Robert Lymon of Massachusetts sold lands in Newark to Jasper Crane. In August, 1675, 107$\frac{1}{2}$ acres were surveyed for Robert Lymon, in seven parcels, home lot, upland, and meadow, as described in the record of surveys, for Newark, and on these acres at a *half-penny per acre* there is now due, if unpaid to the lords proprietors or their heirs, a sum they will never get.

" Robert was also a proprietor of Orange, and the heights of the Watchung mountain, then a rich champagne country peopled with deer, elk and bears, and other creatures with many a fair rising, and prospects all green and verdant." A city of beautiful and princely villas. This investment of Robert could not have been large, for the whole tract was received July 11, 1667, in exchange for " a few handfuls of gunpowder, and some lead, axes, breeches, blankets, guns, kettles, etc. Subsequently the whole slope of the Watchung on the Orange side was purchased for " 2 *guns, 3 coats and 13 cans of rum."*

Milford, Guilford, Brandford and New Haven, in Connecticut, contributed their portion of the people who were to go into this land of " many fair rising forests and meadows," and " be of one heart and consent with God's blessing in endeavoring to carry on other spiritual concernments, as well as their civil and town affairs according to God and godly government."

None of the Connecticut emigrants were allowed to vote or hold office in the new colony, unless they were " members of some or other of the Congregational churches," and it was many years before this sectarian restriction was removed. But then, these people and their descendants have made a good record. Wherever the page of American history is brightest — there the names of these sturdy people reappear. This little group that nestled so harmoniously down in the Orange valley, and whose log huts dotted the romantic slope of Watchung mountain has sent out scores and hundreds to fill the highest places in the various departments of science and art, at the bar, in the pulpit, in the medical profession, in literature, in the senate, in colleges; they have been the pioneers of trade, merchant princes, builders of cities, the defenders of their country through every war, stern patriots — the very *" vim "* of the nation.

Those who took up land on the mountain were Robert Lyman, Samuel Swayne and John Baldwin, 1675; Thomas Johnson, John Ward, Anthony Oliff, Joseph Harrison, 1679. Matthew Williams at the time occupied a tract on on the mountain, and afterwards exchanged some Newark property with the heirs of George Day for the tract on

which he fixed his residence, and which now bears the name
of Williamsville.

In May 20, 1684, Robert Lyman and Hepzibah his wife,
of Northampton, Mass., sold to Jasper Crane for £8 14s. 3d.
44 acres bounded on the north-west of the mountain. The
original document is still extant by which Robert appoints
Sarah Davis, the widow of "his cousin John Ward,"
to settle his affairs in Newark, he being in Northampton;
and that she accomplished the business satisfactorily.

The signature of Robert is associated with others of Northampton, in an effort to restrain and suppress intemperance
by preventing the introduction of ardent spirits and cider
into the town.   In the latter part of life he became reduced
in property, and appears to have been subject to some
mental aberrations which subjected his family to peculiar
trials.   In March, 1691, representations of the state of his
family were made to the county court, in which he is described as being under some "distemperature," and unable
to manage his affairs.   Similar representations were repeatedly made, and the family committed to the care of the
selectmen of the town.   There is no authentic record of
Robert's death.   The tradition in Northampton is that he
became a victim to bis roving, sporting habits, and was found
in the forest frozen where he had fallen in pursuit of his
game.   He m. Hepzibah Bascom.

Children, Third Generation:

29	1	Sarah, b. at Northampton,	Oct. 13, 1663, d. in N. unmarried.
30	2	John,	"	"	Dec. 5, 1664.
31	3	Thomas,	"	"	Dec. 23, 1666.
32	4	Thankful,	"	Jan. 13, 1671, d. early.
33	5	Thankful,	"	"	Oct. 10, 1672.
34	6	Hepzibah,	"	"	Feb. 15, 1674, d. in N. unmarried.
35	7	Preserved,	"	"	April, 1676, m. J. Ellison.
36	8	Wait,	"	"	April 11, 1678, d. May 17, 1697.
37	9	Experience,	"	1679.

Thankful, m. Daniel Hall, the ancestor of Lyman Hall,
Gov. of Georgia, and one of the signers of the Declaration
of Independence.

Experience, m. Henry Cook, of Wallingford. Preserved
is supposed to have m. John Ellison, of Newark, from
whom have descended the Vanderpools, and other distinguished families, in New Jersey. The sons of Robert
appear to have left no issue, and the lineage of Robert, in
the male line at their death, became extinct.

The settlement of Northampton commenced in 1654.

In May 6, 1653, a number of persons petitioned the General Court of Massachusetts to grant them liberty to possess, plant and inhabit this place on the Connectiquot river, called Nonotuck, as their own inheritance; representing that it was a place "suitable to erect a town for the furtherance of the public weal and the propagation of the gospel." Twenty-five families manifested a desire to settle there, "many of whom were of considerable quality for estates, and fit matter for a church." "Townsmen," selectmen, were chosen 1656. In March 18, 1657, the people voted to employ an agent to obtain a minister, and to devise means to prevent the excess of liquors used.

Nonotuck the Indian name for Northampton, including the four Hamptons, was purchased in 1653, by John Pynchon, Esq., for the original planters, 20 in number, from *Wawhillowa, Nenessehalant, Nassicohee,* and four others styled "the chief and proper owners, who all bargained for themselves and the other owners, by their consent." The consideration for the purchase was, "one hundred fathoms of wampum by tale, and ten coats, besides some small gifts in hand paid to the sachems and owners; and also for ploughing up 16 acres of land on the east side of *Quonnecuticut* river the ensuing summer." Sept. 28, 1658, the sachem Umpauchila complained to the commissioners that he had not received so much as he expected. He was accordingly paid an additional sum, and he, by a new deed, released his title to the township.

The inhabitants lived in peace with the Indians 22 years until the famous war with Philip.

The original purchase extended 10 miles on the river and 10 westward, equal to 100 square miles, and included the 4 Hamptons.

The old family homestead, on which Richard settled, was adjacent to the original farm of the Rev. Ebenezer Mather, the first minister of Northampton. This included the ground now occupied by the Shop Row, on the south side of Main street. It appears to have included the homestead owned and occupied by Dr. Hunt a half century since, and the Shop Row, eastward, with the grounds of Gov. Caleb Strong.

The original homestead of Richard became the property of his 2d son John, of his son Benjamin, of his son Joseph, of his son Elisha and of his son Theodore, who sold it in

1827, after it had been in the possession of the family 172 years, through six generations.

The first Moses, grandson of Richard[1] and son of John[2], bought one-half of the Mather farm, and his son, Capt. Moses, bought the other half. The whole became the property of Seth, the 9th child of Capt. Moses. He was unfortunate in business and sold in several parcels the old homestead for the payment of his debts, some time before 1790, and after it had been in possession of the family about 100 years. This farm in 1842, had upon it three dwelling houses, besides the stores and shops in Shop Row, 15 or 20 rods in extent.

The property of Judge Hinckley and of the Hon. Theodore Strong, is said to have been a part of this farm.

Northampton being from the beginning the home of the Lyman family, the cradle from which they have arisen to overrun the whole land, some early notices of them are inserted from the records of the town, illustrative at once of their influence and of the customs of these olden times :

In May, 1654 — was the petition for the laying out of Nonatuck — and yet as early as " Feb. 19, 1660, seven persons were appointed to transcribe the *old records.*" Among these was Richard Lyman.

At a town meeting in 1657 —" It was then voted and agreed that William Holton is desired to solicit the general court & to act and propound several cases that concern the town."—1 — 2 — & 3 to " desire advice what course to take about the preventing of excess in liquors in coming to our town, & of cider; all those present at the making this note, did promise to consent to it, in case the major part of the inhabitants of the town do consent to it. " 25 names were given, & among them that of Robert Lyman.

1658, Jan. 4—" 80 acres of land laid out for the ministry." A committee of 5 to do it, Richard Lyman was second. Jan. 10 — Richard Lyman was one of the three select men, and in March, appointed as " Commissioner to end small causes."

1660, May 15 — Mistake about land upon the "pine plain "— which was drawn for Robert Lyman, also Richard Lyman's portion helped to make up the mistake.

Other commissions include the names of Richard and John Lyman.

1661 — John Lyman chosen constable — a committee to lay out a highway between Robert Lyman and Thomas Hanchett's lots.

1666 — John first mentioned as *Ensign* Lyman.

1669 — Ensign John Lyman chosen surveyor.

1669, April 24—Ensign J. L., appointed Com^{er} to take general list, and carry to Springfield — also on other committees.

1671, Dec. 10th — Satisfaction of Richard Lyman's heirs for damages done by digging trench.

1675 — John Lyman, selectman.

1669, July 27—vote, " that Robert Lyman and any other of the inhabitants of this town, and having common rights in the town, shall have liberty to try to open any place within our bounds, and to make use of any sort of mines or minerals, provided they attend law — and it was a full and clear affirmative vote." *Oct^r* 16th, A town meeting about the " lead mine which Robert Lyman found out," vote — The town gave up all their right. The mine described as " lying about 6 miles off on the w. side of the town."

1681 — Grant to the Mine Company — " to their heirs or assigns "—no further mention of Robert Lyman. On a motion of Richard and Thomas Lyman and others a " liberty to set up Saw mill."

1682 — " John Lyman son of Richard," mentioned in fence regulations.

1688 — Thomas Lyman one of two surveyors of highways.

1690 — Thomas Lyman chosen Select man.

1691, April 24th — Persons to whom homesteads of one acre were granted includes Thomas Lyman.

1692 — John Lyman is mentioned with nine persons dissenting from vote for schoolmaster £40.

1707 — In May, homestead granted to John Lyman, *shoemaker*, and Thomas Lyman.

1702 — To Ensign John Lyman — two home lots for his two eldest sons.

1710 — In fence division land in the meadows to be fenced; Ens^n John L.'s heirs mentioned.

1713 — Lieu^t John L., 41 acres — John L., shoemaker, 16 — Benj. L., 40 — Moses L., 29.

1720 — Plank seats to be made pews ; Benj. Lyman on the committee to build pews. Benjn L., trustee to manage for the town a fund.

5

1724 — Trustee in room of Benj[n] Lyman, deceased.

1733 — Gideon Lyman and Daniel King chosen constables.

1735 — Moses Lyman fence viewer — also chosen (1736) to see to repairs of a bridge by Hurlburt's Mill.

1736–7 — John Lyman, jr., tithing man — Elias Lyman[z], field driver.

1738 — Benj. Lyman, tithing man ; Joseph Lyman, surveyor of ways — Zadoc Lyman, field driver; John Lyman chosen one of the fence viewers, and refusing to serve was fined and paid 20 shillings.

1739 — Ens. John L. mentioned — Unknown. Benj. L. surveyor.

1740 — Among the 8 tithing men were Caleb Strong and Gad Lyman — Field viewer, Simon Lyman; Constable, Abner Lyman.

1742 — Gideon Lyman, fence viewer — Noah Lyman, field driver.

. 1743 — Gad Lyman, fence viewer; Abner Lyman, constable.

1744 — Lieu[t] John Lyman, surveyor of ways.

These mentioned as owning in common fields, 1744 :

Cap[t]. Moses L., Joseph L., William L., Daniel L., Elihu L., Medad L., Benj. L., Gideon L., Gad L., Lieu[t]. John L., 39 acres; Abner L., 21 acres.

1746 — Phinehas Lyman, field driver ; Gad Lyman, constable ; Lieu[t]. James and Abner L., fence viewers.

1746–7 — Nathan L., tithing man — Lieut. John, select man.

1750 — L[t]. Gideon Lyman, select man.

1750 — Gideon Lyman, jr., hayward.

1750 — Gad Lyman, surveyor.

1752 — Gideon L., jr., hayward

1753 — Abner L., tithing man.

1754 Jan. — Seth Lyman — a stray heifer taken to fodder — Seth L., hayward.

1754 — Elias Lyman mentioned.

1754 — Gideon L., on committee for dividing lands.

The sumptuary laws enacted to restrain extravagance in dress are an institution illustrative of the spirit of the times. These laws ordered " that persons whose estates did not exceed 200 pounds, and those dependent upon them, should not wear gold or silver lace, gold or silver buttons, bone lace above 2s. per yard, or silk hoods or scarfs, upon penalty of 10s. for each offense." " At the March court

1676, the jury presented 68 persons from 5 towns in Hampshire, 35 wives and maids, and 30 young men, some for wearing silk and that in a flaunting manner, and others, for long hair, and other extravagances to the offense of sober people."

One of these was Hannah Lyman, of Northampton, 16 years of age, dau. of Richard[2], deceased. The record shows that this young girl possessed an independent, determined will, so characteristic of the Lyman family, flaunting her silks before the court, when arraigned for this very offense. She was prosecuted for wearing silk in a flaunting manner, in an offensive way and garb, not only before, *but when she stood* presented, not only in ordinary, but in extraordinary times; she was fined 10s.

The following racy original phillipic forcibly illustrates the spirit of the times :

" I honour the woman that can honour herselfe with her attire a a good Text alwayes deserves a fair margent ; I am not much offended if I see a trimme far trimmer than shee that wears it ; in a word, whatever Christianity or civility, will allow, I can afford with *London* Measure ; but when I beare a nugiperous gentle dame inquire what dresse the Queen is in this week ; what the nudiustertian fashion of the court; I mean the very newest; with egge to be in it in all haste, whatever it be ; I look at her as the very gizzard of a trifle, the product of a quarter of a cipher, the epitome of nothing, fitter to be kickt, if shee were of a kickable substance, than either honour'd or humour'd. To speak moderately, I truly confesse, it is beyond the ken of my understanding to conceive how those women should have any true grace, or valuable vertue, that have so little wit, as to disfigure themselves with such exotick garbes, as not only dismantles their native lovely lustre, but transclouts them into gant bar-gesse, illshapen, shotten-shell-fish, Egyptian Hyeroglyphicks, or at the best, into French flurts of the pastery, which a proper English woman should scorn with her heels ; it is no marvel they weare drailes on the hinder part of their heads, having nothing as it seems in the forepart, but a few Squirrils' brains to help them frisk from one ill favored fashion to another."—*Simple Cobler of Agawam*, pp 26–27. *Palfrey's Hist.*

It may give a clearer insight into the social and domestic life, in these primitive days to note the current prices of some of the staple articles of sale collected chiefly from the *History of Hadley :* Butter, 6 cents per lb.; beef, $2\frac{2}{3}$; Mutton, 2; flour, $3.50 per bbl.; wheat, 2s. 6d. ; Peas, 2s ; Corn, 1s. 6d. ; oats, 1s. 6d. ; Shad, in 1733, 1 penny ; in 1737 " good fat shad," 2 pence each ; 1767, 100 shad were sold in Hadley, at 1 penny each ; for salmon in Hartford, 1700, 1 penny a pound ; in Northampton 1740, at the same price ;

Horses, 1675 to 1700, 15 to 25 dollars; 1750 to 1775, 7 to 32 dollars. The most valuable horse in the county in 1754, was prized at $66⅔; working oxen, 1680 to 1715, 17 to 28 dollars a yoke; cows, 1700, 6.50 to 9 dollars; 1775, 7 to 11 dollars; fowls, 4 to 6 pence each; eggs, 3 pence a dozen; wild turkeys, 1717; in Northampton, 1s. 4d. each; pigeons from 3 to 6 pence a dozen; venison, 2 to 2½ pence per lb. Choice land, $1.00 an acre, out lots, 25 cents; the salaries of clergymen ranged from 60 to 80 pounds — 150 and 200 dollars, generally paid in produce, *at an advanced price;* marriage fee, 3 shillings — 1692, 25 years later, 4 shillings.

I. BIRTHS OF THE LYMANS IN NORTHAMPTON.

Sarah	11 April, 1654.
John	20 Aug., 1660.
Hannah ...... Richard and Hepzibah...............	8 July, 1660.
Moses. " " "	20 Feb., 1662.
John . Robert and Hepzibah................	5 Dec., 1664.
Dorothy......	4 March, 1665.
Mary..........	2 Jan., 1667.
Experience .. ..,..........	4 Jan., 1668.
Joseph	17 Feb., 1670.
Benjamin....	10 Aug., 1674.
Calah	2 Sept., 1674.
Preserved.... Robert and Hepzibah	April, 1676.
Samuel........ Richard and Elizabeth	April, 1676.
Waitstill....... Robert and Hepzibah...............	14 April, 1678.
Thomas....... Thomas and Ruth.....	13 April, 1679.
Experience .. Robert and Hepzibah	1679.
John..... Richard and Elizabeth...............	6 July, 1680.
Isaac	16 Feb., 1681.
Mindwell .... Peter and Elizabeth	17 April, 1681.
Ebenezer..... Thomas and Ruth....................	17 June, 1682.
Jonathan ..... Richard and Elizabeth ....-1 Jan., 1684.
Elizabeth..... Thomas and Ruth	25 March, 1685.
Richard and Elizabeth	23 March, 1685.
Ann........... Moses and Ann.......................	3 April, 1686.
Noah .... Thomas and Ruth	April, 1687.
Sarah .... John and ———	1688.
Mindwell " "	30 Aug, 1688.
David ... Richard and Elizabeth...............	28 Nov., 1688.
Moses......... son of Moses......................	27 Feb., 1689.
James ... son of Richard	24 Jan., 1690.
Enoch Thomas and Ruth	18 Jan., 1691.
Hannah ...... Moses and Ann.....	2 April, 1692.
John . John and Sarah	26 Jan., 1692.

John	John and Mindwell......................	12 Oct., 1693.
Mercy	Moses and Ann........................	5 Jan., 1694.
Martha........	" "	Sept., 1695.
Abigail	John and Abigail	1 Feb., 1696.
Esther .	John and Mindwell	15 Feb., 1698.
Bethiah	Moses and Ann........................	23 April, 1698.
Nathan........	John and Abigail......................	1 Jan., 1698.
Joseph	Benjamin and Thankful..............	22 Aug., 1699.
Gideon	John and Mindwell	19 March, 1700.
Sarah	Moses and Ann........................	20 Jan., 1700.
Abner	John and Abigail......................	Feb., 1701.
Elias ..	Moses and Ann........................	Feb., 1701.
Job ...	John and Abigail	1 Dec., 1702.
Elizabeth ...	John and Mindwell....................	8 Dec., 1702.
Benjamin.....	Benjamin and Thankful..............	19 Dec., 1702.
Benjamin.....	" " "	4 Jan., 1705.
Joshua	John and Abigail	27 Feb., 1704.
Aaron	Benjamin and Thankful.........	1 April, 1705.
Phineas	John and Mindwell	8 April, 1706.
Nathan	John and Abigail	5 May, 1706.
Eunice........	Benjamin and Thankful..............	6 May, 1707.
Aaron	Thomas and Elizabeth	19 Nov., 1707.
Experience ..	Ebenezer and Experience....,......	17 April, 1708.
Ebenezer.....	" " "	20 Sept., 1709.
Nehemiah ...	John and Mindwell.	15 April, 1710.
Stephen	Ebenezer and Experience............	14 Aug., 1711.
Experience ..	" " "	25 Dec., 1712.
Moses	Moses and Mindwell...................	2 Oct., 1713.
Mindwell.....	Ebenezer and Experience............	13 July, 1714.
Susannah ...	Benjamin and Thankful.............	18 July, 1714.
William......	" " "	12 Dec., 1715.
Elias	Moses and Mindwell...................	30 Sept., 1715.
John	Ebenezer and Experience............	9 April, 1717.
Theodore.....	Moses and Mindwell	22 April, 1717.
Daniel........	Benjamin and Thankful..............	18 April, 1718.
Phebe..	" " "	20 Aug., 1719.
Hannah	Benjamin and Thankful.............	14 July, 1719.
Elisha........	" " "................	10 July, 1720.
Noah.	Moses and Mindwell...................	25 May, 1722.
Medad........	Benjamin and Thankful..............	26 March, 1722.
John..........	John and Abigail,......................	7 Oct., 1723.
Aaron.........	Benjamin and Mary...............	8 Aug., 1727.
Lydia	Abner and Lydia.	17 Aug., 1727.
Eunice	Joseph and Abigail.........	30 May, 1728.
Mary..........	" " "	7 Sept., 1729.
Beulah........	Abner and Lydia......................	17 Aug., 1729.
Mary.	Benjamin and Mary..................	22 Feb., 1730.
Joseph	Joseph and Abigail..................	4 May, 1737.
Elizabeth.....	Abner and Lydia.............	24 Nov., 1731.

Hannah.	Moses and Mindwell....................	31 March, 1731.
Eleazer.......	Joseph and Abigail....................	18 May, 1733.
Eleazer.......	John and Abigail....................	24 Oct., 1735.
Lemuel.......	Benjamin and Mary	17 Aug., 1735.
Leanor	Joseph and Abigail.....:..........	24 Sept., 1737.
Rachel........	Abner and Sarah....................	23 Aug.,1738.
Oliver..........	Gad and Thankful....................	1 April, 1739.
Sarah	Abner and Sarah....................	11 April, 1740.
Naomi........	Gad and Hester....................	17 June, 1740.
Jerusha......	Gad and Thankful....................	16 Nov., 1740.
Elias..........	Elias and Sarah....................	16 Aug., 1740.
Thankful.....	Gad and Thankful....................	9 Jan., 1742-3.
Joel...........	Elias and Hannah....................	16 July, 1742.
Elizabeth.....	Elias and Hannah....................	21 Sept., 1744.
Timothy	Gad and Thankful....................	4 July, 1745.
Abner ..	Abner and Sarah....................	10 Aug., 1746.
Rachel .	William and Rachel.................	7 Aug., 1747.
Eunice	Gad and Thankful	27 May, 1747.
Tryphena ...	" " "	30 April, 1749.
John	John, Jr., and Hannah	8 Sept., 1750.
Rufus.........	John and Hannah	2 Dec., 1751.
Rachel........	William and Jemima.................	22 Nov., 1752.
Hannah	John and Hannah....................	28 Nov., 1754.
Seth	Seth and Catharine....................	12 Sept., 1755.
Hannah	Benjamin and Hannah...............	27 Aug., 1756.
Giles	Seth and Catharine....................	21 Nov., 1757.
Hannah	Elias and Hannah....................	2 March, 1757.
Cornelius.....	William and Jemima.................	7 Jan., 1758.
Phebe	John and Hannah....................	5 Jan., 1759.
Asahel........	William and Jemima.................	8 Feb., 1760.
Erastus	Joseph, Jr. and Mary....................	29 Feb., 1760-1.
Jemina....	William and Jemima	5 Feb., 1761.
Solomon .	Seth and Catharine....................	10 Feb., 1760.
Theodocia	" " "	24 Feb., 1762.
Abigail ..	Oliver and Eleanor....................	18 April, 1762.
Charlotte	" " "	22 Nov., 1763.
Levi	William and Jemima	30 Jan., 1763.
Dorcas	John and Hannah	2 Feb., 1763.
Mehitable ...	" " "	17 Nov., 1764.
Samuel	William and Jemima	12 Jan., 1765.
Susannah ...	John and Hannah	7 July, 1767.
Gad	Oliver and Eleanor......	23 Aug., 1766.
Oliver	" " "	31 May, 1768.
Micah Jones	Eliab and Abigail....................	17 Oct., 1767.
Joseph	Joseph and Mary	22 Oct., 1767.
Submit........	William and Jemima....................	9 Dec., 1767.
Joseph	Abner and Lydia	22 Oct., 1767.
Jerusha	John and Hannah....................	16 Dec., 1768.
Persis........	" " "	19 April, 1771.

Elisha	Elisha and Abigail......................	26 Jan., 1770.
Lewis	" " "	8 June, 1772.
Lydia	" " "	7 Jan., 1775.
Susan	" " "	10 Feb., 1780.
Abigail	" " "	30 Dec. 1782.
Robert	Levi and Lucretia......................	5 April, 1790
Richard	" " "	10 March, 1792.
Clarissa	" " "	10 Jan. 1794.
Lucretia......	" " "	1 Sept., 1795.
Helen........,	William and Jerusha....	March, 1798.
Dwight	" " "	20 Nov., 1795.
Fanny Fowler	Joseph, Jr., and Betsey	3 Aug., 1797.
Elizabeth ...	Levi and Lucretia,......................	19 Aug., 1799.
Elizabeth ...	Joseph and Elizabeth	16 Oct., 1792.
Edwin Dwight	Joseph & Elizabeth Fowler	20 Nov., 1795.
Frances Fowler	" " "	31 Aug., 1797.
Joseph Warren	Samuel and Mary	Jan., 1799.
Samuel Fowler	" " "	3 May, 1799.
John	" " "	31 July, 1801.
Abigail Brocket	Erastus and Abigail	19 Sept. 1801.
Mary	" " "	27 March, 1802.
Jane	" " "	22 April, 1804.

II. MARRIAGES OF LYMANS IN NORTHAMPTON.

David Burt...	Mary Holton	18 Nov., 16 ...
John King.........	Sarah Holton	18 Nov , 1656.
Robert	Hepzebah Bascom.................	15 Nov., 1662.
Hepzebah	John Marsh	7 Oct., 1664.
Sarah	John Marsh	28 Nov., 1666.
Elizabeth	Joshua Pomeroy.................	22 May, 1672.
Richard	Elizabeth Cole.................	26 May, 1675.
Thomas	Ruth (Holton) [Baker]........	1678.
Dorothy.............	Jabez Brackett	2 Nov., 1691.
Benjamin...........	Thankful Pomeroy.	27 Oct., 1698.
Thomas	Elizabeth Parsons....	25 Dec., 1706.
Ebenezer...........	Experience Pimpy	2 Jan., 1706–7.
Ann	Jonathan Rush	11 Dec., 1707.
Moses...............	Mindwell Sheldon	18 Dec., 1712.
James................	Ann Root	31 Dec., 1712.
Martha....	Ebenezer Boshlin..............	1 Dec., 1715
Mary	Samuel Dwight	18 Jan., 1719.
Abigail.	William Boshlin.................	22 Dec., 1720.
Gideon	Esther Strong..	25 Dec., 1723.
Isaac	Thankful Winchell..............	4 Mar. 1723–4.
Esther	Benj. Talcott......................	26 Aug., 1724.
Nathan..	Sarah Webb	12 July, 1733.
Hanna ..	Nathaniel Dwight...............	1734–5.

Phebe.	Caleb Strong......	25 Nov., 1736.
Gad ...	Franklin Pomeroy............	22 June, 1738.
Elias................	Anna Phelps.....................	6 July, 1738.
Abner	Sarah Miller	3 May, 1739.
Luke .	Susannah Hunt..................	21 Jan., 1780
Abigail	Ephraim Worcester..............	2 Feb., 1780.
.Giles..	Phebe Lyman ....·......	24 Feb., 1780.
Theodocia............	Israel Barnhard..................	21 Nov., 1782.
Thomas	Dolly Clark...................... . .	28 Oct., 1784.
Charlotte	Zenas Clark	14 June, 1785.
Justin	Datty Clapp	19 June, 1786.
Lois	Joseph Dewey.....................	8 Jan., 1788.
Levi	Lucretia...........................	Sept., 1789.
John, Jr.,............	Cynthia Dwight..................	4 June, 1789.
Susannah	Obed Averil	25 Feb., 1790.
Betsy	James Molochai, of Goshen...	18 Feb., 1790.
Dorcas	Israel Clark	28 Jan., 1790.
Chloe.................	Daniel Knight	4 Nov., 1791.
Joel	Achsah Parsons...................	29 Dec., 1791.
John, Jr.	Sarah Baker......................	4 July, 1793.
Micah	Elizabeth Sheldon..............	19 Jan , 1794.
Hannah..............	James Breckenbridge	10 Feb., 1795.
Sylvester..	Nancy Clapp	30 Aug., 1797.
Justus	Nancy Covey......................	8 March, 1798.

III. DEATHS OF LYMANS IN NORTHAMPTON.

Johanna Lyman...	....	1 Jan., 1659.
Richard	....	3 June, 1662.
Sarah	....	12 Oct., 1663.
Experience	daughter of John	16 March, 1669.
Bethiah.............	....	14 Nov., 1686.
Kezrah.............	.... -	24 Nov., 1686.
Esther...............	....	4 June, 1689.
Samuel.............	....	12 April, 1690.
Ensign John........	....	20 Aug., 1690.
Hepzibah	....	20 Sept., 1690.
Joseph	....	18 Feb., 1691.
Moses	....	28 Feb , 1691.
Joseph.............	....	18 Feb., 1692.
Sarah	....	17 July, 1694.
Martha.............	....	12 Aug., 1694.
Abigail.............	....	15 April, 1696.
Wait...............	....	17 May, 1697.
Sarah	....	20 Feb., 1700.
Nathan.............	....	11 April, 1700.
Moses..	....	28 Feb., 1701.
Benjamin...........	son of Joseph	22 Jan., 1702.

Job....		14 Jan., 1703.
Hannah		10 Nov., 1703.
Elias		16 Nov., 1703.
Experience		30 Sept., 1708.
Stephen..	son of Ebenezer	22 Feb., 1712.
Abigail..	wife of John	24 Nov., 1714.
Eunice ..	daughter of Benjamin	1 June, 1720.
Lemuel		Feb., 1722.
Lieut. Benjamin...		14 Oct., 1723.
Dorcas	wife of Lieut. John.	21 April, 1725.
John		13 Oct., 1727.
Lydia		Aug 22, 1730.
Experience		20 Nov., 1730.
Lydia	wife of Abraham	2 Dec., 1731.
Lemuel		14 Feb., 1732.
Eleanor	dau. of Joseph	1 June, 1733.
Mindwell.	wife of Lieut. John	8 April, 1735.
Esther	wife of Gideon	22 June, 1740.
Lieut. John		8 Nov., 1740.
Abigail & Hannah	daus. of John, in burning house	8 Dec., 1742.
Sarah	dau. of Asahel	16 Dec., 1742.
Solomon	son of Solomon	27 Jan., 1746.
Rachel	wife of Lieut. William	11 Aug., 1746.
Rachel	dau. of William	18 Aug., 1746.
Elias	son of Elias	24 Nov., 1748.
——	ch. of Benjamin	Jan., 1749.
——	wife of John	Sept., 1750.
Margaretta		28 July, 1752.
Martha	d. of Lieut. Gideon	1 Feb., 1753.
Joshua		4 Oct., 1753.
Noah		12 May, 1754.
——	d. of Seth	28 Sept., 1754.
——		14 Oct., 1754.
Zadock		30 March, 1755.
——	ch. of Benjamin	24 Sept., 1756.
——	wife of Abner	Dec., 1757.
——	ch. of Joseph	19 Nov., 1758.
——	ch. of Joseph	1760.
Asahel	ch. of Capt. William.	9 Nov., 1760.
——	ch. of Gideon	24 March, 1762.
——	Capt. Moses	1 May, 1762.
Benjamin		Jan., 1762.
Elizabeth....	dau. Elias	17 April, 1763.
Joseph		20 Nov. 1763.
——	wife Capt. John	27 July, 1764.
——	ch. of David	30 May, 1765.
——	ch. of David	13 Dec. 1768.
——	ch. of Elisha	25 Sept., 1769.
Capt. James		19 Aug., 1770.
——	ch. of John	

Capt. James........	wife of Capt. T. James.........	15 July, 1773.
Capt. William	....	12 March, or Nov., 1774.
Abner	....	·19 Nov., 1774.
Jerusha	dau. of John	25 Sept., 1774.
Lieut. Gideon	....	3 April, 1775.
———...............	ch. of David	15 April, 1775.
Abigail.............	wife of Joseph	1 May, 1776
———............... ...	ch. of David	1776.
Eleaner	....	1777.
Hannah Allen	wife of Elias.....................	Oct., 1777.
———......	ch. of Joel.......................	12 Sept., 1778
Mindwell..........	w. of Capt. Moses	25 May, 1780.
———...	ch of Abner	1781.
Mary	widow.............................	17 Aug , 1782.
Jemima	....	26 Feb., 1785.
Jonathan	....	28 March, 1786.
———.........	ch. of Elisha	31 July, 1787.
Elias	....	7 April, 1790.
———............... ...	wife of John, Jr., ...1 or	28 May, 1790.
Catharine	widow of Gideon..................	15 March, 1791.
Roxana	dau. of Jonathan	19 March, 1793.
John	son of John	4 Nov., 1797.
Elisha	son of Joseph and Abigail......	13 Aug., 1798.

Two of the sons of Richard[1], Richard[2], and John[2], had each three sons who had issue of several sons; and from these six grandsons of Richard[1] have descended a numerous posterity which have overspread the land. The three grandsons, sons of Richard[2], are Richard[3], Thomas[3]. and John[3]. The three sons of John[2] are John[3], Moses[3] and Benjamin[3]. Richard[3] represents the Lymans in Lebanon, Conn. Thomas[3], the Lymans in Durham, in the same state; the two Johns[3] had their habitat chiefly in Northampton, South Farms and Hockanum, Moses is represented by the Lymans in Goshen and Salisbury, Conn., and in Southampton and Boston, Mass. East and West Hampton were the primary centres of emigration for the descendants of Benjamin[3], the sixth and last grandson. The descendants of each of these six grandsons will be represented under as many subdivisions or parts in the order of seniority, each constituting one part in the general divisions of this work.

Descendants of Richard³.

I. LINEAGE OF SAMUEL⁴, ELDEST SON OF RICHARD³.

Richard,³ the eldest son of Richard², b. in Windsor, Ct., in 1647, m. in Northampton, May 26,1675, Elizabeth, daughter of John Coles, of Hatfield, Mass., and resided in Northampton until 1696, when he removed to Lebanon, Ct., where some of his descendants have continued to reside until the present time; but others have gone out over all the land. They early emigrated to Vermont: from that state some passed into Canada; others westward took their course; and onward still, as new territories and states have arisen, quite to the Pacific ocean.

Richard was not an original proprietor in the *Five Mile purchase* in Lebanon, which was the beginning of the settlement, but an allotment was deeded to him, which he subdivided to his children, some of whom settled in the town and some in the Crank, now Columbia. Here the father himself lived, and died Nov. 4, 1708. No monument marks his resting place.

Children, Fourth Generation :

1 ɪ Samuel, b. April, 1676.
2 ₂ Richard, b. April, 1678; d. 1745.
3 ₃ John, b. July 6, 1680.
4 ₄ Isaac, b. Feb. 20, 1682, probably.
5 ₅ Lieut. Jonathan, b. Jan. 1, 1684; d. Aug. 11, 1753.
6 ₆ Elizabeth, b. March 25, 1685; m. .... Smith.
7 ₇ David, b. Nov. 28, 1688 ; childless.
8 ₈ Josiah, b. Feb. 6, 1690, d. 1760, aged 70 years; left a son, Josiah ; d. in his 27th year, without issue.
9 ₉ Anne, no date; no record whatever is given of this child. She was born in Lebanon, the others in Northampton. The homestead of Richard ² was sold by his son on his removal to Lebanon, to Preserved Clapp of Northampton.

1 SAMUEL⁴, *Richard³*, *Richard²*, *Richard¹*, m. May 9, 1699, Elizabeth Fowler, who d. Feb. 21, 174⅔. *Lebanon.*

Children, Fifth Generation :

11 ɪ Samuel, b. May 22, 1700.
12 ₂ Jabez, b. Oct. 10, 1702.

13 3 Daniel, b. Feb. 18, 1704–5.
14 4 Hannah, b. June 27, 1707; d. young.
15 5 One d. in infancy nameless.

11 SAMUEL[5], m. in Suffield, Ct., Jan. 13, 172⅔, Elizabeth Smith, who d. Feb. 28, 1751. Samuel d. Feb. 4.
1754.   *Lebanon.*
According to another tradition, or record, the wife of
Samuel[3] was Elizabeth *Fowler*, but the improbability that
the names of the wives of both father and son were the
same, casts suspicion on the supposition, and the records
of Suffield justify us in ascribing to the son Elizabeth
Smith as his wife,   *Lebanon, Ct.*

       Children, Sixth Generation.

16 1 Samuel, b. Nov. 8, 1723; resided in Coventry.
17 2 Ichabod, b. 1724; resided in West Hartford.
18 3 James, b. June 3, 1727.
21 4 Eunice, 1733; 5 Desiah, 1735; 6 Dorcas, 1739. Of these
    daughters nothing is known.

16 SAMUEL[6], m. Nov. 7, 1745, Martha Long, of Suffield,
who d. Jan. 8, 1756, aged 33 years.   *Coventry, Ct.*

       Children, Seventh Generation ·

22 1 Phineas,
23 2 Ozias,   } No dates are given, neither does it appear in
24 3 Asa, b. 1750.   what order these were born.
25 4 Roswell, d. in infancy.
26 5 A dau., m. Nathan Hall of Mansfield, Ct. Samuel[5], d. Feb.
    4, 1754; Elizabeth, his wife, d. Feb. 28, 1751.

23 OZIAS[7], *Samuel[6]*, *Samuel[5]*, *Samuel[4]*, *Richard[3]*, *Richard[2]*, *Richard[1]*, b. about 1746 or 1747; m. Nov. 24, 1774,
Ruth Brown; and d. in Coventry about 1806. He is said
to have been subject to insanity for some time previous to
his decease.   *Coventry, Ct.*

       Children, Eighth Generation:

27 1 Ozias, afterwards Jephtha, b. September 18, 1776; lived in
    Dover, Vt.

       Ch. 9th Gen.: 1 Joel, not married; lives in West Dover,
    Vt. 2 James, m. Lydia Esterllett. 3 Abigail, m. A. Bartlett.
    4 Sarah, m. C. Howard. 5 Cynthia, m. Wm. H. Snow. 6
    Laurana, m. Wm. Walker. 7 Amanda E., m. Martin
    Bartlett. 8 Eliz. P., m. J. W. Cook.

36 2 Persis, b. Sept. 11, 1778; no further record.
37 3 William, b. Aug. 21, 1780, in Toland, Conn.

38 4 Jesse, b. Nov. 4, 1782; lived in Brimfield, Mass.
39 5 Edna, b. April 11, 1785; no record.
40 6 Jemima, b. March 18, 1788; no record.

` 37 WILLIAM⁸, removed, in the year 1800, to Wilmington, Vt., d. 1860. He had nine children, six are deceased, names and ages not given. *Wilmington, Vt.*

Children, Ninth Generation .

43 1 Alvah, b. Jan. 26, 1817; a farmer; m. Sept. 7, 1841, Clarissa L. Winchester, of Marlboro, Vt. Wilmington, Vt.
> *Ch.* 10*th Gen.:* 1 d. in infancy, b. Sept. 30, 1842; d. March 24, 1843. 2 Ellen, b. March 8, 1844; m. Dec. 6, 1866, Warren M. Mann. Ashburnham, Mass.
> *Ch.* 11*th Gen.:* 1 Clara H., b. Nov. 30, 1867. 2 Walter L. C., b. Sept. 13, 1869. 3 Morton W., b. Aug. 29, 1847; Gardner, Mass. 4 John M., b. Aug. 2, 1861.
53 2 William E., b. April 25, 1821, South Amherst, Mass; declines all report of his family.
54 3 Jackson I., b .Dec. 2, 1825; m. April 5, 1849, farmer. Sunderland, Vt.
> *Ch.* 10*th Gen.:* 1 Charles A., b. March 16th, 1850. 2 Alvin W., b. Jan. 6, 1853. 3 Warren, b. April 5, 1855. 4 Myron, b. March 3, 1860. 5 Mandus H., b. Sept. 15, 1862.

38 JESSE LYMAN⁸, *Ozias⁷, Samuel⁶, Samuel⁵, Samuel⁴, Richard³, Richard², Richard¹*, 1782–1852, was born in Bolton Conn., Nov. 4th, 1782, married Mary Durkee, of Brimfield, Mass., in Nov. 4th, 1807. They were married at the parsonage in Tolland, Conn. *Bolton, Conn.*

Children, Ninth Generation:

55 1 Mary Holbrook, b. Nov. 4, 1808; d. Dec. 31, 1829.
56 2 Caroline, Sept. 13, 1810.
57 3 Aaron Brown, April 10, 1812.
58 4 Charles Granderson, March 19, 1814.
59 5 Martin Durkee, Nov. 27, 1816.

In 1818 Jesse Lyman removed from Bolton, Conn., to Brimfield, Mass. Children born in Brimfield:

60 6 Nathan Green, March 12, 1820.
61 7 William Henry Harrison, b. July 15, 1824.
62 8 Francis Edward, b. Oct. 10, 1826; d. Dec. 28, 1835.
63 9 A son surviving one week only.

Jesse Lyman, farmer, died in Brimfield, Mass., Aug. 1, 1854, at the age of 72 years.

Mary Durkee, his wife, died in Brimfield, Mass., Jan. 10, 1850, at the age of 65 years.

56 CAROLINE, married Jurien Brackett of Southbridge, Mass.— a manufacturer of cotton goods — settled in Brimfield, Mass., afterwards removed to Racine, Wisconsin, and engaged in agriculture, where they still reside. No children.
Racine, Wis.

• 57 AARON BROWN, stone mason, married Mary Maria Lewis of Vernon, Ct., Oct. 8, 1841.   *Brimfield, Mass.*

Children, Tenth Generation :

65 1 Mary Caroline, b. Oct., 1842.
66 2 Francis Edward, drowned, no date.
67 3 Fannie, d. Oct. 12, 1864.
68 4 Albert Lewis.
69 5 Alfred Lyon.

All born in Brimfield. About the year 1857, they removed to Brookfield, Mass.

68. ALBERT LEWIS, married in New York city, has one daughter the only great-grandchild of Jesse and Mary Lyman.   *New York.*

58 CHARLES GRANDERSON, leather dresser, married Sarah M. Ward, April 7, 1842.   *Brimfield, Mass.*

Children, Tenth Generation :

70 6 Ella Augusta, school teacher, b. Nov. 24, 1844.
71 7 Charles Julius, in a wholesale hosiery establishment, Boston, Mass., b. May 17, 1846.
72 8 Frank Ward, in military school, Leicester, Mass , the present residence of C. G. Lyman, b. March 14, 1852.

59 MARTIN DURKEE, cabinet maker, married Eliza Badger, of Warren, Mass., Nov. 10, 1841. Settled in Brimfield, Mass. He has been superintendent of town farms for a number of years, in Mason, N. H., Lunenburg, Mass.
Templeton, Mass.

Children, Tenth Generation :

74 1 Albert Eugene, clerk for Morgan & Jackson, b. Feb. 18, 1847.
75 2 Myron Everett, fireman on Fitchburg R. R., b. Dec. 16, 1850.
76 3 Willie Hayden, at High School, Templeton, Mass., b. Jan. 10, 1854.
77 4 Ada Lavon, b. Jan. 25, 1853; died in West Townsend, Mass., Jan. 21, 1859, of scarlet fever.

60 NATHAN GREEN, leather dresser, married Mary A. West, of Worcester, Mass., June 17, 1856, where he settled, No children.   *Ottumwa, Iowa.*

61 WILLIAM HENRY HARRISON, teacher of penmanship, and carpenter, married Edna Haskins, of Bolton, Conn., April 23, 1848. Settled in Brimfield, Mass. *Warren, Mass.*

Children, Tenth Generation.

78 1 Marion Rosalie, b. May, 3, 1850; d. at Brimfield, Feb. 2, 1858.
79 2 Elsie Deliza, b. Aug. 23, 1853; d. at Brimfield, May 4, 1869.
80 3 Abbie Jane, b. Feb. 15, 1855; d. at Brimfield, Oct. 6, 1855.
81 4 Frank Sumner, b. at Brimfield, Aug. 2, 1856.
82 5 Lavon Harrington, b. Jan. 18, 1858; d. at Brimfield, Jan. 23, 1865.
83 6 Henry Wilson, b. at Brimfield, Sept. 30, 1860.
84 7 Mary Durkee, b. May 7, 1861; d. at Brimfield, May 11, 1861.
85 8 Ada West, b. Jan. 25, 1863.

24 ASA LYMAN[7], *Samuel[6], Samuel[5], Samuel[4], Richard[3], Richard[2], Richard[1]*, 1755–1718, m. Mary Bowen. *Coventry, Ct.*

Children, Eighth Generation:

86 1 Lydia, b. 1780; m. Mr. Ely; both deceased.
87 2 Asa, b. Dec. 27, 1782; m. Lydia Coleman,; d. 1849, in Iowa; type founder in Chicago.
88 3 Martin, b. 1783; m. Mary Davenport; died in Coventry, Oct. 17, 1859.
89 4 Cynthia, b. 1785; deceased; no records.
90 5 Caroline, b. 1788; m. Solomon Bidwell, of Coventry, Ct., d. Feb. 15, 1866.
    Ch. 9th Gen.: 1 Amelia C., b. 1810; m. Loring Winchester of Coventry, Ct. 2 Jane C., b. 1813; m. Newton Fitch of Coventry, Ct., deceased. 3 Mary, b. 1815; deceased. 4 Nathan L., b. 1825; m. Sarah M. Porter of Coventry. Ct.
95 6 Nathan, b. 1790; of Buffalo, Erie Co., N. Y.
96 7 Diantha, b. 1794; unmarried; lives at Manchester, Ct.
97 8 Alvira, b. 1796; now widow Dickinson of Ravenna, O.
98 9 Harriet, b. 1798; m. a Mr. Clement.

91 NATHAN[8], *Asa[7], Samuel[6], Samuel[5], Samuel[4], Richard[3], Richard[2], Richard[1]*, was born in Coventry, Ct., and married Jane Van Valer, resided in New York for some time and in Boston, and has for many years resided in Buffalo, N. Y., type founder   *Buffalo, N. Y.*

Children, Eighth Generation:

99 1 William E., b. in New York, July 9, 1814.
100 2 Burke, } twins, b. in New York, Nov. 9, 1818.
101 3 John L., }
102 4 Peter S., born in New York, no date.

103 5 Nathan B., b. in Boston, Jan. 14, 1825; these all reside in Buffalo, and are all type founders.

99 WILLIAM E. LYMAN, b. in the city of New York, 9 July, 1814, oldest of ten children, of whom five are living, son of Nathans, m. 7 Oct., 1835, Matilda Babcock, b. April 4, 1814; is now the head of the house in the type founding business; himself one of the most efficient, skillful and thorough type founders in the country. *Buffalo, N. Y.*

Children, Tenth Generation.

103* 1 Emily Cornelia, b. Aug. 9, 1836.

104 2 Cornelius Mortimer, b. Jan. 28, 1842; m. Sept., 1863; druggist and chemist, doing a successful business; fell into irregular habits, lost his business, then by the energies of an indomitable spirit, restored himself and retrieved his loss of means and character.

105 3 Carleton, M.D., b. Jan. 21, 1849. When a schoolboy he was very much criticised for ungrammatical speech and the subject of ridicule; but only saying "We shall see," he persevered, and at the age of 21 was admitted to the bar. Taking "Life with an aim," as his motto, the day is not distant when his scoffers will envy him in that eminence to which they will never attain.

106 4 Mary Josephine, b. Nov. 10, 1852, ⎱ twin daughters, beloved
107 5 Marion Justine,   "   " ⎰ by all who knew them.
Marion d. Feb. 24, 1868; a beautiful child. Amidst all the endearments of life, and in the bloom of youth, touched with the blight of disease and death, she received, with sweet submission, the summons of the pale messenger as her Saviour's gracious call to a nobler life in the spirit world.

100 BURKE[9], m. Margaret Williams, Oct. 8, 1844.

Children, Tenth Generation:

108 1 Livingston J., b. July 2, 1850; resides in Buffalo.
109 2 William C., b. Dec. 8, 1857.
110 3 Nathan F., b. Dec. 28, 1859.
111 4 Francis M., b. March 15, 1866; d. Nov. 9, 1869.
112 5 Edward M., b. Aug. 17, 1869.

101 JOHN L., m. Mary Wise, Sept. 8, 1859.

Children, Tenth Generation:

113 1 Burke W., b. Jan. 18, 1862.

102 PETER S., m. first, Jane Gardner 1843, she d. 1860; he m. 2d, Mary Cook, 1862.

Children, Tenth Generation :
114 1 Annie, b. 1849.
115 2 Lillie, b. 1854.

103 NATHAN B., m. Kate Remsen Bennett, Oct. 22, 1851
Children, Tenth Generation :
116 1 John B., b. July 24, 1853.
117 2 Richard B., b. March, 1857.
118 3 Mary R , b. April 13, 1867.

17 ICHABOD LYMAN[6], *Samuel[5] Samuel[4], Richard[3], Richard[2], Richard[1]*, 1724–1813. His record is quite obscure and uncertain. He lived in West Hartford, a farmer ; and died, according to the records of that place, April 2, 1813, aged 72. The discrepancy between this and the date given above No. 17 we are unable to reconcile. He m. Abigail .., who d. April 10, 1802, in the 60th year of her age. His 2d wife was Honor Casey. *West Hartford.*

Children, Seventh Generation.
119 1 Ruth (probably), who m. Nathaniel Forbes, Jan., 1791.
120 2 A son, who died Oct. 16, 1778, of dysentery.
121 3 A daughter, who died Oct. 20, 1778, of dysentery.
122 4 A child, who died Dec. 7, 1779, of lock jaw.
123 5 Jessie, who m. 1st———Lawrence. She died Dec. 18, 1799, of small pox. He m. 2d, Betsy Whiting, daughter of Allyn Whiting, of West Hartford.
　　Ch 8th Gen.: 1 John, who died in the army. 2 Jesse, who m. Sept. 26, 1818, Betsy J. Sedgwick, daughter of Gad Sedgwick, of W. Hartford. 3 Roxalinda, who m. Ezekiel Woodford is now a widow, and lives with her son, George L. Woodford, in West Winsted, Conn., and has another son, John, living in W. Winsted. 4 Eloisa, who died May 19, 1808, aged 13. 5 A child, died Dec. 2, 1779, of small pox. 6 A child, died Aug. 17, 1779, aged 8 days.
130 6 Timothy, who died Dec., 1810.
131 7 Ichabod, who m. ——— Cole, and had :
　　Ch. 8th Gen.: 1 Joseph. 2 William, who accidentally shot Joseph. 3 Clarissa, b. 1804, who m April 13, 1825, Joseph J. Fielding, and has several children and grandchildren. 4 Mary, who m., Aug. 28, 1832, Walter Hume, Manistee, Mich. 5 Henry, Grand Rapids, Mich. 6 Emily, deceased. 7 Ichabod, East Hartford.

138	8 Samuel.	141	11 Jonathan.
139	9 Daniel.	142	12 Chester.
140	10 Abigail.	143	13 A daughter, name unknown.

Of these six children nothing is known.

126 ROXALINDA, dau. of *Jesse,* son of *Ichabod,*b. June, 18, 1797.; m. Sept. 7, 1825, Ezekiel Woodford, of West Winsted, Conn., now living with her son, George L., in the same place.

Children, Ninth Generation :

144 1 Andrew, d. 6 June, 1826.
145 2 George L., b. Dec. 29, 1827
146 3 John, b. March 4, 1831.

147 Mehitable Lyman, probably dau. of Ichabod, d. in West Hartford, Dec. 9, 1778.

18 JAMES[6], 3d son of *Samuel[5], Samuel[4], Richard[3], Richard[2], Richard[1],* b. 1727, lived in Bolton, now Vernon, Conn. Of his family we have no record. He had a son James[7], residence Bolton, and another Samuel[7], who resided in Glastenbury, where he m. Aug. 24, 1757, Sarah Bartlett.

Children, Eighth Generation

149 1 Sarah, b. April 29, 1758 ; no record.
150 2 Samuel, b. Nov. 28, 1759.
151 3 Isaac, b. May 30, 1762 ; no record.
152 4 Ruth, b. Jan. 1, 1765 ; no record.
153 5 Joel, b. June 21, 1769 ; Dr. Joel of Wilbraham, Mass.
154 6 Irene, b. April 19, 1773 ; no record.

The above data are copied from the records in Glastenbury, and are doubtless correct.

148 JAMES[7], of Vernon, Conn., *James[6], Samuel[5], Samuel[4], Richard[3], Richard[2], Richard[1],* born in Lebanon, lived in Bolton, Conn., a farmer, and appears at some time to have resided also, and d. in Vernon, Conn.

Children, Eighth Generation :

155 1 Samuel, b. Oct., 1772 ; lived and died at Vernon, 1850.
156 2 Jerusha, d. in Vernon ; unmarried.
157 3 Gad, lived in Middlebury, Vt. ; no further record.
158 4 Lemuel, lived and died in Vernon.
159 5 William, b. Oct. 12, 1781 ; resided in Malone, N. Y.
160 6 Eliphalet, b. 1787 ; resided in Vernon.

Another record states that he had " four sons, Chester, John, Samuel, Gad and Lemuel." Perhaps these statements may be reconciled by supposing that he had sons, Chester and John in addition to the five specified above.

We now give the record of Samuels, son of James[7], and brother of William of Malone, N. Y., and of Eliphalet of Vernon, Conn.

150 SAMUEL LYMAN[8], of Bolton, *James[7]*, *James[6]*, *Samuel[5]*, *Samuel[4]*, *Richard[3]*, *Richard[2]*, *Richard[1]*, b. Feb., 1772; when aged 24 years and 4 months, m. June 16, 1796, Sarah Cady, of Bolton, who died June 4, 1797; m. 2d wife, Nov. 27, 1800, Welthy Hartshorn, of Lebanon Crank. At this time he states his age to have been 29 years and 9 months, who died July 19, 1854. Welthy, his wife, died April 11, 1845. *Bolton, Conn.*

Children, Ninth Generation.

161 1 Chester, b. in Tolland, Sept. 9, 1801.
162 2 Sarah Cady, b. in Lebanon Crank, Dec. 26, 1802; d. April, 1870.
163 3 Silas Hartshorn, b. in Columbia, Oct. 20, 1804; deceased; time and place not given.
164 4 Charles, b. in Columbia, Jan. 29, 1806.
165 5 Lucius, b. Jan. 11, 1808; d. Jan. 25, 1808. ⎫
166 6 Lusa, b. Jan. 11, 1808; d. Jan. 29, 1808. ⎬ Triplets.
167 7 Luna, b. Jan. 11, 1808; d. Feb. 9, 1808. ⎭
169 8 Anson, b. Dec. 7, 1810; m., had a dau.; d. Oct. 8, 1855; committed suicide.

161 CHESTER LYMAN[9], m. Sept. 9, 1826, Ann E. Mack, b. Manchester, Conn., April 12, 1804. *Dunlap, Iowa.*

Children, Tenth Generation:

170 1 Mary Ann, b. Nov. 4, 1826; d. June 9, 1839.
171 2 Henry W., b. April 1, 1828, in Manchester, Conn.; m. March 25, 1850, Jane Thompson, E. Haven.
172 3 Elizabeth M., b. March 2, 1830, in Manchester; d. Oct. 4, 1841.
173 4 Charles A., b. Feb. 11, 1832; m. March 28, 1853, Sarah S. Chappell.
      Ch. 11th Gen.: 1 Charles H., b. July 11, 1853; d. Aug. 25, 1854. Alice G., b. Aug. 6, 1856. 3 Andrew, b. ....; d. Oct. 23, 1857. 4 Frank C., b. Sept. 17, 1859. 5 Burton, b. Sept. 20, 1868.
177 5 Caroline D., b. June 24, 1834; d. May 16, 1839.
178 6 Chester J., b. March 25, 1837, Milwaukee; m. Emma J. Moals.
179 7 Albert F., b. Sept. 18, 1840; m., April 20, 1869, Emma Barnum.
180 8 Adelaide, b. April 2, 1843; d. Sept. 1, 1848.
181 9 Edward S., b. April 8, 1845; m. Matilda Teal — farmer. Dunlap, Iowa.
182 10 Franklin P., b. March 20, 1850. Dunlap, Iowa.

Four of these sons were in the Union army in many battles, but all returned unharmed, having left wives and children dependent on them for support.

160 ELIPHALET LYMAN[8], *James[7], James[6], Samuel[5], Samuel[4], Richard[3], Richard[2], Richard[1]*, b. in Vernon, Conn., in 1787; m. Aug. 2, 1807, Nancy Harvey of Windham, b. 1786, d. in Mansfield, Conn., Dec. 6, 1858, aged 72 years, Vernon, Ct. Eliphalet d. in Rockville, Aug. 29, 1859, aged 72 years. *Rockville, Conn.*

Children, Eighth Generation.

183 1 Eliza Ann, b. June 14, 1808, in Westfield, Mass.; d. March 2, 1815.

185 2 Nancy Amanda, b. in Westfield, June 18, 1809; m. Nov. 2, 1826, Joseph H. Brown, Rockville, Conn.
Ch. 9th Gen.: 1 Henry, b. July 28, 1827; d. June 15, 1854. 2 Lucius, b. Sept. 11, 1831. 3 Adelia J., b. Sept. 21, 1844. 4 An infant, b. Feb. 18, d. 19.

189 3 Eliphalet Wadsworth, b. in Tolland, Conn., Jan. 31, 1811; m. Sophia Stearns; 2d, Susan M. Marsh, Clinton, Conn.

190 4 Laura Hovey, b. in Tolland, Nov. 21, 1812; d. in Mansfield, Conn., April 5, 1859, aged 46½ years.

191 5 Gurdon Thompson, b. in Tolland, Sept. 24, 1814; supposed to be deceased.

192 6 Anna Maria, b. in Tolland, Aug. 13, 1810; d. Feb. 16, 1818.

193 7 Anna Maria, b. in T., July 16, 1818; d. March 19, 1820.

194 8 James Robinson, b. July 14, 1820. Has a daughter Emma, Willimantic, Conn.

195 9 Jane, b. in Tolland, Sept. 1, 1822; m. Horace G. Holt.
Ch. 9th Gen.: 1 Jennie L., b. June 4, 1859; d. Dec. 25, 1865, Rockville, Conn.

197 10 Erastus, b. in Vernon, July 24, 1824; m. Amanda Morton, New Haven, Conn.

198 11 Lemuel Warren, b. in Vernon, May 18, 1827; resides Hartford Bridge; m. Cynthia Brainard — A dau. Nellie.

187 LUCIUS EDMUND BROWN, b. Sept. 11, 1831; m. Oct. 7, 1868, Mary J. Irish — A son, Henry Edmund, deceased, *Rockville, Conn.*

188 ADELIA JANE BROWN, b. Sept. 21, 1844; m. Jan. 1, 1868, Joshua Wood — A dau. Minnie Amanda, b. in Rockville, Sept. 4, 1870. *Rockville, Conn.*

171 HENRY W. LYMAN[9], oldest son of Chester, b. in Manchester, Conn., 1 April, 1828; m. 25 Nov., 1850, Anna A. Thompson, East Haven, Conn.; iron founder — private in the late war. *Milwaukee, Wis.*

Children, Tenth Generation:

202 1 Wyllis O., b. 21 Sept., 1854.
203 2 Mary E., b. 20 Oct., 1858.

178 CHESTER LYMAN[9], JR., m. Jan. 24, 1862, Emma J. Moals, of England — private in the late war — iron moulder. *Milwaukee, Wis.*

Children, Tenth Generation.

204 1 Adelaide, b. 23 June, 1864; d, 2 Nov. 1866.
205 2 Ella, b. 22 Feb., 1866.
206 3 Willie, b. 17 Sept., 1869.

159 WILLIAM LYMAN[8], *James[7], James[6], Samuel[5], Samuel[4], Richard[3], Richard[2], Richard[1]*, b. in Vernon, Conn., Oct. 12, 1781; m. Lucy Gilbert, b. Aug. 25, 1777, who d. July 19, 1853; farmer. *Malone, Franklin Co., N. Y.*

Children, Ninth Generation:

207 1 William M., b. March 25, 1804
    Ch. 10th Gen.: 1 Hollon, b. April 28, 1830; d. 1853.
    2 Charles B., b. Feb. 11, 1833. 3 George P., b. July 30,
    1837 ; d. 1862. 4 Wallace G., b. Aug. 17, 1846.
211 2 Lucy, b. Dec. 20, 1805.
212 3 Minrie, b. March 31, 1807 ; d. Sept. 3, 1844.
213 4 Gad, b. Dec. 9, 1808.
214 5 Sophia, b. Jan. 3, 1811.
215 6 Linus, b. Jan. 28, 1813 ; d. Feb. 10, 1865.
216 7 Jerusha, b. May 3, 1815 ; d. Jan. 19, 1833.
217 8 Hannah M., b. Aug. 12, 1817 ; d. 1868.
218 9 Henry M., adopted s., b. May 1, 1825; d. April 24, 1844.

153 DR. JOEL LYMAN[8], son of *Samuel[7]*, who resided in Glastenbury, Conn., *James[6], Samuel[5], Samuel[4], Richard[3]*, lived through life in Wilbraham, Mass., in the practice of his profession; m. Mary Merrick, dau. of Jonathan Merrick of Wilbraham, who d. 1868, more than 90 years of age. *Wilbraham, Mass.*

Children, Ninth Generation:

219 1 Joel Merrick, b. 1796; d. May 26, 1857.
220 2 Samuel, farmer, d. West Martinsburg, N. Y.
221 3 Henry, farmer, Belfast, Alleghany Co., N. Y.
222 4 Charles Pyncheon.
223 5 Mary, m. Charles H. Curtis, Martinsburg, N. Y.

219 JOEL M.[9], son of Dr. Joel of Wilbraham, m. July 1, 1824, Caroline M. McCrage, farmer. *Wilbraham, Mass.*

Children, Tenth Generation:

224 1 William H., b. Nov. 16, 1825, farmer; m. Mary L. Warner, Wilbraham.
225 2 Jane Maria, b. April 17, 1828 ; m. Benj. O. Cutter of Minnesota, June, 1870, San Francisco, Cal.

226 3 Charles W., b. July 10 1830, m. Feb. 24, 1857, Martha
      Deming of South Avon, N. Y., farmer, Northfield, Min.
        Ch. 11th Gen.: 1 Geo. D., b. Oct. 4, 1859.   2 Martha
        Isabel, b. Feb. 6, 1862 ; d. April 12, 1863.   3 Chas.
        Warner, b. April 30, 1864.   4 Edgar Stuart, b. March
        19, 1868.
231 4 George, b. Jan. 10, 1833, m. Louisa C. Kent, Suffield, d.
      Sept. 23, 1864; went south in the late war, contracted
      disease of which he died.   One son William.
232 5 Mary E., b. June 1, 1835; d. Nov. 16, 1859.
233 6 Albert, b. Aug. 6, 1838 ; d. Oct. 21, 1859.
234 7 Edward E., b. Sept., 13, 1845, in mercantile business, Albany,
      N. Y.

163 Silas Hartshorn Lyman[9] second son of *Samuel*[8],
James[7], *James*[6], *James*[5], *Samuel*[4], *Samuel*[3], *Richard*[2], *Richard*[1],
b. in Vernon, Ct., Oct. 20, 1804, m. Feb. 8, 1826, Sophia
Fowler, of Avon, Ct., carpenter.   *Oregon, Ogle Co., Ill.*
     Children, Tenth Generation:
235 1 Sarah, b. 7 Dec., 1826, in Hartford, Ct. ; m. Feb., 1843,
      Edwin Hull ; d. in Rockvale, Ogle Co., Ill., 13 Jan., 1857.
        Ch. 11th Gen.: 1 Edwin, b. Aug. 20, 1846 ; d. Sept.
        30, 1852.   2 Julia E., b. Oct. 24, 1848.
238 2 Harriet, b. April 23, 1828 ; m. March, 1855, John Waffle.
        Ch. 11th Gen.: 1 John Gay, b. 18 Aug., 1857.   2
        Helen Maria, b. June, 19, 1860.   3 Willard Hale, b.
        Aug 5, 1861.   4 Florence, b. Dec. 4, 1864.   5 Hattie
        Nora, b. June 22, 1867.
244 3 Cardelia, b. 23 Nov., 1830, m. March, 1855, Roswell Curtis.
        Ch. 11th Gen.: 1 Hattie Mary, d. in 1856. 2. Wil-
        liam, b. Sept., 1860 ; d. 1861.   3 Carrie, b. May, 1867.
248 4 Silas D., b. 1 March, 1833; m. Nov. 1857, Lucy Lock-
      wood, d. 9 May, 1860.
249 5 Mary Jane, b. 3 Nov., 1835; d. 30 April, 1844.
250 6 Almira, b. 27 Oct., 1837; d. 23 April, 1844.
251 7 Ann Eliza, b. 5 July, 1841 ; m. Feb. 1869, Horace Dexter.
        Ch. 11th Gen.: Horace, b. May 30, 1870.

12 Jabez[5], second son of *Samuel*[4], *Richard*[3], b. Oct. 10,
1702; m. Jan. 29, 1730, Martha Bliss.   The record is, were
"married together" according to the old English form.
                                          Lebanon, Ct.
     Children, Sixth Generation .
259 1 Jabez, b. March 21, 1731; no record.
260 2 Ezekiel, b Oct. 23; bapt. 28, 1733; m. Feb. 10, 1759, Eliza-
      beth Bliss.
261 3 Martha, b. Nov. 15, 1735; m. Josiah Throop, and removed
      to Nova Scotia.

262 4 Israel, b. Nov. 24, 1737; no record.

263 5 Lucy, b. Dec. 19, 1739; d. young.

264 6 Elisha, b. Sept. 22, 1742.

265 7 Elizabeth, b. Oct. 11, 1745, }
    Martha,   "   "   "   " } twins, no further record.

266 8 Jerusha, b. Dec. 4, 1747; no record.

267 9 Eunice, b. May 6, 1752; m. at Lebanon, Conn., Timothy
    Woodworth, in 1783 or '4; removed to Royalton, Vt.; d.
    Oct., 1812. Timothy was in the Revolutionary army; d.
    1835, Royalton.

      Ch. 7th Gen.: 1 William, b. in Lebanon, April 19,
    1783; d. Aug. 22, 1848. 2 Eunice, b. in Royalton, d.
    3 Sarah, d. 4 Lemuel, d. 5 Lyman, d. 6 Polly, d.

260 EZEKIEL[6], eldest son of *Jabez[5], Samuel[4], Richard[3], Richard[2], Richard[1],* b. 183*3*; m. Feb. 10, 1757, Elizabeth Bliss,
of Lebanon; resided in Canterbury; removed to Royalton, Vt., about 1782, where he died at a great age.

                          Canterbury, Conn.; Royalton, Vt.

    Children, Seventh Generation :

273 1 Ezekiel, b. Aug. 18, 1760; m. Mabel Mitchell, of Middle-
    town, Conn.; b. July 17, 1764.

274 2 Daniel, b. .   ...; m. Sally Morse, of Royalton; re-
    moved to Barnston, Canada East. Nothing more is known
    of him, save that he served in the Revolutionary army,
    and received a pension from the government of the U.S.

275 3 Samuel, b. 1764; m. 1st, Prudence Mitchell, of Middletown;
    2d, Hannah, her sister. Resided in Royalton, Middletown,
    Durham, Conn., and Turin, N. Y., where he died in
    June, 1849, aged 85 years.

276 4 Sally, d. unmarried.

277 5 Asa, m. Submit Mitchell, res. West Turin; had a dau. m. to
    David Higby, High Market, Lewis Co., N. Y.

278 6 William, removed to Barnston with his br. Daniel, where his
    history is lost.

279 7 Betsey, m. Garner Rix, of Royalton, and had a numerous
    family.

280 8 Eliphalet, m. Mary Lee, Middletown, Conn.

281 9 Jabez, m., Jan. 24, 1779, Lois Johnson, of Middleton, Conn.
    These children were all b. in Canterbury, Conn., before
    the removal of the family to Royalton.

273 EZEKIEL[7], *Ezekiel[6], Jabez[5], Samuel[4], Richard[3], Richard[2],
Richard,[1]* 1760–1845, July 4th; was a soldier in the
army of the Revolution, and in the meantime, his wife
Mabel Mitchell of Middletown, Ct., supported their little
family by spinning and weaving; a very pious and exemplary Christian woman, and studious scholar; possessing a

cultivated mind and great fondness for poetry, she would, for hours together, repeat the Christian and familiar tunes of former years, even after she had been blind some twenty years. She became totally blind at the age of 62 and· so remained until her death, at the age of 91 years, April, 1848. Through these long years of darkness, she never repined but was always cheerful and industrious, in her blindness weaving linen handkerchiefs.   *Middletown, Ct.*

Children, Eighth Generation:

282 1 Abner, b. June, 12, 1787; m. Eunice Wheeler, 2 sons, 2 daughters, Sandusky, Ohio.

293 2 Eunice, m. Luke Lindsey; 8 daughters 4 sons deceased.

296 3 Betsey E , b. Nov. 10, 1790; m. Trumbull Smith,— 6 sons 6 daughters — d. 1857, West Turin, Lewis Co., N. Y.

308 4 Prudence, b. Nov. 10, 1792; m. Isaac McCrea, 2 sons, 2 daughters, d. Evans Mills, Jefferson Co., N. Y.

313 5 Enoch, b. Feb. 22, 1795; m. Margaret Crego, 4 sons 5 daughters, Turin, Lewis Co., N. Y.

322 6 Isaac, b. July, 12, 1797; m. Cynthia Kent.
    Ch. Ninth Gen.: 1 Louis Jane Lyman, b. Jan. 5, 1821. 2 Watson, b. June 4, 1822. 3 Delia Frances, b. Oct. 24, 1823. 4 James Watson, b. Nov. 9, 1825. 5 Mary Amanda, b. Dec. 31, 1827. 6 Martha Amelia, b. Oct. 19, 1829. 7 Isaac Duane, b. June 25, 1831. 8 Luthera Emeline, b. Feb. 26, 1833. 9 Leonora Adeline, b. March 17, 1835.

333 7 Lydia, b. Jan. 24, 1800; m. Wm. Wheeler, 1 son, 9 daughters, d. N. Y.

344 8 Sally, b. June 12, 1802; m. John W. Hathaway, 2 sons, 4 daughters; d. Dec. 6, 1848, West Turin, N. Y.

351 9 Anne, b. May 13, 1804; m. Elijah Willoughby, 1 son; d. March 1848, Evans Mills.
    All born in the state of New York, Evans Mills, Jefferson Co.

282 ABNER LYMAN[8], *Ezekiel[7]*, *Ezekiel[6]*, *Jabez[5]*, *Samuel[4]*, *Richard[3]*, b. at Middletown, Conn., June 10th, 1789; m. Eunice Wheeler, of Herkimer Co., N. Y.; settled in Sandusky, Ohio, in 1818, captain and major in Ohio militia; served as a private, at Sackett's Harbor, in the war of 1812; d. 1853, aged 66; one of the earliest settlers of Sandusky; a worthy, estimable man, who enjoyed the respect and confidence of all who knew him; millwright and carpenter.   *Sandusky, O.*

Children, Ninth Generation:

353 1 John, b.......; d. Lewis Co., N. Y.

354 2 Sophia, b.. ....; m. Mills.

355 3 William Henry; deceased.

356 4 Hiram Abner.

356 HIRAM LYMAN[9], son of *Abner*[8], *Ezekiel*[7], *Ezekiel*[6], *Jabez*[5], *Samuel*[4], *Richard*[3], b. at Sandusky, Ohio, March 23, 1822; m. at Evans Mills, N. Y., Oct. 8, 1838, Abigail Hinman — machinist and engineer. 7 *Mile House, Erie Co., O.*

Children, Tenth Generation:

357 1 Sophia, b. July 15, 1839; m. June 22, 1862;·L. W. Osborn. Two children.
358 2 Mary E., b. Aug. 19, 1849.

283 EUNICE LYMAN[8], dau. of *Ezekiel*[7], removed from Middletown, Conn., with her parents and grandparents on her mother's side, when 12 years of age, to the Black River country. They traveled in emigrant style, with an ox team and a tented wagon, the carriage of the aged by day, and the lodgings of all by night. This child performed 200 miles of this journey on foot, and discharged the household duties of the family through the summer in the wilderness; m. Jan. 24, 1805, at the age of 16, Luke Lindsey, who d. Dec. 21, 1867. Eunice, d. July 31, 1837.

West Turin, Lewis Co., N. Y.

Children, Ninth Generation:

360 1 Sally, b. Jan. 24, 1808; m. April 26, 1827, Augustus Munson; one son; m. 2d, Campbell Orrick; m. 3d, David Bishop.
361 2 Emily, b. July 18, 1810; m. Dec. 25, 1829, David Munson, Raleigh, Jeff. Co., N. Y.
362 3 Eleanor, b. June 23, 1812; m. Jan. 8, 1833, Asahel Higby; d. April 21, 1858.
363 4 Melissa, b. Oct. 6, 1814; m. Feb. 20, Sidney Hills, Houseville, N. Y.
364 5 Lucy, b. July 9, 1816; m. Oct. 9, 1842, Lot P. Hubbard.
365 6 Susannah, b. June 1, 1818; m. Nov. 10, 1836, Jacob Sharer.
366 7 Harriet, b. March 29, 1820; m. June 20, 1840, Huron Webster; d. Oct. 10, 1856–8.
367 8 Mary Jane, b. May 22, 1822; m. March 24, 1840, Carter Shepard.
368 9 Ellsworth, b. Sept. 19, 1824.
369 10 James Munroe, March 13, 1827.
370 11 Oliver E., b. Feb. 12, 1829.
371 12 Jarvis, b. Dec. 23, 1830.
These 8 daughters all have children, 30 in number.

296 BETSEY E. LYMAN[8], second dau., third child of *Ezekiel*[7], m. Dec. 31, 1807, Trumbull Smith, one of three sons b. at one birth, all of whom were named by Gen. Washington: 1st, Trumbull, after Governor Trumbull; the others being named Greene and George. *W. Turin, N. Y.*

Children, Ninth Generation :
372   1 Lyman, b. Aug. 4, 1809.
373   2 Frances, b. Dec. 6, 1811.
374   3 Harrison, b. June 22, 1813.
375   4 Eldridge, b. April 5, 1816.
376   5 Isaac, b. May, 1818; d. Aug 19, 1851, in Wisconsin.
377   6 Betsey, b. April 9, 1820.
378   7 Royal F., b. March 15, 1822.
379   8 Sally Ann, b. April 28, 1824; d. Feb. 3, 1827.
380   9 Julia Ann, b. June 4, 1827.
381   10 Sally M., b. Sept. 7, 1830; d. May 18, 1834, Vernon, N. Y.
382   11 Catharine A., b. May 24, 1832.
383   12 Emiline, b. April 16, 1834.

351 ANNE LYMAN[8], youngest daughter of *Ezekiel[7]* ; m. Elijah Willoughby, June 15, 1826, and d. March 8, 1848. He d. at Evans Mills, N. Y., Feb. 24, 1846. *Evans Mills.*

Children, Ninth Generation :
384   1 George, b. Oct. 29, 1827 ; m. Oct. 6, 1851, Angeline Stevens. teacher, town clerk, etc., Montague, Lewis Co., N. Y.
      Ch. 10th Gen. :   1 Anna L., b. July 31, 1853.   2 Norman G., b. March 30, 1857.   3 Eugene C., b. Dec. 1, 1858; d. Aug. 5, 1865.   4 Effie M., b. April 2, 1861.   5 Byron E., b. March 7, 1863.   6 Nelson, b. June 7, 1868.

313 ENOCH LYMAN[8], second son and fifth child of *Ezekiel[7]*, at the age of 24 ; m. Margaret Crego, Nov. 4, 1819, in the town of Turin, N. Y. His wife, at her marriage, was but 15 years of age. She was born Oct. 31, 1804, in Conn., and had, with her father's family, migrated from thence to Lewis Co., N. Y. Enoch with his young wife, being in poor circumstances, went boldly into the forests upon Tug Hill, in Turin Co., N. Y., and commenced house-keeping in a log cabin of his own construction. By persevering industry, they made themselves a good, well furnished home in that region, now celebrated for butter-making. Some years after they settled there, their log cabin with most of their household goods caught fire, and burning to the ground in the night time, they barely escaped with their little ones alive. A new and commodious house, which they were then building, was, however, at this time nearly completed and soon after occupied by his family. Being a good hunter and fond of sport, in those early days he furnished his table with the choicest cuts of venison from the adjacent forests, frequently varied with a roast of black bear. Many hours of his old age were spent in narrating

thrilling stories of the chase; and none more thrilling or romantic than true. He was a natural mechanic, and truly termed " Jack of all trades." Though young, he served some months in the war of 1812 and received his military warrant therefor. His wife was a genuine helpmeet, and, as was the custom in those days in that country, spun and wove the flax and wool of their own growing, and by the labor of her own hands kept her large family warmly clothed. Enoch Lyman maintained an exemplary reputation as a citizen, and, at the time of his death, Dec. 8, 1853, aged 58 years, was a member of the old school Baptist Religious Society, in Turin.

Children, Ninth Generation :

391 1 Amanda Jane, b. March 21, 1821; m. Oct. 31, 1839, William Winn, Mohawk, Herkimer Co., N. Y.
392 2 William Abner, b. August 9, 1822.
393 3 Elvira, b. May 10, 1824; m. Feb, 9, 1846, Jay Dexter.
394 4 Virginia, b. Aug. 11, 1826; d. Sept. 21, 1828.
395 5 Lorenzo Branch, b. Sept. 6, 1828.
396 6 Julia S., b. March 19, 1833; d. April 5, 1834.
397 7 Brenton Marcellus, b. August 8, 1838; d. May 27, 1842.
398 8 Hiram Brenton, b. Dec. 19, 1842; unmarried.
399 9 Margaret, b. May 9, 1848.
  All born at Turin, Lewis Co., N. Y.

392 WILLIAM A. LYMAN, son of *Enochs*, and grandson of *Ezekiel*, b. at Turin, Lewis Co., N. Y., Aug. 9, 1822; m. March 16, 1845, Catharine S. Powell of Turin, Lewis Co., N. Y., b. Oct. 20, 1816; d. Sept. 28, 1851; occupation coopering, sawmilling and farming; m. 2d wife, Mary A. Lyman, of Leroy, Lewis Co., N. Y., June 1, 1853.

Ava, Oneida Co.

Children, Tenth Generation :

400 1 Winfield Scott, b. Sept. 13, 1846, in Constableville, N. Y.
401 2 Emily Rosa Ellen, b. Jan. 20, 1850, in Delhi, Wis.
402 3 Isaac E., b. June, 8, 1850; d. Nov. 15, 1854.
403 4 Lorenzo Brenton, b. in Theresa, Jefferson Co.. N. Y., date not given.
404 5 William A., b. in Turin, Lewis Co., N. Y., March 23, 1860.
405 6 Elmer E., b. in Turin, Lewis Co., N. Y., March 8, 1861.
406 7 Delia M., b. in Ava, Oneida Co., N. Y., March 6, 1863, d. March 23, 1863.
407 8 Clarence A., b. in Ava, Oneida Co., July 13, 1865, d. Jan. 8, 1866.
408 9 Jennie May, b. Ava, Oneida Co., N. Y., Jan. 25, 1869.

395 LORENZO BRANCH, the second son of Enoch and Margaret Lyman, m. Mary E. Hawkins, at Waukesha, Wisconsin, Sept. 19, 1858. Being naturally studious in his youth, acquired a liberal academical education, and at the age of nineteen commenced the study of law under the tuition of a prominent lawyer, W. S. Hawkins, at his office in Waukesha, Wis. After pursuing a thorough course of law reading and obtaining a practical acquaintance with the forms of practice in the courts, he was admitted to the bar as an attorney at law in all the state courts of record and United State courts. Under the excitement of the then recent gold discoveries in California, he went to that country "overland" in 1849, and there delved for the precious metal with various fortunes for some eight years, sometimes panning out of his ore one hundred dollars of the dust to the pan and often pocketing a handsome nugget; then for a change and possessing his father's great love for the chase, would go out among the almost countless variety of wild game with which the country abounded — pitch his tent under a live oak and follow a hunter's life and partake of a hunter's fare for months together. At the end of nine years he returned to Wisconsin, married Mary E. Hawkins, the only daughter of his former law tutor, and, as his law partner, resumed the practice of law. He there held many offices of public trust and honor, and was a staunch republican from the birth of that party forward. In 1864 he removed with his family, and settled in the Gallatin valley in Montana Territory, engaged in farming, stock raising and the practice of law, and greatly prospered therein. In 1869 he was appointed by President Grant, register of public lands for that territory.

Children, Tenth Generation:

409 1 A son, b. Jan. 8, 1864; d. in a few weeks.
410 2 Sylvic Rozeffie, b. April 28, 1865, in the Rocky Mountains; by reason of her rosy cheeks, called the Rocky Mountain Rose Bud.
411 3 Herschell Hawkins, b. July 29, 1869.

Mrs. Lyman, d. at Helena City, March 3, 1869. "She was a lady of more than ordinary intelligence, of rare womanly sensibilities, and of qualities of head and heart that endeared her to a large circle of friends and acquaintances, respected and loved by all. Her unexpected and sudden death will be generally lamented, and the widowed husband and orphaned children, in their great bereavement, have the sympathy and condolence of the entire community."

I STILL LIVE.

O, *Thou*, whose love is changeless,
  Both now and evermore ;
Source of all conscious being :
  Thy goodness I adore.
Lord, I would ever praise Thee
  For all Thy love can give ;
But most of all, O, Father !
  I thank Thee that I live.

I live ! O ye who loved me
  Your faith was not in vain ,
Back through the shadowy valley
  I come to you again.
Safe in the love that guides me,
  With fearless feet I tread —
My home is with the angels —
  O, say not I am dead.

Not dead ! O, no, but lifted
  Above all earthly strife ;
Now first I know the meaning,
  And feel the power of life —
The power to rise uncumbered
  By woe, or want, or care ;
To breathe fresh inspiration
  From pure, celestial air ;

To feel that all the tempests
  Of human life have passed,
And that my ark, in safety, rests
  On the mount at last.
To send my soul's great longings,
  Like Noah's dove abroad,
And find them swift returning,
  With a sign of peace from God ;

To soar in fearless freedom
  Through broad, blue, boundless skies
And catch the radiant gleaming
  Of love-lit angel eyes ;
To feel the Father's presence
  Around me, near or far,
And see His radiant glory
  Stretch onwards, star by star ;

To feel those grand upliftings
  That know not space nor time,
To hear all discords ending
  In harmony sublime ;
To know that sin and error
  Are dimly understood,
And that which man calls Evil
  Is undeveloped good ;

To stand in spell-bound rapture
  On some celestial height,
And see God's glorious sunshine
  Dispel the shades of night ;
To feel that all creation
  With love and joy is rife ;—
This, O my earthly loved ones,
  This is Eternal Life !

There, eyes that closed in darkness
  Shall open to the morn ;
nd those whom death had stricken,
  Shall find themselves new-born ;
The lame shall leap with gladness,
  The blind rejoice to see ;
The slave shall know no master,
  And the prisoner shall be free.

There, the worn and heavy-laden
  Their burdens shall lay down ;
There, crosses, borne in meekness,
  At length shall win the crown ;
And lonely hearts that famished
  For sympathy and love,
Shall find a free affection
  In the angel-home above.

O, children of our father !
  Weep not for those who pass,
Like rose leaves gently scattered,
  Like dew-drops from the grass.
Ay, look not down in sadness,
  But fix your gaze on high ;
They only dropped their mantles,
  Their souls can never die.

They live ; and still unbroken
  Is that magnetic chain,
Which, in your tearful blindness,
  You thought was rent in twain.
That chain of love was fashioned
  By more than human art,
And every link is welded
  So firm it cannot part.

They live ! but O, not idly
  To fold their hands to rest,
For they who love God truly,
  Are they who serve Him best ;
Love lightens all their labor,
  And makes all duty sweet ;
Their hands are never weary,
  Nor way-worn are their feet.

Thus by that world of beauty,
  And by that life of love,
And by the holy angels
  Who listen now above,
I pledge my soul's endeavor,
  To do whate'er I can
To bless my sister woman,
  And aid my brother man.

O, Thou, whose love is changeless,
  Both now and evermore,
Source of all conscious being !
  Thy goodness I adore.
Lord, I would ever praise Thee
  For all Thy love can give ;
But most of all, O, Father,
  I thank Thee that I live.

274 DAN or DANIEL LYMAN[7], 2d son of *Ezekiel*[6], m. Sally Morse, of Royalton ; removed to Barnston, Canada East ; subsequent history unknown.

322 Isaac Lyman⁸, *Ezekiel⁷, Ezekiel⁶, Jabez⁵, Samuel⁴, Richard³, Richard², Richard¹*, 1797–1857, m. Feb. 3, 1820, Cynthia Kent, of Suffield, Conn., b. Jan. 19, 1798; d. May 21, 1853 — farmer.   *Turin, Lewis Co., N. Y*

Children, Ninth Generation:

412   1 Louisa J., b. Jan. 5, 1821; m. Oct. 11, 1841, Thomas Murphy.

413   2 Watson, b. June 4, 1822; d. Aug. 17, 1824.

414   3 Delia F., b. Oct. 24, 1823; m. Dec. 30, 1845; Louis Barrett.

415   4 Watson J., b. Nov. 9, 1825; unmarried.

416   5 Mary A., b. Dec. 31, 1827; m. June 1, 1853; William D. Lyman⁹, son of Enoch⁸.

417   6 Martha A., b. Oct. 19, 1829; m. March 8, 1854, Jesse Hamlin.

418   7 Isaac, b. June 25, 1831; d. unmarried, Jan. 15, 1858.

419   8 Luthera E., b. Feb. 26, 1833; d. Dec. 6, 1840.

420   9 Leonora, b. March 17, 1835.

275 Samuel Lyman⁷, 3d son of *Ezekiel⁶, Jabez⁵, Samuel⁴, Richard³, Richard², Richard¹*, 1764–1849; b. in Canterbury; removed with his father to Royalton, Vt., about 1782; in 1786 or '7 m. Prudence Mitchell — farmer; m. 2d wife, Hannah, sister of his first wife; removed to Durham, Conn.   *Middletown, Conn.*

Children, Eighth Generation:

421   1 Calvin, b. in Royalton, 1788; m. Polly Woodworth, who d. about 1862. He still lives in West Turin, Lewis Co., N. Y.; for many years has been insane.

     Ch. 9th Gen.: 1 Anson, res. West Turin; three daus.; history unknown.

422   2 Betsey, b. April 19, 1791; d. in Parishville, N. Y., 1864 aged 73 years.

423   3 Lucy, m. John Howard, of Buffalo, N. Y.; removed further west — nothing more is known of them.

424   4 Samuel, m. Laura Fairbanks, West Turin.

     Ch. 9th Gen.: 1 Herman; 2 Willis.

425   5 Hannah, m. James Green, of Middletown, Conn.; removed probably to Michigan; history unknown.

426   6 Nancy, m. Abram Collins, of Pierpont, St. Lawrence Co., N. Y.

427   7 Mitchell, b. Feb. 14, 1800; a very efficient member of the Presbyterian Church; m. Martha Payne; no children.

Children, second wife:

428   8 William, m. Aug. 1, 1824, Maria W. Griffin of Guilford, Ct., and was killed instantly by the fall of timber on board a vessel.

429   9 Henry, m. Maria Case of Royalton, enlisted in the Mexican war, Muskegon, Mich.

430 10 Charles, m. Sally Myers, of Perry, N. Y., removed to Royal
      Oak, White Lake, Mich.
431 11 Eunice, m. Moses Johnson, of Haddam; d. in Royal Oak,
      Sept. 14, 1842, Utah Ter.
        Ch. 9th Gen.: 1 Eliza Ann. 2 Sarah M. 3 Henry
      L. 4 Margatt. 5 Stephen D. 6 Julia R. Only the last
      two are living. Stephen D. is conductor of the Michigan
      Central R. R. Julia R. m. Horace Fuller, Detroit, Mich.
432 12 Mary, b. Oct. 10, 1811; at Middletown, Conn.; m. William
      Johnson, of Haddam. At the age of 20, removed to
      Perry, Genesee Co., where the husband d. leaving a dau.
      Mary Ann. Mrs. J. then m. in 1834, Lorenzo brother
      of her former husband, and removed to Royal Oak,
      Mich. After a residence there of 12 years, in 1846
      they joined the Mormons and removed to Nauvoo, Ill.,
      now Carthage. Left N. in March for the Indian territory;
      remained in Council Bluffs and vicinity until the spring
      of 1852, then with the Mormons started *en route* for
      the Great Basin in the Rocky Mountains and in
      autumn arrived at Springville, in Utah, 50 miles south
      of Salt Lake City.
        Ch. 9th Gen.: 1 Mary Ann, engaged in trade. 2
      Ellen Amelia. 3 Emily Marinda. These two were b. near
      Council Bluffs, and the latter d. on the way to Utah, aged
      2½ years. 4 William D., now engaged in mining; Col. in
      the Nauvoo region; 4 years alderman in the city of
      Springville. 5 Eunice L., who with Ellen A., is a school
      teacher. 6 Harriet F., tailoress. 7 Julia M., milliner and
      dress maker. 8 John Wesley, carpenter and farmer, a
      good business man.
448 13 Ozias. 14 Mary, both d. young. The children of both
      wives after the decease of their mother were separated
      and lived with friends and relations. Mr. Lyman fell
      into irregular habits, lost his property and d. in Turin,
      N. Y., in June, 1849.

      422 BETSEY LYMAN[8], dau. of *Samuel*,[7] m. Dec. 1816, Gideon
Crandall, farmer; she d. in Parishville, N. Y., 1864.
              Ellsworth, St. Lawrence Co., N. Y.

Children, Ninth Generation.
450 1 Charles, b. Royalton, March 8, 1819, m. 1850; wife's name
      not given, who d. April 19, 1863; no issue; 2d wife,
      m. Dec. 31, 1863, Christina Sanford, farmer. Carrie,
      b. Nov. 22, 1866, d..........Parishville.
451 2 Garner Rix, b. April 2, 1820, m. April 2, 1843, Sophia P.
      Maria Stuard of Ogdensburg—farmer, Ellsworth.

Ch. 10*th Gen.* :　1 James Hopkins, b. Sept. 27, 1846; d. Sept. 17, 1848.　2 Betsey Sophia, b. Dec. 30, 1848. 3 Gardner Brown, b. Nov. 26, 1854.

455　3 George Lyman, b. May 21, 1822; m. July 4, 1849, Drusilla Davidson—farmer.

　　Ch. 10*th Gen.* :　1 Charles, b. June 14, 1841, now in the Rocky Mountains, mining.　2 Andrew D., b. Sept. 7, 1853.　3 Nora, b. Aug. 2, 1864.

459　4 Martin Fuller, b. Sept. 23, 1823; d. Aug. 1839.

461　5 Eliza Ann, b. May 23, 1825 ; m. Feb. 19, 1846, Jacob Anstead, Jr., farmer; d. about 1861, Parishville.

　　Ch. 10*th Gen.* :　1 George A., b. Nov. 14, 1847.　2 Martin Luther, b. May 28, 1849.　3 Margaret A., b. Sept. 7, 1850 ; d. March 24, 1868.　4 Martha E., b. April 30, 1854; d. July 10, 1869.

465　6 Martha M., b. July 23, 1829; m. April 3, 1859, Samuel Maxfield, a man of unusual height and strength, a private in the army of Richmond, at the surrender of Gen. Lee, having left his wife and four small children to join the army, Potsdam, N. Y.

　　Ch. 10*th Gen.* :　1 Charles Crandall, b. April 3, 1860. 2 Fratz S., b. Nov. 20, 1861.　3 Banks.—4 Butler, twins, b. Sept. 15, 1863.　5 William J., b. April 30, 1868.

472　7 Mary, b. 1831, d. in infancy.

428　WILLIAM[8], son of *Samuel[7]*, of Royalton, Vt., *Samuel[7]*, *Ezekiel[6]*, *Jabez[5]*, *Samuel[4]*, *Richard[3]*, *Richard[2]*, *Richard[1]*, b. in Royalton, Feb., 1802; m. May 1, 1824, Wealthy M. Griffin, of Durham, Conn. — farmer.

Children, Ninth Generation :

473　1 Henry Allen, b. July 20, 1825 ; m. July 7, 1850, Sarah Prince, Westport, Conn.,

　　Ch. 10*th Gen.* :　1 Jenette, b. June 16, 1821 ; m. 2d husband, William Patterson, of New Haven, Sept. 14, 1869.

474　2 Mary Charlotte, b. June 15, 1828 ; m. June 26, 1849, Leyden Richardson, New Haven.

475　3 Maria Hannah, b. Jan. 18, 1830 ; m. Dec. 28, 1849, Samuel Farnham.　2d husband Thomas Chapman, machinist, Centreville, Conn., died Oct. 3, 1869, Hamden, Conn.

　　Ch. 10*th Gen.* :　1 Adelia, b. Dec. 17, 1851.　2 Frances W., b. Sept. 7, 1853.

478　4 Julia Ann, b. May 14, 1831; m. April 7, 1849, Norris Andrews, New Haven.

　　Ch. 10*th Gen.* :　1 Charles W., b. April 6, 1850.　2 Louisa J., b. March 23, 1851.　3 Anna M., b. May 28, 1853. 4 John F., b. March 12, 1856.　5 ......b. ......, 16, 1858. 6 Ida L., b....... 16, 1868.

485 5 Oliver William, b. Nov. 16, 1832 ; m. March 18, 1864,
Leona M. Jewell; carpenter, Newark, N. Y.

486 6 Louisa Jane, b. May 16, 1834 ; d. Oct. 19, 1841.

487 7 Gilbert Augustus, b. July 1, 1836; m. May 12, 1862, Hannah Cowls — carpenter, Newark.

488 8 Richard Melvin, b. Feb. 3, 1840; drowned Jan. 12, 1856.

489 9 Urban, b. March 1, 1842 ; m. May 27, 1866, Phebe M.
Barnes, New Haven, Conn.
Ch. 10th Gen. : 1 Emma A., b. July 6, 1869.

491 10 Laviena Elsia, b. Oct. 7, 1843 ; m. Oct. 22, 1865, George
Russell, New York, now New Haven, Conn.

492 11 Lewellyn Eugene, b. Oct. 21, 1845 ; d. April 15, 1855.

493 12 Jenette, b. June 10, 1846.

473 HENRY A. LYMAN[9], son of *William*, was born in Durham, 1825. *Westport.*

Children, Tenth Generation :

494 1 Sarah Alinda, b. Oct. 21, 1851.

495 2 Henry Albertus, b. March 12, 1853.

496 3 Charles Alvin, b. Feb. 11, 1855.

497 4 Charlotte Maria, b. Feb. 22, 1860.

498 5 Araminta Elenora, b. Oct. 27, 1863.

499 6 Mattie Lee, b. Oct. 1, 1866.

500 7 George Alpheus, b. Nov. 26, 1868.

485 OLIVER WILLIAM.

Children, Tenth Generation :

501 1 Frank Eugene, b. May 5, 1864.

502 2 Warren Oliver, b. July 7, 1866.

503 3 William Ellsworth, b. March 14, 1869.

487 GILBERT AUGUSTUS.

Children, Tenth Generation :

504 1 Eugene, b. June 7, 1863.

505 2 Charles A., b. Aug. 3, 1864.

506 3 Mitchell L., b. Jan. 30, 1866.

507 4 Jane, b. May 26, 1867 — all deceased but Mitchell.

426 NANCY LYMAN[8], dau. of *Samuel*[7], m. Abram Collins,
Parishville, July 9, 1826.

Children, Tenth Generation :

508 1 Sarah Ann, b. July, 1828 ; m. Oct. 4, 1848, William H.
Hewit.
Ch. 10th Gen. : 1 Helen, b. May 24, 1851 ; m.
March 22, 1870, Joseph Collett. 2 Emma E., b. April
11, 1857. 3 Louisa J., b Nov. 7, 1858; d. Oct. 6,
185 . . . 4 Gratia, b. March 26, 1863.

513 2 Laura, b. June 28, 1830 ; d. Aug. 17, 1841.

7

514 3 Lyman M., b. Aug. 20, 1833; m. July 4, 1859, Sarah A.
     Hepburn.
          Ch. 10th Gen.: 1 George B., b. Jan. 1, 1861. 2 Ira, b.
     June 22, 1862. 3 Warren A., b. Oct. 16, 1863; d. Dec.
     3, 1865.
518 4 Prudence E., b. Oct. 1, 1835, m. July 21, 1853, Luther
     Burnett.
          Ch. 10th Gen.: 1 Laura E., b. Feb. 8, 1855. 2 John
     Fremont, b. June 6, 1856; d. 1858. 3 Martha, b.
     Sept. 16, 1856. 4 David A., b. Nov. 17, 1864. 5.
     Mary A., b. March, 2, 1866.
524 5 Norman, b. July 28, 1840; m. Oct. 6, 1862, Orpha A.
     Smith, Parishville.
          Ch. 10th Gen.: 1 Henry H., b. Jan. 16, 1864. 2
     Arthur R., b. Feb. 11, 1866. 3 Ella B., b. April 28,
     1868.

279 BETSEY LYMAN[7], dau. of *Ezekiel*[6], b. 18 Nov., 1772;
m. 1790, Garner Rix, and d. Nov. 1, 1851. He d. Aug.
28, 1854, aged 85. Lucy F., 2d wife, d. Dec. 25, 1863.
                                                   Royalton, Vt.
          Children, Eighth Generation :
528 1 Ebenezer, b. Feb. 29, 1792; m. Rhoda Dewey.
          Ch. 9th Gen.: 1 Rachel Ann. 2 Joseph. 3 Rhoda.
     4 Cornelius.
532 2 Rebecca, b. Jan. 23, 1794; m. Darius Dewey.
          Ch. 9th Gen. : 1 Florinda. 2 Garner R.
535 3 Levi, b. June 1, 1796; m. 1829, Lydia M. Mathews, who d.
     1843.
          Ch. 9th Gen.: 1 William M., b. 1831. 2 Mary E., b.
     1833.
538 4 Lemuel, b. May 10, 1798; m. Esther Wild.
          Ch. 9th Gen.: 1 John. 2 A nameless infant. 3
     Mary. 4 Daniel.
545 5 Heman, b. July 25, 1800; m. Betsey Fay.
          Ch. 9th Gen. : 1 George. 2 Albert.
547 6 Calvin, b. May 17, 1802; deceased.
548 7 Florinda, b. April 13, 1804; no further record.
549 8 Daniel, b. Aug. 4, 1806; no record.
550 9 Mary, b. March 12, 1809 ; deceased.
551 10 Joseph, b. April 23, 1811 ; d. in infancy.
552 11 Mary, b. May 18, 1815 ; m. Cyrus Page.
          Ch. 9th Gen. : Willis R.

280 ELIPHALET[7], 6th son of *Ezekiel*[6], *Jabez*[5], *Samuel*[4], *Rich*
ard[3], *Richard*[2], *Richard*[1], 1768 – 1843, was born in Lebanon,

Conn., and removed with his father about 1783 to Royalton, Vt., where he lived a farmer until his death, Nov. 15, 1843. He m. Mary Lee, of Middletown, Conn., b. May 27, 1770; d. at Royalton, March 3, 1857.   *Royalton, Vt.*

Children, Eighth Generation :

553   1 Mary J., b. Dec. 17, 1791 ; m. Luther Howe, of Royalton.
     Ch. 9th Gen.: 1 Lyman. 2 Mary Ann. 3 William Johnson. 4 Storrs Lyman. 5 Diantha. 6 Elizabeth. 7 Louisa. 8 Norman Francis. 9 Mary Jane.

564   2 Elias, b. Aug. 18, 1793 ; m. Pattie Farnham, of Tunbridge, Vt.; died 1864 ; Royalton.
     Ch. 9th Gen.: 1 Martha. 2 William R. 3 Mary. 4 Philip. 5 Sarah. 6 Jennette. 7 Laurie. 8 Eleanor. 9 Susan. 10 Marion. 11 Charlina.

576   3 Garner Rix, b. Oct. 20, 1795 ; m. Caroline Ainsworth, of Tunbridge; d. 1856 ; Royalton.
     Ch. 9th Gen.: 1 Semantha. 2 Garner Rix, Jr. 3 Elizabeth W. 4 John S. 5 Laura A. 6 Mary Jane. 7 Julia Fox. 8 Charlotte S. 9 Gertrude M. 10 Clarence P.

587   4 William Lee, b. Oct. 21, 1798. m. Polly Woodward, of R., d. 1855 ; Polly d. 1843 ; Royalton
     Ch. 9th Gen.: 1 Harriet E. 2 Frederick A. 3 Francis. 4 Mary. 5 Martha. 6 Charlotte.

594   5 Storrs Lee, b. May 1, 1801 ; m. Lydia Hawes, of Chatham, Mass.; Chatham, Mass.
     Ch. 9th Gen.: 1 Laura Augusta. 2 Sophia J. 3 Chas. Henry. 4 Storrs Lee, Jr. 5 Mary Lee.

60 0   6 D. Lee Lyman, M.D., b. at Royalton, Vt., Feb. 2, 1804, read medicine, and graduated ; never practiced ; has represented his native town 2 years ; was state senator for 2 years from Windsor county, Vt.; in the general assembly of the State of Vermont ; m. Betsey Geer Winnock, of Lebanon, N. H., May 21, 1829. She was b. Jan. 3, 1809 ; d. Sept. 7, 1829 ; m. Nancy Fox, of Royalton, Oct. 26, 1836 ; b. April 23, 1804. She d. Sept. 3, 1868.
     Ch. 9th Gen.: 1 Richard Fox. Robert Fox (twins) b. Jan. 11, 1842 ; Richard Fox, d. April 1842 ; Robert Fox, m. Annett, Wolcott, March 3, 1864, Royalton.

281 JABEZ[7], of Royalton, Vt., 7th son of *Ezekiel[6], Jabez[5], Samuel[4], Richard[3], Richard[2], Richard[1]*, b. Aug. 13, 1774 ; m. June 24, 1799, Lois Johnson of Middletown, Conn., dau. of Truelove Johnson ; d. in Royalton, Dec. 26, 1849.
     Royalton, Conn.

Children, Eighth Generation :

603   1 Jabez, b. Dec. 4, 1799 ; m. Abigail Woodbury, Royalton, Conn.

Ch. 9th Gen.: 1 Horace A., resides in Ferresburgh,
Vt. 2 Aurelia L., resides in West Concord, Vt. 3 Charles
A., resides in Royalton, Vt. 4 Daniel W., aged 25, d.
April, 1858 or '9. 5 Amanda C., resides in Lowell,
Mass. 6 Elizabeth R.. Royalton, Vt. 7 Joel F., resides
in Royalton, Vt. 8 Augusta J., resides in Sharon, Vt.
9 Alice J., resides in Sharon, Vt. 10 Edward F., resides
in Royalton, Vt. 11 Abbie R., d. in infancy.

614   2 Mehitabel, b. March 6, 1861 ; m. Tracy Crandall ; Royalton.
615   3 Joel, b. May 20, 1893 ; a millwright, farmer and deacon,
       m. Jan. 18, 1827, Mary Richardson, Barre, Vt. His
       wife d. June 12, 1827, aged 69, Fort Covington, N. Y.
          Ch. 9th Gen.: 1 Mary C. b. Sept. 23, 1834 ; d. Jan.
       1840. 2 Martha R., b. Jan. 1, 1835 ; m. Massena, N. Y.
616   4 Jerusha, b. March 13, 1805 ; m. James Fay of Royalton,
       Potsdam, N. Y.
617   5 William, b. Dec. 18, 1806 ; d. about 1814.
618   6 Alvin, b. Oct. 20, 1809 ; m. Eleanor Huntington, Feb. 1,
       1835 ; Napoli, Cattaraugus Co., N. Y.
          Ch. 9th Gen.: 1 Azro, b. Oct. 28, 1835 ; d. Jan. 14,
       1840. 2 David, b. Oct. 20, 1837 ; d. Jan. 11, 1840.
       3 Augustus, b. Dec. 27, 1839 ; d. July 30, 1842. 4 Au-
       gustus, b May 7, 1843 ; d. June 27, 1849. 5 Joel H.,
       b. Aug. 11, 1845 ; 1st. Lieut. in U. S. army, New York ;
       m. Oct 21, 1868, Cassie Carter of N. Y. City. 6 Mary
       E., b. Oct. 3, 1849. 7 Myra E., b. July 23 ...... ; m.
       Aug. 15, 1869, Oscar Sheldon, North Vineland, N. J.
          Ch. 10th Gen.: 1 Edward Carter ; b. Dec. 24, 1869.
626   7 William, b. April 14, 1814, Bloomington, Grant Co., N. Y.
627   8 Susan, b. Aug. 9, 1816 ; m. George Grow.
628   9 George, b. May 19, 1820 ; m. Rachel Slaughter, Blooming-
       ton, Grant Co., Wisconsin.
629   10 A child, d. in infancy.
          The men of this family are all farmers in good circum-
       stances.

628 GEORGE LYMAN[8], son of *Jabez*[7], of Royalton, Vt., m.
May 23, 1848.   *Bloomington, Grant Co., Wis.*
    Children, Ninth Generation :
630 1 Corydon Dwight, b. March 21, 1849, at Williamstown, Vt.
631 2 Clarence Edwards, b. at W. May 7, 1850.
632 3 Harlan Newell, b. in Patch Grove, Wis., Nov. 9, 1858.
       Bloomington, Grant Co., Wis.
633 4 Ettie Almena, b. in Tafton, Wis., March 9, 1862.

262 ISRAEL[6], 3d son, no report.

264 ELISHA[6], 4th son of *Jabez*[5], *Samuel*[4], *Richard*[3], *Richard*[2], *Richard*[1], m. Sept. 26, 1764, Eunice Lamphear.

Children, Seventh Generation :

638 1 Elisha, b.... ....; settled in New London, Conn.
639 2 Frederic, b.........; Warren, Herkimer Co., N. Y.
640 3 Alvan, b. Nov. 3, 1770; d. Aug. 7, 1853.
641 4 Philota, b ....; m. Bliss.
642 5 Wealtha, b.........; m. Cleland, Warren, Herkimer Co., N. Y.

638 ELISHA[7], *Elisha*[6], *Jabez*[5], *Samuel*[4], *Richard*[3], *Richard*[2], *Richard*[1], b. 1765, d. 1849; settled in New London; resided in Mystic, and in Norwalk, where he died. He joined the Revolutionary army at the age of 14 or 15, and served until his health failed.

Children, Eighth Generation.

643 1 Elisha, supposed residence New London.
644 2 James B., New London, refuses after frequent and urgent solicitations, to give any record of his family; neither has any report been given by Elisha, Luther, and Thaddeus, all of whose residences were or still are in New London. James B. is known to have two sons of adult age.

639 FREDERICK LYMAN[7], *Elisha*[6], *Jabez*[5], *Samuel*[4], *Richard*[3], *Richard*[2], *Richard*[1], removed to Warren, Herkimer Co., N. Y., where he had a family of four sons and one daughter. These sons now reside in Jordansville, in the same county. Of these, no satisfactory account can be obtained. Indirectly, it has been ascertained that the names of these four sons are : 645 Frederick. 646 Dillon. 647 Hubbard. 648 Alvin. 649 Alice.

Children, Eighth Generation :

650 1 FREDERICK.
  Ch. 9th Gen. : 1 Harvey. 2 Leonard. 3 Jane. 4 Marinda.
655 2 DILLON.
  Ch. 9th Gen.: 1 Julia E. 2 Frederick D. 3 Emily W. 4 Jane. 5 Electa.
660 3 HUBBARD, m. Mary Belsham; no dates.

Children, Ninth Generation :

662 1 Merrill, b. Nov. 7, 1823; m. March 27, 1867, Josephine Reynolds, of England — farmer; Rochelle, Ogle Co., Ill.
663 2 Mary, b. Oct. 14, 1868.
664 3 John, b. May 24, 1827; m. Oct. 28, 1855, Reynolds, b. Dec. 25, 1838, in Lancashire, England — farmer; Hicks' Mills N. Y., Franklin, De Kalb Co., Ill.

    Ch. 10th Gen.: 1 Oscar, b. Aug. 26, 1856. 2 Frank, b. June 8, 1858. 3 Hattie, b. June 14, 1863. 4 Carrie, b. June 12, 1868.

669 4 Gilbert, b. in Columbia, Herkimer Co., N. Y., Jan. 8, 1835; m., March 14, 1868, Ann Eliza Bird, of Jackson, Ohio— farmer; Luda, Ogle county, Ill.

    Ch. 10th Gen.: 1 Celeste Ellen, b. Jan. 20, 1869. 2 Orville P. b. Aug. 12, 1870.

670 5 Dutson Lyman, son of Hubbard, b. Aug. 7, 1837; m. Dec. 31, 1862, Mary Jane Schermerhorn, of Richmond, Schoharie Co., N. Y.—farmer and innkeeper, Creston, Ogle Co., Ill.

    Ch. 10th Gen.: 1 Henry Gilbert, b. Oct. 23, 1863; d. Aug. 25, 1865. 2 Harvey Sheridan, b. Dec. 8, 1864; 3 Alice W., b. May 15, 1866; 4 Nelson Hubbard, b. April, 1868; 5 Ida Jane, b. Sept. 15, 1869.

676 6 Daniel.   677 7 Braza.   678 8 Irving.   679 9 Arthur.
    Of these last four children of Hubbard, no record could be obtained.

680 4 ALVIN.

Children, Ninth Generation:

681 1 Jefferson.	684 4 Henry.
682 2 George.	685 5 Harriet.
683 3 James.	686 6 Rhodaite .

673 ALICE W.[8], m. Willis; Cedarville, Herkimer Co., N. Y.

These confused and imperfect data have been obtained with great difficulty. We give them as received, without vouching for their accuracy.

640 ALVAN[7], 3d son of *Elisha[6], Jabez[5], Samuel[4], Rchard[3], Richard[2], Richard[1],* 1770–1853, m. Joanna Maples—blacksmith and farmer, captain of artillery in New London, in the War of 1812, a man of determined spirit, energy and courage; d. Aug. 7, 1863.

Children, Eighth Generation:

687 1 Frances, m. A. W. Manning, resided in Norwich, Conn., Their dau. Julia, m. Beckwith.

689 2 Thomas J., b. Oct. 3, 1809, New London.

691 3 George W., b ......; m. in Cincinnati, Ohio.

692 4 Lawrence L., b. Aug. 25, 1813; has one son George M. m. Oct. 8, 1843.

694 5 Albert G., b. Dec. 13, 1814.

    Ch. 9th Gen.: 1 Eugene, b. Oct. 19, 1842. 2 Thomas A., b. Jan. 29, 1851.

697 6 Lucy, b.........; m. A. D. Gardner, Jewet City, Conn.
   Ch. 9th Gen.: 1 Alfaretta J. 2 Johanna M. 3 Julia
   L. 4 Harriet.
702 7 Abby J., b. Jan. 11, 1824; m. E. B. Manly, Lebanon, Conn.
   Ch. 9th. Gen.: 1 Clarence, b. June 20, 1860. 2.
   Harriet J., b. June 22, 1862. 3 Mary A., b. Nov. 5,
   1865.
   The members of this family whose residence is not
   specified above, reside in Lebanon, Ct.

 12 DANIEL⁵, 3d son of *Samuel⁴*, b. Feb. 18, 1704; m.
1730, Mehitable Porter; d. 1784.   *Coventry.*
   Children, Sixth Generation:
706 1 Mehitable, b. Dec. 12, 1731.
707 2 Zilpah, b. Nov. 14, 1733; m. Thomas Porter, Nov. 1754,
   Coventry.
708 3 Richard, of whom nothing is known.
709 4 Joseph, b. and lived in Coventry; m. 1st, Southard, 2d
   Sally Longfellow; d. 1784, about 50 years of age.
   Ch. 7th Gen.: 1 Joseph, went to England and never
   returned. 2 Nathan, b. 1764, settled in East Windsor,
   Ct., m. Mary Bissell, had 13 children; d. 1826, aged 58,
   East Windsor.
   Ch. 8th Gen.: (1) Harry d. young. (2) Edwin, d. aged
   13. (3) Backus, d. aged 19. (4) Evilina, m. Jeffers,
   had ten children; d. 1865, between 70 and 80 years of
   age. (5) William, d. aged 22. (6) Alford, an itinerant
   Methodist preacher in Michigan, 10 children. (7)
   Mary, b. 1805; m. Barkee, 4 children. (8) Edwin, d.
   aged 27. (9) Charlotte Amelia, m. Henry Dates, Mt.
   Morris, N. Y.; d. aged 27, 2 children. (10) Twins d.
   nameless. (11) Henry Bissel, d. in California; the
   widow and two children are living there; the other two
   children are not given; of the 13 two only are survivors.
751 5 William, resided in Coventry; m. Richardson.
   Ch. 8th Gen.: 1 Jane, bapt. Oct. 21, 1798. 2 Aerauna,
   bapt. Nov. 10, 1799. 3 Alicia, bapt. Oct. 3, 1702. 4
   Idocia, bapt. Aug. 5, 1804. 5 Mary, bapt. Nov. 3,
   1805. 6 Lucy, bapt. Oct. 18, 1807. 7 Nathan T.,
   March, 1811. 8 Julia Ann, Oct. 22, 1815. 9, There is
   a record of Chancey, who d. March 30, 1812, probably
   next older than Julia Ann. Nathan T. lived in Kalamazoo, Mich. A daughter m. and went west; another to
   Vermont, and another to Maine.
760 5 Major Chester, b. 1783, left Connecticut, in early life, lived
   with a brother Stephen in the state of New York, m. and
   settled in Waltham, Mass., received from President

Madison, the appointment of captain of the 9th Regiment of Vermont Infantry; was promoted to major and served through the war of 1812; settled in Troy, N. Y.; represented the town three years in the state legislature; then removed to Swansey, where he still lives in his 88th year, with his third wife.

Ch. 8th Gen.: Eleven in number, six living. 1 Chester, Watertown, Mass. 2 Joseph Groton, N. H. 3 Leon, Swansey. 4 William, killed in the army of the Potomac, wife and two sons in Chelsea, Mass.; one daughter m. Albert Kingsbury, Keene, N. H.; another m. Ebenezer F. Lane, Swansey; and the 3d, Ephraim Whaler, Momence, Ill. 5 Hannah P., b. May 21, 1829, m. Aug. 14, 1850, E. F. Lane.

Ch. 9th Gen.: (1) Henry C., b. Feb. 22, 1852. (2) Hattie M., b. Aug. 15, 1854. (3) Chester L., b. April 9, 1857. (4) Maria F., b. April 20, 1863.

The following record was not received in time to be inserted in its place:

27 JEPHTHA LYMAN,[8] son of *Ozias,*[7] b. 1776; m. Phebe Willis, March 23, 1800, in Connecticut; d. aged 74, in Dover, Vt.

Children, Ninth Generation:

776 1 Jephtha, Jr., b. June 14, 1801; m. Sarah Cummings, Sept. 21, 1830, at Thetford, Vt. He d. Nov., 1862, in Dover, Vt.
     Ch. 10th Gen.: 1 Isaac C., b. Oct. 28, 1831, in Dover, Vt.; m. Mary L. Carpenter, at Tabor, Iowa, July 15, 1858. 2 Sophia E., b. Sept. 21, 1834, in Dover, Vt.; m. Chancey L. Clark, at Tabor, Iowa, April 2, 1862. 3 Monroe E., b. Oct. 10, 1840, in Dover, Vt. 4 Laura P., b. Aug. 8, 1843; m. John H. Fitch at Wilmington, Vt., Jan. 1, 1866.
781 2 Abiah, b. May 12, 1804; m. Avery Bartlett, June, 1829.
     Ch. 9th Gen.: 1 Lydia. 2 Lucretia. 3 Hannah. 4 Harriet. 5 Jane. 6 Julia. 7 Levi.
789 3 Sarah, b. Dec. 4, 1805; m. in Dover, Vt.
     Ch. 9th Gen.: 1 Heli V., b. July 12, 1828, in Dover; m. Candace Sherman, Oct. 29, 1852, at Brimfield, Mass. 2 Minerva S., b. Jan. 21, 1831; m. Solomon Jones, Nov. 21, 1854, Brattleboro, Vt. 3 Harvey C., b. Nov. 8, 1832, in Dover, Vt.; m. Lucy L. Thwing, March 24, 1856, at Brattleboro, Vt. 4 James B., b. June 1834, in Dover; d. Jan., 1842. 5 Hannah C., b. Dec. 12, 1838, in Dover; m. Marcus Pearce, April 19, 1864, at Tabor, Iowa. 6 Joel L., b. March 9, 1842. 7 Lester J., b. Nov. 1, 1845.
797 4 Cynthia, b. Sept. 27, 1808; m. William H. Snow, March, 1856.

798 5 Joel, b. Jan. 22, 1811.
799 6 James, b. Feb. 17, 1813; m. Lydia F. Esterbrook, May 18, 1842.
> *Ch. 9th Gen.:* 1 Franciener, m. Frank R. Mann, Jan., 1861; she d. June 5, 1863.
801 7 Laurana, b. May 20, 1814; m. William Walker, April 1842.
802 8 Amanda L., b. Feb. 10, 1817; m. Martin Bartlett, Sept., 1845.
> *Ch. 9th Gen.:* 1 Addison. 2 Edwin. 3 Henry. 4 James.
807 9 Eliza P., b. Aug. 17, 1819; m. John M. Cook, Nov., 1858.

II. DESCENDANTS OF RICHARD[3], THROUGH RICHARD[4], AND DEA. THOMAS[5].

RICHARD[4], 2d son of *Richard[3]*, *Richard[2]*, *Richard[1]*, was b. at Northampton, in 1678; removed with his family to Leba non, Conn., in 1696; m. April 7, 1700, Mary Woodward; d. June 6, 1746, aged 69, according to these dates. The epitaph on his grave stone in Lebanon, is: "Sacred to the memory of the well beloved Mr. Richard Lyman 4th, who after serving God and his generation faithfully many years, fell asleep in the cradle of death, June 6, 1746, in the 69th year of his age." *Lebanon, Ct.*

Children, Fifth Generation:
1 1 Israel, b. Feb. 22, 1701; d. March 13, 1701.
2 2 Ebenezer, b. Aug. 4, 1702; m. Lydia Wright, no date—farmer, Columbia.
3 3 Thomas, b. July 6, 1704; d. 1783, Lebanon Crank.
4 4 Mary, b. Oct. 27, 1706.
5 5 Hannah, b. Sept. 13, 1708; m. Swetland.
6 6 John, b. Jan. 10, 1711; m. Feb. 25, 1730, Hannah Birchard, who d. June 28, 1746; m. 2d wife, Sept. 3, 1747, Mary Strong of Coventry; d. 1781.
7 7 David, b. 1711; d. 1787.
8 8 Elizabeth, is given in one record without date or further notice of her.
9 9 Richard, b. March 23, 1721. With John and David he enters into covenant with their father and mother to provide for all their temporal wants during their natural lives. He m. June 15, 1758, Ann Bradford, of Haddam, living at that time in Mansfield, where his first two children were b.; then removed to Lebanon where two children were born to him.
> *Ch. 6th Gen.:* 1 Ann, b. April 13, 1759. 2 Richard, b. Sept. 22, 1761, in Mansfield, 3 Joseph Bradford, b. Sept. 1, 1767. 4.........b. Sept. 19, 1769. Nothing more can be found respecting this Richard[5].

8

2 EBENEZER[5], oldest son of *Richard*[4], m. Lydia Wright, date not given—farmer.   *Lebanon, Ct.*

Children, Sixth Generation:

14 1 Lydia, b. March 19, 1725.
15 2 Abigail, b. Dec. 23, 1726.
16 3 Silence, b. Feb. 8, 1728.
17 4 Grace, b. Dec. 6, 1730.
18 5 Rebeckah, such is the orthography of the record, b. May 12, 1733, at Mansfield.
19 6 Mary, b. at M., July 16, 1735. The subsequent history of these two daughters is unknown. The father appears to have returned to his former residence in Lebanon where the other children were born.
20 7 Ann, b. Aug. 4, 1737.
21 8 Elizabeth, b. Jan. 4, 1740.
22 9 Tamer, b. Feb. 9, 1742.
23 10 Ebenezer, b. Jan. 22, 1746.

3 DEA. THOMAS[5], 2d son of *Richard*[4], b. in Lebanon Crank, so called, in 1703; m. in early life Mary Guile, a woman of estimable character, and consistent, uniform and religious life, who died July 4, 1797, in the 90th year of her age. Dea. Thomas Lyman sustained for many years this office in the church in Lebanon Crank, the 2d in L., and by an eminently religious life honored his office in the church, manifesting the power of divine grace and the fruits of a holy life, by uniform communion with God. His epitaph is as follows:" Sacred to the memory of Dea. Thomas Lyman, who died Aug. 13, 1783, in the 80th year of his age. Few have enjoyed more constant communion with heaven; or, at intervals, had greater discoveries of divine things. His life was zealous and exemplary; his death peaceful and triumphant.

> " Behold, my friends, what grace can do for men,   •
> When, by it, they, like babes, are born again."

He died from injuries received by a fall in the bark mill of his tannery.

Inscription on the tomb of his wife :

> " Stop passenger ! see where I lie,
> As you now are so once was I,
> As I am now so you must be
> Prepare for death and follow me."

Children, Sixth Generation:

24 1 Polly, m.. .... Darling ; d. at Gill, Mass., July 27, 1801.
25 2 Sarah, b. 1729 ; unmarried ; d. at her brother Joseph's in East Hartford, Orford parish, July 7, 1801.

26 3 Eunice, m. ......Loomis, had 11 children; d. at Bernardston, Mass., about 1804.

27 4 Thomas, b. 1736; had 3 children: Jesse, Jeremiah and Louisa, (m. ...... Burnet).

28 5 Hannah, m. .. Smith, and settled in Mass., probably in Shelburn.

29 6 Elizabeth, m. ...... Lamb; d. in Coventry, Conn., May 5, 1795, aged 55; her daughter m. Mr. Watch of North Coventry, whose daughter m. Lyman Talcott. Mr. T.'s mother was also a Lyman.

30 7 Rachel, m. . Hunt of Vernon, Conn., and died soon after; left a son, Oliver.

31 8 Joseph, b. in Columbia, Conn., July 6, 1744; settled in the eastern part of Hartford, parish of Orford, now Manchester, where he d. Feb. 20, 1820.

32 9 Benjamin, twin brother of Joseph, settled in Columbia, and d. there in 1871.

33 10 Ruth, m. ...... Edwards, settled in Bernardston, Mass.; d. July 27, 1798; had several children.

34 11 Abigail, b. 1753; m. ...... Fitch, settled in Columbia; d. in Bolton, Dec. 13, 1842. Her husband d. in Columbia many years before. Her son Elijah settled in Bolton, whose son Patten is now living there.

27 THOMAS[6], eldest son of Dea. *Thomas[5]*, m. Anna Manly, Nov. 14, 1759, resided at Columbia, occupation, farmer. The inscription on his monument is as follows:

" In memory of Mr. Thomas Lyman, Jr., who died Nov. 1, 1769, in the 33d year of his age.

" Blessed are the dead that die in the Lord."

Children, Seventh Generation .

36 1 Rachel, b. Feb. 16, 1761; d. 1771.

37 2 Lois, b. April 6, 1762.

38 3 Jesse, b. June 20, 1764, known as Major Jesse.

39 4 Jeremiah, b. Jan. 6, 1766.

40 5 Anna, b. Nov. 14, 1768; m. a Steeter, and they removed with her brother Jeremiah to that part of Ohio, known as New Connecticut, and settled at Twinsburg, Summit Co. Jeremiah had been a soldier in the army of the Revolution, and is supposed to have received bounty lands which he sought to cultivate—previously had settled in Becket, Mass.

41 6 Thomas, b. Jan. 12, 1770, supposed to have removed with his brother Jeremiah to Ohio.

38 Major JESSE LYMAN[7], *Thomas[6]*, *Thomas[5]*, *Richard[4]*, *Richard[3]*, *Richard[2]*, *Richard[1]*, 1764–1814, for his various virtues and his distinguished services to his country as a

patriot warrior, is entitled to the grateful remembrance of his kindred and his countrymen. At the decease of his father in early childhood he was apprenticed to an uncle to learn the trade of tanner and shoemaker. At the age of 16, the earliest period at which he could be enrolled in the Revolutionary army, he enlisted as a private and served under Gen. Washington to the close of the war. He was one of the prison guard when Major André was led out to execution.

After retiring from the army he returned to his native place and industrial pursuits, and m. Mrs. Jerusha Hunt, of Lebanon, who d. Nov. 17, 1838. Of his ten children the first four daughters were b. in Lebanon. He then removed to Vermont, and became a resident of Vergennes, after some two years at Monkton. His occupation through life was that of tanner and currier.

He was a large, well proportioned man, about six feet in height, of lofty, commanding presence. Few men in the army made so noble an appearance in a military dress. His stately person was but an appropriate representation of his lofty patriotism. "Great in soul, he stood unmoved amid the fluctuations of parties and the strife of demagogues; with true independence his manly spirit soared above the meanness of duplicity and the baseness of dishonor. He was sober in his habits, humane of heart and peaceable in life, a kind husband and father, and a useful citizen. His unblemished character defies the invidious attack of envy, malice and detraction."

He was never plaintiff or defendant in any case in court. His character was unimpeachable enough to remain un-unscathed even in the political campaign of the war of 1812, when partizan zeal ran mad. The only impeachment of his character was that he allowed his business to drive him instead of maintaining the mastery of it himself.

After some months service in the war of 1812, Major Lyman returned to his home, but when the enemy invaded the state of New York he volunteered in the service of his country and continued in that service at Plattsburg, until the retreat of Provost. While at Plattsburg, by fatigue and exposure to the severity of the weather by night and by day, he lost his health and returned home, and after a short time, expired at the age of fifty-three years, at his own house, 14 days after his engagement in the battle of Plattsburg.

He left but a small property, having a large family without funds requisite for a large business. He had five sons and five daughters of whom three of each sex are still living, the most of whom are residents in the western states.

Children, Eighth Generation:

42   1 Jerusha L., b. Oct. 15, 1787 ; m. Chas. McNeil, Oct. 11, 1807, who d. Oct. 1864 ; she d. Nov. 7, 1838, Woodford.
43   2 Fanny, b. April 15, 1789 ; m. John McNeil, March, 1817, 2 daus. deceased ; d. Dec. 19, 1869.
44   3 Pamelia, b. Jan. 11, 1791 ; m. Samuel Hurlburt, Jan., 1805, 3 children deceased ; d. Jan. 31, 1840.
45   4 Laura, b. Feb. 24, 1793.   Never married ; d. July 19, 1852.
46   5 Warren, b. March 16, 1796, oldest son of Maj. Jesse, formerly resided in North Augusta, Canada West ; no children ; a worthy citizen and consistent Christian.
47   6 Maria, b. Jan. 31, 1799 ; m. John Lovell, of Amherst, Mass., Jan. 1, 1822.   He d. July 24, 1864.
48   7 George M., b. Feb. 10, 1801 ; never married ; d. May 8, 1828.
49   8 Wm. H., b. Oct 18, 1802 ; m. Louisa Maria Loop, May 28, 1826 ; 2d wife, Julia Sowles, Feb. 7, 1828 ; d. Sept. 17, 1864.
50   9 David, b. July 11, 1806.
51   10 John W., b. Nov. 3, 1809 ; m. Jerusha Newcomb ; no date.

42 JERUSHA LYMAN, dau. of Maj. *Jesse*, b. Oct. 15, 1787 ; d. Oct. 21, 1864 ; m. Charles McNeil of Charlotte, Vt., who was b. Nov. 20, 1782 ; d. Aug. 23, 1860.

Children, Ninth Generation:

52   1 Fanny L., b. June 29, 1808.
53   2 Mary Elizabeth, b. July 14, 1809.
54   3 Nancy Helen, b. Nov. 17, 1810 ; d. Aug. 13, 1859.
55   4 Laura L., b. April 7, 1812 ; m. W. B. Miner, Esq., Jersey-ville, Ill., 4 children : 1 Charles. 2 Nellie E. 3 Frances J. 4 John.
59   5 John L., b. Oct. 10, 1813, a farmer.
60   6 Charles, Jr., b. Dec. 13, 1814.
63   7 David, b. April 21, 1816.
64   8 James Breckenridge, b. Jan. 20, 1818.
65   9 Charlotte, b. Nov. 29, 1819 ; d. Jan. 28, 1839.
66   10 Henry, b. March 3, 1821.
67   11 Jane, b. Dec. 17, 1822.
68   12 George, b. April 15, 1824 ; d. April 18, 1854.
69   13 William, b. May 28, 1826 ; served in the war for the Union in 1861–3 ; was orderly Sergeant in Co.......7th Reg.; the State Militia.
70   14 Ellen, b. July 15, 1827 ; d. Sept. 15, 1827.
71   15 Julia Hunt, b. Oct. 10, 1828.

64 JAMES B. McNEIL, son of Charles McNeil, grandson of Jesse Lyman, of Vergennes, Vt., b. Jan. 20, 1818, in Charlotte, Vt.; m. Sarah Hayard, Dec. 24, 1846, farmer.

Charlotte, Vt.

Children, Tenth Generation:

72 1 Charles H., b. March 3, 1848.
73 2 Henry L., b. Oct. 9, 1849; d. Jan. 21, 1851.
74 3 Frederick R., b. Nov. 17, 1854.
75 4 Sarah L., b. Oct. 24, 1856.
76 5 Ella M., b. Dec. 14, 1858 ; d. Dec. 16, 1858.

47 MARIA, dau. of Major *Jesse*, b. Jan. 31, 1799, John Lovell, Jan. 1, 1822. He d. July 24, 1864. *Amherst, Mass.*

Children, Ninth Generation:

77 1 John, b. Dec. 19, 1825.
78 2 Henry M., b. Dec. 29, 1827.
79 3 Mary J., b. Jan. 14, 1830.
80 4 George W., b. Dec. 30, 1831.
81 5 Jane M., b. April 18, 1840.
82 6 Elizabeth, b. April 3, 1836.

50 DAVID[8], son of Major *Jesse*, lived in Vergennes   He had one son, Henry Clay, who, at the outbreak of the late rebellion, enlisted for the defense of his country; was in the battle of Bull Run, became ill in consequence of the fatigue and exhaustion connected with the retreat; returned to Vergennes, and d. Oct. 4, 1864.

Major Jesse and all his sons and daughters were worthy members of the Congregational church, as are most of their adult descendants — good citizens, lovers of good order and good morals; ready, according to their ability, to assist in every good work.

51 JOHN W. LYMAN[8], son of Major *Jesse*, b. in Vergennes, Vt.; m. March 18, 1840, Jerusha Newcomb, farmer.

Freedom, La Salle Co., Ill.

Children, Ninth Generation:

83 1 John W.; b. Sept. 21, 1844; m. Dec. 24, 1867, Nettie Ford.

III. DESCENDANTS OF RICHARD[3] THROUGH RICHARD[4]
AND DEAS. JOSEPH[6] AND BENJAMIN.[6]

DEA. JOSEPH LYMAN, son of Deacon *Thomas* and *Mary* Lyman — the 8th in the above list — was born in Lebanon, Conn., July 6th, 1744; m. Sarah Edwards—b. March 28th, 1746—dau. of Thomas and Rebecca Edwards,

April 9th, 1767. He settled, the same year, in that part of Hartford, afterwards known as Orford parish, now the town of Manchester. The deeds of some of his land describe it as situated in "Hartford on the east side of the great river, in the tier of lots adjoining Bolton. He was a farmer and tanner; a deacon in the church, and a man of excellent character. He was deranged for many years before his death, which took place Feb. 20th, 1820. His wife died April 2, 1814.

Children, Seventh Generation:

1 1 Daniel, b. Jan. 5, 1768; d. in Dec., 1854.
2 2 A son, b. and d. Jan. 5, 1770.
3 3 Mary, b. May 12, 1771; m. Samuel Rider, and settled in New Hartford, Ct.; d. in New Hartford, Sept. 18, 1796.
4 4 Sarah, b. July 19, 1773; d. Aug. 24, 1793.
5 5 Joseph, b. Aug. 13, 1774; d. July 28, 1842.
6 6 Thomas, b. Sept..8, 1777; d. July 6, 1859.
7 7 Benjamin, b. May 8, 1780; d. Nov. 26, 1858.
8 8 Jesse, b. June 4, 1782; d. July, 1863.
9 9 Chester, b. Dec. 4, 1785; d. May 9, 1864.
10 11 Twins, b. and d. Oct. 7, 1788.
12 12 Salmon, b. March 13, 1791; living, 1872.

1 DANIEL LYMAN[7], 1st son of Dea. *Joseph*, settled a few rods east of his father's, on the Hartford and Providence Turnpike, 10 miles from Hartford city. He m. Lydia Martha Brewster, of Columbia, Conn., about 1794. He was a farmer; a devout man, and of high moral worth. His children, all born at the homestead.

Children, Eighth Generation:

13 1 Milton, b. Manchester, Hartford Co., Nov. 15, 1795.
14 2 Joseph Wadsworth, b. Jan. 8, 1798.
15 3 Daniel Brewster, b. Jan. 26, 1800.
16 4 Mary Annett, b. Oct 23, 1804.
17 5 Jerusha Edwards, b. 1807; d. at home 1842, unmarried.
18 6 Diodate Brockway, b. 1809.
19 7 Lydia Martha, b. Aug. 25, 1813; m. Zenas Loomis, of Coventry, Ct., May 24, 1854; no children. Coventry, Ct.

13 DEA. MILTON LYMAN[8], 1st son of *Daniel*[7], grandson of Dea *Joseph*[6], Marshall, Oneida Co., New York; b. Manchester, Hartford Co., Conn., Nov. 15, 1795; m. Jan. 24, 1819, Rachel Carpenter also of Manchester, Conn. His wife Rachel, d. at Marshall, N. Y., March 21, 1820. He m. for his 2d wife Nov. 15, 1820, Olive Parker, of Marshall, Oneida Co., N. Y. He d. Oct. 16, 1870, at Marshall — wagon maker.

He was 35 years a member of the Congregational Church in Hanover, in the town of Marshall, and for many years one of its deacons.

He could always be relied upon. As a church member and church officer he was sure to be found promptly on all occasions in his place, and both ready and anxious to do whatever he could for the cause of Christ which he loved with his whole heart. In storm and shine he was always the same resolved, consistent, active servant of his master.

When the cause of anti-slavery and of temperance was in ill odor with the great mass of the community around him he stood forth at once as their advocate.

He was also generous in his habits of giving, and sometimes even as it seemed to some of his best friends, beyond his ability.

His habits of body and mind were active and fresh to the last, and he was dismissed from earth without any of the slow decay of age, spending one sabbath joyfully on earth and the next more joyfully in heaven, greatly missed by the little band of church members that worship now without him in the same sanctuary.

While his death is precious in the sight of the Lord, the memory of his life of piety and religious fervor will be ever precious to them.

He had never tasted liquors or tobacco or even tea or coffee, in all his life.

Children, Ninth Generation :

20 1 Harriet Wait, b. at Marshall, Oneida Co., N. Y., Jan. 10, 1820.
21 2 Milton Edwards, b. Nov. 19, 1821.
22 3 Daniel Parker, b. May 17, 1823.
23 4 Aurelia Louisa, b. Oct. 25, 1825 ; d. May 25, 1855, at Marshall, Oneida Co., N. Y.
24 5 Emery Wadsworth, b. Sept , 14, 1827.
25 6 Thomas Spencer, b. Nov. 19, 1832.
26 7 Martha Jane, b. June 2, 1833 ; m. May, 1855, Alfred B. Pitkin, Hartford, Ct., had two daughters.

20 Harriet Wait[9], m. Joseph W. Hamilton, Sept. 1, 1840, who d. at Meaford, Ontario, Canada, Oct. 9, 1867.
Meaford, Ontario, Canada.
Children, Tenth Generation :

27 1 Joseph Henry Hamilton ; b. Oct. 8, 1841 ; m. Caroline Decker, Feb. 15, 1868.
   Ch. 11th Gen.: 1 Lyman Emerson Hamilton, b. June 14, 1869.
28 2 Rachel Angeline, b. July 17, 1843 ; m. Benjamin Franklin Saunders, Jan. 14, 1864.
   Ch. 11th Gen.: 1 Carrie Agnes Saunders, b. Dec. 27, 1867. 2 Hattie Sophronia, b. Jan. 3, 1870.
32 3 Edward Thomas, b. Dec. 4, 1845.
33 4 Milton Clark, b. July 16, 1849.
34 5 Charles Loomis, b. Feb. 3, 1852.
35 6 Harriet Louisa, b. May 16, 1854.

21 MILTON EDWARDS LYMAN[9], Egg Harbor, Door county, Wisconsin, b. in Marshall, Oneida Co., N. Y., Nov. 19, 1821; m. at Milwaukee, Wis., Aug. 21, 1852, Adeline King, b. March 23, 1829. Has held the office of county judge two terms; clerk of the circuit court two terms; county superintendent common schools two terms; town treasurer two terms; town supervisor three terms; town clerk four years; justice of the peace eighteen years; district clerk eight years; occupation, merchant.   *Egg Harbor, Wis.*

Children, Tenth Generation:

36 1 Edward C., b, in Vernon, Ct., June 29, 1844; m. Jan. 3, 1872, Jennie E. Sheldon, dau., of Rev. E. P. Sheldon merchant in Albany and Troy.
37 2 Milton, b. in Marshall, Oneida Co., N. Y.; d. Oct., 1871.
38 3 Olive Parker, Marshall, Oneida Co., N. Y.
39 4 Milton Emory, b. Washington, Door Co, Wis., Feb. 23, 1853; d. Dec. 16, 1871.

22 DANIEL PARKER LYMAN[9], 2d son of *Milton*[8], grandson of *Daniel*[7], South Manchester, Hartford Co. Ct., b. at Marshall, Oneida Co., New York, May 17, 1823; m. at Manchester, Ct., March 31, 1846, Mary Jane, 2d dau. of Dea. Daniel Russell, of Ellington, Tolland Co., Ct. — commercial traveler.   *South Manchester, Ct.*

Children, Tenth Generation:

40 1 Mary Isbella, b. June 9, 1849.
41 2 Ellen Maria, b. July 28, 1851; m. at Manchester, Ct., Jan. 25, 1870, Thomas Broadhurst, of Manchester, Ct.
   Ch. 11th Gen.: 1 Leon Parker, b. June, 1871.
42 3 Carrie Eliza, b. April 21, 1853.
43 4 Katie Louisa, b. Sept. 24, 1856.
44*5 Jessie May, b. Sept. 23, 1861; d. Sept. 16, 1861.

24 EMORY WADSWORTH LYMAN[9], 3d son of *Milton*[8], grandson of *Daniel*[7], Lantan, Van Buren Co., Mich., b. at Marshall, Oneida Co., N. Y., Sept. 4, 1827; m. at Chicago Ill., July 23, 1851, Anna Russell — farmer.
      Lautan, Van Buren Co., Mich.

Children, Tenth Generation:

44 1 Emery Russell, b. at Marshall, N. Y., April 13, 1855.
45 2 Mary Louisa, b. at Meaford, Ont., C. W., Oct. 23, 1856.
46 3 Hattie Jane, b. at Marshall, N. Y., Sept. 10, 1860.

25 THOMAS SPENCER LYMAN[9], 4th son of *Milton*[8], Egg Harbor, Door Co., Wis., b. at Marshall, Oneida Co., N. Y.,

9

Nov. 19, 1832; m. at Waterville, N. Y., Oct. 24, 1857, Mary Fidelia Gilbert, of Marshall — farmer.

Egg Harbor, Door Co., Wis.

Children, 1enth Generation:

47 1 Thomas E., b. at Marshall, N. Y., Oct. 4, 1858.
48 2 Martha, b. at Marshall, N. Y., July 1, 1861.
49 3 Juliette A., b. at Marshall, N. Y., Nov. 18, 1863.
50 4 Daniel H., Egg Harbor, Door Co., Wis., Nov. 19, 1867.
51 5 Mary, Egg Harbor, Door Co., Wis., April.30, 1869.

14 JOSEPH WADSWORTH LYMAN⁸, 2d son of *Daniel⁷*, b. Jan. 8, 1798; m. in Jan. 1824, Electa Loomis of Coventry, b. Feb. 11, 1801, and settled in Stockbridge, Oneida Co., N. Y.— was a blacksmith; a pious man, and a good citizen. He d. June 19, 1860. *Stockbridge, N. Y.*

Children, Ninth Generation:

52 1 Electa Maria, b. Feb. 6, 1827; m. Edward Hill, July 31, 1850; d. April 3, 1851.
53 2 Emerson Wadsworth, b. April 23, 1837; m. Mary Lucretia Francis, Nov., 14, 1860; d. March 15, 1863. His wife d. Feb. 2, 1864. Both children settled near their father in Central New York.

15 DANIEL BREWSTER LYMAN⁸, 3d son of *Daniel⁷*, son of *Joseph⁶*, b. Jan. 26, 1800, graduated at Amherst College in 182..., in preparation for the ministry, but became a teacher. He taught successfully for several years an academy or private school in Glastenbury, and in Berlin, Ct. He married Caroline Hills, April 2, 1835, of East Hartford, b. May 26, 1801, and settled in that town on a farm, where he d. from a fall, Oct. 28, 1846. He was a man of active piety, and an earnest promoter of the religions and educational interests of the community. His widow still occupies the homestead *East Hartford, Ct.*

Children, Ninth Generation:

54 1 Christopher E., b. March 14, 1837; insane, d. Jan. 27, 1867.
55 2 Sarah E., b. Oct. 27, 1838; d. May 17, 1853.
56 3 Helen M., b. Nov. 25, 1840.
57 4 Brewster O., b. March 2, 1842; d. Jan. 24, 1861.

16 MARY ANETTE⁸, b. Oct. 23, 1804; m. Deacon Dan Russell of Ellington, Conn., a farmer, and resided there until some years after his death, when she m. Deacon Austin Loomis, a farmer. *North Amherst, Mass.*

Children, Ninth Generation

58 1 James Milton Russell; b. Aug. 27, 1836; m. Jane Spaulding, Manchester, Conn., July 14, 1858.

Ch. 10th Gen. : 1 Frankie Leon, b. Dec. 7, 1859 ; d.
Sept. 26, 1863, at the age of 3 years 9 months. 2 Raymond,
b. Feb. 5, 1864. 3 Kittie, b. Feb. 27, 1868.

59 2 Robert Lyman Russell, b. June 2, 1838; merchant in Hartford ; m. Jennie Watrous, of Bolton, Conn., Sept. 22, 1803.
Ch 10th Gen.: 1 Robert Dan, d. in infancy.

60 3 Diodate Brockway Russell, b. Nov. 23, 1840, farmer; was
in the war of the rebellion ; m. Ellen Lawrence, of Montague, Mass., Sept., 1864.
Ch. 10th Gen.: 1 Mary.

18 DIODATE BROCKWAY LYMAN[8], b. 1809; was a teacher
of district schools for several winters when a young man,
chiefly in Manchester and East Hartford. He m. Eliza
Vibbert, and, with the exception of a few years in Hartford, he lived on the homestead, until he moved about
1868, to Dunlap in Iowa, where his oldest son Henry had
previously settled. *Dunlap, Iowa.*

Children, Ninth Generation .

61 1 Henry Brewster, b. Feb. 8, 1832, at Manchester, Conn.
62 2 Charles Northrop, b. May 14, 1835, Hartford, Conn.
63 3 Mary Elizabeth, b. Aug. 1, 1837, at Hartford, Conn.
64 4 Albert Russell, b. June 22, 1842, Manchester, Conn.; d.
Oct. 13, 1850, at Manchester, Conn.
65 5 Arthur Wadsworth, b. Oct. 7, 1844, Manchester, Conn.
All the children now living, reside at Dunlap, Iowa, and
are farmers with the exception of the second son. There
are nine grandchildren living; names and dates not given.

62 CHARLES NORTHROP LYMAN[9], son of *Diodate Brockway*[8],
and Eliza Vibbert Lyman, grandson of *Daniel*[7], Manchester, Conn., great grandson of *Dea. Joseph*[6], b. at Hartford,
Conn., May 14, 1835 ; m. Oct. 13, 1863, Miss Eveline
Upson, of New Haven, Conn.—Congregational minister ;
has been pastor there one year and a half, was nearly
six years pastor of the Congregational church of Canton
Center, Conn.; was one year in the army, first as private,
second as chaplain of 20th Regiment Conn. Volunteers.
Dunlap, Iowa.

Children, Tenth Generation :

75 1 Charles Russell, b. Jan. 19, 1867, at Canton Center, Conn.
76 2 Theron Upson, b. Sept. 7, 1869, at Dunlap, Iowa.

19 LYDIA MARTHA, b. Aug. 25, 1813; m. Zenas Loomis
of Coventry, Conn., May 24, 1854; no children.
Coventry, Conn.

55 JOSEPH LYMAN, JR.[7], second son of Dea. *Joseph*[6], son of *Thomas*[5], b. Aug. 13, 1774, m. Anna Dart, dau. of Joseph Dart of Orford, now Manchester, April 12, 1804, d. suddenly, of disease of the heart, July 28, 1842. His widow d. June 2, 1855. He settled, as farmer, about a mile from his father's in Manchester, and resided there through life. He had four sons and five daughters.

Manchester, Conn.

Children, Eighth Generation :

77 1 Joseph, b. Jan. 31, 1805; farmer on the homestead; unmarried; d. June 5, 1865. Paralysed two years before.

78 2 Sarah Edwards, b. Nov. 18, 1806; m. Aaron S. Ingram, farmer, of Bolton, Ct , Sept. 26, 1848, where they still reside. No children.

79 3 Ira, b. Feb. 9, 1808; m. Nov. 1, 1832, Hannah Loomis of Bolton, Conn., b. Dec., 14, 1807 ; settled in Stockbridge, Oneida Co., N. Y., where they had sons.

    Ch. 9th Gen. : Francis Emerson, b. May 20, 1834; d. Aug. 24, 1834. 2 Francis Loomis, b. June 11, 1836 ; d. May 11, 1837. In 1855, they removed to Lowville, Lewis Co., N. Y., where they now live — a wheelwright by trade.

80 4 Loomis, b. Nov. 28, 1809; d. Oct. 1, 1811.

81 5 Anna, b. Feb. 24, 1815; m. Sept. 2, 1868, Henry C. Stoughton, of South Windsor, Conn.; a farmer. Resides there.

82 6 Sybil Loomis, b. April 21, '1818; m. Nov., 27, 1844, William R. Wills, a mason of East Hartford, Conn., where they now reside.

    Ch. 9th Gen.: 1 Emogene, b. Sept. 11, 1845. 2 Luella, b. April 12, 1847 ; d. of hydrophobia, Nov. 11, 1853. 3 Jerome, b. April 15, 1849. 4 Viola, b. April 18, 1825. 5 Chelsea, b. Oct. 20, 1854. 6 Monroe, b. Dec. 9, 1857. 7 Addie, b. Sept. 23, 1859. 8 Everett. 9 Elliott, twins, b. March 16, 1864.

92 7 Eunice, b. Jan., 7, 1820; d. April 13, 1857, at the homestead, unmarried.

93 8 Thomas, b. Jan. 11, 1826. In 1841, went to learn the trade of wheelwright with his brother Ira, in Stockbridge, N. Y. In 1847, went to South Coventry, Ct., m. Dec. 31, 1848, Julia A. Snow, of Ashford, Conn., in 1855; moved to Tamaroa, Perry Co., Ill. He d. Oct. 22, 1856; and his widow d. Oct. 8, 1860.

    Ch. 8th Gen. : 1 Mary Celestia, b. in Coventry, Dec. 26, 1849. 2 Charles Thomas, b. in Tamaroa, June 18, 1856. The children returned to Manchester, and Mary C., m. August 24, 1868, Charles H. Gates, of Manchester. [9th Gen. Edward Leverett, b. July 15, 1869, in South Windsor, Conn.]

96 9 Harriet, b. Oct. 16, 1829 ; m. April 3, 1856, Cornelius
       L. Cheney, of East Hartford, Conn.   They lived several
       years in that place, and then removed to Glastenbury,
       Conn., where they still reside.   Mr. Cheney is a manu-
       facturing optician.
         Ch. 9th Gen. : 1 Robert Herstine, b. March 16, 1857.
       2 Walter Lyman, b. Oct. 13, 1859. 3 Ella Louisa, b.
       Dec. 19, 1869.

    6 THOMAS LYMAN[7], son of Dea. *Joseph[6]*, son of *Thomas[5]*, b.
Sept. 8, 1777 ; m. about 1700, Mabel Millard, of Orford,
East Hartford, dau. of Andrus Millard, and settled in Vernon, N. Y. ; but soon removed to Hanover, a society in
Paris, N. Y., since Marshall, where he resided till his death
July 6, 1859.   His wife d. in 1857,   He was a prosperous
farmer; was among the earliest settlers in that part of
N. Y. ; a leading member of the Methodist church ; a man
of grave demeanor, sound judgment, high integrity, great
moral worth, and wide influence in the community.
                                            Marshall, N. Y.
         Children, Eighth Generation :
100 1 Truman Edwards, b. in 1803; settled in Marshall, N. Y., m.
       Oct. 19, 1826, Electa Parker, of Kirkland, N. Y.
         Ch. 9th Gen.: 1 Orpha Jane, b. Jan. 30, 1828; m.
       J. W. Lewis ; settled in Decatur, Mich. [*Ch. 10th
       Gen.:* (1) Millard E. (2) Henry P. (3) John L.]
       2 Emily Addia, b. March 13, 1830. 3 Mary Electa,
       b. March 9, 1834; m. Ansel A. Skinner, has 1
       son, Ansel Augustus, b. 1860. (4) Thomas Henry,
       b. Feb. 4, 1839, in Grand Travers, Mich. He en-
       listed in the 117th Regiment of New York, State Volun-
       teers at the time of its organization in 1862, and
       served until the close of the war, and was honorably
       discharged; m. Amelia Steele, in Michigan, June 2,
       1870, and has no issue. 5 Truman Edwards, Dec.
       24, 1840 ; d. May 30, 1844. 6 Dwight Edwards, b.
       Oct. 12, 1845 ; m. Sept. 19, 1867, Sarah A. Lasher
       of New Hartford, and removed to Manchester, Conn.,
       where were born their two children ; Frank Pitkin, July
       11, 1868, and Richard Parker, August 19, 1869, machinist.
110 2 Lester B., b. Sept. 19, 1807 ; m. Lois Dyer, Oct., 1829.
         Ch. 9th Gen.: 1 Marcus Livingston, b. July, 1832 ;
       m. Mary Parker. He died in 1858.
         Ch. 10th Gen.: (1) Ella, b. Oct., 1859. (2) Lester, b.
       Dec., 1861. Settled near his father, and was a farmer.
       (3) George, b. Nov. 1863. (4) Marcus E., b. May, 1868·
       (5) Orren.
         Ch. 9th Gen.: 2 Charles Eugene, b. Oct., 1842.

122 3 Louisa, b. 1810; m. June 1843, Thomas J. Walker. Had one daughter, Harriet Augusta, who died at the age of 3 years. Mr. Walker died Aug. 17, 1867.

123 4 Orpha, b. 1812, a deaf mute; m. Nov. 23, 1847, Samuel B. Wyckoff, a deaf mute, had 2 sons, viz., 1 George Lyman, b. Jan. 22, 1849; 2 William, b. Dec. 18, 1852; d. May 13, 1864.

7 BENJAMIN LYMAN[7], son of Dea. *Joseph[6]*, son of *Thomas[5]*, b. May 8, 1780; was a farmer and carriage maker; m. April 18, 1805, Mary Millard, dau. of Andrus Millard. She was b. Feb. 1, 1784, and d. May 20, 1866. He settled at "the Green" in Manchester, half a mile west of his father's, on the Hartford and Providence Turnpike. He was a man of humble piety, of great firmness and simplicity of character, of sound judgment, and strong common sense. He often represented the town in the state legislature, and filled other positions of public trust. Owing to his proverbial candor and practical wisdom, he was constantly consulted as a referee in cases of difficulty in the community, and his decisions were always regarded as eminently judicious and fair. He was extremely modest and retiring, and a man of few words, but these, weighty and to the point. He was universally respected, and not known to have had an enemy. He gathered by his industry and enterprise a handsome property. *Manchester, Conn.*

Children, Eighth Generation:

126 1 Benjamin, Jr., b. May 9, 1807; d. March 3, 1826.

127 2 Mary, b. Jan. 26, 1813; unmarried; resides at the homestead.

128 3 Mabel, b. Nov. 28, 1815; m. June 29, 1837, Aaron Cook of Ashford, Conn.; removed in 1839, to Manchester, where they now reside, near her father's house.

Ch. 9th Gen.: 1 Mabel, b. March 6, 1840. 2 Aaron Jr., b. Sept. 12, 1842; was sergeant in a company of the 25th Regiment Conn. Volunteers, and served creditably in the war of the rebellion, in Louisiana, and elsewhere. He m. Hattie J. Richardson of East Hartford, Sept. 17, 1867. Has a daughter b. Feb. 4, 1870, resides in Manchester. 3 A daughter, b. Feb 15, 1846; and d. same day. 4 Benjamin Lyman, b. Jan. 21, 1848. 5 Mary Elizabeth, b. Nov. 5, 1856.

8 JESSE LYMAN[7], son of Dea. *Joseph[6]*, son of *Thomas[5]*, b. June 4, 1782; m. in 1803, Theodora Dewey of Bolton, Conn., who was b. April 14, 1780. He went to Vernon, N. Y., in 1802, thence to Paris, now Marshall, with his

brother Thomas, and afterwards to Stockbridge, Oneida Co. His was the first white family that settled among the Indians on the Indian reservation in Stockbridge. He was a farmer, and resided in the same place until his death, July 2, 1863. His wife d. Aug. 24, 1858. *Stockbridge, N. Y.*

Children, Eighth Generation :

135 ı Samuel P., b. May 29, 1804; m. Lydia Ann Thomas, of Utica, about 1835 or '6, and settled in that city in the practice of law. He was for a time a law-partner of Daniel Webster, having an office in New York city ; and was associated with him in the Harrison political compaign of 1840. He resided many years in New York city, and was largely engaged in rail road and other business enterprises, though not always with success. The Erie rail road was greatly indebted to his energy in its early development, especially for the aid which it received from the state. He was able, sanguine, fertile in plans, but often disappointed in his expectations, and a loser rather than a gainer in many large speculations in real estate and other property. He d. suddenly at Cold Spring, on the Hudson in the autumn of 1869.

   Ch. 9th Gen.: ı A daughter, Julia, who d. many years age at the age of 15 or 16, and a son, Anson Thomas, who d. about 1867 or '8, at the age of 22 or 23.

139 2 Aurel Theodora, b. Oct. 13, 1805 ; m. Nathan Harvey, farmer, and settled in Smithfield, Madison Co., N. Y.

140 3 Joseph Thomas, b. June 29, 1807 ; d. Sept. 16, 1841 ; unmarried.

141 4 Mary, b. May 24, 1809 ; m. T. C. Clark, farmer, and settled in Pulaski, N. Y. ; d.

142 5 Sarah, b. Dec. 6, 1810 ; m. Ira Goodrich, farmer, and settled in Stockbridge, Madison Co., N. Y.

143 6 Charles Giles, b. Oct. 24, 1813 ; m. Mercy Loomis, and settled in Stockbridge, N. Y., farmer.

144 7 Abby Ann, b. Dec. 14, 1816 ; m. Hiram Whedon, merchant, of Stockbridge, N. Y. ; d. Sept. 8, 1865, a daughter, now a young lady, is living with the widow of Samuel P., in Utica. Mr. Whedon removed many years ago to Rome, N. Y., where he now resides.

146 8 Jesse Welles, b. Nov. 12, 1819 ; m. Minerva Knight, and settled in Hinsdale, Cattaraugus Co., N. Y. ; d. Jan., 1858.

147 9 Emily Jane, b. March 27, 1821 ; d. March 25, 1847 ; unmarried.

148 10 Thomas Addis Emmet, b. July 1, 1825 ; d. May, 1866 ; unmarried.

149 11 Hubert Norton, b. June 10, 1827 ; m. Elvira Smith, and settled in Oswago, Pa. He became a Methodist preacher of ability and success, and has been for some years at or

near Council Bluffs, Iowa, where, owing to ill health, he
is able to preach but little.

9 CHESTER LYMAN⁷, son of Dea. *Joseph⁶*, son of *Thomas⁵*,
b. Dec. 4, 1785; m. Mary Smith, dau. of Samuel Smith of
East Hartford, and Rachel his wife, dau. of Samuel Rockwell of East Windsor, in 1809, and settled a mile north
of his father's, where he built a grist-mill and saw-mill, in
charge of which and a small farm, he spent his life. He
d. there May 10, 1864. His wife d. Aug. 22, 1833; and,
April 10, 1837, he m. Elizabeth Risley of Manchester, who
d. in Aug., 1870. He was a man of exemplary character,
industrious, ingenious, mild in disposition, and of few
words.   *Manchester, Conn.*
    Children, Eighth Generation:
150 1 Emily, b. July 20, 1810; d. March 1, 1822.
151 2 Mary Ann, b May 18, 1812; m. Daniel B. Smith, of Bing-
        hamton, N. Y., in 1847; d. at Binghamton, April 14,
        1851; left no children.
152 3 Chester Smith, b. Jan., 13, 1814; attended a district school
        from seven to thirteen; then a private school a few
        months; in later boyhood, when not at work, occupied
        much in studying by himself astronomy, optics, and
        mathematics, making with a few tools of his father's,
        globes, quadrants, orreries, telescopes, etc., and comput-
        ing the eclipses for many years in advance, and Almanacs
        for 1830 and '31; joined the Congregational church in
        1831; kept school in Manchester S. W. and W. Dis-
        tricts two winters; and in June, 1832, began fitting for
        college at the Ellington school under Judge Hall, living
        in the family of his benefactor, Hon. John H. Brockway;
        entered Yale, August, 1833; in junior year was asso-
        ciated with William M. Evarts and other classmates in
        starting, and afterwards in editing the *Yale Literary
        Magazine,* a monthly periodical still published; in 1837,
        graduated with "oration" rank; superintendent of the
        Ellington School two years; studied theology in the
        Union Theological Seminary, N. Y., and the Theological
        Department of Yale College; ordained pastor of the First
        church in New Britain, Conn., Feb. 14, 1843; health
        failing, resigned, May, 1845, and in October sailed, *via*
        Cape Horn, to the Sandwich Islands; spent a year there,
        and in June, 1847, went to California; engaged chiefly
        in surveying; was among the first to send authentic
        reports of the gold mines to the east; in March, 1850,
        returned, *via* Panama, to New Haven, Conn.; m. June
        20, 1850, Delia Williams Wood, daughter of Hon.
        Joseph Wood of New Haven, and granddaughter of

Chief Justice Oliver Ellsworth; residence ever since in New Haven; in 1858, appointed professor of Industrial Mechanics and Physics in the Sheffield Scientific School of Yale College, taking charge of Physics and Astronomy, and, until 1870, of Mechanical Engineering; spent the summer of 1869, in Europe; since 1859, president, by annual election, of the Connecticut Academy of Arts and Sciences; made Hon. member of the British Association for the Advancement of Science in 1869; occasional contributor to the *American Journal of Science and Art*, the *New Englander*, and other periodicals; since 1858; a deacon of the First or Centre church in New Haven; has preached occasionally.

Ch. 9*th Gen.* : 1 A daughter, b. and d. April 11, 1851. 2 Elizabeth Ellsworth, b. Nov. 11, 1852. 3 William Chester, b. March 15, 1855; d. May 24, 1855. 4 Oliver Ellsworth, b. May 10, 1856. 5 Delia Wood, b. Oct. 3, 1858. 6 Chester Wolcott, b. May 25, 1861.

159 4 Esther, b. May 18, 1817; m. in 1841, William Russell Pease, farmer, son of Deacon Noah Pease, of Ellington, and lived first in Ellington, then in New Brunswick, N. J., till her death, March 10, 1852. Left no children.

160 5 Edwin Howard, b. Feb. 1, 1838; m. Jan. 22, 1862, Mary Jane Goodrich, of Manchester; resided first in Manchester, and in 1864, removed to New Britain, Conn., merchant.

Ch. 9*th Gen.:* 1 Ambrose Burnside, b. March 18, 1863; d. Oct. 26, 1869.

12 SALMON LYMAN[7], son of Dea. *Joseph[6]*, b. March 13, 1791; m. Octa Jones, b. June 24, 1789, dau. of Amos and Aurel Jones, of Colchester, Conn., Nov. 15, 1814. Has always lived at the homestead where he was b., and is now, 1872, the only survivor of his father's family.— horticulturist and farmer. His wife d. Oct. 30, 1868.

Manchester, Conn.

Children, Eighth Generation :

162 1 Maria Louisa, b. Nov. 5, 1815; m. Nov. 1, 1836, Josiah B. Avery, b. May 6, 1814, at Bolton, Conn., cabinet maker; lived many years in Bolton, and for several years past at the old homestead in Manchester.

Ch. 9*th Gen.* : 1 Maria Louisa, b. Sept. 23, 1837; d. Dec. 18, 1850. 2 Julia Adelaide, b. Aug. 3, 1840. 3 Martha Cornelia, b. Dec. 25, 1843; m. Sept. 1, 1867, Walter P. Keeny, has one son Zeno, b. July 12, 1870. 4 Josiah Francis, b. June 20, 1847, machinist. 5 Emily Anna, b. March 19, 1853; d. March 18, 1854.

168 2 A son, b. Jan. 30; d. Jan. 31, 1817.

169 3 Francis Edwards, b. Oct. 23, 1818; d. June 15, 1819.

170 4 Francis Eliab, b. Oct. 27, 1821; m. in 1848, Emily E.
　　　Goodwin, of Hartford, d. Nov. 26, 1850. Manchester.
　　　　Ch. 9th Gen. : 1 Julia Francis, who d. April 24, 1851,
　　　aged 16 months.
172 5 A son, nameless, Nov. 22, 1826.

　　32 Dea. Benjamin Lyman⁶, twin brother of Dea. *Joseph⁵*, a
tanner by trade in Columbia, formerly Lebanon Crank, m.
Elizabeth Collins of the same place, b. 1748; d. Feb. 4,
1826, aged 80. He was an example of the strictest integrity, benevolence and piety. In middle life he became
the subject of insanity, a constitutional tendency peculiar
to several branches of the Lyman family. His derangement took the form of brooding melancholy, in which for
many months he uttered no audible word. In this state
of mind he was induced by much persuasion to attend a
regimental review in Lebanon. From this he returned
apparently a sane man. He conversed freely, returned to the
duties of life and for 18 years enjoyed usual health. He returned from a journey in feeble health, became again deranged, and d. Nov. 16, 1804, aged 60.

　　These twin brothers resembled each other in form and
features so nearly that they were with difficulty distinguished the one from the other. In their mental characteristics and mutual affection they manifested the same
beautiful identity and unity.

　　We now resume the genealogy of Benjamin⁶, twin
brother of Dea. Joseph.

　　In early life, Benjamin m. Elizabeth Collins, of Lebanon
Crank, a woman of exemplary piety, who d. Feb. 4, 1828,
in the 80th year of her age.

　　　　Children, Seventh Generation ·

173 1 Betsey.　　　　　176 4 Benjamin.
174 2 Hannah.　　　　　177 5 Chester.
175 3 Artemas.

　　173 Betsey, b. Nov. 15, 1771; m. Ebenezer Rogers; removed, about 1800, to Washington, Mass., and soon became insane and unable to take care of her family, making
frequent attempts to commit suicide. Late in the afternoon of Friday she walked six or seven miles in a thunder
storm to a friend's house, but remained in a shed by night,
then secreted herself in a swamp where she remained without food until Wednesday, when in extreme exhaustion she
crept to a friend's house, and by careful nursing was restored to health both of body and mind. For many years

she continued in good health; removed in 1828 to the state of New York; became again insane and so continued until her death, Aug. 28, 1849.

174 Hannah, b. Dec. 22, 1773; d. Dec. 2, 1846. Of a reserved, retiring disposition, she lived 17 years by herself in hereditary apartments in her father's house; in Oct., 1845, she went to reside with her brother Benjamin; became insane and so continued until her death.

175 Artemas, b. Aug. 15, 1776; m. Abigail Barston, March, 1802. In 1811 removed to Onondaga, thence to Sweden, N. Y.; there he became a raving maniac on the subject of religion. Conceiving himself to be a messenger of the Lord, when not chained to his cell he would go from house to house, in the dead of night, calling upon the sleepers to awake and flee from the wrath to come. His children, consisting of two sons and two daughters, removed with him to Michigan where he d. in the autumn of 1843. In periods of his sanity he officiated as deacon of the church where he resided. The history of his children is unknown.

176 Benjamin, b. Oct. 30, 1781; m. June 9, 1803, Lydia Barston, and lived through life, almost 70 years, in the same house, within a few rods of the place of his birth. Mrs. L. d. April 15, 1863, a model wife and mother. As her children, nine in number, gathered around the coffin to take the last look of the deceased, and wept, the voice of the venerable and bereaved husband was heard in clear accents, saying: "Suppress your tears! It is the Lord's will. He gave, He hath taken away. Blessed be the name of the Lord." The eldest son responded:

"A shade of gloom is o'er us cast :
A silent voice to us has spoken ;
The silver cord is loosed at last,
The pitcher at the fountain broken,
And all seems sad."

Benjamin, d. Oct. 12, 1871, aged 90 years, less 18 days. His nine children were all present at his funeral—all but one over 50 and three over 60 years of age.

Benjamin Lyman was a kind and affectionate husband and father, revered and beloved by all his children. Such was his moral and religious influence in the training of his household, that none of them have departed from the Christian faith of their father, and all, in a high degree, have maintained blameless lives before the world,

verifying the words of the wise man : " Train up a child in the way
he should go, and when he is old he will not depart from it." He
possessed a good constitution, a strong intellect, a retentive memory,
and a kind and benevolent heart. In manners he was modest, dignified, and gentlemanly. His religion was of the Puritan stamp, not
spasmodic, but even in its course, every day alike. He was consistent and liberal in his views, and yet firm, in what he believed to
be right, and in contending earnestly for the faith once delivered
to the saints. He was a sweet singer, and his presence and help were
often solicited from abroad in times of religious revivals. In 1820,
he assisted the Rev Alfred Wright, missionary to the Choctaws,
in forming the Sunday school in Columbia; was chosen its first superintendent, and held the office some 14 or 15 years in succession.
After his resignation of that office, he became the teacher of a large
adult Bible class, and held it until the infirmities of age rendered it
proper for him reluctantly to retire from his charge. He was an
efficient helper to his pastor, and in his absence, visited at the bed-
side of the sick and dying, sometimes attending funerals, and conducted, with ability, religious meetings in the conference room. When
destitute of a pastor he led the exercises at the church on the sabbath.
He possessed a strong, clear, and sonorous voice, and the old people
loved to hear Dea. Lyman read and pray, as well as sing the songs
of Zion. One lady more than 80 years of age, in looking upon his
form after death, placed her hand upon his brow and exclaimed
" O, how many earnest prayers I have heard from that good man's
lips." He was chosen deacon of the church at 32 years of age, and
officiated in that capacity until disabled through the infirmities of
age. He had but a little education from the schools, but was naturally a student, and improved every opportunity to gain knowledge
from books and from observation. In the prime of life he was an
efficient member of the committee for visiting schools. Poor in
this world's goods, but rich in the endowments of nature's God, he
served his day and generation well. He retained his faculties
nearly unimpaired, until almost four score years of age, after which
his mind gradually decaying, he returned to second childhood, and
at last to partial insanity.

Children, Eighth Generation

181 1 Orville Barston, b. March 14, 1804.
182 2 Benjamin Wight, b. Nov. 28, 1805 ; b. with defective vision,
he succeeded by unwearied efforts in learning to read and
transact business to some extent; united with the church
in 1823 ; still living,
183 3 Lydia, b. June 18, 1807 ; a child of misfortune. In 1827,
the knee was injured by a fall, the cords contracted so
that she could but very imperfectly move even with
crutches; for several years there was a gradual alleviation
of this lameness, then by another fall it was aggravated
to a remediless infirmity — a cripple for life.
184 4 A lifeless infant b. Oct. 17, 1808.

185 5 Samuel Edson, b. Oct. 10, 1810; m. Sept. 24, 1837, Amelia
Dewey, and removed to Barre, N. Y., where his wife was
killed by the fall of a well sweep, Sept. 14, 1839, leaving
an infant child, m. Oct. 20, 1841, Fanny C. Clark, who
d. Jan. 6, 1869; m. March 22, 1871, Mrs. Sarah Lewis.
Ch. 9th Gen.: 1 Edward Payson, b. Dec. 19, 1838; d.
May 31, 1851, a child of uncommon promise. 2 Dwight
A., b. Nov. 11, 1843; m. Sept. 19, 1865, Abbie M. Hunt.
[*Ch. 10th Gen.:* (1) Lizzie D., b. Oct. 19, 1866.
(2) Lillian, b. July 23, 1868.] 3 Samuel Barston, b.
Aug. 28, 1845. 4 Chester Benjamin, b. Sept., 1848;
m. Sept. 20, 1868, Emma J. Webb. [*Ch. 10th Gen.:*
(1) Cora Belle, b. June 20, 1870.] 5 Lydia Amelia,
b. July 1, 1855; d. March 12, 1871. 6 Edward Payson,
b. Nov. 22, 1857.

196 6 Lucina Wright, b. Nov. 20, 1812, long a great sufferer from
an accute chronic disease.

197 7 Elizabeth Collins, b. Feb. 15, 1815; m. Oct. 19, 1834, Elmore
G. Dewey.
Ch. 9th Gen.: 1 Helen A., b. Sept. 21, 1835.
2 Kate A., b. Oct. 27, 1850.

199 8 George Washington, b. May 3, 1817; m. Oct. 20, 1839,
Eunice M. Robertson, who d. of quick consumption,
Dec. 3, 1844; m. Oct. 12, 1845, Emiline Jordan, Hart-
ford, Conn.
Ch. 9th Gen.: (1) Charles K., b. Oct. 30, 1840; m.
May 5, 1870, Hattie C. Rockwood. [*Ch. 10th Gen.:*
(1) Julian G., b. March 1, 1871.] (2) Gabriella C., b.
Aug. 9, 1842; m. Oct. 21, 1868, Robert B. Sturtevant.
[*Ch. 10th Gen.:* (1) Robert F., b. March 14, 1871.]
(3) Albert B., b. July 14, 1846; m. March 22, 1870,
Nettie Vibberts. [*Ch. 10th Gen.:* (1) Hattie A., b.
June 31, 1871.] (4) George B., b. June 28, 1848.
(5) Mary E., b June 9, 1851. (6) Frank W., b. June
24, 1854. (7) Dayton W., b. May 14, 1836. (8) Arthur H., b. Aug. 2, 1859. (9) Hattie A., b. June 15,
1862; d. Oct. 5, 1864. (10) Edward E., b. Dec. 31, 1864.

213 9 Alfred W., b. June 16, 1821; m. Nov. 23, 1845, Elizabeth
C. Hayden.
Ch. 9th Gen.: 1 Richard O., b. Oct. 6, 1852. 2 Wil-
liam A., b. July 1, 1854.

215 10 Harriet Jane, b. Nov. 3, 1824.

181 ORVILLE BARSTON LYMAN[8], son of Dea. *Benjamin*[7], of
Columbia, Ct., b. March 14, 1804; m. Hannah Taber, of
Woodstock, Ct., b. in Westport, Mass., June 5, 1810; d. Nov.
22, 1831. O. B. Lyman united with the church in Columbia
in 1831. He became a scholar in the Sunday school
at the time of its first organization, in June, 1820. With

the exception of attending the common district school, such as they were 50 years ago, about four months in the winter season, until he was eighteen years of age, he was wholly self-educated. His occupation until he was more than 30 years of age, was farming in the summer and teaching school in the winter. His tastes not according fully with farming, he decided, even at this late hour of his life, to change his occupation, and chose the practice of medicine for his future livelihood. He commenced the study of medicine in 1855 by himself; read and examined the works of the different schools, so far as he could obtain them, and finally adopted the theory and practice of the then so-called Thomsonian system, known now as the Eclectic practice, and entered upon its duties Dec., 1837, in the city of Norwich, Ct. At 30 years of age he had no library, with the exception of a few school books. Since then he has gathered a well assorted library of nearly 150 volumes. His practice has been a living one, and he has been blest with more than an average success. He removed from Norwich to Willimantic, Dec., 1852, and followed his profession there with success until April, 1866, when he removed to the city of Hartford, where he still remains in a successful practice. He was superintendent of the Congregational Sunday school in Willimantic, 10 successive years, and also an active member of the church during his stay there.

Hartford, Ct.

Children, Ninth Generation :

216 ɪ Nancy Jane, b. Jan. 9, 1834, at Columbia; d. July 25, 1864, in Willimantic, Ct.

The following lines, occasioned by her death, were written by her father ·

> I cannot make it seem that she is dead,
> Profusely though my stricken heart has bled.
> I cannot make it seem her face is hid,
> No more to smile, beneath the coffin's lid,
> Or, that her voice, so sweetly tuned, is hushed
> And all her hopes of longer life are crushed ;
> Or, that her form lies now below the sod,
> While upward soared the spirit has to God.
> From memory's urn a thought oft steals away,
> Through numerous years, back to the eventful day
> When first I looked at her, my first-born child ;
> With gladness almost passionate and wild
> Back to the time when she encradled lay,
> And fell disease was wasting her away.
> But it was staid, and she was left to grow
> To riper years, and more of life to know.
> With pain and anguish marked were all her years,
> And watered often were with flowing tears ;

And yet I cannot make it seem that death has come,
And called her hence to yonder spirit home.
Oft as I tread the room she called her own,
Now drear and silent, and so very lone,
Where all is seen just as when in her care,
I think I'll see her — but she is not there.
So when I bend over her sacred mound,
Where dust with dust is mingling under ground,
Some still, small voice, seems whispering in my ear:
"Look upward, now, for lo, she is not here!"
As day recedes with coming shades of even,
And as I turn my wandering thoughts to heaven,
And bend the knee and upward look in prayer,
'Tis good to think my daughter's home is there.

217 2 George Restcome, b. Nov. 30, 1835, at Columbia; m. Oct. 9,
1859, Mary A. T. Wagner, of Boston, b. July 20, 1831,
Lahave, Nova Scotia. He d. March 9, 1868, in Boston,
Mass. His disease was softening of the brain, said to be
incurable. His occupation that of burnishing and plating.
He left one child, a daughter, named Cara, b. Dec. 11, 1864.
219 3 Lydia Josephine, b. Oct. 11, 1839, in Norwich, Ct.; m. June
10, 1863, Dr. James O. Fitch, b. April 10, 1833—
-He d. Aug. 28, 1869, in Danbury, Ct.; dentist.

177 CHESTER LYMAN[7], b. Nov. 11, 1784; d. March 16,
1832; m. Nov. 12, 1807, Sophia West, dau. of Samuel West
of Columbia, b. April 26; 1786; d. Nov. 14, 1870. Both
professors of religion, and in their humble walk before
God, gave testimony in favor of Christ and his kingdom
on earth, and had faith to look for the inheritance of
heavenly rest above. She, surviving her husband almost
40 years, retained in a remarkable degree, her faculties of
body and mind. At the age of 84 she was active in
thought, and memory, even to the close of life. With a
few brief hours of illness, she fell asleep never more to
awake on earth.   *Columbia, Ct.*

Children, Eighth Generation:
221 1 Chester W., b. Sept. 25, 1808.
222 2 Sophia C., b. Aug. 8, 1810.
223 3 William C., b. Oct. 11, 1812.

221 CHESTER W. LYMAN[8], son of *Chester*[7], Nov. 13, 1831;
m. Cornelia E. Porter, dau. of Dan Porter, both pro
fessors of religion. He was one of the scholars of the
first sabbath school, organized in 1820, and more than 50
years has been connected with it and has been active in
its service as a scholar, teacher, or superintendent. He
united with the church in 1823, chosen deacon in 1858;
honest and upright in his dealings with men; active and

faithful in all the duties of the office, to which he is called; taking the Bible for his standard and guide; earnest, and stirring in his appeals of divine truth on the heart and conscience; seeking for a higher life manifested in the church of Christ, and its greater enlargement on earth. Not ceasing in kind words of entreaty and expostulation, to warn the impenitent of the error of his ways, and by earnest prayer and supplication, seeking to win souls to Christ.   *Columbia, Ct.*

Children, Ninth Generation :
224 1 Corintha J., b. Jan. 12, 1835.
225 2 Henry E., b. Sept. 26, 1838.

224 CORINTHA J. LYMAN[9], dau. of *Chester W.*[8], m. Aug. 21, 1859, Walter R. Kingsbury, son of Joseph Kingsbury, of Andover, Ct. They soon after their marriage moved to Camp Point, Ill., where she lived a few years and d. Feb. 17, 1864. She, early in life, made a public profession of religion, and during her last sickness she was sustained and comforted with the hope of assurance that heaven would be her home. Her dying message to all her friends was to meet her in heaven.   *Camp Point, Illinois.*

Children, Tenth Generation :
226 1 Charles S. Kingsbury, b. Dec. 20, 1861; d. July 23, 1862.

225 HENRY E. LYMAN[9], son of *Chester W.*[8], m. Aug. 31, 1872, Louisa E. Harris, of Woonsocket, R. I.: professors of religion; a great lover of books, and well read in the history of all nations —farmer.   *Woonsocket, R. I.*

Children, Tenth Generation :
1 Frederick A., b. April 22, 1864.

222 SOPHIA C. LYMAN[8], dau. of *Chester*[7], m. Oct. 14, 1830; John S. Yeomans, of Columbia, both professors of religion; civil engineer, mechanic and farmer, also occupied in public business generally. He has also represented his town and senatorial district, in both branches of the legislature.   *Columbia, Ct.*

Children, Ninth Generation :
227 1 Sophia C. Yeomans, b. June 30, 1832.
228 2 William H. Yeomans, b. July, 1836.

223 WILLIAM C. LYMAN[7], son of *Chesters*, m. Sept. 23, 1839, Mary Ann Phelps, dau. of Oliver Phelps, Hebron, Conn.; members the Episcopal church; immediately moved to

Barre, N. Y., where he died Oct. 23, 1857, where his family still remain—farmer.   *Barre, N. Y.*

Children, Ninth Generation :
229 1 Mary A., b. Oct. 26, 1840.
230 2 Helen J., b. May 5, 1847.
231 3 William D. C., b. Oct. 4, 1853.
232 4 Alice P., b. Nov. 11, 1857.

IV. DESCENDANTS OF RICHARD[3], THROUGH RICHARD[4] AND DEA. JOHN[5]

JOHN LYMAN[5], *Richard[4], Richard[3], Richard[2]*, b. Jan. 21, 1711, m. Hannah Birchard, Feb. 28, 1731; d. Feb. 12, 1781, Hannah, wife of John, d. Jan. 28, 1746; and Sept. 3, 1847. John m. his second wife, Mary Strong b. in Coventry, Ct., March 27, 1717; d. in Brookfield, Vt., 1804. John was a farmer in Lebanon, Ct., a deacon in the Congregational church, an intimate friend of Gov. Jonathan Trumbull, an ardent patriot and strong whig. He was too old and infirm to engage in the war of the Revolution, but sent several of his sons, and it was his daily prayer that the colonies might succeed in their struggles for independence.
Lebanon, Ct.

Children, Sixth Generation :
1 1 Hannah.   5 7 Elijah.
2 2 John.   6 5 Richard.
3 3 Abel.   7 6 Josiah.
4 4 Elias.

These six brothers all moved to Lebanon, N. H., then, Upper Co-os, and John, Abel, Josiah and Elijah removed from there to Vermont.

1 HANNAH[6], b. Dec. 29, 1932; m. Bailey; d. Nov. 8, 1794.

2 JOHN LYMAN[6], *John[5], Richard[4], Richard[3], Richard[2]*, b. Dec. 7, 1740; d. 1830, m. Lucy Phelps, and was one of the first settlers in Brookfield, Vt., in 1782. He served during the war and aided in the capture of Burgoyne; had but one child, who m. Walker Martin.   *Brookfield, Ct.*

3 ABEL LYMAN[6], *John[5], Richard[4], Richard[3], Richard[2]*, b. Jan. 15, 1752; d. Jan. 17, 1823. In 1773 he went to Lebanon and bought land five miles south of where Dartmouth College now stands, and engaged in farming. In 1775 he was commissioned a first lieutenant, and in the

winter of 1775 – '76 commanded a company of militia raised in Grafton, and marched to Quebec, by way of Lake Chamlain, where he joined the army under Arnold, and was engaged in the unsuccessful attempt to capture the city. He was attacked with small pox just before the army commenced to retreat, but kept up, though suffering greatly from the disease, and, by way of Montreal, Lake Champlain and Onion river, arrived at Lebanon in May. In Sept., 1776, he again took command of his company, and in 1777 marched to Saratoga and assisted in the battle and capture of Burgoyne and the army that had driven them out of Canada. He then returned to N. H., and was engaged in guarding the frontiers against the Indians. He m. Hannah Storrs, from Mansfield, Conn. She was b. April 6, 1754, and d. May 31, 1831. They resided in Lebanon until March, 1786, he sold his farm and moved to Brookfield, Vt., and there bought another farm. He and his wife were members of the Congregational church. He held for some time important town offices, and also for a period represented his district in the state legislature.   *Lebanon, N. H.*

Children, Seventh Generation:

9 1 John.
10 2 Abel.
11 3 Azel.
12 4 Alvan.
13 5 Ezra.
14 6 Cornelius.

4 Elias Lyman[6], *John[5], Richard[4], Richard[3], Richard[2], Richard[1]*, b. April 14, 1754; m. Ruth Griswold, of Hartford, Ct., extensively engaged in mercantile business; d. Aug. 1787.   *Lebanon, N. H.*

Children, Seventh Generation:

15 1 Ruth, b..........; m. Dea. Eliphalet Wells of Lebanon, N. H.
     Ch. 8th Gen.: 1 Elizabeth. 2 Rhoda. 3 Lucinda. 4 Elias.
16 2 Lucy, b..........; m. Ozias Allen of Lebanon, N. H.
17 3 Elias, b. July 5, 1778; m. Tryphene Burrows in 1800, who still lives at Woonsocket, R. I., and is 90 years old. He died about 40 years of age.
     Ch. 8th Gen.: 1 Elias, b. in Brookfield, Vt., Sept. 20, 1801; d. 1831. 2 Sophronia, b. in Colebrook, N. H., Aug. 20, 1803; now resides at Woonsocket, R. I. with her widowed mother. 3 Oliver E., b. Colebrook, N. H. July 26, 1808; m. Mary Holt of New Alstead, N. H., 1837, he d. in New Orleans, 1840; left one son Frank P. H., b. 1838, farmer; m. Rebecca Whitcomb, 1856. They have one daughter and two sons.
     Ch. 9th Gen.: George Ellis L. and James Willard L.
25 4 Tryphena, b. at Warner, N. H., Aug. 10, 1810; m. at Lowell, Mass., May 24, 1835, Nathaniel Morrill, b. at Wilmington,

Mass., Nov. 28, 1809; d. at Woonsocket, R. I., Dec. 1, 1842.

Ch. 8th Gen.: 1 Pamelia, b. at Pepperell, Mass., June 10, 1837; d. June 22, 1837. 2 Christina T., b. Nov. 15, 1838, at Pepperell, Mass. 3 William Henry, b. at Woonsocket, R. I., May 15, 1841; d. June 7, 1841.

27 2 Christina T., m. George O. Willard of Natick, Mass., Nov. 28, 1857.

Ch. 9th Gen.: 1 Bertha Eudora, b. at Natick, Mass., Sept. 12, 1858. 2 Carrie Estella, b. at Pawtucket, R. I., Jan. 30, 1861. 3 Florence Augusta, b. at Pawtucket, R. I., Sept. 16, 1863.

32 5 Lucinda, b..........; m. Thomas G. Wells, a physician of Hopkinton, N. H.

Ch. 8th Gen.: 1 Elias, d. in infancy. 2 Thomas Goodwin. 3 Phineas. 4 Dr. Parkhurst Wells, now practicing in Brooklyn. 5 Edwin R. 6 Elias. 7 Lucinda. 8 Maria G. 9 Ruth. 10 Elizabeth.

43 6 Harry, M.D., graduated at Dartmouth Coll., settled in Warren, N. H.; m. 1st, Sarah Bartlett; 2d, Sarah Long, dau. of Dr. Long of Concord, N. H., where he lived and died.

Ch. 8th Gen.: 1 Warren, b. in Hanover, 1808, graduated at Dartmouth; practicing physician in Madison, Ill. 2 Henry. 3 Moses, both d. young.

47 ROSWELL LYMAN[7], *Elias[6], John[5], Richard[4], Richard[3], Richard[2], Richard[1],* b..........; m. Martha Mason, in Lebanon, N.H. March 14, 1810, moved to Vermont, and afterward to the town of Lyman, N. H. where was born their son Amasa M. in 1813. Roswell left home in 1815 and died in New York state. Amasa M. remained in the town of Lyman until 1832, since which time he has lived in the west.

Lyman, N. H.

5 RICHARD LYMAN[6], *John[5], Richard[4], Richard[3], Richard[2],* b. August 12, 1757; d. June, 1802. In 1775, he enlisted in the army and served several years under Gen. Putnam. He ranked as orderly sergeant. He saw the old hero ride down the stone steps, and was with him in several of his most daring and successful enterprises. He was a man of great courage and firmness in the midst of danger. Gen. Putnam once said, that if he only had 1,000 such men as Orderly Lyman he would drive every red-coated Briton out of America in 6 months. He m. Philomela Loomis, d. June 8, 1802. He had 4 sons and 7 daughters. *Lebanon, Ct.*

6 JOSIAH LYMAN⁶, *John⁵, Richard⁴, Richard³, Richard², Richard¹*, b. Aug. 11, 1760. In Sept. 22, 1782, m. Eunice Tiffany. In 1785, he moved to Williamstown, Vt., in 1803, to Brookfield, and afterwards to Randolph. He and his wife were members of the Congregational church. Had 1 son and 3 daughters. *Randolph, Vt.*

Children, Seventh Generation:

59 1 Apama, m. Daniel Child.
60 2 Lois, m. Daniel Washburn.
61 3 Eunice, no record.
62 4 Josiah, studied medicine in Vt., emigrated to Clermont Co., Ohio, one of the pioneer's physicians in the S. W. part of the state; removed 1837, to Greensburg, Indiana, where he d. Jan. 2, 1842.
    Ch. 8th Gen.: 1 David R. 2 Dan Stone. 3 Albert D. 4 James D. Dan Stone studied medicine; m. July 18, 1844, E. C. McClure; no children, Goshen, Clermont Co., Ohio. The other children of Josiah are not living, nor are they known to have left issue.

7 ELIJAH LYMAN⁶, *John⁵, Richard⁴, Richard³, Richard²*, b. March 8, 1764; d. April 12, 1828. When but a youth he was converted and resolved to devote his life to preaching the gospel. He graduated at Dartmouth, in 1786, and was a teacher for some time in the College. He studied theology, and April 8, 1789, was ordained and installed as pastor of the Congregational church at Brookfield, Vt., where he continued to labor 39 years, when he died. During several years of the first of his ministry he was the only Congregational or Presbyterian minister in the north half of the state, and at his own expense he used to spend several weeks every year traveling through the new settlements, organizing churches, preaching and administering the ordinances. He m. M. M. Waterman, of Lebanon, N. H., 1788, and d. at Brookfield, Vt., 1828. His wife d. 1851. *Brookfield, Vt.*

Children, Seventh Generation:

64 1 Mary, b. Dec. 1, 1789; and m. Dan Storrs, Nov. 22, 1813; and is still living in Lebanon, N. H. She has three children.
    Ch. 8th Gen.: 1 Lucinda Storrs, b. Sept. 15, 1814. 2 Dan Storrs, Jr., b. March 5, 1816. 3 Mary A. Storrs, b. Feb. 28, 1819.
68 2 Emily, b. Oct. 15, 1800; m. Albigence Ainsworth, 1822; d. at Northfield, Vt., 1869, leaving one daughter Mary J. Ainsworth.

70 3 Elijah G., b. Dec. 20, 1803; m. Sophia Edson, 1829; d. at
   Brookfield, 1839, leaving one dau. who m. John Griswold
   of Brookfield.

72 4 Walter Harris, b. March 22, 1809; went to Illinois, m. His
   wife d. and he removed to California.

73 5 Louisa, b. April, 1814, m. Milton Bigelow; d. at Brookfield,
   in 1853; leaving 1 daughter, viz.: Emma Louisa
   Bigelow.

9 JOHN LYMAN[7], *Abel*[6], *John*[5], *Richard*[4], *Richard*[3], *Richard*[2],
Richard[1], born in Lebanon, N. H., April 2, 1780; d. Aug. 4,
1865. When 6 years old his parents moved to Brookfield,
Vt. He studied medicine with Dr. Nathaniel Smith, of
Dartmouth, m. Martha Storrs of Lebanon, N. H. and settled as M.D., in New Haven, Vt. In 1817, he moved to
Williston, Vt., and in 1824 to Potsdam, N. Y. In 1832 he
and his brother Azel went on an exploring tour through
the western states, and in the fall of 1833 with 50 others
including in all 5 brothers, viz.: John, Azel, Alvan, Ezra,
and Cornelius, their wives, children and some grandchildren, removed to Sangamon Co., Illinois, traveling in wagons,
spending 8 weeks on the road, and of course observing the
4th commandment by resting from their journey on the
sabbath and meeting for divine worship. Their tents
were pitched, seats provided and the neighbors invited
before sunset on Saturday. John took an active part in
the first anti-slavery movement, and several times came
near being captured while running his train on the " Underground rail road." In his extreme old age he was
very active in business. As a philanthropist he was
energetic and useful. His means were freely given for the
support and spread of the Gospel and for the relief of the
poor and needy.   *Sangamon Co., Ill.*

   Children, Eighth Generation:
75 1 Dea. Henry Pratt, b. Aug. 10, 1805; m. Mercy Sanders of
   Bethel, Vt., Aug., 1833; and removed with his father
   and other relatives to Richland, Sangamon Co., Illinois,
   where he has since been engaged in farming.
      Ch. 9th. Gen.: 1 Calista M., m. Ralph C. Curtiss,
   of Waverly. Their children are: (1) Martha S. (2)
   John S. (3) Laura A. (4) George H. 2 Sarah A., m.
   Rev. James D. Kerr, pastor of the Presbyterian church
   in her native place. Their children are: Grace and
   Henry Paull. 3 Martha S. 4 John S., though very
   young, enlisted, marched with Sherman to the sea. 5
   Laura A. 6 George H.
88 2 Hannah, b. 1808; m. Stephen Childs.

Ch. 9th Gen.: 1 John. 2 Mary, m. George Seely. 3
Martha, m. Franklin Anderson. 4 Stephen. 5 Hannah.
94 3 Benjamin Rush, b. March 10, 1815 ; d. Feb. 16, 1847, moved
from Potsdam to Illinois with his parents, m. Eliza
Estabrook.
Ch. 9th Gen.: 1 Lewis Judd, M.D. 2 Harriet, m.
Edward Smyth. 3 Mary, m. Robert Harford. Eliza afterwards m. Childs and with most of her children are now
in Manhattan, Kansas.
98 4 Martha, b. 1817 ; m. Lewis Judd, of Marine, Illinois, d. 1835.
99 5 Laura, b. 1819 ; m. Augustine Curtiss, of Waverly, Illinois,
where she d. Aug., 1847.
Ch. 9th Gen.: Laura, who m. Wm. Brown.

10 ABEL LYMAN[7], *Abel[6], John[5], Richard[4], Richard[3], Richard[2],
Richard[1]*, b. in Lebanon, N. H., Feb. 12, 1782; d. April 12,
1835; when 4 years old his parents moved to Brookfield,
Vt. In 1810 he m. Dorothy Reed. She d. leaving 4 sons,
and he in 1824 m. Esther Bigelow, by whom he had 4
sons and 2 daughters. When 21 years of age he was 6
feet 4 inches in height, and weighed 210 pounds, and not
a man in Vermont could compete with him in athletic
exercises. He remained on the home farm with his parents.
He was a member of the Congregational church and was,
for a time, a member of the state legislature. His health
failing he visited his brothers in Illinois hoping a change of
climate might prove beneficial, but he continued to decline
and died in Sangamon Co.   *Brookfield, Vt.*
Children, Eighth Generation :
101 1 Azel, b. 1811, in Brookfield ; m. Sarah Lathrop in Braintree,
Vt., where he was a merchant and d. there in 1841,
leaving 1 child. 1 Sarah Azeline, who is now in Watertown, N. Y.
103 2 Rollin, b. June 24, 1813 ; moved to St. Louis, in 1834, and
to Rocheport, Boone Co., Mo., in 1836, engaged for a
time in merchandising ; is now farming ; in 1838 m.
Mary L. Lientz.
Ch. 9th Gen.: 1 Wm. L., b. May 10, 1842. In 1868,
m. Ella Eubank. 2 Hattie E., b. Oct. 29, 1843 ; m.
Alex. Bradford.
106 3 Abel, b. Jan. 22, 1815 ; m. Angeline Edson, West Randolph,
July 3, 1849 ; d. there Dec. 20, 1864.
Ch. 9th Gen.: Harry, b. Sept. 23, 1854.
108 4 John, b. 1818 ; moved to Rocheport, in 1843 ; d. June, 1845.

Dorothy (Abel's first wife) d. in 1822, and in 1824, he m. Esther
Bigelow. Their children were:

109 5 Julius B., b. Nov. 2, 1824 ; was a teacher, a farmer, superintendent of schools, justice of the peace and a member of
the state legislature ; d. June 7, 1865. He m. Ellen
Crane, 1850.
> *Ch. 9th Gen.:* 1 Lucia E., b. March 29, 1851. 2
> M. Louise, b. March 30, 1853. 3 Charles Abel, b. Oct.
> 3, 1856; d. 1859. 4 Arthur, b. Feb. 20, 1859. 5
> Julius B., b. Feb. 23, 1865 ; d. May 13, 1867.

115 6 Cornelius S., b. Feb. 12, 1826; moved to Illinois in 1854; a
farmer ; m. Comfort Mitchell in 1859. Their post office
address is Virden, Macoupin Co., Ill.
> *Ch. 9th Gen.:* 1 Wm. A., b. March 7, 1860. 2 Chas.
> E., b. Nov. 8, 1862. 3 Clara Alice, b. April 28, 1864.
> 4 Clarence, b. Dec., 1865 ; d. 1866. 5 Julius B., b.
> March 4, 1869.

121 7 David, b. April 7, 1828. Resides in Brookfield, Vt.; a
farmer — served three years in the army.

122 8 Dolly T., b. Aug. 18, 1829 ; m. S. S. Abbott, May 14, 1850.
They reside in Brookfield.
> *Ch. 9th Gen.:* 1 Edward, b. Aug. 15, 1853. 2 Solon,
> b. Dec. 8, 1856. 3 Clarence Lyman, b. Aug., 1862.

125 9 George, b. Feb. 18, 1831; moved to Illinois; his address is
Virden ; is a farmer — served three years in Co. D., 73d
Ill. Vols.; m. Minerva J. Collins, Feb. 5, 1868.

127 10 Laura A.

2 AZEL LYMAN[7], *Abel[6], John[5], Richard[4], Richard[3], Richard[2],
Richard[1]*, b. in Lebanon, N. H., Aug. 1, 1784. Before he
was two years old his parents removed to Brookfield, Vt. He
engaged for a time in teaching school. Then he and his
brother Abel bought their father's tannery and spent some
time in the leather business. He m. Roxana Fisk of
Brookfield in 1808. She was also engaged in teaching
school, was b. Dec. 22, 1788, and d. June 7, 1829. In 1810
he sold his interest in the tannery to his brother Abel and
moved to Potsdam, St. Lawrence Co. N. Y., where he built
the 5th dwelling house in the village and also another
tannery. In 1812 St. Lawrence Academy was started and
he was one of the trustees, which office he held till he moved
to Illinois. In 1820 he was appointed deacon of the Presbyterian church and superintendent of the sabbath school.
In 1829–31 he superintended 3 sabbath schools, to do
which he was obliged to travel 18 miles every sabbath. In
1830 he m. his second wife, Mary P. Bates of Potsdam.
In 1832 he and his brother John with their horses and
carriage went on an exploring expedition to the " far west,"
and drove to the Mississippi where the city of Alton now

stands.   In Sept. 1, 1833, with 10 other families he started
for Illinois.   (For account of journey see above in record of
John).   Soon after they arrived, they organized a Presbyterian church and he was appointed one of the elders.
They also organized a Temperance Society and he was
chosen its first president.   In 1835 he spent several months
selling Bibles and distributing tracts.   In 1836 he was employed by the Illinois Sunday School Union.   His field of
labor comprised 35 counties in the southern part of the
state.   He continued in this work 3 years, organized a
great many Sunday schools and started anew many that
had been suspended, and although in a pecuniary point of
view it was an unprofitable, losing business he felt that he
received a rich reward.   In 1851 his dwelling was burned,
he built another and in 1852 sold his farm and purchased
another of 240 acres in Green Valley, Tazewell Co., Illinois.
In 1854 a Presbyterian church was organized and he was
appointed an elder.   He is now, 1872, enjoying good
health though 87 years old.   *Green Valley, Ill.*

Children, Eighth Generation :

128 1 Sophronia, b. Feb. 21, 1809 ; d. Aug. 3, 1810.
129 2 Abel, b. May 3, 1810 ; d. Aug. 1811.
130 3 Mary, b. March 18, 1812 ; d. Aug. 1, 1814.
131 4 Azel Storrs, b. Jan. 23, 1815 ; spent his youth at St. Lawrence
         Academy and in teaching school.   In 1833, he went with
         his relatives to Illinois.   Graduated at Illinois College ;
         taught some ;   published historical chart ; m. Amelia
         Jane Noble, in Cincinnati, Ohio, June 24, 1844.
              Ch. 9th Gen. : 1 Wm. Thornton, b. June 5, 1845 ; m.
         Josephine Fogg, 1869.   2 Edward Matthias, b. April
         14, 1847 ; m. Anna Brinckerhoff, 1868.   3 Mary Kate,
         b. Jan. 22, 1850 ; d. Sept. 29, 1851.   4 Louisa Eliza-
         beth, b. Feb. 17, 1852.   5 Julia Adelaide, Feb. 5, 1854.
         6 Anna Gertrude, b. May 28, 1856.   7 Ella Josephine,
         b. July 30, 1858.   8 Harriet Emma, b. May 6, 1861.
    For the last 15 years his residence has been 212 Second avenue,
New York city.
139 5 Roxana Fisk, b. April 3, 1819, in Potsdam, N. Y.; m. Wm.
         S. Thornton, in Sangamon Co., Illinois, Jan. 1, 1839.
         He d. June 11, 1839 ; and Aug., 1854, she m. Aaron H.
         Palmer, from Middlebury, Vt.   They now reside in
         Chicago, Ill.
140 6 Alvan Earl, b. Aug. 10, 1820 ; d. July 10, 1822.
141 7 Mary Calista, b. March 21, 1824.   Has spent most of her
         life so far in study or in teaching.   She resides with her
         brother's family on 212, 2d avenue, New York.   After
         the death of Roxana Fisk, his first wife, he m. Mary

Paulina Bates of Potsdam, b. Feb. 2, 1809, their children were :

142 8 Ellen Elizabeth, b. April 3, 1831 ; m. in 1852, Simon Simonson from Norway, P. O. address Delavan, Ill.
  Ch. 9th Gen.: 1 Azel L., b. Jan. 17, 1853 ; d. Sept. 4, 1855.
144 9 Emily Eliza, b. April 3, 1833 ; d. July 24, 1836.
145 10 Theron Baldwin, b. June 29, 1836 ; m. Asenath Mundy in 1861.
  Ch. 9th Gen.: 1 Abel E., b. Aug. 22, 1863 ; d. July 27, 1864. 2 Harrie A., b. Dec. 5, 1864. 3 Fred. J., b. Dec. 16, 1866. 4 Richard F., b. May 30, 1868. Their P. O. address is Tallula, Menard Co., Illinois.
149 11 Ova H., b. May 20, 1838 ; d. Feb. 26, 1858.
150 12 Emma E., b. Nov. 5, 1839 ; d. Feb. 20, 1854.
151 13 Abel S., b. May 28, 1841 ; d. Oct. 22, 1842.
152 14 Almira C., b. Feb. 6, 1843 ; m. Charles Parker, May 20, 1866. He was b. in Columbus, Ohio.
  Ch. 9th Gen.: 1 Lyman T., b. March 14, 1867. They reside at Delavan, Illinois.
155 15 Otto B., b. July 23, 1846. P. O. address, Green Valley, Tazewell Co., Illinois.

12 ALVAN LYMAN[7], *Abel*[6], *John*[5], *Richard*[4], *Richard*[3], *Richard*[2], *Richard*[1], b. March 16, 1787 ; d. Oct 6, 1865. In 1810 he bought a farm in Potsdam, N. Y. In 1813, m. Lucy Perrin, of Royalton, Vt. In 1820, he united with the Presbyterian church. In 1833, he moved, with his brothers, to Sangamon Co., Illinois. He had two children, both d. in infancy.
              Richland, Ill.

13 EZRA LYMAN[7], *Abel*[6], *John*[5], *Richard*[4], *Richard*[3], *Richard*[2], *Richard*[1], b. Feb. 23, 1789 ; d. Oct. 1, 1855. In 1811, he m. Mercy Cushman, of Brookfield, Vt., and moved to Potsdam, N. Y., and bought a farm. In 1820, they united with the Presbyterian church. In 1833, moved to Sangamon Co., Ill., with his brothers, as stated above in the record of John. He spent several years in teaching school and farming. He, like all his brothers, was a man of great energy and decision of character, always among the foremost and radical in all efforts for improving the morals or bettering the condition of the people.   *Richland, Ill.*

  Children, Eighth Generation :
156 1 Ezra Cushman, b. May 19, 1814. In 1833 went with his relatives from Potsdam to Sangamon Co , Ill. ; m. Caroline Van Patton, March 28, 1839.

Ch. 9th Gen.: 1 Alvan, b. June 14, 1840; d. March 25, 1847. 2 Hannah Hester, b. Oct. 14, 1841 ; m. Thomas Earnest, Nov. 15, 1863. [*Ch. 10th Gen.*: (1) Carrie Bell, b. Feb. 10, 1856. (2) John William, b. April 29, 1869]. 3 Mary Elizabeth, b. Feb. 23, 1844; m. Robert Morris, Nov. 12, 1867. 4 Cornelius, b. Oct. 14, 1846. 5 Ezra Cushman, b. Oct. 21, 1848. 6 Alvan, b. Jan. 31, 1852. 7 J......D., b. Oct. 7, 1855. 8 Laura Alice, b. Oct. 16, 1859. Farmer, P. O., address, Richland, Sangamon Co., Illinois.

167 2 Mercy S., b. May 19, 1820; m. Jeremiah D. Low, A.M., Oct. 22, 1844.

Ch. 9th Gen.: 1 Cornelia Alice, b. Oct. 16, 1848; d. May 24, 1860. 2 Charles H., b. Oct. 31, 1845. 3 Laura, b. July 17, 1855. Their P. O. address is Springfield, Illinois.

170 3 Betsey, b. and d. in infancy.
171 4 Zeruiah H., b. Jan. 6, 1830.

14 CORNELIUS LYMAN[7], *Abel[6]*, *John[5]*, *Richard[4]*, *Richard[3]*, *Richard[2]*, *Richard[1]*, b. Aug. 10, 1792; d. Jan. 30, 1864; learned the tanner's trade in his father's works; m. Betsey Cushman, of Brookfield. After residing a few years in West Randolph, moved to Potsdam, N. Y., and bought a farm. He, with his wife, united with Presbyterian church in 1820. In 1833, with his family and relatives he moved to Sangamon Co., Illinois. In 1844 he removed with his family to Minnesota. "From the organization of the Presbyterian church, of Stillwater, in 1849, he was a ruling elder, held in great esteem by the church and community. He was an active, useful and consistent Christian, exceedingly affable in disposition, firm and unflinching in his principles.
Stillwater, Minn.

Frontier Life, Reminiscences, etc.—When the elder Cornelius moved there, the country was a wilderness. Where the city of Stillwater now stands—a city of 6,000 or 7,000 inhabitants—there were only three men, and one log shanty. While opening his farm, which was some four miles from what is now the city of Stillwater, his family resided there, camping out in haying time, to cut the wild hay on the prairies; they fell short of provisions, and having nothing but five or six pounds of pork left, his sons went to Stillwater to obtain supplies. The wolves, attracted by the meat, came around his bed; once or twice he drove them away; finally, he put the meat under his pillow for safe keeping, but the wolves carried it off before morning.

He put up a cabin on the bank of the St. Croix in the spring of 1847, and moved up his family. He brought with him a sow and eight pigs, and they finding themselves in a strange place, took refuge under the house. That night the family were awakened by a terrible squealing, and the oldest son, going out to see what the trouble was, beheld a wolf making off with one of the young pigs. He immediately gave chase, but the wolf was too spry for him and escaped. He had but just returned when the pigs sounded the alarm again. He immediately issued forth with intent to kill, but the enemy had retired in good order. Storrs returned to the house, concluding that the wolves, had determined to have the pigs at all hazards, as they did, before morning. The dam, bereft of her young, returned in the morning to the city in grand disgust with frontier life.

The Indians at this time were very numerous, but generally were friendly toward the whites. But the Chippewas and Sioux were continually at war among themselves.

A party of Sioux came to the house one night just at dusk and wanted supper. They had been on the war path and had the scalps of some ten or a dozen Chippewas whom they had killed, that afternoon, some six or seven miles above on the Apple river. No one was at home except Mrs. Lyman. She refused them admittance, but told them they might build their fire out in the yard, which they did; and after supper, they danced their scalp dance, nearly all night. One of the members of that war party is now a missionary among the Sioux.

Children, Eighth Generation :

172 1 Cornelius Storrs, b. May 22, 1815. In 1833 he moved with his parents and relatives to Sangamon Co., Ill.; in 1837 he m. Emily A. Kincaid.

Ch. 9th Gen. : 1 Horace C., b. Jan. 28, 1839. 2 Benjamin F., b. Feb. 5, 1841. 3 Betsey C., b. Nov. 11, 1842. 4 Cornelius S., b. Aug. 28, 1844. 5 Emily A., b. Oct. 23, 1846. 6 Wm. H., b. Dec. 25, 1848. 7 Lucretia, b. Nov. 30, 1850. 8 Eliza J., b. Dec. 14, 1852. 9 Gratia M., b. Dec. 30, 1854. 10 John E., b. Jan. 31, 1857. 11 Rollin, b. Oct. 4, 1859. 12 Walter S., b. Dec. 25, 1862. 13 Thomas, b. Jan. 24, 1865. The address of Cornelius S. and of most of the children is Stillwater, Minnesota. They are farmers on the St. Croix about 3 miles above the city.

186 2 David P., b. March 20, 1822; m. Ann J. Hanna, 1850.
   Ch. 9th Gen.: 1 David H., b. June 24, 1854. 2
   Abel Arthur, b. Aug. 2, 1856. 3 Mary J., b. Feb. 20,
   1861. 4 Oscar C., b. March 1, 1863. 5 Maggie H., b.
   July 6, 1866. They are farmers. P. O. address, Still-
   water, Minn.

6. RICHARD LYMAN[6], *John[5],   Richard[4],   Richard[3], Richard[2],
Richard[1],* AND PHILOMELIA.

Children, Seventh Generation:

192	1 Hill.	198	7 Richard.
193	2 Asa.	199	8 Lydia.
194	3 Philomelia.	200	9 George.
195	4 Sophia.	201	10 Mary.
↑ 196	5 Clarissa.	202	11 Eliza.
197	6 Sarah.		

192 HILL LYMAN[7], b. at Lebanon, N. H., Dec. 24, 1784;
m. Irene Weatherwax, May 15, 1806; d. May, 1815. She
b. Aug. 17, 1784. His family lived in Schaghticoke in
the vicinity of Saratoga Springs, N. Y. At the time of his
death, as for some time previous, he was in the U. S., service as secretary for one of the officers. *Schaghticoke, N. Y.*

Children, Eighth Generation

203 1 Philomelia Eliza, b. Jan. 22, 1807.
204 2 Susannah, b. May 23, 1808.
205 3 Benjamin Franklin, b. March 26, 1810.

193 ASA LYMAN[7], b. in Lebanon, Conn., Nov. 6, 1784;
m. Sarah R. Davis of Canaan, N. H., Aug. 6, 1806. He d.
July, 1847. She was b. March 10, 1786. He was drowned
in the Missouri in 1846, near the present town of Florence
in Nebraska. His children, with one exception, went into
Missouri and nothing more is known of many of them, but
a record of their birth has been preserved—farmer.

Children, Eighth Generation:

206 1 Ziba H., b. Nov., 1807.
207 2 Richard, b. July 29, 1809.
208 3 Asa, b. April 25, 1811. For several years Asa was a resi-
      dent of Mo. At the breaking out of the rebellion he was
      quite wealthy, but was destined to suffer because he could
      not stand by and see the old flag insulted without avowing
      his sentiments in its behalf; living in the very heart of
      rebeldom he was subjected to many insults. His two sons
      joined the Union forces, and then he was driven from

home with his family, and suffered much before reaching
Illinois.

209 4 Sarah, b. Jan. 21, 1813.
210 5 Roswell K., b. Feb. 5, 1815 ; lives in Colton, St. Lawrence
      Co., N. Y. Farmer.
        Ch. 9th Gen.: 1 James W., b. Oct. 8, 1832. 2 Clar-
        issa, b. 1835. 3 Martin P., b. 1847. 4 Orison, b. 1851.
        5 Ettie, b 1859.
211 6 Mary A., b. Feb. 7, 1817.
212 7 Clarissa, b. Jan. 16, 1819.
213 8 William D., b. May 19, 1823.
214 9 George, b. 1825.

210 ROSWELL KIMBALL LYMAN[8], b. in Vermont, Feb. 5,
1815 ; his father moved to Colton, N. Y. while he was a boy.
                                            Colton, N. Y.
        Children, Ninth Generation :
215 1 James W., b. Oct. 18, 1832.
216 2 Clarissa, b. 1835.
217 3 Martin P., b. 1847.
218 4 Orison, b. 1851.
219 5 Ettie, b. 1859.

211 MARY A. LYMAN[8], b. Feb. 7, 1817 ; m. J. D. Roland.
In 1861 at the commencement of the war, she resided in
Mo. When the call for volunteers came, 3 of her sons went ;
while she, being of a daring spirit, often acted in the capacity of a spy, and aided the Union troops in every way
possible. She was instrumental in the capture of a noted
desperado called Jim Anderson, riding 12 miles one dark
rainy night to give information of his whereabouts to a
Union regiment which was quartered that distance from
her home. Many Union boys were relieved by her skillful hands.   *Missouri.*

212 CLARISSA LYMAN[8], b. at Potsdam, N. Y., Jan. 16,
1819 ; m. Lyman Smith 1834, d. 1837 ; m. 2d, Amos Moore,
1840.   *Erie, Kansas.*
        Children, Ninth Generation :
222 1 Ira H. (son by her first marriage). Enlisted in the 61st
        Ill. Infantry, served 3 years.
223 2 Wm. H. (son by her second marriage), b. in 1851. Enlisted in
        the 144th Ill. Infantry, Aug. 12, 1864, as drummer
        when but 13 years of age, and served until the war ended.
224 3 Lyman.   227 6 Sarah.
225 4 Mary.   228 7 Anna.
226 5 Rachel.   229 8 Ellen.

213 WM. D. LYMAN[8], b. May 19, 1823. At the breaking out of the rebellion was a resident of Tenn., and on his refusing to enlist in the rebel army, he was imprisoned; but after being confined 9 months, he succeeded in making his escape and walked 220 miles to the nearest Union forces where he immediately enlisted in the 4th Kentucky Cavalry, in which regiment he faithfully served until the close of the war.   *Tennessee.*

194 PHILOMELIA LYMAN[7], b. Aug. 28, 1786, d. June 9, 1835; m. John Martin, b. May 10, 1813; d. March 3, 1853.

Children, Eighth Generation :

230 1 Richard, b. May 12, 1815; m. Phebe Mower.
       Ch. 9th Gen.: 1 Ann P., b. Sept., 1842. 2 Alice, b. Dec., 1843. 3 Frank—4 Francis, twins, b. Dec., 1845.
231 2 George Loomis, b. Sept., 1817; m. Sarah Jackson.
       Ch. 9th Gen.: 1 Henry, b. 1850. 2 Eva A., b. 1852. 3 Mary Lizzie, b. 1860.
232 3 Lora B., b. April 9, 1819; m. George Jackson.
       Ch. 9th Gen.: 1 Abby Philomelia, b. 1850. 2 Jane, b. 1852. 3 Elbert, b. 1854.
233 4 John Parrish, b. April 24, 1821.

195 SOPHIA LYMAN[7], b. July 30, 1788; d. Jan. 22, 1841; m. James Pike, b. Feb. 14, 1808; d. April 3, 1816.

Children, Eighth Generation :

233*1 Roswell, b. Dec. 16, 1808; d. Dec. 17, 1808.
234 2 Richard L., d. Sept. 14, 1811.
235 3 Mary Armena, b. Feb. 19, 1812; m. Cornelius Robinson, of Chelsea, Vt., Jan. 1862.
       Ch. 9th Gen.: 1 Calista. 2 Lenora. 3 Norman.
236 4 Marinda Fidelia, b. Sept. 2, 1813; m. Henry P. Pope.
237 5 James Lyman, b. Aug. 11, 1815; d. at Lowell, Mass., March 8, 1840. James (father of above) d. and Sophia m. in 1848, Micajah Colburn, of Chelsea, Vt. They had a dau. name unknown.
238 6 Sarah G., b. 1825; m. Alfred Lathrop, 1850. They had one dau., b. 1862.

196 CLARISSA LYMAN[7], b. in Lebanon, N. H., June 27, 1790; d. Feb. 14, 1854; m. John Smith, of Potsdam, N. Y., Sept. 1, 1815, the uncle of the notorious Joe Smith.

Children, Eighth Generation :

239 1 ———— a daughter, who d. unmarried.

240 2 George Albert, b. at Potsdam, N. Y., June 26, 1817; m. Bathsheba W. Bigler, July 25, 1841. He was an early pioneer in the settlement of the territory of Utah, where, with limited advantages of education, he has held various offices of trust and exerted an efficient influence in developing the resources of the country. He held several offices in the early organization of the government; and, especially in the southern section of Utah, was foremost in promoting the culture of the soil and evoking its natural resources. He built the first grist and saw-mill in Iron Co., 22 miles from the nearest mills, and planted extensively fruit trees in the counties of southern Utah. He is president of a company for tunneling a mountain 130 rods to bring water from the lake to a desert tract estimated at about 30,000 acres.

    Ch. 9th Gen.: 1 Geo. A., Jr., b. July 7, 1842; murdered by the Navajoe Indians, Nov. 2, 1860. 2 Bathsheba, b. Aug. 14, 1844; m. Clarence Merrill, Jan. 3, 1861; four children. 3 John, b. at Winter Quarters, Nebraska Ter., April 4, 1847; d. April 4, 1847.

243 3 Caroline Clara, b. at Potsdam, N. Y., June 6, 1820; m. Thos. Callister, Aug. 31, 1845; eight children.

252 4 John Lyman Smith, 2d son of John and Clarissa L. Smith, b. at Potsdam, St. Lawrence Co., N. Y., Nov. 17, 1828; m. Augusta Bowen Cleveland, dau. of John and Sarah Maritta Cleveland, b. in Cincinnati, Ohio, Dec. 7, 1828.

    Ch. 9th Gen.: 1 Isabella, b. June 12, 1846. 2 Augusta Bowen, b. May 23, 1849. 3 Sarah Maritta, b. April 14, 1851; m. M. H. Webb; one child, Clara A. 4 Clarissa Medora, b. May 3, 1853; d. Nov. 3, 1854. 5 John L., Jr., b. Oct. 22, 1855. 6 George Don Alexander, b. April 3, 1859. 7 Lottie Rose, b. Feb. 2, 1861. 8 Sophronia Amanda, b. Sept. 26, 1865.

197 SARAH LYMAN[7], b. May 25, 1792; m. Daniel Flagg, son of Josiah Flagg, of Brookfield, Vt., Nov. 27, 1816; d. April 9, 1869.

    Children, Eighth Generation:

261 1 Louisa, b. March 28, 1819; d. Feb. 18, 1833.

262 2 Ermina, b. Jan. 12, 1825; d. Feb. 17, 1825.

263 3 Josiah Albert, b. Oct. 2, 1827; m. Helen E., daughter of Oramel Williams, of Brookfield, Vt., June 14, 1857; d. Jan. 3, 1859.

264 4 Ermina Williams, b. Sept. 5, 1831; m. June 14, 1857, Geo. F. Kinney, of Plainfield, Vt. He d. Nov. 24, 1862. [*Ch. 9th Gen.:* (1) Alice Ermina, b. Oct. 17, 1861.]

198 RICHARD LYMAN[7], b. Feb. 25, 1794; d. in Canada, Feb. 18, 1861; m. Catharine Lamson, Dec. 7, 1815, dau. of Thos. Lamson, of West Randolph, Vt.

Children, Eighth Generation :

266 1 Thos. Weston, b. Jan. 11, 1817; d. Aug. 9, 1818.
267 2 Richard Lamson, b. Nov. 7, 1818; d. June 8, 1820.
268 3 Catharine, b. at Madrid, N. Y., Oct. 15, 1821; m. Thos. McDowell, of Whitby, C. W., son of Rev. William McDowell, of Whitby, C. W. After the death of Catharine Lamson, Richard m. Elizabeth Jones.
269 4 Thos. Lamson, b. Sept. 25, 1824; m. Sophronia, dau. of Ziba Lyman, of Colton, N. Y., Grinnell, Iowa.
270 5 Eliza Ann, b. at Colbourne, C. W., Feb. 6, 1832; m. L. A. Gansby, of Orono, C. W., July 14, 1853.
271 6 Geo. Washington, b. April 13, 1834.
272 7 Samuel B., b. Jan. 19, 1837; d. June 19, 1857.
273 8 Martha W., b. March 18, 1840.

199 LYDIA LYMAN[7], b. Nov. 22, 1795; d. Nov. 22, 1845; m. Elijah Hawes, Feb. 26, 1816.

Children, Eighth Generation

274 1 Laura, b. June 27, 1817; d. March 21, 1818.
275 2 Emeline, b. Jan. 4, 1820; d. May, 1859; m. Jos. B. Kingsley, of Brookfield, Vt., 1842. They had one son.
     Ch. 9th Gen. : 1 George, b. July 3, 1843.

200 GEORGE LYMAN[7], b. May 17, 1797; d. Aug., 1836, in Missouri, m. Hannah Fairbanks, of Madrid, N. Y.

Children, Eighth Generation :

277 1 Gilbert.   278 2 Mollie.

201 MARY LYMAN[7], b. in Lebanon, N. H., Feb. 18, 1800; d. in Colton, N. Y., Dec. 24, 1868; m. in Madrid, N. Y., July 24, 1822, to Pliny, son of Jos. Hepburn, of that town. He d. March 1, 1866, farmer; they moved March 1830.   *Colton, N. Y.*

Chlidren, Eighth Generation :

279 1 Hannah Philomelia, b. Aug. 30, 1823; m. Feb. 23, 1843 Simon D., son of John Butler, who was b. March 2, 1818; moved March, 1830, to Colton, N. Y., general store keeper.
     Ch. 9th Gen. : 1 Eugene A., b. Oct. 16, 1845; m. Dec. 29, 1865, Ellsworth, N. Y., Harma L., dau. of John Levly, Colton, N. Y., farmer. [*Ch. 10th Gen. :* (1) A son. (2) Edwin A., b. March 8, 1869.] 2 Kittie Emogene, b. Dec. 25, 1850. 3 Ettie C., b. Sept. 22, 1854; d. Sept. 23, 1862.

285 2 Zina Vilroy, b. July 14, 1825; m. July 14, 1851, Helen
Maria, dau. of Ira Selleck, farmer, Colton, St. Lawrence
Co.,.N. Y.
Ch. 9th Gen.: 1 Pliny V., b. Sept. 16, 1859. 2 Darwin B., b. Sept. 28, 1864. 3 Marly L., b. Dec. 6, 1869.
289 3 Charlotte Eliza, b. Jan. 4, 1827; m. Aug. 15, 1844. Edwin H., son of John Butler, manufacturer and dealer in
cloths and woolen goods. Colton, N. Y.
Ch. 9th Gen.: 1 Clarissa M., b. May 24, 1845; m. Dec.
22, 1865, Chas. Ensign, Ellsworth, N. Y., son of Isaac
Mix, Green Bay, Wis., Ex. agent. [*Ch. 10th Gen.:* (1)
Charles E., b. Sept. 27, 1866; d. Nov. 20, 1866. (2)
Hawley McPherson, b. Sept. 26, 1867.] 2 Darwin, b.
June 18, 1846; d. Oct. 13, 1863. 3 Elbert S., b. Sept.
24, 1847; m. in Mich., 1868.
295 4 Lewis Lyman, b. March 2, 1832; m. June 20, 1854, Julia A.
Charles; she d. Feb. 22, 1859, at Remington.
Ch. 9th Gen.: 1 Calla, b. June 20, 1858. Lewis L.
Hepburn, m. Aug. 17, 1859, Lavinia (dau. of Hiram
Fisk). 2 Louis, b. March 7, 1861. 3 Verna, b. Jan. 6,
1863. 4 Melvern, b. July 16, 1868. Occupation, manufacturer of fine guns. Residence. Colton, N. Y.

202 ELIZA LYMAN[7], b. May 25, 1801; d. Feb. 7, 1842;
m. Jabez Fairbanks, of Madrid, N. Y

Children, Eighth Generation:

300 1 Emily, b. about 1826.
301 2 Amos, b. about 1828; d. 1845.
302 3 Edward, b. about 1830; d. April 5, 1830.
303 4 Mary, b. about 1833; m. Feb., 1852, James Bowen, of Ill.
Have one child, a daughter, b. Feb., 1853.
305 5 Jabez, b. about 1836.
307 6 Emily, m. Harvey Marsh, Oct., 1843. Their child, Edward
L., b. Sept., 1846.

V. DESCENDANTS OF RICHARD[3] THROUGH RICHARD[4] AND DAVID[5]

DAVID LYMAN[5], *Richard[4]*, *Richard[3]*, *Richard[2]*, *Richard[1]*,
1711–1787; m. May 27, 1736, Anna Lee, who d. Dec. 15,
1737; m. 2d wife, Mary Benton, of Tolland, March 1, 1740,
who d. May 29, 1741; m. 3d wife, April 8, 1742, Mary
Gittau, of Woodbury, Ct., and removed about 1745, or
1746 to Bethlehem, in Litchfield Co. Mary Gittau was the
dau. of Francis Gittau, a distinguished physician, who was
banished from France during the persecution of the Huguenots in connection with St. Bartholomew's day. Re-

quired to renounce protestantism, or sacrifice all that the heart holds dear on earth, he made the sacrifice for conscience sake. His property, which was ample, was confiscated. His wife, with three young children, was torn from his embrace. Thus destitute and desolate he was banished to a distant foreign country, but he who holds the winds in his fist directed the ship to the shores of England where he was landed. His wife, knowing nothing of his fate, managed to transport her little charge also to England. There, landed on the beach, she sat neglected while others were received by friends or shared the kindness and hospitality of strangers; then raising a loud and bitter cry, she exclaimed: Is there none here who can speak the French language? Attracted by the cry and the accents of his native tongue, a stranger went to her relief and sank into the embrace of his lost, despairing wife, by this surprising providence receiving her with their little ones as alive from the dead! Once more united, an unbroken family in a foreign land, like their Divine Master, they had not where to lay their heads. Still the subjects of penury and of persecution they took refuge in the wilds of America, the home of the oppressed.

The names of their three sons b. in France, were Francis, Ephraim and Joshua. Other children were born to them in America, from whom a numerous posterity have descended worthy of their pious and distinguished ancestry. Mary Gittau, wife of David Lyman, d. in 1803, aged 85 years. He d. Dec. 27, 1787.

Children, Sixth Generation :

1   1 David, issue of the 2d marriage, b. May 20, 1741; d. April 8, 1742..

2   2 John, b. in Lebanon, Feb. 14, 1744.

3   3 David, b. in Bethlehem, May 20, 1747.

4   4 Francis, b. 1755 ; d. in West Andover, Ohio, 1840.

5   5 Josiah, removed to Ashtabula, Ohio, d. many years since, no record.

6   6 Elizabeth, no record.

7   7 Anna, no record.

8   8 A dau., name not given, who m. Steele. This family resided in New Hartford, and, after settling in life, removed 1812, to Andover, Ashtabula Co., Ohio.

2 John Lyman[6], brother of *David*[5], enlisted in the Revolutionary war, was taken prisoner and d. in a British prison, ship near New York, believed by his friends to have been poisoned by the enemy.

3 DAVID LYMAN⁶, 1747–1813, b. May 20, 1747; m. Oct. 20, 1773, Mary Brown of Torringford, a relative of the martyr John Brown and d. in T. where he resided in the latter part of his life, July 29, 1813. Mary his wife d. July 22, 1820. He served some time in the army of the Revolution known as Gen. David; then was honorably discharged to run a grist mill in New Hartford, for the supply of the Revolutionary troops.

Children, Seventh Generation:

9 1 Elijah, b. Aug. 16, 1773; d. Nov. 5, 1819, aged 46.
10 2 David, b. June 14, 1776; d. Feb. 24, 1850, aged 74.
11 3 John, b. Oct. 5, 1778; d. July 20, 1865, aged 87.
12 4 Orange, Rev., July 26, 1780; d. July 16, 1850, aged 71.
13 5 Daniel, b. April 15, 1784; d. July 20, 1846, aged 67.
14 6 Norman, b. Sept. 6, 1787; d. Oct. 20, 1850, aged 65.
15 7 Mary, b. Aug 18, 1789; a venerable lady, m. Mr. Pardee; still living, no children, Torringford, Conn.
16 8 Samuel, b. Feb. 8, 1793; unmarried.

4 FRANCIS LYMAN⁶, *David⁵, Richard⁴, Richard³, Richard², Richard¹*, 1755 – 1840, b. in Bethlehem, Conn.; d. in West Andover, O.; m. Abigail Coles, b. 1760; d. March 23, 1841. They resided in New Hartford, and in 1812 removed to Ohio, suffering the hardships and the trials incident to pioneer life. Their nearest neighbors in one direction were five miles distant, in another eighteen miles. In a case of extreme sickness a dog was sent with a note to their nearest neighbor, who, with a lantern, came by night on foot through the forest to their relief. He d. July 17, 1840, in West Andover, Ashtabula Co., Ohio.

Children, Seventh Generation :

17 1 Anna, b. Dec. 7, 1780; m. Dea. Chester Andrews; d. March 16, 1868, without issue.
18 1 Sally, b. 1782; d. June 18, 1823; unmarried.
19 3 Joshua, d. April 2, 1865, } twins.
20 4 Joseph, died many years ago, }
21 5 Epaphras, b. 1784; m. and settled in Austinsburg; removed to Andover; d. April 11, 1842. The order of the births of of these children is unknown.
22 6 Laura, m. Zadoc Steele.

21 EPAPHRAS was the eldest son and first settler in the township. He came in advance of the family, and for six months labored alone, building a house and making a small clearing. His nearest white neighbor was eighteen miles distant. For his meat he drove with him a young beef

creature, there being no roads for conveying provisions.
He hollowed out a log in which to salt his meat; and with
the few things he could bring on his back, commenced
housekeeping. On returning to his shanty one day, he
found a wolf on the roof eating the heifer's skin which he
had thrown there, to be, as he supposed, out of the way of
such pilferers. At another time, he came home and
noticing, at a little distance, that the door was slightly ajar,
he cautiously advanced, and pushing wide open the door,
an Indian sprang up, rifle in hand, and quickly leveled the
deadly instrument at his breast, at but a few feet distant;
but before the Indian could fire Mr. Lyman sprang upon
him, wrenched the rifle from his hands and quickly overpowered him. The Indian had learned enough of our
language to find words to plead for his life; and, although
he was an old offender, he was dismissed in peace.

Mr. Lyman was a man of good talents who took a promi
nent part in all the affairs of the new settlement, partien
larly all that pertained to the welfare of his fellow men.
The poor found in him a helping, sympathizing friend.
His fund of information was extensive and varied. A man
of sterling integrity: he repeatedly filled offices of trust
and honor. He was born 1784 or 1785, and died 1842 lamented by all who knew him.

Children, Eighth Generation:

23 1 Horatio, b. 1808.
  Ch. 9th Gen.: 1 Reuben. 2 Rufus. 3 Rufus. 4 Minerva. 5 Henry. 6 George. 7 Martha. 8 Louessa. 9 Mary.
  Akron, Mich.
32 2 Betsey, b. 1810; m. George Collins; d. 1869.
  Ch. 9th Gen.: 1 Sophia. 2 Frances C., d. 1870; Min-
  nerith, Tenn.
35 3 Dr. James, b. 1812, the second white child b. in the township, d. 1839. One child, James, Ashtabula, Ohio.
37 4 George, b. 1815.
  Ch. 9th Gen.: 1 Maria. 2 Eurotas. 3 De Witt.
40 5 Lois, b. 1817; m. William Dolph.
  Ch. 9th Gen.: 1 James. 2 Margaret. 3 Lucian. 4 Eliza.
  Akron, Tuscola Co. Mich.
47 6 Willard, b. 1819.
  Ch. 9th Gen: 1 Francis. enlisted when a mere boy
  in the war for the Union, served with great acceptance,
  promoted to Lieut. 2 Charles.
49 7 Edward, b. 1822; no issue.
50 8 Mary, b. 1827; m. L. Tuttle.
  Ch. 9th Gen.: Clagton E., b. 1860.

52 9 Eliza S., b. 1830; m. L. Dorman; no issue.
53 10 Albert H., b. 1831; one child Alice, d.
55 11 Laura N., b. 1834 : m. B. F. Perry, farmer.
    Ch. 9th Gen.: 1 Clara L., b. 1854. 2 Epaphras, b.
    1856. 3 B. F., Jr., b. 1858. 4 Mary E., b. 1860. 5 Maria Laura, b. 1870.

22 LAURA LYMAN[7], dau. of *Francis*[6], b. May 1, 1786; m.
Feb. 11, 1805, Zadoc Steele, of New Hartford, Ct.; moved
to Andover, Ashtabula Co., Ohio, in the spring of 1808. She
d. April 19, 1842. He d. Sept. 27, 1852. *Andover, Ohio.*

Children, Eighth Generation :
61 1 E. Wolcott, b. Oct. 29, 1805; m. Lavinia Johnson, Jan. 7,
    1830, Shirland, Ill.
63 2 William, b. March 24, 1809; m. Caroline Woodruff, of New
    Hartford, Ct.; lives in Homestead, Benzie Co., Mich.
64 3 Frances, b. Sept. 12, 1812; m. Rosetta J. Andrews, of Wayne
    Ohio ; d. in Shirland, Ill., Jan. 31, 1850.
65 4 Almon, b. June 16, 1814; m. Ann Adams, of Brookfield,
    Ohio; d. in Cottonville, Ia., Aug., 1864.
66 5 Harriet, b. June 21, 1816; m. Sept. 8, 1847, Eldad W.
    Merrell, of West Andover, Ohio; d. May 30, 1868.
67 6 Abby C., b. April 25, 1819, unmarried, Andover, Ashtabula
    Co., Ohio.
68 7 Olive, b. Jan. 12, 1822; m. Grove C. Steele, of Cherry Valley,
    Ohio; d. May 12, 1861, no issue.
69 8 Orange, ⎫
70 9 Olive, ⎬ twins, b. Jan. 12, 1822, d. same year.
71 10 Cordelia, b. June 15, 1826; d. March 30, 1831.
72 11 Sarah Ann, b. April 18, 1828; d. April 10, 1831.

61 E. WOLCOTT[8], and LAVINIA JOHNSON STEELE.
                                            Shirland, Ill.
Children, Ninth Generation :
73 1 Orange, b. Dec. 25, 1832; d. Nov, 1864, in the Hospital at
    Chattanooga, Tenn.
74 2 Fayette G., b. Aug. 21, 1834; m. Jan. 1, 1868, Mary A. Chandler, of Clinton, Wis.; one child, Elma, b. Feb. 1, 1870.
75 3 Henry M., b. Sept. 30, 1835; is a lawyer in Winnemucca,
    Nevada.
76 4 Wolcott, b. June, 1837; m. Kate Vallu, of Beloit, Wis., is a
    M.D. in Nevada, one child, Fanny L., b. 1864.
78 5 Martha L., b. April 2, 1841.
79 6 Almon C., b. August 18, 1844; m. Julia Aldrich, July 3,
    1839, a dau., b. Jan. 1871.
81 7 Alma L., b. Jan. 9, 1845; d. Sept. 18, 1865.

63 WILLIAM and CAROLINE WOODRUFF STEELE. *Michigan.*

Children, Ninth Generation:

82 1 Alden P., b. May 16, 1835, Springfield, Ohio.
83 2 George E., b. Oct., 1842 ; m. Lois Judson, of Benzonia, Mich. ;
  is a surveyor and civil engineer, Homestead, Mich.
      Ch. 10*th Gen. :* 1 Louis M., b. March 6, 1867 ; d. Aug.,
      1869. 2 Ray, b. Jan., 1869.

64 FRANCIS and ROSETTA J. A. STEELE.   *Wayne, Ohio.*

Children, Ninth Generation:

86 1 Joseph L., b. June 25, 1837 ; m. in the fall of 1864, Jennie
  White of Davenport, Iowa, lives in Grinnell, Powshick
  Co., Iowa.
      Ch. 10*th Gen. :* 1 Mabel Clare, b. Jan., 1867.
88 2 Sarah Ann, b. March 31, 1840.
89 3 Francis Calvin, b. Aug. 15, 1841 ; m. Myra Fitts, of Gustavus,
  Ohio.
90 4 Claudius B., b. 1844 ; d. in hospital, near Washington, May,
  1863.

65 ALMON and ANN ADAMS STEELE.   *Cottonville, Ia.*

Children, Ninth Generation :

91 1 Harlan P., b. Feb. 18, 1840 ; d. in hospital at Mound City,
  Ill., Jan. 28, 1869.
92 2 Laura A., b. April 3, 1844 ; m. Dec. 2, 1860, Elias Hurd, Cot-
  tonville, Iowa.
93 3 Caroline J., b. March 15, 1846 ; m. July 19, 1866, Samuel Jennings, Buchanan Co., Iowa.
94 4 Zadoc Webster, b. July 25, 1848.
95 5 Hattie C., b. June 21, 1850.
96 6 Quincy A., b. May 9, 1853 ; d. same year.

66 HARRIET STEELE and ELDAD W. MERRELL.
West Andover, Ohio.

Children, Ninth Generation :

97 1 Chester W., b. July 22, 1848.
98 2 Millard F., b. March 16, 1850.
98 3 Francis E., b. Nov. 4, 1851 ; d. Dec. 20, 1862.
100 4 Grove S., b. Jan. 22, 1857.

89 FRANCIS CALVIN and MYRA FITTS STEELE.
Gustavus, Ohio.

Children, Ninth Generation :

101 1 Edith, b. Aug. 15, 1868.

92 LAURA A. STEELE and ELIAS HURD.

Children, Ninth Generation:

102 1 Elijah H., b. Oct. 1, 1863.
103 2 Ann A., b. Sept. 20, 1864.
104 3 Ella, b. Aug. 26, 1868.

93 CAROLINE J. STEELE and SAMUEL JENNINGS.

Children, Ninth Generation:

105 1 Almon L., b. May 20, 1868.
106 2 Charlotte A., b. Oct. 13, 1870.

9 ELIJAH LYMAN[7], *David[6], David[5], John[4], Richard[3], Richard[2], Richard[1]*, was a physician of great excellence and moral worth, who d. in Warren, Litchfield Co., Conn., m. Lorinda Smith.

Children, Eighth Generation:

107 1 Elijah Smith, b. April, 26, 1812; is a physician in Sherburne, Chenango Co., N. Y.; m. Mary White, Jan. 27, 1836.
    2 Lorinda, b. ....still living unmarried.
108   *Ch. 9th Gen :* Elijah Smith and Mary W. Lyman.
109 1 Frances Romeyn, b. Sept. 1, 1837; graduated at the University Med. Coll., N. Y., March 4, 1861; served as assistant and house physician in Bellevue Hospital 2 years, and died in the service of his country at the Harewood Hospital, Washington, D. C. Nov. 14, 1862; a young man of rare talents and great promise.
112 2 William Asa, b. May 23, 1842, a farmer in Sherburne; m. Jan. 1, 1865, Amelia Upham.
    Ch. 10th Gen.: 1 Adeline, b. Oct. 26, 1868. 2 Frank, b. Feb. 6, 1870.
113 3 Henry Clay, b. Sept. 8, 1847; studying medicine for that profession.
114 4 Fayette, b. Oct. 16, 1849; d. Dec. 29, 1851.

10 DAVID LYMAN[7], second son of *David[6]*, 1776 – 1850; m., April 9, 1801, Rhoda P. Belden, b. May 16, 1781 — farmer. *New Hartford.*

Children, Eighth Generation:

115 1 David B., b. at N. H., July 28, 1803; missionary in Hilo, Sandwich Islands.
116 2 George, b. April 18, 1806; m. 1831, Sarah Hart; m. 1837, Emily Hanscom; Cleveland, Ohio.
117 3 Elijah, b. Feb. 6, 1808; Tallmadge, Ohio.
118 4 Edward, b. Aug. 5, 1810; Tallmadge, Ohio.
119 5 Luther F., b. Oct. 1, 1814; Cleveland, Ohio.
120 6 Rhoda P., b. Nov. 22, 1816; m. Luther Miller; d. at Newton Falls, Ohio, Sept. 17, 1864.

126 7 James, b. Feb. 14, 1718; d. May 17, 1818.
127 8 Benjamin, b. July 8, 1819; m., Jan. 15, 1846, Emily
     Turner; Lost Nation, Jackson, Iowa.
         Ch. 9th Gen.: 1 Charles W., b. Oct. 20, 1846. 2 Fi-
     delia, b. June 15, 1850.
129 9 Gaylord P., b. Sept. 6, 1821; Middlebury, Cuyahoga Co.,
     Ohio.
130 10 Julia A., b. May 22, 1822; m. —— Clark; d. Aug 29,
     1826; one child, Franklin A.

115 DAVID BELDEN LYMAN³, *David⁷, David⁶, David⁵, Richard⁴, Richard³, Richard², Richard¹,* b. in New Hartford, Ct.,
July 28, 1803, oldest son of *David⁷,* graduated at Williams
College in 1828, studied theology at Andover Seminary;
m. Nov. 3, 1831, Miss Sarah Joyner, of Royalton, Vt,, and
sailed, shortly after, as a missionary of the American Board
of Commissioners for Foreign Missions to the Sandwich
Islands, where he is still living as principal of the Missionary
High School for the natives at Hilo, Hawaii.

Children, Ninth Generation:
131 1 David Brainerd, b. 1833, d. 1836.
132 2 Henry Munson, b. Nov. 26, 1835.
133 3 Frederick Schwartz, b. July 29, 1837.
134 4 David Brainerd, b. March 27, 1840.
135 5 Rufus Anderson, b. June 23, 1842.
136 6 Ellen Elizabeth, b. Sept. 27, 1845; d. at Chicago, Ill. Jan.
     13, 1868.
138 7 Francis Ogden, b. Aug. 6, 1847.
139 8 Emma Washburn, b. Sept. 16, 1849; residing with her
     brothers in Chicago.

132 HENRY MUNSON LYMAN⁹, b. Nov. 26, 1835, at Hilo,
Hawaii Sandwich Islands; removed to the U. S., A.D.
1854.   Graduated valedictorian, 1858, at Williams College,
Mass.   Graduated valedictorian, 1861, from the College of
Physicians and Surgeons, N. Y.   House Surgeon to Belle-
vue Hospital, N. Y., March, 1861, till April, 1862; acting
Assistant Surgeon, U. S. A., April, 1862, till Feb., 1863; m.
May 27, 1863, Sarah K. Clark, dau. of Rev. E. W. Clark,
one of the earliest missionaries to the Sandwich Islands.
Settled in Chicago, Ill., Nov., 1863, and has there practiced
medicine ever since.   Has one dau. Mary Isabella, b. Feb.
6, 1866.

133 FREDERICK SCHWARTZ LYMAN⁹, b. July, 1837, at Hilo,
Hawaii; m. Feb. 19, 1861, Isabella Chamberlain dau.
of Levi Chamberlain, one of the earliest missionaries to

the Sandwich Islands, now circuit judge of Hawaii. Resides on his plantation in Kau, Hawaii.

Children, Tenth Generation:

141 1 Ellen Goodale, b. Dec. 1, 1862.
142·2 Frederick Snowden, } b. 1863.
143 3 Francis Anderson, }
144 4 Levi Chamberlain, b. at Hilo, Dec. 15, 1866.

134 DAVID BRAINERD LYMAN⁹, b. March 27, 1840, at Hilo, removed to the U. S., June, 1860; graduated at Yale, 1864; graduated at the Harvard Law School, 1866; is now practicing law. *Chicago, Ill.*

135 RUFUS ANDERSON LYMAN⁹, b. June 23, 1842; m. Rebecca Brickwood of Honolulu, Sandwich Islands. Is now the lieutenant governor of the Island of Hawaii.

Children, Tenth Generation:

145 1 Lilian L. H., b. at Hilo, 1866.
146 2 Rufus Anderson, Jr., b. at Hilo, Jan. 14, 1868.

137 FRANCIS OGDEN LYMAN, b. Aug. 6, 1847; removed to the U. S., A.D. 1866; entered Harvard College, A.D. 1867, where he is now pursuing his studies; was one of the famous boat club in the race at Oxford, 1869.

116 GEORGE LYMAN⁸, b. April 17, 1806; m. Sarah Hart, 1831, m. Emily Hanscom, 1867. *Cleveland, Ohio.*

117 ELIJAH LYMAN⁸, b. Feb. 6, 1808; m. Lauretta Freeman, 1837. *Tallmadge, O.*

Children, Ninth Generation:

149 1 Sarah M., b. Oct., 1837; m. O. S. Treat, Oct., 1861; Tallmadge, O.
150 2 George F., b. March, 1841; m. Lizzie F. Lane, Feb., 1870.
151 3 Charles A., b. Oct., 1843; m. Millie Webb, Dec., 1871; Cleveland, O.; m. 2d, Hannah Bingham; m. 3d, Mrs. Musgrove, 1864.
152 4 Alfred E., b. June, 1858; Tallmadge.

118 EDWARD LYMAN, b. Aug. 5, 1810; m. Emily A. Merwin. *Tallmadge, O.*

Children, Ninth Generation:

153 1 Harriet J. 155 3 Josephine.
154 2 Mary E.

121 RHODA P. LYMAN, b. Nov. 22, 1816; m. Luther Miller; d. at Newton Falls, Sept. 16, 1864. *Newton Falls.*

14

Children, Eighth Generation :

156 1 Martha.
157 2 James A.
158 3 Justin E.

159 4 Margaret.
160 5 Emma.

122 BENJAMIN LYMAN, b. July 8, 1819; m. Emily
Turner, 1846.   *Iowa.*

Children, Ninth Generation :

161 1 Charles, b. 1847.

162 2 Fidelia, b. 1849.

123 GAYLORD LYMAN, b. Sept. 6, 1821; m. Betsey Oviatt,
1845.   *Middlebury, O.*

Children, Ninth Generation :

163 1 Porter G., b. 1845.
164 2 Joseph.
165 3 Julia.

166 4 Luther.
167 5 Alice.

124 JULIA A. LYMAN, b. May 4, 1824; m. Alex. Clark,
1845; d. Aug. 28, 1846, leaving one child.

Newton Falls, O.

11 JOHN LYMAN[7], 3d son of *David*[6], b. Oct. 5, 1778; m.
Salome Maltby—farmer.   *New Hartford, Conn.*

Children, Eighth Generation :

169 1 Rev. John Bennett.
170 2 William Maltby.
171 3 Clarinda Mary.
172 4 Salome.
173 5 Marcella.
174 6 Emily.   Marriages and children unknown.

175 7 Laura F.
176 8 David Newton.
177 9 Solomon
178 10 Justin.
179 11 Rufus.

No dates nor further record. Letters have been frequently
written to different parties but no answer has been received.

12 REV. ORANGE LYMAN[7], son of *David*[6], *David*[5], *Richard*[4],
Richard[3], *Richard*[2], *Richard*[1], was a Presbyterian minister,
educated at Williams College, receiving his diploma from
President E. Fitch; he studied theology with Rev. Dr. Porter, of Catskill, N. Y., where he made many warm friends,
among whom was Rev. Samuel J. Mills.   Mr. Lyman
was married Sept. 13, 1814, to a sister of a classmate and
dear friend, Chester Dewey, late of Rochester, N. Y.,
and for many years professor in Williams College, and
in the Rochester University.   His wife's name was Maria
Dewey, dau. of Stephen Dewey of Sheffield, Berkshire
Co., Mass., who reared a large family of children.   She
is still living Jan., 1870.   Mr. Lyman was a man of
great energy of character, sterling worth and eminent

piety. He enjoyed the acquaintance, friendship and confidence of a very large number of the best men of his time; prompted by a desire to do the greatest amount of good, and having a fondness for rural life, he chose the life of a pioneer in the work of the ministry, and from the time when the west meant western New York state, afterwards in north-eastern Ohio, and in the evening of his life in northern Illinois, he was always one of the foremost in the good cause. His wife, one of Berkshire's most gifted daughters, always held up his hands; and his home, though sometimes only a log house, was always graced by her presence and presented the charms of a refined New England home. His latch string was always out, and hundreds of weary brother ministers have found their toilsome life cheered and made bright by only a brief sojourn under his hospitable roof. He was gifted with a very rare fund of anecdotes, always appropriate, and the writer has often, when a boy, sat for hours and listened, as he and some dear old classmate or other cherished friends sat around that cheerful fire, and told over the days of long ago. He died at the good old age of 71, beloved and respected by all who knew him.

Children, Eighth Generation.

188 1 Stephen Dewey, b. in Sharon, Conn., June 23, 1815; is a lawyer, living at Maquoketa, Iowa.

189 2 Cornelia, b. in Vernon, N. Y., July 20, 1818; d. at Vernon, July 26, 1823, aged 5 years and 6 days.

190 3 Henry Martyn, b. at Vernon, N. Y., Oct. 27, 1821; is a farmer at Downer's Grove, Du Page Co., Illinois.

191 4 Thomas, b. in Vernon, N. Y., March 19, 1824, is a real estate agent in Chicago, living at Downer's Grove, Ill.

192 5 Eurotas, b. in Painesville, Ohio, Jan. 12, 1827; d. at Thompson, Ohio, March 1, 1837.

193 6 Mary Elizabeth, b. in Richmond, N. Y., Aug. 6, 1829; d. in Richmond, N. Y., March 27, 1831.

194 7 Edward, b. in Thompson, Ohio, July 3, 1833; d. in Thompson, Ohio, March 4, 1837.

188 STEPHEN DEWEY LYMAN[8], b. Sharon, Conn., June 23, 1815; m. Dec. 29, 1836, Julia House, b. in Chesterfield, Mass., Dec. 24, 1817; d. at Rockton, Ill., Nov. 28, 1854, aged 37, second wife Hannah Matilda Barrows, b. at Middlebury, Vt., Dec. 5, 1824; m. Dec. 25, 1859—lawyer.

Maquoketa, Jackson Co., Ill.

Children, Ninth Generation :

195 1 John H., b. Thompson, Ohio, Jan. 19, 1838 ; m. March 21, 1861, Sarah A. Goodrich, farmer. Downer's Grove, Ill.
Ch. 10*th Gen.* : 1 Charles Dewey, b. Aug. 7, 1862 ; d. July 13, 1866. 2 Julia Maria, b. Jan. 14, 1864.

198 2 Mary Elizabeth, b. in Thompson, Ohio, April 11, 1840·

199 3 Charles Henry, b. in Downer's Grove, Ill., March 6, 1842. Enlisted in the 9th Iowa Infantry, Sept., 1861, served during the war, adjutant of the regiment, health failed, d. Feb. 21, 1868, a loss to the family, the church and country, leaving a precious memorial.

200 4 Helen Cornelia, b. in Shirland, Ill., Nov. 3, 1847.

201 5 Frank Dewey, b. in Rockton, Ill., Nov. 9, 1852.

190 Henry Martyn Lyman[8], son of Rev. Orange and Maria Dewey, m. Miss Lovantia Pease, Sept. 18, 1850, in Painsville, Ohio, by Rev. Mr. Gillet ; Lovantia Pease was b. in Madison, Ohio, Dec. 23, 1821—farmer.
Downer's Grove, Ill.

Children, Ninth Generation :

202 1 Sarah Estella, b. in Downer's Grove, Du Page Co., Ill., March 29, 1852.

203 2 Walter Campbell, b. Feb. 8, 1854—farmer.

191 Thomas Lyman[8], son of *Orange*, m. Dec. 3, 1847, Pierce Ann Clark, b. in Eden, Chautauqua Co., N. Y., Oct. 6, 1822— real estate agent. *Chicago, Ill.*

Children, Ninth Generation :

204 1 Elizabeth Owen, b. at Downer's Grove, Du Page Co., Illinois, Feb. 19, 1849.

205 2 Edward Thomas, b. at Rockton, Winnebago Co., Illinois, Sept. 16, 1850 ; he was drowned in the Maquoketa river, Iowa, July 29, 1861, aged 10 years 10 months 13 days.

206 3 Mary Clark, b. May 9, 1853 ; d. Dec. 10, 1857, aged 4 years 7 months and 1 day.

207 4 Lucia Berry, b. Oct. 28, 1855 ; d. May 9, 1861, aged 5 years, 6 months and 13 days.

208 5 Lincoln Dewey, b. Jan. 7, 1860 ; d. Feb. 14, 1860, aged 5 weeks 3 days.

209 6 Birdie, b. Sept. 22, 1862 ; d. Nov. 19, 1862, aged 8 weeks 3 days.

13 Daniel Lyman[7], 5th son of *David*[6], 1784–1846 ; b. April 18, 1784 ; m. March 12, 1812, Jerusha Merrill ; d. Aug. 20, 1846. *New Hartford, Ct.*

Children, Eighth Generation :

210 1 Frederic, b. March 19, 1813 ; m. Sept. 5, 1848, in New Hartford.

211 2 Henry M., b. Sept. 23, 1814, in Hartford ; m. 1839, Naomi
Carpenter, of Alexandria, Licking Co., Ohio, where he
d. Jan. 3, 1846, St. Albans, Ohio.
> *Ch. 9th Gen.:* 1 Frederic, house carpenter, has two
daughters. 2 Louis, blacksmith, carriage ironing, etc.
3 Henry, blacksmith,, carriage ironing, etc., has one
dau. 4 George M., M.D., grad. 1864, from Medical
Coll., Cincinnati, m. Dec. 27, 1866, Biannia R. Moore,
one dau. b. July 31, 1868, Croton, Licking Co., Ohio.

222 3 Jerusha, b. Nov. 1, 1816 ; d. May 28, 1819.

223 4 Julia, b. Nov. 7, 1818 ; d. Dec. 20. 1829.

224 5 Judson G., b. New Hartford, Ct., Nov. 21, 1820 ; grad. Williams Coll., 1847, Baptist minister in Huntington, Ct., by
failure of health, farmer ; m. June, 1848, Abby B. Clark ;
no children ; adopted sons Walter J., and George E.

228 6 James D., b. Oct. 23, 1823, Torringford, Ct. ; m. Rhoda
Marsh, Nov., 1853 ; m. 2d wife, Mary E. Stone, 1859.

229 7 Jane M., b. Feb. 15, 1826 ; m. June, 1847, Rev. William
W. Baldwin, Wilmington, Ct.
> *Ch. 10th Gen.:* 1 Mary. 2 Arthur L. 3 Ella J.
4 Henry C. d. 5 Julia M. 6 Howard. 7 Ellen F.
8 Martha.

210 FREDERIC LYMAN[8], son of *Daniel[7]*, m. Sept. 5, 1848,
Amanda E. Welsh. New Hartford, Ct.

Children, Ninth Generation :

212 1 Sarah Jane, b. July 5, 1849 ; m. March 5, 1868, Burton N.
Clark, N. Hartford. 2 children.

213 2 Daniel F., b. Aug. 25, 1851 ; d. June 13, 1852.

214 3 Judson M., b. April 25, 1853 ; d. May 7, 1864

215 4 Charlotte A., b. April 23, 1855 ; d. May 7, 1864

216 5 Henrietta, b. April 3, 1857 ; d. May 13, 1864.

217 6 Charles F., b. May 14, 1859 ; d. May 9, 1864. Two of these
children d. the same day and four in one week, all of
scarlet fever.

14 NORMAN LYMAN[7], 6th son of *David[6]*, 1787–1850, who
was b. in Torringford, Litchfield Co., Ct., possessed remarkable and sterling traits of character, deserving a record in
this place.

Dr. Lyman was b. in the parish of Torringford, in Litchfield county, on 6th of September, 1787, and d. in the 64th
year of his age. He early distinguished himself at school by
his great proficiency, being for one year at school, after
which, by his unassisted application, he prepared himself for
entering the junior class at college. After obtaining his
profession, with the cares of a family, and the pressure of
a large professional business, he found time to prosecute

his classical and mathematical studies, until he had attained the full college course, and made himself one of the most perfect scholars of his time.   At the age of 24 years, Dr. Lyman was licensed to practice medicine, by a board of censors; and in 1831, received the honorary degree of doctor of medicine, from Yale College, at the recommendation of the president and fellows of the Connecticut Medical Society.

Dr. Lyman was endowed with faculties of mind which fitted him for eminence in his profession.   He possessed great powers of memory.   When he commenced the study of the Latin and Greek languages, he committed to memory the whole grammar and small *dictionaries* of these languages; and, what would have been to other men a task too irksome to be borne, was to him an easy attainment; his memory was as retentive as it was strong; for we are told, that when a boy, in learning and reading the Bible and Psalm Book, they were so fully committed, that he could recite most of the Testament and every psalm and hymn in the Hymn Book, by giving him the number or first line.   And in reading the Greek Testament, with a Latin translation he *so read it*, that he could recite the whole Testament in the Latin, Greek, and English languages, to the time of his death, and was so familiar with the Greek and Latin classics, that he could recite whole pages, often putting to the blush those who had received a full collegiate education, by his accuracy in classical literature.   His strong and retentive memory, made him the repository of all the great facts and discoveries, both in the natural and medical world, for the last forty years.   It enabled him to gather up all the different systems and theories of medical writers, and the most successful treatment of diseases, from the earliest annals of medicine, to the present time.   He remembered every case of any importance, which he had ever seen, and most of which he had heard.   He practised successfully, for about seventeen years, in Glastenbury, Connecticut, and for the last twenty-two years, in the town of Warren; making thirty-nine years in which he had constantly been engaged in the ordinary duties of his profession. He had thus accumulated a vast fund of medical knowledge, and tested the correctness of different systems of the treatment of diseases, by his own large experience. His mind was, therefore, one great store-house of knowledge, in which nothing was ever *lost*, but so arranged that he could at all times, make those treasures available, by calling them to his aid, on any emergency.   His apprehension had the rapidity of electricity. He saw at a glance the whole case before him in all its bearings; and his far-seeing eye detected at the outset, the point of danger, and he guarded it with the most consummate skill and fidelity, until the danger was past. Hence, in the result of a case, he was never taken by surprise.

Dr. Lyman m. Sept. 12, 1812, Eunice Smith of Litchfield. *Warren, Litchfield Co., Ct.*

Children, Eighth Generation:

238 1 Sidney, M.D., record refused.
239 2 George S., b. in Glastenbury, Aug. 31, 1818; m. Sept. 6, 1841, Mary J. Sackett — farmer, Warren.
  Ch. 9th Gen.: 1 Norman S., b. Oct. 5, 1842; m. Abbie Sheve of Warren. 2 Myron H., b. Jan. 20, 1845; m. J. Watson of Waverly, Ill. 3 Eunice E., b. Jan. 16, 1847; m. Orlando Kingman of Bridgeport, Conn. 4 Edward P., b. Feb. 1, 1856.
244 3 Edward P., M.D., b. in Glastenbury, April 1, 1821; m. Sarah Lemman of Washington, New Preston Soc., Litchfield Co., his own place of residence, actively engaged still, as he has been during the last 28 years, in the practice of medicine and surgery.
  Ch. 9th Gen.: Charles P., b. May 9, 1858.
245 4 Mary, b. 1823; d. 1841.
246 5 Jonathan H., b. 1826; d. Feb. 1, 1852.
247 6 Eunice, b. 1828; d. 1841. Two d. in infancy unrecorded.

They of this branch of the present stock like many others, have been distinguished through successive generations for their adherence to the faith of their fathers, adorning the profession of religion by a consistent, religious life.

VI. DESCENDANTS OF RICHARD[3] THROUGH ISAAC[4] AND CALEB[5].

JOHN LYMAN[4], 3d son of *Richard*[3], was b. July 6, 1680, in Northampton, Mass., removed with his father to Lebanon, Conn., m. July 6, 1710, Hannah Dibble, and d. without issue. *Lebanon Centre.*

ISAAC LYMAN[4], 4th son of *Richard*[3], b. at Northampton, Feb. 16, 1681. From the record of Suffield, Conn., he appears at one time to have lived there; m. 1st wife, Abigail Pomeroy, no date; d. June 3, 1709; 2d, Rebecca Ordway; •3d, Thankful Smith, d. April 26, 1728; 4th, Sarah French Aug. 6, 1745. In Dr. Allen's record, Isaac Lyman and Thankful W. Sachell, m. March 14, 1823. In the records in Northampton Isaac Lyman and Thankful Winchell m. March 4, 172¾. In Dr. G. H. Lyman's record he is said to have left issue, Benjamin, William, Caleb, and Isaac, who m. Winchell. In the Suffield records Caleb son of Isaac of Lebanon which Thankful his wife bare to him April 17, 1728. Thankful Lyman herself d. April 26, 1728—what the real facts may be the reader must decide. *Lebanon, Conn.*

Children, Fifth Generation.

1 1 Isaac, b. 1707; d. 1708.
2 2 Abigail, b. Dec. 25, 1709.
3 3 Caleb, son of Thankful, 3d wife of Isaac, b. in Suffield, Conn., April 16, 1728.
4 4 William, b. Nov. 10, 1730; m. Mary Wright, no further record.
5 5 Benjamin, b. Jan. 30, 1734; d. Sept. 15, 1799, in Bolton. Washington Co., N. Y.
6 6 Isaac, whether father or son, m. Thankful Winchell, and whether Isaac had a second son Isaac are still the subjects of conjecture.

3 CALEB LYMAN[5], 1728-1774, son of Thankful Smith, 3d wife of Isaac, m. Mary Betts, Jan. 2, 1756, by Rev. Solomon Williams, D.D. She d. about 1820 in Vt., aged 93 years.

Children, Sixth Generation:

7 1 David, b. May 20, 1761-1849.
8 2 William, b. March 9, 1764; d. about 1865 in Lebanon, Ct.
9 3 James, b. Oct. 7, 1768, removed to Norwich, Vt., then to Kingsbury, N. Y., one son Portus, no further record.
10 4 Roger, b. March 7, 1773, removed to Norwich, Vt. and d. there 1846; a very tall, stalwart man of imposing appearance and a splendid ⁸inger. His marriage is not recorded, but he d. leaving a family of ten children.

Children, Seventh Generation:

11 1 Laura, d. in Norwich, Vt.
12 2 Louis, without issue.
13 3 Caleb, d. in state of N. Y. had five children, one son, and 4 daughters, names unknown.
14 4 Pamelia, m. Abram Wood of Barre, Vt., removed to Mansfield, where both d. leaving.
    Ch. 8th Gen: 1 Abigail, who m. Nathaniel Dodge, a dau. Abigail. 2 Harvey, he was in the army of 1812, but never returned, supposed to be dead. 3 Theodore, one child. 4 Mary Ann.
20 5 Horace, left Vermont about 1830; when last heard from was living in Maine ten miles north of Ellsworth, had family one or more sons.
22 6 Mary Ann, m. John Carpenter, one son Asa, Stratford, Vt.
23 7 William, removed to Pike Co., Ill., no further record.

24 8 James, lived in Allegheny City, Pa., d. leaving wife and
      three children.
          Ch. 8th Gen.: 1 Eliza, m. Kimball. 2 Olive, m.
      Germain. 3 Lois, husband unknown ; one Lyman is still
      living there doubtless some unrecorded member of his
      family.
28 9 Ira, M.D., Chester Cross Roads, Geauga Co., Ohio.
          Ch. 8th Gen.: 1 Harriet E. 2. Florence. 3. David G.
      4 William G. Alton.
34 10 Chester, m. and d. in Norwich.
          Ch. 8th Gen.: 1 Louisa. 2 Adeline. 3 Louis. 4 Frank.

DAVID LYMAN[6], *Caleb*[5], *Isaac*[4], *Richard*[3], 1761 – 1849, b.
in Lebanon, Conn. ; m. 1785, Submit Gould. At the age
of sixteen he enlisted in the service of his country in the
Revolutionary army, in which he continued six months,
and then learned the trade of carpenter and wheelwright.
In 1789, he removed with his wife and a young child from
Lebanon to Norwich, Vt., with an ox team. In their new settlement they endured the hardships incident to pioneer life,
living in a log cabin for several years, and then removing
into their framed house, in December, before it had been
enclosed with boards without, or duly finished within to
protect them from the inclemency of the winter. Here, in
frugal piety, they lived to a good old age, and died in the
hope of heaven through grace divine, leaving all their
children in the enjoyment of the same Christian hope.
                                                        Norwich, Vt.

          Children, Seventh Generation :
39 1 David, b. in Lebanon, Oct. 19, 1786.
40 2 Orange, b. in Norwich, April 5, 1793.
41 3 Harry, } Twins, b. April 4, 1797.
42 4 Fanny, } Fanny, m. 1817, James Avery, b. 1801 ; d. Nov. 7,
      1850 ; Duxbridge.
          Ch. 8th Gen.: 1 Lydia, b. Aug. 21, 1820 ; m. John
      Hobart ; eight children. 2 Sally, b. Sept. 23, 1822 ;
      m. Simeon Cook, of Thetford, Vt.; four children ; d.
      Aug. 8, 1862. 3 Fannie E., b. March 12, 1824 ; m.
      Jerome B. Jackman, of Thetford, Vt. 4 Park, b.
      March 24, 1826 ; m. Susah E. Adams ; two children.
      5 Harriet, b. Oct. 12, 1828 ; m. James W. Crosby,
      Chicago, Ill. 6 James, b. Feb. 2, 1830 ; m. Ellen Ather-
      ton, Marshfield, Vt.; one child. 7 Lyman, b. 1832.
      8 Lucy, b. July 26, 1840. 9 A nameless infant, no
      date.
52 5 Eunice, b. Jan. 11, 1801 ; m. 1819, Aaron Drake, of Norwich ;
      d. July 9, 1855, at Sugar Grove, Kane Co , Ill., where the
      family now reside.
                        15

53 6 Polly, b. Sept. 28, 1804 ; m. July 8, 1823, Jonathan Smith
        Chelsea, Vt. He d. June 17, 1857.
        Ch. 8th Gen.: 1 George, b. May 7, 1824. 2 Erastus,
        b. Jan. 26, 1827. 3 Fanny P., b. Feb. 4, 1830. 4 Har-
        vey, b. Sept. 18, 1832. 5 Mary, May 28, 1839. The
        sons are both farmers. Harvey, m. Aug. 21, 1853, Judith
        Hill.   Erastus, m. April 7, 1853, Koene Spiller; one
        child, Carrie Smith, b. Nov. 1, 1858.
60 7 Rhoda, b Aug. 22, 1807 ; m. Oct. 15, 1822, Joseph Drake.
        Ch. 8th Gen.: 1 Leonard. 2 Marshall. 3 Lucretia, m.
        April 1, 1831.   4 Rufus Beckwith. [*Ch. 9th Gen.:*
        (1) Charles.   (2) Oscar.   (3) Avery.   (4) Augusta.
        (5) Rhoda.]

    7 DAVID LYMAN[7], m. Martha Goodrich, who d. Feb.,
1842. He d. Oct., 1861 — carpenter and bridge builder.
                                                    Norwich, Vt.
        Children, Eighth Generation :
67 1 Eliza.   71 5 Benjamin.
68 2 Charles.   72 6 Martha.
69 3 Sophronia.   73 7 Daniel.
70 4 Angeline.

    40 ORANGE LYMAN[7], 2d son of *David[6]*, of Norwich, Vt.,
b. 1793 ; m. Mary Smith, d. at Wells River, in the family
of Mrs. Mary Holton, his dau.   *Norwich, Vt.*
        Children, Eighth Generation :
74 1 Emily, b. Jan. 15, 1819 ; m. at Orange, Vt., Oct. 20, 1840,
        Dr. Ira R. Rood, Waterloo, Wis.
        Ch. 9th Gen.: 1 Emily Jane, b. Jan. 3, 1848. 2
        Charles Austin, b. April 14, 1852. 3 Carrie B., b. Sept.
        30, 1856; d. Oct. 25, 1857. 4 Florence Helen, b. May
        11, 1858; d. Jan. 28, 1862.
79 2 Lucius, b. Aug. 5, 1821 ; m. Mary Burgess, Spring Lake,
        Mich.
80 3 Caroline, d. 1853, leaving son and dau.
81 4 Jasper, b Oct. 5, 1824, m. March 12, 1849, Nancy Emery—
        farmer ; North Tunbridge, Vt.
        Ch. 9th Gen.: 1 Florence, b. Nov. 13, 1851 ; d. Oct.
        14, 1868. 2 Frances, b. Oct. 13, 1853. 3 Lucy E., b.
        Aug. 19, 1857. 4 Edward B., b. Feb. 7, 1861.
86 5 David S., b. Jan. 18, 1827 ; m. March 13, 1848, Roxana
        M. Cloud, Norwich, Vt., farmer.
        Ch. 9th Gen.: 1 Mary Lucinda, b. March 30, 1859.
88 6 Mary, no date, m. Harry Holton, Wells River, Vt.
89 7 Albert, now in Teuckee, California, engineer on the C. P.
        rail road.
90 8 A daughter, d. in infancy.

91 9 James or Franklin, now in the southern states, a jeweler. At the outbreak of the rebellion he resided at Little Rock, Ark., from that date nothing is known of him.

79 Lucius Lyman[8], son of Orange[7], of Norwich, Vt., David[6], Caleb[5], Isaac[4], Richard[3], Richard[2], Richard[1], b. Aug. 5, 1821, m. in Chelsey, Vt., April 13, 1843, Mary Burgess of Westmoreland, N. Y. Millwright.

Spring Lake, Ottawa Co., Mich.

Children, Ninth Generation:
92 1 Larietta Maria, b. April 6, 1845.
93 2 Mulfort Eustice, b. Oct. 29, 1846.
94 3 Mary Lorilla, b. April 30, 1849.
95 4 Charles Albert, b. Oct. 1, 1852.
96 5 Caroline Elizabeth, b. Sept. 19, 1854.
97 6 William Henry, b. Nov. 28, 1856.
98 7 Eliza Ann, b. April 2, 1858.
99 8 Harriet Amelia, b. April 12, 1860.
100 9 Clarence D., b. Sept. 1, 1865.
101 10 Alonzo D., b. Sept. 1, 1865.

41 Henry Lyman[7], 3d son of David[6], m. April, 1821, Nancy Wheeler, who d. in Sept. following; m. 2d wife April, 1822, Betsey King—farmer. *Norwich, Vt.*

Children, Eighth Generation:
102 1 George H., b. Feb. 10, 1823.
103 2 Orril H., b. Sept. 4, 1824; m. Jan., 1859, George Willis, d. 1855.
        Ch. 9th Gen.: 1 Emma, b. Oct., 1852. 2 Carrie L., b. 1856.
106 3 Eliza A., b. Aug. 20, 1826; m. May 18, 1846, and d. Aug. 20, 1846.
107 4 Augustus C., b. July 22, 1828.
108 5 Emirath V., b. June 23, 1830.
109 6 Elizabeth Sophia, b. Nov. 18, 1831; m. 1853, J. N. Howard, resides Rutland.
        Ch. 9th Gen.: 1 Harry, b. Nov. 1861.

102 George Lyman[7], farmer, in Thetford, Vt., m. 1847, Emma Ramsdell.

Children, Ninth Generation:
110 1 Eliza, b. June, 1848.
111 2 Emmogene, b. Sept., 1850.
112 3 Eunice, b. Nov., 1853.
113 4 Betsey K., b. Jan., 1859; d. May, 1861.
114 5 Betsey K., b. Aug., 1862.

107 AUGUSTUS C. LYMAN[8], farmer, m. March, 1852, Roxana
Gove.   *Norwich, Vt.*
Children, Ninth Generation:
115 1 An infant, b. Feb., 1855, ḍ. in 3 days.
116 2 Ella F., b. May 25, 1856.
117 3 John C., b. Dec. 7, 1863.
118 4 Harry A., b. Aug. 12, 1868.
119 5 Mary R., b. Nov. 21, 1869.

108 EMIRATH V. LYMAN[8], m. Dec. 1854, J. B. Cloud.
Children, Ninth Generation:
120 1 J. L., b. Feb., 1856.   122 3 Herbert, b. Jan., 1866.
121 2 Jennie, b. May., 1862.

68 CHARLES LYMAN[8], son of *David[7]*, b. Sept. 24, 1813,
m. May 5, 1837; carpenter, builder, mason.   *Chelsea, Vt.*
Children, Ninth Generation:
123 1 Frank, b. in South Royalton, b. Feb. 13, 1838; m. Jan. 1,
       1866.
           Ch. 10th Gen.: 1 Gertrude, b. Feb. 10, 1867. 2
           Estellah, b. 1869.
126 2 John, b. Oct. 28, 1839; m Oct. 20, 1865; carpenter, Chicago.
           Ch. 10th Gen.: 1 Jane, b. Jan. 8, 1867.

VII. DESCENDANTS OF RICHARD[3] THROUGH ISAAC[4]
AND BENJAMIN[5].

1 BENJAMIN LYMAN[5], *Isaac[4], Richard[3], Richard[2], Richard[1],*
1734–1799, 4th son of *Isaac[4]*, removed from Lebanon to Whitingham, Vt., having previously m. Jan. 11, 1759, a widow
Foster whose husband had been killed in the French war;
removed to Bolton, Washington Co., N. Y., and Sept. 15,
1799, was killed by falling from a tree.   *Bolton, N. Y.*
Children, Sixth Generation:
1 1 Isaac, known as Maj. Isaac, b. in Lebanon, Aug. 18, 1759.
2 2 Benjamin, b. March 9, 1761; m. 1782, Polly Temple.
3 3 Eleazar, b Jan. 13, 1767; d. Jan. 11, 1844.
4 4 Silas, date of b. not given, d. March 6, 1802.
5 5 Hannah. 6. Diadama, no date.

MAJ. ISAAC LYMAN[6], *Benjamin[5], Isaac[4], Richard[3], Richard[2],*
1759–1827, was an ensign in the Revolutionary war, was in
the battle of Bennington and other engagements. In the
battle of Lake George he was on a surprise party who
were betrayed by a traitor, and all but about fifteen men
were killed. He resided in Bolton east of Lake George,

removed to Hebron, N. Y., and engaged in the milling business; resided also in Kingston, N. Y., removed 1810 to Lymansville, Potter Co., Penn., where he d. March 10, 1827; m. (1). Edgecombe, March 21, 1782; d. Aug. 22, 1791, aged 28 years. (2). Laura Pierce, Feb. or Jan. 9, 1792. (3). Patience Spofford, March 3, 1809. In his new settlement his only supply of meat was wild game. Grain, flour, provisions, groceries, potatoes, he was obliged to bring on pack horses 50 miles through the forest, until he could raise supplies.

Children, Seventh Generation :

6   1 Sally, b. in Lebanon, March 28, 1783.
7   2 Lydia, b. at Whitingham, March 24, 1785 ; m. Thomas Bellows.
        Ch. 8th Gen. : (1) Dr. E. W. (2) Dilley, b. at Knoxville, Tioga Co., Pa.
8   3 Jonathan, b. in W., Dec. 13, 1784; d. in infancy.
9   4 Charlotte, b. Nov. 29, 1786 ; m. Ira Wells, McKean Co., d. in Madison, Ind.
10 5 Eunice, b. Dec. 17, 1787 ; m. Epaphras Nelson.
        Ch. 8th Gen. : 1 Almeron, Lymansville, Pa.
11 6 John, b. July 7, 1789, Roulette, Pa.

Children of Laura Pierce, 2d m.

12 7 Burrill, b. in Kingston, N.Y., Nov. 10, 1792; d. at R. 1858, aged 66 years.
13 8 Laura, b. Feb. 20, 1794 ; m. Silas McCarty, Dec. 10, 1810, Muncy, Lycoming Co., Pa.
14 9 Harry, M.D., b. in Bolton, N. Y., March 17, 1798.
15 10 Isaac, b. Jan. 15, 1802.
16 11 Otis, b. April 21, 1805, Springville, Mich.

Children of Patience Spofford, 3d m.

17 12 Charles, b. Jan., 13, 1810 ; resides in Michigan, m. Eveline Edgecombe, resided in Mendota, Ill., is a man of culture, visited Europe twice, devotes his time to literature and daily news, quite a politician.
18 13 Eulalia, b. June 6, 1811, the first female b. in Potter Co., m. Woodcock in Almond.
18 14 Milo, b. March 20, 1813; d. March 6, 1830, no family.
20 15 Edwin, b. Dec. 21, 1815 ; m. Maria Clark, Condersport, Potter Co.
21 16 Wm. Lewis, b. Jan. 29, 1818 ; county treasurer two years, m. Hannah Lewis, Sweden, Potter Co., Pa. In addition to these, two infant children d. nameless b. 1795, 1796.

Major Lyman d. March 1, 1827, and in the 67th year of his age at Coudersport, Potter Co., where he had lived through life. More than 70 of his relatives were present at his funeral.

11 John Lyman[7]. 2d son of Maj. *Isaac*[6], resides in Roulette, b. July 7, 1789; m. Sept. 10, 1812, Lucretia Palmer, d. Jan. 13, 1844; m. 2d wife Eley Jackson, Oct. 24, 1844, d. July 21, 1869. Mr. Lyman is known throughout Potter Co., to have been a man for his country, honest, upright, temperate, and industrious; loved and respected by all, never an office seeker. He has served 20 years as justice of the peace, 9 years as county commissioner, and 2 years as county treasurer, besides having held many other minor offices, which he discharged faithfully and with satisfaction to the community.   *Roulette, Pa.*

Children Eighth Generation:

22   1 Sally, b. Feb. 12, 1814; m. Seymour Norton, of Truxton, Cortland Co., N. Y.
23   2 Charlotte, b. June 18, 1815, m. E. H. Burt, McKean Co, Penn., d. March 20, 1842.
24   3 Daniel, b. Oct. 10, 1816, lived but a day.
25   4 Lydia, b. Dec. 15, 1817; m. Ira Fosmer, of Clara, Potter Co.
26   5 John, b. Nov. 19, 1819; m. April, 29, 1846, J. C. Jackson— a physician in Harrisville, Mich.
    Ch. 9th Gen.: 1 Don J., b. Jan. 19, 1848. 2 Victor J., b. Sept. 28, 1851. 3 Hurlburt W., b. Jan. 28, 1859.
30   6 Samuel, b. July 1, 1821; m. Phebe Dingman, d. March 9, 1844.
31   7 Lewis, b. Sept. 16, 1823; m. Eva Weimer, farmer.
32   8 Lucretia, b. June 22, 1826; m. L. Perry, Onondaga Co., N. Y.
33   9 Polly Ann, b. June 24, 1824; m. Abra Taggart.
    Ch. 8th Gen.: 1 Dora. 2 Alva, m. O. R. Webb, resides near Condersport, Penn.
34 10 Lucina, b June 3, 1831; d. Feb. 8, 1844.
35 11 Otis J. P., b. Nov. 6, 1836; m. Rosella Sherwood, March 23, 1863, two sons and one dau.
36 12 Almon N., b. June 13, 1840; d. in the army in Virginia, April 16, 1864.

From Mr. John Lyman we have the following account of frontier life in Potter Co., Penn. William Ayers moved into Potter county, the fall of 1808, six miles east of Coudersport, the county seat of Potter Co. In 1809, Major Isaac Lyman obtained the agency of the land of John Keating & Co., who owned 130,000 acres of land in the county. Mr. Lyman had 150 acres given him, and each of his sons, 50 acres. The first fifty families that settled on their land had fifty acres each by settling thereon, building a house and clearing five acres and residing thereon five years, then they were entitled to a deed, and as much more land as they wished to purchase at two dollars per acre. In Nov., 1809, Mr. Lyman came from Tioga Co., into Potter Co., 42 miles, and laid up a log house twenty by twenty-two feet, put on a roof of shingles four feet long and built up the gable end with the same, split slabs out of pine logs, dressed them with a narrow axe and laid the lower floors, cut out a place for a door and openings for two windows, for two six lighted windows, and laid three-fourths of the upper floor; this was the situation of his house when he moved into it the 16th of March, 1810, at night, with his family, consisting of ten in number. There was not a bushel of grain nor any meat, except wild game, elk, deer, panthers, bears, and wolves; we had to haul our provisions from fifty to seventy-five miles over a very bad road, and some brought on pack horses; where night overtook us there was our tavern, we made our own fires, cooked our own victuals, made our own bed on the ground of hemlock boughs. The landlord was very generous, charged us nothing, but yet the hardships and privations were many. He was married the 10th of Sept., 1812, began life with nothing, having poor health for four years, has had a family of twelve children, and by the help of God is yet alive waiting for the Lord's time to call him home.

12 BURRILL LYMAN[7], 3d son of Maj. *Isaac*[6], m. Jan. 11, 1814; Sybil Beckworth, who d. Jan. 15, 1815; m. July 21, 1816, Dorcas Irons, held for some time the office of Co. Treas., an upright honest man, d. July 23, 1856; his wife Dorcas still lives on the homestead. *Lymansville.*

Children, Eighth Generation :

37   1 Harris, b. July 1, 1817; m. Jan. 25, 1844, Minerva Taggart, and d. at Roulette Nov. 5, 1862; hunter, farmer, merchant.
        Ch. 9th Gen.: 1 Alice L., b. Jan. 6, 1845; d. Aug. 19, 1850. 2 Alva, b. Feb. 4, 1848; d. Dec. 22, 1848. 3 Andrew V., b. Sept. 10, 1853.

40   2 Orrilla, b. Dec. 25, 1818; m. John H. Burt. She was the first white child born in the county.

42   3 Laroy, b. Sept. 5, 1821; m. March 4, 1847, Thankful Card, hunter, trapper, surveyor, farmer, merchant, geologist, Roulette.
        Ch. 9th Gen.: 1 Sybil, b. Nov. 25, 1847. 2 Celestia E., b. Nov. 24, 1848. 3 Isabel, b. May 8, 1850. 4 Milo, b. Feb. 1, 1852.

47   4 Sybil, b. Oct. 1, 1823; d. Jan. 25, 1825.

48   5 Laura, b. March 5, 1826; m. Nov. 29, 1842, George Weimer, farmer.

49   6 Mary Ann, b. June 4, 1828; m. S. P. Reynolds, Esq.

50   7 Prudence, b. Aug. 13, 1830; m. March 13, 1851, William Boyington, former.

51   8 Sarah, b. April 23, 1834; m. J. P. Taggert, assistant judge of the county court.

52   9 Riley, b. July 15, 1836; d. Oct. 25, 1841.

53   10 Marietta D., b. May 27, 1838; d. Oct. 1, 1841.

13 LAURA LYMAN[7], dau. of Maj. *Isaac*[6], m. Nov. 10, 1810; Silas McCarty, carpenter, d. Oct. 15, 1838; she d. Nov. 20, 1864. *Muncy, Pa.*

Children, Eighth Generation:

54 1 Charlotte, b. April 27, 1812; m. June 6, 1836, John Low, one child Lee, d. Oct. 15, 1844.

56 2 Eloisa, b. July 27, 1816 ; m. Nov. 4, 1834, Benjamin Johnson, of Muncy; d. June 8, 1854.

        Ch. 9th Gen.: 1 Mary, d. 1857, aged 18. 2 Harriet, m. Orlo L. Spofford, Driftwood, Pa.

59 3 Lucetta, b. Dec. 30, 1820 ; m. Nov. 18, 1849, Augustus Wilson, six sons, 1 dau.

67 4 Lyman, b. Sept. 30, 1823 ; m. Feb. 28, 1850, Mary Absever, one dau. aged 18 years, farmer, Weatherly, Pa.

69 5 Hiram, b. Dec. 25, 1825; m. April 5, 1847 ; Rebecca Michael. Ch. : 3 sons 3 daughters ; Emma, eldest dau., m. Dec. 1, 1870, Philip K Fisher, farmer.

76 6 Otis, b. March 15, 1828; m. Aug. 20, 1859, Mary Beaber, one dau.

14 DR. HARRY LYMAN[7], 1796–1853, 4th son of Maj. *Isaac*[6], was a man of culture, of thought, of fine figure, and commanding person, and brilliant parts. He graduated at the Med. Coll., in Philadelphia in his 21st year. He engaged in mercantile, in addition to his professional business, and by fraudulent friends became, near the close of life, reduced in his circumstances. He d. at the age of 56 years, Sept. 3, 1854, of a lingering consumption. He m. Dec. 7, 1820, Prudence Jackson, of Hinsdale, Mass.; 2d wife, Fanny DeCorson.

Children, Eighth Generation:

78 1 Andrew Jackson, b. May 12, 1824; m. Eliza Pendleton, Cortlandville, Cortland Co., N. Y., Oct. 15, 1854, a mechanic, now farming at C. A. J. Lyman enlisted in the fall of 1862, in the 10th N. Y. Cavalry, was promoted to Sergeant in Co. L., was in the cavalry arm of service almost two years, and was transferred to the 185th New York Vols., for promotion to 1st Lieutenant in Co. F., where he served until the close of the war, having been in over 20 different general engagements and skirmishes. He sustained several wounds and injuries for which he is upon the U. S. pension list. His occupation is carpenter, and resides in Cortland, Cortland, N. Y.

        Ch. 9th Gen.: 1 Anna Prudence, b. July 1, 1854. 2 Henry Frank, b. Feb. 25, 1856. 3 Harriet Naomi, b. Jan. 29, 1858. 4 William Clark, b. May 23, 1861.

83 2 Chester Corson, b. May 4, 1828 ; m. C. Selina Cory, of Ulysses, Potter Co., Pa., Sept., 1851 ; has of late taken out some very valuable patents ; is decidedly talented as an inventor of complicated machinery, Cleveland, Ohio.

Ch. 9th Gen.: 1 Alice, b. July 30, 1853, a graduate of Edinboro, Erie, Pa., State Normal School of the Musical and Academic Department. 2 Legrand, b. Dec., 1856, has been a student there since five years old.

86   3 Rozellah, b. March 16, 1830 ; m. George W. Webb, of Adelison, Steuben Co., N. Y., Dec. 9, 1849
   Ch. 9th Gen.: 1 Mary. 2 Edney. 3 Gertrude. 4 Eugene. 5 Leeland.

92   4 Bertha M., b. at Coudersport, Potter Co., May 1, 1832, unmarried, teacher and dressmaker, Binghamton, N. Y.

93   5 Grace L., b. at Liberty, McKean Co., Pa., Oct. 15, 1834, graduated at Alford University, July, 1857, taught select and high school, m. J. G. Parkhurst, b. Keene, N. H., has been in mercantile business 20 years in Elkland, Pa., one child Leona, b. Jan. 29, 1868.

94   6 Lorinda, b. at Liberty, Dec. 16, 1837 ; m. Andrew Kelley, Condersport, Potter Co., Pa., March 16, 1855, a mechanic and county clerk of Shippen, Cameron Co., Pa.
   Ch. 9th Gen.: 1 Mary. 2 Willie. 3 Infant nameless.

98   7 Fordyce Allen, b. Nov. 11, 1842 ; m. Viola Badger of Warren, Pa., Oct. 24, 1866, agent for Lyman & Jones of Cleveland, Ohio, one child Jenny.

99   8 Othello, b. Nov. 10, 1846.

100   9 Mordecai, b. May 18, 184......; m. Othella; Ulysses, Cameron Co., Pa.

101   10 Adeloin Joseph, b. Sept. 30, 1851, unmarried, carriage and house painter, Elkland.

15 ISAAC LYMAN[7], Jr., 5th son of Maj. *Isaac*[6], m. Minerva Cole, b. in 1822, who d. in Mercer Co., Pa., in 1839.

Children, Eighth Generation :

106   1 Jane, b. April 17, 1823 ; m. 1838, William Fessenden Brindleville, Orway, Potter Co.

107   2 Eunice, b. March 22, 1824 ; m. 1842, B. W. Skinner; she is deceased.

108   3 Collins C., b. April 23, 1826 ; m. 1852, Alvira Logue.
   Ch. 9th Gen.: 1 Lucina, b. 1853. 2 Anson, b. 1855. 3 Prudence, b. Jan. 18, 1858.

112   4 Prudence, b. Jan. 11, 1828 ; d. 1830.

113   5 Isaac, b. Dec. 2, 1829 ; m. March 25, 1852, Sally Weiderich — farmer, Roulette.
   Ch. 9th Gen.: 1 Jacob W., b. March 21, 1853. 2 Hurd M., b. June 29, 1855. 3 Eldora, b. July 15, 1857. 4 Rosetta, b. Oct. 9, 1859. 5 Chloe, b. March 10, 1862. 6 Alva J., b. Dec. 27, 1863 ; d. May 6, 1868. 7 Roscoe, b. July 8, 1866.

120   6 Silas M., b. June 26, 1831 ; m. 1860, name unknown, 2 sons.

121   7 John M., b. Jan. 8, 1833 ; m. 1855, Barbara Weiderich, Roulette.

16

Ch. 9th Gen.: 1 Watson, b. Nov. 7, 1856. 2 Lenora,
  b. 1859. 3 Jennie, b. 1864. 4 Minnie, b. 1867.

129 8 Gilbert, b. Jan. 9, 1835; m. Lodelia Downey, of Smithport,
    1856, mechanic and farmer, Colegrove P. O., McKean Co.
    4 children, ages and names unknown.

134 9 Henry, b. Jan. 27, 1837; m. in Michigan, killed at the
    battle of Gaines Mills in 1862.

16 OTIS LYMAN[7], 6th son of Maj. *Isaac*, m. April 21,
1805, Sarah Babcock, and resided a farmer in Manchester,
N. Y.; in Oct., 1834, removed to Cambridge, then to
Springville.   *Lenawee Co., Mich.*

Children, Eighth Generation:
135 1 Henry Isaac, b. July 1, 1830.
136 2 Sarah Aurelia, b. Nov. 10, 1831.
137 3 Emily Elizabeth, b. June 12, 1833.
138 4 Josephine Merrit, b. Aug. 1, 1835.
139 5 Silas Lorenzo, b. Dec. 28, 1837.
140 6 Warren Thomas, b. Nov. 23, 1839.
141 7 Granville, b. July 27, 1841.
142 8 Frances Almira, b. Feb. 13, 1844; d. Feb. 21, 1865.
143 9 Theodore Willie, b. Oct. 6, 1849; d. Feb. 21, 1865.
        Ch. 9th Gen.: 1 Frances E. C. Draper, b. June 23,
        1864. 2 Sarah E. King, b. 1864. 3 Granville King,
        b. 1868. 4 Nellie Lyman, b. 1869.

17 CHARLES LYMAN[7], 7th son of Major *Isaac*[6], b. Jan.
13, 1810; m. in 1829, Eveline Edgcombe. The issue of
this marriage is 8 children all living, all b. in Potter Co.—
farmer, but filling various offices in the state and in the
gift of the U. S., among others associate judge of the county
court. The father and sons of this family through all
their public life have seldom been out of office in the Co.
In 1864, Mr. L. removed to Ill., and during that and the
year following traveled in Europe, visiting every state
and a portion of Africa; and in 1869, made short tour in
Europe, visiting Belgium, Prussia and France has also
traveled in Upper and Lower Canada, Nova Scotia, New
Brunswick, and in 20 of the states of our Union.
                          Wapello, Louisa Co., Iowa.

Children, Eighth Generation:
148 1 Charles Eugene, b. Aug. 30, 1829, Henry Co., Iowa.
149 2 William Penn, b. Jan. 26, 1831, Yancton, Dakota Territory.
150 3 Sarah Wells, b. Oct., 1832; m. Hiram Thornton, Mendota,
    Ill., who d. Feb., 1866; no children.
151 4 Maria Mann, b. Dec. 23, 1836; m. Darius Key. 6 children,
    3 living.

152 5 Mary, b. June 3 ....
153 6 Edin, b. Feb. 9, 1840, Chillicothe, Missouri.
154 7 Eliza, b. March 8, 1841, teacher, Mendota, Ill.
155 8 Eulalia, b. May 5, 1843.

20 EDWIN LYMAN[7], 9th son of Major *Isaac[6]*, b. in Lymansville, Potter Co., Dec. 21, 1815 ; m. Jan. 19, 1843, Maria
Clark, b. 1824—farmer.   *Condersport, Potter Co.*

Children, Eighth Generation:

162 1 Ellen M., b. Aug. 19, 1844.
163 2 Hattie, b. April 10, 1859.

21 LEWIS WM. LYMAN[7], 10th son of Maj. *Isaac[6]*, b. in
Lymansville, Jan. 29, 1818; m. Feb. 20, 1839, Hannah
Lewis, farmer.   *Sweden Valley, Potter Co.*

Children, Eighth Generation:

164 1 Thomas Benton, June 28, 1840 ; m., Feb. 1, 1865, Mary
      Jane Guiles, of Monroe, Ashtabula Co., Ohio, b. July
      11, 1839, carpenter and cabinet maker, Sweden Valley,
      Potter Co.
        Ch. 9th Gen.: 1 Ray S., Jan. 14, 1866. 2 Jesse
        Guiles, b. Dec. 6, 1867. 3 Arthur Mann, Feb. 21, 1870.
168 2 Albert G., Aug. 8, 1844, Sweden.
169 3 Arthur, b. April 19, 1847, Potter Co.
170 4 Eustin Milo, b. Jan. 1, 1853 ; d. Feb., 1854.
171 5 Charles, b. May 10, 1856 ; d. Nov. 18, 1862.
172 6 Willie, b. Dec. 8, 1862.

We give this family in Lock Haven, Pa., a place here
because they seem to be related to the lineage of Major
Isaac Lyman.

The tradition of the family is that their *grandfather Eleazer* was a son of one Major Lyman, an officer of the Revolution, that this Eleazer, b. in Mass. m. Betsey Raymond—
that he removed to Tioga Co., N. Y., where he lived a
farmer until 1850. They had 3 sons and 6 daughters

One of these sons was Eleazer, Jr., the father of the present
family, who m. Sally Payne said to be from Mass. The
issue of this marriage was 4 sons and 2 daughters. He
removed to Alleghany Co., and studied medicine, and then
established himself in Great Bend, Susquehannah Co., Pa.,
as a physician and surgeon. He was killed by his horse at
the age of 42 in 1845. His wife d. in 1839.

A sister of this Dr. Lyman m. Ex-Governor Blair of
Michigan.

The oldest son of Dr. Lyman, C. A. Lyman, Esq., a
lawyer in Lock Haven, enlisted in 1861 as Capt. of a Co.,

in the 7th Pa. R. C., and participated in many of the great battles of the Peninsula and the Potomac, and was promoted to the rank of Maj. and Col. He is 51 years of age and has a family of six children.

The second son, C. E. Lyman, is a mechanic and manufacturer. Another brother with himself and his son enlisted early in the war of the rebellion all distinguished for their bravery in many battles, the brother and son were killed when leading the forlorn hope in storming Fort Fisher. The surviving brothers were frequently raised in rank for their dauntless courage and effective service in many battles, never laying down their arms until victory was achieved and the rebellion quelled.

Few families have a more patriotic and honorable record. Some one, we hope, more fortunate than ourselves, will be able to establish their true relations to their kindred, whom all the Lyman family would gladly welcome to their brotherhood.

2 BENJAMIN LYMAN⁶, 1761–1846, 2d son of *Benjamin⁵, Isaac⁴, Richard⁴,* removed about 1800, to Canada West and resided in the town of Kitley, farmer. He was a magistrate for many years and also a school teacher. He served in the army during the Revolution and drew a pension from the American government until his death. He was b. apparently in Whitingham, Vt., since famous as the birth place of Brigham Young, president of the Mormons, and d. June 2, 1846, aged 85. His wife, Polly Temple, d. Dec. 5, 1844, aged 81.

Children, Seventh Generation :

173 1 Clarissa, b. in Whitingham, May 23, 1783, appears to have d. young.
174 2 Barnabas, b. July 15, 1784; d. 1865.
175 3 Jonathan, b. June 12, 1786
176 4 Polly, b. June 15, 1788; m. William Hoyl; d. 1865, Canada West.
177 5 Calvin, b. April 21, 1790, Michigan.
178 6 Anna, b. March 8, 1792; m. Aaron Allen, Avon, C. W.
179 7 Zina, b. Feb. 19, 1794; d. April 29, 1795.
180 8 Melinda, b. June 1, 1797.
181 9 Benjamin, b. May, 1799, Morganville, N. Y.
182 10 Joseph, b. March 17, 1801.
183 11 Horace, b. Oct. 6, 1803, Michigan.
184 12 John C., b. Sept. 25, 1807.

The first 5 were b. in Whitingham, the last 2 in Kitley, Benjamin in Hartford, N. Y., Joseph in Canada.

2 BARNABAS LYMAN[7], eldest son of *Benjamin*[6], appears to have resided in Kitley, but of his residence and m. no record is given.

Children, Eighth Generation :

185 1 Clarissa, b. Aug., 1810 ; d. 1866.
186 2 Robert F., b. Feb. 9, 1811, Widder Station.
187 3 John Calvin.   191 7 Anna.
188 4 Maria.   192 8 Barnabas.
189 5 Stephen.   193 9 William, Rev., Mimosa, C.W.
190 6 Luther.

14 ROBERT F. LYMAN[8], son of *Barnabas*[7], was b. at Kitley, near Brockville, Canada West, Feb. 9, 1811; m. June 11, 1835, Lucy Kennedy.   *Widder Station, Ontario.*

Children, Ninth Generation :

194 1 Morris, b. at Georgetown, Ontario, Sept. 19, 1836 ; m. Aug. 6, 1858, Rachel Ward—builder, Widder Station.
     Ch. 10th Gen. : 1 Morris B., b. at Port Franks, Sept. 22, 1860. 2 Lillian, b. at Widder Station, June 15, 1862. 3 Robert George, b. at W. S., May 20, 1868.
198 2 Rev. Barnabas, b. at Camboro, Aug. 15, 1840 ; m. Aug., 1865, Georgiana Bailey, who d. June 7, 1866; m. April 5, 1868 ; Maria Prource, minister in the Methodist Episcopal church.
199 3 Robert N., May 7, 1842 ; Feb. 23, 1863—Lucretia Ward, farmer.
     Ch. 10th Gen. : 1 Emerson, b. Jan., 1864. 2 Lucy L., April 1, 1868.
200 4 Albert, b. March 22, 1845 ; d. March 8, 1851.
201 5 Joseph B., b. Jan. 20, 1847 ; d. March 7, 1851.
202 6 Sylvester, b. June 7, 1849, farmer.
203 7 Jacob S., b. April 20, 1852.
204 8 Sarah S., Oct. 20, 1854.
205 9 Samuel J., June 16, 1863.

187 JOHN CALVIN LYMAN[8], 2d son of *Barnabas*[7], m. 1840, at Esquiring, Ont., Susannah Kennedy, who d. 1862; m. 2d wife, Anna Cisbe.   *Michigan.*

Children, Ninth Generation :

206 1 Sarah Susannah, b. April 6, 1841 ; m. July 22, 1858, Richard Laird.
207 2 Clarissa, b. March 30. 1850.
208 3 Gilbert D., b. Sept. 3, 1851.
209 4 Martha, b. Sept. 4, 1853.
210 5 Luther W., b. Aug. 18, 1856.
211 6 Horatio B., b. Aug. 13, 1859.

189 Stephen Lyman[8], *Barnabas[7], Benjamin[6], Benjamin[5], Isaac[4], Richard[3], Richard[2], Richard[1]*, b. in Kitley, Aug. 22, 1815; m. May 6, 1856, Elizabeth Odell— farmer.

Kitley, Canada West.

Children, Ninth Generation :

212 1 Mary Ann, b. Aug. 1, 1858.
213 2 Charles Stinson, b. Aug. 15, 1861.
214 3 Sarah Jane, b. Sept. 7, 1863.
215 4 Margaret Ellen, b. Dec. 24, 1866.

190 Luther Lyman[8], son of *Barnabas[7]*, b. in Penfield, N. Y., April 4, 1821; m. Sept. 21, 1843, Susanna Wackhaner, d. Aug. 3, 1854; m. Aug. 20, 1861, Mary Keer, 2d wife.

Children, Ninth Generation:

216 1 Harriet, b. July 17, 1844.
217 2 Huldah, b. Oct. 11, 1846.
218 3 Isaac B., b. Dec. 24, 1849.
219 4 Mary Elizabeth, b. Feb. 28, 1864.

191 Anna Lyman[8], dau. of *Barnabas[7], Benjamin[6], Benjamin[5], Isaac[4], Richard[3], Richard[2], Richard[1]*, b. in Penfield, N. Y., Oct. 21, 1816; m. Nov. 27, 1836, James Allen.

Children, Ninth Generation :

220 1 John, b. Sept. 15, 1837.
221 2 Betsey, b. Feb. 7, 1839.
222 3 William Levi, b. Dec. 28, 1840.
223 4 Adam Luther, b. Dec. 26, 1842.
224 5 Samuel, b. Nov. 20, 1844.
225 6 Lucy Jane, b. Dec. 11, 1846.
226 7 James Bush, b. Jan. 7, 1849.
227 8 Ebenezer Pratt, b. Nov. 9, 1850.
228 9 Peter Miller, b. Oct. 18, 1852.
229 10 Joseph Allen, b. Oct. 20, 1854.
230 11 Israel, b. Sept. 28, 1856.
231 12 Anna Sophia, b. Nov. 16, 1858.
232 13 Benoni, b. Feb., 1861.

293 Rev. William Lyman[8], youngest son of *Barnabas[7]*, b. at Chinguacoutchy, Ontario, July 6, 1827; m. Jan. 24, 1850, Sarah Masoles, who d. Feb. 12, 1855; m. 2d wife, Nov. 13, 1856, Hannah L. Morden. *Mimosa, Ontario, C. W.*

Children, Ninth Generation :

233 1 Martha, b. Oct. 10, 1850.
234 2 Robert, b. at E., Nov. 6, 1852.

175 JONATHAN LYMAN[7], 2d son of *Benjamin*[6], lived in Kitley, d. May 10, 1860, aged almost 74 years.

Kitley, Co. of Leeds.

Children, Eighth Generation :

235 1 Lucinda, b. April 13, 1815.
236 2 Clarinda, b. Sept. 30, 1816.
237 3 Zina, b. March 1, 1819, resides Kitley.
238 4 Alvah C., b. June 18, 1824, Kitley, C. W.

235 LUCINDA LYMAN[8], m. Edward Bissel. *Aquota, C. W*

Children, Ninth Generation :

239 1 Lyman.
240 2 G. W.
241 3 William.
242 4 Ellen.
243 5 Adalia.
244 6 Mary.

236 CLARINDA LYMAN[8], m. Duncan Livingston. *Kitley.*

Children, Ninth Generation :

245 1 Miles.
246 2 Morton.
247 3 Lawson.
248 4 Eucador.
249 5 William.

237 ZINA LYMAN[8], son of *Jonathan*[7], grandson of *Benjamin*[6], Kitley, m. Sally Marshall. *Toledo, Ontario, C. W.*

Children, Ninth Generation ·

250 1 Leonard, b. 1847.
251 2 Charles, b. 1855.

177 CALVIN LYMAN[7], 3d son of *Benjamin*[6], no record further has been obtained, he is reported to have removed to Michigan, but his residence is unknown.

Children, Eighth Generation :

252 1 Lovina M., b. July 13, 1814 ; m. Daniel Clark, farmer.
    Ch. 9th Gen. : 1 Charles. 2 George. 3 Franklin. 4 Mary, d. 5 Edward.
255 2 Lorenzo D., b. Sept. 10, 1815 ; m. June 1, 1861, Hannah Cilley.
    Ch. 9th Gen. : 1 Lorenzo D., b. Oct. 11, 1843 ; d. Aug. 1, 1856. 2 Hannah A., b. Jan. 25, 1847. 3 Sarah E., b. Oct. 11, 1854. 4 Mary F., b. May 26, 1858. 5 Edwin C., b. June 25, 1862. 6 William L., b. Jan. 11, 1866.
262 3 Louisa A., b. March 6, 1817 ; m. Benjamin Pevoir, Parkville, St. Joseph, Mich.
    Ch. 9th Gen. : 1 Mary E., m. Coy Hinbash, Schoolcraft, Mich. 2 William, m. Jane Call or Carol. 3 Charles, m. Carrie Fisher, Chicago. 4 Lewis, m. Susan Fiske. 5 Emma, m. Dr. McElrath, Parkville, Mich.

268   4 Lurett E., b. April 26, 1818 ; m. Charles Carlisle, Leoni-
          das, St. Joseph, Mich.
            Ch. 9th Gen. : 1 Mary E., m. Frederic Thiebaud, one
          child.   2 Charles.   3 Harriet.
272   5 Lewis B., b. Feb. 6, 1820 ; m. Nov. 3, 1844, Mary Wight-
          man, Mendon, St. Joseph Co., Mich.
            Ch. 9th Gen. : 1 Frances, b. 1846 ; m. Rodney E.,
          Fletcher, Mendon, Mich.   2 M ..... b. 1853.   3 Myrta,
          b. 1861, d.
275   6 Luther C., b. July 26, 1821 ; m. Melvina Strong, Three
          Rivers, Mich.
            Ch. 9th Gen.: 1 Emma, b. 1850; m. Marten Haulbiel,
          Della, Fulton Co., Ohio.
            Ch. 10th Gen. : (1) Mier.   (2) Ellen, d.
280   7 Lorena L., b. July 23, 1823, d. in infancy.
281   8 Leonard, birth not given, d. in infancy.
282   9 Luria, b. April 26, 1828 ; d. young.
283   10 Lucinda Ann, b. April 26, 1828 ; m. Joseph Russell,
          farmer, Centerville, St. Joseph, Mich.
            Ch. 9th Gen.: 1 Elvin.   2 Frederic.   3—4. infants, d.
287 •11 Leroy N., b. Oct. 11, 1830 ; m. Rosètta Miner—farmer,
          Kansas.
            Ch. 9th Gen. : (1) Lurietta, b. 1855.   (2) William,
          b. 1858.   3, 4, 5. nameless, d. young.

181 BENJAMIN LYMAN[7], *Benjamin[6], Benjamin[5], Isaac[4], Rich-
ard[3], Richard[2], Richard[1],* b. in Hartford, Washington Co.,
N. Y., May 6, 1799 ; m. in Webster, Monroe Co., N. Y.,
Aug. 15, 1836, Harriet Cleveland —blacksmith.
                    Morganville, Genesee Co., N. Y

  Children, Eighth Generation :
293   1 Martha, b. in Brighton, N. Y., Aug. 31, 1837.
294   2 Mary E., b. in Batavia, N. Y., Feb. 12, 1841.
295   3 Albert, b. in Bethany, N. Y., Sept. 11, 1843.
296   4 Infant, b. in Bethany, N. Y., Aug. 28, 1845.
297   5 Infant, b. in Bethany, N. Y., Jan. 25, 1847.

182 JOSEPH LYMAN[7], 6th son of *Benjamin[6],* Kitley, C. W.
                                      Western States.
  Children, Eighth Generation.
298   1 Ariel.   302   5 Sylvester.
299   2 Alanson.   303   6 Lavina.
300   3 Clarinda.   304   7 Benson.
301   4 Jesse.

183 HORACE LYMAN[7], 7th son of *Benjamin[6],* of Kitley,
C. W.   *Lapier, Lapier Co., Michigan.*

Children, Eighth Generation:

305 1 Almon.
306 2 Arden.
307 3 Daniel.
308 4 Lineus.
309 5 Eliza Ann.

310 6 Melbourn.
311 7 Malcom.
312 8 Willard.
313 9 Delorme.

3 ELEAZER LYMAN⁶, *Benjamin⁵, Isaac⁴, Richard³, Richard²,
Richard¹*, 1767–1844. Eleazer Lyman was b. in Lebanon,
Conn., Jan. 30, 1767 ; d. at Poultney, Rutland Co., Vt.,
Jan. 11, 1844, aged 77 ; by profession a carpenter ; served
as orderly to his brother, Major Isaac Lyman, in the war of
the Revolution ; m. Clarissa Hitchcock, of Springfield,
Mass., b. in the year 1770 ; d. at Castleton, April 11, 1838,
aged 69 years, and 10 months, having reared 12 children.

Children, Seventh Generation :

314 1 Lura, ⎫ twins.
315 2 Sarah, ⎬ Born at Windham Co., Vt., Aug. 24, 1789.
Sarah d. in infancy. Lura m. for her first husband, W. F.
Weston, by whom she had two sons, Cyra L. and Benjamin F. ; for her second husband, Gen. Arms, who
served in the war of 1812 ; now living as his widow, with
her son, B. F. Weston, in Kaneville, Kane Co., Ill.
319 3 Gad Lyman, b. at Whitingham, Jan. 5, 1791 ; was killed by
a fall from the roof of a barn at Pawlet, Vt., June 3, 1806,
aged 17 ;' buried at Rupert.
320 3 Ambrose, b. at Whitingham, Jan. 12, 1742 ; d. at Jersey
Shore, Lycoming Co., Penn , Oct., 1822. Went as a
volunteer to Plattsburg, near the close of the war of
1812 ; m. Oct. 7, 1810, Lucia Hart near Utica, both d. in
Lycoming Co., Penn., in early life.
Ch..8th Gen.: 1 Edwin Clark, b. May 12, 1817 ; d.
1835, or '36 2 James W., son of Ambrose, m. Feb.
11, 1841, Hannah B. Ganhart ; an elder for many
years in the M. E. church — gardener, Oconomowoc,
Wis. *Ch. 9th Gen.:* (1) Albert Clark, b. March 1,
1842 ; m. Dec. 28, 1864, Jennie Ritche, who d. Dec. 8,
1868. [*Ch. 10th Gen.:* (1) Jennie, b. March 5, 1866,
2 Willie, b. Oct. 19, 1868.] (2) Anna Maria, b. April
1, 1844 ; m. Jan. 2, 1865, Josiah Leslie, no children.
(3) Mary Catharina, b. Aug. 25, 1847 ; m. Jan. 1, 1867,
Abram J. Cole, no children. (4) James Hope, b. Oct.
2, 1855. (5) Eddy Ellsworth, b. June 26, 1864). 3
Lucia Jane, b. July 15, 1821 ; m. Behren, Hazleton, Pa.,
[*Ch. 9th Gen. :*] (1) John. (2) Samuel. (3) Willie.]
334 5 Eleazer, Jr., b. at Whitingham, March 30, 1795 ; now
living in Oswago, Potter Co., Penn. By profession, car-

17

penter and joiner; soldier in the war of 1812 (orderly
sergeant), under the veteran, Gen. Scott; m. for first wife,
Mary Dudley, of Rutland Co., Vt., by whom he had seven
children, two d. in infancy. For second wife, Mary E.
Hollister, of Pawlet, Rutland Co., Vt., March 6, 1833, by
whom he had five children.

   Ch. 8th Gen.: By first marriage, two d. in infancy,
three m. and d.; no record. Five children by second
marriage. 6 Lucy L., b. June 2, 1818; m. Roland
Marshall, who lost a son in the Union army, and has one
son, Francis H., and one daughter, Mary L., now
living. 7 Benjamin F., b. March 21, 1822; was in the
Union army (16th Penn. Cavalry); m. Sophia Wood, of
Fairhaven, Vt.; she has five children. [*Ch. 9th Gen.:*
(1) Mary S. (2) Helen S. (3) Don F. (4) Samuel
Fayette. (5) George H.] 8 Jennie M., b. March 13, 1834;
H. O. Yale, of Wellsville, N. Y.; has two children. [*Ch.
9th Gen.:* (1) Charles H. (2) Mary L.] 9 Sarah M., b.
July 13, 1836; m. Walter Wells, of Oswago, Pa.; has
four children. [*Ch. 9th Gen.:* (1) Arthur G. (2) Ernest
L. (3) Myrtle W. (4) Walter John.] 10 A. Sidney, b.
April 28, 1840; was in the Union army, in the cavalry
stationed at Newbern, North Carolina); m. Rachel Taggart; has three children. [*Ch. 9th Gen.:* (1) May E.
(2) Maurice W. (3) Maud R.] 11 Lucretia E., b. April
11, 1844; dressmaker in West Milton, Wisconsin. 12 Ashbel A., b. Sept. 9, 1846; d. Feb. 3, 1853, buried in Oswago, Potter Co., Pa.

347 6 Silas Lyman, b. at Whitingham, Sept. 23, 1796; d. 1819,
   at Jersey Shore, Lycoming Co., Pa., when but three
   months married; carpenter and joiner; went as a volunteer to Plattsburg, near the close of the war of 1812.
      Ch. 8th Gen.: 1 Francis. 2 Mary. 3 Marcus, d.
   of a fever in the Union army in the late rebellion.

348 7 Clarissa, b. at Whitingham, Dec. 25, 1797; m. Truman
   Loveland, of Castleton; went west and d. Of her family
   nothing is known.

349 8 Sally, b. at Whitingham, 1798; for first husband, m. Dan
   Moulton, of Castleton, by whom she had one child. For
   second husband, m. Dr. Hall; went west and died.

350 9 Isaac, b. at Hartford, Washington Co., N. Y., July 6,
   1800, by profession, carpenter and joiner, m. Achsah
   Ames, of Ira, Rutland Co., Vt., Feb. 27, 1824; m. 2d
   wife, Elizabeth Hill, of West Rutland, Oct. 29, 1851.
      Ch. 9th Gen.: 1 Emily Jane, b. Feb. 17, 1824; m.
   Hiram D. Rudd, of Middletown, Sept. 5, 1846, now residing in Kaneville, Kane Co., Illinois, no children.
   Her husband served for three years in the Union army.
   2 William Carlos, b. Jan. 16, 1827; m. Marina Rock-

well, of Middletown, Vt., Nov. 27, 1845; 2d wife, Lois
M. Sanborn, of Lowell, Vt., Oct. 27, 1855, by whom
he has 4 children. [*Ch. 9th Gen.:* (1) Milo Bradley,
b. Feb. 24, 1856. (2) Laura Augusta, b. Jan. 19, 1857.
(3) William Albert, b. April 29, 1865. (4) Judson
Carlos, Feb. 9, 1867, now living in Concord, Michigan,
by profession, carpenter, and joiner. He went to Michigan, in 1860, entered the army in the spring of 1865,
mustered out at its close, the same year.] 3 Ambrose
Hawley, b. Feb. 5, 1831; m. Sarah Ensign, of Poultney,
November 16, 1853. [*Ch. 9th Gen.:* (1) Blanche
Isabel, b. July 10, 1858. (2) Katie Louise, b. July
19, 1863. He now resides in Concord, Mich., by
profession, carpenter and joiner, joined the Mechanic's
regiment, raised in Mich., and served some three years in
the Union army]. 4 Laura A., b. Sept. 15, 1837; m.
Henry M. Rose, of Illinois, Sept. 17, 1862, one child.
[*Ch. 9th. Gen.:* George Lyman Rose, now living in
Prarie Pond, DeKalb Co., Ill.] 5 Milo W, b. April 8,
1839; m Mary Turner, of Sudbury, Vt., July 29, 1863,
one child. [*Ch. 9th Gen.:* (1) Charles Milo, b. May
10, 1869, now living in Rutland, Vt., by profession
carpenter and joiner. He responded to the call of the
president for 75,000 men, was gone 3 months, then re-
enlisted as a veteran for 9 months, was in the battle of
Gettysburg and Big Bethel.] 6 Harriet N., b. Sept. 3.
1852; m. Scott Hunter, of Argyle, Washington Co.,
N. Y., Nov. 24, 1870, now residing in West Rutland,
Rutland Co., Vt.

365 10 Hiram, was b. at Rupert, Aug. 25, 1803; m. 4 times, dates
not known. Has three children living, and one d. in the
Union army, carpenter, Castleton, Vt. *Ch. 9th Gen.:*
1 Washington Franklin, Kaneville, Ill. 2 Lura, m. Hiram
Aldridge, Whitehall. 3 Warren. 4 John F., lost in the
army, drowned in Virginia, foraging.

370 11 Betsey, b. at Rupert, April 8, 1806; m. Josiah Wheaton,
of Castleton. [*Ch. 9th Gen.:* (1) William. (2) Lura,
(3) Clarissa. They are all living in Kaneville, Kane Co.,
Illinois.] Carpenter and joiner, Kaneville.

374 12 William, b. at Rupert, April 6, 1811; d. at Castleton, Sept.
26, 1829, aged 18. Was killed by falling from the
scaffolding of a church.

4 Dea. SILAS LYMAN[6], 4th son of *Benjamin[5]*, probably b.
about 1766; in Whitingham, soon after the removal of
the family from Lebanon. He resided occasionally in Hartford, N. Y., in Bolton, and Hebron, then in Rupert, Vt., and
last at Loraine, Jefferson Co., N. Y. Here, as elsewhere, he
struggled with all the hardships incident to the settlement

of a new country, often carrying provisions for his family 6 or 8 miles on his shoulders through the woods. By these exhausting hardships and exposure he contracted disease which after a year and a half ended in a quick consumption of which he d. March 6, 1812, leaving to his family and friends a sure and certain hope that he rested from his labors with them that die in the Lord. He m. Parnee Brown, dau. of Wm. B.   *Loraine, Jefferson Co., N. Y.*

Children, Seventh Generation

375   1 Vashti, b. Feb., 1792, Watertown, N. Y. unmarried.
376   2 Parnee, b. 1793, Fredonia, N. Y., known as widow Stephens.
377   3 Silas, b. July 24, 1794, farmer, deacon of the church, Pulaski, N. Y.
378   4 Parthenia, m. Lamfear in Penn.
379   5 Orin, no date, m. Miss Hosford.
380   6 Calvin, b. June 10, 1800, Westfield, N. Y.
381   7 Luther, b. June 10, 1800; m. Betsey Stedman.
382   8 William B., m. Orrins, Utica, N. Y.
383   9 Benjamin F., m. Clarissa Chase, Buffalo, N. Y., both deceased.
384   10 John Preston, b. 1806 or 1807, at Lyman, Jeff. Co., N. Y., d. in Pulaski.

377 Dea. SILAS LYMAN⁷, son of Dea. *Silas⁶*, resides in Pulaski, Oswego Co., N. Y., farmer, m. Jan. 26, 1817, Cynthia Waugh. On the death of his father, at the age of 17 the care of the family devolved on him. By industry and severe economy they were supported and debts paid. He was on the lines through the war of 1812, and promoted through several grades to the rank of lieut. col., in the 55th Regiment of N. Y. Militia. In his protracted life of toil he has turned his hand to various occupations besides farming, milling, coopering, shoemaking, &c. For 50 years he has been a consistent professor of religion, thoroughly loyal, a firm supporter of the temperance and anti slavery reformations, prayerfully seeking to live peaceably with all men, fearing God and keeping his commandments.   *Pulaski, N. Y.*

Children, Eighth Generation:

385   1 Gilbert, b. Dec. 4, 1817; m. June 1, 1742, Mary B. Frink, d. Sept. 11, 1845, in Wisconsin. His wife d. June 5, of the same year leaving an infant Antoinette, who has lived in the family of Dea. Lyman, as child and grandchild.
386   2 Irene, b. July 3, 1819; m. Oct. 1, 1840, Bernice L. Doane. *Ch. 9th Gen.:* 1 Sattira M., b. May 19, 1842; d. March 14, 1865. 2 Frederick S., b. March 12, 1844; m.

May 1, 1867, Mary E. Mills, aged 18. [*Ch.* 10*th Gen.:* (1) Alice J., b. Jan. 22, 1868.] 3 Alice M., b. Oct. 10, 1846; d. Oct. 17, 1866. 4 Sidney T., b. Dec. 9, 1848.

Fred S. Doane enlisted May 1, 1861, as drummer boy in company B, 32d New York Vols., for the term of 2 years, regiment organized on Staten Island, shipped for Washington in June, crossed the Potomac day after Col. Elsworth was shot at Alexandria; at 1st Bull Run and through the Peninsula campaign under McClellan, in Franklin's grand division. Returned to Alexandria in time for 2d Bull Run, sick in Seminary Hospital, Georgetown, D. C., during Antietam, 1st and 2d Fredericksburgh, and until regiment was discharged in New York city May 1, 1863. Returned home remained 6 months, reinlisted into the 147th Regular Brass Band which was then at Culpepper, Va., and from there to the battle of the Wilderness, to the surrender of Lee at Petersburgh; was transferred to 3d brigade band, 3d division, 5th Army Corps —at Washington at the grand review, and July 5, shipped for Albany and then discharged.

391 3 Parnee, b. April 15, 1822; m. March 15, 1843, Willard W. Huson, farmer, Sheboygan Falls, Wisconsin.

    Ch. 9*th Gen.:* 1 William B., b. Jan. 16, 1844. 2 H. H., b. May 11, 1845. 3 G., b. Feb. 18, 1847. 4 William Wilford, b. June 5, 1849. 5 Debro, b. Sept. 26, 1851; d. Jan. 5, 1860. 6 George, b. Sept. 6, 1854.

398 4 Sarah, b. Jan. 16, 1825; m. March 16, 1846, William H. Johnson, resides in Minneapolis, Minn.

    Ch. 10*th Gen.:* (1) Jasper J.

400 5 Mary, b. March 24, 1829; m. Dec. 30, 1847, Jeremiah Gardner, Sheboygan Falls, Wis.

    Ch. 9*th Gen.:* 1 Harriet A., b. Feb. 16, 1849. 2 Francis W., b. Jan. 11, 1853. 3 Fredrick H., b. Oct. 8, 1855. 4 Edward E., b. Sept. 25, 1858. 5 Henry, b. Dec. 17, 1860. 6 Minnie Evelyn, b. Sept. 10, 1864; m. June 1, 1869, at Sheboygan Falls, Wis., Emmitt A. Little.

407 6 Sophronia, b. at Loraine, Jeff. Co. N. Y., Aug. 11, 1831; m. Henry E. Allen of Loraine, Sept. 25, 1848.

    Ch. 9*th Gen.:* 1 Ellen E., b. Aug. 7, 1851. 2 Elias H., b. Jan. 17, 1854. Henry E. Allen, husband of Sophronia, d. in Sharon, Wis., Nov. 8, 1858; m. Wm. Allen of Sharon, Wis., April 17, 1860, where they now live.

408 7 Silas, deceased, dates not given.

411 8 Amanda, b. at Loraine, Sept. 6, 1835; m. George B. Boomer, of Euclid, Oswego Co., N. Y., July, 1868. They have one dau., b. 1869.

413 9 John N., M.D., b. at Loraine, April 3, 1838; m. Fanny F. Meacham, of Pulaski, Oswego Co., N. Y., March 5, 1862. He entered the service in Aug., 1861, as medical cadet, not having graduated in medicine; stationed at Seminary Hospital, Georgetown, D. C., graduated in March, 1862, at National Medical College, Washington, D. C., was shortly after appointed acting assistant Surgeon U. S. A. also commissioned 1st assistant Surgeon, 61st N. Y. Vols. stationed at Convalescent Camp, Va., during winter of 1862 and '63, and in summer of 1863, promoted to surgeon to the Third U. S. Colored Regiment, being the *first surgeon* appointed to a colored regiment, by the president of the United States, and in accepting this position, joined hands with a brave set of officers, men who were not only willing to face the black flag, by the side of black men, but also to face public opinion that their country might be truly free. He was at the battle of 2d Bull Run, Antietam, and on Morris Island, where many of the regiment were killed and wounded, in pushing forward our works, against Fort Wagoner, which it will be remembered the " rebels " " slid out of " in the night. Here he was taken with typhoid fever, and after a severe and protracted illness on account of which he was sent to Hospital in Beaufort, and in Jan., 1864, received an honorable discharge on account of physical disability.

Ch. 9th Gen. : 1 Frankie B., b. June 4, 1865. 2 Flora M., b. May 17, 1867, Cincinnati, Ohio.

416 10 Henry H., b. at Loraine, April 15, 1841; m. Flora Clark of Pulaski, N. Y., in 1862 or 1863, who d. in 1865; m. second wife, Emily Bennett, in 1867, one child. [*Ch. 9th Gen. :* Anna, b. March, 1868.] He entered the army Aug. 21, 1862, private Co. C., 147th Regiment, New York Vols., commissioned Feb., 1863, 2d lieut. commissioned adjutant of the regiment Feb , 1864. Participated in the battles of Chancellorsville, Gettysburg, Haymarket, Mine Run and Wilderness, where he was taken prisoner, May 5, was kept at Macon, Savannah, and Charleston, most of the time, was one of our officers who were under *our fire* in the old Charleston jail, and of course suffered fearfully at the hands of our " erring brothers " as did all others who fell into their hands, was exchanged May 5, 1865, and discharged with the regiment June 7, 1865. Brevetted major, Sept., 1866.

381 LUTHER LYMAN⁷, 4th son of Dea. *Silas⁶*, m. Nov. 7, 1827, Betsey Stedman, b. at Loraine, N. Y., Jan. 5, 1807 — farmer; d. Jan. 20, 1869.   *Sheboygan Falls, Wis.*

Children, Eighth Generation:

418 1 Martha, b. Feb. 22, 1829 ; m. at Sacketts Harbor, N. Y.,
July 4, 1846, Levi Eastman, who d. Oct. 18, 1864.
Ch. 9th Gen.: 1 Seymour L.— 2 Edward, twins, b. in
Rodman, Jefferson Co., N. Y., July 21, 1851. 3 Nora, b.
in. Rodman, May 29, 1861. 4 Willie, b. in Plymouth,
Sheboygan Co., Wis., Aug. 13. 1864 ; d. Sept. 30, 1865.

423 2 Sophia, b. July 20, 1831 ; m. at Smithville, Jefferson Co.,
N. Y., July 4, 1852, David Reed.
Ch. 9th Gen.: 1 Emory, b. in Loraine, N. Y., Sept.
21, 1853. 2 Clarence, b. at Sheboygan Falls, Wis., Sept.
30, 1858. 4 Lettie J., b. at Sheboygan Falls, April 26,
1861. 4 Jennie, b. at the falls, Dec. 1, 1865.

429. 3 William B., b. Dec. 15, 1833 ; enlisted in the service of his
country, Sept. 15, 1861, in the first regiment of volunteers ; was honorably promoted to various ranks and mortally wounded in the battle of Chickamauga ; removed to
Louisville, Ky., by a tedious journey of twelve days,
where he d. Jan. 10, 1864.

429 4 Semantha, b. May 31, 1836 ; m. at Rodman, July 3, 1853.
Dennis Eastman.
Ch. 9th Gen.: 1 Nettie, b, at Rodman, March 6, 1855 ;
d. April 9, 1862. 2 Henry W., b. at Rodman, Oct. 6,
1857. 3 Charles A., b. Aug. 9, 1861, at Lyndon, Wis,
4 Herman, b. at Lyndon, Jan. 26, 1866.

434 5 Vashti, b. June 14, 1839 ; res. Sheboygan Falls, Wis.

435 6 Julia, b. April 26, 1842 ; m. at Sheboygan Falls, March 10,
1862, De Witt Sweeting.
Ch. 9th Gen.: 1 Flora Bell, b. Nov. 23, 1862. 2 Charles
D., b. Oct. 30, 1864. 3 Ella J., b. Oct. 16, 1866.
4 William H., b. Nov. 23, 1868 ; all b. at Sheboygan
Falls.

440 7 Birney G., b. June 26, 1845.

441 8 Timothy Preston, b. May 24, 1849.

442 9 Harrison H., b. July 28, 1851.

VIII. DESCENDANTS OF RICHARD[3], THROUGH LIEUT. JONATHAN[4].

Lieut. JONATHAN LYMAN[4], 5th son of *Richard[3]*, b. 1684,
removed with his father from Northampton, Mass., to Lebanon, Conn., A.D. 1696, where he lived a farmer and m.
Lydia Loomis, who d. July 10, 1775. He d. at Lebanon,
Conn. 1753. *Lebanon, Conn.*

Children, Fifth Generation:

1 1 Jonathan, b. Sept. 19, 1708 ; d. early.

2 2 Lydia, b. Nov. 23, 1709 ; m. Thomas Webster, Aug. 17, 1727.

3   3 Jonathan, b. April 23, 1712.
4   4 Sarah, b. Jan. 24, 1713 ; m. William Hunt, Dec. 19, 1734.
5   5 Hannah, b. Feb. 15. 1715 ; m. Simeon Hunt, July 29, 1736.
6   6 Joseph, b. July 3, 1718.
7   7 Jacob, } twins, b. May 4, 1721.   Rachel, m. May 15, 1745,
8   8 Rachel, }   Edmund Grandy.   Jacob, m. June 26, 1745,
            Mehitable Burhnell.
9   9 Zeriah, b. April 14, 1723 ; m. Samuel Bushnell, Oct. 5, 1743.
10 10 Elijah, b. July 21, 1727 ; m. Esther Clark, Dec. 14, 1749.
11 11 Anna, b. Jan. 28, 1731; m. May 19, 1748, Isaiah Tiffany,
            of Norwich, Ct., and had a daughter b. July 11, 1769, who
            m. a Robinson, and d. at Lebanon, Sept. 1, 1871, aged
            one hundred and two years, one month, and twenty days,
            the oldest on record in the book, and the last survivor of
            the sixth generation.   She was familiarly acquainted with
            many of the officers of the Revolutionary war, and recalled
            to the last of life the names and personal appearance of
            many of the officers of a legion of French cavalry who in
            1780, were for some time stationed in her native place.
            This venerable woman is the sole representative of the great
            Lyman Family, not less perhaps than 15,000 in number
            who has attained to the age of one hundred years.

1 Jonathan Lyman[5], m. Bethiah Clark, Oct. 2, 1735 ;
resided in Lebanon, Conn.; was a farmer, also a tanner
and currier; d. July 28, 1792, aged 80   *Lebanon, Conn.*

   Children, Sixth Generation :
12   1 Jonathan, b. May 8, 1737.
12   2 William, b. Aug. 12, 1838.
14   3 Rachel, b. March 20, 1740 ; m. —— Emmons, Nov. 2, 1791.
15   4 Bethiah, b. Oct. 15, 1741 ; m. Joseph Leach, Oct. 17, 1765.
16   5 Lydia. b. Dec. 11, 1743 ; d. 1750.
17   6 Sarah, b. Jan. 8, 1747 ; d. 1750.
18   7 Joseph, b. April 3, 1749.
19   8 Lydia, b. Aug. 1, 1751; m. Elias Peck, Oct. 4, 1787.
20   9 Eliphalet, b. March 5, 1754.
21   10 David, b May 11, 1756 ; d. May 14, 1760.
22   11 Asa, b. Oct. 31, 1757.

12 Rev. Jonathan Lyman, b. May 8, 1737; graduated
at Yale College 1858; was tutor from 1760 to '65. He d.
in Springfield, May 4, 1766, while on his way from Hatfield to visit his friends in Lebanon, Conn.; a young man
of remarkable endowments and rare attainments. His
funeral sermon was preached at Springfield, by the Rev.
Mr. Breck. An oration was also delivered in Hatfield, by
Ebenezer Baldwin, Esq., of New Haven. At college he

outshone his equals, and justly acquired the character of a first-rate scholar in all branches of academic learning, alike conspicuous and beloved as a friend, a gentleman, a scholar and a Christian. He never married.

15 BETHIAH LYMAN⁶, m. Joseph Leach, Oct. 17, 1765.

Children, Ninth Generation:

24 1 Jonathan, b. Oct. 6, 1756; d. April 14, 1767.
25 2 Jonathan, b. June 21. 1768; d. Jan. 12, 1790, aged 21.
26 3 Joseph, b. March 3, 1770.
27 4 Isaac, b. May 2, 1772; d. April 4, 1773.
28 5 Isaac, b. April 9. 1774.
29 6 Amos, b. April, 1777.
30 7 Bethiah, b. June 25, 1781.

13 WILLIAM LYMAN⁶, *Jonathan⁵, Jonathan⁴, Richard³, Richard², Richard¹,* 1738–1827; m. Mary Parker of Lebanon, Feb. 12, 1761, " by Rev. Solomon Williams, D.D." Resided in Lebanon, was a farmer, tanner and currier, also a shoemaker, &c. He was an esteemed member of the Congregational church, and during his latter days manifested the zeal, faith, and submission of a ripe Christian. In his advanced age, he was accustomed to go to church in a " one horse shay," driving for many years the same old black horse. The horse declined faster than his master, and was put upon the superannuated list, but his habits had become fixed and he would still go to meeting. If confined on the sabbath he manifested great uneasiness, and when the gate was opened, trotted down to the meeting house and stood at his post until the meeting ended; and then returned remaining in perfect contentment while going to church regularly on the sabbath. A horse in Amherst, Mass., well known to the author, for many years, conveyed an aged couple to meeting in a similar " shay " repeatedly going without a driver by similar force of habit, stopping at the horse block, then going to the stall.

In the life time of Mr. Lyman a heated controversy arose in Lebanon about the location of a church, which illustrates the spirit of the times; and, with circumstantial variations, stands as an example of controversies often enacted in New England, on similar occasions.

In the height of their excitement one party set fire to the old " meeting-house," but failing in their object, the other party committed an equal sacrilege on the old church with their axes, breaking up the pews and hewing the

18

timbers.   On the sabbath following, the contending parties
met in the school house for public worship.   Their pastor
proposed to these discordant assailants of himself and his
church to sing the 74th Psalm as paraphrased by Dr. Watts:

> Will God forever cast us off?
> His wrath forever smoke
> Against the people of his love
> His little chosen flock?

> How are the seats of worship broke!
> They tear the building down ;
> And he that deals the heaviest stroke
> Procures the chief renown.

> With flames they threaten to destroy
> Thy children in their rest,
> Come, let us burn at once, they cry
> The temple and the priest.

The chorister, an active agent in the sacrilege, confused
and trembling, set his pitch pipe, the tuning instrument of
the day, upon B flat, and sounded the note, but had no
voice to lead the song.   The result was that two churches
were erected a mile apart, and two feeble antagonistic as-
semblies formed, who might have remained a powerful
central church harmoniously meeting for worship in the great
congregation age after age.

Mary, wife of William Lyman, d. June 8, .1792, and
he m. Theodah Williams, Oct. 24, 1793.   She d. Oct. 2,
1821.   William Lyman, d. April 2, 1827.   *Lebanon, Ct.*

Children, Seventh Generation :

31 1 Molly, b. June 28, 1762.
32 2 William, b. Sept. 5, 1764.
33 3 Sarah, b. Oct. 2, 1766 ; d. 1791.
34 4 Elizabeth, b. Sept. 1, 1768.
35 5 Clarissa, b. Oct. 31, 1771.
36 6 Jonathan, b. Oct. 15, 1773 ; d. 1798.
37 7 Asa, b. Feb. 24, 1777.
38 8 Lydia, b. Nov. 28, 1781.
39 9 Joseph, b. Aug. 15, 1783.

31 MOLLY[7], eldest dau. of *William and Mary Lyman*[6], m.
Zabdiel Hyde, Dec. 8th, 1785, Lebanon afterwards in Bath,
Me. ; d. May 15, 1842.   She d. Aug. 31, 1815.   *Bath, Me.*

Children, Eighth Generation :

40 1 Zabdial, b. Sept. 24, 1786.
41 2 William, b. May 27, 1788.

42   3 Jonathan Lyman, b. Jan. 15, 1790.
43   4 Henry, b. Aug. 25, 1791.
44   5 Gershom, b. Oct. 2, 1793.
45   6 Maria, b. June 10, 1796.
46   7 Henrietta, b. Feb. 11, 1798.
47   8 Edwin Augustus, b. April 23, 1800 ; d. April 14, 1811.
48   9 Lucy Philomela, b. Jan. 26, 1802.
49 10 Elijah Clark, b. Nov. 29, 1804.

40 ZABDIAL HYDE[8], m. Julia Ely, Sept. 24, 1812. He
d. Oct. 27, 1851, New York city. His wife d. Aug. 1870.

41 DEA. WILLIAM HYDE[8], m. Julia Douglass. He d.
Aug. 18, 1870. Resided in Bangor, Me., wife still living.

42 JONATHAN LYMAN HYDE[8], m. Laura Ely, dau. of Rev.
Zebulon Ely of Lebanon. Part of his life he resided in
Pittsfield, and was a teacher in the High School. Afterward
he went to Missouri where he d. Oct. 21, 1851. *Missouri.*

43 DEA. HENRY HYDE[8], m. 1st, Maria Hyde, of Lebanon,
June 8, 1818; d. Jan., 1820; m. 2d, Elizabeth Herrick
Lovett, Nov. 6, 1827.   *Bath, Me.*
          Children, Ninth Generation :
50 1 William Lyman, b. Dec. 27, 1819.
51 2 Elizabeth Maria, b. Feb. 11, 1829 ; d. April, 1835. •
52 3 Henry Augustus, b. Nov. 20, 1831.
53 4 John Wallace, b. Oct. 26, 1835; d. Jan. 12, 1837.

44 GERSHOM HYDE[8], m. Sarah Hyde, of Lebanon, Jan.
3, 1821.   *Bath, Me.*
          Children, Ninth Generation :
54 1 Maria, m. E. K. Alden, of South Boston, Mass.
55 2 Sarah, m. Rev. J. J. Hill, home missionary, formerly at the
        West.
56 3 Abby Ann, m. Rev. G. F. Magoun, of Iowa College, and for
        many years president.
57 4 Harriet.

45 MARIA HYDE, m. Asa Palmer, May 11, 1826.
                                                  Bath, Me.
          Children, Ninth Generation :
58 1 Edward Stanton, b. April 20, 1827.
59 2 Henry Edwin, b. June 17, 1829.
60 3 Asa Clark, b. Feb. 12, 1830.
61 4 Maria Hyde, b. June 30, 1832 ; d. Nov., 1841.
62 5 Lois Caroline, b. June 3, 1834.
63 6 Gershom Hyde, b. March 2, 1836.

64 7 Henrietta, b. July 2, 1838.
65 8 Mercy Julia, b. Oct. 28, 1840.

46 HENRIETTA HYDE, m. Samuel Donnell, July 2, 1820;
d. Oct. 15, 1825. He m. Lucy P. Hyde, April 11, 1827;
Samuel Donnell, d. Dec. 17, 1837; Lucy P. Donnell m.
again, Ebenezer Arnold, Dec. 13, 1843.   *Bath, Me.*

Children, Ninth Generation .
66 1 Matey Lyman, b. April 22, 1821.
67 2 Calvin Chaddoc, b. Sept. 17, 1824; d. 1826.
68 3 Henrietta H., b. Jan. 5, 1828.
69 4 Jane Barstow, b. Sept. 7, 1829.
70 5 Laura Ely, b. Oct. 11, 1832; d 1836.
71 6 Calvin Chaddoc, b. June 24, 1836.
72 7 Henry C. Arnold, b. Nov. 27, 1844; d. 1870; wife still living.

49 ELIJAH C. HYDE, m. Adaline Lyman, 1830.   *New York.*
Children, Ninth Generation :
73 1 Anna.   76 4 C. W. Gillam.
74 2 Rhoda.   77 5 Lucy.
75 3 Robert.

32 Rev. WILLIAM LYMAN[7], D.D., of Millington, a parish
in the town of East Haddam, Conn. son of William Lyman
of Lebanon, Conn., b. at Lebanon, 6th Sept., 1764, educated
at Yale College where he graduated in the class of 1786,
served a brief term as tutor in his *alma mater.* He was a
chaplain with the troops under Gen. Shepard, during the
Shays rebellion.

Dr. Lyman was a man of uncommon bodily strength;
and 288℔s. weight.

He settled in Millington in the year 1784, where he remained thirty-six years in an uninterrupted pastorate. He
afterwards removed to western New York, where he continued ministerial labors, in the churches of Mount Morris
and Le Roy for a time. He died at Arcade, N. Y., in Nov.,
1832.

At his installation in Millington he was quite young, in
fact, and still younger in appearance. His trial sermon
before the ordaining council, was highly satisfactory, insomuch that a member ventured the suggestion that a more
experienced hand than his had been employed upon it.

Mr. Lyman was a good preacher and was made more
impressive by the uncommon compass of his voice. He
was never fatigued by speaking. He has been known to
speak nine hours in a day. The power of his voice was a

quality that aided to individualize him.   When it fell to him to preach the "election sermon" at Hartford, a gentleman on his way to that city invited his neighbor in Farmington to go with him to hear and see the proceedings.

"No," said he, "I am very busy, but when the hour comes, I am going up into the mountain to hear the sermon"—10 miles distant.

Dr. Lyman sat as a prince in his parish in virtue of the influence that he had fairly earned, and a remnant is still left of those who ardently cherish his memory.   Many of his occasional sermons were published.   Some of them remain in the memory of his people.   Upon a funeral occasion, when there was no preacher present, a lady who had committed to memory one of Dr. Lyman's funeral sermons, upon invitation, repeated it, and thus all the proper rites of the occasion were filled.   He m. Rhoda Huntington, Dec. 24, 1789.   She was b. at Lebanon, Ct., June 11, 1767.

Children, Eighth Generation :

78   1 Sarah, b. Jan. 26, 1791 ; m. Nathan Barlow.
79   2 Bethiah, b. July 12, 1792 ; m. Allen Ayrault, Sept. 9, 1822, of Geneseo, N. Y.
80   3 William, b. Nov. 8, 1793 ; m. Nancy Jones, Feb. 5, 1821 ; Moscow, N. Y.
81   4 Rhoda, b. March 10, 1796 ; d. March 16, 1798.
82   5 Rhoda H., b. July 5, 1801; m. Col. C. O. Shepard, Dec., 1836; d. Sept. 22, 1859.
83   6 Huntington, b. April 25, 1803 ; m. Frances Kingman, April 25, 1839.
84   7 Adeline Cornelia, b. Oct. 23, 1804; m. Elijah C. Hyde, Jersey City.
85   8 Lucretia Caroline, b. July 6, 1806 ; m. Col. Reuben Sleeper, 1827 ; Mt. Morris, N. Y.
86   9 Ralston Walley, b. Oct. 4, 1809 ; m. Harriet N. Tracy, 1833, and Lucinda Parker, Jan. 23, 1862 ; Arcade, N. Y.
87   10 Mary Barker, b. Oct. 4, 1812 ; m. Wm. Bond, Dec. 15, 1841 ; d. July 1, 1850.

80 WILLIAM LYMAN[8], b. Nov. 6, 1793 ; m. Nancy Jones Feb. 5, 1821.   *Moscow, N. Y.*

Children, Ninth Generation :

89   1 William, b. May 21, 1822, one child, no name, b. Jan. 1, 1870.
90   2 Ann, b. Jan. 20, 1824 ; d. March 22, 1843.
91   3 Jane, b. Jan. 3, 1826 ; Nov. 1, 1840.
92   4 Mary, b. Dec. 10, 1828 ; m. Cutler and Shepard.
93   5 Julia, b. Nov. 12, 1830 ; m. Prettyman, lives at Chicago.
94   6 Harriet, b. May 15, 1835.
95   7 Sarah, b. March 10, 1838 ; m. Watkins.
96   8 Robert, b. Feb. 8, 1842, cashier at Titusville.

83 RHODA H. LYMAN[8], m. Charles O. Shepard, of Arcade,
N. Y., Dec., 1836.

Children, Ninth Generation:

97 1 Mary Shepard, b. 1839; m. James B. Parker in 1859; Buffalo, N. Y.; has two sons.

98 2 Charles Otis Shepard, b. 1842; served as lieut. in the war of
the rebellion; was appointed in 1869 as consul to Japan;
Yedo, Japan.

98 COL. CHARLES OTIS SHEPARD, U. S. consul at Yedo,
Japan, son of Charles Otis Shepard and Rhoda H. Lyman Shepard, of Arcade, N. Y.; was b. at Arcade, 1842.
He enlisted in the early days of the rebellion, and was soon
promoted to a lieutenancy, in which capacity he served
during the war. His aptness as a drill-master and clerk
led to heavy drafts upon his energies. He returned home
to Buffalo. He labored in the organization of the "frontier
police," and enstamped upon that organization the seal of
his genius. He became a colonel. He threw himself into.
the canvass, which resulted in the election of Gen. Grant to
the presidency. Under the administration to whose accession he had contributed, he was appointed consul at
Japan, to reside at Yedo. The running down of the
U. S. ship Oneida off the coast of Japan, called the consul
to vigorous but unsuccessful efforts to save the crew. In the
disaster by explosion at Yedo, in which Missionary Cornes,
his wife and child were destroyed, Consul Shepard exerted himself to better effect. When Hon. W. H. Seward
visited Japan, the pleasure of entertaining him, on account
of sickness in the family of the American minister, devolved upon Consul Shepard; and thus, when Mr. Seward
went into the presence of the Mikado, Mr. Shepard was
also admitted — an honor never before attained by one of
his rank. Mr. Shepard, though the youngest, is one of the
most efficient and useful of American consuls.

Yedo, Japan.

83 REV. HUNTINGTON LYMAN[7], was the 2d son of Rev.
William Lyman, D.D., of Millington, where he was b.
April 25, 1803. His parents desired to give him a collegiate education, and to that end some progress was made
in the study of the Latin classics. Pecuniary stringency
following the war of 1812, however, interrupted the plan,
and Huntington entered a clerkship opened to him by his
older brother in Sparta, and in Moscow, N. Y. After
completing his apprenticeship he became a partner of that

brother, and pursued a prosperous business for seven years in China, N. Y. At this stage of his life he became in the military line, inspector of brigade.

In 1831, the Amer. S. School Union being desirous to fill the valley of the Mississippi with Sunday schools, invited Mr. Lyman to enter their service and to have charge of the Sunday school depository at New Orleans; which he did. The influence of the climate was unfriendly and compelled him after severe sickness to abandon his position and return to a northern latitude.

On his way, he met at Cincinnati, friends who had gathered with the purpose of entering Lane Seminary which was awaiting the arrival of Dr. Beecher and other professors. The proposal was here made to Mr. Lyman, to join those who were to constitute the first theological class of the new institution. Although the difficulties in the way of this step were great, they were overcome. After spending a short time in the preparatory course, Mr. Lyman was admitted as a member of the first formed class of that seminary, not on a college diploma but on the score of " general attainments."

Two years of happy sociality and earnest study under beloved teachers ensued.

American slavery was at that day an apple of discord and a theme of public debate. The institution was anti-slavery in all its parts, but it was divided upon the question of colonization. A great majority of the students were for unconditional abolition, and opposed to the scheme of colonization. This difference, through the action of the executive committee became the occasion of a rupture. The executive committee, persons unknown to the students prepared a code of laws which a majority of the students, thought oppressive, and decided not to enter for another term under them. Mr. Lyman was one of those who for this cause took letters of dismission.

He immediately became a member of Oberlin Theological Seminary, where he completed his studies. He was ordained in 1836. He accepted a commission from the American Anti-slavery Society, and as a lecturer, performed for it, in stormy times, a brief service. Then he became pastor of a church in Buffalo, N. Y. In 1845, he removed to the territory of Wisconsin. As a home missionary, he spent at Sheboygan the greater part of the fifteen years of his life in that region. Returning in 1860, to New York, he has up to this date, 1872, devoted him-

self to the duties of his profession, at Marathon, N. Y.
When the rebellion broke out, Mr. Lyman exerted all his
powers to rally loyal soldiers and to sustain and cheer
those at the front. He m. Frances Kingman, April 25,
1839.   *Marathon, N. Y.*
        Children, Ninth Generation:
89 I Theodore Weld, b. Jan. 25, 1840; a farmer in Homer, N. Y.

   85 LUCRETIA C. LYMAN[8], m. Reuben Sleeper, Esq., of Mount
Morris, N. Y. April 8, 1827.   *Mount Morris, N. Y.*
        Children, Ninth Generation:
99 1 Caroline Augusta, b. Aug. 5, 1830; d. May 27, 1832.
100 2 Lucretia Maria, b. March 5, 1832; m. H. Kellogg, April,
        1854, merchant, Jackson, Mich.
101.3 Caroline Louisa, Aug. 28, 1834; d. Feb. 25, 1837.
102 4 Emma Cornelia, b. Nov. 26, 1836, wife of W. G. King, d.
        May 5, 1865.
103 5 William Lyman, Nov. 18, 1838; d. Dec. 1, 1838.
104 6 Albert Huntington, b. July 2, 1841; d. June 29, 1842.
105 7 Frank Hamilton, b. July 27, 1846·

   86 RALSTON WALLEY LYMAN[8], son of *Rev. Wm. Lyman,
D.D.*, of Castile, New York, m. Harriet N. Tracy, in
1833, and m. Lucinda Parker, Jan. 23, 1862, merchant.
                                         Castile N. Y.
        Children, Ninth Generation:
106 I Theodore Huntington, b. Aug. 13, 1835; m. May 8, 1866,
        Armira W. Clough (widow), merchant, Castile, N. Y.
107 2 Robert Ralston, b. June 13, 1837; m. Sarah A. Hubbard,
        Feb. 14, 1865, farmer, Valmont, Col. Ter.
108 3 Jacob Pierce, b. Feb. 14, 1844, professor, Grinnell, Ia.
109 4 Ralston Parker, b. Oct. 1, 1869; son of second wife.

   87 MARY B. LYMAN[8], dau. of *Rev. Wm. Lyman, D.D.*,
m. William Bond of Geneseo, N. Y., Dec. 15, 1841.
        Children, Ninth Generation:
110 1 Nella, b. Nov. 1843, Geneseo, N. Y.
111 2 Mary, b. May, 1846. teacher in Female Seminary, Buffalo, N.Y.
112 3 Carrie Bond,   } twins.
113 4 Nancy H. Bond, } b. July 1, 1850. Nancy H., d. 1863.

   106 THEODORE H. LYMAN[9].   *Castile, N. Y*
        Children, Tenth Generation:
115 I Harriet Caroline, b. Aug. 6, 1868.
115 2 Myrta Alice, b. Jan. 27, 1870.

   107 ROBERT RALSTON LYMAN[9].

Children, Tenth Generation.

116 ı Harriet Gratia, b. Jan. 11, 1870.
117 2 Henry A., b. March 7, 1871.

34 Elizabeth Lyman[7], b. 1768; m. Carey Throop, Nov.
26, 1788; d. Feb. 27, 1834; he d. Nov. 26, 1830; his grandchildren are numerous — scythe maker. *Norwich, Conn.*
' *Children, Eighth Generation :*
118 ı Sally, b. Sept. 7, 1790; d. March, 1804.
119 2 Betsey Lyman, b. Nov. 29, 1793; m. Coit; d. Oct. 30, 1860.
120 3 Carey b. March 22, 1797; d. Sept. 15, 1821.
121 4 Mary, b. April 5, 1799; d. July 1, 1808.
122 5 Jonathan T., b. June 28, 1801; d. May 17, 1860.
123 6 William, b. July 16, 1802.
124 7 Thomas L., b. June 16, 1804; d. Oct. 26, 1860.
125 8 Joseph, b. June 14, 1808; d. 1809.
126 9 Sarah Maria, b. March 18, 1812; d. July, 1844.

35 Clarissa Lyman[7], b. 1770; m. 1795, Isaac Leech, a
saddler; d. Feb. 4, 1863, at Fayetteville, N. Y
Fayetteville.
Children, Eighth Generation :
128 ı Clarissa, b. Nov. 14, 1796; m. Daniel Evans, of Fayetteville.
129 2 Mary L., b. Dec. 15, 1798; m. Lucius Evans, of Fayetteville.
130 3 Joseph, b. June, 27, 1806; lives at McGrawville.
131 4 Sarah Bethiah, b. July 5, 1810; m. Dr. Lord, April 27, 1852.
132 5 Amos Leech, b. June 18, 1812; d. at Virgil, N. Y., 1864.
Of the above, Clarissa, Mary and Amos have children and grandchildren.

37 Rev. Asa Lyman[7], b. Feb. 24, 1777, at Lebanon,
Conn.; d. at Clinton, N. Y., 1836; m. Mary Benedict, Jan.
1, 1800. She was a dau. of Aaron Benedict of Middlebury Conn.; d. 1865. Mr. Lyman graduated at Yale
College about 1797, was ordained about the year 1800, to
the Congregational ministry. Very early in his ministerial
career, which opened with much promise, he was compelled by ill health to abandon his calling and undertake
that of teaching. Returning health led him to resume
the duties of the profession he so much loved, only to be
again compelled to return to the office of a teacher of
youth. In 1820, he had a boarding school at Jamaica,
L.I., in 1825, preached at Chatham, N. J., in 1828, he
removed to New York city editing for a time the *Youth s
Journal*, removed in 1832, to Buffalo, N. Y., had a boar -
ing school in Skeneateles; in 1834, removed to Clinton, at
19

which place he d. in 1836. All his life he was struggling against the inroads of pulmonary disease, resuming ministerial labor whenever an improvement in his health or a change of climate encouraged him to do so. For many years before his death he did not attempt any regular charge, officiating only occasionally as he found himself able. He taught at Kennebunk, Boston, Buffalo and Clinton.   *Clinton, N. Y.*

Children, Eighth Generation:

132   1 Sereno Edwards, b. 1802; d. an infant.
133   2 Elizabeth Trowbridge, b. 1803; m. Robert Smith, d. without issue.
134   3 Mary Ann Benedict, b. 1806; m. 1837, Rev. Ebenezer Mead, a Presbyterian minister of Le Roy, N. Y., where he d. in 1841.
135   4 Caroline Barker, b. 1807.
136   5 Louisa Shipman, b. 1810.
137   6 Julia Douglass, b. 1813; d. 1837.
138   7 Theodore Benedict, b. Feb. 15, 1816.
139   8 Dwight Edwards, b. 1818, educated at Columbia College, Roman Priest, Baltimore.

138 THEODORE BENEDICT LYMAN[8], D.D., b. at Brighton, Feb., 1816, graduated at Hamilton College, N. Y., 1837, entered the General Theological Seminary of the Protestant Episcopal church in 1837, and was ordained in Baltimore, in 1840. From 1840 to 1850, he was rector of St. John's church, Hagerstown, Md. From 1850 to 1860, he was rector of Trinity church, Pittsburgh. From 1860 to 1870, he was residing in Europe and during a part of that time was acting as American Chaplain in Rome, Italy. Since December, 1870, he has been rector of Trinity church, San Francisco. Dr. Lyman was m. in 1845, Anna Margaret Albert, of Baltimore.

San Francisco, Cal.

Children, Ninth Generation:

140   1 Albert Benedict.   143   4 Theodore Benedict.
141   2 Fanny Augusta.   144   5 Augustus Julian.
142   3 William Whittingham.   145   6 Anna Cornelia.

38 LYDIA LYMAN[7], dau. of *William Lyman* of Lebanon, b. 1781; m. Joseph Parsons of Enfield, Conn., July 24, 1832; d. May 7. 1849. He died in 1837. She was a woman of excellent social qualities and of very good sense when at home in the country. But in the city she made many grotesque failures, one of which is here related. While visiting in New York, she was attracted, by a notice

of a meeting of the Bible Society, at the City Hotel. At the hour appointed she was working her way through the crowd in the streets to the place appointed. Arriving at the hall, she found it already crowded. On descending, she met the usual throng in Broadway, all going, *as she supposed, to the Bible meeting.* Her own disappointment being fresh in mind, she addressed first one and then another group: " You can't get in." This address was only returned by a look of curiosity while the crowd swept on. Finding that her well intended effort made no impression, she said: " Well, try it if you will, but I've just been there, and the hall is full." *Enfield, Conn.*

39 JOSEPH LYMAN[7], *William*[6], *Jonathan*[5], *Jonathan*[4], *Richard*[3], *Richard*[2], *Richard*[1], 1783 – 1860; m. Clarissa Rockwell, May 1, 1808; she d. Jan. 6, 1855, aged 74; he d. Aug. 21, 1860, aged 77. *Lebanon, Ct.*

Children, Eighth Generation :
146 1 Jonathan, b. Aug. 10 1810; living in Lebanon.
147 2 Sereno, b. May 28, 1812.
148 3 William, b. Dec. 11, 1814,
149 4 Jane, b. Nov. 24, 1816; living in Lebanon.
150 5 Rhoda, b. April 26, 1819; d. June 22, 1846.
151 6 Sarah, b. Sept. 17, 1821 ; living in Lebanon.

147 SERENO LYMAN[8], m. Mrs. Mary Adams, at Defiance, Ohio, March 18, 1845; he d. at Big Grove, Iowa, Aug. 13, 1857; his widow is still living in Defiance, Ohio. *Defiance.*

Children, Ninth Generation :
152 1 Clarissa, b. Sept. 3, 1849 ; d. April 9, 1854.

148 WILLIAM LYMAN[8], m. Sarah Pierce, of Lyons, Mich., March 20, 1839.

Children, Ninth Generation :
153 1 Joseph, b. Sept. 13, 1840; known as Major Joseph — lawyer ; m. Josie E. M. Smith, July 28, 1869 ; she d. Jan. 15, 1870 ; Council Bluffs, Iowa.
154 2 Sereno, b. March 6, 1742 ; m. Eunice Reynolds, July 25, 1869, Big Grove, Iowa.
155 3 William, b. Oct. 27, 1844.
156 4 Emily, b. Feb. 5, 1848 ; d. March, 1848.
157 5 Rufus, b. Oct. 21, 1850.
158 6 Rhoda, b. Aug. 28, 1853.
159 7 Lucy Anna, b. Jan. 10, 1863.
The above children living were born at Defiance, Ohio, except Joseph, who was born at Lyons, Mich., and Lucy Anna, Big Grove, Iowa. *Defiance, O.*

153 JOSEPH LYMAN[9], *William*[8], *Joseph*[7], *William*[6], *Jonathan*[5], *Jonathan*[4], *Richard*[3], *Richard*[2], *Richard*[1]. The martial character of the sons of William Lyman of Iowa, is worthy of record. Three of his sons served against the rebellion with Iowa troops, bravely and with distinction. The two younger sons were not old enough to serve at the commencement of the war.

Joseph, however, the eldest, enlisted as a private at the breaking out of the war. Failing to secure a position in the 1st Iowa Regt. of Infantry, the company to which Joseph belonged, became a part of the 4th Iowa Cavalry as "Co. E." After serving as private and corporal of cavalry until Nov., 1862, a commission came unexpectedly from the Gov. appointing him adjutant of the 29th Regt. of Infantry, which he accepted. He was the youngest officer, and, with few exceptions, the youngest man in the Regt. The only vacancy occurring in the offices above him was that of major, to which by general voice, Mr. Lyman was promoted. In 1864, Maj. Lyman was in the staff of Gen. S. A. Rice, and was by the side of that officer when he received his mortal wound. During the last year of the war Maj. Lyman served as adjutant general in the staff of Maj. General F. Steele. Major Lyman was mustered out of service in 1865, after the surrender of the rebel armies. Desirous to retain him in the military service, a commission in the regular army was sent him which he declined. Maj. Lyman was in very active service which led him, with the exception of N. and S. Carolina and Va., into all the rebel states. Aside from frequent skirmishes the following is the list of battles in which he participated, Helena, Ark., July 4, 1863; Little Rock, Sept. 10, 1863; Terre Noir Creek, April, 1864; Prairie De Anne, April 1864; Camden, April, 1864; Saline River, April, 1864; Bluff Springs, Fl., March, 1865; siege of Mobile, April 29, 1865. During more than four years service at the front Maj. Lyman was never wounded, though he had two horses killed under him.

Sereno and William, brothers of the foregoing Major Lyman, becoming of sufficient age, enlisted in 1864 in Co. C, in the same—24th Regt.—with their brother, where they served to the end of the war. A commission as captain of a negro company was tendered to Sereno, which, as it involved the necessity of serving longer than the duration of the war, was for that reason declined. *Council Bluffs, Ia.*

19 Rev. JOSEPH LYMAN[6], D.D., of Hatfield, was b. April 14, 1749, at Lebanon, and was the son of Jonathan and Bethia Lyman. He m. Oct. 15, 1772, Hannah Huntington, dau. of Simon and Sarah of Lebanon, Ct. Graduated at Yale, in 1769, with high honors. After a popular tutorship there, he was ordained 4th March, 1772, pastor of the Congregational church in Hatfield, Mass., where, for over half a century he served the church and society, with great ability, and wielded a marked influence among the ministry and churches of western Massachusetts. He used to ascribe much of his pastoral success, to his wife, whose ruling aim seemed to be, to promote his usefulness. He was one of the most commanding men in the ministry, in his day; and in nothing of a worldly nature, did he show more power over his contemporaries, than in giving shape to pulpit influence, during our Revolutionary struggle. His colleague, Rev. Dr. Waterbury, late of Boston, speaking of him, as he was in the last two years of his life, makes this just estimate of his character, and this is said after he had passed into a state of bodily infirmity, which, to use his forcible language, " gave to him, the aspect, somewhat, of a magnificient ruin. The heavy column, and the broad span of the arch, told, even in their dilapidation, the scale of grandeur, upon which the whole structure had been reared. The Roman cast of his features, his expressive eye, his simplicity of language, and manner, struck me very forcibly upon my first introduction to him." " This great and good man" d. March 27, 1828. He had seven children, only two of which survived him.

For 56 years Dr. Lyman was pastor of the church in Hatfield; a man of mark in his day, of great originality and decision of character, he exerted for many years a commanding influence in the state, especially in ecclesiastical councils, in settling controversies in the churches and theological discussions; many candidates for the ministry resorted to him for instruction in theology. From 1823 to 1826 he was president of the A. B. C. F. M.; the degree of S. T. D., he received from Williams College. Many anecdotes are related of him illustrative of his character and influence, of which the following may be given :

While he was ever true and faithful to the gospel, he was roused to great zeal and activity in promoting the revolution which resulted in the independence of our country.

He was associated with Caleb Strong and Isaiah Thomas in writing and publishing letters of the most stirring character. Nor did he fail in private, or in public, to exert all his powers in rousing and keeping alive the patriotism of the people. But his actions and his utterances, in this direction, did not fail to awaken opposition. A leading man of the parish was of different politics, and, of course, became indignant that his young minister should thwart and counteract him. Able to bear it no longer, he came one day into the parson's study, and, in an excited manner, exclaimed, "Mr. Lyman, I have gotten you here as my minister, and now you rise up against me. I shall not bear it." Mr. Lyman at once arose, assuming an attitude, at least as erect and commanding as his assailant, and said : " Sir, you have governed this town, and to a great extent, the county for a long time, but I now inform you there is one you will never govern." The rebuker, wrathful but abashed, hastened out of the room. But to his credit, be it said, after a little time he returned with an apology, and showed his nobility by saying: " Mr. Lyman, I shall ever honor your independence, and be more your friend than ever on account of it."

" Very soon after my own settlement in the ministry," says a cotemporary, " Dr. Lyman stopped for a few minutes at my house, saying as he came in, ' I am an Old Testament man, and call on ministers.' This was the introduction to my acquaintance with one whom I ever found cordial, interesting and instructive to an uncommon degree. What I particularly remember of his first call was, that after the door was quite closed at his departure, he came back and said, in a fatherly but most impressive manner, ' You are beginning the ministry, and I want to give you one charge ; always make Saturday *noon* your last limit for the full preparation of your sabbath sermons. Do this that you may relax, and refresh yourself in the afternoon ; have your nerves in such a state that you can sleep; and be in a proper physical condition for the labors of the pulpit.'

" I will add that my own experience, and the contrary experience of many of my brethren, have fully confirmed me in the wisdom and importance of the rule thus given me at my front door, more than fifty years ago."

Dr. Lyman m. Oct. 15, 1772, Hannah, dau. of Simon Huntington of Lebanon, Ct.; b. in Lebanon in 1749, she d. Aug. 10, 1829, aged 80 years. Dr. Lyman d. March 27, 1828, aged 79.   *Hatfield, Mass.*

Children, Seventh Generation :

160 1 Hannah, b. July 20, 1773; m. June 23, 1796, Colton Part-
ridge, of Hatfield, d. May 10, 1835, leaving nine children
living at her decease, one dau. m. David Whitney of
Northampton.

161 2 Fanny, b. April 7, 1775; m. Rev. E. Johns, of Canandaigua,
June 19, 1810; one son.

162 3 Joseph, b. June 2, 1777; d. 1784.

163 4 A son, b. Feb. 15, 1779; d. nameless.

164 5 Bethiah, b. 1780; d. 1787.

165 6 Jonathan Huntington, b. June 13, 1783.

166 7 Eunice, b. Feb. 28, 1786; d. young.

93 JONATHAN HUNTINGTON LYMAN[7], son of Dr. *Joseph*[6],
graduate of Yale College, 1802, removed to Northampton
in 1807, lawyer, m. Oct. 10, 1808, Sophia, dau. of Hon.
Samuel Hinckley of N. She d. April 6, 1839, aged 51
years and 6 months.

Children, Eighth Generation :

167 1 Joseph, b. at Northampton, Mass., July 14, 1809; m. Mary
A. Clarke, of West Haven, Conn., May 25, 1836, lawyer, Englewood, N. J.

 Ch. 9th Gen. : 1 Sophia, b. July 21, 1837; d. Sept.
6, 1837. 2 Samuel Hinckley, b. Jan. 26, 1839. 3 George
Clark, b. Sept. 20, 1840. 4 Joseph, July 26, 1843.

172 2 Samuel Hinckley, name changed to Sam. Lyman Hinckley, in
1831; b. Aug. 11, 1810, graduate of Williams Coll.   He
d. in Paris Dec. 1871; m. Henrietta E. Rose of Sumpter-
ville, S. C., who d. Dec. 20, 1838; m. 1849, Ann L.
Parker, Boston, now lives in Boston.

 Ch. 9th Gen.: By 1st wife one son, Henry Rose, b.
Oct. 20, 1828; graduated Yale, 1859; lieut. in Mass.
Cavalry during the rebellion; m. June 2, 1866, Mary, dau.
of Dr. Benjamin Barrett, of Northampton, where he now
lives, by profession a lawyer.   Samuel's 2d wife, Anna
C. Parker, was dau. of Hon. Samuel D. Parker, of
Boston.   By 2d wife: 1 Samuel Parker, b. Jan. 17,
1850, now undergraduate at Harvard. 2 Susan Green-
ough, b. May 15, 1851. 3 Robert Cutler, b. April 3,
1853. 4 Anna Cordelia, b. Dec. 15, 1857; d. Oct. 12,
1865.

178 3 Sally Outram, b. May 19, 1812; m. Dec. 30, 1834, Richard
L. Allen, of Buffalo, removed to New York City.   He d.
in Stockholm, Sweden, in 1870.

 Ch. 9th Gen. : 1 Richard Hinckley, b. Aug. 4, 1838,
now merchant in New York. 2 Mary Isabella, b. Dec.
2' 1840. 3 Huntington Lyman, b. June 6, 1843; d.
June 8, 1844. 4 Arthur Huntington, b. Oct. 20, 1851.

183 4 John Chester, b. Aug. 8, 1813, graduate of Harvard, 1833;
m. Jan. 24, 1854, Mary, dau. of Hon. Matthias Morris,

Ch. 9th Gen.: 1 John Huntington, b. at Philadelphia, Jan. 22, 1856; d. Dec. 1, 1857. 2 William Morris, b. at Philadelphia, Feb. 1, 1857; d. Aug. 12, 1857. 3 Arthur Meredith, b. at Doylestown, Oct. 8, 1858; d. Aug. 4, 1859. 4 Richard Morris, b. at Doylestown, Oct. 11, 1859. 5 Marion, b. at Doylestown, March 18, 1861. 6 Sophia Hinckley, b. at Doylestown, July 7, 1864. 7 Robert Huntington, b. at Doylestown, June 17, 1867.

191 5 Sophia Ann, b. April 14, 1815; m. Oct. 1, 1835, G. W. Phipps, d. Feb. 20, 1860.

Ch. 9th Gen.: 1 Frank Huntington, b. Aug. 9, 1843, graduated West Point 1863, now Bvt. Capt. U.S.A.; m. June 11, 1867, Louisa Hart Patterson, of St. Louis. 2 Ellen, b. Aug. 6, 1845.

194 6 Jonathan Huntington, b. Aug. 18, 1816, graduated M.D., at the University of Penn., 1840; m. 1847, Julia Dwight, of New Haven, m. Jan. 2, 1855; 2d wife, Mary Dwight, sister of his 1st wife. His wives, were daughters of Timothy Dwight of New Haven, and granddaughters on paternal side of President Timothy Dwight, and on maternal side of Gov. Caleb Strong. By 2d wife no issue.

Ch. 9th Gen.: 1 Edward Huntington, b. Oct. 14, 1848; d Feb. 17, 1852. 2 John Chester, b. May 27, 1851. 3 Francis Hinckley, b. Jan. 19, 1853; d. at San Benediction Hospital in the city of Para, Brazil, July 20, 1871, of yellow fever. He went to South America to study the natural history of the country, having very strongly-developed tastes in that direction, and his friends hoped much from the results of his expedition.

198 7 George Hinckley, b. Feb. 1, 1818; d. Feb. 11, 1819.

199 8 George Hinckley, b. July 18, 1819, graduated, M.D., University of Penn., 1843, removed to Boston 1845, Lt. Col., and medical inspector U.S.A., from 1861 to 1865; m. Oct. 14, 1846, Maria Cornelia Ritchie, dau. of Hon. James T. Austin, granddaughter of Elbridge Gerry, vice president of U. S. She d. Dec. 6, 1846. Dr. Lyman was senior brigade surgeon of U. S. Vols., being the 1st appointed in 1861, by commission from the president, and in 1863, appointed to Regular Army, as lieut. col., and medical inspector, thus from the first being highest in rank of all appointments in said service of the army from civil life. The mother of Maria C. R. was Catharine Gerry, dau. of Gov. Elbridge Gerry, Vice President U. S.

Ch. 9th Gen.: James Trecothick Austin, b. Aug. 27th 1847; d. May 6, 1850. 2 Catharine Maria, b. Oct. 11, 1848. 3 George Hinckley, b. Dec. 13, 1850. 4 Gerry Austin, March 5, 1855. 5 Bessie Huntington, b. Sept. 16, 1856.

205 9 David Hinckley, b. Nov. 21, 1820; graduated at Harvard, 1839; m. Sophia Doughty of Ravenna, Ohio; removed to Cleveland, Ohio, 1867, now lives in Pittsburg, Penn., a lawyer, and editor of *Pittsburg Gazette.*
> *Ch. 9th Gen.:* 1 Sophia Hinckley, b. Dec. 25, 1845; d. Nov. 12, 1848. 2 Katie Hinckley, b. Dec. 16, 1847; d. June 24, 1848. 3 Charles Hinckley, b. April 14, 1849, now cadet at Naval Academy, Annapolis. 4 Nellie and 5 Clara, b. Aug. 16, 1851; Clara, d. July 1852, and Nellie, d. Jan. 1853.

211 10 Hannah Huntington, b. Dec 15, 1821; m. Aug. 9, 1849, Rev. Charles Mason, D.D., pastor of Grace church, Boston, and son of Hon. Jeremiah Mason.
> *Ch. 9th Gen.:* 1 Anna Sophia L., b. Oct. 4, 1853. 2 Charles Jeremiah, b. Sept. 25, 1855. 3 Harriet Sargent, b. May 2, 1858. Her husband Charles Mason, d. March 23, 1862. She was his 2d wife, his first wife being Susan, dau. of Hon. Amos Lawrence by whom he had: [*Ch. 9th Gen.:* (1) Amos Lawrence. (2) Susan. (3) (4) Mary and Sarah, twins.]

218 11 Martha Prince, b. March 13, 1823; m. Oct. 4, 1860, L. F. S. Foster, of Norwich, Ct., lately senator and vice president of U. S., no issue.

220 12 Frances Sophia, b. March 12, 1824; m. May 5, 1853, W. W. Morland, M.D., of Boston, no issue.

221 13 Eleanor Dorothy Strong, b. Nov. 25, 1825; m. Oct. 5, 1858, T. J. Trist, of Philadelphia. Mute from early childhood, and her husband also mute, is now instructor in Deaf Mute Institution, of Philadelphia. He is great-grandson of Thomas Jefferson, his mother being Miss Randolph, of Va.

20 Rev. ELIPHALET LYMAN[6], 1753–1836, 4th son of *Jonathan[5], Jonathan[4], Richard[3],* b. in Lebanon, March 1753, graduated at Yale, 1776; studied theology in New Haven, Conn., settled as pastor of the church in Woodstock, 1779, which office he sustained until 1821; d. Feb. 2, 1836; m. 1779, Hannah Huntington, of Norwich, b. April 28, 1753; d. April 19, 1836. The pastor and his wife are buried in the church-yard with his people whom he served so long and so well, at Woodstock, Windham, Ct.

He was never detained from his pastoral duties on the Lord's day, by sickness, during his connection with the church. He was a liberal donor to all the benevolent institutions of his day. In 1820, the society contemplated building a new church, and at a meeting of the society for that purpose, it was proposed that a committee should first settle their accounts with their pastor. The committee accordingly attended to the settlement, and found, that there were certain sums left unpaid for the last sixteen years, which several sums, with the interest upon each to the time of settlement amounted to the sum of three thousand and three hundred dollars, Mr. Lyman, then told the committee, if they would give him a note for three hundred dollars he would cancel the obligation.

Children, Seventh Generation :

222   1 Hannah, b. June 15, 1780; d. June, 1864.
223   2 Eliphalet, b. Aug. 1781; d. about 1858.
224   3 John, b. July 3, 1783; d. Aug. 10, 1783.
225   4 Daniel, b. Sept. 5, 1784; d. March 5, 1870.
226   5 Polly, b. July 22, 1786.
227   6 Lucy, b. May 2, 1788; d. Jan. 6, 1791.
228   7 Asa, b. Oct. 15, 1789; d. March 25, 1789.
229   8 Asa, b. Feb. 19, 1792; d. Oct. 4, 1831.
230   9 Joseph, b. Aug. 26, 1794.
231   10 Huntington, b. March 8, 1797; d. Jan. 25, 1798.

222 HANNAH LYMAN[7], m. Chester May, of Woodstock, Dec. 24, 1806. He d. June, 1855. She d. June, 1864, buried in Woodstock, Ct.

Children, Eighth Generation :

232   1 Lucy, b. Nov. 22, 1807; d. Dec. 23, 1807.
233   2 Silas, b. Feb. 7, 1809; m. Harriet, dau. of Henry Perry, of Woodstock.
234   3 Lydia, b. Sept. 20, 1810.
235   4 Mary Ann, b. June 4, 1812; m. John Paine, of W., 1836.
236   5 Annette Maria, b. Oct. 29, 1813; m. Robert D. Fowler, of Canterbury, 1864.
237 6 Harriette, b. Feb. 28, 1815; d. May 11, 1825.
238 7 Eliphalet, b. Nov. 15, 1816; m. Harriet L. Stone, 1847.
239 8 Hannah, b. Dec. 8, 1819.
240 9 Nancy, b. March 18, 1823; m. Nathaniel Child, 1847.

223 DR. ELIPHALET LYMAN[7], eldest son of Rev. *Eliphalet[6]*, b. in Woodstock, Ct., May, 1781; was educated at Dartmouth College, Oct., 1805; m. Abigail, dau. of Rev. Sylvanus Ripley, of Hanover, N. H.; d. July 19, 1858; she d. June 10, 1827.

Children, Eighth Generation.

241   1 Annette Maria, b. at Stafford, Ct., Aug. 6, 1805; m. John Crockers, of Eaton, N. H., 1822; d. May 5, 1830.
242   2 Sylvanus Ripley, b. at Fryeburg, Me., Dec. 27, 1807; m. Caroline Beck, of Portland, Aug. 12, 1830; she d Sept., 1839; m. 2d wife, Christiana Blanchard, of Portland, Me., Aug. 4, 1842.

Ch. 9th Gen. : 1 Thomas Ripley, b. Sept. 21, 1832; m.
Anna A. Dow, Sept. 8, 1857. 2 Caroline Abigail, b.
Sept. 26, 1832; d. Aug. 7, 1833. 3 Caroline Martha, b.
May 19, 1835; d. May 16, 1840. 4 Henry Wheelock,
b. April 21, 1837; d. Aug. 14, 1838. 5 Caroline Beck,
b. July 23, 1839; d. March 14, 1840. 6 Ellen Blanchard, b. March 14, 1844; m. Henry Littlefield, Dec. 15,
1868. 7 Abby Ripley, b. Dec. 9, 1845. 8 Annie
Wheelock, b. April 30, 1849. 9 James Philips, b. Feb.
7, 1851. 10 Elizabeth D., b. Aug. 18, 1855. 11 Edward
Wheelock, b. Aug. 14, 1857; d. Jan. 15, 1863.

254 3 Elizabeth Huntington, b. at Fryeburg, Me., March 29, 1808.
. m. Jabez D. Philbrick, of Lancaster, N. H., Feb. 16, 1831.
255 4 James Wheelock, b. at Danville, Vt., May, 1810; m. 1833,
McMary Ring, of Lebanon, Me.

Ch. 9th Gen. : Mary Annette, b. April, 1834; d. Jan.,
1866. 2 Charles W., b. Jan., 1836, at Memphis, Tenn.
3 Lucy Abbie, b. Feb., 1842; Daniel Longfellow, 1861;
res. Machias, Me.

259 5 Caroline Abigail, b. at Guildhall, Vt., March 22, 1812; m.
April 20, 1842, Samuel Reynolds, of Griggsville, Ill.
260 6 Edward Huntington, b. at Lancaster, N. H., June 7, 1814;
was drowned in the Connecticut river, at S. Hadley, May,
1832.
261 7 Charles Philips, b. at Lancaster, June 3, 1816; m. Caroline
May, of Milton, Vt., June, 1851; d. in Jacksonville, Ill.,
Aug., 1862; she d. in Milton, Vt., Feb. 16, 1863.

Ch. 9th Gen. : 1 Lizzie Huntington, b. in St. Louis,
Mo., May 28, 1852. 2 Edward Huntington, b. in Griggsville, Ill., May 22, 1854. 3. Charles Philips, b. in Ho-
boken, N. J., May 23, 1856. 4 Walter Ray, b. in Ho-
boken, N. J., Nov. 6, 1857, d. Aug. 1855. 5 Arthur
W., b. in Griggsville, Ill., Aug. 17, 1859.

225 DANIEL LYMAN[7], M.D., was born in Woodstock,
Ct., Sept. 5, 1784, and what is a little remarkable, was taken
to church on the day of his birth—it being the sabbath—
and baptized by his father Eliphalet Lyman who was pastor
of the Congregational church in that village for 40 years.
Daniel fitted for college in the Woodstock Academy, and at
the time of his death was the only living member of the first
class which left that institution. He entered Yale about
the year 1805. He stood high in that institution as a
scholar, took an active part in debate and other exercises
connected with some one of the literary societies which
flourished there. During the latter part of his senior year
he was attacked with an affection of the heart, which ne-
cessitated his laying aside his studies for some months, so

that he failed to graduate with his class. He pursued a regular course in the medical department of Dartmouth under the instruction of the celebrated Dr. Smith. He was a remarkably apt scholar to whatever department of study he turned his attention. He commenced the practice of medicine and surgery in his native village, about the year 1809 or 1810, in which calling he had a wide and very successful practice for 40 years. He administered to the bodies of his fellow citizens of the surrounding region, for almost the identical period of time which it was the privilege of his honored father to prescribe for their spiritual maladies. He made a specialty of cases of epilepsy in the treatment of which he had remarkable success, having patients from every state of the Union. And he was not without honor in other departments : he held the office of judge of probate for several successive terms, during which time he had the decision of several very intricate cases. One case in particular on which he could get no light from high authority which he consulted, he at length decided according to his best judgment, which judgment was afterward confirmed and made the law of the state in such cases by legislative enactment. He had an almost intuitive perception and insight, into the merits of any matter brought before him. He was justice of the peace for many years. He feared no man. No flatteries, no bribes, no insinuations, no threats could move him a hair's breadth from what he considered a straight line. Of firm nerve, of undaunted courage, he was a terror to evil doers. He entered heartily into all matters of public, social, civil, or religious interest. In temperance he early advocated the principle of total abstinence, and delivered a stirring address in his own town in 1835, in which he advocated this platform as the only safe one. An earnest Christian, a zealous patriot, he possessed a clear head, a guileless heart, a tender conscience : he has left to his children the precious legacy of a good name. He was united in m. June 26, 1811, with Miss Frances M. Eldridge, of Brookline, Conn., and d. March 5, 1870.   *Woodstock, Conn.*

Children, Eighth Generation :
267   1 Edward E., b. April 8, 1812 ; d. in infancy.
268   2 Edwin H., twin brother, d. Dec. 20, 1835.
269   3 Gurdon E., b. Feb. 10, 1814 ; m. June 1, 1846, Sarah H.
        Bugbie ; Providence, R. I.
            Ch. 9th Gen. : 1 Hattie E., b. June 27, 1851. 2 Mary
        E., b. Dec. 29, 1854.

272   4 Francis M., b. April 4, 1816; Woodstock, Conn.
274   5 Harriet A., b. March 26, 1818; m. June 26, 1850, Edward
          A. Huntington ; Norwich, Conn.
275   6 Caroline L., b. July 28, 1820 ; m. Nov. 24, 1852, Rev.
          David Breed ; Abingdon, Conn.
              Ch. 9th Gen.: 1 Mary L., b. Sept. 18, 1853.   2 Caro-
          line C., b. Oct. 14, 1859.
277   7 Daniel F., b. Aug. 23, 1822 ; d. March 13, 1826.
278   8 James E., b. Oct. 11, 1824 ; m. Oct. 11, 1855, Lucinda
          Bacon ; Providence, R. I.
279   9 Daniel F., b. Jan. 30, 1827; m. June 9, 1858, Maria L.
          Bowers ; Providence, R. I.
280 10 Lucy M., b. June 20, 1828 ; Woodstock, Conn.
281 11 Asa, b. April 10, 1833 ; m. Nov. 7, 1866, Elizabeth P.
          Cutts ; Providence, R. I.
              Ch. 9th Gen.: 1 Rolfe M., b. April 4, 1868.   2 An
          infant son, b. Nov. 10, 1869.

Literary and Clerical Character of the Lebanon Lymans.

This branch is represented in the ministry of every
church from the democratic Congregational to the imperial
Roman Catholic inclusive.   Two families have educated
each two sons for the ministry ; and another, three for the
same office.   Those only, who, with the control of moderate
means, have battled with the task of educating publicly
their sons, can appreciate the zeal and persistence required
for its accomplishment.

Almost, without exception, the Lymans have survived the
severities of their curriculum, and emerged from their college course, *mens sana in corpore sano*, sound in body and in
mind.   As a characteristic illustration it may be remarked
that the colonial laws of college were very different from
those which are borne by republican students of the present day.   One of those old laws having a reference to the
proper dignity of the seniors, allowed that class to exact
menial service from the freshmen.   The freshmen split
wood, made fires, brushed boots, and carried parcels for
their superiors.   A pompous senior, as his classmate passed
his door, said to him, " Lyman, as you are going by the
cricket ground, please send me a dozen freshmen."   Mr.
Lyman executed the order to the letter and was at
pains to wait until the full number of freshmen was found
and marshalled.   When they presented themselves at his

door, the senior was taken aback by the array. All the errand he could make, was, the conveyance of his six pieces to the laundress.

Other incidents of college life are omitted for want of space.

IX. DESCENDANTS OF RICHARD³ THROUGH JACOB⁵ ELIJAH⁵ AND JOSIAH⁴

JACOB LYMAN⁵, *Jonathan⁴, Richard³, Richard², Richard¹*, b. in Lebanon, Conn., May 4, 1721; d. 1802; m. Mehitable Bushnell, of Lebanon, Ct., June 26, 1745. This marriage is recorded in Lebanon. Probably they removed directly to Andover, Ct., for in May following, their oldest child was b. there.   *Andover, Conn.*

Children, Sixth Generation:

1   1 Jacob, b. May 6, 1746 settled in Bolton, Conn.
2   2 Mehitable, b. June 22, 1748; m. Abner Badger.
3   3 Sarah, b. June 9, 1750; m. Adonijah Jones, they had one dau. Sarah.
5   4 Irene, b. May 3, 1752; m. Jonathan Hutchinson, d. Jan. 19, 1794. They had two children Jonathan and Irena.
8   5 Josiah, b. Oct. 15, 1755; d. Sept. 5, 1776, in the army of U. S. A. of camp distemper, in the 21st year of his age.
9   6 Abiathar, b. Jan. 15, 1758.
10 7 Hannah, b. March 28, 1760.
11 8 Silas, b. Dec. 20, 1762.
12 9 Anne, b. Jan. 31, 1766; m. Sept. 1786, Jonathan Whelden; they had 7 children, 4 are living 3 are dead, 4 grand-children, 4 great grandchildren, Williamstown, Mass.
28 10 Submit, b. Sept. 14, 1770; m. John Little, Columbia, Ct., d. March 31, 1842, in 71st year of her age. These children were all b. in Andover. The family record reads: Our honored grandfather, Jacob Lyman⁵, departed this life Jan. 15, A.D., 1802, in the 81st year of his age, farmer and tanner. Our honored grandmother Mehitable Lyman departed this life May 11, A.D. 1814, in the 89th year of her age, Andover, Ct.

1 DEA. JACOB LYMAN⁶, son of *Jacob⁵*, was b. Andover, Ct., May 6, 1746; m. Dec. 19, 1771, Mary Woodward, who d. Oct. 17, 1814 — farmer; d. March 25, 1819.   *Bolton, Ct.*

Children, Seventh Generation:

29 1 Jacob, b. March 15, 1773; m. Joanna Bolles; d. April 12, 1858; his wife d. about 1850.

30 2 A son d. nameless, July 27, 1779.
31 3 Junia, b. July 14, 1782 ; d. March 23, 1799.
32 4 Mary, b. Sept. 26, 1785 ; d. unmarried, Dec. 1, 1844.

29 JACOB LYMAN[7], son of *Dea. Jacob[6]*, farmer and tanner.
Bolton, Conn.
Children, Eighth Generation :
33 1 Joanna, b. June 12, 1804 ; m. Joseph Eaton, date unknown ;
has five children.
39 2 Jacob, b. Sept. 20, 1805.
40 3 Ezra, b. April 30, 1807; m. May 4, 1831, Deborah Hall
carpenter, Bolton.
41 4 Elisha, b. June 20, 1809 ; d. July 12, 1809.
42 5 Elijah, b. June 20, 1809 ; d. Oct. 11, 1816.
43 6 Sophia, b. Feb. 8, 1812 ; m. Oliver Chapman ; d. May 25,
1854 ; unmarried.
44 7 Mary, b. Oct. 16, 1816 ; m. Gallup ; several children.

39 JACOB LYMAN[8], son of *Jacob[7]*, farmer ; res. where he
was b. in Bolton, and occupies the farm which has been
owned and cultivated by this family near 100 years. He
m. Nov. 26, 1835, Dorcas Chapman.
Children, Ninth Generation :
45 1 Almira, b. Oct. 27, 1836, in Bolton ; m. July 10, 1859, John
Lord ; has five children ; res. Marlboro, Ct.
51 2 Margarette, b. Aug. 28, 1838 ; m. Nov. 28, 1860, Elisha M
Burdick, of Vernon, Ct. ; three children.
56 3 William, b. Feb. 8, 1840 ; m. May 16, 1862, Martha — cabinet
maker ; served in the 1st Conn. Cav. during the late war ;
one child ; N. Y. City.
57 4 George, b. Sept. 13, 1841 ; m. Sept. 18, 1867, Maria A. Dins-
boro ; an officer in the police of New York city ; served in
the 12th Marine Corps during the late war.
58 5 Dea. Charles, b. April 10, 1843 ; m. June 10, 1865, Amitia
B. Campbell, of Hartford — an officer in the 14th Conn.
Volunteers in the late war ; now a lawyer ; in the Treasury
Department, D. C. ; one child.
Ch. 10th Gen. : 1 Ella C., b. Jan. 4, 1870.
60 6 Benjamin, b. Dec 14, 1845 ; m. Nov. 17, 1869, Nancy Bowers,
of Rockville, Ct. ; a mason in Bolton.
61 7 Norman, b. Feb. 22, 1848 — farmer ; Bolton.
62 8 John, b. Aug. 25, 1850 — farmer ; Bolton.

40 EZRA LYMAN[8], son of *Jacob[7]*, a farmer. *Bolton.*
Children, Ninth Generation :
63 1 Walter C., b. Jan. 30, 1835 ; m. July 4, 1863, Ann Bolin —
farmer ; Old Saybrook, Ct.

64 2 Jane, b. March 15, 1837; m. Jan. 31, 1855, William A. Stan-
      nard, of West Saybrook; one son.
66 3 Henry H., b. Oct. 2, 1841; enlisted in Co. R., 10th Regt.,
      Conn. Volunteers, Sept. 1861; killed in front of Peters-
      burg, Va., Sept. 13, 1864.
67 4 Mary A., b. Dec. 14, 1843.
68 5 Clarissa A., b. June 8, 1848.
69 6 John F., Nov. 5, 1853.
70 7 Emily C., b. Jan. 2, 1857.

9 Abiathar Lyman[6], son of *Jacob Lyman[5]*, was b. Jan.
15, 1758; m. Joannah Loomis — b. Oct. 1, 1758 — Dec. 25,
1782 — tanner and currier, also farmer.   *Andover.*

A Copy of their Marriage Certificate.

" This certifies that Abiathar Lyman and Joannah Loomis,
both of Andover, were married together* December 25,
1782.   " Samuel Lockwood, Pastor. "

Our Family Record reads, namely:

" Our honored mother, Joannah Lyman, departed this life
July 1st, 1837, in the 80th year of her age.

" Our honored father, Abiathar Lyman, departed this life
Sept. 19, 1842, in the 85th year of his age. "

Children, Seventh Generation:

71 1 Josiah, b. Dec. 21, 1783; health poor; d. Sept. 12, 1848, aged
      64 years, 8 months and 22 days; unmarried.
72 2 Nathan, b. Oct. 25, 1785; was baptized June 26, 1809; was
      chosen deacon Nov. 17, 1820; ordained Dec. 14, follow-
      ing; m., the second time, to Mrs. Clarissa House, Nov.
      25, 1846; d. Oct. 8, 1850, aged 65. Deacon Lyman,
      though born and educated in the Congregational faith,
      yet from conviction became a Baptist, and was the first
      person immersed upon a profession of faith in Christ in
      the town. In his theology he was strictly Calvinistic,
      but earnest in all the practical duties of the gospel. He
      made the Bible supreme and final in his faith and practice.
      He loved the church and consecrated his abilities to its
      support and edification. He was very faithful in prayer
      and exhortation, and in the absence of a pastor led the
      worship of the sanctuary, to the comfort of the church
      and satisfaction of the congregation. In a very decided
      sense it may be said of him, that he used the office of a
      deacon well and purchased to himself a good degree and
      great boldness in the faith. He was a good man; an

---

* " Married together " is the accredited expression in the old English records.

obliging neighbor, loving husband and father; an humble Christian and an honored servant of the church of God.

73 3 Delia, b. May 19, 1787 ; 84 years old, able to ride to church, a mile, on the sabbath; will be 85, May 19, 1872; unmarried.

74 4 Joannah, b. Dec. 1, 1789 ; m. Sylvester Jones, of Coventry; res. West Groton, N. Y. ; they had six children.

81 6 Ele, b. Dec. 28, 1793 — farmer.

82 7 Cyrus, b. May 16, 1796.

72 NATHAN LYMAN[7], son of *Abiathar*[6], b. in Andover, Ct., Oct. 25, 1785, m. May 31, 1810, Asenath Sprague, Andover, Ct. He was chosen deacon, Nov. 17, 1820, and was publicly set apart to that office by ordination, Dec. 14, following; m. for 2d wife, Mrs. Clarissa House, both of Andover, Ct., Nov. 25th, 1846. Asenath, d. Sept. 19, 1842, of consumption, aged 54. She was a worthy member of the Baptist Church. Nathan, d. Oct. 8, 1850, aged 65 years.

Children, Eighth Generation :

83 1 Nathan Bradley, b. May 14, 1812. He was chosen deacon, soon after the decease of his father; m. April 6th, 1836, Lucy Huntington House,— farmer, Andover, Ct.
   Ch. 9th Gen.: 1 Albert House, b. Jan. 22, 1837 ; occupation, commercial traveler, Andover, Ct.

84 2 Marcia, b. April 23, 1814, and d. Aug. 10, 1842, of consumption, in the triumph of faith in Jesus Christ, 28 years old.

85 3 Abiathar Milton, b. Aug. 22d, 1816; d. Dec. 4, 1821, of croup, in the 6th year of his age, a son of more than ordinary promise.

81 ELE LYMAN[7], son of *Abiathar*[6], was born in Andover, Conn., Dec. 28, 1793. In 1814 he was drafted into the army of the U. S., and served about three months in the vicinity of New London. He learned the hatter's trade and worked at it, also had a farm which he cultivated. He m. Hannah Darrow, who d. July 31, 1854, aged 44. He d. April 21, 1856, aged 62; both d. in Coventry.

Coventry, Ct.

Children, Eighth Generation :

87 1 Marcus E., b. Jan. 7, 1837.

88 2 Abner A., b. Jan., 1839; m. Hattie E. Austin of Suffield, Ct., Oct. 23, 1861; three children — farmer; Suffield, Ct.
   Ch. 9th Gen.: 1 Jennie C., b. at Windsor Locks, Ct. April 15, 1862. 2 Ellen M., b. in Suffield, Ct., Sept. 28, 1864. 3 Addie B., b. in Enfield, Ct., Sept. 23, 1869.

21

89 3 Adoniràm Judson, b. March 28, 1840; m. Artie L. Sykes,
        of Suffield, Conn., Nov. 4, 1869; res. in Suffield, Conn.;
        brought up as a farmer; has been successful in peddling
        tinware for four or five years ; returned to farming.
90 4 Maria H., b. Aug. 12, 1842; res. in Hartford, Conn.
91 5 Theron O., Dec. 24, 1844; res. in Coventry; works on a farm.
92 6 Eleazer Hunt, b. March 24, 1846. He enlisted into a regi-
        ment of heavy artillery in Mass., served in it and got an
        honorable discharge — slater ; Hartford, Conn.
93 7 Ella M., b. July 24, 1848 ; Hartford, Conn.
94 8 Leroy D., b. March 14, 1850 ; Norwalk, Ohio — farmer.
95 9 Asa F., b. Dec. 3, 1851 ; d. April 22, 1853 ; all b. in Coventry.

87 MARCUS E. LYMAN[8], son of *Ele*[7], m. Emma Hunt,
1860. He enlisted in the town of Farmington, Sept. 20, in the
16th Regiment of Conn. Volunteers, Co. K ; after a week's
sickness at Prince Street Hospital, Alexandria, Va., he d.
Dec. 16, 1862, nearly 26 years old — farmer. *Berlin, Conn.*

Child, Ninth Generation:
96 1 Nellie E., b. Nov. 22, 1862, at Berlin; Conn.

82 CYRUS LYMAN[7], son of *Abiathar*[6] was b. in Andover,
Conn., May 17, 1796 ; was m. Tolland, Conn., to Mary
Tillinghast, Feb, 4, 1824. They lived in Andover, Conn.,
until Sept., 1847, when they moved to Norwalk, Ohio.
He was counting much on being at that great family
meeting at Mt. Tom; but as he was starting into the
village on May 25th, to make some preparations in view of
his trip east, his horse took fright and overturned his carriage, killing him instantly, and severely wounding his wife
and daughter. Mr. L. was 70 years old, and an excellent
Christian man, a member of the Baptist church for twenty
years.   *Norwalk, Ohio.*
Children, Eighth Generation :
99 1 Mary Elizabeth, b. in Andover, Conn., Feb. 12, 1825; m.
        in Norwalk, O., to Milton F. Remington, a machinist,
        March 31, 1852 ; had four children.
          Ch. 9th Gen. : 1 Emma Jane, b in Norwalk, Ohio,
        Aug. 1, 1853. 2 Alice Maria, b. in Norwalk, Ohio, Feb.
        8, 1856; d. Dec. 23, 1862. 3 Cornelia Augusta b. in
        Norwalk, Ohio, April 10, 1860. 4 Frank Rich, b. in
        Adrian, Mich., Nov. 2, 1865.
104 2 Sarah Maria, b. in Andover, Ct., May 12, 1729; m. in Nor-
        walk, O., to James Indicott, March 6, 1860 — carpenter
        and joiner; has two children.
          Ch. 9th Gen. : 1 Mary Ina, b. in Norwalk, O., Dec.
        17, 1860. 2 Arthur Lyman, b. in Norwalk, O., March
        28, 1869.

107 3 Martha Jane, b. in Andover, Ct., June 7, 1833; was m. to
Samuel Barnes, in Norwalk, O., Sept. 7, 1852; has two
children.
Ch. 9th Gen.: 1 Leslie Lyman, b. in Norwalk, Oct
22, 1855. 2 Eugene Platt, b. in Norwalk, O., Aug. 13
1862.

11 SILAS LYMAN[6], son of *Jacob L.*[5], of Andover, was
drafted at the age of 16 years and served three months in
the army of the U.S., b. Dec. 20, 1762; m. 1790, Lydia
Hutchinson, b. July 5, 1764, in Granby, Ct. She d. July
5, 1833; he d. Feb. 8, 1838.

Children, Seventh Generation :
110 1 Lydia, b. Aug. 1, 1791; m. David Grover, resides in Bingham,
Potter Co., Pa., had 7 children.
118 2 Laura, b. Aug., 1793; m. Isaac Bronson, had 8 children.
126 3 Sherburn, b. Sept. 24, 1798; m. Lydia Ticknor, d. Dec.,
1841, in Willimantic, a blacksmith.
Ch. 8th Gen.: 1 Clarissa, b. Oct. 12, 1819; d. March
8, 1840. 2 Elizabeth, b. Sept. 15, 1822; m. Aug. 22,
1842, Henry M. Prentice. 3 Henry, b. no date; d. Nov.
1, 1847. 4 Huldah, b. May 25, 1829; m. Sept. 22,
1846, Joseph Dunham. 5 Charles, b. Oct. 5, 1841.
132 4 Levina, b. June 12, 1800; m. Amasa Jones, resides in Andover,
Ct., had 4 children.
137 5 Flavel, b. Dec. 23, 1807.
138 6 Harvey, b. July 3, 1810.

131 CHARLES LYMAN[8], works in a mill, cotton or woolen,
enlisted into the 5th Reg. Conn. Volunteers, Company B,
1st brigade, 1st division, 12th Army Corps, had an honorable discharge; m. April 2, 1865, Luthera Hall.
Ch. 9th Gen.: 1 Charles Francois, b. May 16, 1866.

137 FLAVEL LYMAN[7], m. June 28, 1832, Harriet Cogswell—farmer.
Children, Eighth Generation :
142 1 William, b. April 5, 1832.
143 2 Amoret, b. June 16, 1834; d. Jan., 1850.
144 3 Enos, b. May 13, 1842.
145 4 Egla Medora, b. Jan. 24, 1851.

142 WILLIAM LYMAN[8], in the service of a Mass. Reg., in
the battle of Wilderness and before Petersburg until the
taking of Richmond, then honorably discharged in Mass.

144 ENOS LYMAN[8], enlisted into the navy for one year,
afterwards enlisted into a Mass. Reg., was taken prisoner at

Cedar Mountain, taken to Richmond, exchanged, then sent west to fight Indians; stationed at Omaha.

138 HARVEY LYMAN[7], shoemaker and farmer, m. Oct. 16, 1835, Anna Trapp. She d. Oct. 22, 1839, m. 2d wife March, 1841, Almira Holt.   *Wilmington, Ct.*

   Children, Eighth Generation
146 1 Angeline A., b. Aug. 19, 1836.
147 2 Julia A., b. Feb. 26, 1844; d. April 1, 1848.
148 3 Lewellyn, b. Sept. 1, 1846; d. Aug. 22, 1858.
149 4 Julius A., b. Aug. 14, 1849, carpenter and joiner, resides Andover, Conn.
150 5 Clark H., b. Jan. 6, 1855.

ELIJAH LYMAN[5], youngest son of Lieut. *Jonathan[4]*, resided in Coventry, m. Dec. 4, 1749, Esther Clark, physician.   *Coventry, Conn.*

   Children, Sixth Generation :
1 1 Esther, b. July 4, 1750.
2 2 Gershom C., Rev., D.D., b. Jan. 18. 1753.
3 3 Lucy, b. July 16, 1756; m. Dr. John Waldo; no further record.

3 GERSHOM CLARK LYMAN[6], D.D., b. in Coventry, Ct., was graduated at Yale, 1773, was ordained and consecrated the first pastor and minister of the Cong. church at Marlborough, Vt., Dec. 9, 1777. He d. April 13, 1813, in the 61st year of his age and 35th of his ministry. At the time of his death he was pastor of the Cong. church in M., Vt., was an only son and had two sisters, Esther and Lucy. His wife Lucy, d. March 16, 1831, aged 78 years.

   Children, Seventh Generation, :
4 1 Henry.   7 4 Lucy.
5 2 William.   8 5 Elijah.
6 3 Esther.   9 6 Clark.

8 ELIJAH LYMAN[7], son of *Gershom[6]*, b. Jan. 12, 1781; m. 1st, Irene Whitney, date unknown, d. Sept. 27, 1820; 2d, Margaret Pope, date of marriage and death unknown.

   Children, Eighth Generation :
11 1 Harriet, b. July 17, 1803; m. Wheeler Cole; d date unknown, Strongsville, O.
12 2 Hollis, b. Dec. 12, 1804; d. Dec. 1820.
13 3 Julia Ann, b. June 22, 1807; m. Thatcher Avery, April 18, 1825, Strongsville, O.
14 4 Elijah, b. Jan. 26, 1810.
15 5 Esther, b. Nov. 22, 1811; d. Aug., 1828.

16 6 Irene, b. Sept. 23, 1814; m. Theodore Hale, Jan. 1, 1835, Oberlin, O.
17 7 Lucy Hubbard, b. March 27, 1816; m. Benoni Bartlett, Jan. 24, 1836, Strongsville, O.
18 8 Tamar Whitney, b. June 27, 1818; m. Joseph Reed, April 5, 1843, Fairview, O.
19 9 Sophia, b. June 29, 1820; d. Oct. 30, 1828.
20 10 Hollis, b. Oct. 31, 1824; d. Oct. 30, 1828.
21 11 Ardelia Pope, b. Aug. 12, 1826; m. Curtis, Woodworth, O.

14 Elijah Lyman[8], son of *Elijah*[7], and grandson of *Gershom*[6], b. Jan. 26, 1810; m. 1st Lucy Stevens, May 26, 1831, who d. Sept. 20, 1845; 2d, Achsah C. Bancroft, Sept. 1, 1846.   *Strongville, O.*

Children, Ninth Generation:
22 1 Newell Deming, b. June 6, 1833; d. Nov. 16, 1833.
23 2 Amelia Maria, b. Feb. 15, 1835; m. Frederick Nash, Sept. 1, 1862.
24 3 George Whitney, b. Nov. 22, 1837; m. April 3, 1862, Sarah O. Rogers.
        Ch. 10th Gen.: (1) Minnie I., b. Sept. 22, 1864. (2) Mary May, b. June 12, 1866.
25 4 Mary Eliza, b. Oct. 6, 1839; d. Aug. 5, 1865.

13 Julia Ann Lyman[8], m. Thatcher Avery, April 18, 1825.   *Strongsville, O.*
Children, Ninth Generation:
26 1 Lyman, b. April 29, 1826; deceased.
27 2 Elijah Lyman, b. Aug. 17, 1828; deceased.
28 3 Mary Sanborn, b. March 6, 1830; deceased.
29 4 George, b. Aug. 18, 1832.
30 5 Sarah, b. July 4, 1834; deceased. •
31 6 Irene Lyman, b. Oct. 6, 1839.
32 7 Hollis L., b. Dec. 13, 1841.

16 Irene Lyman[8], m. Theodore Hale Jan. 1, 1835.
Children, Ninth Generation:
34 1 Sarah I. b. Dec. 22, 1835.
35 2 Elijah T., b. Nov. 22, 1837; deceased.
36 3 Julia A.., b. June 13, 1840; deceased.
37 4 Sophia L., b. April 22, 1845.
38 5 Nettie C., b. Aug. 16, 1847.
39 6 Celia E., b. July 12, 1852.
40 7 Flora E., b. Feb. 19, 1854.
41 8 Myra A., b. March 5, 1856.

17 LUCY H. LYMAN[8], m. Jan. 27, 1836, Benoni Bartlett.

Children, Ninth Generation :

42 1 Delia S., b. Feb. 21, 1837 ; deceased.
43 2 Henry H., b. Aug. 22, 1840.
44 3 Harriet E., b. Nov. 18, 1845.
45 4 Louis B., b. Nov. 4, 1852.

18 TAMAR W. LYMAN[8], m. Joseph Reed, April 5, 1843.

Children, Ninth Generation :

46 1 Francis E., b. Feb. 13, 1844 ; deceased.
47 2 Joseph, b. Feb. 7, 1846.
48 3 John H., b. July 19, 1847.
49 4 Sophia L., b. March 17, 1849.
50 5 Mary I., b. Feb. 27, 1850.
51 6 Frederick N., b. Nov. 20, 1851 ; deceased.
52 7 Frederick N., b. July 14, 1853.
53 8 Julia A., b. July 18, 1855 ; deceased.
54 9 Charly T., b. Jan. 8, 1857. ·

55 JOSIAH LYMAN[4], son of *Richard*[3], b. Feb. 6, 1690; m. Nov. 25, 1717, Sarah Loomis ; d. Feb. 6, 1790. *Epitaph*— He was endowed with good natural ability, steady temper, sound judgment and witnessed a good profession.

Columbia, Conn.

Children, Fifth Generation :

56 1 Esther, b. Sept. 17, 1718.
57 2 Josiah, b. March 4, 1721; d. Sept. 25, 1747, " the only and well beloved son of Josiah[2] "
58 3 Anna, b. March 18, 1724.

PART IV.

Descendants of Dea. Thomas[3].

1 THOMAS LYMAN[3], *Richard[2]*, *Richard[1]*, 1649–1725; the 2d son of the 2d Richard; b. in Windsor, Conn., about 1649; moved with his parents to Northampton about 1656, where he m. 1678, Ruth, widow of Joseph Baker and daughter of William Holton. By her marriage with Mr. Baker, in 1663, she had had six children, the eldest of whom, Joseph, b. Jan. 20, 1665, was, with his father, killed by the Indians, Oct. 29, 1675. Dea. Thomas[3], had, according to Savage, six children, two of whom—Elizabeth and Enoch— are mentioned by him alone, and do not appear in the Durham records. He moved, in 1708 or '9, to Durham, Conn., which, for three or four generations thereafter, was the headquarters of this branch of the Lyman family. His wife Ruth and a part of his children came with him; he was one of the early settlers; one of the first deacons; a representative of the town several sessions; and d. there July 15, 1725, aged 75. The date of Mrs. Ruth Lyman's death is unknown. Both signed the covenant pledge at the settlement of the Rev. Nathaniel Chauncey, the first minister of Durham, Dec. 30, 1710. The letter of dismission and recommendation from Dr. Solomon Stoddard is preserved and is here copied: "To Mr. Nathaniel Chauncey and the brethren at Durham that are about to enter into a church state: Ensign Thomas Liman, who is one of your inhabitants, has desired letters of dismission for himself and wife, accordingly we do recommend them to your holy communion; he is in covenant with us; she is in full communion; both without offense. We desire that God would make them blessings among you, and prosper your beginings that a foundation may be laid for the conversion and edification of many, thus requesting your prayers for us, we remain your brethren in the fellowship of the gospel. Solomon Stoddard in the name and consent of the church in Northampton. N. Hampton, Jan. 16, 17$\frac{10}{11}$."
The six children of Thomas[3] were "

Children, Fourth Generation:

1 1 Thomas[4]; 1678—; had 3 children, Aaron, Elizabeth, Thomas.
2 2 Mindwell[4]; 1680–1758; m. John Harris; s. p.

3 3 Ebenezer⁴ ; 1682–1762 ; had 7 children, Experience, Ebenezer,
       Stephen, Experience, Mindwell, John, Hannah.
4 4 Elizabeth⁴ ; this name is found only in Savage.
5 5 Noah⁴; 1686–1728 ; had Noah⁵, Gen. Phineas⁵, Rev. Jonathan⁵.
6 6 Enoch⁴ ; b. Jan. 18, 1691, found only in Savage ; he may have
       d. young; no date of any kind ; no record of marriage ; does
       not appear in the Durham records, though the names of
       his three brothers appeared there repeatedly. This
       Enoch Lyman appears to have removed early to Glasten-
       bury, where he m. Dinah, dau. of Samuel Smith, b. Oct.
       28, 1697. He appears to have inherited property from
       his wife and to have been a large landholder. He sells
       land at different times for £80, 70, 450, 150, 55, 120,
       and releases to Samuel his brother-in-law, 234 acres for
       £120, buys in 1733 land for £550, appears to have d.
       between 1745–8, leaving a dau. Dinah and a son
       Samuel.

8 Samuel Lyman⁵, son of *Enoch⁴*, m. Aug. 24, 1757 ;
Sarah Bartlett, and at a late period in life to have removed
to Bolton, Conn.

Children, Sixth Generation :

7 1 Samuel⁶ ; b. Nov. 28, 1759.   12 4 Joel ; b. June 21, 1769.
8 2 Isaac⁶ ; b. May 30, 1762.   13 5 Irene ; b. April 19, 1773.
9 3 Ruth⁶ ; b. Jan. 1766.

2 Thomas Lyman⁴, *Thomas³, Richard², Richard¹*, b. at
Northampton, 13 April, 1678 ; m. Elizabeth ......, in North-
ampou, where his first child was b. ; removed to Durham,
with his father or soon after his father ; was representative
four sessions or more ; date of death not known. His three
children were :

Children, Fifth Generation :

10 1 Aaron⁵ ; b. in Northampton, Nov. 19, 1707 ; had a dau. bap-
       tized in Durham, Nov., 1731.
11 2 Elizabeth⁵; baptized in Durham, April 5, 1713. (*Hist. of
       Durham* 253.)

2 3 Thomas⁵; 1714 – 1761 ; bapt. 13 Feb. ; d. April 2761 ; had
       7 children : Sarah, Elizabeth, Thomas, Ann, Abel, James,
       Daniel.

3 Ebenezer Lyman⁴, *Thomas³, Richard², Richard¹*, 1682 –
1762, b. at Northampton, 1682 ; removed to Durham several
years after his father, not earlier than 1717, not later than
1719 ; his wife was Experience Pomeroy ; m. Jan. 2, 1706 ;
lived near the north line of Durham, on the west or lower
side of the Durham road formerly called " Crooked Lane ; "

purchased land in 1837 over the line, in Middlefield, with his brother Noah. He removed about 1740, to Torrington, having been preceded by his son Ebenezer[5], who was the first settler of that town, 1737. The father and son were among the first members of the Congregational church at its organization, Oct. 21, 1741, and the father was chosen deacon Jan. 1, 1742. His name appears on a deed of Eph. Coe to John Lyman, dated April 11, 1748, as witness, and again subscribed to the acknowledgment as justice of the peace. He was probably, at the time, on a visit to his son John, in Middlefield. He was representative from Durham, 1737. He d. in Torrington, in 1762, aged 80. His 8 children were ·

Children, Fifth Generation

13 1 Moses[5]. We learn from Moses[7] that his father, Phineas[6] was a cousin of Col. David[6], which makes Moses[5] a brother of John[5] and son of Ebenezer[4]; we assume that he was the oldest child of Ebenezer[4], Thomas[3], Richard[2], Richard[1], 1707–1796.

14 2 Experience[5]; b. in Northampton, April 17, 1708; d. Sept. 30, 1708.

15 3 Ebenezer[5]; b. in Northampton, Sept. 20, 1709; had 6 children: Caleb, Ebenezer, Sarah, Esther, Elizabeth, Rhoda, and Ruth.

16 4 Stephen[5]; b. in Northampton, Aug. 14, 1711.

17 5 Experience[5]; b. in Northampton, Dec. 25, 1712.

18 6 Mindwell[5]; b. in Northampton, July 13, 1714; bp. in Durham, Sept. 15, 1718 (*History of D.*, 255); m. Oct. 29, 1741, Jacob Strong, Jr., 6 children. — *Strong Family*, vol. I, p. 123.

    Ch. 6th Gen.: 1 Mindwell; b. July 28, 1742. 2 Experience, b. and d. Aug. 13, 1743. 3 Abigail, b. Jan. 27, 1745–6; m. May 6, 1785. Ebenezer Stoddard, of Torrington, had 2 children. [*Ch. 7th Gen.:* (1) Phena, b. March 18, 1786. (2) Anne, b. May 8, 1787.] 4 Experience, b. March 28, 1749–50. 5 Elizabeth, b. Sept. 10, 1755; d. Jan. 2, 1756. 6 Mary, b. July 2, 1757.

27 7 John[5]; 1717–1763; had 8 children: John, Catharine, Hannah, John, David, Esther, Elihu, Phineas.

28 8 Hannah[5]; bp. in D., June 30, 1723 (*Hist. of D.*. 259); m. Asahel Strong, of Torrington; d. Feb. 19, 1771.

    Ch. 6th Gen.: Asahel, Jr., b. April 17, O. S., 28 N. S. 1750; d. Jan. 6, 1831. 2 Hannah, b. Nov. 30, 1753; m. John Miner, Winchester, Conn. 3 Dorcas, b. Feb. 27, 1758; m. Hezekiah Beecher, of Bethlehem. 4 Chloe, b. Dec. 4, 1763; m. David Holmes, of Russell, Mass. 5 David, b. May. 31, 1768.

5 NOAH LYMAN[4], *Thomas*[3], *Richard*[2], *Richard*[1], 1686–1728 ; b. in Northampton about 1686, says Stearns ; m. Elizabeth...... ; bought July 7, 1719, 14 acres near Durham line, in connection with his brother Ebenezer. He d. 1728, when his widow Elizabeth petitioned court (Middletown records) to divide the 14 acres with Ebenezer ; heirs in interest, Noah, Jr., Phineas and Jonathan. Left 3 children, viz

Children, Fifth Generation :

33 1 Noah[5] ; 1713–1756 ; had 3 children : Noah, Elizabeth, Miles.
34 2 Phineas[5] (Gen.) ; 1715–1775 ; had eight children : Phineas, Gamaliel, Dwight, Thaddeus, Thompson, Oliver, Eleanor, Experience, Thompson.
35 3 Jonathan[5] (Rev.) ; 1717–1763 ; his children were : Noah, Russell, Jonathan, David, Mary.

9 THOMAS LYMAN[5], *Thomas*[4], *Thomas*[3], *Richard*[2], *Richard*[1], b. and d. in Durham ; baptized Feb. 13, 1714–15 (*Hist. of D.*, 253). He m. Ann......; will dated Feb. 17, 1757 ; inventory Sept. 4, 1761 ; d. April 20, 1761. His widow Ann d. Jan. 17, 1772. His children were :

Children, Sixth Generation :

36 1 Sarah[6] ; Mrs. Benton, baptized May 31, 1741 (*Hist. of D.*, 279).
37 2 Elizabeth[6] ; bapt. March 11, 1743–4 (*Hist. of D.* 283) ; m. Ezra Baldwin of D., March 16, 1764.
38 3 Thomas[6] ; bapt. Feb. 16, 1745–6 ; had 3 children : George, Henry, Elizabeth.
39 4 Ann[6] ; bapt. Jan. 14, 1747–8 (*Hist. D.*, 287) ; m. David Talcott 1767, and had a family.
40 5 Abel[6] ; 1749–1828 ; had 4 children : Sophia, Frances, Dwight, James.
41 6 James[6] ; b. Jan. 10, 1753.
42 7 Daniel[6] ; (col. and judge) ; 1756–1830 ; Y. C. 1776 ; had 13 children.

13 MOSES LYMAN[5], lived in Wallingford, Conn., where he m. Jan. 10, 1733, Ruth Hickox ; she d. Aug. 12, 1734, when he m. 2d, June, 1735, Ruth Gaylord. He removed to Southington, Ct., about 1740, and was admitted to the Congregational church there, Nov. 8, 1841 ; Ruth his second wife, d. in Southington, Aug. 21, 1751, in her 35th year, when he m. 3d, Sarah ......, who d. Jan. 28, 1765, in her 46th. He d. in Southington, March 3, 1796.

Children, Sixth Generation :

43 1 Moses[6] ; b. 20 Jan. 1734, by 1st wife, d. March 17, 1734.
44 2 Ruth[6] ; b. 23 March, 1736, by 2d wife ; she m. 2 Feb., 1758, Samuel Woodruff, of Southington, who d. 7 July, 1816,

in his 82d year; she d. 9 Aug., 1829, aged 93; 10 children.

45 3 Moses[6] baptized in Southington, Feb. 13, 1743; m. Abigail Blackston of Branford, Conn., she was his second wife; he settled in Cheshire, Mass., where he d. about 1812, aged 64. He left no sons.

46 4 Sarah[6]; bp. Jan. 6, 1745, in Southington.

47 5 Lois[6]; bp. Feb. 15, 1747, in Southington.

48 6 Hannah[6]; bp. July 3, 1749, in Southington.

49 7 Noah[6]; bp. Oct. 13, 1751, in Southington.

50 8 Phinehas[6]; bp. May 4, 1755, in Southington.

51 9 Sarah[6]; bp. July 16, 1757; d. Jan. 1, 1758.

Moses Lyman had a son who d. in the campaign in 1759, probably b. in the interval between 1736–43, his name and date of birth have not been found.

33 Noah Lyman[6], son of *Moses[6]*, was b. 1751, in South-ington, and was baptized there, not long after birth, Oct. 19, 1751, by Rev. Jeremiah Curtis, pastor of the Congregational church. He m. Dec. 9, 1785, Rachel Johnson; he lived in the south part of Southington, Conn., at what is called "south end," and was by occupation a stone mason; he d. Oct. 11, 1830, aged 72 years. Rachel, his widow, d. Sept. 13, 1836, aged 77 years. Their children ·

Children, Seventh Generation :

52 1 Emma[7]; b. .....; d. Feb. 15, 1794, in her 5th year.

53 2 Emma[7]; b........; m. March 20, 1825, Oliver Lewis, she was his second wife; they removed to the west where she d.

34 Phineas Lyman[6], son of *Moses[5]*, baptized May 4, 1755, in Southington, Conn., where he was b. not long before; m. (1) Huldah Berry, who d. m. (2) Mabel, widow of Ezra Munson. He d. in Meriden, Conn., 1825, aged 71 years.

Children, Seventh Generation .

54 1 Berry[7]; b........; m. 1st Esther Cowles; m. 2d Charity Parker.

55 2 Phineas[7]; b........; d. 1810, aged 23 years, unmarried.

56 3 Moses[7]; b. Jan. 30, 1835; m. Laura Butler.

57 4 Sarah[7]; b........; m. Liberty Perkins of Meriden; d. 1825, aged 44.

58 5 Anna[7]; b........; never m.; d. aged 70.

59 6 Eda[7]; b · m. Moses Baldwin.

54 Berry Lyman[7], son of *Phineas[6]*, m. Esther, daughter of Timothy Cowles of Meriden; who d. in 1804, when he m. 2d Charity Parker. He d. 1820, aged 41 years.

Children, Eighth Generation:

60 1 Huldah³, b. by 1st wife, m. Joel Bartholomew of Meriden.
61 2 William³, b. by 2d wife is m. and resides in New York state.

56 MOSES LYMAN⁷, son of *Phinehas⁶*, b. Jan. 30, 1795, in Meriden, m. Oct. 19, 1820, Laura, daughter of Samuel Butler of Meriden. He resides in Berlin, Kensington Soc., Conn., and is a farmer by occupation. Laura (his wife) d. March 4, 1870, aged 72 years.

Child, Eighth Generation:

61* 1 Henry R. Lyman, b. April 11, 1825.

61* HENRY R. LYMAN⁸, only child of Moses and Laura (Butler) Lyman, was b. April 11, 1825, in Meriden; m. Sept. 23, 1851, Lucy Hart of Kensington, daughter of Samuel and Lucy (Dickinson) Hart. She was b. Dec. 13, 1830, in Kensington. He resides at Montevallo, Shelby Co., Ala., where he has been for several years extensively engaged in mercantile business.

Children, Ninth Generation:

62 1 Mary⁹, b. Feb. 14, 1853.
63 2 Catharine⁹, b. July 14, 1855; d. 1857.
64 3 Laura⁹, b. April 5, 1857.   67 6 Hattie⁹, b. April 27, 1865.
65 4 Henry⁹, b. Jan. 10, 1860.   68 7 Willie⁹, b. Oct. 27, 1867.
66 5 Edward⁹, b. July 7, 1862.

15 EBENEZER LYMAN⁵, *Ebenezer⁴, Thomas³, Richard², Richard¹*, born at Northampton Sept. 20, 1709; probably came from N. with his father about 1718 or 1719; and m. according to Stearns, Elizabeth, a daughter of Noadiah Seward, about 1733; she soon d.; and about 1734 he m. Sarah. According to Barber's *Hist. Coll.* (496) he was the first settler of Torrington, 1737, whither he removed in that year "with a young family of three persons only." His granddaughter, Mrs. Hannah L. Ingersoll of Rochester, N. Y., says: "My grandfather Ebenezer came to Torrington before it was settled, purchased a large tract of land, hence the name Lyman Brook, which ran so far on his land. After a few persons came into the place, they built a fort on my grandfather's land, and every night resorted to it to sleep. In the day time they hoed their corn and cut their hay, with their guns by their side." She goes on to say that he had 2 sons and 5 daughters, viz.

Children, Sixth Generation:

69 1 Caleb⁶; 1747–1810; who by 1st wife, Hannah Loomis, had 5 children: Medad⁷, Sybil⁷, Eleanor⁷, Rhoda⁷, George⁷, and by 2d wife had Hannah.

70 2 Ebenezer[6]; who removed to Vermont; b. March 17, 1750; d. March 7, 1813; m. Ann......and had 5 children, viz. *Ch. 7th Gen.* : 1 Ebenezer[7] ; m. Clarissa Loomis and d. March 13, 1813. 2 Laura[7]; b. Oct. 17, 1788; m. Feb. 28, 1808, George Wadsworth; d. at Plattsburg, Jan. 2, 1863. [*Ch. 8th Gen.:* (1) Roxala. (2) Desius. (3) Laura. (4) George. (5) Hiram. (6) Nicholas. (7) Daniel.] 3 Phineas[7]; no dates. 4 Ann Amanda[7]; m. Russell Harrington, at Burlington, Vt., March 17, 1810. [*Ch. 8th Gen.:* (1) Charles. (2) Juliette. (3) Donald. (4) Marrien. (5) Edward.] 5 Roxana[7]; b. Oct. 15, 1777, no further date. Ann, the mother d. March 14, 1813.

87 3 Sarah[6]; m. Joel Wetmore.
88 4 Esther[6]; m. Nehemiah Lewis, some of their descendants live in Bridgeport, Conn.
89 5 Ruth[6]; m. Ashbel North, dau. Roxana[7] son Phineas[7] Esq.
90 6 Rhoda[6]; m. Nathaniel Hayden.
91 7 Mary[6]; m. a Mr. Tuttle and settled in Windsor, Ct.

Ebenezer Lyman[5], d. about 1751, at the age of 42; this date is recovered by means of the following singular tradition, preserved by his grandson, Geo. Lyman, of Wadsworth, Ohio, who writes to his sister, under date of Feb. 4, 1869, ·as follows : " Our grandfather lost his life in the following manner : He, with two other men, went from home on a hunting expedition expecting to be gone from home several days. It was in the winter. When they arrived at the place where they expected to stop awhile, it being night, they built a fire against a large rock, and lay down by it to sleep. While thus situated, the fire operated on the rock and a very large portion fell over directly on our grandfather and so badly bruised him he did not long survive. Father, Caleb[6], b. 1747, was then about four years old ; so that the death of Ebenezer[5], first settler of Torrington, occurred about 1751.

27 JOHN LYMAN[5], *Ebenezer[4], Thomas[3], Richard[2], Richard[1]*, 1717–1763; b. at Northampton, April 9, 1717; came with parents to Durham, 1719, or a little earlier; m. Sept. 13, 1739, Hope Hawley, dau. of Jehiel Hawley, and Hope Stow Hawley, of Middletown and Durham, they lived on the boundary line, and granddaughter of the Rev. Samuel Stow, of Middletown, who owned much land in Middlefield, " some of which descended to John Lyman's wife." Hope Hawley Lyman was baptized by the Rev. N. Chauncey, July 18, 1719. While still described in legal documents as " of Durham" John[5], purchased of

tenor, 36 acres of land with a mansion house, March 14, 1741. The next month, Hope, wife of John[5], buys April 6, 1741, of Eph. Coe, 25 acres for £200, directly west of the previous purchase, now called "swamp pasture." And so John[5], and his wife go on buying, as shown by 14 curious old deeds, till they have 165 acres, which cost £1,623. He d. in 1763. His 8 children were:

Children, Sixth Generation:

97 1 John[6]; 1740, d. young.
98 2 Catharine[5]; bp. at Durham, Nov. 8, 1741; m. Lot Benton, of Guilford.
99 3 Hannah[6]; bp. at Durham, June 19, 1743; m. Rev. Mr. Williston, of West Haven.
100 4 John[6]; bp. Jan. 13, 1744–45; d. young.
101 5 David[6]; 1746–1815; had 10 children: Polly, Phineas, David, William, Esther, Alanson, Sally, Urania, Andrew, Elihu.
102 6 Esther[6]; b. Feb. 17, 1749; m. Mr. Beecher and was the mother of Dr. Lyman Beecher.
103 7 Elihu[6]; b. about 1751; a physician, and d. at the south.
104 8 Phineas[6].

33 NOAH LYMAN[5], *Noah[4], Thomas[3], Richard[2], Richard[1]*, 1713–1756; baptized in Durham, Jan. 24, 171¾; m. Sarah ......; d. 1756; widow Sarah, administratrix, April 5, 1756; inventory June 5, 1756, estate £831; 3 minor children; widow m. 2d husband, Robert Atkins, March 23, 1758. His children were:

Children, Sixth Generation:

105 1 Noah[6]; bapt. at Durham, June 21, 1747; had 3 children: Noah[7], Electa, Miles[7].
106 2 Elizabeth[6]; bapt. at Durham, Nov. 5, 1749; m. ...... Norton; d. very old in Harpersfield, N. Y.
107 3 Miles[6].

34 Gen. PHINEAS LYMAN[5], *Noah[4], Thomas[3], Richard[2], Richard[1]*, 1715–1775; bapt. in Durham, March 6, 1715; graduated at Yale, 1738, and was one of the Berkley scholars; tutor 1739; studied law and settled in Suffield, where he kept a law school. "Endowed with great abilities he soon rose to distinguished eminence in his profession," and "was at the head of the bar of Hampshire county," Suffield being then a part of Massachusetts. In 1750, after the transfer of Suffield to Connecticut, he was representative to the general assembly, and in 1753 assistant. In 1755, he was major general and commander-in-chief of the 5,000 Connecticut forces, and actual commander of the American force sent to the Canadian war. At the important

battle of Lake George, Sept. 8, 1755, Gen. Johnson having retired to his tent after "receiving a flesh wound in his thigh at the commencement of the battle," the command devolved on Gen. Lyman, who, says Dr. Dwight in his *Travels*, vol. III, 349, "immediately stationed himself in front of the breast-work, and there, during five hours, amid the thickest danger, issued his orders to every part of the army, with a serenity few acquire." At length the French were repulsed on all sides, and their commander, Baron Dieskau, an able general, was taken prisoner. Gen. Johnson, though he acknowledged in conversation that the victory was won chiefly by Gen. Lyman, *did not mention him in his dispatches.* The news of the victory arriving in England when the government was discouraged by Braddock's defeat of two months before, revived the hopes of king and country, and gave a new turn to the fortunes of the war. Johnson's claims being immediately urged in the right quarter, Lyman's name being as yet unheard of in England, he received the thanks of parliament, and £5,000, and a baronetcy. After the close of the war, which this and other services of Gen. Lyman had contributed to render successful and glorious, he went to England, where he remained eleven years and where his solicitations for recognition and reward were fruitless, or nearly so. He returned in 1774, cherishing some faint hope of recompense in a projected settlement of Mississippi and the Yazoo lands; but d. in 1775, in West Florida, on his way to the new colony. Besides Dwight's *Travels*, vols. I and III, see *Mass. Hist. Collections*, vol. VII, 1st series, 108–115; also Fowler's *Hist. of Durham*, 108–9. Gen. Lyman m. Oct. 7, 1742, Eleanor Dwight, aunt of President Dwight, and had 8 children, viz:

Children, Sixth Generation:

108　1 Phineas[6]; 1743–1775, b. at Suffield, Sept. 21, 1743; Y. C., 1763; received a commission in the British army which he relinquished for the study of the law; at length, in failing health, he accompanied his father to West Florida where he d., and was soon followed to the grave by his discouraged father. "The next year, 1776," says Dr. Dwight, *Travels*, I, letter XXXI, "Mrs. Lyman, wife of Gen. Phineas[5], together with all the surviving family except the second son, embarked for the same country, accompanied by her only brother, Col. Dwight. Within a few months after their arrival she d., and her brother the next summer. The rest of the family continued in West Florida until it was invaded and conquered by the Spaniards in 1781 and 1782."

109 2 Gamaliel Dwight⁶, b. April 4, 1745. " Brilliant, gay, and ingenious beyond most of mankind, he received while in England a military commission, and, a little before the commencement of the American war, was required to join his regiment at Boston. He continued in the army until 1782; and then, with a heart nearly torpid with disappointment, sold his commission and came to Suffield," where his fine mind " languished into lethargy and insensibility," and ere long " he fell a victim to this mental consumption."--- Dwight's *Travels*, I, 280.

110 3 Thaddeus⁶; b. March 16, 1746.
111 4 Thompson⁶; b. Nov. 10, 1752; d. Aug. 9, 1755.
112 5 Oliver⁶; b. Jan. 22, 1755.
113 6 Eleanor⁶; b. Dec. 13, 1756.
114 7 Experience⁶; b. Nov., 1758.
115 8 Thompson⁶; b. Dec. 22, 1760.

35 Rev. JONATHAN LYMAN⁵, *Noah⁴, Thomas³, Richard², Richard¹*, 1717–1763; brother of Gen. Phineas; baptized at Durham, April 21, 1717; a graduate of Y.C. 1742; preached in Middlefield, 6 sabbaths 1745; installed at Oxford, Ct., 1745; m. Abigail.........; was the first minister of that part of Derby which, since 1798, has formed the town of Oxford. He served for some time in the Revolutionary war as captain of a company. The following records may show in what consideration he was held :

To all persons to whom these presents shall come, I Samuel Wheeler send greeting. Know ye that I yᵉ said Samuel Wheeler of Oxford, in Derby, in the county of New Haven and colony of Connecticut in New England, do for, and in consideration of love, good will and respect which I have, and do bare towards the Rev. Mr. Jonathan Lyman, pastor of the Church of Oxford, in Derby, in the county and colony aforesaid in New England; have given and granted by these presents do fully and clearly and absolutely give and grant unto the said Rev. Mr. Jonathan Lyman, his heirs and assigns forever, a certain parcel of land lying in Derby, parish of Oxford, near the meeting house. (Then follows a description of the land) : Sept. 10, 1746. April 21, 1747, John Lumm gives him a piece of land : " For and in consideration of the good will and respect that I have and do bare to the Rev. Jonathan Lyman for encouragement to him in his settlement, in yᵉ work of the ministry with us, which consideration is to my good and full satisfaction." His children were :

Children, Sixth Generation :

116 1 Noah Russell⁶
117 2 Jonathan⁶; b......; d. about 1790 in Derby; m. 1781, Sarah Davis, of Derby; had 3 children : Russell⁷, Jonathan⁷, Mary⁷ (Mrs. Samuel Basset), who d. Oct. 25, 1835.
118 3 David⁶.   119 4 Mary⁶.

38 THOMAS LYMAN[6], *Thomas[5]*, *Thomas[4]*, *Thomas[3]*, *Richard[2]*, *Richard[1]*, 1746-1832; lived in Durham on the ancestral farm where he d. June 6, 1832, aged 86. Prof. Fowler in his *History of Durham*, 190, says of him : " he was a man of great intelligence and extensive reading; dignified in manners and impressive in conversation. It is not impossible that he and some others were influenced in their opinions by the writings of Priestly and Price. So much pleased was Mr. Jefferson with him, that he gave him an invitation to spend a week with him at Monticello, which he accepted very much to his satisfaction. He was with Gen. Phineas Lyman in one of his expeditions to the south. He was a delegate to the convention that formed the constitution of Connecticut." His 3 children were

Children, Seventh Generation :

120 1 George[7]; 1776—; who had 4 children : Edward, Thomas, Frederick, Daniel.

121 2 Betsey[7]; s. p.

122 3 Henry[7]; 1782-1852 ; s. p., d. Aug. 28, 1852, on the farm of his forefathers for 4 generations.

40 ABEL LYMAN[6], *Thomas[5]*, *Thomas[4]*, *Thomas[3]*, *Richard[2]*, *Richard[1]*, 1749-1828, brother of the preceding; baptized Feb. 10, 1749-50 ; freeman 1778 ; m. Adah Picket, March 15, 1790. Representative 1818 ; d. 1828; had 4 children, viz :

Children, Seventh Generation :

123 1 Sophia[7], b. Dec. 3, 1790 ; m. Daniel Dimmock, Jr.

124 2 Frances Amelia[7] ; b. March 4, 1793.

125 3 Dwight Alpheus[7] ; b. Jan. 14, 1797.

126 4 James[7]; b. June 28, 1815.

42 DANIEL LYMAN[6], *Thomas[5]*, *Thomas[4]*, *Thomas[3]*, *Richard[2]*, *Richard[1]*, 1756-1830 ; graduate of Y. C. 1776 ; colonel in the Continental army ; lawyer, judge, and chief-justice; assisted at the capture of Ticonderoga, Crown point, and St John's ; was at the battle of White Plains, and had a horse shot under him ; was a member of the Hartford Convention, and a president of the Society of Cincinnati. In Fowler's *History of Durham*, he is spoken of as an "able advocate, a firm, intelligent, and high-minded man; " "he retired from the law many years before his death and spent the latter part of his life at a pleasant seat near Providence, R. I.," d. 1830, aged 74 y. 8 mo. and 20 d. ; m. Jan. 10, 1782, Mary Wanton, dau. of John Wanton of Newport, R. I., and had 13 children :

23

Children, Seventh Generation :

127   1 Annie Maria[7]; b. Nov. 13, 1782; m. July 4, 1802, R. K. Randolph of Virginia.

128   2 Harriet[7]; b. March 16, 1784 ; m. Oct. 29, 1807, Benjamin Hazard of Newport, lawyer.

129   3 Margaret[7]; b. Nov. 24, 1786; m. Nov. 5, 1827, Samuel Arnold of Smithfield, manufacturer ; she d. May 18, 1865.

130   4 Polly[7] (or Mary); b. Oct. 7, 1788 ; m. July 7, 1808, Jacob Dunwell of the Island of Madeira, merchant.

131   5 Eliza[7]; b. May 30, 1790; not married.

132   6 Thomas[7]; b. Dec. 20, 1791; unmarried; merchant; d. Nov. 4, 1832.

133   7 John Wanton[7]; b. May 10, 1793 ; merchant and manufacturer; m. Nov. 14, 1832, Eliza, dau. of Seth Wheaton, Esq., of Providence, R. I.

134   8 Daniel[7]; b. Sept. 28, 1794; unmarried ; merchant; d. Aug. 4, 1822.

135   9 Henry Bull[7]; b. Nov. 13, 1795; manufacturer; m. Caroline, dau. of Elisha Dyer of Providence, March 2, 1829; have one son, Daniel W.[8], b. Jan. 24, 1844.

136   10 Louisa[7]; b. April 16, 1797 ; m. Dr. George H. Tillinghast of Providence, Oct. 16, 1825; d. Feb. 10, 1869.

137   11 Sally[7]; b. Feb. 14, 1799 ; m. Governor L. H. Arnold, June 23, 1819; d. Feb. 19, 1837.

138   12 Julia Maria[7]; b. Aug. 30, 1801; m. John H. Easton of Newport, Sept. 18, 1826.

139   13 Emily[7]; b. Dec. 23, 1804; d. Aug. 29, 1805.

69 CALEB LYMAN[6], *Ebenezer[5], Ebenezer[4], Thomas[3], Richard[2], Richard[1]*, 1747–1810; second cousin of the preceding; lived and d. in Torrington, on his father's farm; m. first Hannah Loomis, by whom he had 5 children, and second, Mrs. Delight Marsh, by whom he had one child, a dau.; names of children as below, few dates having been ascertained :

Child, Seventh Generation :

140   1 Medad[7]; a lawyer in Vt.; m. Eliza Rich; had children, Medad[8], Eliza[8], George[8], and Riley[8], b. in Torrington, 1789; m. Christina Case of Simsbury, Ct., still living farmer ; he d. 1847, Torrington, Ct.

Children, Ninth Generation :

141   1 Erastus[9]; b. 1819; d. 1847.

142   2 Hiram[9]; b. Oct. 18, 1823; m. May 7, 1848, Julia M. Ostrum, who d. April 30, 1858 ; m. 2d wife Nov. 23, 1859, clock manufacturer, Thomaston, Ct.
    Ch. 10th Gen.:   1 Ora S.; b. Jan. 10, 1861.   2 Mary A. ; b. March 16, 1857.

145   3 Adeline[9]; b. April 2, 1831; m. Burritt Tuttle of Woodbury; d. 1857.

146 4 Edward[9]; b. Oct. 4, 1835; m. Nov. 5, 1857, Ellen M. Potter,
of Litchfield, who d. Sept. 29, 1865; m. 2d wife May 28,
1867, Henrietta E. Blood, of Stratford, who d. March
18, 1869; m. Caroline H. Brinsmade of New Haven
constructing engineer and draftsman, New Haven, Ct.
Ch. 10th Gen.: 1 Wilbur S.; b. Feb. 22, 1863. 2
Charles H. b. March 27, 1871.

Children, Seventh Generation :
149 2 Sybil[7]; m. Mr. Beach; settled in Washington; had 2 daughters.
150 3 Eleanor[7]; m. Joseph Hurlburt of Charlotte, Vt, d. early and
left a daughter.
151 4 Rhoda[7]; m. also Joseph Hurlburt, and had 3 children : Medad, lost in steamer in Lake Erie; Elvira, and George.
152 5 George[7]; b. Aug. 1, 1790; m. Feb. 22, 1812, Ophelia Cook.
153 6 Hannah[7]; m. Rev. Alvan Ingersoll, Jan. 13, 1825; had 6
children :
Ch. 8th Gen.: 1 Sarah Lucinda, b. Nov. 24, 1825.
2 Jonathan Edwards, b. Nov. 16, 1827. 3 George, b.
Feb. 13, 1830. 4 Mary Elizabeth, b. July 18, 1832.
5 Charles Finney, b. Feb. 5, 1835, was 1st lieutenant in
2d Ohio cavalry, and d. Dec. 13, 1861, aged 26. 6 Emily
Louisa, b. May 9, 1839.

87 Sarah Lyman[6], b. 1740; m. Nov. 23, 1763, Joel Wetmore, of Middletown, and lived in Torrington, both
"owned covenant" March 10, 1765. Mr. W. d. Feb., 1814,
aged 75; Mrs. W., d. 1832, aged 92.

Children, Seventh Generation :
160 1 Olive; b. March 10, 1765; m. July 13, 1786, Ezra Hayden,
of Windsor, Conn.; d. Nov., 1848, aged 83.
161 2 Ebenezer, b. 1766; bp. Dec. 28, 1766, Torrington.
162 3 John Pomeroy, b. Jan. 15, 1770, in Norfolk, Conn.; m. Nov.,
1795, Miriam Dibble; 2d wife, Mirah Atwater, Burlington, Vt.
163 4 Melicent; b. Jan. 10, 1772; m. Jan., 1791, Capt. Thomas
Watson, New Hartford, Ct.
164 5 Sarah; m. Giles Whiting, Torrington, Ct.

101 David Lyman[6], *John[5]*, *Ebenezer[4]*, *Thomas[3] Richard[2]*,
Richard[1], 1746–1815; first cousin of Caleb[6], and Ebenezer[6],
and second cousin of Col. Daniel[6] and Thomas[6], of Durham,
lived and d. on the Lyman farm in Middlefield; b. Jan. 6,
1746; m. May 20, 1777, Sarah Comstock of Norwalk, Conn.,
selectman, col. of militia; d. Feb. 28, 1815, aged 69. Mrs.
L., d. Feb. 28, 1835, aged 78. "Estate" says Stearns
"$30,412, liabilities $20,069, leaving but moderate inherit-

ance, after paying so large an amount of debts, to widow
and 9 children." He had 10 children.

Children, Seventh Generation:

165 1 Polly[7]; b. May 3, 1778; d. March 1852; m. Feb. 27, 1803,
Aaron Robinson of Bennington, Vt. Had 8 children,
viz: 1 Phineas Lyman; 2 Sally Hopkins—Mrs. Black-
more. 3 William; 4 Catharine; 5 Charles; 6 Esther
M; 7 Semanthe Mrs. Edward H. Swift; 8 Moses.

166 2 Phineas[7]; 1779–1799; b. Oct. 25, 1779.

167 3 David[7]; 1781–1811; m. May 1, 1803, Sophia Park. Children: Alanson and Sophia—Mrs. Atwater.

168 4 William[7]; 1783–1869; 7 children; Phineas; Adeline;
Elizabeth; David; Sarah; Elihu; Adeline.

169 5 Esther[7]; b. July 31, 1785; d. 1816; m. Reuben Brush,
Sept. 11, 1808; had 3 children: Henry, who lives in
Ottawa, Ill.; Catharine—Mrs. Philo Doolittle of Burling-
ton, Vt.); Charles, who d. in Leghorn, Italy.

170 6 Alanson[7]; 1787–1836; m. Nov. 20, 1810, Sina Coe; had
Roswell D., Henry, and Sena.

171 7 Sally[7]; b. Oct. 27, 1789; m. Jan. 20, 1816, Abner Miller;
children, Jennette, Mrs. Southworth; Sarah C.; Helena;
Urania; Giles, a lawyer in Chicago; Esther; Mary.

172 8 Urania[7]; b. Jan. 21, 1792; m. May, 1818, David Buttolph,
Esq.; children, David, Jane.

173 9 Andrew[7]; b. Dec. 31, 1794; m. Jan. 4, 1816, Ann Hall;
children, William W.[8], and 3 others.

174 10 Elihu[7]; 1797–1825.

103 ELIHU LYMAN[6], *John[5], Ebenezer[4], Thomas[3], Richard[2],
Richard[1]*, b. about 1751; a physician and d. at the south;
left 2 children, Alfred and Maria. Maria[7], lived and d.
unmarried in Middlefield. Alfred[7], also lived and d. in
Middlefield; m .... Camp, left a dau. Annis, who m.
James Thrall, a soldier in the war of 1861–5.

105 NOAH LYMAN[6], *Noah[5], Noah[4], Thomas[3], Richard[2],
Richard[1]*, bp. at Durham, June 21, 1747. had 3 children.

Children, Seventh Generation:

177 1 Noah[7]; m. Lucy Bishop, of Richmond, afterwards of Berkshire,
N. Y., had 5 children, only 2 of whom are living: Nancy[8],
and George[8], who lives in New Albany.

178 2 Electa[7]; m. Levi Branch, of Richmond, Mass., had 11 children of whom 5 are living, Eunice[8], Sally[8], Nancy[8],
Harriet[8], Eliza[8]. 1 Eleanor[8]; m, Brown, she d. Had
10 children, 5 sons and 5 daus. 2 Eunice[8]; m. Waldo.
Has had 4 children, 1 son and 3 daus., 1 son and 1 dau.
living. 3 Sally[8]; m. Smith, 4 children, 3 sons and 1
dau. 4 Levi[8]. 5 Lucy[8]; m. Chapman, and is d. Had

4 daus. and 1 son, 3 living. 6 Nancy[8]; m. Hammond. Had 10 children, 6 sons and 4 daus. 1 dead. 7 Harvey[8]. 8 Harriet[3]; m. Porter. Had 4 children, 3 sons and 1 dau. 1 son and 1 dau. living.. 9 Eliza[3]; m. Denison. Had 1 child is dead. 10 Henry[3]. 11 Mary[8].

191 3 Miles[7]; no dates, had 3 children, a son[3], 2 daus[3], only one living, residence unknown.

117 JONATHAN LYMAN[6], *Rev. Jonathan[5], Noah[4], Thomas[3], Richard[2], Richard[1]*, date of birth not known, d. about 1790, in Derby; m. 1781, Sarah Davis, of Derby, who d. June 19, 1847, at Schodack Landing, Rensselaer Co., N. Y., at the age of 90. The children of Jonathan[6] were :

Children, Seventh Generation :

192 1 Russell[7]; b. Dec. 7, 1784, at Derby; d. Aug. 11, 1802.
193 2 Jonathan[7]; b. June 7, 1786, at Derby; d. Dec. 5, 1856, at Schodack Landing, N. Y.; had 6 children by 1st wife, viz · Charles Russell[8], John[8], James[8], John[8], Davis[8], Sarah[8].
194 3 Mary[7]; b. Dec. 17, 1788, at Derby; d. Oct. 25, 1835; m. April, 1809, Samuel Bassett of Derby.

120 GEORGE LYMAN[7], *Thomas[6], Thomas[5], Thomas[4], Thomas[3], Richard[2], Richard[1]*, b. 1776; had 4 children, three by his 1st wife, and one by his 2d. *Wadsworth, Medina Co., Ohio.*

Children, Eighth Generation :

195 1 Edward[8], b. 1802 ; went to sea and never heard from more.
196 2 Thomas W.[8], b. April 23, 1810; d. April 7, 1862; m. Rachel Brocket ; one child, Mary R.[9], b. Feb. 5, 1847 ; m. Dec. 10, 1863, Wm. D. Goodrich, of Pulaski, N. Y. They have two children. 1 Charlie[10], b. Sept. 1, 1864. 2 Nellie E.[10], b. July 11, 1868.
198 3 Fredrick[8], b. Oct. 11, 1812 ; d. July 29, 1869, aged 57 ; m. Nov. 27, 1846, Mary Miner, 4 children. Ellen, Geo. H., Malbee, Fannie.
199 4 Daniel[8].

122 HENRY LYMAN[7], *Thomas[6], Thomas[5], Thomas[4], Thomas[3], Richard[2], Richard[1]*, 1782–1852, b. May 30, 1782; d. Aug. 28, 1852 ; lived unmarried, as did his sister Betsey, on the farm which had been the home of his forefathers for 4 generations. Before the death of his father, Thomas[6], he had lived in Middletown, in mercantile business.

135 HENRY BULL LYMAN[7], *Daniel[6], Thomas[5], Thomas[4], Thomas[3], Richard[2], Richard[1]*, b. Nov. 18, 1795; manufacturer; m. March 2, 1829, Caroline, dau. of Elisha Dyer of Providence, R. I., had one child.

Child, Eighth Generation :

200 1 Daniel Wanton[8]; b. Jan. 24, 1844.

152   GEORGE   LYMAN[7],   *Caleb[6]*,   *Ebenezer[5]*,   *Ebenezer[4]*, *Thomas[3]*, *Richard[2]*, *Richard[1]*, b. Aug. 1, 1790; m. Feb. 22, 1812; Ophelia Cook, b. Jan. 3, 1794.

Children, Eighth Generation:

201 1 Emily C.[8]; b. Dec. 22, 1812; d. at the age of 25.
202 2 Cornelius N.[8]; b. May 14, 1819; now living and practicing medicine in Wadsworth, Medina Co., Ohio. George[8], removed to Wadsworth, Ohio, in 1817, "before there was an acre of land cleared," and there is "only one man left who was here when we came;" so he writes.

167 DAVID LYMAN[7], *David[6]*, *John[5]*, *Ebenezer[4]*, *Thomas[3]*, *Richard[2]*, *Richard[1]*, 1782–1811; b. Sept. 3, 1781; d. March 15, 1811; m. May 1, 1803, Sophia Park, sister of the late excellent William Park of Woodford, Vt. She was b. April 25, 1783, and d. June 9, 1836. David[7], lived in Woodford, and had 4 children.

Child, Eighth Generation:

203 1 Emmeline Sophia[8]; b. April 25, 1804, Mrs. Atwater.
204 2 Phineas[8]; b. Jan. 25, 1806; d. Jan. 25, 1806.
205 3 Alanson P.[8]; b. Dec. 4, 1806; a lawyer in Bennington, Vt.
206 4 Sally Alma[8]; b. Jan, 27, 1810; d. Nov. 13, 1830.

ᵧ 168 WILLIAM LYMAN[7], *David[6]*, *John[5]*, *Ebenezer[4]*, *Thomas[3]*, *Richard[2]*, *Richard[1]*, 1783–1869; the patriarch of Middlefield; his life prolonged to his 86th year, was as good and active and useful as it was long lived, and d. on the Lyman farm; a deacon of the Congregational church; an early, earnest, and steadfast abolitionist, from the time of the mobs of 1836 and ever afterward; m. Oct. 20, 1807, Alma Coe who was b. March 25, 1786. Elisha[6], Joseph[5], Joseph[4], John[3], Robert[2], Robert[1], of Suffolk, England, b, 1596. Dea. William[7], d. of lung fever, easily and peacefully, Jan. 29, 1869, at the age of 85 years and nearly 6 months, having been born Aug. 21, 1783. He outlived all his seven children except two, David and Sarah. His children were:

Children, Eighth Generation:

207 1 Phineas[8]; b. Oct. 15, 1808; d. Feb. 13, 1826.
208 2 Adeline[8]; b. Feb. 9, 1810; d. Aug. 6, 1826.
209 3 Elizabeth[8]; 1812–1851; b. Sept. 9, 1812; d. July 10, 1851; m. Rev. Charles L. Mills, Sept. 5, left 2 children: Lyman Allan[9], b. Feb. 25, 1841, who m. Jane Andrews June, 1866, and has a son Herbert Lee[10], b. Feb., 1868; and Catharine Elizabeth[9], b. June 4, 1844.
210 4 David[8]; b. Oct. 19, 1820; has nine children.
212 5 Sarah[8]; b. Feb. 8, 1823; m. May 15, 1845, James T. Dickinson[7], Horace[6], Lemuel[5], John[4], John[3], Nathaniel[2] Nathaniel[1].

213 6 Elihu E.[8]; b. March 2, 1825; d. of consumption, April 2, 1848.
214 7 Adeline Uranias; b. May 17, 1828; d. of consumption, July 5, 1849.

170 ALANSON LYMAN[7], *David[6], John[5], Ebenezer[4], Thomas[3], Richard[2], Richard[1]*, 1787–1836; m. Nov, 20, 1810, Sina Coe, and had Roswell D.[8]; m. 2d. Lavinia Bartholomew, and had Henry[8], Sina C.[8], and Charles C[8]. The 4 children of Alanson[7], were:
Children, Eighth Generation:
215 1 Roswell D.[8]; b. Jan. 6, 1814; lives unmarried in Ottawa, Ill.
216 2 Henry[8]; lives in Scotland, Canada West.
217 3 Sina C.[8]; b. 1820; m. Franklin Gould, and has 4 children: Louisa[9], Edward[9], Elizabeth[9], Nelly[9]; lives in Brantford, Canada West.
218 4 Charles C.[8]

173 ANDREW LYMAN[7], *David[6], John[5], Ebenezer[4], Thomas[3], Richard[2], Richard[1]*, b. Dec. 13, 1794; m. Jan. 4, 1861, Ann Hall; had 4 children, viz:
Children, Eighth Generation:
219 1 Elizabeth Ann[8]; b. May 4, 1818; d. April 25, 1833.
220 2 William W[8]; b. March 29, 1821; lives in Meriden, Conn.
221 3 Francis Kirtland[8]; b. Jan. 30, 1825; d. Aug. 9, 1825.
222 4 Sarah Cornelia[8]; b. June 2, 1826; d. Feb. 22, 1831.

175 ALFRED .LYMAN[7], *Elihu[6], John[5], Ebenezer[4], Thomas[3], Richard[2], Richard[1]*, lived and d. in Middlefield, leaving 1 child, viz:
Children, Eighth Generation:
223 Annis[8]; a daughter who m. James Thrall, a soldier of the war of 1861–5.

193 JONATHAN LYMAN[7], *Jonathan[6], Rev. Jonathan[5], Noah[4], Thomas[3], Richard[2], Richard[1]*, b. at Derby, June 7, 1786; removed to Albany, N. Y., 1815; m. Martha Brown of Albany, Jan. 1, 1818; she d. Dec. 3, 1836. He m. 2d, Maria Burbans of Bethlehem, N. Y., 11 Sept. 1839; d. at Schodack Landing, N. Y., Dec. 5, 1856. His children were:
Chlidren, Eighth Gneration:
224 1 Charles Russell[8]; b. Oct. 10, 1818; m. Angeline Spencer.
225 2 John[8]; b. at Albany, June 15, 1821; d. Sept. 27, 1822.
226 3 James[8]; b. at Albany, June 15, 1821; m. Mary Greig.
227 4 John[8]; b. at Albany, Jan. 14, 1825; m. Lucy Read.
228 5 Davis[8]; b. at Albany, Dec. 6, 1830; d. Aug. 11, 1831.
229 6 Sarah[8]; b. at Albany, Nov. 13, 1833; d. May 19, 1837.

198 Frederick Lyman[8], *George*[7], *Thomas*[6], *Thomas*[5], *Thomas*[4], *Thomas*[3], *Richard*[2], *Richard*[1], 1812–1869, b. Oct. 11, 1812; m. Nov. 27, 1846, Mary Miner; d. July 29, 1869, aged 57, d. in Durham on the ancestral farm, his children forming the seventh generation on the same farm. He left 4 children ·

Children, Ninth Generation :

230 1 Ellen F.[9]; b. March 8, 1848. Age 22 years.
231 2 George H.[9]; b. June 28, 1849. Age 21.
232 3 Mattie A.[9]; b. Dec. 30, 1852. Age 18.
233 4 Fannie S.[9]; b. Jan. 5, 1865. Age 5.

200 Daniel Wanton Lyman[8], *Henry Bull*[7], *Daniel*[6], *Thomas*[5], *Thomas*[4], *Thomas*[3], *Richard*[2], *Richard*[1], b. Jan. 24, 1844, son of Henry Bull[7] and Caroline Lyman, and grandson of Col. Daniel[6].

202 Cornelius N. Lyman[8], *George*[7], *Caleb*[6], *Ebenezer*[5], *Ebenezer*[4], *Thomas*[3], *Richard*[2], *Richard*[1], b. May 14, 1819; a physician in Wadsworth, Medina Co., Ohio.

205 Alanson P. Lyman[8], *David*[7], *David*[6], *John*[5], *Ebenezer*[4], *Thomas*[3], *Richard*[2], *Richard*[1], b. Dec. 4, 1806; a lawyer in Bennington, Vt.; m. March 1, 1838, Lucina Harrington, who was b. Jan. 7, 1817; their children are:

Children, Ninth Generation :

234 1 Ellen E[9]; b. Dec. 31, 1840; m. Sept. 5, 1860, John V. Hall; children, Florence[10], b. July 6, 1861, Edward John[10], b. July 14, 1866.
237 2 John S.[9] (1st.); b. Sept. 30, 1842; d. Sept. 26, 1843.
238 3 John S.[9] (2d); b. Nov. 5, 1845.

210 David Lyman[8], *William*[7], *David*[6], *John*[5], *Ebenezer*[4], *Thomas*[3], *Richard*[2], *Richard*[1], b. Oct. 19, 1820; lived on the farm of his forefathers on which—including his children— five generations of Lymans have lived and are living; was president of the New Haven, Middletown and Willimantic Railroad. He m. Jan. 30, 1849, Catharine Elizabeth Hart, b. May 9, 1826, whose lineage is traced back to England as follows: (William[6], 1788–1862; Thomas[5], 1762–1829; Thomas[4], 1723–1813; John[3], 1632–1731; Thomas[2]; Stephen Hart[1]). They have had nine children, six sons and three daughters, viz

Children, Ninth Generation :

239 1 Mary Elizabeth[9]; b. Dec. 2, 1850.
240 2 Harriet Augusta[9]; b. Sept. 9, 1852.
241 3 William[9]; b. May 3, 1854.

242 4 Henry[9]; b. March 3, 1856.
243 5 Charles Elihu[9]; b. Nov. 3, 1857.
244 6 John[9]; b. Sept. 1, 1860.
245 7 James[9]; b. Sept. 1, 1862.
246 8 Adeline[9]; b. Sept. 24, 1864.
247 9 David[9]; b. April 5, 1867.

David Lymans, was b. in Middlefield, Conn., then a part of Middletown, Conn., on the 19th of October, 1820 ; and d. in Middlefield, 24th of Jan., 1871, at the age of 50 years and 3 months. From the numerous biographical notices which appeared in the journals of New Haven, Hartford, Middletown, and other places, we select and abridge the following, published in *The Free Press* of Bennington, Vt., Feb. 4, 1871:

From his parents, persons of uncommon physical vigor, of more than ordinary intellectual capacity, and of the strongest moral and religious convictions, Mr. Lyman inherited a permanent capital in the business of living a good life — that sound, physical, mental and moral constitution which has stood him in so good stead through his eminently useful career. He received in his youth what was then considered a good common school education, supplemented by a little academical instruction. At the age of nineteen he was sent by the Messrs. Trowbridge of New Haven to Kentucky to purchase mules for the West India market, and by them and the house of Alsop & Chauncey of New York, was kept at this work for some years. For a short time he followed it too on his own account. At twenty-seven he was appointed to the trusteeship of a large estate, and, by the conditions of the will of the testator, was not required to give the bonds usual in such cases. In the management of this trust, which he held up to the time of his death, his great capacity for business was constantly called into requisition. Not long after his acceptance of the trust, a legal controversy arose concerning certain dispositions of the will. This controversy ran through the highest courts of Connecticut and New York, and the U. S. Circuit Court for the District of Connecticut. At the end of ten years of expensive litigation, in which some of the most distinguished lawyers of the land had been employed on one side or the other, Judge Nelson of the U. S. Supreme Court, in giving a decision in the case at New Haven, said of him : " His conduct presents a conspicuous instance of great capacity, fidelity and success in the discharge of the difficult and responsible duties confided to him by the deceased under the will, and calls for the commendation of this court. We have rarely known an instance of such faithful, conscientious, and accurate performance of the duties of a trustee ; and in view of the fact that trust estates are so often, through incompetency or unfaithfulness, wasted, we feel it our duty to give the conduct of this trustee the marked approval of this court."

Mr. Lyman's chief business, from which he received, for ten years previous to his death, a large annual income, was the manufacture of clothes-wringers by a manufacturing company, in which he held a controlling interest. For the last four years, however, he had had little to do with its active management, his whole time having been completely absorbed — so completely as to have shortened his days — by his interest in the new line of railroad from New Haven to Middletown, and thence to Willimantic, the aim of which was, by connecting the two points of New Haven and Willimantic, to form a shorter line between New York and Boston. To build a rail road is not usually difficult when the money is at hand, but financial matters in this case were not the chief difficulties to be encountered. The Connecticut river was to be bridged at Middletown, and to this the most powerful interests in the state were opposed. The river towns above the proposed bridge; the competing lines of rail road already in existence; and, more than all, the city of Hartford, the city *par excellence* of judicious care for its own interests, were the parties the new rail road would have to contend with, and which twenty years before had defeated the very project Mr. Lyman proposed to accomplish. A man of less pluck, less ability, and less enthusiasm and hope, would have stopped even before he had begun. For two years he worked before the Connecticut legislature for a charter for the bridge and failed. The interests against him were too powerful for any one man or corporation. But nothing daunted, he went to Congress, and obtained the right to bridge the river, and the work was commenced. How he has labored since then, through doubt and discouragement, through evil and good report, through the lukewarmness of friends, and the open attacks of enemies, cannot be narrated here. All admit, friends and foes, that nobody else could have built the road at this time, or during the present generation. The two cities of Middletown and New Haven know and appreciate his labors. As a slight tribute to his memory, their corporate authorities passed each a series of resolutions, and attended his funeral at Middlefield. One of the New Haven resolutions was as follows:

" *Resolved,* That in the death of David Lyman, the public at large are called upon to deplore the loss of a true man, eminently faithful in the discharge of every duty; attending to every trust committed to his care; genial, earnest, full of hope, inspiring others with his enthusiasm; who carried to substantial completion that great enterprise, the Air Line Railroad, a work of inestimable benefit to this city, and which will ever endure as a monument to him, illustrative of his sagacity, perseverance, and indomitable energies."

The magnetism of the man was something remarkable. He inspired all with whom he came in contact, with his own enthusiasm and with interest and confidence in himself. He had that "hopeful, buoyant temper," that "cheerfulness and hopefulness which are reported to belong to the real Lyman stock," and to which Henry Ward Beecher, himself a Lyman in part, alluded in a characteristic letter to the Lyman gathering at Northampton, in 1869.

Too soon has the grave closed over him. In the prime of life, in the midst of his usefulness, with the most promising future before him, he is cut down, a sacrifice to the work he had undertaken. Less than a week before his death, he left his home against the wishes of his family to attend to important railroad business. He returned to it never to leave it alive. His disease was typhoid fever, which progressed favorably until congestion of the lungs set in, which proved fatal. Of his own knowledge he was soon conscious of approaching dissolution; and, as was said by an eye-witness of the scene, "he set about the business of dying as about a rail road or any other business that had to be done." He was completely self-possessed to the last, his mind clear and composed to an unwonted degree. During the last few hours he was unable to articulate, but continued to communicate his thoughts and wishes by writing. He was in no pain, as he frequently signified by words or signs. He retained something of his great physical strength to the end, the grasp of his hand, only a few minutes before his death, seeming as powerful as ever, while his smile was quite the same that had won so many hearts. He breathed his last, with pencil in hand, endeavoring to complete a few more cheering words to surviving friends.

Farewell, kind friend,'dutiful son, loving husband, affection' ate father, faithful citizen, public benefactor, too soon, farewell!

The *Hearth and Home*, of March 17, 1871, which contains one of the best likenesses of Mr. Lyman, says of him that : "No man had warmer friends and none better deserved them, while few could command so great respect from those opposed to measures he advocated. His unremitting labors undoubtedly caused the acute disease which hurried him to the grave. With ordinary work to do, he seemed to have the constitution of an octogenarian, and himself expected long life. But he murmured not when the summons came — his life had been a preparation for a better sphere.

220 WILLIAM W. LYMAN[8], *Andrew[7]*, *David[6]*, *John[5]*, *Ebenezer[4]*, *Thomas[3]*, *Richard[2]*, *Richard[1]*, son of *Andrew[7]*, and Ann Hall; b. March 29, 1821, in Woodford, Vt.; m. Roxana G. Frary, Sept. 5, 1814; lives in West Meriden, Ct.; manufacturer, is first cousin of David[8], and Alanson P.[8], and Roswell D.[8]; has one child, a daughter, viz.

    Child, Ninth Generation :
248 1 Josephine G.[9]; b. June 14, 1847 ; m. May 5, 1868, Henry Warren, of Watertown, Conn., manufacturer. New Haven, Conn.

215 ROSWELL D. LYMAN[8], *Alanson[7]*, *David[6]*, *John[5]*, *Ebenezer[4]*, *Thomas[3]*, *Richard[2]*, *Richard[1]*, b. Jan. 6, 1814; his mother was Sina Coe, sister of Mrs. William Lyman[7]; he lives, unmarried, in Ottawa, Ill.

216 HENRY LYMAN[8], *Alanson[7]*, *David[6]*, *John[5]*, *Ebenezer[4]*, *Thomas[3]*, *Richard[2]*, *Richard[1]*, his mother was Lavinia Bartholomew, second wife of Alanson[7]; he lives, unmarried, in Scotland, Canada West, a sister of Mrs. Goold, has 4 children.   *Brantford, Canada West.*

224 CHARLES RUSSELL LYMAN[8], *Jonathan[7]*, *Jonathan[6]*, *Rev. Jonathan[5]*, *Noah[4]*, *Thomas[3]*, *Richard[2]*, *Richard[1]*, b. at Albany, N. Y., Oct. 10, 1818; m. Oct. 5, 1841, Angeline Spencer, of Albany; his children are:

    Children, Ninth Generation :
249 1 Sarah Davis[9]; b. Feb. 20, 1843; d. April 5, 1843.
250 2 Russell[9]; b. June 4, 1846.
251 3 Mary Augusta[6], b. Aug. 19, 1850.
252 4 Edward Spencer[9]; b. Feb. 22, 1853; d. May 28, 1854.

226 JAMES LYMAN[8], *Jonathan[7]*, *Jonathan[6]*, *Rev. Jonathan[5]*, *Noah[4]*, *Thomas[3]*, *Richard[2]*, *Richard[1]*, b. at Albany, N. Y., June 15, 1821; m. April, 1848, Mary Greig, of Elmira, N. Y. His children are :

Children, Ninth Generation :
253 1 Charles Russell[9] ; b........., Elmira, N. Y.
254 2 John[9] ; b........., Elmira, N. Y.

225 JOHN LYMAN[8], *Jonathan[7]*, *Jonathan[6]*, *Rev. Jonathan[5]*, *Noah[4]*, *Thomas[3]*, *Richard[2]*, *Richard[1]*, b. at Albany, N. Y., Jan. 14, 1825; m. Dec. 16, 1858, Lucy Reed, of Schodack Landing, N. Y., d. May 5, 1864, at Schodack Landing, N. Y. His children are:

Children, Ninth Generation :
255 1 Frank[9]; b. Dec. 23, 1859, at Schodack Landing, N. Y.
256 2 Charles Russell[9] ; b. Jan., 1861; d. Aug. 12, 1862.
257 3 Jno. Reed[9] ; b. April 16, 1864.

250 RUSSELL LYMAN[9], *Charles Russell[8]*, *Jonathan[7]*, *Jonathan[6]*, *Rev. Jonathan[5]*, *Noah[4]*, *Thomas[3]*, *Richard[2]*, *Richard[1]*, b. June 4, 1846, at Albany, N. Y.; son of Charles Russells.

The entire number of descendants of Thomas[3], may be estimated at 400, or more.

PART V.

Descendants of John³ son of Richard².

JOHN LYMAN³, son of *Richard²*, was b. in Windsor, Ct., in 1655; lived in Northampton; m. Abigail .   ; d. Oct. 13, 1727, aged 72, as appears on his grave-stone, distinguished from others of the same name by the addition of " Richard's son."

Children, Fourth Generation:

1 1 Abigail, b. in Northampton, March 12, 1696; d. April 15, 1696.
2 2 Abigail, b. in Northampton, Feb. 1, 1697.
3 3 Nathan, b. in Northampton, Jan. 1, 1699; d. April 11, 1700. It is inferred that this death, taken from Northampton records is the one whose birth is here given, because there was a second Nathan in this family, b. in 1706, and this Nathan must have d. before that time.
4 4 James, b. in Northampton, 1700 , m. Ann, who d., according to monument in the cemetery, July 15, 1773, in her 83d year. On the stone is inscribed " Ann, wife of Capt. James." On the stone to Capt. James, is inscribed: " Capt. James Lyman, died Sept. 25, 1769, in his 70th year." They left no children.
5 5 Abner, b. in Northampton, Feb. 1, 1701 ; m. 1st, Lydia ....
and had the following children :
Ch. 5th Gen.: 1 Lydia, b. Aug. 17, 1727; d. Aug. 22, 1731. 2 Beulah, b. Aug., 1729; m. Obadiah Janes, of Easthampton, who d. in 1817, having had no children. 3 Elizabeth, b. Nov. 24, 1731. Abner Lyman m. 2d, Sarah Miller, May 3, 1739, and had children ; she d. Sept. 28, 1756. 4 Sarah, b. April 11, 1740. 5 Abner, b. Aug. 16, 1746.
11 6 Job, b. in Northampton, Dec. 1, 1702; May, 1703.
12 7 Joshua, b. in Northampton, Feb. 27, 1704 ; m. 1st, Sarah Narmon, and 2d, Esther
13 8 Nathan, b. in Northampton, May 5, 1706; m. Sarah Webb, of Hadley, who d. 1788, aged 72. He d. in Southampton, Oct. 16, 1784, aged 78, leaving no children. He settled in Southampton in 1733, one year after the first two families, and was a member of the church formed in 1743.

12 LIEUT. JOSHUA LYMAN⁴, son of *John³*, was b. Feb. 27, 1704. At the time of his marriage he was said to be of

Northampton; but subsequently his residence was in North-field, where he was one of the first settlers ; he m. Sarah Narmon, of Suffield, Conn., Oct. 1, 1729, and 2d, Esther ... The first five were the children of Sarah ; he d. 1777, aged 73.

Children, Fifth Generation ·

14 ɪ Simeon, b. Nov. 26, 1730 ; m. Sarah Field, of Sunderland.
15 2 John, b. Dec. 27, 1732 ; m. Martha Hannum.
16 3 Joshua, b. March 10, 1734. As no information can be gained regarding this person, it seems probable that this Joshua Lyman whose death is recorded as occurring Oct. 14, 1753, is the same.
17 4 Seth, b. Feb. 1, 1736 ; m. Eunice Graves.
18 5 Mary, b. Sept. 22, 1738 ; d. Sept. 1, 1739.
19 6 Sarah, b. Jan. 15, 1740.
20 7 Mary, b. Aug. 15, 1742 ; d. Nov. 5, 1749.
21 8 James, b. June 9, 1747.
22 9 Esther, b. June 12, 1752 ; m. Reuben Frizzell, of Leyden, Mass. ; no children.

14 SIMEON LYMAN[5], eldest son of Lieut. *Joshua[4]*, was b. Nov. 26, 1730. He was a farmer living in a pleasant part of Northfield street and owning a meadow and outlands, as also land in Winchester. In the early part of his life he lived much in a fort on account of Indian troubles. He m. Sarah Field, of Sunderland. He d. May 19, 1799, aged 78. His wife, Sarah, d. Nov. 28, 1797, aged 63.

Children, Sixth Generation:

23 ɪ Mary, b. May 29, 1756 ; m. May 16, 1781, Solomon Holton, b. April 8, 1755, at Northfield, Mass. He d. Aug. 9, 1824; she d. Feb. 10, 1840. They lived in Winchester, N. H., of which place he was an early settler He was a lieutenant in the Revolutionary war·

Ch. 7th Gen.: ɪ Bohan, b. March 28, 1782 ; m. May 19, 1811, Lucy Butler, b. at Winchester, N. H., Jan. 7, 1785 ; he d. March 13, 1854; she d. June 26, 1867, Winchester, N. H. 2 Irene, b. Feb. 9, 1784 ; m. March 9, 1808, at Winchester, N. H., Elihu Wright, b. May 9, 1782 — farmer; Northfield, Mass. 3 Polly or Mary, b. July 8, 1786, at Northfield, Mass.; m. Col. Medad Alexander, in Northfield and Chauncey Beach, of Hebron, Ct., b. Sept. 18, 1786. 4 Elihu, b. Jan. 1, 1789, at Winchester, N. H.; m. Dec. 9, 1816, W. Persis, b. July 12, 1792; she d. Jan. 23, 1855 ; he d. July 9, 1861 — farmer ; Winchester, N. H. 5 Harris, b. April 15, 1791 ; d. April 26, 1791, Winchester, N. H. 6 Esther, b. March 6, 1792 ; m. 1816, at Glover, Vt., Ralph Corey, of Plain-

field, Ct., b. Feb. 2, 1790; d. July 18, 1866 — farmer;
she d. Aug. 25, 1837; Albany, Vt.

30 2 Persis, b. Aug. 7, 1758; m. Joseph Smead; had one dau.,
Sarah who d. young.

31 3 Joshua, b. Oct. 12, 1760; m. Catharine Hammond.

32 4 Joseph, b. Jan. 23, 1763; m. Elizabeth Luscombe.

33 5 Simeon, b. Dec. 8, 1764; d. at Northfield, May 19, 1809.

34 6 Submit, b. July 11, 1767; m. George Dennison; no children.

35 7 Sarah, b. Sept. 13, 1769; m. James Strobridge, of Tru-
mansburg, N. Y.; d. Feb. 16, 1833. They had six
children :
   Ch. 7th Gen.: 1 Sarah. 2 Lyman, b. Jan. 31, 1793.
   3 Sophia. 4 Henry. 5 Ellen. 6 Fanny.

42 8 Timothy, b. Sept. 22, 1771.

43 9 Penelope, b. July 26, 1774; m. Hezekiah Mattoon; she d.
Aug. 13, 1849; she had six children :
   Ch. 7th Gen.: 1 Mary M., b. Jan. 27, 1807, North-
field. 2 Hezekiah, b. Dec. 22, 1808, Northfield. 3 Lucia
A., b. Nov. 20, 1810; d. Oct. 25, 1832. 4 Julia M., b.
Dec. 14, 1812; d. Nov. 8, 1856. 5 Sarah E., b. June 11,
1815; res. at Huntsville, Ala. 6 John L., b. April 18,
1817; res. at Northfield.

50 10 Elisha, b. Aug. 13, 1778; m. Margaret Luscombe.

15 JOHN LYMAN[5], second son of Lieut. *Joshua[4]*, *John[3]*,
Richard[2]. *Richard[2]*, 1732–1811, b. Dec. 27, 1732, at Fort
Dummer. He came from Northfield to Southampton, that
he might take care of his uncle Nathan; m. Martha Hannum, of East Hampton, and d. Oct. 28, 1811, aged 78. She
d. Sept. 16, 1814, aged 77.

John, usually called Dea. Lyman, was a farmer, a vigorous and active man. On one occasion he went on snow
shoes to what is since called Huntington, eight or ten miles
over the hills, where he shot a deer, and returned at evening, bringing or dragging the deer. One of its antlers is
still in possession of his granddaughter.

Prof. B. B. Edwards has recorded of him in a note to
his address at the centennial celebration at Southampton,
1841: " Dea. John Lyman was a man of great weight of
character, and exemplariness of life. He was equally remarkable for his wit and his wisdom, and was among the
ablest and most useful men who have resided in town."

Rev. John Woodbridge, in an article printed as " Reminiscences of an Old Man," wrote: " On the grave stone of
Dea. Lyman, that good man so familiar with some of the
best writings of the Puritans, particularly the works of
Flavel, that the thoughts they gave him seemed infused into

nis very being, moulding and establishing his principles, and regulating and sustaining the even tenor of his life, is inscribed with the utmost pertinency the divine sentence : ' Blessed are the peace makers,' &c.   If tumults ever arose and serious divisions were threatened in the town, his gentle voice for many years was a charm to command silence and allay the elements of strife.

The children of Dea. John Lyman were Sarah, Martha, Nathan, John, long known as Maj. Lyman, Achsah, Asa, who d. in infancy, and Asa.

Children, Sixth Generation :

51 1 Sarah, b. Sept. 1761, m. Stephen Wright, of Easthampton.
    Ch. 7th Gen. : 1 John, m. Tryphena Clark, of Easthampton. Their children are Tryphena, who m. 1st, Quartus Lyman, left one child John ; m 2d, Lewis Clapp, of Easthampton.   2 Sarah, m. Zenas Clark, of Easthampton. [*Ch. 8th Gen. :* (1) Lewis, who m. Clapp, and has one child : Maloille, m. at the West but now lives in Easthampton and has children. (2) Climena, living with her parents. (3) Sarah, m. Hervey Smith of West Springfield. (4) Zenas, m. and is living in Easthampton.] 3 Lucy, m. John Wright of Easthampton. 4 Sheldon d. unmarried in early manhood. The Wrights and others, descendants of Dea. John Lyman of Southampton above named are respectable citizens of Easthampton.

61 2 Martha L., b. Sept. 14, 1763 ; m. Joel Burt of Westhampton ; d. Jan. 24, 1835.   *Ch. 7th Gen. :* 1 Levi Burt, b. May 18, 1891 ; m. Betsey Hale, dau. of Rev. Enoch Hale. [*Ch. 8th Gen. :* (1) Lyman, d. leaving children. (2) Martha, m. an Edwards and d. leaving children. (3) Joel, m. an Edwards, has children. (4) Sarah, m. a Clapp, has children. (5) Enoch, lost at the burning of the Central American returning from California. (6) Franklin, graduated at Amherst College and d. in Michigan. (7) George, m. and has children.] 2 Joel, b. March 12, 1796, graduated at Dartmouth College in 1821, studied medicine at the south, practiced at Benton, Alabama, where he d. Nov., 1859. 3 Nathan, b Sept. 26, 1800 ; m. Climena Bates of Westhampton [*Ch. 8th Gen. :* (1) Helen, m. in West Springfield. (2) Caroline, teaching in Springfield. (3) Achsah, who m. a Montague in Westhampton. 4 George, b. Dec. 2, 1802, graduated at Amherst College in 1825, was a merchant in Benton, Alabama, where he d. Never m. These Burts have been respectable citizens of Westhampton.

76 ₃ Nathan, son of Dea. John L., b. April, 1766, was injured by a kick from a horse, some years before his death, and was afterwards subject to fits. He d. Jan. 2, 1799, aged 33.

77 ₄ John, long known as Major Lyman, b. Sept. 1769 ; m. Eunice Ely, of West Springfield, Jan., 1796. Major Lyman d. Sept. 25, 1847, aged 78 ; his wife d. eleven months earlier, aged 74. Of Major Lyman and his wife, Prof. B. B. Edwards wrote : " They were among the most interesting people whom I knew in all that region. The major would have made a governor or judge in other circumstances. " He was upright and reliable, was town treasurer for twenty years, when he declined the office. He was also one of the selectmen of Southampton for many years, and honored as an exemplary Christian and a wise counsellor in the church of which he was long a member. Like his father, he was a man of wit and sound judgment. When Major Lyman was a small boy he sometimes wished for better clothing. The deacon said to him, " You must remember you are a poor man's son ; " but John could not see it. Not long after, a friend from a distance wishing to see the deacon, went out into the field where he was at work, his young son being with him. The father wished the boy's dress had a more respectable appearance, and apologized to his friend. The boy looked at the stranger and said : " I'm a poor man's son, sir ; poor man's son." One night in autumn, when John and some friends were regaling themselves with delicious peaches that loaded the trees, his father, hearing a noise and supposing that thieves were taking the fruit, opened the the door and said : " John, where's my gun ? " " Behind the door, father, " was the prompt reply of John. The deacon withdrew. His family, his laborers and friends were often cheered by a sally of wit, a pleasant joke or unexpected repartee. His children were

Ch. 7th Gen.: ₁ A daughter, who d. in infancy. ₂ Nathan. ₃ Eunice. ₄ John ; all of whom resembled their father in these traits of character.

82 Asa Lyman⁶, youngest child of Dea. *John* and Martha, b. Jan. 12, 1778 ; m. Charity Burt, in 1810 ; d. Feb. 10, 1839.   *Southampton.*

17 Capt. Seth Lyman⁵, *Joshua⁴, John³, John², Richard¹,* 1736–1817, 4th son of Lieut. Joshua, was b. Feb. 1, 1736. He lived in Northfield out of the street ¾ of a mile N. E. of Simeon. He d. Oct. 14, 1817, aged 81, farmer. He m. Eunice Graves of Sunderland, Mass., Oct. 23, 1760. She was b. Jan. 25, 1741, and d. Oct. 1, 1801, aged 60. 2d wife's name unknown, no issue.   *Northfield, Mass.*

Children, Sixth Generation :

83 1 Tertius, b. Nov. 2, 1761; m. Eunice Houghton.

84 2 Phineas, b. Nov. 13, 1763; m. Hannah Houghton.

85 3 Lucy, b. Feb. 17, 1766; m. Israel Russell of Sunderland, Mass;
     d. Dec. 6, 1852, in Winchester, N. H.

86 4 Eunice, b. April 17, 1770; no further record.

87 5 Seth, b. Sept. 8, 1772; m. Betsey Page.

88 6 Samuel, b. March 28, 1775; m. Sarah Smith.

89 7 Nancy or Naomi, b. Aug. 17, 1777; m. Ebenezer Bancroft,
     of Northfield.

90 8 Aaron Graves, b. Dec. 2, 1780; m. Cynthia Lyman, dau. of
     Israel Lyman, of Hockanum.

91 9 Molly or Polly, b. June 2, 1783; m. George Alexander, of
     Bernardston.

21 COL. JAMES LYMAN[5], youngest son of Lieut. *Joshua*[4],
was b. Jan. 9, 1747. He lived in Northfield, and d. Jan.
25, 1804. He m. 1st, Mary Crouch Nash, who d. March
22, 1777, aged 29 years, had 4 children. He m. 2d, Abigail Wright, who d. Aug. 12, 1829, aged 71.

Northfield, Mass.

Children, Sixth Generation.

92   1 Luther, b. Jan. 15, 1769, lived in Kinderhook, N. Y., and
      d. without family.

93   2 Princess, b. June 22, 1771; m. .....Root, and removed to the
      state of New York (west).

94   3 Aretas, b. Feb. 4, 1773; m.

95   4 James, b. Feb. 28, 1775, lived in Thomaston, Me., and d.
      without family.

96   5 Gad, b. Dec. 17, 1782, studied law with Esq. Upham of New
      Salem, and d. unmarried, aged 23.

97   6 Polly, b. Dec. 5, 1783; d. unmarried at Northfield, Aug.
      17, 1848, aged 64.

98   7 Robert, b. March 20, 1785; d. Sept. 29, 1795, aged 10
      years.

99   8 Richard, b. July 14, 1786; m. Abigail Janes.

100 9 Twins, { Thomas, b. Dec. 18, 1787; m Zana Johnson.
101 10   { Henry, b. Dec. 18, 1787; m. Lucy Field.

102 11 Rodolphus, b. April 19, 1790; m. Bethiah Robbins.

103 12 Abigail, b. July 19, 1791; m. David Clark of Northfield;
      d. without children July 3, 1824.

31 DEA. JOSHUA LYMAN[6], eldest son of *Simeon*[5], *Joshua*[4],
John[3], *Richard*[2], *Richard*[1], 1760–1840, was b. Oct. 12, 1760.
"He was an enterprising, industrious man. At 21 his father
gave him 100 acres of wild land in Winchester, N. H., and
an axe." His diligence was rewarded with the respect of
his townsmen. He was 11 years one of the selectmen,

40 years Dea. of the Congregational church, was, with his son among the founders of the town library. Was in the war of the Revolution, as a substitute for his father, at the age of 18. He m. Catharine Hammond, Dec. 18, 1760, had seven children; m. 2d Sally Houghton. He d. 1840, or 1841.   *Winchester, N. H.*

Children, Seventh Generation :

104 1 Elias, b. Oct. 10, 1788. He was teacher and law student, d. unmarried, at Lyons, N. Y., Aug. 11 or 27, 1817.
105 2 Asahel, b. March 7, 1790; m. Lucy Bartlett.
106 3 Rufus, b. Aug. 15, 1793; m. Sophia Field.
107 4 Abel, b. Nov. 29, 1795 ; m. Catharine Van Voorhis.
108 5 Sally, b. 1802; m. Leonard Smith in 1820. He d. in 1837, Winchester, N. H.
          Ch. 8th Gen.: 1 Henry S., m., had 5 children, 4 daus. and one son. 1 Leonard R. Smith. 2 Rebecca, d. 3 Sylvia, m, John Morgan. 4 Catharine, m. Henry Richardson, Boston, Mass.
118 6 Catharine, b. 1803; m.........Cook, Hadley, Mass.
          Ch. 8th Gen.: 1 Henry. 2 Rufus, d. in the Union army at Newburn, aged 21 years. 3 Julia, m. Amasa Davis, Hinsdale, N. H.
122 7 Sophia, b. 1805; d. Dec. 14, 1827.

32 JOSEPH LYMAN[6], second son of *Simeon[5], Joshua[4], John[3], Richard[2], Richard[1]*, 1763–1832, b. Jan. 23, 1763 ; m. Elizabeth Luscombe, Dec. 16, 1809, and d. Dec. 21, 1832. His wife d. Oct. 25, 1855.   *Northfield, Mass.*

Children, Seventh Generation:

123 1 Joseph, b. Nov. 9, 1810; m. Rebecca Page.
124 2 Simeon, b. May 1, 1812; m. Julia F. Harris.
125 3 Robert, b. Feb. 14, 1814 ; m. 1st Sarah Miner, 2d Mrs. Dunbar, Nov. 28, 1867. Clinton, Mass.
126 4 Charles, b. Feb. 10, 1816, Petaluma, California.
127 5 John, b. Dec. 1, 1819 ; d. April 7, 1860, at Northfield.
128 6 Elizabeth, b. Oct. 18, 1852; m. Marshall Lee, Jan. 30, 1853,
          Ch. 8th Gen.: 1 Ida E. 2 Emma D., Vernon, Vt.
          3 Forrest M. 4 Minnie S. 5 Charles F.
134 7 Margaret, b. Dec. 26, 1824; m. George N. Felton, Dec. 25, 1856 ; d. May 11, 1867, Northfield.
          Ch. 8th Gen.: 1 Maryetta M. 2 George W. 3 Annie F.
          4 Effie G.

33 SIMEON LYMAN[6], third son of *Simeon[5], Joshua[4], John[3], Richard[2], Richard[1]*, b. Dec. 8, 1764 ; m. 1792, Diadama Allen, who d. aged 79. He d. 1845, aged 81.   *Walpole, N. H.*

Children, Seventh Generation:

139 1 Levi, b. June 28, 1793 ; m. Jan. 14, 1824, Lovice Weer, who
        d. May 3, 1869, aged 72, no children.
140 2 Allen, b. Oct. 14, 1794 ; m. Jan., 1824, Bicknell.
        Ch. 8th Gen.: one d. in infancy. 2 Lorena, b. 1836;
        d. June 3, 1854. 3 Allen. Stockholm, St. Lawrence Co.,
        N. Y.
144 3 Jessie, b. April 5, 1797 ; d. June 21, 1822.
145 4 Lorena, b. June 3, 1801 ; m. Feb., 1827, Amos Bicknell, two
        children deceased.
146 5 Diana, b. Feb. 17, 1806; m. Nov. 16, 1831, Daniel Ross.
        Ch. 8th Gen.: 1 Lorena, b. 1838; d. 1854. A son
        still lives.

42 TIMOTHY LYMAN[6], fourth son of *Simeon[5]*, was b. Sept.
22, 1771. He was a farmer in Glover, Vermont. He m.
Ruby Beach, April 1, 1804, and d. July 7, 1836. His
wife was b. Feb. 10, 1780, and still lives in Glover, retaining
her activity and her mental faculties in a remarkable degree.   *Glover, Vt.*

Children, Seventh Generation :

149 1 Timothy, b. Feb. 19, 1805; m. Maria E. Hazen.
150 2 Ruby, b. Sept. 15, 1807 ; m. Lewis Barber, a farmer, July
        17, 1839. Had four children.
        Ch. 8th Gen.: 1 Helen M., b. July 30, 1841; m.
        Charles Cook, Nov. 26, 1868, resides in Glover. 2 Ly-
        man, b. April 30, 1846. 3 Ann, b. July 15, 1848. 4
        David, b. July 30, 1852.
155 3 Eliza, b. Aug. 15, 1811; m. John Clark, a farmer, April 24,
        1833.
        Ch. 8th Gen.: 1 Eleanor R., b. Nov. 2, 1835; m. Elias
        O. Randall, merchant, Sept. 23, 1860, res. Glover. 2
        John T., b. Dec. 27, 1837 ; d. Nov. 19, 1860. 3 Harriet
        B., b. Aug. 27, 1842; m. Dan Mason, Capt. of Volunteers,
        March 20, 1865. He d. in the U. S. service. 4 Alson,
        b. June 9, 1845. 5 Hannah, b. Dec. 22, 1819.
160 4 George, b. Oct. 27, 1814; d. Aug. 16, 1835.
161 5 Sarah, b. Jan. 17, 1818 ; m. Charles Parker, farmer, Oct.
        27, 1847, removed to Albany, and afterward to Pepper-
        rell, Mass., where she d. Dec. 20, 1863, leaving 1 dau.
        Addie, b. Nov., 1852.
163 5 Mary, b. Nov. 9, 1820 ; m. Asahel Buswell, farmer, March
        27, 1861, removed to Barton, Vt., one child Fidelia, b.
        Aug. 2, 1861.

50 ELISHA LYMAN[6], fifth son of *Simeon[5]*, was b. Aug. 13,
1778 ; m. Margaret Luscombe, May 30, 1805. She d. Oct.
6, 1811. He d. Dec. 28, 1858

Children, Seventh Generation :

165 1 Adaline, b. Feb. 18, 1806; d. Feb. 24, 1806.

166 2 Frances M., b. May 7, 1807; m. Henry McLallan, Aug 31, 1831.

> *Ch. 9th Gen. :* 1 James, b. July 20, 1832. 2 Amanda L., b. Sept. 2, 1834. 3 Elisha L., b. Feb. 2, 1836. 4 Margaret A., b. Nov. 28, 1837. 5 Clarissa M., Feb. 14, 1839. 6 Henry M., b. April 22, 1840. 7 Henry, Aug. 2, 1841. 8 John, b. Sept. 22, 1842. 9 Eliott, b. Jan. 6, 1844. 10 Mary, b. April 27, 1845. 11 Frances M., b. May 2, 1846. 12 Ellen, b. Nov., 1848.

178 3 Amanda Ann, b. Sept. 12, 1809 ; m. Walter Field, Feb. 28, 1849.

> *Ch. 9th Gen. :* 1 Clarissa M., b. March 15, 1850 ; d. March 8, 1854.

81 JOHN LYMAN[6], son of Dea. *John*[5] and *Martha*, was b. Sept 5, 1769, in Southampton, Mass., known as Maj. Lyman, m. Eunice Ely, of W. Springfield, in 1795, and he d. Sept. 25, 1847, aged 78.

Children, Seventh Generation :

180 1 Daughter, b. and d. Nov., 1796.

181 2 Nathan, b. April 22, 1801.

182 3 Eunice, b. Aug. 11, 1806 ; m. Col. Elisha Edwards, of Southampton, March 21, 1839. Col. Edwards represented the town in the state legislature several years, was a long time school committee, also justice of the peace, and engaged in public business much of his life. Col. Edwards, d. April 26, 1867, aged 74.

183 4 John, b. Oct. 5, 1808 ; d. unmarried in St. Augustine, aged 26.

82 ASA LYMAN[6], youngest child of Dea. *John*[5] and *Martha*, was b. Jan. 12, 1778. He resided in Southampton. He m. Charity Burt in 1810, and d. Feb. 10, 1839.

Children, Seventh Generation .

184 1 Samuel, b. July 16, 1811 ; m. Lucetta Burt.

185 2 Dorcas H., b. June 15, 1813 ; m. Mann Loomis, of Southampton.

> *Ch. 8th Gen. :* 1 Helen D., b. Feb. 21, 1840 ; m. Albert Frary. They have one son. 2 Isabella. 3 Maria D., b. Nov. 23, 1851.

189 3 Charity, b. Nov. 7, 1817 ; d. Feb. 29, 1818.

190 4 Charity, b. Oct. 6, 1819 ; d. June 26, 1826.

191 5 Martha, b. Sept. 8, 1822 ; m. Milton Clark, of Southampton.

> *Ch. 8th Gen. :* 1 Abby M., b. Jan. 13, 1848. 2 Lysander L., b. Jan. 11, 1850. 3 Charles N., b. May 19, 1852. 4 Martha L., b. Nov. 13, 1862.

83 TERTIUS LYMAN⁶, first child of Capt. *Seth⁵*, b. Nov. 2, 1761. He went from Northfield to Winchester, in the first settlement of that town. He m. 1st, Eunice Houghton, April 16, 1787, by her he had five children; she d. July 11, 1810. He m. 2d Hannah Foster, Nov. 27, 1810, by whom he had one son, she d. Jan. 3, 1863.

Winchester, N. H.

Children, Seventh Generation:

193 1 Freedom, b. Feb. 15, 1788; m. Simeon Page.
   Ch. 8th Gen.: 1 Allen, d. young. 2 Warren, m. and had 4 children. 3 Thomas, had 4 children. 4 Allen. 5 Lewis, d. young. 6 Seth. 7 A dau, d. young. 8 William, unmarried.
210 2 Fanny, b. Feb. 5, 1790; m. Bartholomew Kendrick, of Winchester, who was b. Dec. 20, 1786, one child Eunice b. May 25, 1813: m. Elisha Smith.
212 3 Eunice, b. Aug. 3, 1792; d. Aug. 1, 1794.
213 4 Eunice, b. Aug. 20, 1795; m. Zephaniah Thomas; d. June 6, 1850.
214 5 Atta, b. Oct. 13, 1797; m. William Smith.
215 6 Anson, b. Aug. 2, 1799; m. Catharine R. Murdock.
216 7 Tertius Alexander, b. March 13, 1812; m. Sarah P. Codding.

84 PHINEAS LYMAN⁶, 2d son of Capt. *Seth,⁵* b. Nov. 13, 1763. He went to reside in Winchester, at the same time as his brother Tertius and his cousin Joshua—farmer; m. Hannah Houghton, April 21, 1788. She was b. Jan. 28, 1771; and d. Feb. 20, 1814. Phineas L., m. Sarah Morse, of Winchester, N. H., d. Aug. 24, 1814; she was b. Jan. 25, 1771; and d. June 18, 1849. He d. Sept. 20, 1840.

Winchester, N. H.

Children, Seventh Generation:

217 1 Alba, b. April 11, 1789; m. 1st, Sally Codding, Jan. 1, 1818, she was b. July 13, 1788; d. Nov. 25, in the 34th year of her age. He m. 2d, Aurelia Whiting, Sept. 8, 1825. She was b. July 28, 1795; d. June 3, 1831, in the 36th year of her age. He m. 3d, Lucy Johnson, April 18, 1832. She was b. Dec. 11, 1800; d. Jan. 17, 1840, aged 40 years. He m. 4th, Lucinda Smith, Sept. 17, 1840. She was b. Jan. 20, 1795. He d. March 9, 1843, in the 54th year of his age.
   Ch. 8th Gen.: 1 A dau. b. Jan. 21, 1819; d. Jan. 22, 1819. 2 Erastus Houghton, b. Sept. 19, 1820. 3 A son, b. Nov. 22, 1821. 4 Harry Whiting, b. May 5, 1826. 5 Sarah Aurelia, b. March 24, 1828; m. March 10, 1853, William C. Trim, Elkland, Pa. [*Ch. 9th Gen.:* (1) Cora J., b. April 11, 1854. (2) Benjamin F., b. Nov. 21, 1856. (3) George S., b. June 13, 1857. (4) Hobart F., b. July 11, 1859. (5) W. W., b. March 20, 1861.

(6) Lora C., b. Nov. 24, 1868. 6 Charles Luther, b. April 8, 1830.] 7 Mary Lucy, b. March 12, 1833. 8 Lyndia Myra, b. Dec. 1, 1837; d. Oct. 2, 1859.

232 2 Ella, b. April 11, 1791; d. Aug. 19, 1793, at Winchester, N. H.

233 3 Ella, b. Aug. 21, 1793; m. Nov. 1, 1821, Clarissa Cook.

234 4 Luther, b. Feb. 24, 1796; m. Sarah M. Wooley; d. Aug. 10, 1842.

235 5 Calvin, b. July 20, 1798 ; m. Sophronia White.

236 6 Polly, b. April 1, 1801; m........Bliss, Royalton, Mass.; d. Nov. 6, 1852.

237 7 Lynda, b. Sept. 16, 1803 ; unmarried, Winchester.

238 8 Myra, b. July 1, 1806 ; unmarried ; d. May 8, 1863.

239 9 Seth, b. Jan. 18, 1809; d. Jan. 14, 1815, aged 6 years.

87 SETH LYMAN[6], third son of Capt. *Seth*[5], b. Sept. 8, 1772, in Northfield — farmer ; removed to Herkimer Co., N. Y.; d. Feb. 24, 1858.

Children, Seventh Generation :

246 1 Elvira, b. in Northfield, Jan. 3, 1796; m. Sept 13, 1814, Daniel Fisher; d. in Michigan; had two daughters, one, Mary, m. .... Cutler, Hillsdale, Mich.

249 2 Elizabeth or Betsey, b. Sept. 1, 1797; m. Feb. 1, 1820, John Bartlett, of Guilford, N. Y.; removed to Greene, Chenango Co., N. Y — carpenter and joiner; d. March 26, 1857; his wife d. March 15, 1857.

Ch. 8th Gen.: 1 Seth, b. Oct. 12, 1821; m., Nov. 19, 1845, Jane Moffatt. *Ch. 9th Gen.:* (1) Mary E., b. Nov. 30, 1846; m. Nov. 1, 1865, Devilla Robinson. [*Ch. 10th Gen.:* (1) Addie Jane, b. July 9, 1867. (2) Raymond D., b. May 6, 1869.] (2) John L., b. Feb. 6, 1854. (3) George L., b. Jan. 14, 1857. (4) Willard R., May . ..., Greene, Chenango Co., N. Y. 2 Elvira, b. Sept. 23, 1823; d. Sept. 12, 1844. 3 Diadama, b. June 8, 1826 ; m. Oct. 21, 1847, Ransom Page. *Ch. 9th Gen.:* (1) Addie E., b. Jan. 6, 1849 ; m. Oct. 23, 1867, Hugh Skillin. [*Ch. 10th Gen. :* (1) Gracie, b. Oct. 10, 1870.] (2) Eugene A., b. March 27, 1852.

262 3 Esther, b. June 24, 1779 ; m. Dec. 21, 1826, Francis Griswold; d. Oct. 4, 1871.]

Ch. 8th Gen.: 1 Frances, b. Jan. 15, 1829 ; m. Aug. 11, 1861, Sarah E. March. *Ch. 9th Gen.:* (1) Allah M., b. June 1, 1863. (2) Alexander, b. Dec. 31, 1830 ; m. Oct. 4, 1851, Esther March. [*Ch. 10th Gen.:* (1) James, b. Nov. 20, 1852. (2) Frank, b. July 21, 1855. (3) Hattie I., b. March 16, 1857. (4) Dwight M., b. Jan. 15, 1859 ; Middleville, Herkimer Co., N. Y.]

269 4 Seth, b. May 5, 1801; d. Oct. 11, 1803.

270 5 Henry, b. in Northfield, May 19, 1803.

271 6 Sophia, b.......; m. Feb. 28, 1826, Jeremiah Winston.
    Ch. 8th Gen.: 1 Polly, b. March 27, 1827 ; m. June
    20, 1848, Charles McCuller. [*Ch. 9th Gen.:* (1)
    Harry, b. 1849. (2) Horace, b. 1855. (3) Clifford, b.
    1865. (4) Hugh D., b. 1871. New Ohio, Broom Co.,
    N. Y.] 2 Ruth, b. June 26, 1832; m. Jan. 1, 1857,
    James Shaver. [*Ch. 9th Gen.:* (1) Eugene, b. March
    25, 1858. (2) George, b. Jan. 21, 1861. (3) Fernando,
    W., b. Nov. 21, 1863.]
281 7 Sarah, b. Jan. 15, 1806.

. 88 SAMUEL LYMAN⁶, 4th son of Capt. *Seth⁵*, was b. in
Northfield, March 28, 1775. He married Sarah Smith,
who was b. in Winchester, N. H., Oct. 3, 1778; d. Dec. 1,
1803. He d. in Northfield, Nov. 6, 1823. His widow m.
Samuel Smith, of Granby, Mass., and d. Aug. 11, 1857.
Northfield, Mass.

Children, Seventh Generation :
282 1 Warren, b. Aug. 23, 1805 ; m. Elvira..........
283 2 Samuel Jewett, b. Sept. 27, 1807 ; m. Sarah L. Gray.
284 3 Arad, b. May 12, 1810, was partner in a business firm in
    Columbus, Ga.; d. in New York city.

90 AARON GRAVES LYMAN⁶, 5th son of Capt. *Seth⁵*, was b.
Dec. 2, 1780. He m. Cynthia Lyman, dau. of Israel of
Hockanum, Jan. 14, 1806; d. April 15, 1841. *Northfield.*

Children, Seventh Generation :
285 1 Aaron G., b. May 27, 1808, resides at Hadley, unmarried.
286 2 Seth Heaman, b. Dec. 21, 1809 ; d. Sept. 14, 1822.
287 3 George Beals, b. Oct. 11, 1811 ; d. Sept. 9, 1822.
288 4 Mary Ann, b. June 3, 1814 ; m. William Stebbins ; d. Aug.
    8, 1865.
289 5 Cynthia, b. Jan. 26, 1816 ; d. July 27, 1830.
290 6 Israel, b. June 5, 1818 ; m. Sophronia W. Lyman, dau. of
    Calvin.
291 7 Elijah W., b. Aug. 20, 1820; d. Sept. 12, 1822.
292 8 Elijah S. G., b. May 7, 1824 ; m. Louisa C. Lyman, dau. of
    Calvin.

94 ARETAS LYMAN⁶, 2d son of Col. *James⁵*, b. Feb. 4,
1773, in Northfield. Many letters of inquiry have been
written but no information has been obtained respecting
this man. His history is a perfect blank.

99 RICHARD LYMAN⁶, sixth son of Col. *James⁵*, b. July
14, 1786, farmer, lived in Northfield ; m. Abigail Janes, of
Easthampton, Sept. 10, 1815 or '13, an exemplary, hospitable, Christian woman. *Northfield, Mass.*

Children, Seventh Generation:

293 1 James, b. June 14, 1814 ; m. Mary Stratton.

294 2 Jonathan, b. Dec. 26, 1815 ; m. 1st, Harriet Woodward ; 2d, Charlotte Holton.

295 3 Mary, b. Nov. 5, 1818; m. James Brazier, Sept. 11, 1844, of Benton, Ala., formerly of Boston and Groton, Mass., first teacher, then merchant.

> *Ch. 8th Gen.:* 1 Frances Ellen, b. Jan. 29, 1846, at Benton, Ala. 2 William Henry, b. Dec. 29, 1849. 3 Lyman Varnum, b. June 24, 1851. 4 Mary Saltonstall, b. Aug. 4, 1852. 5 James, b. Sept. 18, 1859.

301 4 Gad Cornelius, b. Dec. 5, 1819 ; m. Fanny Wright, of Northfield ; 2d, Rosina Marsh of Springfield, Vt., no children.

302 5 William, b. March 26, 1822; m. Eliza M. Wilson, of Ala., Aug., 1860 : one child Hattie, b. Aug., 1861, went to Alabama in 1847 ; d. Dec. 21, 1863, taught several years then engaged in mercantile business.

304 6 Aaron, b. Nov. 15, 1826, went to Alabama, in 1843, first as teacher, then as merchant; d. Oct. 16, 1848, in N. Y., on his return from a visit home.

305 7 Albert Richard, b. Oct. 5, 1829 ; m. Frances Brooks of Brattleboro.

306 8 Edwin L., b. Nov. 20, 1830 ; m. Rhoda M. Bridge, b. Aug. 23, 1832.

> *Ch. 8th Gen.:* 1 George A., b. Sept. 14, 1856. 2 Maria A., b. July 28, 1858. 3 Henry, b. Nov. 7, 1860, farmer, Northfield, Mass.

307 9 Warren Fay, b. April 22, 1833, went to Alabama, in 1853, taught school 10 or 12 years ; since that has been engaged in the book and stationery business ; m. July, 1860, Jennie E. Stone, of Calmadge, Ala.

> *Ch. 8th Gen.:* 1 Henry, b. Aug. 25, 1861; d. May 1862. 2 Lucy Abigail, b. Sept. 16, 1863. 3 Mary Helen, b. 1865 ; d. in a few days.

100 CAPT. THOMAS LYMAN[6], son of Col. *James*[5], was b. Dec. 18, 1788. He with his twin brother was apprenticed to Dwight Lyman, on the death of their father. He commenced business as a hatter, in Keene, N. H., and afterwards removed to Northfield, in 1812, where he continued in business 30 years, purchased a farm in Vernon, Vt., where he removed April 12, 1844, and remained until March 22, 1862, since which he has resided with his son-in-law Dr. William S. Severance, in Greenfield, Mass. He m. Zama Johnson, of Vernon, Vt., May 19, 1829. She d. at the residence of Dr. Severance, Shelburne Falls, Jan. 17, 1862.   *Greenfield, Mass.*

Children, Seventh Generation.

314 1 Thomas Henry, b. Feb. 14, 1830 ; m. Nancy W. Morgan ; d. 1860.
315 2 Martha Elizabeth, b. Oct. 17, 1831 ; m. Wm. S. Severance, M.D., of Leyden, Mass., Nov. 24, 1853. They resided at Shelburne Falls, afterwards Greenfield.
      Ch. 8th Gen. : 1 William, b. Sept. 17, 1858. 2 Wilhelmina, b. March 1, 1866, in Greenfield, Mass., 3 Charles Dori, b. Dec. 18, 1868.
316 3 Theodore Edson, b. Aug. 16, 1833 ; d. the same day.
317 4 Charles Alfred, b. June 30, 1838 ; d. June 21, 1861.
318 5 William Dwight, b. Oct. 30, 1840 ; d. March 10, 1860.

101 HENRY LYMAN⁶, son of Col. *James⁵*, twin brother of Capt. Thomas, moved from Palmer, Mass., to Wisconsin in 1846, and settled in Ashippun, Dodge Co., Wis. He m. Lucy Field, of Northfield, March 11, 1813 ; d. June 24, 1854.   *Ashippun, Wis.*

Children, Seventh Generation :

322 1 Sarah E., b. Jan. 8, 1815.
323 2 Henry J., b. Aug. 19, 1816.
324 3 George G., b. Jan. 26, 1819.
325 4 Lucy, b. March 16, 1821.
326 5 Marilla, b. Oct. 30, 1823.
327 6 Mary Ann, b. Nov. 22, 1824.
328 7 John F., b. Nov. 2, 1826.
329 8 Abner F., b. March 8, 1829.
330 9 Waldo F., b. July 1, 1831.
331 10 Juliette A., b. March 16, 1833.

102 RODOLPHUS LYMAN⁶, youngest son of Col. *James⁵*, was b. in Northfield, April 23, 1790, or 91. In 1835, he removed from Northfield, to Somerset, Vt., from there to Dover, and thence to Stratton, and to Sunderland. He d. in Bennington, Vt., Sept. 17 or 18, 1866. He m. Aug. 17, 1791, Bethiah Robbins, in Northfield, Mass., April 24, 1810.

Children, Seventh Generation.

332 1 Eldridge; b. Nov. 1, 1811 ; m. Elvira Simmonds.
333 2 Maria, b. Feb. 10, 1813 ; d. in Northfield, Feb. 19, 1821.
334 3 Rufus, b. Sept. 3, 1815.
335 4 Fanny W., b. May 17, 1817 ; m. Edward M. Pratt ; has one child ; Manchester, Vt.
337 5 Robert Thomas, b. May 6, 1819.
338 6 Rodolphus, b. April 23, 1821.
339 7 Lucia Ann, b. March 31, 1823 ; m. Oscar J. Northrop ; has one child ; Bennington, Vt.

341 8 Lucius, b. March 31, 1823 ; m. Oct. 15, 1855, Laura Fills —
farmer ; W. Wardsboro.

342 9 Bethiah, b. May 14, 1825 ; m. Merritt Hawkins ; two
children ; Sunderland, Vt.

345 10 Ann Maria, b. April 16, 1827 ; m. Milton Stevens, of
Shushan, N. Y. ; d. Aug. 31, 1868.

346 11 Elisha, b. March 26, 1829 ; m. Henrietta Ingram.

347 12 Eliza Jane, b. March 26, 1833 ; m. William Ferguson ; has
three children ; Rutland, Vt.

105 ASAHEL LYMAN[7], second son of Deacon *Joshua*[6] and
Catharine Hammond, b. March 7, 1790 ; m. Lucy Bartlett,
March 1, 1819 ; d. Aug. 26, 1867. *Winchester, N. H.,*

Children, Eighth Generation :

351 1 Elias, b. Dec. 18, 1819.

352 2 Clark, b. June 12, 1821 ; d. March 23, 1847, at Palmyra,
N. Y.

353 3 Leonard, b. Feb. 28, 1824.

354 4 Henry, b. Sept. 29, 1826.

355 5 Julietta, b. Aug. 5, 1828 ; m. Amos B. Davis ; d. Oct. 11,
1852, Winchester, N. H.

356 6 Antoinette, b. Oct. 31, 1830 ; m. S. F. Hamilton ; d. Jan. 22,
1862, at Chicopee, Mass.

357 7 Clarissa, b. Aug. 20, 1833.

106 RUFUS LYMAN[7], 3d son of Dea. *Joshua*[6] and
Catharine Hammond, b. Aug. 15, 1793, removed when
quite young to Whitestown, Oneida Co., New York ;
learned the cabinet, chair and carriage making business ;
m. Sophia Field, native of Keene, N. H., lived at Utica,
and vicinity, moved to Ill., where he soon d., left two sons
and two daus. who d. before twenty years of age. The sons
1st, Luther H., at Palmyra, Wisconsin, a farmer. 2d, Henry
in California. *Oneida Co., N. Y.*

107 ABEL LYMAN[7], fourth son of Dea. *Joshua*[6], and
Catharine H., b. Nov. 29, 1795. He removed to western
New York, Oct., 1816 ; m. Catharine Van Voorhis, Aug. 23,
1837. Resides in Lyons, N. Y.

Child, Eighth Generation :

362 1 William Remsen, b. July 2, 1828 ; m. April, 1866, Mary
Campbell, of New Orleans, came to N. O., in 1856, was
a student at Harvard College in 1860, left there when
Louisiana seceded from the Union, was in the Con-
federate army from the beginning to end of war. As captain
of Infantry under Jackson, for 3 years ; as captain of
artillery at the close of the war. Since the war he has

been in banking business in N. O., is a member of the Presbyterian church.

Ch. 9th Gen.: 1 Lillian Townsend, d., aged 4 years.
2 Charles Wood, d., aged 2 years.

123 JOSEPH LYMAN[7], eldest son of *Joseph Lyman[6]*, and Elizabeth Luscombe, was b. Nov. 9, 1810. He m. Rebecca Page, March 9, 1837. *Northfield, Mass.*

Children, Eighth Generation:
365 1 Harriet, b. April 1, 1838 ; d. Sept. 21, 1838.
366 2 Elizabeth, b. Feb. 27, 1839; d. Dec. 1, 1846.
367 3 Maryetta, b. Sept. 13, 1840 ; d. Nov. 23, 1846.
368 4 Augusta P., b. Oct. 29, 1842.
369 5 Frances, b. March 3, 1845 ; d. Jan. 5, 1847.

124 SIMEON LYMAN[7], second son of *Joseph[6]*, and Elizabeth Lyman, was b. May 1, 1812. He m. Julia F. Harris, Nov. 24, 1753.

125 ROBERT LYMAN[7], third son of *Joseph[6]*, and Elizabeth was b. Feb. 14, 1814 ; m. 1st Sarah Miner, 2d Mrs. Dunbar, Nov. 28, 1867. He resides in Clinton, Mass.

Child, Eighth Generation:
370 1 Charles Robert, b. in Clinton, Nov. 7, 1869.

127 JOHN LYMAN[7], fifth son of *Joseph[6]*, and Elizabeth, was b. Dec. 1, 1819 ; m. Malinda Smith, April 17, 1851. He d. at Northfield, April 7, 1860.

Children, Eighth Generation:
371 1 Laura M., b. July 5, 1862.
372 2 Milton J., b. June 15, 1856.
373 3 Jennie M., b. Oct. 24, 1857 ; d. Nov. 5, 1857.
374 4 Hollis C.

149 TIMOTHY LYMAN[7], eldest son of *Timothy* and *Ruby Lyman[6]*, b. Feb. 19, 1805, m. Maria E. Hazen, June 2, 1831—farmer. *Glover, Vt.*

Children, Eighth Generation:
375 1 George, b. Feb. 28, 1832 ; d. Dec. 31, 1851.
376 2 Rhoda S., b. March 6, 1834 ; m. Elijah Hovey, July 4, 1857, a merchant, removed to Albany, Vt., and subsequently to Iowa.
377 3 Elijah B., b. July 31, 1835 ; d. Feb. 23, 1865.
378 4 Nelson H., b. Nov. 23, 1845, Glover, Vt.
379 5 Julia M., b. May 20, 1848 ; m. Charles Skinner, June 3, 1868 ; a farmer, and removed to Barton, Vt.
380 6 Newell T., b. June 12, 1850, Glover, Vt.
381 7 Clara D., b. June 28, 1853, Glover, Vt.

79 NATHAN LYMAN[7], son of *John[6]* and Eunice Ely, b. April 22, 1801. He lived some years in Rochester, N. Y., where he m. Abigail Cleveland, Jan., 1829, she d. there in 1836, or '40· He returned to Southampton, where he d. Aug. 17, 1866-7. *Southampton, Mass.*

Children, Eighth Generation.

382 1 Elizabeth, b. Jan., 1830; d. in infancy.
383 2 John Cleveland, b. about 1831; d. April 10, 1846, aged 16.
384 3 Nathan Henry, b. Jan., 1833; m. Julia Sheldon.
   Ch. 9th Gen.: 1 Orrie, b. Aug. 11, 1861; d. Aug. 26, 1864. 2 Willifred, b. Aug. 4, 1863. 3 Winnefred, b. Aug. 4, 1863; d. July 19, 1864. 4 Clifford, b. Nov. 24, 1864.
389 4 Benjamin, b. May, 1835; d. in infancy.

184 SAMUEL LYMAN[7], son of *Asa[6]* and Charity Burt, b. July 16, 1811; m. Lucretia Burt, of Southampton, Sept. 1, 1831. *Illinois.*

Children, Eighth Generation:

390 1 Samuel Burt, b. Nov. 20, 1833; m. Semantha M. Harris, May, 1815; enlisted in the army in 1861; served four years.
   Ch. 9th Gen.: 1 Lewis E., b. Jan. 14, 1866. 2 Samuel W., b. Jan. 14. 1869.
393 2 John Danforth, b. Feb. 12, 1836; entered the army Aug. 1, 1861; d. of pneumonia, at Bentonville, Arkansas, March 5, 1862.
394 3 George E., b. Oct. 29, 1840; d. Nov. 15, 1840.
395 4 George P., b. Jan. 29, 1843; entered the army May, 1863; served six months; m Helen M. Searl, Oct. 16, 1866.
396 5 Edward M., b. May 23, 1850.

215 ANSON LYMAN[7], son of *Tertius[6]*, b. Aug. 2, 1799; m. Catharine R. Murdock, Dec. 9, 1823; d. Oct. 24, 1834. His wife d. May 7, 1844. *Winchester, N. H.*

Children, Eighth Generation:

397 1 Lucy Maria, b. Nov. 27, 1824; d. Feb. 2, 1825.
398 2 Lucy Ann, b. Feb. 23. 1826; m. at Winchester, N. H., William Parker, of Keene, Sept. 14, 1847.
   Ch. 9th Gen.: 1 Emma Catharine, b. in Orange, Mass., July 10, 1848. 2 Endreas, b. in Palmer, Dec. 23, 1850; d. March 27, 1865. 3 Willie Anson, b. Dec. 29, 1865.
405 2 Catharine Augusta, b. Dec. 28, 1827; d. Jan. 25, 1859; .m. Nov. 29, 1849, Charles W. Hastings, of Orange.
   Ch. 9th Gen.: 1 Nellie Maria, b. Sept. 2, 1851. 2 Flora Marion, b. May 6, 1856.
406 4 Benjamin Murdock, b. Jan. 13, 1830; d. April 11, 1865; m. Dec. 9, 1852, Sara D. Hastings, of Orange, Mass.

Ch. 9th Gen.: 1 Cora, b. Oct. 9, 1853; d. March 17, 1855. 2 Cora, b. Sept. 3, 1855. 3 Anson, July 19, 1858. 4 Charlie, b. July 2, 1869; d. July 19, 1864.

410 5 Marshall Houghton, b. Dec. 25, 1831; m. Jan. 10, 1856, Margaret Ellen Bradbury, of Boston, Mass.
> *Ch. 9th Gen.:* 1 Ellen Houghton, b. Dec. 10, 1856; d. Sept. 18, 1857. 2 Fanny Kendrick, b. in Winchester, N. H., April 19, 1869.

216 TERTIUS ALEXANDER LYMAN[7], son of *Tertius*[6], b. March 13, 1812. In 1827 he left his home as an apprentice to the carpenter and joiner's trade, which business he followed with success until 1856 when he moved with his family to Lee, Ill., where he engaged in farming. He m. Sarah P. Codding, March 13, 1834. *Lee Centre, Ill.*

Children, Eighth Generation:

413 1 Sarah A., b. Sept. 30, 1835; m. Charles Wilbur, March 22, 1865. Allen's Grove, Wis.
414 2 George Alexander, b. June 26, 1838; m. Mary E. Jones, of Bradford, Ill.
> *Ch. 9th Gen.:* 1 James, b. Oct. 17, 1866. 2 Alexander. 3 George Richard, b. Dec. 1, 1871.
418 3 Levi Hall, b. June 1, 1841; Frances Bruce, of Allen's Grove. China, Ill.
419 4 Climea Osgood, b. June 24, 1843; d. July 11, 1843.
420 5 Cyrus Osgood, b. June 24, 1843; m. Jane Elizabeth Evetts, has one dau. b. April 5, 1868. He served in the Union army the last two years of the war.

233 ELLA LYMAN[7], *Phineas*[6], *Capt. Seth*[5], *Joshua*[4], *John*[3], *Richard*[2], *Richard*[1], farmer and carpenter, a private in the war of 1812, resided in Winchester, N. H., m. Aug. 12, 1835, Lucy Murdock, of Winchester, b. Sept. 9, 1799.
Hudson, Wis.

Children, Eighth Generation:

422 1 An infant, name and date not given.
423 2 Lucius C., b. Jan. 24, 1823; m. Nov. 26, 1846, Martha Upham — blacksmith; Winchester.
> *Ch. 9th Gen.:* 1 Hattie C., b. July 14, 1855.
425 3 Nancy Ann, b. April 23, 1824.
426 4 Phineas H., b. Nov. 14, 1826.
427 5 Frances A., b. Oct. 6, 1836.
428 6 Charlie, an adopted child, motherless, friendless, no kindred or acquaintance; original name Richardson.

426 PHINEAS LYMAN[8], son of *Ella*[7], m. at Beloit, Wis., Cora M. Griswold, of Homer, N. Y., who d. Aug. 1, 1861, in the asylum for the insane, Madison, Wis.; m. 2d,

Nov., 1862, Leathy A. Anderson — farmer and cabinet
maker.   *Menominee, Wis.*
Children, Ninth Generation :
429 1 Ella C., b. July 22, 1852.   432 4 Earle, b. Dec., 1865.
430 2 Effie M., b. Aug. 7, 1857.   433 5 Mary.
431 3 Lynda, b. May, 1863.   434 6 Seth.
The last two are given without dates.

234 LUTHER LYMAN[7], fourth son of *Phineas*[6], b. Feb. 24,
1796; m. Sarah M. Wooley, of Winchester, Feb. 24, 1818,
located in Northfield, Mass., but removed about 1820 to
Ellington, Ct., was there a short time, also again in Northfield, and thence to Templeton, Mass., in 1822, where he d.
Aug. 8, 1842.   Mrs. S. M. Lyman moved to Fitchburg, in
1855, where she now lives. She was b. in Northfield, Sept.
6, 1796.   *Fitchburg, Mass.*
        Children, Eighth Generation :
435 1 Hannah Elizabeth, b. Oct. 20, 1818; m. Samuel Kinsman
        of Thetford, Vt., May 23, 1860; lived in Lowell; he d.
        in Thetford, Jan. 26, 1865.
436 2 Luther Houghton, b. June 19, 1820, in Northfield, Mass.; d.
        in Winchester, N. H., Aug. 1, 1825.
437 3 Amasa Lloyd, b. March 1, 1823, in Templeton; m. Jan. 30,
        1849.
        Ch. 9th Gen. : 1 Clara Estelle, b. in Fitchburg, Feb. 8,
        1850. 2 Arthur, b. May 19, 1850; d. in Sandusky, O.,
        Aug. 19, 1863. 3 Alice Helen, b. May 8, 1854, in San-
        dusky. 4 Edwin L., b. Oct. 20, 1856. 5 Mary Lees, b.
        Dec., 1864. 6 Grace, b. Sept. 1, 1866; d. Oct., 1866.
444 4 Welthea Burt, b. Dec. 13, 1824.
445 5 Luther Houghton, b. April 14, 1827, drowned while skating
        on Thanksgiving day, Nov. 28, 1839.
446 6 Sarah Ann, b. May 11, 1829 ; m. Charles W. Pollard, now
        of New York.
        Ch. 9th Gen. : 1 Agnes L., b. March 14, 1863. 2
        Edith M., b. July 17, 1865.
448 7 Edwin Augustus, b. Oct. 31, 1832 ; d. in Templeton, Sept. 18,
        1840.
449 8 Estelle Marie, b. Dec. 13, 1837 ; d. Sept. 1, 1840.

235 CALVIN LYMAN[7], fifth son of *Phineas*[6], b. July 20, 1798.
He resides in Winchester, N. H.   He m. Sophronia White,
Sept. 9, 1841.   She was b. March 15, 1795, and d. March
6, 1869; m. 2d, Miranda Burnap, of Brattleboro, Vt., b. in
Guildhall, Vt., Sept. 21, 1806.   *Winchester, N. H.*
        Children, Ninth Generation :
450 1 Sophronia W., b. April 9, 1820 ; m. Israel Lyman, Sept. 9,
        1841. Northfield, Mass.

451 2 Louisa C., b. March 6, 1823; m. Elijah S. G. Lyman, Sept.
10, 1846, and d. Feb. 26, 1867, at Northfield, Mass.

452 3 Calvin, b. April 30, 1830; d. July 25, 1831.

453 4 Mary, b. April 7, 1833.

270 HENRY LYMAN[7], Seth[6], Capt. Seth[5], Joshua[4], John[3],
Richard[2], Richard[1], 1800 – 1867; m. Jan. 9, 1828, Prudence
Willey, b. June 10, 1804; d. Feb. 20, 1859. He d. Aug.
30, 1867 — farmer. Granby, Mass.

Children, Eighth Generation:

454 1 Mary M., b. Feb. 11, 1822; m. Dec. 27, 1853, George Nut-
ting, of Hatfield.
Ch. 9th Gen.: 1 Oliver G., b. Oct. 5, 1856. 2 Dwight
C., b. March 17, 1861. 3 William L., b. Oct. 12, 1867.

458 2 Eliza A., b. Nov. 10, 1834; m. May 3, 1854, William Taylor,
of Belchertown; d. July 24, 1870.
Ch. 9th Gen.: 1 Elmon R., b. March 20, 1857. 2 Alvin
L., b. July 27, 1860. 3 Ellen S., b. Dec. 28, 1864.

462 3 Charles F., b. Feb. 8, 1837 — farmer; Granby.

463 4 Dwight C., b. July 4, 1839.

464 5 Nancy J , b. June 25, 1845; m. Oct. 9, 1860, Alexander H.
Randall, of Belchertown; d. Aug. 26, 1869.
Ch. 9th Gen.: 1 Charles H., b. Aug. 8, 1861. 2 Mary
Jane, b. July 5, 1869.

282 WARREN LYMAN[7], son of Samuel[6], and Sarah Smith
was b. in Northfield, Aug. 23, 1805. He went to Texas
in 1832, and was surveyor of land for the government.
He d. in Texas, Nov. 18, 1837. He m. June 22, 1826,
Eliza Stebbins, who now resides in South Hadley Falls.
Texas.

Children, Eighth Generation:

467 1 Sarah, b. Jan. 27, 1827; m. Simon G. Southworth, Chicopee,
Mass.
Ch. 9th Gen.: 1 Henry L., b. Jan. 6, 1851. 2 Arad,
b. Aug. 29, 1853. 3 Mary Elizabeth, b. April 18, 1859.
4 Ozrel A., b. July 16, 1863. 5 George E., b. Dec. 25,
1866.

473 2 Maria Eliza, b. Oct. 3, 1828; m. Horace Hatfield, South
Hadley Falls.
Ch. 9th Gen.: 1 Sarah E , b. Oct. 16, 1848. 2 Mary
A., b. May 17, 1853. 3 Hattie Maria, b. Aug. 1, 1855.
4 Frank W., b. Feb. 4, 1862. 5 Lottie E., b. March 17,
1869.

479 3 Henry Clay, b. Nov. 18, 1830; d. Jan. 4, 1836.

480 4 George Warren, b. March 15, 1833; m. Sarah Flavilla Lyman,
dau. of Samuel J., now resides in New Orleans, planter,
paymaster, 2d Alabama Cavalry extended service in Montgomery Co., in 1861.

27

Ch. 9th Gen.: 1 Eugene Montgomery, b. in New Orleans, March 19, 1865; d. July 2, 1867. 2 Mary Eliza, b. in Chicopee. Mass., Dec. 17, 1866. 3 George A., b. in New Orleans, Jan. 27, 1868. New Iberia, La.

484 5 William Henry, b. July 18, 1838; d. Oct. 31, 1855, Chicopee.

485 4 Mary Henrietta, b. July 18, 1838. Is a teacher in Chicopee, Mass.

283 SAMUEL JEWETT LYMAN[7], second son of *Samuel[6]*, was b. Sept. 27, 1807. He resides in Keene, N. H.; m. Sarah L. Gray, of Templeton, Mass., April 12, 1831 : she d. July 26, 1836. He m. 2d, Elizabeth T. Gray, Dec. 30, 1868.
Keene, N. H.

Children, Eighth Generation :

486 1 Delia Ann, b. June 27, 1834; m. William K. Taylor, in Warwick, Mass., Sept. 20, 1853.

487 2 Edward Emerson, b. Oct. 26, 1836, in Hubbardston, Mass.; m. Rosanna Willis.

488 3 Sarah F., b. July 1, 1840, in Templeton, Mass.; m. Geo. W. ·Lyman, N. Orleans, in Springfield, Mass., March, 1864.

489 4 Albert G., b. Aug. 2, 1842, in Hubbardston, Mass.

490 5 Samuel J., b. June 13, 1844, in Warwick; m. Anna Maynard, Aug. 20, 1867.

491 6 Elizabeth G., b. Aug. 13, 1851.

290 ISRAEL LYMAN[7], son of *Aaron[6] G.*, b. June 5, 1818. He resides in Northfield; m. Sophronia Lyman, dau. of Calvin Lyman.   *Northfield, Mass.*

Children, Eighth Generation :

492 1 Cynthia, b. Feb. 9, 1844.

493 2 Francis J., b. July 2, 1846; d. April 8, 1848.

494 3 Elliot J., b. Dec. 8, 1848.

292 ELIJAH S. G. LYMAN[7], youngest son of *Aaron G.[6]*, was b. May 7, 1824; m. Louisa Lyman, dau. of Calvin Lyman, Sept. 10, 1846, she d. Feb. 26, 1867. He m. 2d, Lodusky M. Rugg; b. Aug. 4, 1869, or June 10, 1868.
Northfield, Mass.

Children, Eighth Generation :

495 1 Andrew E., b. July 26, 1848.

496 2 Arthur H., b. May 7, 1854.

497 3 Frank W., b. Aug. 15, 1858; d. May 16, 1860.

293 JAMES LYMAN[7], eldest son of *Richard[6]*, and Abigail Janes, was b. June 14, 1814, resides in Northfield, is farmer and drover; m. Mary F. Stratton, June 10, 1839, she d. May 21, 1865.   *Northfield, Mass.*

Children, Eighth Generation :

498 1 Mary Jane, b. May 3, 1842 ; d. Oct. 9, 1859.
499 2 James Edward, b. Feb. 14, 1848, resides in Iowa.
500 3 Frances Harvey, b. Jan 14, 1850.
501 4 Albert Willis, b. Feb. 26, 1853 ; d. Feb. 7, 1854.

294 JONATHAN LYMAN[7], second son of *Richard[6]* and Abigail, was b. Dec. 26, 1815. He m. 1st, Harriet Woodward, March 25, 1838. She d. and he m. 2d, Charlotte Holton, Nov. 18, 1847, who d. Oct. 16, 1865. He m. 3d, Elizabeth R. Phelps, Sept. 30, 1868. Is a farmer. *Northfield, Mass.*

Children, Eighth Generation :

502 1 Alfred H., b. Feb. 11, 1839 ; d. Sept. 15, 1840.
503 2 Mary Harriet, b. Jan. 11, 1841 ; m. James W. Faxon, of
        Boston, Mass., May 1, 1865.
            Ch. 9th Gen.: 1 Adeline Lyman, b. Sept. 2, 1866,
        resided at Northfield.
504 3 Jonathan Alfred, b. July 19, 1843 ; m. Sarah Jane Howard, of
        Winchester, N. H., Nov., 1862, resided Northfield, Mass.
            Ch. 8th Gen.: 1 Harriet Jane, b. Sept. 12, 1864.
        2 Gilbert Howard, b. Feb. 10, 1867. 3 Jonathan, b.
        Sept. 2, 1868
508 4 Harriet Abbie, b. Sept. 2, 1868 ; resides with her father.

323 HENRY J. LYMAN[7], eldest son of *Henry Lyman[6]* and Lucy Field, was b. Aug. 19, 1816.

332 ELBRIDGE LYMAN[7], eldest son of *Rodolphus[6]*, b. Nov. 1, 1811 ; m. Nov. 29, 1834, Elvira Simonds ; b. Sept. 27, 1811—dealer in boots and shoes.   *Rushville, N. Y.*

Children, Eighth Generation :

509 1 Eleanor A., b. Dec. 27, 1837.
510 2 Melissa A., b. Sept. 26, 1845.

334 RUFUS LYMAN[7], son of *Rodolphus[6]*, b. Sept. 3, 1815 ; m. Oct. 15, 1839, Tryphena Pike, b. Dec. 3, 1817 — is a farmer and lumberman.   *Stratton, Vt.*

Children, Eighth Generation :

511 1 Fidelia S., b. Oct. 20, 1840.
512 2 William R., b. May 25, 1845.

336 ROBERT THOMAS LYMAN[7], b. May 6, 1816 ; m. Feb., 1850, Angeline Mear, b. Dec. 19. 1828—trader in butter and eggs.   *Waterloo, Ind.*

Children, Eighth Generation :

513 1 Milton S., b. Dec. 21, 1855.
514 2 Annie Mary, b. April 9, 1859.
515 3 Elma A., b. July 27, 1861.

338 RODOLPHUS LYMAN[7], Jr., b. April 23, 1821; m. March 28, 1843, Julia A. Galusha—farmer.   *Clayton, Mich.*

Children, Eighth Generation:

516 1 Robert C., b. June 18, 1844.
517 2 Lettie E., b. Oct. 8, 1848.

346 ELISHA LYMAN[7], youngest son of *Rodolphus[6]*, b. March 26, 1827; m. Jan. 1, 1856, Henrietta Ingram.

Children, Eighth Generation :

518 1 Minnie A., b. March 11, 1858.
519 2 Willie J., b. Nov. 2, 1864.

PART VI.

Descendants of John³, son of John².

JOHN LYMAN³, eldest son of *John²* and Dorcas, was b. in Northampton. He lived in the part of the town called the South Farms, and kept a public house near Smith's Ferry. He m. Mindwell Pomeroy, April 19, 1687; she was b. Feb. 24, 1666; was daughter of Mary Woodford Sheldon, of Northampton, and widow of John Pomeroy, to whom she was m. April 30, 1684. John Lyman d. Nov. 8, 1740, aged 80, and his wife d. April 8, 1735, aged 69.

Northampton, South Farms.

Children, Fourth Generation :

1 1 Mindwell, b. Aug. 30, 1688.
2 2 Dorcas, b. 1690.
3 3 Hannah, b. April 2, 1692.
4 4 John, b. Oct. 12, 1693 ; m. Abigail Moseley.
5 5 Esther, b. Feb. 15, 1698.
6 6 Gideon, b. March 19, 1700.
7 7 Elizabeth, b. Dec. 8, 1702.
8 8 Phineas, b. May, 1706 ; d. at Yale College, 1726.
9 9 Elias, b. May, 1710.
10 10 Gad, b. May, 1713.

4 JOHN LYMAN⁴, eldest son of *John³* and Mindwell, *John²*, *Richard¹*, was b. Oct. 12, 1693. He lived many years on the plain, so called, where his children were b. The house of this third John, usually called Capt., was burned with his two daughters near midnight Dec. 8–9, 1747. This it is said was one cause of his removal to Hockanum about 1745, where he made large purchases of land. He m. Abigail Mosely of Westfield in 1718, who d. Nov. 9, 1750 ; and 2d, widow Theoda Sheldon, formerly Hunt. He d. Nov. 9, 1797. *Hockanum, Mass.*

Children, Fifth Generation :

11 1 Zadoc, b. 1719 ; m. Sarah Clark.
12 2 Mindwell, b. 1721 ; m. Ebenezer Pomeroy ; d. Oct. 9, 1797.
13 3 John, b. Oct. 7, 1723 ; m. Hannah Strong.
14 4 Abigail, b. 1725 ; burned to death.
15 5 Dorcas, b. 1727 ; m. 1st, Noah Clapp ; and 2d, Josiah Moody.
16 6 Sarah, b. 1730 ; m. Supply Clapp.
17 7 Hannah, b. 1733 ; burned to death.

18 8 Eleanor, b. 1735 ; m. 1st, Stephen Pomeroy ; 2d, Oliver Morton.
19 9 Caleb, b. June 21, 1738 ; baptized July 2, 1738 ; m. 1763
     Mehitable Strong, removed to New York state, and had
     a son Caleb, Jr., m. Azubah Cooley, and a daughter
     Martha.

6 Lieut. GIDEON LYMAN[4], second son of *John*[3] and Mindwell, b.......1700. He lived and d. in Northampton. He
took an active interest in public affairs and held several town
offices. He m. 1st, Esther Strong, Dec. 25, 1723, and
2d, Catharine, widow of Nathaniel Phelps of Springfield,
Vt., and dau. of John King of Northfield, who d. March
15, 1791, in the 90th year of her age. Monument in the Cemetery.   *Northampton.*
         Children, Fifth Generation ·
21 1 Phineas, b. about 1725 ; m. 1st, Joanna Eastman ; 2d, widow
     Elizabeth Hawley.
22 2 Gideon, b. about 1730 ; m. Eunice Clark.
23 3 Martha, b. 1734 ; d. according to grave stone, July 28, 1753,
     aged 19 years.
24 4 Elijah, bp. Aug. 8, 1736 ; m. Esther Pomeroy.

9 ELIAS LYMAN[4], third son of *John*[3] and Mindwell, b.
May 15, 1710, at the South Farms, Northampton. He succeeded his father, was among those who were called out
for the defence of Bennington in the Revolutionary war,
in his business a farmer and keeper of public house. He
d. April 17, 1790. He m. Hannah Allen, dau. of Dea.
Samuel Allen, of Northampton, April 8, 1736 ; she was b.
1714, and d. Oct. 1717. ·   *Northampton, South Farms.*
         Children, Fifth Generation
25 1 Hannah, bp. May 15, 1737 ; m. Joseph Clapp.
     Ch. 6th Gen.: 1 Elizabeth, who m. Phelps. 2 Joseph.
     3 Thaddeus, who had children : [*Ch. 7th Gen. :* (1)
     Philena, m. Clark. (2) Theodore. (3) Thaddeus. (4)
     Luther. (5) Mary, m. Merritt. (6) Elvira, m. Bart-
     lett.] 4 Luther. 5 Isaac. 6 Rufus.
38 2 Rachel, bp. Aug. 27, 1738 ; m. Jonathan Strong, of North-
     ampton.
     Ch. 6th Gen. : 1 Jonathan. [*Ch. 7th Gen. :* (1) Eliza-
     beth. (2) Rachel. (3) Jonathan. (4) Calvin. (5)
     George.] 2 Asahel. 3 Elisha. [*Ch. 7th Gen.:* (1)
     Mary. (2) Henry. (3) Ebenezer. (4) Elisha.] 4
     Samuel.
52 3 Elias, b. Aug. 18, 1740 ; m. Hannah Clapp, of Easthampton.
53 4 Joel, b. 1742 ; m. Mary Eastman, of Granby.
54 5 Elizabeth, b. Sept. 29, 1744 ; d. June, 1762.

55 6 Sarah, b. 1746; m. John Strong, of Southampton; d. 1778, aged 32 years.

    Ch. 6th Gen.: 1 John. 2 Phineas, m. Eunice Lyman, 1797. [*Ch. 7th Gen.:* (1) Elizabeth. (2) Eunice (3) Pamelia, m. Rev. Sumner G. Clapp. (4) Phineas. (5) Noah Lyman. (6) Mary. (7) Horace. (8) Francis A.] 3 Sarah, m. Josiah Parsons of N. [*Ch. 7th Gen.:* (1) Fanny, m. Clark. (2) Sally, m. Wright. (3) Lyman (4) Betsey. (5) Josiah. (6) Chauncey. (7) Julia.] 4 Mary.

76 7 Mindwell, b............; m. Dr. Sylvester Woodbridge, of Southampton.

    Ch. 6th Gen.: 1 Rev. John, D.D [*Ch. 7th Gen.:* (1) Mary. (2) Mindwell. (3) Susan. (4) Charlotte. (5) Emmeline. (6) Loisa. (7) Rebecca. (8) Octavia.] 2 Rev. Sylvester of New Orleans, who m. Elizabeth Gould. [*Ch. 7th Gen.:* (1) Rev. Sylvester of Benicia, Cal. (2) Jahleell. (3) Prof. Samuel, of the Theological Sem. New Brunswick, N. J. (4) Rev. John, Saratoga Springs.] 3 Mindwell, m. Rev. Vinson Gould, of Southampton, Sept. 9, 1808. [*Ch. 7th Gen.:* (1) Brewster. (2) Lyman. (3) Mary, m. Rev. A. W. McClure. (4) Mindwell Lyman, m. 1843, Rev. John Patton, Phil. (5) Rachel. (6) Sarah. (7) David. (8) Sarah. (9) Margaret.]

101 8 Jonathan, b. 1748; m. Lois Clapp, of East Hampton.

10 GAD LYMAN[4], youngest son of *John*[3] and Mindwell, was b. Feb. 13, 1713, lived in Northampton until late in life when he went to Goshen, Mass., where he d. Oct. 24, 1791. He m. Thankful Pomeroy, June 22, 1738, who d. Aug. 12, 1790, aged 79.   *Goshen, Mass.*

    Children, Fifth Generation:

102 1 Oliver, b. April 1, 1739; m. Eleanor Lyman.

103 2 Jerusha, b. Nov. 16, 1740.

104 3 Thankful, b. Jan. 9, 1742.

105 4 Timothy, b. July 4, or 25, 1745, or 6; m. Hannah Colson.

106 5 Eunice, b. March 27, 1747; m. 1st, Rev. Mr. Mills; 2d, ... Southworth.

107 6 Tryphena, b. April 30, 1749; m. 1st, ...Williams; 2d, ... Dutton of Northfield.

11 ZADOC LYMAN[5], eldest son of *John*[4] and Abigail, was b. in 1719, he lived in Hockanum, and kept a public house. He m. Sarah Clark, dau. of Ebenezer Clark and d. Oct. 14, 1754, leaving four children, Sarah; m. for her second husband John Wright, of Northampton; by him she had three children, and d. in 1795, in Williamsburg, Mass.

        Hockanum, Mass.

Children, Sixth Generation :

108 1 Israel, b. Feb. 7, 1746, in Hockanum ; m. Rachel Beals.
109 2 Azariah, b. Dec., 1747 ; m. Jemima Kingsley.
110 3 Abigail, b....... 1751 ; m. Ephraim Wright, of Westhamp-
        ton.
111 4 Luke, b....... 1753 ; m. Susanna Hunt.

13 JOHN LYMAN[5], second son of *John*[4] and Abigail, was
b. Oct. 7, 1723, he lived in Northampton on the old homestead on the plain. He m. Hannah Strong, dau. of Jonathan Strong. She was b. April 8, 1729, and d. April 15,
1801, aged 72 years. He d. Nov. 4, 1797, aged 74. His
eldest son, and three of his daughters were deaf mutes.

South Farms.

Children, Sixth Generation :

112 1 John, b. Sept. 8, 1850 ; m. 1st, Cynthia Dwight ; m. 2d, Sarah
        Baker.
113 2 Rufus, b. Dec., 1851.
114 3 Hannah, b. Nov. 28, 1754 ; m. Joseph Eastman, d. Aug.
        21, 1830, aged 76.
115 4 Thomas, b. Dec. 18, 1756 ; m. Dorothy Clark.
116 5 Phœbe, b. Jan. 5, 1759 ; m. Giles Lyman — d. Feb. 25,
        1829, aged 70.
117 6 Asahel, b. March 11, 1761 ; d. Aug. 10, 1770, aged nine
        years.
118 7 Dorcas, b. Feb. 7, 1763 ; m. Jan. 28, 1780, to Dea. Israel
        Clark, of Sunderland, afterwards of Hawley and North-
        ampton.
119 8 Mehitable, b. Nov. 17, 1764 ; m. David Cone, of Westmin-
        ster, Vt., and d. Oct. 11, 1827, aged 63.
120 9 Susanna, b. July 20, 1767 ; m. Ovid Avery, of Westminster,
        Vt., she was a deaf mute had 8 children who were care-
        fully raised by her.
129 10 Jerusha, b. June 16, 1768 ; d. Dec. 19, 1774.
130 11 Persis, b. April 19, 1791 ; d. April 19, 1826, aged 55,
        she was a deaf mute.
131 12 Anne, b. Feb. 7, 1773 ; d. July 19, 1839, a deaf mute,
        aged 66.

19 CALEB LYMAN[5], third son of *John*[4] and Abigail, b. June
21, 1738 ; m. Mehitable Strong Jan. 25, 1766, and d.
Mehitable was b. Feb. 17, 1743 ; d. Feb. 27, 1800.

Hadley, Mass.

Children, Sixth Generation :

132 1 Isaac, b. April 24, 1769, in Hadley. He was called Doctor.
133 2 Martha, b. March 25, 1771, in Hadley, drowned in Conn.
        river, Jan. 17, 1779.
134 3 Caleb, b. July 31, 1775, in Hadley ; m. Azubah Cooley.

21 PHINEAS LYMAN⁵, eldest son of *Lieut. Gideon⁴, John³, John², Richard¹*, b. about 1725; m. 1st, Joanna Eastman, April 5, 1750. She d. Feb. 5, 1759, in her 29th year, and he m. 2d, Elizabeth Hawley, widow of Elisha.   *Northampton.*

Children, Sixth Generation:

135 1 Phineas, b. Jan. 22, 1750; committed suicide, April 23, 1779.
136 2 Timothy, b. Aug. 15, 1753; m. Elizabeth Pomeroy.
137 3 Elisha, b. Sept. 23, 1756; committed suicide by hanging previous to 1792.

22 GIDEON LYMAN⁵, second son of Lieut. *Gideon⁴*, was b. in Northfield, about 1730; m. Eunice Clark, and d. about 1752.   *Northfield, Mass.*

Children, Sixth Generation.

138 1 Gideon, b. Jan. 26, 1758; m. Dolly Spencer. ·
139 2 Eunice, b. Nov. 8, 1760; m. Sprague and lived with her mother in Northampton.

24 ELIJAH LYMAN⁵, youngest son of *Lieut. Gideon⁴*, was bp. Aug. 8, 1736; m. Esther Pomeroy.   *Northampton.*

Children, Sixth Generation:

140 1 Elijah, bp. Sept. 7, 1771; d. Aug. 24, 1778.
141 2 Esther, m. Elijah Arms.
142 3 Martha, m. Jacob Smith, in 1795.

52 ELIAS LYMAN⁵, eldest son of *Elias⁴* and Hannah, *John³, John², Richard¹*, b. Aug. 18, 1740, at Northampton, S. Farms. He built a house about a mile north of his father's, not far from the Rock Ferry; here all his children were b. He was a farmer and kept a public house. He m. Hannah Clapp, dau. of Jonathan Clapp, of Easthampton, Oct. 25, 1764. She was b. June 25, 1742, and d. Aug. 1813. He d. March 2, 1816.   *South Farms.*

Children, Sixth Generation:

143 1 Justin, b. Oct. 17, 1765; m. Martha Clapp.
144 2 Elias, b. Feb. 23, 1768; m. Anna White.
145 3 Gaius, b. Nov. 24, 1769; m. Submit Field.
146 4 Elizabeth, b. Oct. 31, 1771; m. Capt. Malachi James, of Goshen. Mass., Feb. 18, 1790. He was b. July 9, 1707, and d. Aug. 24, 1849.
        Ch. 7th Gen.: 1 Sophia, b. Nov. 18, 1791; m. Thomas Sears, May 11, 1815; d. at Chelsea, Michigan. [*Ch. 8th Gen.* : (1) Darwin R., d. young. (2) Claudius W., b. Nov. 8, 1817. (3) Frances M. (4) Sophia A. (5) Thomas S., d. young. (6) Clarissa C. (7) Thomas S. (8) Elizabeth L. (9) Sarah James. (10) Mary.] 2

28

Enoch, b. Dec. 8, 1793; m. A. R. Dwight, Jan. 18 1827; d. at Ann Arbor, Michigan, Feb. 28, 1867. [*Ch. 8th Gen.:* (1) Henry. (2) Lyman. (3) Martha. (4) Mary. (5) Enoch Dwight. 3 Lyman b. March 23, 1796; m. Maria C. Goodrich, March 17, 1825. He d. Dec. 16, 1830, at Bellefonte, Alabama, leaving two daughters (since dead) Elizabeth and Rhoda G. 4 Maria, b. July 2, 1799; m. Samuel Howes, of Ashfield. 5 Clarissa, b. May 18, 1801; m. Josiah D. Whitney, of Northampton, Oct. 13, 1834. [*Ch 8th Gen.:* (1) James L., b. Nov. 28, 1835, grad. at Yale in 1856, prof. of mining, &c., Harvard. (2) Alice, d. in infancy. (3) Alice L., b. Dec. 17, 1840. (4) Harvy, M., b. Jan. 6, 1843, grad. at Yale, 1864, professor of rhetoric, English Literature, Beloit College, Wisconsin. 6 Luther, b. July 13, 1803. 7 Lewis, b. May 8, 1805; m. Cerintha Wells. [*Ch. 8th Gen.:* (1) Darwin R. (2) Lewis Whitney. (3) John Wells. (4) William H. H. (5) Isabella.] 8 Elizabeth, b. Nov. 22, 1810; m. A. L. Babcock, has one son James L. 9 Rachel L., b. Nov. 15, 1812; m. David Storrs, June 1845, had one child David Williams, b. Oct. 20, 1846.

182 5 Hannah, b. Dec. 18, 1773; m. Daniel Breckenridge, of Bennington, Vt. She d. at Bennington, Nov., 1811.

> *Ch. 7th Gen.:* 1 Lyman. 2 Daniel. 3 Justin. 4 James. 5 Mary. 6 Julia. 7 Cecilia. 8 Normand. 9 Lewis.

192 6 Asahel, b. April 10, 1776; m. Lucy Parsons.

193 7 Simeon, b. Dec. 3, 1777; unmarried. He graduated at Dartmouth College, in 1802. Went to London, as secretary to Gen. William Lyman. After his return was in the employ of his brothers J. and E. Lyman, made several voyages to foreign ports as supercargo in their vessels. He was twice captured by privateers, met with perils by land and by sea; on his return voyage he was wrecked, continuing ten days on the wreck. His constitution became enfeebled and after a few years of service in the business of his brothers in New York, he became a resident of Hartford, Conn., where he d. April 12, 1832.

194 8 Rachel, b. Nov. 4, 1779; d. at Northampton, Feb. 19, 1808; unmarried.

195 9 Job, b. Dec. 9, 1781; m. Mary Parrot Hall.

53 JOEL LYMAN[5], second son of *Elias*[4], and Hannah Allen, b. about 1742; m. Mary Eastman, of Granby, and d. Oct. 10, 1801, in his 60th year.   *Northampton.*

Children, Sixth Generation:

196 1 Joel, b. 1765; d. Sept. 5, 1778 (as by stone in Cemetery).

197 2 Mayr, b. 1778, aged 10 years, 1 month.

198 3 Mary, b. 1768; m. John Dickinson, of Granby, Mass.
> *Ch. 7th Gen.:* 1 John H., in the ministry and d. in Plainville, Conn. 2 Abby, m. George Salisbury at the west and removed to Oregon, where they both died, leaving 3 children. 3 Margaret, m. George Underwood of Hillsdale, Mich. and d. leaving one son who came to the Williston Seminary and d. there.

206 4 Elizabeth, b. Sept. 9, 1785; m. David Bassett, Nov. 2, 1813.
> *Ch. 7th Gen.:* 1 Justin, b. July 22, 1814; d. Aug. 20, 1846. 2 Joel L., b. Feb. 17, 1817; d. Aug. 8, 1817. 3 Elizabeth, b. July 21, 1818; d. April 22, 1838. 4 Hannah, b. Nov. 14, 1821; d. May 14, 1838. 5 Joel L., b. Jan. 13, 1825.

101 JONATHAN LYMAN[5], youngest son of *Elias*[4], and Hannah Allen, b., 1748; d. March 28, 1788; m. Lois Clapp, of Easthampton, a lineal descendant from Capt. Roger Clapp, who came from Salem, Devonshire, England, 1630, the ancestor of the Clapps in America. *Northampton.*

> *Children, Sixth Generation.*

212 1 Jonathan, b. Oct. 12, 1775; m. Clarissa Clapp.
213 2 Sally, b. Sept. 9, 1777; m. Luther Wright, of Easthampton, a farmer, was dea. in Congregational church, and d. Jan. 1, 1860. She d. Nov. 29, 1866.
> *Ch. 7th Gen.:* 1 Luther, b. Nov. 24, 1796. 2 Roxana, m. a Marsh, and d. in 1836, leaving no issue. 3 Sarah d. in 1818, aged 18 years. 4 Theodore Lyman, b. Oct. 7, 1806, has six children. Beloit, Wis. 5 Julia Semantha, m. an Avery, had 8 children. Easthampton, Mass. 6 Lois Clarissa, b. Jan. 15, 1817; m. C. Lord, 2 children.

234 3 Sylvester, b. Dec. 11, 1775; m. Nancy Clapp, Aug. 30, 1797.
235 4 Clarissa, b. Jan. 1, 1780; m. Elisha Warner, of Southampton, d. in Easthampton, in the spring of 1865, no issue.
236 5 Roxana, d. young.
237 6 Sophia, m. Daniel King of Northampton.
> *Ch. 7th Gen.:* 1 Lyman. 2 William. 3 Daniel. 4 Edward. 5 Clarissa. 6 Sophia.

214 LUTHER WRIGHT[7], son of *Luther*[6] and Sally Lyman, m. Oct. 8, 1829, Emeline G. Colton, of Long Meadow, Mass. d. Sept. 5, 1870. She d. March 6, 1863.
> *Easthampton, Mass.*

Rev. Luther Wright, son of Luther and Sarah Lyman Wright, was b. in Easthampton, Nov. 21, 1796, on the spot where he died. Was fitted for college at Phillips Academy in Andover, Mass. Admitted to Yale College in New Haven, Conn., in 1818. Graduated in 1822. Was principal of an Academy in Maryland from Sept.

1822 to Aug., 1824. Began to study theology in New Haven in the autumn of 1824. Was tutor in Yale College from March, 1825 to Sept., 1828. Was licensed to preach in 1828. Was for a time professor of Latin and Greek in the Military Academy at Middletown, Conn. : but after a few months' service resigned the office, because the place, from its associations with war, was not congenial to his views and feelings. Was m. Oct. 1829, to Emeline Gregory, daughter of Samuel and Anne G. Colton of Longmeadow, Mass., who died, greatly beloved and lamented, March 6, 1863. Was associated with Judge Hall, in 1829, in establishing the Classical School at Ellington, Conn. Was principal of the Academy at Leicester, Mass., from Sept. 1833 to Oct. 1839, when in consequence of broken health, induced by labors above measure, he resigned his place, and returned with his family to his native town, in hope of recovering, if possible, by farm labor, his physical strength, and that he might nourish, with filial assiduities, his aged father and mother.

He was principal of the Williston Seminary from its opening Oct. 1, 1841, to July, 1849.

After resigning his place in the Seminary, Mr. Wright was for several years engaged in giving instruction to private students in classical learning—a labor of love with him; and his soul broke for the longings it had unto it at all times. In the closing day of his last sickness, amid his wanderings of mind, those who watched around his bed-side found him fancying himself engaged in his favorite toil, teaching Greek. It is estimated that in the various positions held by him as a teacher, he has had under his care and tuition an aggregate of four thousand pupils. Of these pupils there are those now occupying positions of eminent usefulness whom *we* have heard frankly and thankfully confessing, that for all that they are and have done, they are indebted, under God, to Luther Wright.

Mr. Wright became a Christian while a member of Yale College, and joined the church in that institution. His conversion, in respect of its immediate and instrumental cause, he attributed to Mr. Nettleton's whispering in his ear the three words, " Be in earnest," at an inquiry meeting, in a season of revival in Yale College. His convictions of sin were pungent, and that thorough " law work " gave depth and fervor to his piety as seen in after years.

Coming to Easthampton from Leicester, Mr. and Mrs. Wright brought letters from the church there, and joined the church July 5, 1840. He was chosen deacon of this church May 14, 1857, and continued to discharge the duties of that office till the day of his death. Was chosen member of the church committee June 28, 1866. Has served during several years as member of the parish committee. Has been the treasurer of the church since his election to the office of deacon. Has many times been sent with the pastor to neighboring churches to serve on ecclesiastical councils.

In his humility he requested that upon his tomb-stone should be placed no title, but simply his name. And so, in conclusion, as was

said of Henry Kirke White, I should say of my friend and father—
LUTHER WRIGHT, " His monument shall be his name alone."

Child, Eighth Generation :

244	1 Sarah Emeline, b. Nov. 5, 1831.
245	2 Ellen Louisa, b. June 6, 1834.
246	3 Luther Lyman, b. Aug. 13, 1826 ; m. Oct. 17, 1866, no
	children.
247	4 Arthur Colton, b. Sept. 7, 1839 ; d. Feb. 28, 1866.

102 OLIVER LYMAN[5], eldest son *Gad*[4] and Thankful, was
born April 1, 1739. He was called Capt. He resided in
Northampton in the early part of his life, being mentioned
as there Oct. 6, 1767. He m. Eleanor Lyman, dau. of
Joseph. He removed to Charlotte, Vermont, and d. there.
Charlotte, Vt.

Children, Sixth Generation :

248	1 Abigail, b. April 18, 1762 ; m. Ephraim Wooster, of Litch-
	field, in 1781.
		Ch. 7th Gen.: 1 Eleanor, who m. Josph Harrington,
	of Burlington, Vt., had 2 children, Lyman, and Laura.
	2 Fanny, m. Rev. Mason Knappen, who was settled in
	Orwell, Vt., several years, his wife died there, had two
	children, Fanny, and Philander. 3 Lyman, m. Anne
	Pease, of Charlotte Vt., dau. of Wm. Pease.
		Ch. 8th Gen.: 1 Marianne, m. Mr. Rice, of Charlotte,
	and had 3 children, m. 2d, Mr. Hooker, of Poultney. 2
	Guy. 3 Sarah.
262	2 Charlotte, b. Nov. 22, 1763 ; m. Ezra Clark, June 14, 1785.
		Ch. 7th Gen.: 1 Charlotte, m. Oliver Hubbell, a
	lawyer of Charlotte, Vt. 2 Frances. 3 Lewis. 4 and
	5 Martha and Charles, both d. unmarried, Charles, at
	Burlington, Vt. 6 Zenas, settled in Potsdam, Vt., and
	had six children. 7 Theodore, settled in Vergennes.
	8 George, removed to Albany. 9 and 10 Marianne, 1st
	d. in infancy, and Marianne 2d m. Mr. Harris, of
	Middlebury.
279	3 Gad, b. Aug. 23, 1766 ; m. Prudence Bill of Huntington,
	Mass.
280	4 Oliver, b. May 31, 1768 ; d. unmarried at the age of 25 in
	1793, in New Jersey.
281	5 Medad, b. March 18, 1770 ; m. Anne Clapp, dau. of Benja-
	min C., of Easthampton.
282	6 Jared, b. Sept. 6, 1772 ; Zeruiah [This name has been given
	by some as Jeremiah] Birch, and removed to Char-
	lotte, Vt.
283	7 Eleanor, b. June 25, 1775 ; d. 1777.

105 LT. TIMOTHY LYMAN[5], 2d son of *Gad*[4] and Thankful,
b. July 25, 1745. He was son of the early settlers of

Goshen, Mass. He m. Hannah Colson, who was b. Nov. 30, 1743. He d. in Goshen, Feb. 23, 1818. [The record of Frederic W. Lyman, of Kanosha, Wis., gives the date Feb. 18, as the death of Lt. Timothy, but others and the tomb stone give it the 23.] His wife d. Feb. 7, 1818, aged 74.   . *Goshen, Mass.*

Children, Sixth Generation :

284 1 Thankful, b. May 6, 1771; d. 1777.
285 2 Jerusha, b. March 6, 1773; m. George Salmon, and d. at Fulton, N. Y., about 1858 or '9·
286 3 John Colson, b. Jan. 20, 1775; m. Susan Burgess.
287 4 Mary, b. Feb. 1, 1777 ; d. April 29, 1777.
288 5 William, b. Feb. 21, 1778 ; m. Agnes, dau. of Hugh Mitchell, Esq.
289 6 Timothy, b Jan. 20, 1780 ; m. Hannah White, dau. of Wm. White, Esq., who was among the first settlers of Goshen, and d. Dec. 26, 1831, no children.
290 7 Francis, b. Feb. 3, 1781; m. Helen Mitchell, dau. of Hugh Mitchell, Esq.
291 8 Thomas, b. Feb. 12, 1783; m. Dorcas Smith, Goshen.
292 9 Abigail, b. about 1788; m. Dr. Daniel Parce, d. March 1, 1868, aged 80.

108 ISRAEL LYMAN[6], eldest son of *Zadoc*[5] and Sarah, b. in Hockanum, Feb. 7, 1746. He m. Rachel Beals, Jan. 4, 1770. She was b. June 8, 1747; d. Dec. 27, 1824. He d. June 8, 1830.   *Hockanum, Mass.·* •

Children, Seventh Generation :

293 1 Sarah, b. Sept. 12, 1770 : m. Stephen Johnson, d. Sept. 19, 1835.
294 2 Rachel, b. March 10, 1772; m. Elijah Montague, in 1784; d. Sept. 27, 1803.
      Ch. 8th Gen.: 1 Wealthy. 2 Moses. 3 Obed. 4 Sarah, all m. and had children.
299 3 Zadoc Samuel, b. March 26, 1774; m. Hannah Watson.·
300 4 Israel, b. Aug. 9, 1775; d. Aug. 10, 1775.
301 5 Israel, b. Oct. 17, 1776 ; m. Sally Moody.
302 6 Achsah, b. April 27, 1778 ; m. Chester Clark ; d. Nov. 21, 1819.
303 7 Cynthia, b. April 8, 1780; m. Aaron Graves Lyman, of Northfield, and d. Dec. 2, 1839.
304 8 Amaziah. b. Feb. 13, 1782 ; Elizabeth Alford, of S. Hadley.
305 9 Hannah, b. Oct. 9, 1783; m. Perez Smith, of South Hadley, she had a numerous family one of them was George Lyman. She d. in 1861.
306 10 Elijah, b. Nov. 13, 1785; d. June 30, 1786.
307 11 Elijah, b. May 23, 1787 ; m. Hadassah Moody, of S. Hadley.

D. Clarke.

308 12 Enos b. Jan. 2, 1790; m. Lydia Wadsworth. Hadley.
309 13 George, b. Dec. 13, 1792; m. Laura Wadsworth.

109 Azariah Lyman[6], second son of *Zadoc[5]* and Sarah,
was b. Dec. 1747. He went to Westhampton, m. Jemima
Kingsley, the dau. of Samuel Kingsley, of Southampton,
March 17, 1774. She d. Jan 6, 1866 aged 91 years.
He d. Oct. 23, 1833, aged 86.   *Westhampton.*

   Children, Seventh Generation :

310 1 Jemima, b. Feb. 19, 1775; m. Jonathan Clark, March 10,
    1796. She d. Oct. 31, 1839.
      Ch. 8th Gen : 1 Rev. Dorus, D.D., b. Jan. 2, 1797 ; m.
      Hannah A. Bliss, and had 5 children. 2 Tertius Strong,
      b. Dec. 17, 1799 ; m. Almira A. Marshall, and had three
      children. 3 Adolphus, b. in 1803 ; d. aged 2 years. 4
      Sarah, b. in 1805 ; d. 1833. 5 Jemima, b. in 1807 ; d.
      young. 6 Lucina, b. in 1809 ; m. 1st. Hiram Bell, 2d;
      William M. Wilson. 7 Sophia, b. in 1811; d. Jan. 13,
      1829.
326 2 Azariah, b. Dec. 6, 1777 ; m. Rhoda Rust.
327 3 Elihu, b. Oct. 16, 1779 ; m. Hannah Judd.
328 4 Sophia, b. Dec. 21; m. 1st, Oliver Hastings in 1815 ; 2d,
    Solomon Ferry, d. Aug. 26, 1832.
      Ch. 8th Gen. : 1 A son, b. Dec. 26, 1816 ; d. same day.
      2 Fidelia Lyman, b. Jan. 2, 1818 ; m. Rev. William Ho-
      garth, of Geneva, N. Y. 3 Sophia, b. April 5, 1822 ;
      m. Wm Strong, of Northampton and had 10 ch
      4 Julia Ann, b. April 12, 1824 , m. Frederick A. Spencer
      of Westfield, Mass.
352 5 ... b. March 6, 1784 ; d. June 21, 1788, from the effects
    of scalding.
353 6 Infant, b. Oct. 31, 1788 ; d. same day.
354 7 Jesse, b. March 9, 1789 ; m. Lucy Kingsley.

111 Luke Lyman[6], 3d son of *Zadoc[5]*, and *Sarah*, was b.
Jan. 8, 1753. He m. Susanna Hunt, dau. of Joel Hunt,
Dec. 21, 1780. She was b. July 2, 1760 ; d. Dec. 20, 1829.
He d. Jan. 12, 1825.   *Hockanum.*

   Children, Seventh Generation :

355 1 Sylvester, b. Jan. 27, 1782; m. Elizabeth Wright.
356 2 Electa, b. March 19, 1784 ; m. Abner Wright, Oct. 10, 1810 ;
    d. Oct. 1, 1850.
      Ch. 8th Gen. : 1 William L. Wright, who resides in
      Hartford, Conn. [*Ch. 9th Gen. :* (1) Edwin. (2) Har-
      riet. (3) Fowler. (4) Julia. (5) Maria. (6) Enoch
      Phelps. (7) Martha.]
360 3 Luke Clark, b. Dec. 1, 1785 ; d. Aug. 14, 1790.

D. Clarke.

308 12 Enos, b. Jan. 2, 1790; m. Lydia Wadsworth. Hadley.
309 13 George, b. Dec. 13, 1792; m. Laura Wadsworth.

109 AZARIAH LYMAN⁶, second son of *Zadoc⁵* and Sarah, was b. Dec. 1747. He went to Westhampton, m. Jemima Kingsley, the dau. of Samuel Kingsley, of Southampton, March 17, 1774. She d. Jan. 6, 1839, aged 91 years. He d. Oct. 28, 1833, aged 86.   *Westhampton.*

Children, Seventh Generation :
310 1 Jemima, b. Feb. 19, 1775; m. Jonathan Clark, March 10,
       1796. She d. Oct. 31, 1839.
       Ch. 8th Gen : 1 Rev. Dorus, D.D., b. Jan. 2, 1797 ; m.
       Hannah A. Bliss, and had 5 children.   2 Tertius Strong,
       b. Dec. 17, 1799 ; m. Almira A. Marshall, and had three
       children.   3 Adolphus, b. in 1803 ; d. aged 2 years.   4
       Sarah, b. in 1805 ; d. 1833.   5 Jemima, b. in 1807 ; d.
       young. 6 Lucina, b. in 1809 ; m. 1st, Hiram Bell, 2d,
       William M. Wilson. 7 Sophia, b. in 1811; d. Jan. 13,
       1829.
326 2 Azariah, b. Dec. 6, 1777 ; m. Rhoda Rust.
327 3 Elihu, b. Oct. 16, 1779 ; m. Hannah Judd.
328 4 Sophia, b. Dec. 21 ; m. 1st, Oliver Hastings in 1815 ; 2d,
       . Solomon Ferry, d. Aug. 26, 1832.
       Ch. 8th Gen.: 1 A son, b. Dec. 26, 1816 ; d. same day.
       2 Fidelia Lyman, b. Jan. 2, 1818 ; m. Rev. William Ho-
       garth, of Geneva, N. Y.   3 Sophia, b. April 5, 1822 ;
       m. Wm. Strong, of Northampton and had 10 children.
       4 Julia Ann, b. April 12, 1824 ; m. Frederick A. Spencer
       of Westfield, Mass.
352 5 Jesse, b. March 6, 1784 ; d. June 21, 1788, from the effects
       of scalding.
353 6 Infant, b. Oct. 31, 1788 ; d. same day.
354 7 Jesse, b. March 9, 1789 ; m. Lucy Kingsley.

111 LUKE LYMAN⁶, 3d son of *Zadoc⁵*, and *Sarah*, was b. Jan. 8, 1753. He m. Susanna Hunt, dau. of Joel Hunt, Dec. 21, 1780. She was b. July 2, 1760 ; d. Dec. 20, 1829. He d. Jan. 12, 1825.   *Hockanum.*

Children, Seventh Generation :
355 1 Sylvester, b. Jan. 27, 1782; m. Elizabeth Wright.
356 2 Electa, b. March 19, 1784; m. Abner Wright, Oct. 10, 1810 ;
       d. Oct. 1, 1850.
       Ch. 8th Gen. : 1 William L. Wright, who resides in
       Hartford, Conn. [*Ch. 9th Gen.:* (1) Edwin. (2) Har-
       riet. (3) Fowler. (4) Julia. (5) Maria. (6) Enoch
       Phelps. (7) Martha.]
360 3 Luke Clark, b. Dec. 1, 1785 ; d. Aug. 14, 1790.

361 4 Asenath, b. Feb. 13, 1788; m. Cecil Jewett, Nov., 1811; d. March 26, 1846.

369 5 Susanna, b. March 24, 1790; m. Epaphras Clark, Feb. 7, 1811; d. Oct. 16, 1822.
    Ch. 8th Gen.: 1 Maria Theresa, b. May 31, 1811; d. Nov. 11, 1822. 2 Susanna, b. March 10, 1812; m. Wm. A. Tomlinson. 3 Henry Hunt, b. May 28, 1815, resided Baltimore, Md. 4 Wm. Lewis, b. May 10, 1817; d. Feb. 18, 1822. 5 Samuel Barnard, b. Aug. 16, 1819, resided Norfolk, Va. 6 Wm. Lewis, b. Jan. 30, 1832, resided Middleton, Ct.

376 6 Luke Clark, b. Feb. 21, 1792; m. Sarah Dummer.

377 7 Horace, b. June 9, 1784; m. Electa Day.

378 8 Mary, b. Sept. 4, 1796; m. Wm. W. Naramore, June 19, 1821, who d. Jan. 18, 1868. She resides in Derby, Conn.
    Ch. 8th Gen.: 1 William, Bridgeport, Conn. 2 Robert, Birmingham, Conn. 3 Joseph, engaged in the manufactory of Wallace & Son, Ansonia. 4 Mary, m. Mr. Gilbert, of Derby.

112 JOHN LYMAN⁶, eldest son of *John⁵*, and Hannah Strong, *John⁴*, *John³*, *John²*, *Richard¹*, was b. Sept. 8, 1750. He resided in Northampton, on the plain so called on the homestead when the old house was burned in 1742. He m. 1st, Cynthia Dwight, June 4, 1789. She d. May 28, 1790. He m. 2d, Sarah Baker, July 4, 1793, she d. Jan. 27, 1834, aged 82 years. He d. March 11, 1808. *South Farms.*

Child, Seventh Generation:

383 1 Cynthia Dwight, b. ......; m. Titus Smith, and lived in Granby.

113 RUFUS LYMAN⁶, second son of *John⁵* and Hannah, was b. in Northampton, Dec. 13, 1751, and d. June 5, 1807, aged 56. He m. Martha Burt, of Southampton, 1774, she d. Aug. 1, 1827, aged 76. *Westhampton.*

Children, Seventh Generation

384 1 Jerusha, b. Feb. 12, 1775; m. Samuel Rhoades, March, 1807, had four sons, and two daughters; she d. Aug. 25, 1844. Montville, Ohio.

391 2 Asahel, b. April 16, 1777; m. Esther Strong.

392 3 Rufus, b. Jan. 19, 1779; m. Sophia Montague.

393 4 Martha, b. Aug. 30, 1780; m. Luther Wright, had 1 son and 3 daughters; d. Sept. 19, 1847.

398 5 Enoch, b. June 13, 1782; m. Silence Edwards.

399 6 Tryphena, b. April 18, 1784; m. Elihu Seals, had 3 sons and 2 daughters, d. April 5, 1855.

405 7 Nancy, b. April 3, 1786; m. Amasa Strong, 4 sons and 2 daughters.

412   8 Sereno, b. Feb. 2, 1788; m. 1st, Mary Clark, Sept. 16, 1813;
        she d. Jan. 13, 1818.   He m. 2d, Deborah James, March
        11, 1819.
413   9 James Harvey, b. Oct. 29, 1789; m. Charlotte Miller, had
        1 son Warren Smith, who was b. Jan 11, 1821; and d.
        Oct. 10, 1843. He d. March 5, 1842.
415 10 John Burt. b. April 4, 1792; m. 1st, Ruth Strong, who d.
    .   Dec. 5, 1857; he m. 2d, Naomi Joy.
416 11 Liberty, b. June 22, 1794; m. Lucinda Sikes.   All of these
        were b. in Westhampton.

115 THOMAS LYMAN⁶, third son of *John⁵* and Hannah, b.
Dec. 18, 1756.   He m. Dorothy Clark, Oct. 28, 1784,
She d. March 7, 1843, aged 83.   Mrs. L. was a woman of
exemplary piety and was the subject of a small volume
styled, *Light and Cloud.*   He d. April 15, 1845, aged 88.
  This family had five pairs of twins, 11 children in 10
years.   *Westhampton.*
        Children, Seventh Generation:
417   1 Thomas, b. Aug. 15, 1785; m. Betsey Clapp.
418   2 Dolly, b. Oct. 23, 1786; m. Dea. Eleazer Judd, of Westhamp-
        ton, Sept. 29, 1808; and d. Aug. 3, 1866, aged 79.
        Ch. 8th Gen.: 1 Juliette Juturna, b. Aug. 24, 1809; m.
        John W. Dunlap, May 1, 1837; d. Aug. 29, 1841. 2
        Anna Thompson, b. Jan. 24, 1811; m. Asa C. Edwards,
        Dec. 3, 1835, and d. Feb. 17, 1837. 3 Silence Sheldon,
        b. Jan. 22, 1814; and d. April 6, 1840. 4 Jonathan
        Sheldon, b. Feb. 4, 1816, graduated at Williams College
        1839, and at the Theological Institute of Conn., in 1842.
        He m. Emily E. Wolcott, of Agawam, Nov. 16, 1843,
        and Emily C. Smith, of Terryville, Ct., May, 1862.   Was
        ordained and installed pastor of the 2d Congregational
        Church in Whately, Oct. 12, 1843, and was dismissed at
        his own request, in Oct., 1855, and installed pastor of
        the Congregational Church in Middlebury, Ct., June 25,
        1856, and died while pastor of the church, May 11, 1864,
        aged 48 years. 5 Dorothy Lyman, b. Feb. 7, 1818; m.
        Charles H. Robertson, of Charlotte Co., Va., July 3,
        1849. 6 Eleazer, b. April 13, 1821; m. Sophia C. San-
        derson, of Whately, Jan. 24, 1855.   Resides in Sunder-
        land. 7 Ada, b. Feb. 5, 1824; d. Nov. 1, 1847. 8
        Princess M., b. June 6, 1826.   Resides (in 1868) with
        her sister in Virginia. 9 Solomon Stoddard, b. March
        14, 1829; m. Mary A. Bates, of Saybrook, Ct., Aug. 21,
        1859.   Resides in Springfield, Mass.
428   3 Polly, twin of Dolly, m. George Bennet,; d. Oct. 3, 1839.
429   4 Thaddeus, b. Sept. 21, 1789; m. Sarah V. Schoonmaker.
        29

430 5 Alpheus, b. Sept. 21, 1789 ; unmarried ; d. in Northampton,
        Jan. 6, 1864, aged 74.
431 6 Betsey, b. April 20, 1792, (mate d.) ; m. Noah Clark, Nov.
        3, 1813 ; d. July 14, 1864, aged 74.
            Ch. 8th Gen.: 1 Elizabeth, m. Alanson Bugbee.
        2 Noah B. 3 George.
435 7 Phebe, b. Sept. 17, 1795, (mate d.) ; m. Timothy Clark,
        March 15, 1817.
            Ch. 8th Gen.: 1 William Judd, b. Jan. 16, 1818 ; ˙
        d. young. 2 Anson B. 3 Sarah Theresa. 4 Mary Lyman.

120 CALEB LYMAN⁶, b. July 31, 1775 ; m. Azubah Cooley
Aug. 30, 1793. He d. March 13, 1862, Azubah ; d. April
26, 1839.   *Lorraine, N. Y.*
        Children, Seventh Generation :
440 1 Martha, b. June 13, 1800 ; d. Aug. 22, 1851.
441 2 Elam, b. Feb. 9, 1803 ; m. Susan Wiswell, b. Nov. 22, 1802.
442 3 John, b. June 1, 1805 ; d. March 19, 1813.
443 4 Caleb S., b. May 17, 1807 ; d. June 5, 1861.
444 5 Oshea G., b. Nov. 8, 1808 ; d. April 13, 1829.
445 6 Azubah, b. Oct. 10, 1813 ; m. Lorraine ; d. April 12, 1830.
446 7 Betsey W., b. Oct. 31, 1815 ; m. Walter W. Stewart, July
        30, 1857, Lorraine, Jefferson Co., N. Y.

441 ELAM LYMAN⁸, m. Susan Wiswell, lived a farmer.
                                             Lorraine, N. Y.
        Children, Ninth Generation :
447 1 John M., b. Aug. 13, 1825 ; m. Hannah S. Contan.
448 2 Adelia Ann, b. March 28, 1827.
449 3 Martha M., b. Feb. 23, 1829.
450 4 Samuel O., b. Oct. 30, 1830 ; d. April 8, 1852.
451 5 Lois A., b. July 7, 1833 ; m. Bateman, d. Dec. 2, 1866.
452 6 Mary J., b. Dec. 27, 1835.
453 7 Elam S., b. Aug. 5, 1838 ; m. March 1, 1859, Mary C.
        Weatherbee.
            Ch. 10th Gen.: 1 Hattie A. B., b. March 10, 1860. 2
        Lois B., b. Dec. 16, 1866 ; d. Oct. 7, 1867. 3 Frank C.,
        b. July 29, 1869.
457 8 Alsaminia M., b. Nov. 19, 1841 ; d. Sept. 7, 1843.
458 9 William O., b. March 29, 1844.
459 10 Joseph M., b. April 23, 1848. Lorraine, N. Y.

447 JOHN M. LYMAN⁸, *Elam⁷, Caleb⁶, Caleb⁵, John⁴, John³,
John², Richard¹,* farmer.   *Lorraine.*
        Children, Ninth Generation :
460 1 William E., b. July 19, 1849.
461 2 Elizabeth, b. Oct. 7, 1855.
462 3 John, b. April 13, 1857.
463 4 Susan, b. Oct. 4, 1859.

464 5 Juliette, b. May 28, 1862.
465 6 Fanny, b. Aug. 5, 1865.

449 MARTHA M. LYMAN⁸, dau. of *Elam⁷*, m. July 4, 1850,
Marenno Jewrell — farmer.   *Sandy Creek, N. Y.*
    Children, Ninth Generation.
466 1 Edward, b. April 21, 1852.
467 2 Ada Maria, b. Dec. 29, 1858.
468 3 Mary A., b. Sept. 27, 1861.
469 4 Mattie A., b. Nov. 1, 1865.

443 CALEB S. LYMAN⁸, son of *Caleb⁷, Israel⁶, Caleb⁵, John⁴,
John³, John², Richard¹*, b. May 17, 1807; m. Oct. 23,
1829, Theda Butler, b. Dec. 31, 1803; d. June 27, 1869,
Caleb S., d. June 5, 1865, farmer.   *Adams, N. Y.*
    Children, Ninth Generation :
475 1 Oshea G., b. Oct. 5, 1830 ; m. Feb. 19, 1853, Sarah C.
        Wheeler, b. Nov. 26, 1832— farmer. Raymond, Stearns
        Co., Minnesota.
            Ch. 10th Gen.: 1 Theda S., b. June 9, 1855.
        2 Emma, b. July 21, 1857. 3 Ellen D., b. April
        10, 1860. 4 Sarah C., b. Feb. 22, 1863. 5 Daniel B.,
        b. Feb. 28, 1866; d. Nov. 8, 1868.
476 2 Henry C., b. April 11, 1833 ; m. July 31, 1858, Sarah
        Smith—farmer, Raymond, Stearns Co., Minn.
            Ch. 10th Gen.: 1 Angeline E., b. April 1, 1859. 2
        Martha A., b. April 11, 1860. 3 Caleb S., b. Nov. 1,
        1862. 4 Arthur E., b. May 3, 1868.
481 3 Caleb N., b. March 14, 1835 ; m. July 28, 1861.
482 4 David L., b. April 14, 1837 ; m. Sept. 6, 1859, Ellen D.
        Duncan, b. June 9, 1837; d. Feb. 28, 1860 ; m. 2d,
        wife, Aug. 29, 1863, Ellen S. Heath, b. Sept. 9, 1842.
        Jefferson Co., N. Y.
            Ch. 10th Gen.: 1 Carrie L., b. Oct. 5, 1869. Adams,
        N. Y.
483 5 Virgil C., b. May 12, 1839 ; m. Amanda M.
484 6 Sylvanus L., b. Sept. 29, 1841 ; m. Jan. 21, 1869, Emma
        Clarke, b. May 1, 1848, has one son Daniel B., b. May
        3, 1870.
485 7 Abigail C., b. May 4, 1844 ; m. Oct. 31, 1866, Franklin
        Farmer.
486 8 Daniel B., b. Dec. 4, 1846; d. March 11, 1849.

134 TIMOTHY LYMAN⁶, second son of *Phineas* and Joanna
Eastman, b. Aug. 15, 1753, m. Elizabeth Pomeroy, June 1,

1780, who after his death m. Ebenezer Clark of Lunenburg, Vt. Timothy Lyman, d. June 12, 1792.

Children, Seventh Generation .

487 1 Joanna, b. prob., May 4, 1782 ; m. Abel Brown of Springfield and about 1739, removed to Wisconsin. This
entire family appears to have removed to Wis. where all
further trace of them is lost.

488 2 Elizabeth, bp. March 29, 1784 ; she was a cripple.

489 3 Phineas, bp. Feb. 20, 1786.

490 4 Naomi, b. March 17, 1787 ; m. Asa Clark of Lunenburg, Vt.

491 5 Elihu, b. July, 1789, went to Vt., thence to Wisconsin.

136 GIDEON LYMAN⁶, only son of *Gideon⁵* b. Jan. 26,
1758, in Northampton. His father d. when he was about
4 years old and he lived with his uncle Elijah. He was a
soldier in the Revolutionary army for about six months,
was near by at the surrender of Burgoyne. He went to
Vermont about 1780, on a farm given him by his uncle at
the foot of Mt. Ascutney in Wethersfield. He m. Dolly
Spencer, of Clermont, N. H., in 1782. He removed to
Lynn, Penn.

In 1803, in a tract of land 6 miles square in Susquehannah Co., Pa., which had been purchased for a half bushel of
silver dollars, his farm had been purchased for an indif-
ferent horse and saddle. For many miles he cut his way
for his team through an unbroken forest, and reached his
destination with fifty cents capital to begin life in this wilderness, subsisting upon game and wild fruits until he
could clear the grounds for crops. The title being invalid,
he bought 200 acres at one dollar an acre. Here he reared
in competence a family of eleven children, all of whom
lived to a good old age and several had numerous families ;
two had 12 children, two had 10, one had 8, and another
9. He d. May 22, 1824, leaving more than 126 descendants, children and grandchildren.

Children, Seventh Generation:

492 1 Elijah, b. Aug. 20, 1783 ; m. Prudence Carrier.

493 2 Dolly, b. Aug. 9, 1785 ; m. John Oakley, Feb. 13, 1806 ; still
living, has no children.

494 3 Gideon, b. Aug. 9, 1785 ; m. Keziah Earll.

495 4 Joseph Arvin, b. May 18, 1788 ; m. Anna Hall

496 5 Naomi, b. Jan. 22, 1790 ; m. Elisha Newman, March 5,
1809, had 2 daus. and m. 2d Frank Spencer, her cousin
Nov. 27, 1813.
  Ch. 8th Gen.: 1 Naomi, b. May 20, 1814. 2 Eunice,
b. May 11, 1816. 3 Benjamin N., b. May 17, 1818.

4 Francis, b. June 22, 1820. 5 Mary Ann, b. July 11, 1822. 6 Henry Ashley, b. Oct. 21, 1824. 7 Lyman Clark, b. Feb. 4, 1826. 8 Hume, b. Dec. 21, 1828. 9 Eveline, b. April 15, 1831. 10 Caroline, b. April 15, 1831. 1, 3, 5, 6, 9, 10, still living.

509 6 Eunice, b. April 22, 1792 ; m. Julius Cogswell.

Ch. 8th Gen. : 1 Theodore, b. Sept. 28, 1817. 2 William, b. June 27, 1819. 3 Dolly, b. June 9, 1821. 4 Charles Wesley, b. April 21, 1823. 5 Edward Spencer, b. July 18, 1825. 6 Emily Anna, b. Sept. 3, 1828. 7 Gideon Lyman, b. March 1, 1831. 8 James Theodore, b. Aug. 20, 1833.

518 7 Mehitable, b. April 24, 1794; m. Wm. Taylor, April 29, 1812.

Ch. 8th Gen. : 1 Gideon Lyman, b. May 14, 1813. 2 Elizabeth, b. April 6, 1815. 3 Francis B., b. Feb. 15, 1817. 4 Lucinda, b. April 14, 1819. 5 Lewis S., b. Nov. 25, 1821. 6 John Griffin, b. June 3, 1824. 7 Dolly Amarilla, b. Feb. 12, 1827. 8 Helen Sophronia, b. Nov. 3, 1829. 9 Elijah Wells, b. Oct. 6, 1833. 10 Davis Jackson, b. Sept. 4, 1836.

529 8 Samuel, b. Jan. 26, 1796; m. Eunice Earll.

530 9 John Bennet, b. May 2, 1798; m. 1st, Abigail Newman, 2d, Sarah Brace.

531 10 Lucinda, b. May 6, 1800 ; m. Henry Ellsworth, April 3, 1838.

Ch. 8th Gen. : 1 Joseph, b. March 30, 1839—still living near Lynn, Pa.

533 11 Prentis, b. Sept. 28, 1802; m. Eliza Milburn.

141 JUSTIN LYMAN[6], *Elias*[5], *Elias*[4], *John*[3], *John*[2], *Richard*[1], 1765–1834, eldest son of Elias 2d and Hannah Clapp, was b. Oct. 17, 1765. He early left his father's farm to engage in business first on the river at which time he lived a little distance from his father near the Rock Ferry. About 1797 or '8, he removed to Hartford and in connection with his brother Elias established the firm of J. & E. Lyman, which for many years carried on an extensive and prosperous trade both inland and foreign. About 1804, he moved to New York, but after retiring from business, he returned to Hartford, Conn., where he d. April 27, 1834. He m. 1st, Martha Clapp, of Northampton, June 19, 1786. She d. in Hartford, Conn., Aug. 9, 1798, in her 35th year. He m. 2d, Fanny Goodwin, widow of Capt. Goodwin, of Middletown, Ct., Feb. 1805. He had three children by his first wife. *Hartford, Conn.*

Children, Seventh Generation :

534 1 Lorinda, b. 1788 ; d. July 23, 1794.

535 ₂ Theodore, b. 1790; Oct. 8, 1812. He was educated at Dartmouth College and commenced the study of law at Litchfield, Conn., but his health declined and he d. with consumption on his way to New York, at Fairfield, Conn.

535 ₃ Patty, b. about 1792 ; d. Dec. 7, 1793, aged 11 months.

142 ELIAS LYMAN⁶, second son of *Elias*⁵ and Hannah Clapp was born Feb. 23, 1768. He established himself in trade at Wethersfield, Vt., about 1790. His store was burned and he commenced business at Hartford, Vt., now White River Junction. He engaged in cotton manufacture, one of the earliest in the state and in connection with his brother Justin in New York, and a branch in Hartford did an extensive business in provisions and country produce, gaining what was considered at that period great wealth. He married Anna White of Hatfield, Mass., Dec. 30, 1790. He died Nov. 22, 1830, aged 62. She was born Dec. 14, 1771, and died Feb. 11, 1844, aged 72.

White River Junction, Vt.

Children, Seventh Generation :

537 ₁ Lewis, b. Dec. 17, 1791; m. Mary Blake Bruce.

538 ₂ Fanny, Aug. 26, 1793; m. Charles Dodd, of Hartford, Ct., Oct. 14, 1812; d. Feb. 25, 1816.

    Ch. 8th Gen. : ₁ Frances, b. Sept. 9, 1813; m. James Brewer 2d of Springfield, have 2 children. ₂ Charles, b. Feb. 15, 1815 ; d. Aug. 11, 1825.

541 ₃ Normand, b. Feb. 23, 1795 ; m. Elizabeth Walker, still living in Hartford.

542 ₂ Wyllys, b, May 15, 1797; m. Sarah B. Marsh.

543 ₃ Anna, b. Nov. 18, 1798; m. Charles Dodd (his 2d wife) June 19, 1822. He d. May 21, 1844 or 1856.

    Ch. 8th Gen. : ₁ Elias Lyman, b. June 24, 1823 ; d. Aug. 18, 1843. ₂ Charles, b. Oct. 25, 1825 ; d. Aug. 12, 1831. ₃ Anna Lyman, b. Nov. 28, 1827 ; m. George T. Bond, June 1, 1854. ₄ Mary Elizabeth, b. May 15, 1833; m. Adrian H. Bement, Sept. 26, 1860, ₅ Jane, b. Jan. 29, 1836; d. April 22, 1837. Mrs. Anna Dodd, m. 2d, Dr. James Spaulding, of Montpelier, Vt., and d. Dec. 11, 1856. He d. March 15, 1858.

549 ₆ Elias, b. July 8, 1800.

550 ₇ Horace, b, March 16, 1802 ; d. Aug. 20, 1814.

551 ₈ Theodore, b. Oct. 27, 1803 ; d. aged 18 hours.

552 ₉ Clementine, b. Sept. 19, 1804 ; m. Joseph F. Tilden now of Rochester, N. Y., Jan. 16. 1828, at Hartford, Vt. He was b. at Hartford, Vt., March 2, 1797.

    Ch. 8th Gen. : ₁ Clementine Lyman, b. Oct. 24, 1828, at Rochester, Vt., was m. at Newberry, Vt., Aug. 3, 1853, to Wm. Alling of Rochester, N. Y., and had one ·

child, Joseph Tilden, b. at Rochester, N. Y., Jan. 19, 1855. 2 Josiah, b. Feb. 14, 1830. 3 Anna Elizabeth, b. Dec. 16, 1832; d. August, 1869. 4 Hannah Lyman, b. May 26, 1835.

558 10 George, b. April 6, 1806; m. Minerva Briggs.

559 11 Charles, b. Oct. 5, 1808; m. Maria Spaulding.

560 12 Simeon, b. Aug. 16, 1810; m. Lucinda Hall.

561 13 Hannah, July 7, 1813; m. George S. Kendrick of Lebanon, N. H., June 30, 1836, and died there March 14, 1857, aged 43.

Ch. 8th Gen.: 1 Martha Jane, b. March 20, 1837; m. Charles P. Alden, Nov. 21, 1861. [*Ch. 9th Gen.* (1) George K., b. Feb. 10, 1863; d. March 22, 1863. (2) Ralph P., b. July 20, 1865. (3) Helen E., b. Dec. 7, 1866.] 2 Elizabeth, b. Aug. 11, 1839. 3 Edmund, P., b. Feb. 1, 1849.

568 14 Jane, b. Aug. 7, 1816; m. Harvey King of Montpelier, Vt., July 12, 1844; d. April 11, 1852, aged 35.

Ch. 8th Gen.: 1 Jane Lyman, b. Aug. 10, 1845; m. Benjamin W. Hoyt, Dec. 10, 1868. 2. Fanny Brewer, b. Sept. 6, 1849.

143 GAIUS LYMAN[6], 3d son of *Elias[5]* and Hannah Clapp, b. Nov. 24, 1769, succeeded his brother Justin, in the occupation of the Rock House for several years. In 1804, he removed to Hartford, Conn. He traded in lumber and West India goods. He d. in Hartford, Jan. 4, 1845, aged 75. He m. Jan. 18, 1797, Submit Field, dau. of Dea. Joseph Field of Sunderland, Mass., who was b. June 17, 1774, and d. in Hartford, April 27, 1846, aged 72

Hartford, Conn.

Children, Seventh Generation :

571 1 Elhanan Winchester, b. Feb. 27, 1799; m. Maria Farnsworth.

572 2 Christopher Columbus, b. Dec. 28, 1800; m. Cecilia Breckenridge.

573 3 Orra Almira, b. Jan. 3, 1803; m. James G. Bolles, who d. March 29, 1871.

574 4 Julia Etta, b. March 26, 1805; d. Feb. 2, 1871, Hartford, Ct.

575 5 Emma Submit, b. June 15, 1807; d. Nov. 7, 1807.

576 6 Jane Rachel, b. Oct. 2, 1808; d. June 3, 1842.

577 7 Hannah Submit, b. March 12, 1812; m. Chester Judson, April 20, 1831; d. June 10, 1835. She had one dau. Jane Lyman, b. May 16, 1832.

579 8 Theodore, b. April 29, 1814; m. Mary L. Nichols of Bridgeport, Ct., May 20, 1835; she was b. Feb. 22, 1816, one son Theodore, b. Sept. 2, 1836; d. May, 1840.

Deacon James G. Bolles, the husband of Orra A., was the son of Rev. Matthew Bolles, and was born in Eastford now Ashford, Conn.,

Jan. 17th, 1802. When a lad of about fifteen years of age, he went into the printing office of the *Bridgeport Farmer*, under the late Mr. Stiles Nichols, and continued there until he was twenty. Afterwards Mr. Bolles was the publisher of the *Christian Watchman* in Boston, but, not finding his physical strength equal to the demand there made upon it, he came to Hartford about 1825, and engaged in the dry goods business. Subsequently, he took up Fire Insurance, as the great business which he made emphatically his life's work, so far as his secular occupation was concerned. For a number of years he was the respected secretary of the Hartford Fire Insurance Company. When the North American Company was organized in 1857, he was made its president, and held the position for some time. He was a director of that company at the time of his decease. He was among the oldest, if not the oldest underwriter in the city. During the administration of President Lincoln, Mr. Bolles was collector of Internal Revenue for the first district in this State; but was removed by President Johnson. In 1855, he was elected major of the Governor's Foot Guard. Several times Mr. Bolles traveled in Europe, and he was on the eve of making another tour with his family, at the time of his decease.

Having been an example of a pure and blameless life, and a faithful attendant on the duties of religion, his conversion at the age of 40 years was a remarkable illustration of the reality of the new and nobler life to which one is born by grace divine. All were constrained to see and admire the change in Mr. Bolles, to which all his subsequent life gave witness.

Mr. Bolles was baptized Jan. 24, 1841, and from that date to his death, he has been a most faithful friend to the church. He was elected to the deaconship, Feb. 4th, 1845. He gave largely for the support of the preaching of the gospel, and was glad to have a share in the benevolent operations of the day. Dea. Bolles was a generous contributor all our objects of Christian benevolence. In addition, he left by will, to the First Baptist church $10,000; to the Connecticut Baptist State Convention, $10,000; to the Connecticut Baptist Education Society, $10,000; and to the Hartford Hospital, $10,000.

Mr. Bolles was a man of great purity of life and uprightness of character, amiable and gentle in all the relations of life, but firm in principle. He was a devoted Christian, in connection with the Baptist church. He was a man generally beloved, his advice was sought, his counsel was sound and valuable; he was especially friendly to young men, and always ready to help them to an honorable start in life. Very many who read this paragraph will recall his always friendly words, his charity, his kindly manner, his efficient help. He was a man beloved and trusted; true in his political life, true in his friendships, liberal and upright. Hartford owes its honorable reputation to such men. We profit by his example and mourn his loss — a Christian gentleman, one of nature's noblemen, all the more ennobled by grace divine.

MISS JULIA E. LYMAN.—The following obituary is abridged from that which was presented at the last Reunion of the Lyman Family ·

> Soft as the lunar ray that sleeps
> Upon the bosom of the peaceful lake;
> Or dewy eve distilling sweet
> On vernal flowers; or breath of morn,
> On od'rous wings ascending from the east
> With melody of birds—so soft and sweet,
> Is memory of those we loved.

Forty years ago, and more, you might have seen in one of the Lyman families of Connecticut, a very slight delicate girl, studious and accurate as a scholar, sedate, conscientious, fond of books, but not given to as abundant use of the tongue, as some of her sex are reported to be. That fine, quiet, scholarly girl, early formed a loving attachment to the Lyman name. She never would change that name for any other. Born in it, she lived and died in it.

She early manifested talent for business: a mind clear, quick, accurate and retentive. Fortunately for us, while yet a girl, she became interested in the Lyman genealogy. That interest increased with the increase of years. She felt, as well she might, that the Lyman, like many other families, were sustaining a great loss, by a criminal ignorance and neglect of their worthy ancestors.

It is a noble work to help save a family name from an ignoble oblivion. She engaged in it with Christian zeal and love, and persevered in it at the cost of time and money and perhaps of life itself.

The chart of the Lyman family, so highly valued by us, is wholly the work of her hands. None, save he who has tried it, knows how much work, *hard* work, is requisite to prepare such a chart. The sources of information for it are fourfold: 1st. Ancient colonial and municipal records. 2d. Old monuments and grave stones. 3d. Old family and church records. 4th. Old folks of sound memory and clear mind. All these she consulted as extensively as her health and strength would permit, years and years ago. Before many of us had ever been baptized into the Lyman name, she might have been seen collecting and correcting these materials, writing and visiting various places in Connecticut, Massachusetts and Vermont; examining old saffron-colored records and parchments, rubbing off the ancient moss from old tombstones, that she might read the name and the date thereon, asking for the sacred old family record, and talking with the "*old folks*," about persons, that their childhood memories could recall. All these facts, she would set down in their order, until she had collected the indisputable data, out of which, to construct this wonderful chart-wheel. where we can all trace our own families as belonging to the branch of Richard Lyman, who came from High Ongar, to establish a name in America. Let us remember, too, that all this was a *work of love;* no money tempted her; she always peremptorily refused all pecuniary aid. She would not even share with others, the expense of her journeys and correspondence in this matter.

30

She *would work*, disinterestedly, from love of the work, and love of the family.

For all we have enjoyed of union and reunion of the Lyman brotherhood, we are, in no small degree, indebted to her patient, life-long labors. By the letters she had written, the facts she had collected, and the interest she had helped to excite in our family history, she has done more than any one else to create the demand, among the Lymans, for our reunion, and for such a history as we hope to have. It is sad to think, that by these assiduous labors, she hastened her end. Self-sacrifice, and Christian love for others, seemed the law of her life. She had cast her anchor within the vail; she died in faith, she sleeps in Jesus, our Lord and Master in whom the whole family in Heaven and earth is named.

The following extract is from the letter of a sister, who speaks from a full heart ·

"The chart she commenced many years ago. When a prospect opened of a genealogical record of the whole Lyman family, being combined in a book, her assiduities increased, and her labors expanded. Innumerable notes of names and families multiplied upon her desk, like leaves of the forest, communicating with persons of the Lyman name and connection, in almost every part of the Union, and beyond. They were labors of love, and I know of no other motive, that ever led her to undertake or carry it on, and though her frame was slight and delicate, and her health never good, often very poor, yet she had a fund of mental resolution which induced her to go on in her efforts, far beyond what she had strength to sustain. The chart she wrote, and rewrote, many times, and it was a work she enjoyed. But the difficulty of getting it rightly engraved, was one she could not control, as she could her own hand: and it saddens me to remember, how severely this work told upon her health, which was at that time very feeble. After her part of the work was finished, her health steadily declined; such intense and long-continued labor, combined with active disease of body, showed their sad effects. The last few months of her life were seasons of great sufferings, which she bore with sweet Christian patience.

"Her views of herself, were very lowly; but this did not remove her from the Rock, Christ Jesus, on whom her faith rested. It may not be thought proper, for one so nearly related, to dilate upon the excellencies of her character, but, surely, none knew as well as myself, how beautiful that character was. A person so disinterested and so conscientious, is rarely seen; self-sacrifice was the law of. her life. Life was joyless to her when she could not communicate some good to some of her kind. · Her energies were not all spent upon the work of which we have been speaking, but scattered all along her pathway in life, she found many ways of doing good, in a quiet and unobtrusive manner, and it is a sweet solace to me to believe that the influence of her lovely example, is not lost in the little world in which she moved. Her memory will be cherished, in the hearts of all, who knew her well."

192 ASAHEL LYMAN[7], fourth son of *Elias*[6] and Hannah Clapp, b. April 10, 1776, resided with his father on the homestead and after the death of his father continued to carry on the farm with increasing success until his death March 5, 1864, at the age of nearly 88. He m. Oct., 1804. Lucy Parsons, dau. of Joel Parsons, of Conway, Mass., b. Aug. 3, 1782. Mrs. Lucy Lyman is still living with Mrs. J. P. Williston, her only child. *Northampton, Mass.*

Child, Eighth Generation:

580 1 Cecilia, b. Aug. 6, 1805; m. John Payson Williston, of East-hampton; who d. Jan. 4, 1872, Northampton, Mass.

Ch. 9th Gen.: 1 Asahel, b. Dec. 17, 1827; d. March 9, 1832. 2 John Payson, b. Nov. 19, 1829; d. Sept. 13, 1834. 3 Lucy, b. Oct. 6, 1832. 4 A. Lyman, 2d, b. Dec. 13, 1834; m. Sarah Stoddard. June 12, 1861. [*Ch. 10th Gen.:* (1) May, b. May 7, 1863; died May 12, 1863. (2) John Payson, b. May 23, 1864. (3) Lucy, b. Aug. 7, 1866. (4) Robert Lyman, b. Jan. 12, 1869. (5) Bessie, b Feb. 27, 1871.] 5 Lucy, 2d, b. Nov. 5, 1836; d. Nov. 3, 1842. 6 Sarah Birdsye, b. Nov. 14, 1838; d. Jan. 1, 1843. 7 Hannah More, b. Aug. 11, 1841; m. Aug. 11, 1864, Rev. George S. Bishop, of Newburgh. N. Y. [*Ch. 10th Gen.:* (1) William Samuel. (2) Margaret Williston.]

Mr. Williston, son of Rev. Payson Williston and brother of Hon. Samuel Williston, entered into business in Northampton as a druggist and grocer, and later in life was an extensive cotton manufacturer. Also the original inventor and only manufacturer of Payson's indelible ink. In his business he was successful from the start. He was sagacious and far-seeing, and planned for a campaign of a lifetime, rather than for the present. Such was his clearness of perception, his knowledge of correct business principles, and his capacity to adhere to them, that he seldom if ever, made a failure of any enterprise he engaged in. He was a director of the Northampton Bank for many years, a director of the Holyoke Water Power Co., and at one time was a selectman of the town.

He early engaged in true temperance reform; was active and prominent in the Washingtonian movement. Bold, defiant, aggressive, he pursued the evil with tireless zeal, and summoned to his aid whatever of assistance his wealth could command. During this protracted controversy his barn was twice destroyed by an incendiary fire, and his house likewise fired and partially consumed. His life was an unfailing testimony to his faith in his temperance principles, for he practiced himself what he earnestly counseled and demanded of others.

He was also the early and devoted friend of the anti-slavery cause. This he espoused in its infancy, when it was unpopular and even obnoxious to the general New England public. Regardless of fear or favor, he pushed it onward, demanding that slavery should be discussed and denounced in our halls and pulpits. Here also he practiced what he preached, and the fleeing fugitive slave, who often came this way on the route to Canada, found in him a faithful friend. His roof sheltered, his table fed, his sympathy cheered, his purse assisted, the fleeing bondman. His house thus became widely known as one of the depots of the " underground railroad," which conveyed so many people from a land of slavery to a land of liberty, in fact rather than in name.

But perhaps Mr. Williston was best known to this community for his large, though unostentatious charities. In his early years he espoused the Christian religion, and his long life was conspicuous for his faithful following of the teachings of Christ. Benevolence he regarded as one of the Christian principles, and with religious fidelity he practiced it. Soon after he entered upon his business life he resolved to appropriate whatever he should make each year in excess of $500, during the period of ten years, to benevolent objects. At the end of that time, he found he had nothing to give, and he then resolved to devote to charitable objects one-tenth of his income, be it more or less. This resolution he more than fulfilled, and during the later years of his life he gave away in charities his entire income. The public little know, nor will it ever be apprised of, the full extent of his charitable contributions, for he gave in secret, and never with a view to notoriety. The widow, the orphan, the lonely and forsaken ones, have been helped by him when help was precious. He also assisted many poor young men to commence business, or aided them when involved in difficulty. His heart was open and his hand ready whenever he could see that the call was a worthy one. He also aided many young men to educate themselves. He espoused the cause of a poor colored boy, and educated him at his own expense, until he graduated at Oberlin College.

Mr. Williston was for a long series of years an active and leading member of the first church and society in this town, and in 1838 was chosen one of the deacons of the church, retaining the office to the day of his decease, a period of 34 years.

Although often at variance with the public in dealing with questions of policy or principle, he yet retained at all times the entire respect and confidence of the people. His great boldness, his wonderful perseverance, his unyielding devotion to whatever he believed to be right, his hatred of shams and whatever seemed to be false, and above all, his incorruptible integrity, rendered him a remarkable power in the community, and his influence here will be felt long after the present generation shall have passed away. He may truly be regarded one of the most remarkable men that ever lived in Northampton. His was a life of earnest purpose, of courageous effort, of strict, methodical adherence to principle. Such a life is a life of power and of lasting influence. Modest, retiring, conscientious and unswerving in principle, eminently successful in business and unostentatious in his charities, he is an illustrious example of a good and faithful servant of his Master.

Mr. Williston was m. in March, 1827, to Miss Cecilia, only daughter of the late Asahel Lyman, of this town, who survives him. Their children have been nine in number ; seven died almost in infancy, the oldest being only five years old, and two are now living : Asahel L. Williston of Florence, now and for a number of years, the general manager of the Greenville Manufacturing Company, and Hannah, wife of Rev. George S. Bishop, settled over a Congregational Church in Newburg, N. Y. They have also an adopted son, Rev. Martin L. Williston, settled over a Congregational church at Flushing, L. I.

195 Job Lyman⁶, sixth son of *Elias⁵*, 2d, and Hannah Clapp, b. at Northampton, Mass., Dec, 9. 1781.

Children, Seventh Generation

594 1 Louisa, b. Dec. 2, 1823 ; m. Robert W. Traip, of Boston ; had one daughter, who d. young.
595 2 Edward, b. Jan. 21, 1826 ; m. Minerva Lyman.

Hon. Job Lyman inherited from his Puritan ancestors a rugged strength of moral principle which served throughout the changes and vicissitudes of modern skepticism to retain, intact, the early faith of New England ; a faith, which, however stern in theory, when blended with the warm, generous impulses of his· heart, became a religion that irradiated to the close of the life of the gentle pilgrim ! Exceeding by nineteen years the allotted three score and ten, Mr. Lyman illustrated in the ever gentle courtesy of his demeanor, the dignity of the " *old school!*" and the daily life of colonial times. Breaking away from the agricultural and mercantile traditions of his family, the younger brother made a bold move to secure to himself the advantages of a liberal education, and entered Dartmouth College when he graduated in 1804; classmate of Daniel Webster. He studied law at Windsor and Haverhill, N. H., and located for the practice of his profession at Woodstock, Vt., where he spent the prime of an honorable and useful career.

He early became connected with various important public interests ; serving as cashier in the Old Vermont State Bank throughout its existence, and as president of the Woodstock Bank for many years.

He was court auditor of Windsor Co., for a long period and a member of the governor's council. As a member of the Congregational church, he sustained a prominent position, and in every relation of life, whether private or public, was known as an industrious, successful and honest man.

In 1850 he removed to Burlington, Vt , retiring from all business, to spend the rest of his days in the family of his son Edward, whose affectionate care, coupled with that of his only daughter, Mrs. Traip, made pleasant the declining years of life.

Mr. Lyman married a daughter of Judge Lot Hall, of Westminster, who died, sincerely mourned, seven years previous to the death of her husband.

Mr. Lyman retained to the last his cordial interest in public and national affairs. Throughout the long and sometimes doubtful struggle of our late civil war, he remained a cheerful, unwavering supporter of the government; and, although too aged and infirm to place himself within the lists, sent a stalwart substitute to battle in behalf of his principles.

One of the most pleasing incidents that marked the last years of this venerable old man, was his ability to be present at the centennial commencement of his *alma mater* — Dartmouth College — where as the oldest graduate present, one of sixty five years' standing, he was the most noticed of the Alumni.

Extreme weakness prevented his attendance at the Lyman pic-nic the August following, but his cordial letter of greeting and encouragement was not lacking on that occasion.

He took a lively interest in the growth and prosperity of Burlington and in many charitable institutions, prominent among which was the Home for the Destitute, which realized from his generosity a tangible and munificent benefit.

He fulfilled with conscientious strictness his duty as a citizen, not forgetting the important duty of voting, even when gathering years might well have excused him.

His last illness was brief, terminating on the 2d day, Sept. 10, 1870. He passed away ripe in years, rich in the garnered experience of an useful life, known to all as a patriotic and worthy citizen, a sincere Christian and a friend whose aid and sympathy were surest when the need was the most pressing; and those who have known him long and intimately, felt, in connection with the purity and gentleness of his heart, that he might well have exclaimed with the unfortunate Josephine of France : " I have never willingly caused a tear to flow."

212 JONATHAN LYMAN[6], eldest son of *Jonathan[5]*, *Elias[4]*, *John[3]*, *John[2]*, *Richard[1]*, 1778–1860, m. Lois Clapp, was born Oct. 12, 1775. This is probably the date of Sylvester's birth in Northampton. He removed to Vergennes, Vt. He m. 2d, Clarissa Clapp, of Easthampton, in Nelson, N. H., Jan. 24, 1796. He d. in N. Ferrisburg, Feb. 3, 1860. She was b. Feb. 22, 1776, and d. Oct. 5, 1867, aged 91.

Children, Seventh Generation :

596 1 Roxana, b. Sept. 4, 1797 ; m. Dennis Barney, March 7, 1819, had one son, George Lyman, b. March 5, 1820, went to Ill., in 1835. Mr. Barney, d. Nov. 11, 1844. She returned to Vt., and m. 2d, L. N. Brown, May 6, 1856, resides at Williston, Vt.

598 2 Theodore Dwight, b. July 28, 1799 ; m. Betsey Fuller.

599 3 Edmund, b. March 28, 1803 ; m. Hannah L. Forman, March 18, 1835 ; d. Nov. 30, 1847, without children.

600 4 Louisa Maria, b. June 10, 1807; m. Alanson B. Martin,
Dec. 28, 1835, went to Potsdam, N. Y., her husband d.
She returned to Vt., and N. Ferrisburg.

601 5 Jonathan, b. March 19, 1810, m.

602 6 Fanny, b. June 2, 1813.

603 7 Clarissa Amelia, b. Oct. 24, 1816; m. Avery W. Billings,
April 25, 1850, has one child, Lois Abby, b. March 30,
1851. N. Ferrisburg, Vt.

246 SYLVESTER LYMAN[6], second son of *Jonathan*[5] and
Lois, was b. Dec. 11, 1775. He m. Aug. 30, 1797, Nancy
Clapp, who was b. Oct. 8, 1777, and d. in Albany, Feb.
25, or 23, 1842. Sylvester Lyman d. May 19, 1839.

Children, Seventh Generation:

605 1 George, b. July 20, 1796, drowned in Lake Nicaragua in
1825.

606 2 Ann, b. Sept. 4, 1798; m. Dr. C. H. Picket and d. in Ohio
in 1829. He d. in 1850.
Ch. 9th Gen. 1 Albert L., who d. in 1851. 2 Frances,
who d. 3 Mary, m. M. L. Converse, N. Y. 4 Ann, m.
resides in Conn.

611 3 Lavinia, b. March 6, 1801; d. May 15, 1801.

612 4 Edward, b. March 20, 1802; d. Aug. 14, 1825.

613 5 Henry, b. Sept. 3, 1804; d. Sept. 6.

614 6 William, b. May 20, 1806; m. Anna L. Wood, Sept. 8,
1841; d. Nov. 8; 1845, grad. with highest honor at
Union Coll., also at Princeton Theological Sem., d. April
10, 1858, no children.

615 7 Sylvester, b. Sept. 20, 1808; d. Dec. 1, 1808.

616 8 James, b. Nov. 20, 1810; d. Nov. 23, 1810.

617 9 Henry, b. March 14, 1811; m. Mrs. Hannah D. Learned,
near Boston.

618 10 Sylvester, b. April 20, 1813; m. Miss Goodyear, New York
City, 1 dau. Elvira.

620 11 James Harvey, b. Oct. 28, 1815; m. Louisa Tardrew, and
d. Dec. 6, 1853, in California, no children.

621 12 Charles H. P., b. March 5, 1818; d. April 26, 1818.

622 13 Charles Harvey P., b. June 16, 1819; m. Mary E. Green.

279 GAD LYMAN[6], eldest son of *Oliver*[5], and Eleanor,
was b. Aug. 23, 1766. He m. Prudence Bill, of Huntington, Mass. Both d. in one week of yellow fever at Charlotte, Vt., in Feb. 1813.

Children, Seventh Generation:

623 1 Wealthy,...... m. Orrin Smith, of Charlotte, Vt., had six
children.

630 2 Oliver, m. Ann Linnberry, in 1823; removed to Ohio.

Ch. 8th Gen.: 1 William, b. in Tunbury, Ohio, Sept.
9, 1828; m. Dec. 17, 1855, Mary Hotchkiss Tailor.
Mt. Giliard, Ohio. [*Ch. 9th Gen.:* (1) Minnie, b. July
12, 1856. (2) Oliver G., b. Oct. 17, 1858. (3) Edwin
A., b. April 30, 1864.]

635 3 Fanny, m. Bingham, of Charlotte, Vt., resides Frederictown,
Knox Co., Ohio.

636 4 Ann, m. Bryant of Hinesburg, Vt., and removed to Canandaigua, N. Y., had three children.

640 5 David Bill, b. May 13, 1804; m. Lucretia Smith, killed by
explosion on Erie railroad, April 14, 1852.

641 6 Frederic. Marrietta, Ohio.

642 7 Gad, b. June 21, 1810; m. Cecilia Smith, Dec. 12, 1833,
removed to Burlington, Vt., is engineer in the Harlem
railroad. White Plains

Ch. 8th Gen.: (1) Mary, b. Oct. 21, 1834. (2) Lucy,
b. Jan. 2, 1837. Is a soldier's widow. (3) Josephine,
b. Feb. 10, 1849; unmarried.

281 Medad Lyman[6], third son of *Oliver*[5] and Eleanor,
was b. March 18, 1770; m. Anne Clapp, dau. of Benjamin
Clapp, of Easthampton, who d. Dec. 13, 1802, and he m.
2d Mrs. Olive Mead, Dec. 5, 1805. Medad Lyman d. Feb.
5, 1803.

Children, Seventh Generation ·

646 1 Minerva, b. March 3, 1797.

647 2 Son, d. young.

648 3 Dau., d. young.

649 4 Sophia, b. Sept. 21, 1800; m. Abel Kittredge, of Nelson,
N. H.

Ch. 8th Gen: 1 Sophia, b. 1823; m. Rev. French.
[*Ch. 9th Gen.:* (1) Nancy (2) James, is a widow and
city missionary in Boston, Mass.] 2 Edward Lyman.
3 Charles, d. young. 4 Samuel Farrington, Mrs. Sophia
Kittredge, d. May, 1839, and Abel Kittredge, m. 2d,
Anne M. Lyman.

656 5 Anne M., b. Dec. 5, 1802; d. May 18, 1803.

657 6 Anne M., b. Oct. 25, 1806; m. Abel Kittredge.

Ch. 8th Gen.: 1 Minot Mellville, b. 1840. 2 Charles d.
young. 3 Henry, b. Nov. 20, 1843.

282 Jared Lyman[6], fourth son of *Oliver*[5] and Eleanor, b.
Sept. 6, 1772; m. Zeruiah Birch; removed to Charlotte,
Vt., thence to Bridport, where he d. Jan. 26, 1813.

Children, Seventh Generation :

661 1 William.　　　　　　　　662 2 Medad.

286 JOHN C. LYMAN[6], eldest son of Lieut. *Timothy[5]*, *Gad[4]*, *John[3]*, *John[2]*, *Richard[1]*, 1775 – 1854, b. Jan. 20, 1775 ; m. Susan Burgess, Nov. 7, 1799. He lived in Goshen until 1826, then he removed to Cummington, Mass.; his wife d. there the 26th of June following; he m. again Nov. 7, 1827; he d. March 12, 1854, aged 79.   *Cummington.*

Children, Seventh Generation:

663 1 Adam C., b. Oct. 21, 1800 ; d. Oct., 1822.
664 2 Christa, b. May 5, 1805 ; m. Lewis Ford, Sept. 11, 1832. They lived in Cummington several years, then they removed to Ohio, where she d. July 28, 1862.
665 3 Benjamin B., b. Sept. 17, 1807 ; m. Roxana Packard, Oct. 14, 1832.
666 4 Hannah C., b. Feb. 29, 1810 ; m. F. W. Whitman, Cleveland, Ohio, Oct. 14, 1832.
667 5 Susan M., b. Aug. 11, 1813 ; m. Orrin Bryant, Aug. 11, 1833 ; d. Oct., 1833.

288 WILLIAM LYMAN[6], second son of Lt. *Timothy[5]*, b. Feb. 21, 1778. He learned the tailor's trade of Sylvester Lyman, of Northampton. He settled in Schenectady, had a store there; he m. Dec. 18, 1791, Agnes, the dau. of Hugh Mitchell, Esq., of Canajoharie, and d. at Schenectady, N. Y., in 1861. She d. Dec. 1860, buried on 69th anniversary of her marriage.   *Schenectady, N. Y.*

Children, Seventh Generation:

668 1 Agnes, b. 1815 ; m. 1841, John Foster Prof. in Union College, and d. 1855.
       Ch. 8th Gen.: 1 Helen M., now in Cambridge, N. Y.
       2 Agnes Lyman, d. 1868

290 FRANCIS LYMAN[6], fourth son of Lt. *Timothy[5]*, was b. Feb. 3, 1781. He was a farmer in Goshen, a deacon in the Congregational church, and on his monument is inscribed : " An Israelite indeed, in whom is no guile." He m. Helen Mitchell, dau. of Hugh Mitchell, Esq. She d. May 26, 1831, aged 42. He m. 2d, Lucinda Parsons April 10, 1839. She was b. April 12, 1802, is living still in Goshen. Francis Lyman, d. July 5, 1851.
          Goshen, Mass.

Children, Seventh Generation:

671 1 William, b. Aug. 3, 1810 ; m. ....; his wife died, he m. 2d .... He was educated at Union College, studied medicine, went to the West. He was a surgeon in Gen. Grant's army during the campaign from Pittsburg Landing to the taking of Vicksburg. He d. in Rockford, Ill., Dec., 1866.

31

672 2 Hugh Mitchell, b. Oct. 21, 1814; m. Sarah Kingman of Worthington, has one daughter Helen Agness. He d. 1869.

674 3 Timothy P., b. Aug. 7, 1834; m. wid. Jennie Rice of Haydenville, Oct. 14, 1865, has one child Lizzie Knowlton. He joined the army in 1861, and continued through the war, became 2d lieutenant.

676 4 Helen L., b. March 24, 1838, resides in Goshen.

677 5 Mary Clark, b. May 1, 1840; d. Oct. 6, 1844.

678 6 Francis Henry, b. Jan. 26, 1844; d. Sept. 9, 1844.

291 THOMAS LYMAN⁶, fifth son of Lt. *Timothy⁵*, was b. Feb. 12, 1783; m. Dorcas Smith, in 1812, or '13; d. 1822.

Goshen, Mass.

Children, Seventh Generation :

679 1 Mary Ann, b. Sept. 21, 1814; d. March 9, 1822.

680 2 Thankful Pomeroy, b. Dec. 12, 1815; m. Zimri Newell, Nov., 1837.

681 3 Frederic William, b. March 31, 1817; m. Sarah Naramore.

682 4 Charlotte Augusta, b. Sept. 30, 1818; m. Edwin A. Carpenter, Nov., 1837.

683 5 Timothy Sumner, b. May 8, 1820; d. Dec. 26, 1829.

684 6 Thomas Colson, b. March 11, 1822; d. Jan. 10, 1830.

299 ZADOC S. LYMAN⁷, eldest son of *Israel⁶* and Rachel, *Zadoc⁵, John⁴, John³, John² Richard¹*, 1774 – 1849, was b. March 26, 1774, d. Dec. 8, 1849. He kept a tavern many years at Hockanum. He m. Hannah Watson of Windsor, Ct., Jan. 26, 1797. She was b. July 21, 1768, and d. Dec. 17, 1845.

Hockanum.

Children, Eighth Generation :

685 1 Samuel Watson, b. Nov. 13, 1797; m. Purly Hubbard.

686 2 Lucretia, b. March 20, 1799; m. July 2, 1851, Elijah Clark of Plainfield, Mass.

687 3 William, b. Oct. 22, 1800; m. Amanda White.

688 4 Horace, b. Oct. 14, 1802; m. Elvira Hubbard.

689 5 Zadoc Moseley, b. July 12, 1804; m. Mary Smith.

690 6 Rodney, b. June 10, 1806; m. Melissa Fuller in 1831. Is a grazier and resides at Pine Run, Genesee Co., Mich., no children.

691 7 Charles, b. Sept. 9, 1808; d. July 16, 1810.

692 8 Charles, b. Aug. 12, 1810; m. Mary D. Holmes, 1833.

     Ch. 9th Gen.: 1 Mary. 2 Hannah, who m. E. Clark, of Plainfield.

694 9 Frederic, b. Oct, 3, 1813; m. Caroline Whitten.

301 ISRAEL LYMAN⁷, was b. Oct. 17, 1776. He was a farmer in Hockanum, m. Sarah Moody, May 13, 1802, and

d. Aug. 4, 1836. Sarah his wife was b. May 12, 1782, and
d. March 17, 1848. *Hockanum.*

Children, Eighth Generation .

696   1 Alonzo, b. March 16, 1803 ; m. Amelia Moody.
697   2 Keziah Moody, b. Jan. 19, 1805 ; m. Moses Hubbard of Sunderland, a farmer.
698   3 Maria, b. Nov. 2, 1806 ; m. May 10, 1831. Brown went to Michigan, d. June 24, or 28, 1833, had one child d. in infancy.
700   4 Almon, b. July 29, 1808 ; m. Clarissa Burnett.
701   5 Israel Franklin, b. Sept. 12, 1810.
702   6 A son, b. Feb. 8, 1813 ; d. Feb. 11, 1813.
703   7 Harvey, b. Aug. 26, 1814 ; m.
704   8 Hadassar, b. Oct. 27, 1816 ; m. Henry E. Bartlett, of Hadley ; d. Oct. 11, 1846.
705   9 Mary Pomeroy, b. Nov. 12, 1819 ; d. Jan. 29, 1820.
706   10 A son, b. Oct. 4, 1821 ; d. Oct. 7, 1821.
707   11 Elijah Austin, b. Feb. 22, 1823 ; m. Sophronia Pease.
708   12 Edward Mason, b. May 13, 1825 ; m. 1st, Caroline Blodgett ; 2d, Mrs. Eliza Hopkins.

304 AMAZIAH LYMAN[7], son of *Israel[6]* and Rachel, b. Feb. 13, 1782; m. Elizabeth Alvord, of S. Hadley. *Hockanum.*

Children, Eighth Generation :

709   1 Rachel, b. July 5, 1806 ; m. Baxter Wilder of Chesterfield.
710   2 Luther Alvord, b Jan. 1, 1808 ; m. Esther L. Ewings.
711   3 Edwin Waitstill, b. May 22, 1809 ; m. Lois A. Forbes.
712   4 Elizabeth, b. March 6, 1811 ; d. Nov. 12, 1812.
713   5 Elizabeth Serussa, b. Nov. 23, 1812 ; d. Oct. 31, 1813.
714   6 Harriet Sophia, b. Jan. 22, 1814 ; d. Aug. 8, 1840.
715   7 Amaziah Henry, b. Sept. 24, 1816 ; d. Nov. 25, 1850.
716   8 Joseph Willard, b. March 7, 1818 ; d. May 9, 1841.
717   9 Cornelius, b. March 11, 1821 ; d. Dec. 20, 1841.
718   10 Julius, b. Jan. 20, 1823 ; d. March 21, 1825.
719   11 Elizabeth Serina, b. Dec. 31, 1825 ; d. July 13, 1843.

308 ENOS LYMAN[7], twelfth child of *Israel[6]* and Rachel, was b. Jan. 2, 1790. He m. Lydia Wadsworth, of Ellington, Ct., Jan. 29, 1817, and d. Sept. 22, 1848. She is still living in Hockanum. *Hockanum.*

Children, Eighth Generation :

720   1 Harriet H., b. March 31, 1820 ; m. Wm. E. Mather, of Northampton.
      Ch. 9th Gen. : 1 Frank C., b. Aug. 28, 1849. 2 John L., b. Jan. 9, 1851. 3 Dwight C., b. Oct. 28, 1852. 4 George H., b. April 17, 1859 ; d. Nov. 13, 1861.
725   2 Wadsworth P., b. May 10, 1822.

726 ₃ Romanta N., b. March 14, 1824.
727 ₄ Enos Dwight, b. July 4, 1826 ; d. Jan. 24, at Mormon Island, Cal.
728 ₅ Francis A., b. Oct. 7, 1828 ; d. July 18, 1829.
729 ₆ Francis A., b. Dec. 6, 1830 ; m. Mary Boynton.
730 ₇ Samuel A., b. May 31, 1834 ; d. Nov. 1, 1838.
731 ₈ Lucius A., b. May 29, 1837; d. March 27, 1839.

309 GEORGE LYMAN⁷, youngest child of *Israel⁶* and Rachel, b. Dec. 13, 1792; m. Laura W......, who d. Jan. 19, 1872. He d. in Ellington, Ct., April 14, 1866.   *Ellington, Ct.*
Children, Eighth Generation :
732 ₁ Lorenzo W., b. Sept. 18, 1820 ; m. Sarah Williams.
733 ₂ John, b. April 17, 1822 ; m. Julia A. Smith ; he was a farmer and lived in Amherst, Mass. ; d. March 1, 1859.
734 ₃ Laura S., b. Nov. 19, 1823 ; d. June 25, 1825.
735 ₄ George J., b. Sept. 13, 1826 ; m. Pamelia J. Taylor ; res. S. Hadley.
736 ₅ Laura S., b. July 6, 1828 ; d. Nov., 1838.
737 ₆ Warren Israel, b. Oct. 19, 1830 ; m Emeline Elizabeth Miller, of Kensington, June 11, 1854, lived in South Hadley and Hadley. He was carpenter and joiner, and wagon maker. In 1861, at the call for 300,000 volunteers, after the peninsular campaign, he enlisted in the government service for three years ; was in the battle of Fredericksburg under Burnside, also in the famous mud march, or Burnside's second attempt to move on Fredericksburg, in which he was disabled, and was honorably discharged May 28, 1862. In Nov., 1862, he removed to Springfield, and engaged in introducing the Independent Steam Engine, an ingenious and useful machine of his own invention.
    Ch. 9th Gen.: ₁ Clara Elizabeth, b. March 8, 1855.
    ₂ Emma Julia, b Oct. 12, 1866 ; d. May 25, 1860.
    ₃ Lewis Warren, b. Jan. 16, 1865.
738 ₇ David, b. Aug. 7, 1835 ; farmer; m. Hattie J. Smith, April 27, 1859 ; had one child.
    Ch. 9th Gen.: ₁ George Henry, b. Sept. 1, 1860 ; d. Nov. 1, 1860 ; res. in Hadley.

326 AZARIAH LYMAN⁷, 2d son of *Azariah⁶* and Jemima, was born Dec, 6, 1777; m. Rhoda Rust, Nov. 27, 1799. She was b. April 5, 1778, and d. Nov. 17, 1809. He m. 2d, Sarah Bartlett, Jan. 8, 1811. She was b. May 24, 1784, and d. May 14, 1859. He d. May 12, 1857.
Children, Eighth Generation :
743 ₁ Fidelia, b. Aug. 9, 1800 ; d. March 8, 1817, in Huntington, Mass.

744 2 Sophronia, b. June 14, 1802; m. May 23, 1826, John Fellows, b. Feb. 20, 1801, in Chester, O.

> *Ch. 9th Gen.:* 1 John Parker, b. Feb. 16, 1827. 2 Dwight, b. Nov. 23, 1828. 3 Dorus, b. Sept. 20, 1830, in Chester, O. 4 Julia, b. Nov. 28, 1833, in Kirtland, O. 5 John Lyman, b. May 31, 1842, in Newburgh, Ia. 6 Orrin, b. July 20, 1843, in Youngstown, O. (1868).

751 3 Roxana, b. Sept. 9, 1804; m. Alonzo Melvin, b. Oct. 2, 1794; m. in Chester, O., Nov. 27, 1825.

> *Ch. 9th Gen :* 1 Fidelia Lyman, b. Aug. 3, 1826, in Chester, O. 2 Martha Maria, b. May 24, 1827, in Chester, O. 3 Addison Smith, b. Sept. 22, 1829; m. Cordelia McKenney, b. in Chester, O. 4 Shepard Knapp, b. Aug. 13, 1830. 5 Fordyce Rust, b. July 23, 1832. 6 Sarah Elizabeth, b. Aug. 24, 1834. 7 Reuben Lyman, b. Oct. 12, 1836. 8 Elihu Oliver, b. July 27, 1838. 9 Dunton Taylor, b. Oct. 23, 1840. 10 Alonzo Austin, b. Aug. 10, 1842. 11 Roenna Coysilda, b. Sept. 3, 1844. 12 Edward Payson, b. Oct. 21, 1846. 13 Henry Martyn, b. Sept. 17, 1850, Brooklyn, Wis.

765 4 Rhoda, b. Sept. 2, 1806; m. Seth Frissel, in Chester, O., Jan. 2, 1833; b. Dec. 12, 1799. A farmer Chester, O.

> *Ch. 9th Gen.:* 1 Electa Foot, b. Jan. 15, 1834. 2 Thomas Botter, b. Oct. 5, 1836. 3 Elizabeth, b. Dec. 5, 1839. 4 Franklin Kitteridge, b. April 10, 1847; d. May 23, 1864, in the army Co. C. Ohio Artillery. 5 Augustus Watkins, b. Aug. 14, 1849.

771 5 Mary, b. Oct. 22, 1809; m. in Chester, O., Jan. 3, 1830, Solomon C. Ferry, b. in Easthampton, Mass., Sept. 9, 1806. A farmer in Chester, O.

> *Ch. 9th Gen.:* 1 Marcus Chalmers, b. Sept. 17, 1830. 2 Solomon Alanson, b. Nov. 2, 1833. 3 Lucina Parnell, b. March 11, 1834. 4 Solomon C., b. Nov. 7, 1836. 5 Emily Rocina, b. Aug. 20, 1839. 6 Sophia Melissa, b. Jan. 23, 1842. 7 Lyman Solomon, b. Aug. 3, 1845. 8 Nelson C., b. Feb. 1, 1847. 9 Dora Maria, b. Aug. 10, 1850.

781 6 Newman Rust, b. Nov. 12, 1811, in Westhampton, Mass.

782 7 Elihu Oliver, b. June 12, 1817, in Norwich. (Huntington, Mass.)

783 8 Melissa, b. Aug. 27, 1818; m. Aug. 3, 1846, Enoch Winslow Page, b. July 4, 1824, Bloomfield, N. Y.

> *Ch. 8th Gen.:* 1 Lyman Eliot, b. May 26, 1854, in N. Y. 1 Emily Sarah, b. March 9, 1857. 3 Melissa Susan, b. Sept. 30, 1860.

787 9 Osman Azariah, b. Sept. 23, 1824; graduated at the Western Reserve Coll., in 1844, studied law, admitted to the bar Dec. 25, 1846. Practiced law at Greenville, O., six years in partnership with Mr. Bell, afterwards in Dayton,

and in New York ; left the law in 1860 ; studied theology ; served as Chaplain in the army with the 41st Reg., Ohio Vols., and with the 93d at the battles of Shiloh, siege of Corinth, and battle of Stone river ; resigned on account of impaired health, became pastor of Euclid St. Church of Cleveland, O., May, 1868.

Rev. Dr. O. A. Lyman, of the Euclid Street Presbyterian church, Cleveland, Ohio, was struck with paralysis while attending a special meeting of Presbytery in the Second Presbyterian church. He was the prosecutor in a trial, which has occupied the attention of the Presbytery for some time, and he had been engaged for parts of two days in examining witnesses, and had just made his argument in a quiet manner, though with some evidence of painful feeling in the discharge of the duty. While sitting a chair he slipped to the floor, and when lifted up was found to be entirely paralyzed on his right side. Excellent medical attendance was immediately at hand, and he was soon taken to his house. He remained helpless and unconscious till death, and the event produced great pain throughout the city. He was in the early prime of his powers, and had won the highest respect of the community.

327 Elihu Lyman[7], 2d son of *Azariah*[6] and Jemima, was b. Oct. 17, 1779 ; m. Hannah Judd, of Westhampton, Dec. 16, 1802. He d. in Westhampton, Mass., April 24, 1815, aged 35. His widow Hannah, m. Dec. 26, 1833, Ahira Lyman, of Easthampton, who was b. Dec. 10, 1790. Ahira Lyman, d. in Easthampton, Nov. 1, 1835 ; she d. Feb. 16, 1865.

> *Children, Eighth Generation.*

788 1 Clarissa Judd, b. March, 12, 1806 ; m. Rev. John H. Bisbee, of Chesterfield, May 5, 1804. He was b. Jan. 23, 1805.
> Ch. 9th Gen.: 1 Lucy Hooker, b. Feb. 16, 1835, in Middlefield, Mass. 2 Mary Howe, b. Feb. 3, 1837. 3 Jane Lyman, b. Aug. 5, 1840, in Worthington. 4 Julia Judd, b. July 25, 1842. 5 John Jay, b. Dec. 1, 1744. 6 Clara Lyman, b. Feb. 13, 1847.

795 2 Theresa, b. Aug. 29, 1810 ; m. Ahira Lyman, Feb, 6, 1840. Ahira was b. Oct. 13, 1807.
> Ch. 9th Gen.: 1 Henry, b. July 31, 1832. 2 Gaius Burt, b. July 19, 1836. (1) Francis Burt, b. Dec. 8, 1840. (2) Arthur Judad, b. July 30, 1842. (3) Albert Ahira, b. Dec. 27, 1845. (4) Richard, b. Sept. 8, 1847. (5) Bobert Worthington, b. Sept. 27, 1850. (6) Willie, b. May 22, 1854.

796 3 George, b. Nov. 19, 1812, in Westhampton ; m. Lucina Phelps.

354 JESSIE LYMAN[7], b. March 9, 1789, in Westhampton; m. Jan. 2, 1817, Lucy Kingsley, b. Dec. 14, 1794.

Children, Eighth Generation:

797 1 An infant, b. April 2, 1820.
798 2 Maria Elma, b. Nov. 23, 1831; m. March 31, 1852, Edward H. Norton, b. Jan. 24, 1824. He d. at Albion, N. J., April 13, 1867.
   Ch. 9th Gen.: 1 An infant, b. Oct. 4, 1858. 2 Charles Henry, b. Sept. 4, 1859, in Batavia, N. Y.
801 3 Elihu Eustice, b. Nov. 21, 1824; d. Aug. 21, 1827.
802 4 William Eustice, b. Oct. 28, 1828; m. Mary E. Orcutt.
803 5 Sylvester, b. June 1, 1830; d. April 10, 1833.

355 SYLVESTER LYMAN[7], eldest son of *Luke[6]* and Susanna, b. Dec. 27, 1782. He m. Harriet Elizabeth Wright, Dec. 28, 1808. He d. Aug. 26, 1853. His wife d. Sept. 16, 1861.

Children, Eighth Generation:

804 1 Moses, harness and trunk maker; d. in Springfield.
805 2 Charles, farmer; d. in Northampton.
806 3 Martha, m. Rev. George Sheldon, of Plainfield, N. J.; d. at Princeton, N. J. No dates are given; no record of children; Charleston, S. C.

376 LUKE C. LYMAN[7], second son of *Luke[6]* and Susanna, b. in Northampton on the plain now called Bridge street, Feb. 21, 1792, and m. Sarah Dummer, dau. of Capt. Stephen Dummer, of New Haven, Conn., Dec. 25, 1817.
Jersey City, N. J.

Children, Eighth Generation:

807 1 George Dummer, b. Jan. 31, 1822; m. A. A. Wenman.
808 2 Sarah Elizabeth, b. Oct. 14, 1823; d. Jan. 25, 1829.
809 3 Henry Augustus, b. Nov. 26, 1826; m. M. C. Cory.
810 4 Sarah Elizabeth, b. Nov. 25, 1828; m. Uzal Cory, June 10, 1857, in Jersey City, N. J.
   Ch. 9th Gen.: 1 Frances Lyman, b. March 20, 1862. 2 Herbert Dummer, b. Dec. 4, 1866.

377 HORACE LYMAN[7], son of *Luke[6]* and Susanna, b. June 9, 1795, and m. Electa Day, Dec. 1, 1819. He d. March 24, 1859. *Northampton.*

Children, Eighth Generation:

813 1 Fanny Woodbury, b. Oct. 24, 1820; m. Ozro A. Hillman, March 5, 1845, and d. April 7, 1852.
   Ch. 9th Gen.: 1 Susan L., b. Nov. 23, 1846. 2 Frank W., b. Aug., 1851, all b. at Northampton.
816 2 Isaac, b. Aug. 4, 1822; d. Aug. 15, 1831.
817 3 Luke, b. Nov. 1, 1824; m. Elizabeth B. Hartung.

818 4 Isabella, b. March 10, 1827; m. Lucas Bridgeman, of Northampton, Sept. 16, 1862, no children.
819 5 Sylvester, b. Oct. 26, 1828; d. Jan. 28, 1829, in N.
820 6 Horace, b. Dec. 6, 1829; d. Sept. 27, 1832, in N.

391 ASAHEL LYMAN[7], eldest son of *Rufus[6], John[5], John[4], John[3], John[2], Richard[1]*, 1777–1811, and Martha Burt, was b. April 16, 1777; and m. Esther Strong, Dec. 5, 1798, and d. Sept. 18, 1811. She was b. April 29, and d. Feb. 13, 1824.   *Norwich, Mass.*
       Children, Eighth Generation :
821 1 Dexter, b. Sept. 24, 1800; d. Jan. 2, 1816.
822 2 A son, b. March 6, 1802; d. April 13, 1802.
823 3 Peuuniah, b. Nov. 2, 1804; m. Thomas Elwell.
824 4 Malissa, b. July 22, 1806; d. Oct. 20, 1806.
825 5 Dorcas, b. Jan. 3, 1808; m. Micah R. Barr.
826 6 A son, b. June 22, 1809; d. same day.

392 RUFUS LYMAN[7], second son of *Rufus[6]* and Martha, was b. Jan. 19, 1779; and m. Sophia Montague, Nov. 28, 1805. She was b. Aug. 30, 1785; and d. April 1, 1857. He d. March 7, 1860.   *Norwich, Mass.*
       Children, Eighth Generation :
827 1 Ashley, b. July 12, 1806.
828 2 Moses M., b. Sept. 15, 1809; m. Cynthia B. Tucker.
829 3 William G., b. June 8, 1812.
830 4 Linus M., b. Dec. 13, 1817; d. March 5, 1838.
831 5 Rufus E., b. Oct. 4, 1821.
832 6 Laura S., b. Aug. 7, 1829.

398 ENOCH LYMAN[7], third son of *Rufus[6]* and Martha, was b. June 13, 1782, and m. Nov. 18, 1804, Silence Edwards. She was b. July 13, 1784, and d. Sept. 14, 1864. He d. March 29, 1849.   *Norwich, Mass.*
       Children, Eighth Generation :
833 1 A son d. in infancy.
834 2 Mary E., b. May 10, 1810; m. John Fisk, now living.
835 3 Silence J., b. Dec. 29, 1814; d. April 27, 1865, single.
836 4 Philomela T., b. Aug. 24, 1818; m. Samuel W. Fisher April 17, 1847; d. July 23, 1858.
837 5 Enoch H., b. Oct. 28, 1822; m. Amoret R. Judd, Nov. 16, 1862; has a son Washington Hooker, b. April 12, 1848. South Deerfield, Mass.

412 SERENO LYMAN[7], fourth son of *Rufus[6]* and Martha, was b. Feb. 2, 1788, and m. Mary Clark, Sept. 17, 1813.

She d. Jan. 13, 1818, and he m. 2d, Deborah James, March 12, 1819. She was b. Dec. 6, 1789, and d. Sept. 6, 1868.

Norwich, Mass.

Children, Eighth Generation ·

838 1 Asahel W., b. July 22, 1815.
839 2 Sereno C., b. Jan. 6, 1818.
840 3 Sereno D., b. Sept. 10, 1822.
841 4 Mary C., b. May 22, 1825.
842 5 William J., b. June 28, 1827.
843 6 Francis O., b. July 7, 1830.
844 7 Edward P., b. May 27, 1834, all b. in Norwich, Mass.

415 JOHN BURT LYMAN[7], 6th son of *Rufus[6]*, of West-hampton, Mass., b. April 4, 1792; m. Feb. 2, 1815, Ruth Strong, dau. of Waitstill Strong, of Southampton, who was b. Feb. 29, 1783, and d. Dec. 5, 1856.

Norwich, Mass.

Children, Eighth Generation :

845 1 Mary Strong, b. July 27, 1818.
846 2 Dexter, b. Sept. 10, 1821 ; m. Mary L. Clark, of Southampton.
847 3 Jairus Joy, b. Aug. 24, 1823.
848 4 John, b. Dec. 30, 1825, all b. in Norwich, Mass.

416 LIBERTY LYMAN[7], 7th son of *Rufus[6]*, b. June 22, 1794; m. Lucinda Sykes, in 1816. She was b. Oct. 16, 1796, resided 18 years in Blandford, removed 1839, to Shiawassee, Michigan, then a wilderness, suffering many privations going 25 miles to mill, subject to ill health from fever and ague.   *Shiawassee, Mich.*

Children, Eighth Generation :

849 1 Pliny Sykes, b. April 29, 1818; m.   Has two sons.
      Ch. 9th Gen.: 1 Pliny Orrenda. 2 Sereno Burt.
852 2 Catharine, b. Jan. 15, 1820; m. Samuel Brown, has 6 children.
853 3 Sylvester, b. Feb. 26, 1822; m. has one dau. — farmer in California.
854 4 Romanzo, b. April 4, 1824.
      Ch. 9th Gen.: 1 George. 2 Liberty. 3 Henry M., farmer in California.
857 5 Anna Sybella, b. Feb. 23, 1826 ; m. Charles C. Lockwood, who d. in 1856.
858 6 Calvin Waldo, b. March 8, 1828 ; d. Jan. 20, 1848.
860 7 Lucinda, b. March 6, 1830 ; m. R. J. Hastings, d. March 16, 1857, left one son Lyman, who d. aged 10 days.
862 8 Sereno Burt, b. April 5, 1832 ; farmer in California. Was in the war in the state service three years, is unmarried.

32

863   9 Edson Liberty, b. May 12, 1834 ; m. has 2 daughters, a farmer.
866   10 James Henry, b. April 30, 1837 ; m. served 4½ years in the war, was honorably discharged, reenlisted, was made sergeant, Iowa.

417 THOMAS LYMAN[7], oldest son of *Thomas[6]* and Dorothy, was b. Aug. 15, 1785 ; m. Betsey Clapp of Southampton, Dec. 1, 1813 ; d. Oct. 24, 1850, aged 65. *Onondaga, N. Y.*

Children, Eighth Generation:

867   1 Eliza Jane, b. March 4, 1815, at Southampton ; m. Joseph C. Kenyon in Onondaga, and d. June 25, 1843.
868   2 Francis, b. July 27, 1816 ; m. Mrs. Betsey Taylor, April 20, 1847, at Marcellus, N. Y., and died Jan. 21, 1865, in Syracuse. Had son Frank who d. April 12, 1866, aged 14 years.
870   3 Julia Ann, b. May 9, 1818 ; m. Wm. A. Graves, Northampton, April 6, 1841.
871   4 Mary Strong, b. Nov. 6, 1819 ; m. Davis Baker of Onondaga, March 15, 1841, d. Nov. 23, 1841, at Marcellus.
872   5 John C., b. April 2, 1821, at Westhampton ; m. Aug. 9, 1853, Ruth Ann Abbott, who d. Jan. 13, 1857, in Auburn, N. Y. ; m. 2d Viola Curtiss, Nov. 22, 1861, at Skeneateles, N. Y., is a druggist in Newcastle, C. W.
873   6 Perez C., b. March 22, 1823, at Otisco, N. Y. ; m. Oct. 15, 1857, to Caroline F. Mudge at Greenville, Alabama, a merchant about to remove to Topeka, Kansas.
874   7 Dorothy C., b. Jan. 9, 1825 ; m. Oct. 20, 1846, to P. Dean Howe ; a farmer in Marcellus.
875   8 Helen A., b. Feb. 11, 1827 ; m. Nov. 21, 1850, at Onondaga, to Theodore Hall, a farmer.
876   9 Margaret C., Nov. 16, 1828 ; m. Feb. 23, 1859, to Henry Colton of Marcellus, a farmer.
877   10 Thomas J., b. Sept. 30, 1830 ; m. Aurelia Van Inwegen, Oct. 3, 1859, in Sodus, N. Y. He is a merchant in Phelps, Ontario Co., N. Y.
878   11 Frederick A., b. Sept. 3, 1833 ; m. Dec. 24, 1862, in Jordan, N. Y.. to Jennie Phillips, who d. Feb. 10, 1864, at Marcellus ; he m. 2d Mrs. Mary Woodford, Oct. 3d, 1865. He is a lawyer, resides in Syracuse, N. Y.
879   12 Harriet A., b. Dec. 1, 1836 ; m. Charles H. Forman, April 9, 1856. He is a dentist in Syracuse, N. Y.

429 THADDEUS LYMAN[7], second son of *Thomas,* and Dorothy, was b. in Southampton, Mass., Sept. 21, 1789, m. Sarah G. Schoonmaker, of Newark, N. J., Nov. 6, 1817; is a manufacturer of saddlery hardware, etc. *Newark, N. J.*

Children, Eighth Generation :

880 1 Theodore Dwight, b. Aug. 13, 1818; d. Aug. 18, 1819.
881 2 Sarah Elizabeth, b. June 16, 1820; m. David A. Nichols,
merchant of Flanders, N. Y., Sept. 25, 1844.
882 3 William Henry, b. March 21, 1822; m. Georgiana G. W.
Bleeker.
883 4 Margaret Vantilburg, b. May 22, 1824.
884 5 Mary Alida, b. June 22, 1826; m. Thomas A. Staymor, of
Brooklyn, N. Y., Oct. 21, 1858. Is at present, 1869,
collector of customs, at St. Marks, Newport, Florida.
Ch. 9th Gen. : 1 Charles Dudley, b. July 26, 1859.
886 6 Anna Josephine, b. May 25, 1833; m. Theodore H. Silvery,
of Newark, May 17, 1859. Is an officer in the Custom
House, Newark, N. J.
Ch. 9th Gen. : 1 Annie Margaret, b. March 15, 1860.
2 Frederic Lyman, b. March 28, 1862. 3 Isabella Davis,
b. Nov. 18, 1867.

470 ELIJAH LYMAN[7], son of *Gideon[6]* and Dolly Spencer,
b. Aug. 20, 1783, in Wethersfield, Vt. He removed to
Susquehanna Co., Penn., when at the age of nineteen, and
from there to Rushford, N. Y., in April, 1816 or '17· He
m. Prudency Carrier, of Hebron, Conn., Sept. 22, 1802,
and is still living in Rushford. She d. March 2, 1857.

Rushford, N. Y.

Children, Eighth Generation

890 1 Reuben, b. March 14, 1808.
891 2 Emily E., Oct. 24, 1810; m. Albert Wood, Jan., 1829.
Ch. 9th Gen. : 1 John Wiley, b. Oct. 29, 1829. 2 Albert Wood, d. Nov., 1850; Rushford, N. Y.
894 3 P. Maranda, b. Feb. 23, 1812; m. in 1834, Aaron Eaton, b.
in Pa., March 12, 1809, and d. Dec. 26, 1852.
Ch. 9th Gen. : 1 Cyrus, b. Oct. 3, 1835. 2 Emma
E., b. Aug. 27, 1842. 3 Myra A., b. April 1, 1850.
898 4 Dolly C., b. Feb. 9, 1815; m. Wm. Baxter Bradford, May
3, 18 —, Kalamazoo, Mich.
899 5 Alonzo H., b. Dec. 11, 1817; m. Mary A. Miller.
900 6 Sally A., b. April 13, 1820; m. Charles Perry Cady, Feb.
25, 1841. He was b. at Rushford, N. Y., Jan. 1, 1820.
Ch. 9th Gen. : 1 Lucy Jane, b. Feb. 20. 1843. 2
Sophia Prudency, b. Feb. 21, 1846. 3 Matthew Patrick,
b. Jan. 29, 1849. 4 Charles Henry, b. June 20, 1851.
5 Esbon, b. May 20, 1854. 6 Grace Eliza, b. Jan. 13,
1858. 7 Edwin Lyman, b. May 22, 1860. 8 Hattie, b.
May 5, 1862.
909 7 G. Dinsmore, b. June 1, 1823, unmarried, Rushford.
910 8 Gideon S., b. Jan. 22, 1826; m. Theresa Taylor.

472 GIDEON LYMAN[7], the second son of *Gideon*[6] and Dolly, b. Aug. 9, 1785. He m. Keziah Earl of Wyoming, Penn., Jan. 9, 1811. He owned and tilled a farm adjoining his father's on the south-west where his children were all b. Keziah his wife d. Aug. 13, 1831; m. 2d, Harriet Lee, of Wyoming, Sept. 1, 1831. He d. Sept. 11, 1841.

Wyoming, Pa.

Children, Eighth Generation :

911 1 Lewellyn, b. June 14, 1812.
912 2 Landis, b. Nov. 10, 1814.
913 3 George, b. May 25, 1817; d. April 4, 1840.
914 4 Fanny, b. Sept. 19, 1820; m. Zara Travis, Sept. 8, 1837. She lives in Burlington, Bradford Co., Penn.; her oldest son is blind, and her husband has been a cripple for several years.

Ch. 9th Gen.: 1 George, b. Nov. 19, 1840. 2 Keziah E., b. Oct. 22, 1842. 3 Landis Lewis, b. Jan. 25. 1844; was in the Union army and a prisoner in Andersonville, where he came near losing his life. 4 Delilah Maria, b. July 10, 1847. 5 Harriet Elizabeth, b. Nov. 8, 1850. 6 Mary Helen, b. July 30, 1853. 7 Myson Welton, b. May 21, 1855.

922 5 Sarah, b. May 6, 1836.

473 JOSEPH ARVIN LYMAN[7], 3d son of *Gideon*[6] and Dolly, was b. May 18, 1788. He m. Anna Hall, of Genesee, N. Y., Aug. 5, 1812. He lives on a farm taken from the old homestead on the south. *Wyoming, Pa.*

Children, Eighth Generation :

923 1 Mary Ann, b. Oct. 8, 1813; d. May 25, 1815.
924 2 Mary, b. April 22, 1815; m. David Daley, Oct. 1, 1856.
925 3 Densmore, b. June 30, 1819; d. Oct. 13, 1819.
926 4 Elihu Hall, b. Aug. 17, 1823.
927 5 Joseph Walter, b. Aug, 17, 1823; m. Abzara Margarette Myers, Jan. 2, 1854. He is a physician residing in Tunkhannock, Wyoming Co., Penn.
928 6 Keziah, b. Feb 17, 1827; m. Willis Walker, March 11, 1851, one child Josephine E., b. April 21, 1854.
929 7 Roxena Ashley, b. Jan. 23, 1830; d. Jan. 22, 1834.
930 8 Charles Harris, b. Nov. 23, 1832; d. May 28, 1833.

529 SAMUEL LYMAN[7], fourth son of *Gideon*[6] and Dolly, was b. Jan. 26, 1796. He m. Phebe Earll of Wyoming, July 8, 1815, she d. Feb. 8, 1820; he m. 2d, Eunice Earll her sister, Sept. 28, 1820. She was the mother of all the children. He m. after her death Sept. 14, 1851, a widow, Harriet Overfield, Nov., 1863. He d. Feb. 1, 1867. He

lived on a farm taken from the N. W., part of the old homestead, was also a Methodist minister. *Wyoming, Pa.*

Children, Eighth Generation:

931 1 Phebe, b. May 5, 1822; m. Wm. Garrison, Sept. 8, 1840.
        Ch. *9th Gen.*: 1 Catharine, b. Aug. 9, 1743. 2 Lucinda Ellsworth, b. May 29, 1847. 3 Samuel Lyman, b. Aug. 14, 1849. 4 Eunice Ann, b. April 3, 1855. 5 Benjamin, b. Feb. 18, 1859.
937 2 Elijah, b. Sept. 11, 1824; d. May 17, 1725.
938 3 Elisha Bibbins, b. Feb. 1, 1826.
939 4 George Earll, b. Sept. 18, 1828.
940 5 James, b. Sept. 14, 1830; d. April 7, 1832.
941 6 Lewis Otis, b. March 11, 1833; d. May 1, 1834.
942 7 Benjamin, b. Jan. 26, 1835.
943 8 Theron Stark, b. Feb. 11, 1837.
944 9 Mary Elizabeth, b. April 16, 1839; m. Archibald Sheldon.
945 10 Ruth Elizabeth, b. April 6, 1841; d. April 26, 1841.
946 11 Gideon, b. July 16, 1842.
947 12 Joseph Arvin, b. Sept. 11, 1845; m. Katura Bunnell, Sept. 20, 1866, child Mary Adelaide, b. March 5, 1867. He lives on a farm taken from his father's on the north. Wyoming, Penn.

530 JOHN B. LYMAN[7], fifth son of *Gideon*[6] and Dolly, was b. May 2, 1798; m. 1st, Abigail Newman, of Luzerne Co. Penn., Oct. 6, 1824. She d. July 31, 1825; and he m. 2d, Sarah Almira Brace, of Genesee, N. Y., March 8, 1827. He is a farmer and lives on a part of the old homestead.
                                     Wyoming, Penn.

Children, Eighth Generation:

949 1 Gideon Clark, b. Jan. 13, 1828; d. Aug. 27, 1858.
950 2 Marvin Brace, b. April 15, 1830; m. Jane Ellen Avery.
951 3 Abigail, b. Oct. 1, 1832; m. Anson Asel Margott, May 23, 1850.
        Ch. *7th Gen.*: 1 Esek Palmer, b. Sept. 17, 1851. 2 Ella Gertrude, b. March 11, 1853. 3 Landis Lansing, b. July 12, 1855. 4 Kate, b. Nov. 9, 1860; d. March 10, 1862. 5 John Lyman, b. Dec. 9, 1863. 6 Frederic, b. Oct. 16, 1866.
958 4 James Hodge, b. Nov. 20, 1834; m. Maria Gorham.
959 5 Charles Stanley, b. April 25, 1837, killed in battle in Georgia near Lafayette, Sept. 14, 1863.
960 6 Anna Minerva, b. Aug. 22, 1839.
961 7 George Loomis, b. Dec. 3, 1842; d. July 15, 1847.
962 8 Thomas Wilcox, b. Jan. 27, 1845; unmarried, is teaching and preparing for college, was in Kilpatrick's cavalry in Sherman's march through the Southern states.
963 9 John Oakley, b. March 30, 1848, is a carpenter.

533 PRENTIS LYMAN[7], youngest son of *Gideon*[6] and Dolly, was b. Sept. 28, 1802, a farmer owning a farm adjoining the old homestead on the west. He m. Eliza Milburn, of Brooklyn, Pa., July 13, 1826. She d. June 11, 1863, and he m. 2d, widow Esther Safford—family name Smith.

Meshoppen, Wyoming Co., Pa.

Children, Eighth Generation:

964 1 Sarah Abigail, b. Jan. 26, 1830; m. Wm. Packer, d. Sept. 22, 1867, no children.
965 2 Elijah, b. April 12, 1832; m. Adelia Honeywood Wheeler.
966 3 Bloomfield Milborn, b. July 3, 1834.
967 4 Anna, b. June 28, 1839; m. Theron Lyman.

537 LEWIS LYMAN[7], eldest son of *Elias*[6] and Anna, was b. in Hatfield, Mass., Dec. 17, 1791. He was connected with his father in the mercantile business in Hartford, Vt. He m. March 1, 1821, Mary Blake Bruce of Boston, Mass., and d. Jan. 29, 1837. His wife d. May 3, 1864. *Hartford, Vt.*

Children, Eighth Generation:

968 1 Sarah Blake, b. April 24, 1823; m. Sawyer S. Stone of Boston, Jan. 12, 1858, residence White River Junction.
969 2 Mary Jane, b. Aug. 18, 1825; m. Samuel J. Allen, M.D., June 11, 1844.
    Ch. 9th Gen.: 1 Samuel J., b. April 30, 1845. 2 Lewis Lyman, b. Feb. 15, 1847; d. March 4, 1847. 3 Frederick Lyman, b. July 7, 1849. 4 Harry Bruce, b. Sept. 30, 1858.
974 3 Lewis, b. Sept. 11, 1827.
975 4 Annie, b. Sept. 30, 1829.
976 5 Elias, b. Nov. 19, 1831; d. Jan. 21, 1850, at Hartford, Vt.
977 6 Henry Bruce, b. Dec. 3, 1833; d. Feb. 6, 1834.
978 7 Frances Dodd, b. Dec. 8, 1834; d Sept. 10, 1861.
979 8 Maria Bruce, b. July 8, 1837.

541 NORMAND LYMAN[7], second son of *Elias*[6] and Anna, b. in Hartford, Vt., Feb. 23, 1795, is a merchant in Hartford, Conn., m. Elizabeth Walker, of Providence, R. I., Dec. 22, 1824, who d. in Hartford, Feb. 16, 1865, aged 63. *Hartford, Conn.*

Children, Eighth Generation:

980 1 Albert, b. Nov. 16, 1825, in Hartford, Conn.
981 2 Normand, b. July 31, 1827.
982 3 Frances Elizabeth, b. Dec. 14, 1828; d. Oct. 16, 1829.
983 4 Sarah Coles, b. Aug. 1, 1830.
984 5 Thomas Coles, b. June 15, 1832.
985 6 Anna, b. Aug. 24, 1834.
986 7 Susan Walker, b. Aug. 19, 1836.

987 8 Jane, b. Jan. 17, 1839; m. May 19, 1869, R. B. Goodyear,
    M.D., North Haven, Conn.
988 9 Elizabeth, b. Jan. 5, 1843; m. William Stocking, May 19,
    1869, editor, Detroit, Mich.

542 WYLLIS LYMAN[7], third son of *Elias*[6] and Anna,
b. May 5, 1797; was educated at Dartmouth and Yale
Colleges; studied law at the Harvard Law School; commenced the practice of his profession in Hartford, Vt., and
afterwards removed to Burlington, Vt.   He m. Sarah
Marsh, daughter of Hon. Charles Marsh, of Woodstock. He
d. at Burlington, Dec. 1, 1862, aged 65.

Children, Eighth Generation:
990 1, 2 Two boys, d. in infancy.
991 3 Wyllis, Jr., b. at Hartford, Vt., in April, 1830; he studied
    and practiced law until the breaking out of the rebellion,
    in which he served as adjutant and major in the 10th
    Vermont Regiment until its close.   He was appointed
    captain in the regular army in 1866, and has since con-
    tinued in the service.   He was m. in New York, in
    1861.
    Ch. 9th Gen.: 1 Charles, b. 1862.   2 Susan Mary, b.
    1869.
994 3 Susan Marsh, b. at Hartford, Vt., Oct 19, 1831; m. Aug.,
    1852, Hon. George F. Edmunds, of Burlington, Vt.
    Ch. 8th Gen.: (1) Mary Mayhu, b. in Burlington,
    Vt., in 1854.   (2) Julia Maynard, b. in Burlington,
    Vt., in 1861.

549 ELIAS LYMAN[7], 4th son of *Elias*[6] and Anna, b.
July 8, 1800; m. Cornelia J. Hall, of Troy, N. Y., April
14, 1842. She was b. at Greenfield, Mass., Aug. 15, 1820.
Burlington, Vt.

Children, Eighth Generation:
997 1 Ellen C., b. Jan. 19, 1843; m. Charles E. Allen, Oct. 31,
    1867, Burlington.
998 2 A son, b. Sept., 1847; d. aged six weeks.
999 3 Elias, b. Oct. 22, 1849, a student in the University, Burling-
    ton, Vt.

Elias Lyman, of Burlington, Vermont, was born July 8, 1800,
at Hartford, Vermont, to which place his parents removed from
Massachusetts at an early day. His father, whose name he bore,
and who was the *third* of that name in direct descent, was a prominent landholder in Vermont. His mother was Anna White of
Hatfield, Mass. Mr. Lyman was the sixth child of a family of
eight sons and five daughters, of whom but three of the former and
one of the latter are living. At the age of twenty-one he commenced

business as a merchant, in Norwich, Vermont, where his energy and ability secured for him results so favorable, that he soon after enlarged his business by opening branch stores in Enosburgh and Thetford, Vermont, and Hanover, New Hampshire.

In 1831 his fellow citizens of Norwich selected him as their representative in the legislature of the state, in which capacity he served during each succeeding year, until his removal in 1834 to Burlington.

In 1842 he was m. to Cornelia J., second dau. of Timothy and Lucinda Hall, of Troy, N. Y., by whom he had two children, Ellen C., wife of Charles E. Allen, Esq., of Burlington, and Elias. At Burlington he engaged in successful mercantile pursuits for several years, till at length increasing bodily infirmities resulting eventually in the paralysis of the lower limbs, compelled him to withdraw from active duties, and in 1850, retired from business to the quiet life of home. But although thus rendered unable to engage personally in active pursuits, he still and throughout his life maintained a great interest in them, and continued his connection with various important business and social enterprises. As a business man he bore a reputation for untiring energy, sound judgment, and scrupulous honesty. Uniformly courteous with a manner quiet and unassuming, and ever exhibiting a marked degree of kindness and regard for the welfare of others, he possessed the love as well as the confidence of all who knew him.

His private life was an example of patience, cheerfulness and affection under his severe affliction. During the last ten years of his life he was unable to move about without assistance, but his perfect resignation and forgetfulness of self, in his consideration for others, are a sunny memory in the hearts of all who were intimately associated with him. He was an earnest member of the Protestant Episcopal church, and for thirty years he was one of the vestrymen of St. Paul's, Burlington.

In the summer of 1870, his disease, which had thus far been marked by a progress so gradual as to be almost imperceptible, reached the vital organs ; and after five weeks of entire prostration, which were borne, as had been all his other trials, without a word of murmuring, he quietly entered into his rest on Monday, September 5th, 1870. As we remember him, the words of an American poet emphasized by his own whitened locks, come to mind :

> " His youth was innocent ; his riper age
> Marked with some act of goodness every day ;
> And watched by eyes that loved him; calm and sage,
> Faded his late declining years away.
> Cheerfully he gave his being up, and went
> To share the holy rest that waits a life well spent."

558 GEORGE LYMAN[7], son of *Elias*[6] and Anna, b. April 6, 1806, resides on the homestead at White River Junction, is post master ; m. Minerva Briggs at Rochester, Vt., Dec. 30, 1828. *White River Junction.*

Children, Eighth Generation :

1000 1 George Briggs, b. Oct. 19, 1829, at Royalton, Vt.; d. at Hartford, Aug. 21, 1865.

1001 2 Elias, b. Jan. 5, 1831 ; m. in Rochester,Vt., Dec. 14, 1858, Addie Trask of Rochester. He is president of the First National Bank, Kewanee, Henry Co., Ill.
Ch. 9th Gen.: 1 Nellie, b. Oct. 31, 1863. 2 Lizzie Louisa, b. Feb. 17, 1870.

1004 3 Minerva B., b. Sept. 18, 1832; m. Edward Lyman, of Burlington, Oct. 25, 1853.

1005 4 Julia, b. Oct. 2, 1834 ; m. George A. King, Aug. 30, 1855, Virginia City, Nev.

1006 5 Henry, b. Aug. 15, 1836; d. in Royalton, March 23, 1840.

1007 6 Dean Briggs, b. March 15, 1838 ; m. Ellen L. C. Smith of Alton, Ill., Dec. 18, 1865, Washoe City, Nev.

1008 7 James Edward, b. April 24, 1841 ; d. Sept. 4, 1842, at Norwich, Vt.

1009 8 Edward, b. Aug. 4, 1843, at Norwich, enlisted in Co. F, Reg. U. S. sharp shooters, served in nearly all the battles of the army of the Potomac until mortally wounded in front of Petersburg, Va., June 20, 1864; d. at City Point, June 24, 1864.

1010 9 Lizzie Briggs, b. April 25, 1846.

1011 10 Louisa Homer, b. Nov. 22, 1849, at Hartford, White River Junction.

1012 11 William Henry, b. June 3, 1852.

559 Charles Lyman[7], son of *Elias*[6] and Anna, b. Oct. 5, 1808. Was a merchant in Montpelier, Vt., m. Maria W. Spaulding, b. Sept. 18, 1818, m. Dec. 6, 1837 ; present occupation, chief of the dead letter office. *Washington, D. C.*

Children, Eighth Generation :

1013 1 Charles W., b. Aug. 21, 1838 ; m. Charlotte Virginia Hobletzell of Cumberland, Md. He entered the army in the late war, was captain of the Indianapolis Guard ; was transferred to Gen. Grant's staff as chief quarter master, where he served until Gen. Grant was transferred to the army of the Potomac. He remained in the army until the close of the war, then engaged in business in Shelby, Ohio, where he d. Oct. 10, 1866.
Ch. 9th Gen. : 1 Charles, b. 1864 ; d. aged 6 months. 2 Charles, b. Oct. 8, 1865.

1016 2 Maria, b. Feb. 23, 1842.

1017 3 Sarah Collins, b. Sept. 30, 1842 ; d. March, 1856.

1018 4 John Spaulding, b. Aug. 21, 1848 ; d. Aug. 22, 1859, by drowning in a river.

1019 5 Fanny Dodd, b. July 26, 1850.

33

560 SIMEON LYMAN[7], youngest son of *Elias[6]* and Anna, b. Aug. 16, 1810. He was a merchant at Hartford, Vt., and afterwards for a short time in Cincinnati, O., thence removed to Montpelier, Vt., where he d. Oct. 1, 1855. He m. Lucinda Hall, of Troy, N. Y. *Montpelier, Vt.*

Children, Eighth Generation:

1020 1 Anna Lucinda, b. 1845; m. L. L. Lawrence, May 1, 1867; d. Nov. 14, same year, at Burlington.

1021 2 Florence, b. 1849. Burlington.

571 ELHANAN WINCHESTER LYMAN[7], eldest son of *Gaius[6]* and Submit, was b. Feb. 27, 1799. He m. Maria Farnsworth, Nov. 14, 1822. He commenced trade and engaged in ship building in Steuben, Me., but his health failing he returned to Hartford, from which place he made several voyages, in the cold seasons, to the West Indies. He d. in Hartford, Sept. 1, 1827. *Hartford, Conn.*

Children, Eighth Generation:

1022 1 Frederic, b. Sept. 19, 1823, in Steuben, Me.; m. Caroline Willis.

1023 2 Emma, b. Nov. 27, 1825, in Hartford, Ct.; d. 1826.

1024 3 Caroline, b. Jan. 20, 1827, in Hartford, Ct.; d. May 29, 1827.

572 CHRISTOPHER COLUMBUS LYMAN[7], second son of *Gaius[6]* and Submit, was b. Dec. 28, 1800; m. Cecilia Breckenridge, in Bennington, Vt., Sept. 6, 1830; she d. in Hartford, Ct., Feb. 20, 1870. *Hartford, Conn.*

Children, Eighth Generation:

1025 1 Cecilia, b. 1831; d. Aug. 1, 1832.

1026 2 Theodore, b. Jan. 4, 1834.

1027 3 Cecilia, b. Oct. 14, 1837; d. March 24, 1842.

1028 4 Mary, b. Sept. 30, 1842; d. April 21, 1844.

595 EDWARD LYMAN[7], son of *Job[6]*, was b. Jan. 21, 1826, is a merchant in Burlington, Vt., m. Minerva B. Lyman, Oct. 25, 1853. *Burlington, Vt.*

Children, Eighth Generation:

1029 1 Mary Louise, b. Nov. 26, 1856; d. March 14, 1862.

1030 2 Minnie E., b. June 9, 1861.

598 THEODORE DWIGHT LYMAN[7], son of *Jonathan[6]* and Clarissa, was b. July 28, 1799; m. Betsey Fuller, March 12, 1829. He resided in Vermont until 1865, when he removed to South Troy, Minn., where he now resides. *South Troy, Minn.*

Children, Eighth Generation:

1031 1 Charles H., b. Dec. 24, 1829 ; m. Emroy J. Carpenter.

1032 2 Elias A., b. Aug. 18, 1831 ; m. Clara S. Prior.

1033 3 Ellen Mary, b. Aug. 31, 1833 ; d. Feb. 25, 1837.

1034 4 Frederic F., b. Nov. 2, 1836 ; m. Ellen Horsford.

1035 5 Sarah A., b. Aug. 30, 1838 ; m. A. P. Newell, Oct. 13, 1867.

1036 6 Maryetta, b. March 12, 1842 ; m. Dec. 22, 1867, William H. Anderson.

1037 7 Theodore D., b. Oct 18, 1845 ; m. Martha Bullock, April 18, 1868.

1038 8 Jonathan C., b. April 6, 1848.

601 JONATHAN LYMAN[7], youngest son of *Jonathan[6]* and Clarissa, was b. March 19, 1810. He removed from Vermont, to Kansas, about 1838. *Centreville, Kans.*

Children, Eighth Generation:

1039 1 Charles Henry, b. March 19, 1841, resided near Pine Bluff, Ark., enlisted into the Union army in 1861, and served with honor during the war, having been promoted to 2d Lieut. in the Reg. Army; was at Wilson's Creek, Mo., when Gen. Lyon, fell.

1040 2 William Arms, b. March 8, 1843, enlisted in the Union Army, in 1861, and served until the close of the war under Gen. Albert Lee, in Tenn., Miss., and Alabama, and was in numerous engagements elsewhere, resides Centreville, Kans.

1041 3 Edmund, b. Nov. 16, 1844.

1042 4 Frances M., b. June 24, 1846 ; m. June, 1869.

1043 5 Ellen J., b. Feb. 16, 1849 ; m. Aug. 24, 1869.

1044 6 Loesa A., b. Nov. 29, 1850 ; m. Nov. 29, 1868.

1045 7 Julia A., b. July 21, 1852 ; m. July 24, 1869.

1046 8 Sylvester C., Jan. 11, 1854.

1047 9 Emma R., b. Feb. 13, 1856 ; d. March 13, 1856.

1048 10 Jonathan F., b. Aug. 22, 1858 ; d. March 13, 1859.

1049 11 Estella C., b. Aug. 25, 1862.

622 CHARLES HARVEY PICKET LYMAN[7] son of *Sylvester[6]*, and Ann, was b. June 16, 1819. He m. June 27, 1854, Mary Elizabeth Green, b. April 11, 1824. Dry goods merchant, head clerk of Field, Lighter & Co. *Chicago, Ill.*

Children, Eighth Generation:

1050 1 William Henry, b. Nov. 26, 1845 ; was a Lieut. in the army in the war.

1051 2 George Sylvester, b. Dec. 16, 1847 ; d. Nov. 20, 1848.

1052 3 Caroline Louisa, b. Jan. 7, 1850.

1053 4 John Townsend, b. March 10, 1852 ; d. Jan. 15, 1857, mortally wounded on the eve of the 14th.

1054 5 Griffin Green, b. March 27, 1854 ; d. April 2, 1854.

1055 6 Charles Edward, b. July 7, 1855 ; d. March 10, 1858.
1056 7 James Harvey, b. Oct. 31, 1857.
1057 8 Sylvester, b. April 18, 1860.
1058 9 Thomas Tileston, b. Jan. 20, 1863.

This notice of the family of Sylvester Lyman, coming to hand too late to be inserted in its proper place, is given in connection with that of his surviving son, Charles Harvey Picket Lyman.—See p. 269.

Sylvester Lyman was b. at the old homestead near Smith's Ferry at the foot of Mount Tom, m. in Northampton, commenced business in " Shop Row," afterwards removed to Boston, opened dry goods business.   After the war of 1812, and declaration of peace, removed to Ohio, where he remained several years and then returned and settled in Pittsfield, Mass., where he resided some 10 or 12 years, was prostrated by lithiasis, went to Albany, N. Y., for a surgical operation, which he survived only 6 weeks ; and was buried in the family plat in the Albany Rural Cemetery.   He was a man of medium height, though his father measured over six feet, blue eyes and light complexion, of remarkable purity of character, uniformity of disposition, of great endurance and appli- cation, courteous and gentlemanly in his manner, warm-hearted and a true friend, of whom the companion of his pilgrimage after his decease often testified, that for more than forty years she had borne with him the vicissitudes of life, yet in all that time he never spoke one unkind word to her.

Nancy Clapp, his wife, was born at the old homestead, which is still standing in South street, Northampton, daughter of Ebenezer Clapp ; of deep piety, warm affections ; governing by a look, never by *words* or *blows ;* a consistent member, through her whole life, of the Congregational church.   She survived her husband but two years, and is buried by her side.   The writer of this owes his first religious impressions to her constant practice of retiring with him up to the period of his leaving home, in his early boyhood, to her private chamber and then on bended knee commending him in prayer to God's mercy and protection.

George Lyman, the eldest son, was b. in Northampton.   He was a man of more than ordinary ability, was pronounced in his day, the " most elegant man in Boston."   His height was 5ft. 11 inches, well built, dark hair, hazel eyes, straight as an arrow, polished and grace- ful, a warm friend, but quick to resent insult.   His history was one of peculiar interest to his family, more remarkable than fiction, but too lengthy to narrate here.   In 1824, he embarked in a commer- cial enterprise, in connection with the opening up of the Nicaragua canal, by the British government, in Central America.   The expedi- tion was unfortunate.   While crossing Lake Nicaragua, a storm arose, and the merchandise was thrown overboard, and, though an expert swimmer and urged to make an effort to save his life, he nevertheless simply wrapped his cloak around him and went down with the vessel.   Only one escaped to tell the tale.

Wm. Lyman, was b. in Boston. Shortly after the emigration of his parents to Ohio, he returned to Massachusetts, for the purpose of entering a store, and traveled alone on foot over the Aleghanies and safely reached his destination, being then only 13 years of age. About 1830 he went to Albany, N. Y., and shortly after established the well known firm of Lyman & Hanford, which for many years maintained an enviable reputation. He d. suddenly in the spring of 1858, of congestion of the lungs, and is buried by the side of his wife, father and mother. He left no issue.

Henry Lyman, was b. in Boston, graduated at Union College with the valedictory honors; passed through Princeton Theological Seminary, and after serving acceptably a number of years in the ministry, took up his residence in New York. He d. of pneumonia, Jan. 31, 1872, and is buried by the side of his wife in his family vault, at Forest Hill Cemetery, West Roxbury, near Boston, Massachusetts. He left no issue.

Sylvester Lyman, of New York, and C. H. P. Lyman, of Chicago, are the only surviving members of the family.

630 OLIVER LYMAN[7], eldest son of Gad[6], b. in Charlotte, Vt., in 1796, moved to Genoa, Ohio, 1818, m. Ann Linnberry of Geneva, Delaware Co., O., 1823. He was killed by being thrown from a wagon near Columbus, Ohio, in 1843. *Genoa, Ohio.*

Children, Eighth Generation :

1059 1 Medad.
1060 2 Ambrose.
1061 3 William, lives in Mt. Gilead, Ohio.
1062 4 Edwin, Franklin Co., O.
1063 5 Wealthy, m. John Cook.
1064 6 Prudence, lives in Henry Co., Iowa.
1065 7 Sophia, m. Allen Echels, a farmer in Morrow Co., Ia.
1066 8 Gad, resides N. London, Iowa.
1067 9 Nancy.

640 DAVID BILL LYMAN[7], 2d son of Gad[6], b. May 13, 1804; m. Lucretia Smith, at Williston, Vt. He was killed by the explosion of a locomotive on the Erie R. R., April 16, 1852. They had children, 2 sons and 5 daughters. *Charlotte, Vt.*

Children, Eighth Generation :

1068 1 Frederic Augustus, b. Nov. 15, 1828; d. in July 17, 1855.
1069 2 John Smith, b. Aug. 5, 1831, is in South America. Daughters' names not given.

641 FREDERIC LYMAN[7], third son of Gad[6], b. 1807; m., lives in Ohio.

Children, Eighth Generation :

1075	1 Son d. in infancy.	1079	5 Rhoda, Columbus.
1076	2 Oliver, d. in Anderson­ville prison.	1080	6 Delia, Newark—single.
		1081	7 Harriet, m. Kendall.
1077	3 Philip, lives in Chicago.	1082	8 Frances, m. Brown.
1078	4 Luke b. near Sandusky, O., farmer.	1083	9 Antoinette, unmarried.
		1084	10 Maria, Delaware Co , O.

665 Benjamin B. Lyman⁷, son of *John C.*⁶ and Susan Burgess, b. Sept. 17, 1867, m. Roxana Packard, Oct. 14, 1832.   *Cummington, Mass.*

Children, Eighth Generation :

1085 1 Agnes S., b. May 30, 1834; m. William E. Tower of Cum­mington, Nov. 22, 1831, one child Edith M., b. April 22, 1837.

1087 2 William C., b. Dec. 18, 1836; m. May 22, 1866, Kate Ham­lin of Elkhorn, Wis.. He studied medicine and served as a surgeon in the U. S. Navy; settled in Chicago where he is now practicing medicine, no children.

1088 3 Philander P., b. Aug. 27, 1838; m. Mary W. Robinson, Nov. 29, 1856, one child, Ada E., b. Oct. 29, 1867,

1090 4 Flora J., b. Jan. 31, 1840; m. C. W. Steeter, Feb. 22, 1862, one child Frederic W., b. March 17, 1867. Cum­mington, Mass.

1092 5 Darwin Eugene, b. July 26, 1846, Cummington, Mass.

681 Frederic Wm. Lyman⁷, son of *Thomas*⁶ and Dorcas Smith, b. March 31, 1817; m. Sarah Worthington Nara­more, Feb. 8, 1844.   *Kenosha, Wis.*

Children, Eighth Generation.

1093 1 Frank Henry, b. June 26, 1845.
1094 2 Agnes Smith, b. March 14, 1847.
1095 3 Elizabeth Bardwell, b. Dec. 5, 1851.
1096 4 Frederic P., b. March 31, 1861.
1097 5 Richard Salmon, b. July 12, 1867.

685 Samuel Watson Lyman⁸, eldest son of *Zadoc*⁷ and Hannah Watson, b. Nov. 13, 1797; m. 1st, Purly Hub­bard, b. May 2, 1796, and d. Sept. 12, 1833; m. 2d, Mary Ann Campbell, March 13, 1839, now living in Oconomowoc, Wis. He moved to Wis., 1846. He d. May 27, 1856.   *Oconomowoc, Wis.*

Children, Ninth Generation :

1098 1 Lucretia Elvira, b. Sept. 16, 1820; m. Thomas Wells of Hustiford, Wis.; d. April 8, 1858.

1099 2 Marcia Ann, b. Dec. 3, 1822; m. Israel F. Lyman, Spring­field, Mass.

Ch. 10*th Gen.:* 1 Edward, b. Sept. 11, 1825; d. Sept. 2, 1827. 2 Edward H., b. Sept. 10, 1828; d. Aug. 11, 1829.

1100 3 Sarah Jane, b. July 29, 1830; m. Dexter Bellows, Chicopee, Mass.
1101 4 William Campbell, b. Dec. 17, 1839, Oconomowoc, Wis.
1102 5 Mary Eliza, b. March 2, 1842.
1103 6 Charles Moseley Watson, b. Sept. 8, 1844; d. in Nebraska, June 24, 1867.
1104 7 Lois Ada, b. March 10, 1851.
1105 8 Ella Annette, d. June 19, 1855.

687 WILLIAM LYMAN[8], second son of *Zadoc[7], Israel[6], Zadoc[5] John[4], John[3], John[2], Richard[1]*, b. in Hadley, Mass., Nov. 22, 1800; m. Oct., 1823, Amanda White, of South Hadley; she was b. July 10, 1797. He was murdered in Rochester, N. Y., Nov. 23, 1837, by Baron, who waylaid him on returning from the bank. *South Hadley, Mass.*

Children, Ninth Generation:
1106 1 Theodore W., b. Sept. 26, 1826; m. Sept. 11, 1850, Elizabeth S., of New York; one child, Austin S., b. Jan. 27, 1852. She d. Jan. 25, 1853; m. 2d, Jan 27, 1858, Henrietta S. Ware.
　　Ch. 10*th Gen.:* 1 Charles W., b. Jan. 7, 1859. 2 Francis, b. Sept. 20, 1862.
1111 2 Joseph Austin, b. Nov. 14, 1828; m. Lizzie Hale, of Gill, Mass., July 4, 1863.
1112 3 Mary Amanda, b. Oct. 16, 1833; d. May 14, 1849.
1113 4 William Wirt, b. April 30, 1834; m. March 8, 1859, Lucy J. Snow.
　　Ch. 8*th Gen.:* 1 George S., b. Feb. 1, 1860. 2 Mary A., b. Oct. 22, 1862.

688 HORACE LYMAN[8], 3d son of *Zadoc[7]*, b. Oct. 14, 1802; Elvira Hubbard, May 2, 1827. She was dau. of Elisha and Achsah Hubbard, and was b. Oct. 16, 1802. *Sunderland, Mass.*

Children, Ninth Generation:
1115 1 Eliza Hubbard, b. March 17, 1828; m. Jan. 10, 1850, John M. Smith, of Sunderland.
1116 2 Helen Elvira, b. March 4, 1830; m. Whitney L. Warner, June 16, 1851, of Greenfield.
1117 3 Jane Louisa, b. Feb. 28, 1832; d. Jan. 2, 1833.
1118 4 Edward Elisha, b. Dec. 13, 1834, a lawyer of Greenfield.
1119 5 Henry William, b. Nov. 24, 1838; d. May 17, 1855.
1120 6 Jane Louisa, b. June 1, 1841, resides at Sunderland.

694 FREDERIC LYMAN[8], youngest son of *Zadoc*[7], was b. Oct. 3, 1813. He m. Caroline Whitten, Jan. 3, 1842.

Kansas.

Children, Ninth Generation:

1121 1 Charles Frederic, b. Nov. 24, 1842. He joined the 8th Kansas Regt. in 1862, was in several battles in Sherman's march through Georgia, was killed at Atlanta, July 24, 1864.

1122 2 Mary Delano, b. Dec. 22, 1844, in Hadley; m. Enoch G. Crabbe, of Kansas.

1123 3 William, b. May 7, 1848; d. July 14, 1867.

1124 4 Melzar Whitten, b. March 9, 1851.

1125 5 Helen Elizabeth, b. June 26, 1854.

1126 6 Hannah Watson, b. Dec. 29, 1864.

696 ALONZO LYMAN[8], eldest son of *Israel*[7] and Sarah Moody, b. March 16, 1803. He m. Amelia Moody of S. Hadley, and d. Sept. 25, 1840, was a farmer, left 4 children which his widow placed with the Shakers in Enfield.

South Hadley, Mass.

Children, Ninth Generation.

1127 1 Eli Dyer, b. Nov. 13, 1829; d. in Kansas, burned in his cabin, which had caught fire.

1128 2 Harriet Amelia, b. Sept. 23, 1831.

1129 3 Seth Alonzo, b. Feb. 2, 1834.

1130 4 Sarah Rachel, b. Sept. 22, 1836; m. Franklin Hubbard, of Adrian, Mich., has two daughters, resides in Toledo, O.

1131 5 Edward Israel, b. Feb. 9, 1839; m. Estelle McIntyre.

Ch. 10*th Gen.* : 1 Frank A., b. May 25, 1866. 2 Mary Estella, b. May 20, 1870.

700 ALMON LYMAN[8], son of *Israel*[7], b. March 16, 1808; m. Clarissa Burnett of S. Hadley, d. Sept. 25, 1840.

South Hadley, Mass.

Children, Ninth Generation:

1136 1 Sarah Maria, b. Nov. 10, 1830.

1137 2 Alden Burnett, b. Aug. 2, 1835, resides with the Shakers in Enfield, Conn.

1138 3 Clarissa Keziah, b. Sept. 14, 1837; m. John W. Copley, New York.

701 ISRAEL FRANKLIN[8], son of *Israel*[7] b. Sept. 11, 1810. He m. 1st, Catharine A. Mann; 2d. Marcia Ann Lyman; and 3d, Margaret E. Harmon.

Children, Ninth Generation:

1139 1 William Arnold, b. July 27, 1841, d. Feb. 19, 1844, in Michigan.

1140 2 Auret Mann, b. Jan. 23, 1843, m. Nellie M. Tower, May 4, 1865. South Hadley, Mass.

    Ch. 10th Gen.: 1 Franklin Mann, b. April 23, 1870.

1142 3 Moses Watson, b. Dec. 20, 1850.

1143 4 Henry Dexter, b. Nov. 24, 1855.

1144 5 Lizzie Marcia, b. May 26, 1867.

  703 HARVEY LYMAN[8], b. in South Hadley, Aug. 26, 1814, son of *Israel[7], Israel[6], Zadoc[5], John[4], John[3], John[2], Richard[1]*. His mother's name was Sally Moody. His father had about a hundred acre farm, including the Rock Ferry between Mt. Tom and Holyoke. At the age of 16, 1831, he joined the Congregational church in South Hadley. In 1835, he received faith in the Shaker religion, and in April, 1837, he with his mother, Elijah and Edward, joined the Shakers at Enfield, Ct. He remained a private member until 1841, when he was promoted to a trustee; in 1846, he was appointed one of the elders, whose duty it was to oversee all business, particularly to receive new members and the confessions of the fraternity. In 1850, he became somewhat dissatisfied; and having formed an attachment to the second eldress, Mary Ann White, both found means *to look unutterable things* which they were not permitted to express, and in June 24, 1854, he and the eldress found themselves in Springfield, made one by marriage. He carried on the grocery business until Nov., 1857, when with his family he went to California, but returned in about four months, making a loss of about 1,000 dollars.

  From that time he has conducted a successful grocery business in Springfield, in several places from which with his rents, he receives a handsome income.

  To him and his wife the Lyman family are indebted chiefly for their union Aug. 10, 1869, and reunion, Aug. 30, 1871. At a picnic the proposal of a similar social gathering of the Lymans was suggested by Mrs. Lyman, and he was designated to carry it into effect; which was happily and successfully accomplished. The facilities for the reunion in 1871, were chiefly provided by the same, and we may hope that these have inaugurated the stated meetings of the family in future years. *Springfield, Mass.*

  Children, Ninth Generation:

1145 1 Charles Harvey, b. April 31, 1855.

1146 2 George Edward, b. May 7, 1857.

1147 3 John White, b. Feb. 9, 1862.

707 ELIJAH AUSTIN LYMAN[8], son of *Israel[7]*, b. Feb. 22, 1823; m. Sophronia Pease, Dec. 28, 1845. *Easthampton.*

Children, Ninth Generation.

1148 1 Byron Austin, b. Sept. 30, 1847; d. Aug. 28, 1851. ·
1149 2 Leona Maria, b. Dec. 2, 1849.
1150 3 Jerome Albert, b. Dec. 7, 1851.
1151 4 William Edwin, b. Sept. 21, 1857.
1152 5 Arthur Leroy, b. March 30, 1862; d. Aug. 2, 1863.

708 EDWARD MASON LYMAN[8], youngest son of *Israel[7]*, b. May 13, 1825; m. Caroline Blodgett; 2d, Mrs. Eliza Hopkins. *Springfield, Mass.*

Children, Ninth Generation:

1153 1 Gilbert Edward, b. Feb. 2, 1856; d. Dec. 2, 1859.
1154 2 John Alonzo, b. March 12, 1857.
1155 3 Herbert Mason, b. Dec. 6, 1868. Second wife Eliza Hopkins, m. June 9, 1868.
1156 4 Alice May, b. April 3, 1869.

710 LUTHER ALVORD LYMAN[8], eldest son of *Amaziah[7]*, b. Jan. 1, 1808; m. Esther L. Ewings, Oct. 31, 1831, is a farmer. *South Hadley, Mass.*

Children, Ninth Generation:

1157 1 Mary Sophia, b. Aug. 17, 1832; m. Francis W. Fisk of Amherst.
    Ch. 10th Gen.: 1 Mary Etta. 3 Frankie Edgar, d. July 10, 1862. 3 Frank Luther.
1161 2 Sarah Sarina, b. June 9, 1837.

711 EDWIN WAITSTILL[8], son of *Amaziah[7]*, b. May 22, 1809; m. Lois A. Forks, Dec. 6, 1839; d. Jan. 12, 1855. *South Hadley, Mass.*

Children, Ninth Generation.

1162 1 Charles Austin, b. Feb. 1, 1841, enlisted in the 37th Mass. Regt.; was in a rebel prison 11 months.
1163 2 Joseph Cornelius, b. Sept. 3, 1843; d. Oct. 19, 1862.
1164 3 Ansel Adelbert, b. Aug. 1, 1847.
1165 4 Elizabeth Ann, b. June 14, 1851; d. March 29, 1852.

715 AMAZIAH HENRY LYMAN[8], son of *Amaziah[7]*, b. Sept. 24, 1816; m. March 17, 1841, and 2d, Oct. 10, 1843. He d. Nov. 25, 1850.

Children, Ninth Generation:

1166 1 Eugene Henry, b. Aug. 10, 1844
1167 2 Irving Laroy, b. Jan. 16, 1846; m. July 10, 1871, at Springfield, Mass., Elizabeth Belville of Munroe, Butler Co., Ohio, removed to Lincoln, Nebraska.

725 WADSWORTH PORTER LYMAN[8], eldest son of *Enos*[7] b. May 10, 1822, at Hadley, m. Sept. 6, 1846, Roby Ann Morton of Ellington, Ct. He is a successful house carpenter and resided in Ruggles in Ashland Co., Ohio, from which place he removed to Franklin Co., Tenn., where he owns a farm. *Tullahoma, Coffee Co., Tenn.*

Children, Ninth Generation :

1168　1 Clarence H., b. Nov. 9, 1847 ; enlisted at the age of sixteen in Bat. D, Ohio Reg. Light Artillery ; was with Gen. Sherman, from Knoxville to Atlanta, Ga. ; was in the battles around Nashville to N. Carolina ; at the capture of Wilmington, &c. ; discharged July 3, 1865.

1169　2 Edgar Enos, b. at Rockville, Ct., July 29, 1850; d. Aug. 29, 1851.

1170　3 Charles Dwight, b. Aug. 31, 1857, at Ruggles, Ohio.

1171　4 Harriet Louisa, b. Oct. 26, 1858

1172　5 Frank A., b. Jan. 19, 1862.

726 ROMANTA N. LYMAN[8], second son of *Enos*[7], was b. March 14, 1824. He m. 1st,.............. of Northampton ; 2d, Mary A. Phelps, Feb. 6, 1848. *Hadley, Mass.*

Children, Ninth Generation :

1173　1 Lorrin A., b. March, 1848; d. Sept. 22, 1848.

1174　2 Lorrin A., b. July 29, 1849.

1175　3 Eddie A., b. Dec. 6, 1851.

1176　4 Enos P., b. July 30, 1858.

729 FRANCIS A. LYMAN[8], son of *Enos*[7], b. Dec. 6, 1830 ; m. Mary B. Boynton, of Hadley　　*Hadley, Mass.*

Children, Ninth Generation ·

1177　1 Alfred D., b. Oct., 1856.

1178　2 Francis R., b. March 22, 1859.

1179　3 Arthur L.

1180　4 Edward M., b. Jan. 20, 1864.

732 LORENZO W. LYMAN[8], eldest son of *George*[7] and Laura, was b. Sept. 18, 1820, is a farmer. He m. Sarah Williams, of Huntington, Oct. 30, 1844, she d. July 1858.

Hadley, Mass.

Children, Ninth Generation :

1181　1 Clara Sarina, b. Sept. 19, 1845 ; d. Aug. 15, 1847.

1182　2 Erskine Leroy, July 12, 1847.

1183　3 George Morris, b. June 6, 1849.

1184　4 Ella Williams, b. July 6, 1851.

1185　5 Laura Irena, b. Dec. 16, 1853.

1186　6 John, b. April 7, 1856.

1187　7 Lorenza Edson, b. April 15, 1858.

781 Newman Rust Lyman[8], eldest son of *Azariah*[7] and
Sarah, was b. Nov. 12, 1811, in Westhampton, Mass.; m.
Julia Ann Hunt, b. at Westhampton, July 30, 1820.   They
were m. in Chester, Geauga Co., Ohio, April 23, 1839.
                                                    Chester, O.
Children, Ninth Generation :
1188 1 Henry Newman, b. June 2, 1840; d. Nov. 12, 1864.
1189 2 Mary Emmeline, b. March 18, 1842; d. Dec. 16, 1864.
1190 3 Alonzo Hunt, b. Jan. 16, 1847, merchant, resides in Cleve-
        land, Ohio.
1191 4 Elihu Osman, b. March 12, 1852; d. Nov. 9, 1864.
1192 5 Charles Edward, b. May 3, 1859.
1193 6 Infant son, b. May 4, 1860; d. same day.

782 Elihu Oliver Lyman[8], 2d son of *Azariah*[7] and Sarah,
was b. in Huntington, Mass., June 12, 1817; m. Feb. 2,
1842, Emily Adams Ranney, b. Jan. 27, 1823, in Chester,
Ohio, is a farmer and merchant in Chester, Geauga
Co., O., lives on the old homestead of his late father which
was bought there in 1823.   *Chester, O.*
Children, Ninth Generation :
1194 1 Flora Emily, b. Oct. 24, 1842; m. Corwin Brackly, in
        Chester.
1195 2 Thomas Stow Ranney, b. Feb. 23, 1844; d. May 3, from
        the kick of a horse May 1.
1196 3 Frances Melissa, b. Feb. 21, 1846; d. April 9, 1846.
1197 4 Frances Eliza, b. March 30, 1847; d. Dec. 22, 1847.
1198 5 Tertius Cornelius, b. Sept. 4, 1850; d. Feb. 5, 1852.
1199 6 Ernest Chalmers, b. Jan. 11, 1852.
1200 7 Elmer Morris, b. Dec. 9, 1853.
1201 8 Clara Theresa, b. May 26, 1855; d. May 18, 1867.
1202 9 Elsie Ada, b. March 21, 1857.
1203 10 Alice Loesa, b. May 18, 1858.
1204 11 Elgin Osmer, b. July 2, 1862.
1205 12 Celia Ellen, b. March 17, 1864.

796 Rev. George Lyman[8], son of *Elihu*[7], was b. in
Westhampton, Nov. 19, 1812; m. Maria Lucina Phelps,
in Brooklyn, N. Y., Dec. 25, 1851; b. in Westhampton,
May 29, 1823.   He graduated at Amherst College, in 1837,
at Andover Theological Sem., 1841.   Taught in Va.,
next 2 years.   Preached in S. Deerfield, in the winter of
1844-5, in Charlemont, in 1845-6, in Norwich, from Oct.,
1846 to 1867, at S. Deerfield, from May, 1848 to Dec., 1849.
Ordained and installed in Sutton, Mass., Nov. 12, 1851.
Congregational minister.   *South Amherst, Mass.*

Children, Ninth Generation .

1206 1 Maria Phelps, b. Nov. 7, 1852, in Sutton.
1207 2 Mary Montague, b. Nov. 30, 1855 ; d. Feb. 16, 1858.
1208 3 George, b. Oct. 16, 1857 ; d. April 4, 1860.
1209 4 William Judd, b. March 16, 1860; d. Aug. 27, 1862.
1210 5 Franklin Clarke, b. July 15, 1862.

802 WILLIAM EUSTICE LYMAN[8], son of *Jesse Lyman[7]*, was b. in Westhampton, Oct. 28, 1848. He m. Nov. 13, 1851, Mary E. Orcutt, b. June 15, 1829, dau. of Dr. Henry Orcutt, of Westhampton — farmer. *Westhampton.*

Children, Ninth Generation :

1211 1 Lillie Bell, b. Aug. 3, 1852 ; d. from scalding, Feb. 1, 1855.
1212 2 Ella, b. Oct. 14, 1856; d. May 27, 1857.
1213 3 Myra Elma, b. May 10, 1858.
1214 4 Annie Field, b. Nov. 21, 1862.
1215 5 William Hervey, b. May 15, 1866.
1216 6 Lizzie Rogers, b. Nov., 1869, and d. at the age of 9 months.

807 GEORGE D. LYMAN[8], son of *Luke C.[7]*, b. Jan. 31, 1822. He resides in Tenifly, N. J., and was the originator and manager of the New York Bank Clearing House, m. A. A. Wenman, of New York, June 1, 1848. *Tenifly, N. J.*

Children, Ninth Generation :

1216* 1 Agnes Adele, b. Oct. 8, 1849.
1217 2 George Frederic, b. Dec. 1, 1851.
1218 3 Henry Augustus, b. Nov. 14, 1853.
1219 4 Frances Russell, deceased, no date.
1220 5 Mara Addine, b. July 1, 1857
1221 6 William Camp, b. Jan. 19, d.
1222 7 Frances Russell, b. Aug. 7, 1860.
1223 8 William Hunt, b. Dec. 23.
1224 9 Frank Terry, b. Dec. 25.
1225 10 Edward Lloyd, b. Jan. 19.
1226 11 Sarah Dummer, b. Aug. 7.

809 HENRY AUGUSTUS LYMAN[8], son of *Luke C.[7]*, b. Nov. 26, 1826 ; m. Mary Clementia Cory, Oct. 13, 1850, in Jersey City, N. J. *Englewood, N. J.*

Children, Ninth Generation :

1227 1 Stuart, b. June 15, 1860.
1228 2 Julia Cleveland, b. Dec. 12, 1861.
1229 3 Mary Clementine, b. June 14, 1865.
1230 4 Sarah Dummer, b. Sept, 22, 1867.

817 LUKE LYMAN[8], son of *Horace[7]* and Electa, b. Nov. 1, 1824; m. Elizabeth B. Hartung, Nov. 1, 1848. Elizabeth,

was b. at S. Mansfield, Ct., Sept. 28, 1828; and d. Oct. 24, 1865; m. 2d, Sarah Catharine Hartung, May 30, 1867. He was commissioned as Lt. Col., 27th Mass. Regiment, in the late war; brevetted Col. and Brig. Gen. for meritorious conduct, for his bravery and officer-like bearing in various battles, collector of internal revenue.

Northampton, Mass.

Children, Ninth Generation:

1231 ı Susan Hartung, b. Nov. 18, 1849.
1232 2 Catharine Brown, b. April 15, 1852.
1233 3 Fannie Day, b. Jan. 8, 1855; d. Oct. 13, 1859.
1234 4 Lizzie Bell, b. Nov. 25, 1856; d. Sept. 6, 1857.

827 ASHLEY LYMAN⁸, eldest son of *Rufus⁷*, b. July 12, 1805; m. Caroline Kirkland, Oct. 16, 1832, in Huntington, Mass. She was b. March 13, 1808.

Huntington, Mass.

Children, Ninth Generation:

1235 ı A son, b. July 4, 1836; d. same day.
1236 2 Eliza C., b. Feb. 24, 1840.
1237 3 Samuel K., b. Feb. 23, 1843.
1238 4 Infant son, b. May 4, 1844; d. May 8, 1844. All in Huntington.

828 MOSES M. LYMAN⁸ second, son of *Rufus⁷*, b. Sept. 15, 1809; m. Cynthia Tucker, Dec. 31, 1833.

Children, Ninth Generation:

1239 ı Julina, b. Sept. 28, 1234; m. Alfred D. Jones, March 7, 1860, Adams Co., O., have had three children who all d. young.
1243 2 Martha M., b. May 14, 1840; m. Sereno B. Bodman, Oct. 22, 1865. They have one daughter and one son.
1246 3 Moses M., b. Dec 21, 1842; d. Jan. 5, 1843.
1247 4 A son, b. Jan. 7, 1847, d. same day.
1248 5 Arthur M., b. Oct. 2, 1849.
1249 6 Oscar S., b. Jan. 13, 1852; d. Jan. 22, 1854.
1250 7 Eva Mary, b. Jan. 28, 1860; d. May 29, 1860.

829 WILLIAM GRAVES LYMAN⁸, third son of *Rufus⁷*, b. June 8, 1812; m. Clarissa Louisa Doane, who d. in 1839; he m. 2d, Amity Shaw; 3d, Olive Mears; 4th, Mrs. Gill.

Children, Ninth Generation:

1251 ı Sophia, b. Dec. 13, 1835; m. Palmer.
1252 2 Ellen Eliza, b. April 13, 1837; m. Benjamin Stuart Butterfield, April 15, 1852.
        Ch. 10th Gen.: ı Ellen, b. May 2, 1853. 2 Nathaniel W., b. Aug. 17, 1854, d. 3 Mary E., d. 4 Benjamin S., b Nov. 12, 1857, d. 5 Benjamin H., b. Feb. 37, 1858, d.

6 Mary, b. Jan. 12, 1861. 7 Elizabeth, b. Feb. 14, 1866.
8 Ashley, b. July 12, 1867. 9 Clarissa Ellen, b. Sept. 4, 1869.

1262 3 William Graves, Jr., b. Dec. 12, 1848 ; m. Sophia Allen. Table Rock, Nebraska.

1263 4 Eona Christina, b. Aug. 9, 1862.

831 RUFUS EARL LYMAN[8], son of *Rufus*[7] b. Oct. 4, 1821; m. July 12, 1849, Sophia Axtell. *Huntington, Mass.*

Children, Ninth Generation :

1264 1 Eugene E., b. Feb. 2, 1851 ; d. April 5, 1854.
1265 2 Henry A., b. May 6, 1856.
1266 3 Libbie S., b. Oct. 1, 1857.
1267 4 Harlie S., b. March 8, 1863.

837 ENOCH H. LYMAN[8], son of *Enoch*[7], and Silence Ed wards, b. Oct. 28, 1822 ; m. Amoret R. Judd, Nov. 16, 1862. Has one son Washington Hooker, b. April 12, 1848. *South Deerfield, Mass.*

846 DEXTER LYMAN[8], son of *John Burt*[7], m. Nov. 22, 1848, Mary L., dau. of Elisha Clark, of Southampton. *Norwich, Mass.*

Children, Ninth Generation :

1268 1 George Dexter, b. March 16, 1850.
1269 2 Myra Ellen, b. Oct. 21, 1855 ; d. July 8, 1857, killed by being thrown from a wagon.
1270 3 Myron Clark, b. Oct. 2, 1858.
1271 4 James Burt, b. Feb. 3, 1861.

847 JAIRUS JOY LYMAN[8], son of *John Burt*[7], b. in Hunt-ington, Mass., Aug. 24, 1823 ; m. Cyrene C. Moore, June 29, 1867. *Huntington, Mass.*

Children, Ninth Generation

1272 1 Rosella C., b. March 18, 1848.
1273 2 Ruth S., b. Oct. 1, 1851.
1274 3 Emma R., b. Nov. 17, 1854.
1275 4 Arabell S., Feb. 1, 1857.
1276 5 John Wilson, b. Aug. 26, 1864. All b. in Huntington.

848 JOHN BURT LYMAN[8], b. Dec. 30, 1825 ; was m. May 15, 1850, to Lutheria Elizabeth, dau. of Samuel Ellis, who was b. at Norwich, Oct. 22, 1826 ; and d. Aug. 26, 1861. He enlisted in the army Dec. 15, 1863, as a private in Co. K, 1st Mass. Heavy Artillery. He was in the battle near Spottsylvania Court-House and fell mortally wounded May 18, and was carried to Fredericksburg, and d. May 21, 1864. *Huntington, Mass.*

Children, Ninth Generation :
1277 1 Elbert, b. March 16, 1851; d. in Norwich, Oct. 7, 1851.
1278 2 Asahel Hubert, b. April 17, 1853, in Huntington.
1279 3 Catharine Elizabeth, b. June 3, 1859.

872 JOHN C. LYMAN[8], son of *Thomas*[7], was b. at Westhampton, Mass., April 2, 1821; m. Ruth Ann Abbott, Aug. 9, 1854. She d. Jan. 13, 1858; m. 2d, Viola Curtis, Nov. 26, 1861, dealer in drugs.   *Newcastle, Canada West.*
Children, Ninth Generation :
1280 1 Willis J., b. Dec. 5, 1857 ; d March 11, 1858.
1281 2 Mary, b. April 22, 1865.

873 PERES C. LYMAN[8], son of *Thomas*[7], b. at Otisco, N. Y., March 23, 1823; m. in Greenville, Ala., Oct. 15, 1857, to Caroline Mudge,—merchant, and farmer.
                                                    Eugene, Kansas.
Children, Ninth Generation
1282 1 William F., b. Aug. 17, 1848, at Grenville, Ala.
1283 2 Thomas Jefferson, b. July 2, 1861.
1284 3 Frank, b. Sept. 18; 1863.
1285 4 Charles Peres, b. Sept. 2, 1866.

890 REUBEN LYMAN[8], eldest son of *Elijah*[7] and Prudency Carrier, was b. in Springville, Sus. Co., Penn., March 14, 1808, he m. Mary C. Kimball, Oct. 14, 1832.   She was b. in Windsor, Vt., Feb. 26, 1812.   His father's family went to Rushford, N. Y., and Reuben went from there to Ill., in 1857   *Fairbury, Ill.*
Children, Ninth Generation:
1285* 1 Nathan E., b. Nov. 17, 1834, in Rushford, N. Y.
1286 2 Lydia L., b. March 7, 1838.
1287 3 Edson W., b. 19, 1841, in Farmersville, N. Y.
1288 4 Densa M., b. Sept. 5, 1850, in Farmersville, N. Y.

899 ALONZO H. LYMAN[8], second son of *Elijah*[7], b. Dec. 11, 1817, in Rushford, m. Oct. 18, 1841, Mary A. Miller, b. in Avon, N. Y., Sept. 14, 1822.   *Rushford, N. Y.*
Children, Ninth Generation :
1 89 1 Infant daughter, b. July ...; d. the day of her birth.
1290 2 Sarah A., b. Feb. 15, 1843.
1291 3 Ella, b. Sept. 20, 1847.

910 GIDEON S. LYMAN[8], son of *Elijah*[7], b. in Rushford, Jan. 22, 1825; m. Theresa Taylor, b. in Farmersville, Feb. 8, 1825, Sept. 18, 1868.   *Rushford, N. Y.*

Children, Ninth Generation:

1292 1 Keziah, b. June 22, 1849.
1293 2 Harriet, b. Aug. 17, 1850.
1294 3 Elijah, b. Jan. 22. 1852.
1295 4 Dayton, b. April 10, 1853.
1296 5 Miranda, b. Dec. 12, 1854.
1297 6 Addie, b. June 24, 1860.
1298 7 Elbert, b. July 30, 1863; d. April 6, 1864. } Twins.
1299 8 Albert, b. July 30, 1863; d. April 2, 1864. }
1300 9 Pliny, b. Nov. 6, 1864.
1301 10 Annette, b. Oct. 2,, 1867.

911 LEWELLYN LYMAN[8], eldest son of *Gideon[7]* and Ke-
ziah, b. June 14, 1812; m. Julia Ann adopted dau. of
Mr. Coburn, of Warren, Bradford Co., Penn. He was a
Methodist preacher, and also a school teacher. He d. Feb.
12, 1840.   *Wyoming, Susquehanna Co., Pa.*
Children, Ninth Generation:

1302 1 James French, b. Oct. 8, 1837.
1303 2 Mary Coburn, b. Sept. 29, 1837; m. Clark, of Waverly,
        Bremer Co., Iowa.

912 LANDIS LYMAN[8], eldest son of *Gideon[7]* and Keziah,
b. Nov. 10, 1814. He m. Eliza Saunders, May 22, 1836.
He lives on the farm originally owned by Samuel.
                           Wyoming, Susquehanna Co., Pa.
Children, Ninth Generation:

1304 1 Wilber Fisk, b. July 7, 1839.
1305 2 Adelaide Stark, b. May 11, 1842; m. Solomon Bunnell,
        April 1, 1864.
        Ch. 10th Gen.: 1 Minnie, b. April 7, 1868.
1307 3 Lucy Adeline, b. Dec. 13, 1845; m. Rev. Luther Peck,
        May 15, 1867, has one child, b. Feb. 27, 1868.
1309 4 Prentis Herbert, b. May 21, 1858; d. April 28, 1864.

926 ELIHU HALL LYMAN[8], son of *Joseph A.[7]* and Anna,
b. Aug. 17, 1828; m. Sarah Smith of Washington, Wyo
ming Co., Penn., March 26, 1865.   *Wyoming, Pa*
Children, Ninth Generation:

1310 1 Lewellyn, b. March 1, 1841; d. March 13, same year.
1311 2 Narcissa Jenette, b. Feb. 13, 1847; m. Elma Alger, Feb.
        12, 1868.
1312 3 Amelia Gertrude, b. March 6, 1853.
1313 4 Eudoxia Ethleen, b. March 8, 1860.

938 ELISHA BIBBINS LYMAN[3], eldest son of *Samuel[7]* and
Eunice, b. Feb. 1, 1826; m. Sarah Ann B. McLain, March

35

18, 1851. He is a farmer, and lives a half mile east of the old homestead. *Wyoming, Pa.*

Children, Ninth Generation:

1314 1 Lewellyn Ready, b. Dec. 25, 1851.
1315 2 Joseph Finley, b. Sept. 17, 1852.
1316 3 Samuel McLain, b. Jan. 17, 1856.
1317 4 Ella Euphemia, b. July 27, 1857.
1318 5 Mary Routh, b. Oct. 30, 1863.
1319 6 Jerry Albert, b. Jan. 27, 1866.

939 GEORGE E. LYMAN[8], son of *Samuel[7]*, b. Sept. 18, 1828; m. Sarah Elizabeth Kintner, Oct. 6, 1850. Is a farmer living in Cere Gordo Co., Iowa. He was in the Union ramy in the war. *Cere Gordo Co., Ia.*

Children, Ninth Generation:

1319* 1 Lucretia Malvina, b. Dec. 10, 1851.
1320 2 Myron Wells, b. April 3, 1853.

943 THERON S. LYMAN[8], son of *Samuel[7]*, b. Feb. 11, 1837; m. Anna Lyman, Jan. 23, 1861. He lives on the farm formerly owned by his father, and is a blacksmith.
Wyoming, Pa.

Children, Ninth Generation:

1321 1 Ina Blanchard, b. April 22, 1862.
1322 2 Lewis Otis, b. May 23, 1866.

946 GIDEON LYMAN[8], son of *Samuel[7]*, b. July 16, 1842; m. Lydia A. Bunnell, June 9, 1866. He lives on a farm joining Theron's on the south. He also is engaged in teaching and preaching. He was a soldier in the war.

Child, Ninth Generation:

1323 1 John Passmore, b. May 30, 1867.

949 GIDEON CLARK LYMAN[8], eldest son of *John[7]* and Sarah Brace Lyman, b. Jan. 13, 1828; m. Jemima Knapp, of Springville, Pa., was a lawyer and attempted farming. He d. Aug. 27, 1858. *Springville, Pa.*

Children, Ninth Generation:

1324 1 Berkley, b. June 5, 1853.
1325 2 Victor, b. March 12, 1856.

950 MARVIN BRACE LYMAN[8], second son of *John[7]* and Sarah B., b. April 15, 1830; m. Jane Ellen Avery, of Washington, Pa., March 26, 1856, lives on a farm one mile west of the old homestead, is a mason by trade. He was a soldier in the Union army in the war—in the battles

of Chancellorsville, Gettysburg, Shephardstown, etc., until
after the surrender of Lee. *Wyoming, Pa.*

Children, Ninth Generation :

1326 1 Lamont, b. Jan. 9, 1858; d. March 15, 1858.
1327 2 Auvergne Lamont, b. Jan. 27, 1859; d. July 7, 1863.
1328 3 Stanley Avery, b. Nov. 2, 1867.

958 JAMES HODGE LYMAN[8], third son of *John[7]*, was b. in
Lynn, Pa., Nov. 20, 1834, is a farmer, lives on the old homestead first occupied by his grandfather. He m. Maria Gorham, July 5, 1860, she d. Jan. 12, 1864. He m. 2d Mary
Amey, June, 1865. *Lynn, Pa.*

Children, Ninth Generation

1329 1 Bernice, b. Aug. 28, 1861; d. Feb. 29, 1862.
1330 2 Anna Minerva, b. April 8, 1863.

965 ELIJAH LYMAN[8], eldest son of *Prentis[7]*, was b. in
Lynn, Pa., April 12, 1832, is a farmer, living on the place
formerly occupied by his father. He m. Adelia Honeywood Wheeler, of Meshoppen, Pa., March 16, 1858.
Lynn, Pa.

Children, Ninth Generation :

1331 1 Florence Effa, b. June 2, 1859.
1332 2 Frank Brownell, b. April 25, 1861.
1333 3 Alfred Grow, b. April 28, 1863.
1334 4 Noble, b. Nov. 27, 1866; d. June 7, 1868.
1335 5 Harry, b. Nov. 26, 1868.

966 BLOOMFIELD MILLBURN LYMAN[8], second son of *Prentis[7]*,
b. in Lynn, Pa., July 3, 1834; is a farmer, living about
two miles west of his brother, is also a mason. He m.
Martha Isadore McLain, Dec. 5, 1860. *Lynn, Pa.*

Children, Ninth Generation :

1336 1 Archer Kent, b. Feb. 20, 1861.
1337 2 Charles Fremont, b. Oct. 11, 1863.

980 ALBERT LYMAN[8], eldest son of *Normand[7]*, b. in Hartford,
Conn., Nov. 16, 1825; m. 1st, Eliza Fuller, June 19, 1851,
she d. He m. 2d, Elizabeth Prentice, Feb. 12, 1856, at
Hartford — merchant. *New York city.*

Children, Ninth Generation .

1338 1 William Prentice, b. Aug. 26 1857, at Troy, N. Y.
1339 2 Sarah Elizabeth, b. Nov. 12, 1859.

981 NORMAND LYMAN[8], JR., second son of *Normand[7]*, b.
July 31, 1827. He m. Louisa G. Wickham, at Hartford,
April 24, 1849. *Hartford, Conn.*

Children, Ninth Generation :

1340 1 Wyllis, b. April 10, 1850, at Hartford; d. Oct 8, 1851.
1341 2 Louisa, b. March 16, 1852, at Hartford; d. Oct.18, 1867.
1342 3 Normand, b. Dec. 5, 1854.
1343 4 James Walter, b Dec. 10, 1856.

984 Thomas C. Lyman[8], youngest son of *Normand[7]*, was b. June 15, 1832; m. Lois Manly, of Brooklyn, N. Y., June 26, 1856.   *Brooklyn, N. Y.*

Children, Ninth Generation ·

1344 1 Laura Cornelia, b. June 21, 1857, at Brooklyn, N. Y.
1345 2 Robert Manley, b. Aug. 6, 1862.
1346 3 Lois Manley, b. Nov. 19, 1863.
1347 4 Eliza Brown, b. Feb. 5, 1867.

1022 Frederic Lyman[8], son of *E. Winchester[7]*, b. Sept. 19, 1823, m. Caroline Willis, of Portland, Me., merchant, New York city.   *Orange, N. J.*

Children, Ninth Generation :

1348 1 Clarissa May, b. June 26, 1856.
1349 2 Caroline, b. April 4, 1858.
1350 3 Frederic, b. April 21, 1860; d. 1761.
1351 4 Frank, b. Nov. 28, 1861.
1352 5 Emily, b. Nov. 24, 1863 ; d. Oct. 4, 1865.
1353 6 Percy, b. Sept. 27, 1865.
1354 7 Helen, b. Aug. 19, 1867.
1355 8 Alice, b. June 14, 1869.

1031 Charles H. Lyman[8], son of *Theodore D.[7]* and Betsey, was b. Dec. 24, 1829, m. Emory J. Carpenter.
                                        Minnesota.

Children, Ninth Generation :

1356 1 James O.   ·1358 3 Cora Adelaide.
1357 2 Charles H.

1032 Elias A. Lyman[8], second son of *Theodore D.[7]* and Betsey, was b. Aug. 18, 1831, m. Clara S. Prior.

Children, Ninth Generation :

1359 1 Alice Betsey.   1361 3 Elias Armintos.
1360 2 Ellen Mary.

1034 Frederic F. Lyman[8], third son of *Theodore D.[7]* and Betsey, was b. Nov. 2, 1836 ; m. Ellen Horsford, Feb. 18, 1862.

Children, Ninth Generation :

1362 1 Mary Ellen.   1363 2 Destinah Betsey.

1285* NATHAN E. LYMAN[9], *Reubens, Elijah[7], Gideon[6], Gideon[5], Gideon[4], John[3], John[2], Richard[1]*, banker, m. March 30, 1837, Rachel A. Weaver.   *Fairbury, Ill.*

Children, Tenth Generation:

1365 ɪ Minnie, b. Dec. 8, 1860.
1366 2 Adelbert, b. March 13, 1867.
1367 3 Grace, b. July 31, 1869.

1286 LYDIA L. LYMAN[9], m. Jackson B. Young.

Children, Tenth Generation:

1368 1 Nelson, b. March 22, 1867.
1369 2 Homer, b. April 5, 1869.

1287 EDSON W. LYMAN[9], m. Oct., 1866, Frankie Snow. Edson early enlisted in the war against the rebels, declined promotion repeatedly offered, marched as a private through Kentucky, skirmishing with the rebels; and, at Perryville, in battle against Gen. Bragg, lost his left arm. After leaving the army, studied law, engaged successfully in his profession at Pontiac, Ill., and now resides in Fairbury, where parents and children are now gathered. The father and mother, with all their children near, all identified with whatever is good and true, all living active Christians, having not one missing from their circle, and with groups of grandchildren growing up around them, seem in most things un usually blessed, and ready for a ripe, happy old age,—a pleasant retrospect over a useful, well spent life, a cheerful waiting for the tide that shall carry them out to the " home beyond the river."   *Fairbury, Ill.*

Children, Tenth Generation:

1370 1 Winifred, b. March 4, 1869.

PART VII.

Descendants of Moses³, son of John².

MOSES LYMAN³, *John²*, *Richard¹*, 1662–1701, b. in North-ampton, Mass., Feb. 20, 1662; d. Feb. 25, 1701; m. Ann ...., said to be from Long Island.

Children, Fourth Generation:

1 1 Ann, b. April 3, 1686; d. young.
2 2 Moses, 2d, b. Feb. 27, 1689; known as Captain Moses.
3 3 Hannah, b. April 2, 1692; d. young.
4 4 Martha, b. June 5, 1694; d. young.
5 5 Martha, 2d, b. Sept., 1695; m. Ebenezer or Eleazer Bartlett.
6 6 Bethia, b. April 23, 1698; m. Ebenezer or Eleazer Hawley.
7 7 Sarah, b. Jan. 20, 1700; d. young.
8 8 Elias, b. Feb., 1701; d. young.

Only three of these eight children lived to adult age. He died February 28, 1701, aged 39. His widow m. Jonathan Rust.

2 CAPT. MOSES⁴, *Moses³*, *John²*, *Richard¹*, 1689–1762, b. Feb. 27, 1689; m. Mindwell Sheldon, Dec. 13, 1712, and d. March 24, 1762, aged 73 years. She d. May 23, 1780, aged 88. Moses, the only son who left issue, became thus the ancestor of a very numerous posterity, including all that follow in this division of the Lyman family. His descendants exceed those of any of this generation, the great-grandsons of Richard.

Children, Fifth Generation:

9 1 Dea. Moses, b. Oct. 2, 1713; d. 1768.
10 2 Elias, b. Sept. 30, 1715; d. 1803.
11 3 Theodosia, b. 1717; d. early.
12 4 Phebe, b. Aug. 20, 1719; a sensible, resolute woman, to whom Gov. Strong owed his talents quite as much as to his father; m. Caleb Strong, father of Gov. Strong, d. Jan. 5, 1802.
13 5 Noah, b. May 25, 1722; d. May 12, 1754, unmarried.
14 6 Rev. Isaac, b. Feb. 25, 1725, ancestor of a distinguished lineage in and near Boston.
15 7 Simeon, birth not given in the records of Northampton.
16 8 Hannah, b. March 31, 1731; m. Elijah Hunt, no children.
17 9 Seth, m., had issue; descendants still in Genesee and Oswego, N. Y.

18 10 Job, b. Sept. 21, 1734, grad. Yale, 1756, eight sons and two daus.; two of the sons were publicly educated at Yale Coll. Five of these sons became the ancestors of a very numerous and influential line of descendants.

9 Dea. MOSES LYMAN[5], 1st son of Capt. *Moses*[4], m. Sarah, Hayden or Heighton, of Windsor, Conn., March 24, 1742 She was b. Sept. 17, 1716, and d. in Goshen, Ct., Aug. 27, 1808, aged 92. He removed to Goshen, Conn., in the autumn of 1739, one of the earliest inhabitants of the place, the settlement having been begun the year preceding. He d. Jan. 6, 1768, aged 55, the ancestor of a distinguished and noble lineage, an honor to the name and the whole Lyman family.   *Goshen, Ct.*

Children, Sixth Generation :

19 1 Col. Moses 4th, b. March 20, 1743 ; m. Ruth Collins, dau. of Wm. Collins of Guilford.
20 2 Sarah, b. Sept. 29, 1744 ; m. Rev. Daniel Collins, son of Daniel Collins of Guilford, many years pastor of the church in Lanesboro, Mass. They had 4 sons and 5 daus. Their descendants are numerous, settled chiefly in the Western states.
21 3 Anne, b. March 1, 1746 ; m. Gideon Wheeler, resided at Lanesboro. *Ch. 7th Gen. :* Ruth, m. Mr. Savage, chief justice of the state of N. Y., and member of Congress. She d. in Albany, 1837, aged 81, funeral services by Dr. Sprague. She had two daus., one of whom m. Judge Shaw of Lanesboro, Mass., chief justice of the state and member of congress.
22 4 Samuel, b. Jan. 25, 1749 ; m. Mary Pynchon of Springfield. *Ch. 7th Gen. :* 1 Charles P., m. Miss Chapin, and d. soon after his marriage. 2 Samuel, was a graduate from Yale College, by request of his father, studied divinity, but not with design of becoming a preacher. He then studied law, and was admitted to the bar in Litchfield, Conn., and m. Clarissa Gates, of Belchertown, Mass. He went to Hartford, and opened an office as a lawyer and with flattering prospects of success, but shortly had an appointment in the *pay table* office. In that business he continued until he left the state. While in Massachusetts, he was a judge of the circuit court in that state, and a member of the first congress convened under the constitution of the U. S. He d. at the age of 55 years, leaving six children, their record not given. 3 Mary, m. Mr. Emery, captain of a ship in the East India trade ; d. at Springfield, leaving 3 children.
35 5 Hannah, b. June 25, 1751 ; m. Epaphras Sheldon, Jr., of Torrington ; d. at Putney, Steuben Co., N. Y., leaving 3 sons and one dau.

39 6 Esther, b. Sept. 16, 1754; m. Samuel Baldwin, of Har-
rinton, resided at Whitestown, N. Y., d. there leaving 3
sons.

40 7 Phebe, b. Dec 29, 1756; m. David Ellsworth, of Windsor,
brother of Judge Ellsworth, lived and d. there leaving
3 sons and 3 daus.

Dea. Moses Lyman, bought and cleared two 50 acre lots for his
farm, on Town Hill, where he built first, a log house, and, in time,
a framed house, which again gave place to the brick house on the
homestead, which was occupied by his grandson, Moses Lyman,
Esq. This house is still in the possession of the family, and has
been occupied by the first son of the same name to the present time.

At the town meeting, Dec. 6, 1739, Mr. Lyman, then 26 years
of age, was appointed collector and treasurer, a grand juror, in 1744,
tything man, in 1743; in 1746, one of committee of six for the settlement of the Rev. Mr. Heaton, as pastor of the church, with whom
he in connection with others was soon in controversy respecting his
Armenian sentiments, as they alleged. This controversy resulted in
the dismissal of Mr. Heaton, in June, 1753. In May, 1759, Mr.
Lyman was chosen deacon of the church which office he continued
to hold through life, about nine years.

Dea. Lyman, and his wife are characterized as religious, exemplary,
industrious, economical and liberal to the poor. He was remarkable
for his endeavors to make peace and reconcile difficulties, of sound
judgment and for many years a magistrate, he exercised a controlling
influence in the town. It is said of Mr. Lyman that he was a father to
the poor, eyes to the blind, and feet to the lame, relieving the fatherless and helpless, and making the widow's heart to sing for joy.

He was a magistrate many years. As the representative of the
town in the general assembly he attended 14 sessions. His judgment was good and much depended on. His intellectual acquire-
ments and improvements in the knowledge of things, human and
divine, were superior.

SABBATH HOUSES.— The Sabbath-day houses of that age were a
characteristic institution which has passed away with the generation
that frequented them. Dea. Lyman was one of the first to erect one of
these near the church. They were built for the accommodation
of families during the intermission of public worship. The families of the proprietors were the first and principal occupants, but
the houses were open also to other worshipers. Here the entire
family were expected to spend the hour of intermission. The deacon was accustomed to bring the dinner for his family in his saddle
bags on horseback. The dinner was spread upon a small table, and
a wooden bottle supplied them drink. Mr. Buell, who was a joint
proprietor of the house, usually asked the blessing and the deacon
returned thanks. All arose from their seats when the blessing was

asked, and when the thanks were returned. After dinner, the children were expected to occupy the time in reading some religious book for the edification of the company. The room was ceiled; and with a liberal supply of dry wood, all were made comfortable in the coldest season. Stoves were a luxury then unknown.

19 Col. Moses Lyman[6], m. Ruth Collins, dau. of William Collins, of Guilford, Ct., who d. June 8, 1775. After a period of 12 years, during which his mother had the care of the family, he m. for 2d wife the widow of Jesse Judd of Litchfield, dau. of Capt. Jonathan Buell, of Goshen, with whom he had been intimate from childhood. Col. Lyman was a farmer, and occupied the homestead of his father.through life. He d. Sept. 29, 1829, aged 87; his 2d wife d. Oct. 7, 1835, aged 73. *Goshen, Ct.*

Children, Seventh Generation:

51 1 Moses, b. April 16, 1768.
52 2 Daniel, b. June 11, 1769.
53 3 Samuel, b. July 23, 1770.
54 4 Erastus, b. Nov. 1, 1773.
55 5 Mary, b. June 27, 1787. } Children of Mary B. Judd.
56 6 Darius, b. July 19,1789. }

In the militia, Col. Lyman held in succession every grade of office from that of corporal to colonel. During the war he was frequently in the army, sometimes by draft, sometimes as a volunteer on sudden alarms. He went with the recruits from Goshen, to join the Northern army, before the surrender of Burgoyne. When the call came to the town for troops in the Revolutionary war, his company was called together. When formed in line they were told how many men were wanted and those willing to volunteer were requested to step forward. *Every man* in the company marched to the front. Then every fifth man was ordered to the rear and those were taken.

Col. Lyman was commander of a body of troops stationed on the night of the 7th of Oct., 1777, to watch the movements of Burgoyne's army, and was the first to inform Gen. Gates, on the morning of the 8th, that they had deserted their camp. In consideration of his important services, he was honored with the duty of conveying to Gen. Washington personally the first intelligence of the battle of Saratoga, and the surrender of the British, under Burgoyne. He was also commander of the guard over the illustrious and gallant captive Major Andrè, at and previous to the time of his execution.

In civil life, Col. Lyman sustained many offices in the gift of the town. He was a man of strong mind and great energy and decision of character, of the strictest integrity, conscientious in the observance of the sabbath and of the daily worship of God in his family. Though not a professor of religion, vice and immorality never failed to meet his frown and stern rebuke. By his infirmities in advanced life he was, for several years, confined to his house, and d. Sept. 29, 1829, aged 87 years. His second wife d. in Milton Society, Litchfield, Oct. 7, 1835, aged 93.

51 MOSES LYMAN[7], b. April 16, 1768; m. Jan. 21, 1796, Elizabeth Buck of Litchfield, Milton Society. He 'd. May 22, 1844, aged 77 years.   *Goshen, Ct.*

     Children, Eighth Generation.

57 1 Lucretia, b. Feb. 13, 1801; a communicant in the church May 5, 1822; m. Jan. 18, 1826, Caleb Day, Esq., Catskill, N. Y.

     Ch. 9th Gen.: 1 Moses Lyman, b. Nov. 3, 1826; d. April 29, 1833. 2 Caleb Atwater, b. Oct. 23, 1829, book keeper and cashier, Chicago, Ill. 3 Edward Lyman, b. Feb. 2, 1835; m. Laura Williams of Cleveland, Ohio—manufacturer. [*Ch. 10th Gen.:* (1) Laura, b. June, 1865, Kent, Ohio.] 4 Elizabeth Henrietta, b. March 27, 1837; d. March, 1858. 5 Ellen Augusta, b. July 15, 1840; m. June, 1863, Benjamin Way, druggist, Catskill, N. Y.

64 2 Moses, b. Oct. 1, 1810; m. May 6, 1834, Mary Ann Holley of Salisbury, Ct.; many years a merchant, now an iron manufacturer, Goshen.

     Ch. 9th Gen.: 1 Moses, b. in Goshen, Conn., Aug. 20, 1836; m. Dec. 31, 1863, Ellen A. Douglas, dau. of Edwin A. Douglas of Mauch Chunk, Penn., at Windsor Locks, Conn. He now resides in Waverly, New York. He graduated at Brown University, Providence, R. I., in Sept., 1858. Served in the 15th Vermont Vols., in 1862–3. [*Ch. 10th Gen.:* (1) Moses, b. July 17, 1865, at Windsor Locks, Conn., the eighth Moses Lyman, the first, b. in regular succession. (2) Isabel Douglas, b. March 21, 1867, at Waverly, New York. (3) Harriet Deyton, b. July 27, 1870.] 2 Mary, b. in Goshen, Aug. 15, 1839; m. June 15, 1865; Philip Wells, of Brattleboro, Vt., now resides in Amenia, Dutchess county, New York. 3 Alice, b. in Goshen, Conn., May 15, 1845. 4 Richard, b. in Goshen, Conn., June 27, 1848; d. Dec. 24, 1851, aged 3 years and 6 months. 4 Holley Porter, b. in Goshen, Conn., Jan. 22, 1855. He was injured by falling from his horse on Dec. 2, 1865; and d. on the 5th, aged 10 years and 10 months.

Col. Moses[7], m. Jan. 21, 1796, Elizabeth Buell, of Litchfield, Milton Society, dau. of Ira Buell. He had in a remarkable degree the characteristics of his father and his ancestors, a man of commanding influence and foremost standing in society, a thorough and successful business man, firm supporter of the gospel, though not a professor of religion. He engaged extensively in commercial pursuits, first in partnership with Elihu Lewis, of Goshen, from 1793 to 1797, then with his brother Erastus, until 1827, when they dissolved their partnership by dividing their property into equal parts as nearly as possible and bidding for the choice, which fell to Erastus at a premium of 400 dollars. From this time to their decease, each cultivated his own farm. He was a man of superior mind, much above mediocrity. His manners were polished and he was distinguished for politeness.

In mercantile pursuits he was a correct and successful business man. Through a long course of years he successively sustained most if not all the offices in the gift of the town. He represented the town many times in the General Assembly and long acted as a civil magistrate.

52 DR. DANIEL LYMAN[7], second son of Col. *Moses[6]*, m. Sarah Brag, dau. of Rev. Mr. Brag, of Guilford, resided as a physician at Norfolk, Conn., and d. at Guilford, while on a visit there, leaving one child, Sarah, b. Feb. 21, 1792; m. Rev. Munson C. Gaylord, April 18, 1816. Dr. Daniel Lyman was a man of great promise in his profession, d. young. *Norfolk, Conn.*

Children, Ninth Generation:
73 1 Samuel, b. March 18, 1818.
74 2 Sarah, b. March 18, 1821.
75 3 Cornelia, b. April 25, 1824.

53 SAMUEL LYMAN[7], 3d son of *Col. L.[6]*, m. Sarah Webster, Nov. 20, 1799, who d. at Newark, N. J., April 2, 1848, aged 72. Both united with the church in Goshen, July 1, 1827. He resided a farmer in Goshen, a man of superior talents, education and character, honorable and beloved in his family and the community with whom he lived. He d. April 28, 1842, aged 72, much respected and beloved. His talents were of a high order, and his education good for his time. He sustained many offices in the gift of the town, and was several times representative. *Goshen, Ct.*

Children, Eighth Generation:
76 1 Eliza, b. Oct. 1, 1800, united with the church, March 7, 1817; m. Nov. 7, 1832, James B. Pineo, of Newark, N. J.
      Ch. 9th Gen.: 1 Samuel L., b. Sept. 22, 1835. 2 Mary E., b. Aug. 7, 1837. 3 James C., b. July 17, 1839. 4 William M., b. May 31, 1842; d. Aug. 4, 1843.

54 ERASTUS LYMAN[7], 4th son of *Col. L.[6]*, m. Abigail, dau. of Ephraim Starr of Goshen, Sept. 8, 1803, both united with the church Jan. 1, 1832, and resided through

life in Goshen. Mr. L., like others of the family, was a man of distinguished abilities, energetic, methodical and successful in business, eminently distinguished for his piety and benevolence, and his deep interest in the affairs of the church and the town. In the course of his life he filled almost all the offices of the church, the society and the town. Towards the close of his active life, he remarked to a friend that he transacted more business for others than. for himself. He was the friend of the, friendless, the protector of the widow and the orphan, and the ready advisor of all who sought his counsel. He d. Dec. 20, 1854, aged 81. His wife d. Jan. 22, 1855, aged 77.   *Goshen, Ct.*

Children, Eighth Generation:

81 1 Horatio Nelson, b. May 2, 1804.
82 2 Lucy, b. Dec. 19, 1805; m. May 16, 1831, Dr. De Forest, of Watertown, a graduate of Yale College, 1826. She was an exemplary Christian and d. in the faith, Aug. 3, 1855. *Ch. 9th Gen.:* 1 John Lyman, b. Feb. 27, 1832; d. Sept. 17, 1832. 2 Erastus Lyman, b. June 27, 1834.
85 3 Jane M., b. Feb. 7, 1808, united with the church Aug. 28, 1831, and m. Oct. 4, of the same year Alexander H. Holley, of Salisbury, Conn.; July 20, 1832, she gave birth to Alexander Lyman, and d. Sept. 8, in the peace and serenity of Christian faith and hope.
87 4 Rev. Ephraim, b. June 3, 1810.
88 5 William, b. Oct. 2, 1812.
89 6 Abigail, b. Sept. 4, 1814, New Haven, Conn., unmarried.
90 7 Erastus, b. Nov. 29, 1816.
91 8 Frederick, b. Dec. 7, 1819.
92 9 Samuel, b. July 29, 1822, unmarried, New York.

Erastus Lyman[7], a man and a Christian of no ordinary stature, has fallen in our midst; of uncommon capacity and of inestimable value to the community. Self-made, or rather made by circumstances incident to a life of bold business adventure in all parts of this country as it was fifty years ago; with more than an average amount of natural endowments, actuated under the pressure and the promptings of an indomitable purpose, he rose to prominence and an influence indicative of his character. In him, as a man with remarkable physical energy, were combined great mental activity and a strong moral sense. He became associated with the prominent men of this country and state, in conducting and adjusting important business matters, and enjoyed a high reputation abroad as a counselor and an executor in financial affairs.

We can point our young men to his regularity and punctuality at every place where duty called him, to his readiness for every good word and work, to his promptness in saying and doing whatever he had to say or do; and to his ready and cheerful response to almost every call of charity, and say to them: " Go ye and do likewise."

81 HORATIO N. LYMAN[8], m. 1st, Marana Elizabeth Chapin, of Goshen, May 9, 1836, who d. Jan. 26, 1846; m. 2d wife, June 4, 1850, Juliet North, widow of Wm. North, of Elmira, N. Y. After a residence in Goshen of some 20 years from his first marriage he removed to Waterbury, Ct.

New Haven, Conn.

Children, Ninth Generation:

93 1 Jane E., b. July 11, 1837.
94 2 Henry Alexander, b. Sept. 5, 1839; m. Sept. 12, 1866, in Westminster, London, by Rev. Samuel Martin, to Isabella Maria, dau. of F. K. Faulls, Esq., of London; residence of Mr. Lyman, Roma Villa, Upper Norwood.
95 3 Josephena Maria, b. Oct. 2, 1841.
96 4 Abby, an infant, b. June 13, 1843, d. soon.
97 5 William Thompson, b. March 5, 1851; d. Feb. 15, 1853.
98 6 George Nelson, b. Aug. 29, 1852; d. at Goshen, Feb. 19, 1853.
99 7 Edward Norman, b. July 1, 1855; d. at Waterbury, Oct. 29, 1855.

Henry Alexander Lyman, b. Sept. 5, 1839. Removed with his father from Goshen, to Waterbury, Conn., from thence to New York city, Jan. 1, 1859. Became a citizen of New York, by registration in Nov., 1860. Emigrated to London, England, in the same month and year, and settled at Upper Norwood, in the county of Surrey. Connected in business, as resident partner at London, with the brothers of his father's second wife, William S., and Charles H. Thomson, who had commercial houses in New York, London, Paris, and Brussels. Compiled the pedigree of the Lymans in England, and completed the writing of the same in Nov., in the year of our Lord one thousand eighteen hundred and sixty-nine.

Mr. Lyman has in his possession a large quantity of interesting documents relative to the Leman, *alias* Lyman, family, and their estates; consisting of letters, deeds, wills, proofs, certified copies of registers, pedigrees, etc., etc. Also a full and interesting historical pedigree of Elizabeth Lambert, dau. and heiress of Henry Lambert, of High Ongar, Co. Essex, time Henry VI, and wife to Thomas Lyman, of Navistoke, Co. Essex, showing her descent from Sir Radulphus Lambert, Knt., grandson of Lambert, count of Loraine and Mons, who came into England with his kinsman, William the Conqueror, and was present at the battle of Hastings. Also the pedigree of Johanna, sister and co-heiress of Gilbert d'Umphreville, earl of Kyme, the famous soldier in the French wars, time Henry IV and Henry V, and who was slain with Thomas, Duke of Clarence and others 1421; who m. Sir Thomas Lambert, Knt., of Owlton, and showing her descent from Sir Robert d'Umphreville, Lord of Tours and Vian, in Normandy, commonly called "Robert with the Beard," and who was kinsman to William the Conqueror, with whom he came into England, and who in the 10th year of his reign gave him the forest of Riddlesdale, with all its castles, manors, lands and woods. Also, the pedigree of Matilda, Countess of Angus, in her own right, who m. Gilbert d'Umphreville, earl of Angus, Lord Umphreville, Baron of Padhoe, Lord of Riddlesdale, time Ed. I, and showing her descent from Malcolm, 5th earl of Angus, living 1225, who m. Mary, dau. and heiress of Sir Humphrey Berkeley, Knt., and who was the son of Duncan, 4th earl of Angus, who was the son of Gilchrist, 3d earl of Angus, who had command of the Scottish forces, and defeated the English in their invasion of Cumberland, and who m. Maud, sometimes called Majory, sister of William the Lion, king of Scotland, and David, earl of Huntingdon, and dau. of Henry, prince of Scotland, who was the son of David I, king of Scotland, who was the son of Malcolm III, king of Scotland, who was slain at Alnwick Castle, Co. Northumberland, A.D., 1093.   *Roma Villa Upper Norwood.*

87 REV. EPHRAIM LYMAN[8], b. June 3, 1810; graduate of Yale College, 1832; member of College church; ordained over the church and society of Plymouth, Ct., Oct. 28, 1835; m. Hannah D. Richards, of New London, Oct. 2, 1839; dismissed June 8, 1851; installed at Washington, Ct., June 30, 1852; dismissed on account of long continued ill health, June 7, 1863; removed to Northampton, Mass., May, 1864, and joined the old church of which his great-grandfather was a member.   *Northampton, Mass.*

Children, Ninth Generation:

100   1 Lucy De Forest, b. at Plymouth, Conn., Jan. 15, 1841; unmarried and lives at home.

101   2 Ann Eliza, b. at Plymouth, Conn., Nov. 24, 1842; d. at Washington, Conn., Feb. 8, 1857, aged 14.

102   3 George Richards, b. at Plymouth, Conn., Dec. 27, 1841, unmarried, in the drug and apothecary business in Minneapolis, Minn.

103   4 Ellen Hart, b. at Plymouth, Conn., Feb. 14, 1847; unmarried, and lives at home.

104   5 Frederick Wolcott, b. at Plymouth, Conn., June 18, 1849; unmarried, and lives at home.

105   6 Hart W., b. at Plymouth, Conn., Dec. 8, 1851; now a member of Yale College.

106   7 Richard Huntington, b. at Washington, Conn., Sept. 22, 1854, d. at Washington, Conn., Sept. 5, 1860.

107   8 Jane Richards, b. at Washington, Conn., Feb. 3, 1827; d. at Washington, Conn., Dec. 12, 1862.

88 WILLIAM LYMAN[8], fifth child of *Erastus*[7], m. March 19, 1834, Mary Ann Ives, of Goshen.   *El Paso, Ill.*

Children, Ninth Generation:

108   1 Horatio Nelson, b. Feb. 10, 1835, in Goshen; d. Jan. 29, 1865; El Paso, Ill.

109 2 John De Forest, b. June 18, 1836; d. at El Paso, Sept. 9, 1867.
110 3 Edgar William, b. Jan. 14, 1838.
111 3 Mary Abby, b. Oct. 30, 1841.
112 5 Daniel, b. Oct. 1844; d. in camp at Alexandria, Va., Nov. 2, 1862, aged 18; member of Co. C., 19th Regt. Conn. Vols.
113 6 Lucy Starr, b. Sept. 1, 1846; d. at El Paso, Aug. 30, 1866.
114 7 Helen Frances, b. 30, 1851; d. at Goshen, March 11, 1863.
115 8 Alfred, b. July 24, 1853.

90 ERASTUS LYMAN⁸, seventh child of *Erastus*⁷, m. May 6, 1846, Abigail Wade.   *New York city.*

Child, Ninth Generation:
116 1 Erastus, b. Jan. 20, 1847, at New York.

The following sketch of Mr. Lyman's career in business is taken from one of the journals of the day.

Among the most intelligent and efficient members of the business community of the city of New York may be named Erastus Lyman, Esq. He was b. at Goshen, Litchfield county, Connecticut, Nov. 29th, 1817. He is the son of the late Erastus Lyman, of Connecticut, who was a merchant in that state for over forty years, and also a prominent politician and holder of several state offices. After the close of his political career, he turned his attention to farming, and d. from an accident at the age of eighty-six years. His son Erastus lived on the farm, and devoted himself to the care of the horses and cattle, and, in the summer, worked in the harvest-field.

At the age of twelve years, he left home for New Haven, with the view of taking some preparatory studies. In a few months, however, his health failed, and he was obliged to go into the mountain districts, where he again gave his attention to agricultural pursuits. Having regained his health, he returned to New Haven, where he entered a retail store, in which he remained some two years.

He commenced at the lowest round of the ladder, fearing neither drudgery nor toil, and at once developed a great tact for business. He had found the exact sphere in which he could best develop his talents and energies. Bargaining and selling, speculation and enterprise, system and energy, all appealed to qualities which he possessed in a most marked degree.

At length he determined to seek a wider field in the city of New York. Entering the employment of one of the then leading dry-goods houses, he threw his whole energy and mind into the duties of the position. This, in the beginning, was a very inferior one; but, true to his antecedents in New Haven, it did not prevent him from aspiring to the highest. He applied himself with a diligence that did not go unrewarded. He rose from from clerkship to clerkship, until he became the head salesman of the house. He was noted as one of the most clear-headed, enterprising clerks of his day, and for a geniality and integrity of character that secured to him popularity and respect among the whole mercantile community. He formed a very intimate and extensive business acquaintance throughout the south and southwest.

Depending chiefly upon this acquaintance, and his reputation for energy and integrity, he finally embarked in business on his own account. He established a grocery, jobbing and commission business, and became a large receiver of cotton, and other southern products. From year to year his business increased, until it became one of the most extensive in New York. At a later date, he organized the Knickerbocker Life Insurance Company, of which he became, and still is, president. This was in 1853, and he has now held the presidency of the company for over nineteen years. The organization and successful management of such an institution as a life insurance company requires very high business capability. In this case Mr. Lyman has met these requirements to the utmost degree. The whole system of organization and business has been arranged and developed under his personal direction. He has held no sinecure office, but one which called for the highest general business ability as well as knowledge as to this particular branch, and a personal resolution which could defy and overcome every kind of obstacle.

In his business character Mr. Lyman is remarkable for great executive powers, reliable judgment, and system and order in regard to all that he directs or undertakes. He has a keen and critical observation; nothing escapes him that he ought to see or know, and still he does not seem to be giving more than the ordinary attention to matters. In fact, thoroughness, energy, intelligence and system are purely force of habit with him. As a clerk, as a merchant, and now, in his executive capacity, his success has been based on these, rather than, as with so many, upon mere shrewdness and good fortune. His whole life has been a settled plan and purpose, followed with zeal and courage, and wherein action and reason have ever been made to accord. His character will bear this close analysis, for it is a strong and peculiar one. Those who come under its influence soon feel its scope and power, and to the superficial observer, he appears not less the master of will.

91 FREDERICK LYMAN[8], son of *Erastus*[7], m. Sept. 14, 1843, Julia Gold, of Goshen, both members of the church in Goshen—farmer and merchant. *Somerville, N. J.*
  Children, Ninth Generation:
117 1 Samuel Gold, b. June 26, 1846 ; d. Oct. 24, 1846.
118 2 Anna Elizabeth, b. Sept. 13, 1847.
119 3 Frederick Gold, b. Aug. 27, 1850.
120 4 Sarah M., b. Oct. 21, 1852.
121 5 Theodore, b. Nov. 19, 1858 ; d. Dec. 31, 1858.
122 6 Edward C., b. June 16, 1860 ; d. Aug. 5, 1862.
123 7 Charles Reckard, adopted son, b. June 17, 1860.

55 MARY LYMAN[7], dau. of Col. *Moses*[6], b. June 27, 1787; m. April 30, 1811, Amos Morris Collins, son of Dea. William Collins, of Litchfield, Conn., resided in Blanford, Mass., until 1819.   *Hartford, Ct.*

Children, Eighth Generation :

123*1 William, b. Feb. 10, 1812 ; m. Harriet Rierson.
124 2 Morris, b. Oct. 15, 1813 ; m. Martha Blatchford.
125 3 Erastus, b. Feb. 12, 1815 ; m. Mary S. Atwood.
126 4 Charles, b. April 2, 1817 ; m. Mary Hull Terry.
127 5 Edward, b. Nov. 5, 1820 ; d. Aug. 4, 1820.
128 6 Maria Elizabeth, b. Nov. 25, 1822 ; m. Rev. Caleb Strong, of Montreal, resides now in New Haven, Ct.
129 7 Henry, b. Jan. 7, 1827 ; d. Aug. 22, 1828.
130 8 Mary Francis, b. June 13, 1829.

56 The Hon. DARIUS LYMAN[7], m. Dec. 13, 1818, Huldah O. Hudson, widow of Ira Hudson, Ohio, b. Aug. 8, 1793, who d. Aug. 15, 1832; 2d, Lucy Ann Walbridge, of Geneva, N. Y., dau. of Almon Rose, of the same place.
                                          Ravenna, O.

Children, Eighth Generation :

131 1 Mary Ann, b. June 4, 1819 ; d. July 4, 1820.
132 2 Darius, b. June 6, 1826; m. Oct. 26, 1847, Betsey C. Converse, Parkman, Geauga Co., Ohio.
        Ch. 9th Gen. : 1 Clement Longstreet, b. Oct. 14, 1848. 2 Henry Darius, b. April 12, 1852.
135 3 Laura, b. Sept. 6, 1823 ; m. Nov. 1, 1842, Wm. S. C. Otis, Esq
        Ch. 9th Gen. : 1 Lucy L., b. June 17, 1844 ; d. July 24, 1845. 2 May, b. June 14, 1847. 3 Alla, b. May 11, 1851. 4 William Lyman, b. May 6, 1853. 5 Grace, b. July 19, 1855. 6 Edith, b. June 29, 1861, Cleveland, Ohio.
142 4 William, b. July 23, 1827 ; m. June 3, 1854, Margaret Moore, d. Aug. 18, 1865 ; he d. July 8, 1868.
        Ch. 9th Gen. : 1 John D., b   .. ; d. Sept. 9, 1869 ; a young man of great promise. 2 Laura Otis, b. Nov. 8, 1865. El Paso, Ill.
145 5 Mary Rose, issue of 2d marriage, b. Sept. 28, 1835 ; m. Oct. 14, 1857, Edmund B. Hood.
        Ch. 9th Gen. : 1 Edmund, b. Aug. 18, 1858. 2 William C. b. June, 1866.
148 6 Anna Haskel b. Nov. 3, 1839 ; m. Oct. 1, 1861, George W. Woodworth, no children.

Hon. Darius Lyman 7 died at the residence of his son-in-law, W. S. C. Otis, Esq., in Cleveland, Ohio, December 13th, 1865, aged seventy-six years and five months. He was born in Goshen, Litchfield county, Conn., July 19, 1789. His father, Col. Moses Lyman, was an officer in the army of the Revolution, and commanded a regiment at the battle of Saratoga; and as a mark of honor for meritorious services, he was deputed to convey to General Washington the official report of that important victory. His uncle, the Hon. Samuel Lyman, was a member of the first congress elected under the constitution of the United States.

Mr. Lyman was reared upon a farm, where he was taught those habits of industry, economy, self-reliance and self-control, and those principles of virtue, which constitute the foundation of true manly character. He early manifested a desire for, and determined to obtain a liberal education. After the usual preparation, he entered Williams College, and graduated in 1810. While a member of college, he wrote out and solemnly adopted, on his nineteenth birthday, the following resolution as the rule of his life :

" *Goshen, Connecticut, July* 19, 1808.

" The will of God shall be my rule of life."

Shortly after his graduation, he entered the law school at Litchfield, then under the charge of Judge Gould, where, by diligent attention to his studies, and the spotless purity of his life, he won the respect and affection of his distinguished teacher, and of all those associated with him. While connected with the law school, he wrote out and adopted this further rule of life :

" *Litchfield, Connecticut, December* 12, 1812.

" The Prince of Peace shall be my Guide."

After leaving the law school at Litchfield, Mr. Lyman proceeded to Pittsburgh, Pa., where he spent several months in the office of the Hon. Henry Baldwin, one of the justices of the Supreme Court of the United States, in order more fully to perfect himself in his legal studies. From thence, in the early part of the year 1814, he emigrated to Ohio, was admitted to the bar, and established himself permanently at Ravenna, Portage county. Here, before he had tried a single cause, he adopted and wrote out the following resolution, as the daily rule of his professional life :

" *Ravenna, Ohio, April* 25, 1814.

" Having adopted the profession of the law to procure a livelihood, I will practice it through life, always governed by a lofty and sacred sense of honor and perfect rectitude. I will do all the good I can to those with whom I may be called to associate. I will never allow myself to indulge a feeling of revenge, either for insult or injury."

These " rules of life " he always carried about his person, and he paid to them such practical obedience, that all might see, and none mistake, his principles of action ; and neither in domestic, private, professional nor public life, was he ever known to depart from this law which he had prescribed to himself. It might well be said of him that he was upright before God and man.

Though by temperament unobtrusive and retiring, Mr. Lyman was frequently called to occupy public stations. In 1816 he was elected to the lower branch of the State Legislature ; was reelected in 1817; and in 1818 he was elected state senator. In 1828 he was again elected senator, and was re-elected in 1830, when, at the close of his term, he declined a re-election. In 1833 he was the candidate of the Anti-Masonic and National Republican parties for governor. In 1850 he was again elected senator. Mr. Lyman had much to do in moulding the legislation of his adopted state; and among the prominent public measures, to the success of which his influence greatly contributed, was the construction of the Ohio canal, and the adjustment of the difficulty relative to the boundary between the states of Ohio and Michigan.

In 1854, Mr. Lyman was elected probate judge of Portage county, which office he continued to hold for three successive terms. As an illustration of his conscientious attention to his official duties, it may be mentioned that during the entire period of nine years, he was absent from his office but fourteen days.

Judge Lyman also took an active interest in the educational, moral and religious improvement of the community in which he lived, and always contributed liberally of his time and means to their support. He was for many years an efficient member of the board of trustees of Western Reserve College. He was the very earliest advocate of the temperance cause, when nearly all his cotemporaries were openly and actively hostile to the movement; he was the uniform and firm opponent of slavery and of oppression in every shape, advocating and successfully defending the right of free speech when assailed by violence. He aided in organizing the First Congregational church and society in Ravenna, and was one of the trustees of the society for a period of nearly twenty-five years.

Judge Lyman possessed a clear, well-balanced and discriminating mind, inflexible uprightness and unsullied purity of heart, and great decision of character, united with the most refined gentleness and tenderness, and a dignity of mind and manner peculiarly his own. Such a rare combination of virtues and qualities constantly drew to his home a large circle of cherished and valued friends, to whom he always dispensed a generous hospitality. It was here — in the bosom of his family and among his friends — that he shone the brightest and took captive the affections; it was here that he was most loved, revered and cherished; and in that inner circle, especially, his death created a vacuum which can never be filled.

Average of those who had children from the 2d to the 7th generation 6.83. No. of children in families of the 3d, 4th, and 5th generations 6.38; of the 6th 7th, and 8th generations 4.208.

II. DESCENDANTS OF MOSES[3], THROUGH DEA. ELIAS[5], OF SOUTHAMPTON, MASS.

10 DEA. ELIAS LYMAN[5], *Moses*[4], *Moses*[3], *John*[2], *Richard*[1], 1715, 1803, 2d son of Capt. Moses Lyman, of Northampton,

one of the first settlers of the second precinct, now Southampton, was b. in Northampton, Sept. 30, 1715, the 2d
son of Capt. Moses L., grandson of Moses and great-grandson of John, the son of Richard.[1]   He m. Anne Phelps, of
Northampton, and after a long and useful life, d. in S.
Feb. 18, 1803, aged 88 years. He was early chosen deacon
of the church ; was a delegate to the provincial congress,
at Concord, Mass., Oct. 11, 1768 ; with several of the town
was one of a committee of correspondence ; and in 1775,
was a member of the provincial congress which met at
Cambridge. He was a frequent member of the legislature,
and one of a committee of safety in the Revolutionary war,
in addition to many important offices in which he was employed during his long and useful life. By his only surviving grandchild, his tall, stout and venerable form, grave
and sedate demeanor, are distinctly remembered as commanding the reverential regard of his family and his friends.
He reared a family of seven children, two daughters and
five sons. His descendants are very numerous, exerting
a commanding influence in the various occupations and
professional pursuits of life. Anne, his wife, d. Nov. 18,
1791, aged 72. He d. at the advanced age of 88 years.

Southampton, Mass

Children, Sixth Generation :

1 1 Stephen, b. in Northampton, Sept. 8, 1742; m. Ann Blair,
Oct. 3, 1770 ; m. 2d, Widow Anna Clark, July 10, 1776.
2 2 Timothy, b. Dec. 31, 1744, N. S.; m. Dorothy Kenney, of
Worthington, Mass., Aug. 18, 1769.
3 3 Eunice, b. Nov. 25, 1749, of great personal beauty ; m. Lemuel Pomeroy, of Southampton, from whom have descended
the Pomeroys of Pittsfield, Mass.
4 4 Anne, b. 1751; lived unmarried ; greatly given to reading and
theological discussions; d. in Southampton, according to
one record, Jan. 5; another, May 3, 1792, aged 41 years.
5 5 Elias, b. June 27, 1752, lived near his father's farm in the
western part of the town, remembered as a large cor-
pulent man, facetious, jocose, full of mirthfulness, killed
May 26, 1804, by falling from a young horse unaccustomed
to the saddle.
6 6 Noah, b. 1754, enlisted in the army of the Revolutionary war,
returned enfeebled by disease and d. at Southampton,
Jan. 2, 1778, aged 24.
7 7 Joel, b. Sept. 20, 1758; m. Achsah Parsons, of Northampton,
Dec. 19, 1791, farmer on the homestead of his father
through life.

The settlement of Southampton was begun near a century later
than that of Northampton, on a meadow within the limits of the

town. The Pomeroys appear to have made some improvements early in the eighteenth century. The tradition is that they built their first houses in 1722 or 1724. The first meeting on record of the proprietors was held March 21, 1730. This was an adjournment from Jan. 31. In this a committee was appointed to make an equitable division and assignment of the land to the original proprietors. The division was made by lot to thirty individuals, on condition that they should make improvements and erect buildings within a specified time. In Dec. 22, 1732, Ensign John Baker and Moses Lyman, of Northampton, were appointed by that town to lay out a highway so as to accommodate the new settlement. That year two houses had been erected in the precinct.

In May, 1733, fourteen families from Northampton joined the settlement, of whom one was that of Nathan Lyman, son of John and grandson of Richard. He built a house near the present residence of Dea. Samuel Lyman. During three or four succeeding years, fourteen additional settlers took up their residence in the precinct, among whom was Elias Lyman then 17 years of age and grandson of Moses mentioned above. The new settlement was incorporated into the second precinct of N., July 23, 1741. The petition to the general court for this purpose was signed by 35, who requested to be set off with usual privileges, and that a tax of six-pence per acre should be laid on the whole of their tract, being 14,000 acres that they might be enabled to build a meeting house, settle a minister and have the worship of God among themselves.

In 1743, the number of ratable polls was 31, and the valuation of the whole settlement £750 7s., in 1750 the polls were 62 and the valuation £1205 2s. 9d. Their meeting house was not completed until several years later. The church was first occupied for worship by the people sitting on the sills of the house. In Jan., 1753, a committee was appointed to "dignify the seats and the pews." At the ordination of the Rev. Mr. Judd, their pastor, in 1743, the church consisted of 63 members, 32 males and 31 females, comprising almost every adult in the town. The Rev. Jonathan Edwards was the preacher on the occasion. For settlement, Mr. Judd had 200 acres in land, 100 pounds old tenor in money, and 125 pounds in work ; for salary 130 pounds for 3 years, then an increase of 5 pounds a year until the salary amounted to 170 pounds a year.

For several years the inhabitants were fearfully molested by the Indians. When they walked in the road or went into the woods in search of their cattle, every man carried his weapons with him, and in their labor in the fields some kept watch in rotation as sentinels to prevent surprise. A stockade or palisade of stakes was set around certain houses to which the families fled for safety upon an alarm from the Indians. All lived in constant terror and several fell victims to the tomahawk and scalping knife of the savages. In 1748 the settlements were broken up and abandoned for some time to the ravages of the Indians. In addition to these terrors from the Indians, the labor of the husbandman failed by reason of frost and droughts; in 1746, a severe frost on 12th of August killed almost their entire crop of corn; in 1749, there was no rain except one small shower from March until wheat harvest. Not a handful of hay could be gathered at the time of haying, but the rains in autumn gave a good crop of rowen. These details have been selected from the Centennial Address of the Rev. B. B. Edwards, to illustrate the perils, hardships and self-denials with which our forefathers established their settlements " for the furtherance of the public weal and the propagation of the gospel."

They were subject not only to the relentless wars with savages at home, but with foreign foes in the French war, for a series of years. When in 1745, Cape Breton was reduced by New England forces under Gen. Pepperill, Elias Lyman went from Southampton, as a private in this expedition. In the expedition to Crown Point, in 1755, in the capitulation of Fort William Henry, followed by the treacherous massacre of the garrison and soldiers, in 1757, in the siege of Ticonderoga, 1758, and in the capture, we believe, of Quebec, by Wolfe, 1759, the inhabitants of this town were represented by their quota of men. Then again these military sufferings and sacrifices were soon followed by the accummulated horrors of the Revolutionary war.

1 DEA. STEPHEN LYMAN⁶, eldest son of *Elias⁵*, *Moses⁴*, *Moses³*, *John²*, *Richard¹*, 1742 – 1812, Southampton, was b. in Northampton, Sept. 8, 1742. His father, soon after his birth, removed to Southampton, where he lived till about the year 1767; he then removed to Merryfield, afterwards named Chester, where he lived and cleared the land which was then a wilderness, being one of the first settlers in the town.

He married, Oct. 23, 1770, Anna Blair, of Western Mass. He raised a family of ten children, and died Dec. 11, 1810, aged 70 years; Anna, his wife, died Dec. 16, 1768. His second wife was Hannah Clark, of Southampton, m. July 10, 1786.   *Chester, Mass.*

Children, Seventh Genertion .

8	1	Gaius, b. July 15, 1771; d. June 13, 1841.
9	2	Crispus, b. March 27, 1773; b. Jan. 11, 1855.
10	3	Stephen, b. Jan. 25, 1775 ; d. July 15, 1810.
11	4	Clarissa, b. Oct. 10, 1776; d. Jan. 27, 1843.
12	5	Noah, b. Oct. 2, 1778; d. Dec. 11, 1866.
13	6	Burnham, b. April 22, 1780; d. Jan. 18, 1828.
14	7	Chester, b. March 22, 1782 ; d. Sept. 4, 1854.
15	8	Anna, b. Jan. 7, 1784; d. Nov. 4, 1827.
16	9	Electa, b. Dec. 7, 1785; d. Feb. 17, 1865.
17	10	Samuel, b. May 2, 1787, still living in full health in his 86th year.

Dea. Stephen, and his brother Timothy began public life together as the first settlers of Murrayfield, now Chester, a mountain town, 17 miles west of Southampton, their native place. Tall, stalwart young men, with strong hands and hearts, they went out into the wilds together and cleared from the native forest adjoining farms on which they lived through life. Their way was through an unbroken forest with no track for their guide but that of the bears and the deer. A single camp chest contained their frugal outfit, a few loaves of brown Boston bread, a cheese, a ball of butter and two or three tow shirts, each grasping one handle of the chest with one hand and carrying his axe in the other, they set forward in 1763, for their wild mountain land home. As they rested at frequent intervals they marked the trees with their axes to guide their way back to their native place. Their farms were given them on condition that each one, within the space of three years from June, 1762, should build a dwelling house on his lot, 24ft. by 18 and 7 feet stud, and have 7 acres well cleared, and brought to English grass, or ploughed, and actually settled, by a family on the farm, and continue such family for a period of six years, and within 8 years settle a Protestant minister. Stephen and Timothy, are recorded among those who organized the Congregational church in Chester, Nov. 14, 1769, of which the former was the first deacon.

8 Gaius Lyman[7], m. Tryphena Clark of Southampton, Aug. 18, 1793, removed to Southampton where he lived and cultivated a farm where all his children were b. and he d. *Chester, Mass.*

Children, Eighth Generation :

18   1 Gad C., b. April 9, 1796, South Hadley Falls.
19   2 Hannah, b. May 20, 1798; m. April 14, 1841, James K. Sheldon, a merchant of Southampton—no children.
20   3 Anna, b. Sept. 9, 1800, d. July 11, 1801.
21   4 Anna, b. May 20, 1802; d. June 7, 1803.
22   5 Gaius, b. April 12, 1804, Southampton.
23   6 Tryphena, b. Feb. 23, 1808; m. Aug., 1839, Joel Miller, of Hadley Falls, deputy sheriff,—no children.
24   7 Catharine E., b. June 3, 1811.
25   8 Harriet N., b. June 29, 1814; a school teacher for about 30 years at South Hadley Falls; she d. at Southampton, April 18, 1868.

18 Gad C. Lyman, m. Fanny Danks, of Southampton, March 5, 1839, he traded as a merchant a number of years in Southampton; afterwards went to Boston, and is now retired a gentleman of leisure. *Boston, Mass.*

Child, Ninth Generation :

26   1 Fanny, b. Nov. 28, 1830, d. Jan. 15, 1848.

22 GAIUS LYMAN[8], JR., a merchant and farmer; m. Silence Loomis, of Southampton, Oct. 7, 1828.

Southampton, Mass.

Children, Ninth Generation:

27 1 Francis A., b. Aug. 10, 1801; m. Augustus Bates, Nov. 26, 1852; d. June 21, 1853— no children.
28 2 Henry G., b. Aug. 29, 1833; d. May 16, 1852.
29 3 John C., b. April 21, 1840; d. April 23, 1851.
30 4 Edward B., b. June 14, 1847; m. 1871—one child.

24 CATHARINE E. LYMAN[8], m. Aug. 1, 1839, Timothy P. Bates, of Southampton, a deacon in the Congregational church and a farmer. *Southampton, Mass.*

Child, Ninth Generation:

32 1 Augustus B., b. March 31, 1842; m. Nov., 1865, L. M. Smith,— 4 children, 3 deceased.

9 CRISPUS LYMAN[7], m. Adah Smith, Jan. 24, 1796— farmer, d. in Ohio. *Chester, Mass.*

Children, Eighth Generation.

37 1 John, b. March 22, 1798; d. Sept. 23, 1802. Adah his wife d., 1798, 2d wife Betsey Smith, m. April 3, 1799.
38 2 Jason W., b. in 1800; d. Sept. 20, 1802.
39 3 Sarah, b. Sept. 26, 1802; m. Dryden Cressy, of Cherry Valley, Ohio, Sept. 21, 1841.
       Ch. 9th Gen. : 1 Eliza A., b. Oct. 3, 1842. 2 Sarah E., b. Feb. 24, 1846; Crown Point, N. Y.
42 4 Nancy, b. April 12, 1804; m. Henry R. Hoisington, Sept. 21, 1831.
43 5 Sophronia, b. May 12, 1807; m. May 6, 1827, John L. Bell, M.D., Williamstown, one son Lyman F., b. Aug. 31, 1830; m. in 1850; O. Burns Sophronia m. Moses Lyman, Dec. 7, 1836.
       Ch. 9th Gen.: 1 Nancy, b. Nov. 28, 1837; d. Jan. 12, 1859. 2 Amelia W., b. Aug. 12, 1844; m. 1871, ... Gleason, of Hinsdale, Mass.
47 1 Ambrose B., b. June 14, 1811; m. Nov. 16, 1836, Eliza B. Searl, Cincinnati, O.
       Ch. 8th Gen.: 1 Richard H., b. Nov. 21, 1843. 1 Ambrose W., b. Aug. 30, 1848. 3 Herbert W., b. Sept. 12, 1852.

42 NANCY LYMAN,[8] dau. of *Crispus*, m. Sept. 21, 1831, Rev. H. R. Hoisington, missionary. *Madras.*

Children, Ninth Generation ·

51 1 Sarah E., b. Jan. 7, 1835; m. May 20, 1868, Rev. F. A. Stoddard, Kansas, d. May, 1871.

52 2 Henry R., b. Oct. 4, 1836; m. Oct. 17, 1865, Rev. M. Fenton,
of Circleville, Ohio, two children.
53 3 Samuel L., b. Feb. 15, 1838 ; d. at Madras, Nov. 5, 1839.
54 4 Joseph K., b. Dec. 29, 1840; d. at sea, March 11, 1842.
55 5 Lucy W., b. Oct. 21, 1842; m. June 23, 1863, Rev. W. H.
Clark, N. Y.
> *Ch. 10th Gen. :* 1 Nancy L., b. Oct. 4, 1864. 2 Lucy
> H., b. Jan. 25, 1867.
58 6 Ann Maria, b. July 25, 1846; m. April 15, 1867. William
B. Porter, Esq., Warren, Ohio, dau. of Sarah, b. Jan.
27, 1868.

Rev. Mr. Hoisington, after a missionary life of about 10 years,
returned on account of ill health, and finally settled at Center Brook,
Conn., where he d. suddenly of paralysis, of which he was seized
in the pulpit while ministering to his congregation on the sabbath.

10 STEPHEN LYMAN[7], m. Betsey Witt, of Chester, Sept.
19, 1799 —farmer— d. July 13, 1810.   *Chester, Mass.*

Children, Eighth Generation:

59 1 Aurelia, b. ...... 1801 ; m. 1822, William Stone, no children;
d. Aug. 31, 1871.
60 2 Wealthy, b. April 2, 1804 ; d. Oct., 1814.
61 3 Ashley W., b. 1806; m. April 11, 1850, Laura Wright.
> *Ch. 9th Gen.:* 1 George S., b. Feb. 11, 1833; m.
> July, 1859. [*Ch. 10th Gen.:* (1) Laura, b. Feb. 22,
> 1850; d. Feb. 6, 1854. (2) Laura, b. April 13, 1854.
> (3) William S., b. July 6, 1861. (4) James W., b. Oct.
> 3, 1863. (5) George W., b. July 8, 1866.]

11 CLARISSA[7], dau. of Dea. *Stephen*[6], m. Sept. 22, 1796,
Israel Searl, of Southampton.   *Southampton, Mass.*

Children, Eighth Generation:

68 1 Lyman B., b. Sept. 27, 1798; killed by being caught in a bark
mill, Aug. 12, 1837.
69 2 Harmony B., b. Aug. 16, 1800 ; m. Feb. 14, 1828, Flavius
Moore, of Montgomery.
> *Ch. 9th Gen.:* 1 Frances, b. Dec. 23, 1823 ; m. May
> 10, 1848, Augustus Moore. [*Ch. 10th Gen.:* (1) Alice
> F., b. Dec. 13, 1850. (2) Hattie A., b. March 4, 1859.
> (3) Clifton A., b. Nov. 12, 1861.] 2 Lyman B., b. Nov.
> 30, 1837 ; m. March 31, 1863, Keren H. Bates, of West-
> field. [*Ch. 10th Gen.:* (1) A daughter. (2) Lewis L.,
> b. Feb. 28, 1860.] 3 Celia E., b. Aug. 17, 1839. 4 Emma
> K., b. March 23, 1845; adopted by H. W. Lyman; d.
> Sept. 21, 1854.
78 3 Clarissa, daughter of J. Searl, b. Oct. 5, 1802 ; d. Sept. 23,
1838.

38

79 4 Electa A., b. Oct. 6, 1805; m. April 14, 1842, Joel Lyman,
     of Southampton.
80 5 Israel W., b. April 8, 1808; d. Oct. 18, 1834, a missionary in
     Africa.
81 6 Ann N., b. April 14, 1812; m. May 13, 1834, John Wright,
     2d, of Easthampton; d. Jan. 4, 1855.
          Ch. 9th Gen.: 1 Emily B., b. Sept. 3, 1835; m. May
          15, 1866, L. S. Clark, of Easthampton. 2 Watson H., b.
          May 3, 1840; m. Lucy Hannum, May 23, 1866. [*Ch.*
          10th Gen.: 1 Herbert W., b. Nov. 23, 1867. 2
          Mary C., b. Nov. 3, 1844. School teacher.]
85 7 Wharton D., b. April 12, 1814.
86 8 Stephen E., b. Feb. 9, 1817.

85 **Wharton D. Searl**[8], m. Mary Lyman, Sept. 18,
1844.   *Southampton, Mass.*
     Children, Ninth Generation:
87 1 Lyman W. Searl, b. June 18, 1846, unmarried.
88 2 Josephine E., b. May 10, 1848; m. Edward Bell, Oct. 30,
     1867, Southampton.
89 3 Mary L., b. Aug. 16, 1851, teacher.
90 4 Ella N., b. April 30, 1858; d. May 7, 1859.
91 5 Ida D., b. April 28, 1860.

86 **Stephen E. Searl**[8], m. Henrietta A. Bliss, May 6,
1846.   *Southampton, Mass.*
     Children, Ninth Generation:
92 1 Clara J., b. May 15, 1848, teacher.
93 2 Edward B., b. Aug. 21, 1850.
94 3 Isabella H., b. March 1, 1858. } twins.
95 4 Nellie, b. March 1, 1858.   }
96 5 Arthur L., b. July 28, 1860.

12 **Noah Lyman**[7], 4th son of Deacon *Stephen*[6], m. Clarissa
Granger, of Worthington, March 19, 1804, who d. June
30, 1828, he lived a few years in Norwich, Mass., then removed to Columbia, N. H., about 1812, where most of his
children were b. For a gun and a horse he bought a large
tract of wild land, on which he lived through life. His 2d
wife, mother of his last two children, was Olive Day, date
of m. not given.   *Columbia, N. H.*
     Children, Eighth Generation:
97 1 John S., b. Oct. 30, 1801.
98 2 Elias, b. May 25, 1804.
99 3 Elvira, b. May 23, 1806.
100 4 Stephen, b. June 22, 1808; d. March 22, 1839.
101 5 Wharton, b. Nov. 17, 1810.
102 6 Noah, b. Jan. 30, 1813; d. April 19, 1851.

103 7 Caleb S., b. June, 23, 1815; he was killed in a personal
difficulty in Bayou Sara, La., in 1861. A man of giant
strength and stature. He had the frame of a Greek
athlete and could have thrown the discus against Ajax
himself. He was very far from being a quarrelsome or
bad man, but he often interposed his strength to prevent
difficulties. He was always doing generous and self-
sacrificing things, and was a pet among men of rude life.
104 8 William G., b. Sept. 4, 1817.
105 9 George B., b. Jan. 20, 1819.
106 10 Clarissa A., b. Aug. 5, 1823
107 11 Charles C., b. Sept. 20, 1825.
108 12 Olive, b. June 4, 1829 ; deceased.
109 13 Marian, b. Dec. 15, 1831; no further record.

97 JOHN S. LYMAN[8], son of *Noah[7]*, m. Emily Schapp, Jan.
27, 1831 — farmer.   *Columbia, N. H.*

Children, Ninth Generation

110 1 Diana, m. Charles H. Smith; one child.
    Ch. 10*th Gen. :* 1 Lydia, b. Oct. 27, 1851.
112 2 John, b. July 4, 1834; killed in the battle of Cedar Moun-
    tain, Aug. 20, 1862.
113 3 Prudentia Ann, b. April 26, 1836 ; d. Feb. 9, 1838.
114 4 Cassandana, b. Jan. 10, 1838 ; m. Sarah Austin, of Roxbury,
    Mass., Nov. 28, 1867.
115 5 Lucretia A., b. Oct. 24, 1839 ; m. Dela Vining.
    Ch. 10*th Gen.:* 1 Fred, b. Nov. 26, 1863. 2 Sarah
    D., b. in 1866.
118 6 William C., b. June 20, 1845.
119 7 Elvira, b. March 30, 1848 ; d. June 14, 1862.
120 8 Horace G., b. Sept. 23, 1851.

98 ELIAS LYMAN[8], 2d son of *Noah[7]* and Clarissa C. Smith,
b. Oct. 9, 1828,—farmer, postmaster.   *Lemington, Vt.*

Children, Ninth Generation :

121 1 Charles C., b. June 6, 1829 ; m. Delia A. Buffington, Oct.
    8, 1852 ; d. Nov. 15, 1856.
    Ch. 10*th Gen :* 1 Ida Isabella, b. May 5, 1854. 2
    Minnie, b. June 30, 1866 ; d. March 11, 1868
124 2 Russell, b. Aug. 2, 1830 ; m. Lizzie A. Stewart, Aug. 15,
    1857.
    Ch. 10*th Gen. :* Maud, b. July 12, 1858 ; he d. July
    13, 1863, mechanic, Lowell, Mass.
126 3 Cyrus E., b. Oct. 10, 1831 ; m. Mary A. Parker, Dec. 15,
    1863, manufacturer of head stones, Canada East.
    Ch. 10*th Gen.:* 1 Alice, b. May 14, 1865. 2 Minnie,
    b. June 30, 1866; d. March 11, 1868.
129 4 Laura L., b. Dec. 5, 1832 ; m. Mills D. F. Blodget, Sept.
    24, 1866.

99 Elvira Lyman[8], was m. to Joseph A. Martin, of Columbia, New Hampshire, July 8, 1827.　　*Columbia, N. H.*

Children, Ninth Generation :

138　1 Charles A., b. March 18, 1828.　He was killed on a railroad in Ohio, Jan. 26, 1862.

139　2 George L., b. May 7, 1829; m. to Olive Haynes, in 1860, one son George, b. in 1864.

140　3 Lizzie B., b. March 29, 1831; m. April 6, 1858, Peletiah M. Greedy, of Lowell, Mass.

141　4 John D., b. Dec. 16, 1833; m. Caroline Thompson, in 1858. They have four children, names unknown.

146　5 Julia A., b. Sept. 16, 1835; m. Dec. 31, 1855, to Robinson S. Gamsby.　She is now a widow.

147　6 Parthena B., b. Nov. 22, 1837; m. Henry Harris, April 24, 1860.

　　　Ch. 10th　Gen.: 1 Charles H., b. Feb. 12, 1862. 2 Henry H., b. March 10, 1868.

150　7 Andrew, b. Oct. 22, 1838; d. April 1, 1839.

151　8 Augusta A., b. Jan. 1, 1839; m. to Henry H. Adams, Dec. 22, 1863; one son Durant, b. Dec., 1865.

153　9 Jane E., b. March 24, 1842.

154　10 Clara L., b. June 17, 1845; m. George Parsons, May 12, 1868.

155　11 Ella A., b. March 17, 1846.

156　12 Adah E., b. Feb. 26, 1849.

157　13 Fred W., b. April 16, 1851.

158　14 Arabella, b. May 31, 1854.

100 Stephen Lyman[8], son of *Noah[7]*, m. Caroline M. Smith, Aug. 18, 1833; d. March 22, 1839, leaving three daughters
Columbia, Mass.

Children, Ninth Generation :

159　1 Lucia, b. Jan. 17, 1834; m. A. L. Day, of Columbia, N. H., Nov. 12, 1852.

　　　Ch. 10th Gen.: 1 Lizzie E., b. Nov. 5, 1853. 2 Herbert A., b. April 13, 1855.　3 Alma C., b. March 21, 1857.　4 Jennie E., b. Feb. 11, 1859.　5 Ervine N., b. June 28, 1863; d. April 5, 1864. 6 Myra P., b. March 31, 1868.

166　2 Adaline, b. April 27, 1836; m. Charles C. Stoddart, Nov. 24, 1853.

　　　Ch. 10th Gen.: 1 Adah, b. Jan. 9, 1855. 2 Effie A., b. April 29, 1857.　3 Charles E., b. Jan. 9, 1859. 4 George R., b. Oct. 15, 1861. 5 Elmer E., Jan. 9, 1863.　6 Cecil A., b. April 19, 1865.

173　3 Phebe D., b. June 15, 1838; m. Stephen Tileston, June 27, 1858.

Ch. 10*th Gen.:* 1 Harriet A., b. July 1, 1859. 2 Ellen
A., b. July 6, 1861. 3 Elvira B., b. Aug. 25, 1863.
4 Lucia L., b. Feb. 6, 1866.

101 WHARTON LYMAN[8], son of Noah[7], was b. in West
Hampton, Nov. 17, 1810; m. to Ann Maria Bliss, of West
Springfield, Oct. 11, 1838. He is a mechanic and rail road
builder. *Centerville, Ind.*
    Children, Ninth Generation:
178 1 George B., b. Dec. 16, 1841; d. Dec. 14, 1865.
179 2 Ann Maria, b. Jan. 24, 1844; m. at Centerville, Ind., Aug.
    13, 1863, Oliver W. Coggswell.
180 3 Freddie W., b. March 29, 1846; m. May 11, 1867, Marinda
    Shoemaker; one son.
        Ch. 10*th Gen.:* 1 George Curtiss, b. May 1, 1868.
182 4 Eva Clara, b. Nov. 5, 1852, all b. in West Springfield.
183 5 Jane Nora, b. in Centreville, Ind., July 11, 1863.

102 NOAH LYMAN[8], son of *Noah[7]*, m. to Charlotte Blodget.
    Children, Ninth Generation:
184 1 Sarah. 186 3 Noah, d. in infancy.
185 2 Emma.

104 WILLIAM G. LYMAN[8], son of *Noah[7]*, m. Eliza Fuller,
Aug. 31, 1847. *North Stratford, N. H.*
    Children, Ninth Generation:
187 1 Harriet. 189 3 Julia.
188 2 Emma. 190 4 Lola.

105 GEORGE B. LYMAN[8], son of *Noah[7]*, m. Sarah J. Bates,
of Cincinnati, Feb. 13, 1849 — merchant. *Xenia, Ohio.*
    Children, Ninth Generation:
191 1 William G., b. July, 1850.
192 2 Edward A., b. July, 1853.
193 3 Mattack B., b. March, 1857.
194 4 Jennie E., b. March, 1860.
195 5 Harriet B., b. July, 1863.

106 CLARISSA A. LYMAN[8], dau. of *Noah[7]*, m. William
Franklin Ripley, Sept. 23, 1850. She has two children
living in Cambridgeport, Mass. *Cambridgeport, Mass.*
    Children, Ninth Generation:
196 1 Frank, b. Oct. 10, 1852, in Lowell.
197 2 Maria M., b. Oct 22, 1860.

107 CHARLES CHAUNCEY[8], son of *Noah[7]*, m. to Electa M.
Buzzard, of Spartansburg, Indiana, Dec. 11, 1859.

Child, Ninth Generation .

198 1 Charlie, b. Oct. 17, 1762; d. July 20, 1863.

13 BURNHAM LYMAN[7], 5th son of Dea. *Stephen[6]*, m. at
Batavia, New York, Charity Blodget, Sept. 9, 1807
                                                    Ohio.

Children, Eighth Generation :

199 1 Lucinda, b. at Batavia, New York, Nov. 9, 1808; m. William
          Durand, March 20, 1828, of Concord, Ohio.
          Ch. 9th Gen. : 1 Melvina A., b. at Mentor, Ohio, July
          22, 1829. 2 Horace C., b. July 25, 1833. 3 Cordelia
          L., b. July 2, 1837. One grandchild, name not given.

204 2 Electa, b. at Batavia, New York, June 17, 1811; m. Otis
          Wood, of Mentor, Ohio, April 3, 1831.
          Ch. 9th Gen. : 1 Marion G., b. at Perry, Ohio, June
          14, 1833. 2 Ann Maria, b. Dec. 5, 1840. 3 Electa L.,
          b. Jan. 17, 1848, one grandchild, name not given.

209 3 Charity, b. at Kingsville, Ohio, June 15, 1814; m. Dennis
          Griffin, 1832.
          Ch. 9th Gen. : 1 Arrilla, b. at Hannibal, Ohio, 1833.
          2 Heman. 3 Edward, and 4 Edwin, twins. 5 Thomas.
          6 William.

215 4 Andrew B., b. at Concord, Ohio, Aug. 28, 1815.
          Ch. 9th Gen. : 1 David C., b. Jan. 11, 1861. 2 Pattie
          F., b. Oct. 24, 1863,   .

218 5 George B., b. at Kingsville, Ohio, Aug. 28, 1818 ; m. Mary
          Whitten, of Ypsilanti, Mich., Nov. 6, 1841.
          Ch. 9th Gen. : 1 Marion M., b. Aug. 9, 1842. 2 Sa-
          repta C., b. June 20, 1844. 3 Anna E., b. Oct. 5, 1846.
          4 Burnham, b Feb. 11, 1848. 5 Andrew A., b. Feb.
          15, 1852. 6 Leroy W., b. July 24, 1856. 7 Otis Wil-
          liam, b. Aug. 28, 1861. 8 Eddy Lincoln, b. March 2,
          1863. 9 Frederick A., b. March 2, 1866.

228 6 Ann S., b. in Concord, Ohio, Dec. 15, 1827 ; m. June 8,
          1847. Augustus A. Pike, M.D. ; d. May 4, 1849, in
          Perry Lake county, Ohio, leaving a dau. Ann M. Pike,   .
          now a young lady of rare comeliness of person and accom-
          plishments.

Andrew B. Lyman[3], M.D. was at an early age bereaved of both his
parents, and by his unaided efforts carved his way to distinction
and usefulness, in the medical profession.   After several changes,
he settled in Richmond, Kentucky, where he is successfully engaged
in his profession.   Faithful among the faithless in the great rebellion,
he remained true to his country and to the cause of freedom, and
early volunteered in defense of his country's flag.   For over two
years his services were given to the federal government, in the care
of the sick and wounded, and for a portion of the time he was on
the medical staff, under General Saunders.   His own house was in-

vaded by rebel soldiers under Morgan, and the life of his venerable father-in-law, 80 years of age, was saved by the noble wife and daughter, throwing herself before the weapon of the assassin who cowered in view of her dauntless heroism and spared the life of the patriot patriarch. Dr. Lyman m. May 19, 1858, Isabel Field, of Richmond, Ky.

The aged father, E. H. Field, saved by the heroic daring of this daughter, was a loyal Kentuckian, who in those days that tried men's souls, nobly dared at his great age—to rally around his country's flag, for her defense against the traitor rebels of his native state ; to take his gun and join the horse-guards for the protection and preservation of the Union, for which his father Capt. Henry Field had bled and died, in the terrible battle of Blue Licks. The mother of Mrs. Lyman was a sister of Col. Irvin, who lost his life at Fort Meigs, while bravely leading his regiment against the British and the savages in the war of the revolution. Such is the noble and gallant blood that runs in the veins of the heroic, devoted daughter.

14 CHESTER LYMAN[7], 6th son of Dea. *Stephen*[6], m. Abigail Wilcox, Oct. 25, 1806—a farmer, lived and d. in his native place.   *Chester, Mass.*

Children, Eighth Generation :

230 1 George W., b. Jan. 2, 1808.
231 2 Abigail B , b. July 10, 1809.
232 3 Julia A., b. Dec. 20, 1813.
233 4 Horatio W., b. Nov. 1, 1815 ; m. Sept. 11, 1844, Redexa S.
        Moore, of Montgomery, no children.
            Ch. 9th Gen.: 1 Hattie A., an adopted dau. Nov.
            b. 12, 1861.
235 5 Henry S., b. June 7, 1817, never m.
236 6 Mary B., b. Jan. 26, 1821, d. young.
237 7 Mary B., b. Nov. 22, 1822 ; d. at Madison, Ohio, May 22,
        1836.
238 8 Annie, b. August 21, 1825 ; d. June 21, 1836.
239 9 Genette O., b. March 16, 1830.

230 GEORGE W.[8], m. Susan B. Wood, of Chester, Oct. 2, 1834. A merchant a number of years in Middlefield, Mass., afterwards pursued the business in Springfield, and Troy, N. Y.   *Madison, Ohio.*

Children, Ninth Generation :

240 1 Alida W., b. Feb. 1, 1839, at Chester, Mass. ; she grew
        physically and mentally strong, graduating at the high
        school, Springfield, Mass., receiving her diploma at the
        age of 17 ; m. at the age of 21, Charles H. Bigelow, of
        Troy, N. Y., at this date lives in St. Paul, Minnesota.
        They have 3 children, Emma, George, Charles. Mr.

Bigelow is a very prosperous business man, at St. Paul, Minn.

244 2 Charles W., b. at Middlefield, Mass., Sept. 2, 1843. From Madison, Ohio, at the age of eighteen, he enlisted in the 1st Regt. of Ohio Artillery, battery C. At the battle of Mill Springs, he proved his courage by voluntarily seizing a rifle and running into the hottest of the fight till the rebels fled, taking and yet keeping as a trophy Zollicoffer's watch and chain. After two years, he re-enlisted as a veteran, went through the southern campaign with Sherman, and was honorably discharged at the close of the war, since which time to the present he has been engaged in the lumber business at Chicago, a faithful and strictly moral man ; not married. .

245 3 Nathan W., b. at Middlefield, Mass., Aug. 22, 1845, obtaining a good commercial education, went to Chicago as clerk and bookkeeper in a wholesale house. Enlisted at Chicago as a 100 day man, was private secretary of the commanding general, while in service, returned to his place and is now head salesman of and traveling agent for the house, not married.

246 4 S. Elizabeth, b. Jan. 1, 1851, at Springfield, Mass. Graduated in 1870 or '71, at Oberlin, Ohio.

231 ABIGAIL R. LYMAN[8], dau. of *Chester*[7], m. Feb. 28, 1831, her cousin Franklin Toogood, son of Anna Lyman, sister of Chester.   *Chester, Mass.*

Children, Ninth Generation :

247 1 Abigail Augusta, b. Feb. 4, 1832 ; m. May 22, 1851, Sylvester Alderman.

    Ch. 10*th Gen.:* 1 Abbie A., b. July 20, 1852. 2 Hattie M., b. Sept. 1, 1855. 3 Norman F., b. July 15, 1859. 4 Wilhecucia, b. Oct. 16, 1867.

252 2 Cornelia, b. Sept. 30, 1833 ; m. Aug. 3, 1854, Henry Billings, of Springfield, Mass.

    Ch. 10*th Gen.:* 1 Charles H., b. May 9, 1855. 2 Abbie C., b. Sept. 29, 1860.

255 3 William F., b. June 2, 1835 ; m. Jan. 1, 1862, Alzina Williams ; resides in Illinois.

    Ch. 10*th Gen.:* 1 Franklin W., b. Jan. 26, 1863. 2 Albert Lee, b. July 7, 1864. 3 Herbert Edward, b. Sept. 5, 1865 ; d. Sept. 12, 1865. 4 Infant, b. Sept. 12, 1866.

260 4 Lyman Oaks, b. May 12, 1838 ; m. May 16, 1860, Antoinette Campbell ; one child.

    Ch. 10*th Gen.:* 1 Hettie.

262 5 George Dwight, b. Dec. 29, 1839 ; m. Nov. 15, 1862, Lucy Williams ; Illinois.

Ch. 10th Gen.: 1 Jesse, b. Jan. 12, 1864; d. Oct. 13, 1865.

264 6 Mary A., b. March 20, 1843; m. Aug. 11, 1862, Albert F. Mears.

239 GENETIE O. LYMAN[8], m. May 20, 1851, Andrew M. Eames, of Troy, N. Y. *Troy, N. Y.*
Children, Ninth Generation:
265 1 Carrie, b. Oct. 4, 1852.
266 3 Nellie, b. Jan. 16, 1854.
267 3 Lizzie, b. Sept. 3, 1855.

15 ANNA LYMAN[7], dau. of Dea. Stephen, m. William O. Toogood, July 1, 1802 of Chester, where they lived and d.; he cultivated a farm, and made cider brandy and potash. *Chester, Mass.*
Children, Eighth Generation:
268 1 Franklin, b. Feb. 7, 1803; d. Sept., 1849.
269 2 Mary, b. Oct. 31, 1807.
270 3 Mariah J., b. March 12, 1810; d. Dec. 18, 186/.
271 4 Anna S., b. July 12, 1817.

269 MARY TOOGOOD, m. Alonzo Smith, of Chester, May 27, 1837. *Chester, Mass.*
Child, Ninth Generation
272 1 Franklin, b. May 17, 1838; m. Ellen Cannon, Nov. 10, 1859.
Ch. 10th Gen.: 1 Luther S., b. Aug. 17, 1861.

270 MARIAH J. TOOGOOD, m. Orin Percival, June 15, 1827. *Chester, Mass.*
Children, Ninth Generation:
273 1 William, b. April 7, 1829; m. June 7, 1849, Paulina Langdon.
274 2 Mary Ann, b. June 4, 1837; m. May 28, 1863, Samuel Drag.
Ch. 10th Gen.: 1 Arista, b. Aug. 20, 1852.

271 ANNA S. TOOGOOD, m. Nathan Samuels, Aug. 22, 1838. *Chester, Mass.*
Children, Ninth Generation:
275 1 Lewis, b. June 30, 1839; m. Dec. 8, 1864.
276 2 Albert N., b. Nov. 5, 1841; m. Sept. 25, 1865.
277 3 Amelia A., b. Jan. 3, 1846.

16 ELECTA LYMAN[7], dau. of Dea. *Stephen[6]*, m. John Elder of Chester, Oct. 8, 1805. He was for a number of years a deacon in the church in Chester, and d. Feb. 15, 1859, with his armor on, ready to depart. *Chester, Mass.*

Children, Eighth Generation :

278   1 Lyman M., b. May 1, 1807; d. at Little Rock, Arkansas,
        m. April, 1829, Charlotte Whipple, of Chester, Mass.
          Ch. 9th Gen. : 1 Marcus Maro, b. Oct. 23, 1839, at
          Chester.
279   2 Electa, Jan. 14, 1809; d. March 30, 1809.
280   3 John B., b. Nov. 9, 1810; m. Dinah Tucker, of Chicopee,
        June 15, 1854.
          Ch. 8th Gen. : 1 Sarah Ann, b. May 19, 1855. 2 Hat-
          tie, b. Feb. 26, 1861. 3 John J., b. July 10, 1862.
281   4 Stephen, b. March 10, 1813; d. Aug. 17, 1814.
282   5 Electa S., b. Nov. 31, 1814; m. April 26, 1840, Heman
        Moody, of Belchertown, Mass.; d. Aug. 2, 1841.
283   6 Harriet A., b. Dec. 18, 1816; m. Nov. 25, 1838, William
        P. Masters, post master and mail carrier at Chester, Mass.,
        d. Nov. 27, 1848.
284   7 Corinth E., b. Sept. 23, 1818; d. April 14, 1843.
285   8 Stephen N., b. Oct. 15, 1820; m. Jan. 20, 1846, Abigail
        Noony of Chester—a farmer, in Berlin, Conn.
          Ch. 9th Gen : 1 Maria A.   2 Earnest.   3 James.
          4 Lilly A.
286   9 Sarah A., b. May 10, 1822; m. Nov. 28, 1840; Alvah
        Foot, no children, d. June 3, 1850, Chester.
287 10 Brainard A., b. June 28, 1824; d. Jan. 19, 1825.
288 11 Brainard P., b. Feb. 4, 1828; m. Lucy Jane, Loverigewer.
          Ch. 10th Gen. : 1 Maria Jane b. Oct. 19, 1855; d.
          Feb. 22, 1863 — Chester.

17 SAMUEL LYMAN[7], youngest child of Dea. *Stephen[7]*,
b. May 21, 1787, issue of his second marriage to Hannah
Clark, m. Miriam S. Tinker of Chester, Oct. 26, 1809. He
lived in Chester, his native town; followed the occupation
of a farmer; was an officer and spent some time in Col. Enos
Foot's regiment of militia at South Boston in the war of
1814; was not engaged in any battle; after he came home,
he was promoted from one office in the militia to another,
to that of colonel of the 4th Regt., 1st brigade and 4th
division of the militia of Massachusetts. He held the
office of justice of the peace for Hampden and Hampshire counties for about 42 years or until he was 80 years
old. He removed from Chester to Southampton in April,
1842. He was Dea. of the Congregational Church in
Chester for more than 20 years, and after his removal to
Southampton, was again rechosen to this office. Children
by his wife Miriam S., ten in number, were all b. in
Chester.   *Southampton, Mass.*

Children, Eighth Generation:

289 1 Harriet, b. Oct. 10, 1810; d. Aug. 18, 1860.
290 2 Stephen, b. Dec. 24, 1811.
291 3 Wealthy, b. May 13, 1816; d. Jan. 25, 1821.
292 4 Miriam B., b. Jan. 4, 1819.
293 5 Samuel T., b. Sept. 18, 1820; d. Oct. 18, 1823.
294 6 Rufus, b. Oct. 5, 1822.
295 7 Samuel T., b. Aug. 5, 1824.
296 8 Emma S., b. July 31, 1826.
297 9 Charles B., b. Oct. 22, 1828.
298 10 Myra E., b. July 27, 1833.

289 HARRIET LYMAN^8, m. Nov. 6, 1833, Garry Munson, a merchant. *Chester, Mass.*

Children, Ninth Generation:

299 1 Myron A., b. May 5, 1835. He received a liberal education at Amherst, studied at the Theological Seminary at Andover, spent some months traveling in Europe, is now settled as pastor over the Congregational church in Pittsford, Vt.

300 2 Edward G., b. Sept. 23, 1839; a merchant, m. Caroline Brewster, of Waterford, N. Y., no children.

301 3 Horace W., b. Dec. 24, 1840; m. Nancy Avory, of Westfield, May 28, 1863. He lives in the town of Liberty, Susquehanna county, Penn., a dealer in hides and leather.
     Ch. 10th Gen.: 1 Wilson A., b. Sept. 29, 1864. 2 Emma H., b. Jan. 19, 1868. 3 Garry, b. 1870.

305 4 Homer W., b. Dec. 24, 1840; a merchant in Huntington, Mass., m. Addie Stanton, of Huntington, May 28, 1867; no children.

306 5 Samuel, b. June 14, 1844; m. Susan Hopkins, of Albany, May 21, 1868. He now lives in Albany, N. Y., a linen merchant.
     Ch. 10th Gen.: 1 Harriet, b. March 8, 1869. 2 Annie H., b. 1871.

309 6 Emma, b. Sept. 23, 1849; d. Oct. 14, 1863.

310 7 Cleora, b. May 8, 1852, is now attending school at Andover, Mass.

290 STEPHEN LYMAN^8, m. Julia S. Searl, of Chester, April 28, 1830. Lives in Southampton, grocer and R. R. agent. *Southampton, Mass.*

Children, Ninth Generation:

311 Martha L., b. Dec. 8, 1838; m. George R. Edwards, of Southampton, Dec., 1864, he was a officer stationed at Alexandria near the city of Washington in the great southern rebellion.
     Ch. 10th Gen.: 1 Josephine, b. Sept. 22, 1869; d. April 1, 1870.

313 2 Harriet E., b. Dec. 14, 1843 ; d. Sept. 3, 1844.
814 3 Harriet E., b. Feb. 12, 1846.
315 4 Stephen W., b. Oct. 10, 1850.
316 5 Freddie, b. Dec. 31, 1853.

Hattie E. Lyman, was m. June 20, 1871, to Wm. R. Stocking. He was ordained at Westfield on the June 19, as a missionary to Ooroomiah, in Persia; they sailed from N. Y., the 9th of August, 1871, and arrived at the place of destination in just ten weeks from the time of starting in good health and spirits.

292 MIRIAM B. LYMAN, m. Francis A. Strong of Southampton, Nov. 27, 1845; soon after marriage removed to, Ripon, Wisconsin. He is a miller, farmer, and dealer in flour. *Ripon, Wis.*

Children, Ninth Generation :
317 1 Eunice L., b. March 14, 1849
318 2 Louis H., b. April 25, 1852.
319 3 Sarah E., b. Oct. 20, 1854; d. July 5, 1865.
320 4 Abbie A., b. June 22, 1856.

294 RUFUS LYMAN[8], son of Dea. *Samuel*[7], m. Oct. 9, 1849, Sarah A. Bartlett of Southampton, a carpenter and joiner, lived a few years in Ripon. *Unionville, Ct.*

Children, Ninth Generation :
321 1 A dau., b. March 26, 1854.; d. March 28, 1854.
322 2 Clarence M., b. in Ripon, Wis., March 2, 1859.
323 3 Herbert B., b. in Southampton, March 15, 1863.

295 SAMUEL T. LYMAN[8], 3d son of Dea. *Samuel*[7], m. April 19, 1849, Augusta N. Kirkland, of Agawam, teacher, merchant, post master, and express agent. *Huntington, Mass.*

Children, Ninth Generation :
324 1 Charles P., b. Agawam, Dec. 25, 1851.
325 2, 3 Ellen A., and Emma, b. March 19, 1854, both d. in infancy.
327 4 Eugene K., b. Feb. 1, 1857, in Huntington.
328 5 Cassius S., b. March 2, 1860, at Huntington.
329 6 Robert H., b. March 3, 1864.

296 EMMA S. LYMAN[8], dau. of Dea. *Samuel*[7], m. Sept. 14, 1848, Samuel N. Coleman, farmer. *East Hartford, Mass.*

Children, Ninth Generation :
330 1 Frank B., b. Sept., 1849, merchant, Springfield.
331 2 Emerson N., b. July 26, 1851, farmer.
332 3 Carrie M., b. June 30, 1853 ; d. Sept. 16, 1855.
333 4 Ellen J., b. Aug. 16, 1855.

297 CHARLES B. LYMAN[8], 4th son of Dea. *Samuel*[7], m. May 8, 1851, L. Angeline Avery, farmer. *Southampton, Mass.*

Children, Ninth Generation :

334 1 Arthur W., b. April 20, 1852.
335 2 Flora A., b. Jan. 10, 1863 ; d. March 25, 1864.
336 3 Charlie L., b. May 11, 1865.

298 MYRA E. LYMAN[8], dau. of Dea. Samuel[7], m. Dec. 30, 1858, Solomon Richards, dealer in grain and flour.

Unionville, Ct.

Child, Ninth Generation :

337 1 George L., b. June 1, 1863.

Dea. Samuel Lyman, the youngest son of Dea. Stephen, now 86 years of age, has collected and recorded the genealogy of 337 of his kindred, the descendants of his father in just 100 years — the most prolific on record, in this, genealogy, of the whole lineage of the Lyman family.

2 TIMOTHY LYMAN[6], 2d son of Dea. Elias[5], Moses[4], Moses[3], John[2], Richard[1], 1744–1815. With his brother Stephen settled in Chester on adjacent farms, then a wilderness, where he lived through life highly esteemed as a man of strong native talent, an influential citizen holding various offices in the town, and a consistent Christian. His usefulness and happiness were overshadowed by peculiar mental aberrations in the last years of his life. He d. Oct. 12, 1815, aged 71; his wife Dorothy Kinney, b. Jan. 10, 1752, d. Dec. 11, 1829, aged 78. *Chester, Mass.*

Children, Seventh Generation :

338 1 Susannah, b. Nov. 6, 1770 ; m. 1789, Joseph Clapp, of Easthampton, a merchant of that place many years, and a prominent citizen. With one exception he held the office of town clerk longer than any citizen of the town. In 1810, he retired from mercantile life, and in 1830, removed to Homer, N. Y., where several of his children resided. He d. July 11, 1839, aged 74 years. His wife d. July 18, 1842, aged 72 years.

339 2 Achsah, b. Feb. 27, 1774 ; m. July 19, 1792, Dr. William Coleman, of Middlefield, Mass.

In 1816, Achsah and family removed to West Hartford, Conn.; in 1821, to Pittsfield, Mass.; in May, 1868, removed to Oberlin, Ohio, where she resided with her daughters in good health and a green old age, verging on 95 years, having been a housekeeper 76 years and a widow 10 years, after completing almost 66 years of married life with Dr. Coleman. So far as appears in this genealogy, she attained to the greatest age of any of the Lyman family. This venerable woman died Dec. 7, 1868, after an illness of a day or two. She was truly a mother in Israel. In early life she made a public profession of faith in her Saviour, and her whole subsequent life was one of unobstrusive but devoted piety. She retained the full possession of her faculties to the very last; and her dying hour, full of peace and joy, was the fitting close of a Christian course that extended beyond the number of years ordinarily allotted to human life.

> Cold in the dust the perished heart must lie,
> But that which warmed it once can never die.

340 3 Theodosia, b. Nov. 16, 1775, m. Jasper Brewster, lived several years in Washington, where were born four sons and one dau., in 1817; removed to Madison, Lake Co., Ohio, where Dea. B. died, Sept. 15, 1824, aged 55 years. Mrs. B. died April 1, 1851, aged 75 years.

341 4 Dorothy, b. April 24, 1780, m. Oct. 4, 1804, Edward Taylor of Montgomery, Mass., d. 1866.

342 5 Timothy, b. Aug. 30, 1782; m. Experience Bardwell, Jan. 6, 1808; lived on the homestead in Chester; died Dec. 22, 1837, aged 55.

343 6 Asahel, b. April 2, 1785; m. Jan. 23, 1810, Dolly Blair of Blandford, Mass. Engaged in mercantile life in several places.

The marriage of Timothy Lyman and Dorothy Kinney was one of the first, perhaps the first, in the town of Worthington, Mass., adjoining Chester, on the north-east. The town was not yet incorporated, neither do any records of the precinct run back to this period. Col. Kinney, the father of Dorothy, from Preston, Conn., had removed his family consisting of several daus. of adult age, into his log cabin inclosing a single compartment comprising kitchen, parlor and lodgings for the household, very inconvenient for the entertainment of lover and friend and the reciprocal expression of the " conscious flame." But the address of these wood nymphs was equal to the emergency. Lumber they had none, but the birch bark of the forest carefully prepared, afforded a substitute of silvery tint and polish that might grace the wainscoting of a princely parlor; and with their birch bark partitions they extemporized a cosy parlor for the reception of their friends. Within this birch bark parlor one hundred and two years since a youthful virtuous pair, with native energy and character competent for higher scenes, pledged their mutual faith and love, and were m. May 18, 1769. The husband was a man of rare ability, quick discernment, and sound judgment, very ready in repartee and capable of the keenest irony.

338 SUSANNAH LYMAN[7], m. Joseph Clapp of Easthampton, in 1789, who d. July 11, 1839, aged 74 years. She d. July 18, 1842, aged 72 years.   Homer, N. Y.

Children, Eighth Generation:

344 1 Eunice, b. Jan. 23, 1790; m. Edward Hunt, lived in various places, in N. Y.; d. in Camillus, about 1848.

    Ch. 9th Gen.: Three sons and a dau. 1 Harriet, who d. at Syracuse, one son d. young; two reside in Syracuse.

345   2 Hannah, b. April 11, 1792; m. Timothy Pomeroy, Feb. 4, 1810; resides in Buffalo, N. Y., and has resided in various places in western parts of N. Y.

346   3 Joseph, b. Oct. 10, 1793; d. early.

347   4 Susannah, b. Dec. 8, 1794; m. Jared Babcock; d. Oct. 15, 1835; Homer, N. Y.; had three sons and one daughter, who has one child of the tenth generation.

348   5 Joseph, b. July 8, 1796; removed to Homer, N. Y.; m. Sarah Bassett; d. March 13 1869.
      Ch. 9th Gen. : 1 Justin B.. had one daughter of the 10th generation.

349   6 Harriet, b. May 1,1798; m. July 14,1818,Thomas McKnight, sheriff of Cortland Co., N. Y., who d. Sept. 2, 1836.

350   7 Sumner G., b. March 10, 1800; a graduate from Yale College, 1822, settled in the ministry successively in Enfield, Mass., Chickopee, Mass., St. Johnsbury, Vt., and Sturbridge, Mass. Resided in Dorchester, Mass.; m. Pamelia Strong, Southampton, Mass. Two children, Frances Amelia and Henry Lyman.

351   8 Almira, b. Jan. 23, 1802; m. Charles McKnight of Truxton, N. Y.

352   9 Eliza, b. June 17, 1805; m. J. Babcock, of Homer — no children.

353   10 Alonzo, b. Oct. 15, 1808; married — no children.

354   11 Alender, b. Jan. 28, 1811; a graduate from Amherst College, 1837; studied theology at Andover; taught in Worthington and Pittsfield, Mass., and in Miss.; without any assignable cause his usefulness was interrupted by mental derangement; d. at Northampton, March 3, 1866, in the asylum for the insane, where he had lived many years.

Sumner Gallup Clapp, Cong. clergyman, b. in Easthampton, Mass., March 10, 1800; fitted for college at Plainfield, Mass., with Rev. Moses Hallock; at Amherst Academy, and then at Hartford Academy with Rev. Lyman Coleman; principal 1823–4 of Lincoln Academy, Newcastle, Me. Graduated at Yale Coll.,1824. Studied theology in Andover; pastor 1824–7; pastor Cong. Church in Enfield, Mass., 1828–37; Mass., of Third Cong. Church, Cabotville, Mass., 1837–50; pastor of South Cong. Church, St. Johnsbury, Vt., 1850–5; pastor of Cong. Church, Sturbridge, Mass., 1856–62; then preached one year in Lyndon, Vt.; his health failing, he ceased preaching in 1865. Married in 1829, Pamelia, dau. of Phinehas and Eunice Strong, of Southampton, Mass., by whom he had two children; Frances Amelia, b. Nov. 2, 1831, who is married to Franklin, son of Gov. E. Fairbanks, of St. Johnsbury, Vt., and has had three children, one only now surviving.—Henry Lyman, b. Aug. 2, 1836, was in Amherst College till junior year, when he was obliged by ill health to leave; now of the firm of Fairbanks & Co., 118 Milk street, Boston, and is m. to Susie Taintor, of Brookfield, Mass. After enjoying, through several of his declining years, the quiet home in Dorchester, Mass., provided for him by his children, died at his son's house in Boston, Jan. 20, 1869, aged sixty-eight years. He was "a faithful, true-hearted and most affectionate servant of Christ, and wherever he dwelt attracted the confidence and love of many hearts."

The close of life was serene, cheerfully bearing the burden of ill health, endearing himself by his sweet and modest worth to all around, he waited for the summons, which came suddenly at last, but not too suddenly for one who long had felt that "The Lord's appointment is the servant's hour." His record is on high; and though his labors have ended, his words of truth and love will long remain to bless those to whom he ministered.

345 HANNAH CLAPP[8], m. Timothy Pomeroy. *Buffalo, N. Y.*

Children, Ninth Generation :

355 1 Watson J., b. March 16, 1813, a farmer in Dwight Co., Ill., has had 9 children of the 10th generation, two sons in the army, one was severely wounded in the battle at Chickamauga.

356 2 Timothy Lyman, b. Sept. 16, 1815, is a Methodist minister in Ill., has had six children of the 10th generation; two sons enlisted in the army at the first call of their country, served through the war and returned unscathed. Two more noble boys never served in their country's defense; more than this, they are good soldiers of the cross of Christ.

357 3 Emerson C., b. March 10, 1818; m. Sept. 1, 1851, Jane E. Lyon, Otisco, N. Y., resides in Ill., a professional teacher, has 2 children of the 10th generation.

358 4 Angeline, b. March 20, 1820; m. Henry Baker, one of the earliest volunteers for the defense of the country; d. in Jackson, Tenn., July 5, 1862, of disease contracted in the army.

    Ch. 10th Gen.: 1 An only son, enlisted in the service of the country at its last call.

359 5 Worcester E., b. Sept. 9, 1822; d. young, June 18, 1826.

360 6 Eveline, b. Sept. 6, 1824; m. E. B. Collins, of Enfield, Mass.; no children.

361 7 Worcester E., b. Oct. 4, 1826; d. April 29, 1863 — mechanic; has four children of the 10th generation.

349 HARRIET CLAPP[8], m. Thomas McKnight. *Ripon, Wis.*

Children, Ninth Generation

362 1 Harriet C., b. May 28, 1820; m. Jan. 18, 1843, Rev. Perly Wark, Wisconsin.

    Ch. 10th Gen.: 1 Edward P., b. Jan. 27, 1845; d. Nov. 24, 1853. 2 Wayland C., b. Nov. 9, 1847; d. June 5, 1851. 3 Lawrence McKnight, b. Nov. 5, 1851; d. April 16, 1855. 4 Charles P., b. Dec. 13, 1854.

363 2 Albina E., b. Jan. 20, 1823 ; m. March 31, 1842, Hiram H.
   Meade, banker in Ripon, Wisconsin.
      Ch. 10*th Gen.* : 1 Elizabeth H., b. June 23, 1846.
   2 Louisa, b. Dec. 6, 1849.
364 3 Sophronia J., b. July 19, 1826 ; m. Aug. 1, 1851, Ripon, Wis.
      Ch. 10*th Gen.* : 1 Nelson C., b. Nov. 13, 1852 ; d. Jan.
   13, 1864.
356 5 Sarah E., b. Oct. 5, 1828; m. Sept 16, 1847, George N. Lyman,
   son of Asahel Lyman, a merchant and farmer, Ripon, Wis.
      Ch. 10*th Gen.* : 1 Ceylon E., b. Oct. 13, 1849. 2
   Hattie F., b. May 23, 1852. 3 Alice E., b. June 17,
   1856 ; d. Aug. 17, 1858. 4 George N., Jr., b. June 11,
   1861.
367 5 Susan S., b. March 6, 1833 ; m. Sept. 12, 1854, Edward P.
   Brockway, banker in Ripon.
      Ch. 10*th Gen.* : 1 William S., b. Dec. 29, 1855. 2
   Mary O., b. Jan. 4, 1858.
370 6 Sumner J., b. April 2, 1836 — a lumber merchant. Hanni-
   bal, Missouri.

351 ALMIRA CLAPP[8], b. Jan. 23, 1802 ; m. Charles Mc-
Knight, of Truxton, N. Y.   *Truxton, N. Y.*
      Children, Ninth Generation :
371 1 Lyman, d. in California.
372 2 Alonzo, merchant, d. in Springfield, Mass.
373 3 John,   } both merchants in Springfield, in extensive busi-
374 4 William, }   ness, both married.
375 5 Mrs. Newell, lives in Springfield.
376 6 Mrs. Shedd, d. in Springfield, leaving two sons of 10th gen.
377 7 Mrs. Coats, Homer, N. Y.
378 8 Mrs. Hawley, Springfield.
379 9 A daughter, unmarried.

339 ACHSAH LYMAN[7], m. July 19, 1792, William Coleman,
M.D., of Middlefield, Mass., who d. at Pittsfield, Mass.,
April 22, 1858, in the 93d year of his age. She d. at
Oberlin, Ohio, Dec. 7, 1868, in the 95th year of her age.
      Children, Eighth Generation
389 1 William, b. Jan. 15, 1794; d. at Montrose. Lee Co., Iowa,
   May 5, 1859. Lydia Kilborn, his wife, d. Dec. 29, 1856.
      Ch. 9*th Gen.* : 1 George, b. May 5, 1825. Fort
   Madison, Iowa.
381 2 Rev. Lyman, D.D., b. June 14, 1796; graduated at Yale,
   1817; m. Sept. 21, 1826, Maria Flynt, of Munson, Mass.,
   who d. Jan. 11, 1871.
382 3 Sarah, b. May 16, 1799; m July 26, 1832, L. L. Rice, of
   Ravenna, Ohio.
      Ch. 9*th Gen.* : 1 Mary Sophronia, b. Nov. 29, 1838;
   graduated at Oberlin ; m. at Oberlin, Ohio, Aug 5, 1869,

John M. Whitney, M. D., and lives at Honolulu, Sandwich Islands. 2 Rev. William Holden, b. Jan. 4, 1841; grad. Oberlin College, studied theology there; m. at Oberlin, April 25, 1867, Libbie P. Kinney.

    Ch. 10th Gen.: 1 Lewis George, b. Feb. 6, 1868; d. Aug. 29, 1868. 2 Harold Kinney, b. Dec. 8, 1869, Oberlin, Ohio.

383 ̃4 Sophronia, b. Jan. 19, 1802, ; d. Feb. 24, 1826.

384 5 Fanny, b. May 20, 1804.

380 WILLIAM COLEMAN[8], b. Jan. 15, 1794; d. at Montrose, Lee Co., Iowa, May 5, 1859.

    Children, Ninth Generation :

385 1 George Lyman, b. May 5, 1825, Fort Madison, Iowa.

    Ch. 10th Gen. : 1 Charles K., b. Oct. 25, 1855. 2 Edward N.. b. Jan. 31, 1861. 3 William H., b. Jan. 8, 1865. 4 George H., b Jan. 24, 1867.

381 REV. LYMAN COLEMAN[8], D. D., b. June 14, 1796, grad. from Yale, 1817. On leaving college, was three years in the Latin Grammar School at Hartford, Ct., then four and a half years tutor in Yale College; studied theology there; was seven years pastor of the church in Belchertown, Mass.; afterwards five years principal of the Burr Seminary, Vt., and subsequently five years principal of the English department of Phillips Academy, in Andover, Mass.; spent the year 1842–3 in study in Germany, and in travel. Since then has resided at Amherst, Mass., three years, at Princeton, N. J., two years, and in Phila.; nine years, in connection with different literary institutions; at Princeton, as professor of German in the college from which he received the degree of S.T.D. Author of the *Antiquities of the Christian Church*, a translation and compilation from Augusti, and other German authors; of the *Apostolical and Primitive Church, Popular in its Government, and Simple in its Worship ; Historical Geography of the Bible ; Ancient Christianity Exemplified in the Private Life of the Primitive Christians and in the Original Institutions, Offices, Ordinances, and Rites of the Church*; and an *Historical Text Book and Atlas of Biblical Geography*, a large 8vo, *A Manual on Prelacy, and Ritualism. The Apostolical and Primitive Church — Popular in its Government, simple and informal in its Worship.* 12mo; *Genealogy of the Lyman Family.* These, with one exception, have been republished in England. To these may be added several articles published in American Quarterlies: *Historical Sketch of the Christian Sabbath ; Pagan Origin of the Festivals of the Church ; Eusebius as an*

Desert, past and present compared; Samaritans, a Remnant of the Ten Tribes; The Great Crevasse of the Jordan and the Red Sea. Traveled in 1856-7 one year in Europe, Egypt, the Desert and Palestine. For several years has been Prof. of Ancient Languages in Lafayette College, Easton, Pa.

Easton, Pa.

Children, Ninth Generation:

386 1 Olivia, b. Oct. 10, 1827; d. Sept. 28, 1847.
387 2 Eliza M., b. Jan , 1832; m. June 6, 1861, Rev. J. L. Dudley, of Middletown, Conn.; d. June 3, 1871, at Milwaukee, Wis.

340 THEODOSIA LYMAN[7], m. Jasper Brewster, who d. Sept. 15, 1824, aged 55 years. She d. April 1, 1851, aged 75 years. *Madison, O.*

Children, Eighth Generation ·

388 1 Jasper, b. Nov. 9, 1797; m. 1st, Lucetta Freeman, Sept. 1832, Madison, O.
　　Ch. 9th Gen : 1 Mary L., b. Aug. 17, 1833 2 Jasper Lyman, b. 1835; d. Oct. 4, 1838. 3 Emily, b Sept., 1837; d. Oct. 9, 1838. 4 Jasper F., b. ...... 1843; d. July 1, 1844; m. 2d, April 18, 1865, Mrs. Rebecca T. Safford.
392 2 Sidney L., b. in Washington, Mass., Dec. 2, 1799; m. 1st, Sarah Withrow, June 28, 1831. She d. Oct. 17, 1838; m. 2d, Ann Kennell, d. May 3, 1850; m. 3d, Catharine E. Smith, d. March 6, 1854. Sidney L., d. April 25, 1864.
　　Ch. 9th Gen.: By 1st m. 1 Samuel, b. May 14, 1832; d. March 26, 1844. 2 Lucia, b. April 25, 1834; m. Silas W. Camp, Feb. 20, 1853, had one son William. 3 George, b. Sept. 27, 1836; m. Mary J. Hannon, Nov., 1858, had one dau. By 3d m. 4 Samuel Dwight, b. Aug. 6, 1851.
397 3 Marshall, b. in Washington, Mass., 1802; m. Chloe Smith, 1836, in Madison, Ohio; they have six children, one daughter and five sons; graduated at Williams College.
406 4 Emerson Wadsworth, b. Washington, Mass., April 2, 1804; m. Harriet Keep, Jan., 1838, Madison, Ohio.
　　Ch. 9th Gen.: 1 Julia, b. Oct. 19, 1838. 2 Oliver R., b. March 9, 1841; soldier in the 105th Ohio Regt.; wounded in battle; d. Oct. 18, 1862, at Perryville, Kentucky. 3 Robert L., b. Oct. 4, 1843. 4 Joseph W., b. Dec. 17, 1846; d. Feb. 2, 1850. 5 Jenett, b. Nov. 6, 1850.
412 5 Mary Amanda, only daughter of Dea. Jasper and Theodosia L. Brewster, b. April 26, 1807; m. May 17, 1836, Philander Raymond, of N. Y., Brady's Bend, Pa., and Bowling Green, Ohio.

Ch. 7th Gen.: 1 Brewster Gray, b. Nov. 7, 1839, New York; d. July 4, 1857, a modest, sober, lovely youth, dutiful and reverential to his parents, affectionate to all, with an eager thirst for knowledge, and maturity of mind beyond his years. He was a ready proficient in his studies, and at his decease was prepared to enter college with rare promise of future usefulness in the ministry. 2 Alanson Dwight, b. March 8, 1842, at Brady's Bend. Armstrong Co., Pa.; d. July 10, 1857. 3 Mary Celestia, b. Dec. 12, 1843, in Brady's Bend, Armstrong Co., Pa, 4 Henry Scott, b. May 15, 1847, in Brady's Bend, Armstrong Co., Pa., d. Feb. 18, 1848. 5 William Conrad, b. Dec. 17, 1848, in Brady's Bend, Armstrong Co., Pa.; d. at Unionville, Ohio, July 7, 1857. 6 Henry Sidney, b. March 6, 1851, at Orleans Furnace, Sugar Creek, Venango Co., Pa.

389 Mary L. Brewster[9], dau. of *Jasper*[8], m. Philo T. Safford, Oct. 11, 1860.	*Madison, O.*

Children, Tenth Generation :

419 1 Kate L., b. Aug. 11, 1861.
420 2 Grace, b. Feb. 8, 1863.
421 3 Bertha, b. April 8, 1865.
422 4 Mary, b. Jan. 15, 1868.

341 Dorothy Lyman[7], m. Edward Taylor, of Montgomery, Mass., who d. 1866.	*Huntington, Mass.*

Children, Eighth Generation :

423 1 Eunice Nash, b. July 29, 1805; d. Oct. 13, 1829.
424 2 Julia, b. Dec. 9, 1807; d. March 13, 1870, at Huntington, Mass., leaving 8 or 10,000 dollars for different objects of charity.
425 3 Jonathan L., b. Dec. 23, 1812; d. Oct. 11, 1827.
426 4 Edward M., b. June 2, 1817; m. Ellen Copeland, Oct. 10, 1860, Saginaw City, Michigan.
    Ch. 9th Gen.: 1 Edward, b. March 14, 1863. 2 Henry C., b. Dec. 19, 1865.

342 Timothy Lyman[7], m. Exprience Bardwell, Jan. 6, 1808. He d. Dec. 22, 1837, aged 55 yrs.	*Chester, Mass.*

Children, Eighth Generation :

429 1 Washington, b. June 6, 1810; m. Dec. 1, 1844, Harriet B. Rowzee, of Uniontown, Ky. He has lived in Kentucky, engaged in agricultural pursuits, d. Aug. 20, 1870, at Tangepaho or Union Landing, La., no children.
430 2 Louisa, b. April 8, 1813; m. May 1, 1832, Warren A. Reed, resided in Belchertown, and Northampton, Mass. and d. in Troy, N.Y., Sept. 10, 1845.

Ch. 9th Gen.: 1 Sarah L., b. March 24, 1834; m. Jan. 1, 1856, Thomas J. Dowty. Fort Adams, Miss. 2 Lyman Coleman, b, June 7, 1838, a grad. from Jacksonville Coll., Ill., engaged in teaching at the south, joined the rebel army, was many months a prisoner near Columbus, Ohio, now teaching a school in Louisiana. 3 George S., b. Dec. 1, 1840; d. Sept. 1, 1841. 4 Ellen Loraine, b. July 19, 1843; m. Aug. 30, 1864, Seth Lathrop, of South Hadley, Mass. 5 Elizabeth W., b. March 13, 1846.

436 3 Edward, b. July 30, 1815, unmarried.

437 4 Sarah, b. Aug. 14, 1817; d. Nov. 25, 1826.

438 5 Timothy, b. Aug. 28, 1819; was graduated from Amherst College in 1844; ordained 1850, and for fifteen years a missionary in the west and south; installed in Killingworth, Conn,, in 1866; m. June 15, 1854, Valeria Van Reed Rinehart, who d. Oct. 11, 1857; m. July 9, 1860, Helen Durand; dismissed from the church in Killingworth in 1869; acting pasotr of the church in Southwick, Mass.

Ch. 9th Gen.: 1 William B., b. May 8, 1855. 2 John Van Reed, b. June 13, 1857.

441 6 Wealthy, b. Oct. 6, 1821; d. July 19, 1841.

442 7 Ebenezer E., b. May 14, 1824; d. April 11, 1839.

443 8 Joseph B., b. Oct. 6, 1829; a graduate from Yale College, 1850, studied law in Tenn., m. July 14, 1858, Laura E. Baker, from Maine, settled in New Orleans in the profession of law to avoid conscription, engaged as commissary in the rebel army, March, 1863; in Sept., 1868, after many adventures made his way through the rebel lines and joined his family in Boston, who had made their escape by sea from New Orleans. In 1865, settled in Stamford, Conn., where he was engaged in literary efforts as a profession.

Ch. 9th Gen.: 1 Alexandria Steele, b. in N. O., April 8, 1860. 2 Charles Washington, b. in N. O., Nov. 5, 1861. 3 Harriette Frances, b. Dec. 12 1864; d. Feb. 15, 1865. 4 Laura Eugena, b. Dec. 24, 1866. 5 Carrie F., b. in 1869. 6 Joseph B., Jr., b. in 1870. 7 Clarence A., b. in 1870.

Joseph B. Lyman, d. suddenly at Richmond Hill, L. I., Jan. 28, 1872. He was from childhood a great reader and good scholar. Had an original turn of mind and when a child greatly amused the neighbors by his smart sayings and philosophical turn of mind. He was early inclined to study for college and was willing to make great sacrifices to fit for college and support himself while there.

He taught for two or three years at the south, and studied law and was admitted to the bar, in New Orleans. He was ambitious and a very careful and diligent student. He was just beginning to gain a position in his profession when the war broke out, which eventually drove him north, impoverished and disappointed. He was remarkably cheerful in misfortune. Always looking on the bright side and when he went to New York, in 1864, he had nothing but his head and hands to depend upon. He had no one to introduce him, or to help him into a position, or support him and his increasing family till he could get a start. He wrote articles for newspapers on topics of interest, depending upon their own merits to introduce them. They were, many of them, published, though the writer was unknown. He made a demand for his writing by their true merit. He wrote most of the sketches of that very popular book *The Women of the War*, though his name does not appear. He also wrote several articles on agriculture and together with his wife, published *The Philosophy of Housekeeping*, and soon became the agricultural editor of the *New York Tribune*.

Extract from the Weekly Tribune.

" These experimental essays brought him into communication with New York journalism, and he came to this city to begin the useful and successful career which has been suddenly cut short by death. He acted for two years as agricultural editor of the *World*, next became managing editor of *Hearth and Home*, from which position he came to the *Tribune*, where he filled for the last four years of his life, with unusual energy and intelligence the chair of agricultural editor. He traveled extensively west and south, and his conscientiousness and sagacity made his lettters especially valuable. He was a prominent member of the Farmer's Club and Rural Club, and in honorary capacity connected with many horticultural and agricultural societies. The Farmer's Club afforded him congenial means of diffusing practical knowledge on current subjects. This club owes largely its importance and usefulness to his zealous cooperation." He was a very hard working man, would undertake what would seem impossible to other men. In all his labors for the diffusion of knowledge and progress in agriculture, he was imbued with the thought that he was doing good. He was for many years a professing Christian. In his last sickness when inquired of, by his wife, about his feelings, his reply was, ' Christ has been the head centre of my faith, for 20 years, I have no fear.' "

343 ASAHEL LYMAN[7], son of *Timothy[6]*, of Chester, Mass., b. in Chester, 1785; d. at Cortlandville, N. Y., Feb. 19, 1847, aged 67; m. Jan. 23, 1810, to Miss Dolly Blair, daughter of Rufus Blair, of Blandford, Mass., who was b. March 3, 1787; d. Aug. 17, 1856, aged 69 years and 5 months. Both were members of the Presbyterian church at Cortlandville, N. Y. After marriage they resided about two years in Worthington, Mass., removed to Milford, N. Y., for a short time, from thence to Brookfield, N. Y., and in 1815,

to Cortlandville, where they resided to the day of their
death.   *Cortlandville, N. Y.*

Children, Eighth Generation. :

450 1 Dolly Ann Frances, b. at Worthington, Mass., Oct. 26, 1810;
m. Ceylon North, of Fly Creek, N. Y., July 17, 1833,
resided after marriage at Fly Creek, N. Y., until 1859,
moved to Ripon, Wisconsin, where they resided until
1864, moved to Oswego, N. Y., where they now reside.
Both are members of the Congregational church in
Oswego. In general commission business, firm of C.
North & Son.

Ch. 8th Gen. : 1 Charles Gilbert. 2 Frances Amelia,
d. ; a young lady greatly beloved, a charming example of
youthful piety. 3 Clayton Henry. 4, and 5 Albert and
Asahel, twins.

456 2 Asahel Phelps, b. at Brookfield, N. Y., Jan. 23, 1814; m.
Cynthia Higby, dau. of Anson Higby at Fly Creek, Oct.
26, 1837, resided at Cortlandville, N. Y., after m. engaged in mercantile business until about 1845, moved
to Sheboygan, Wisconsin, where he now resides, engaged
in shipping and farming business. Attends the Presbyterian church of which Mrs. Lyman is a member. They
have one son.

Ch. 9th Gen. : Sylvester Blair, b. in Cortlandville,
N. Y., about 1839, m. Alice Higby, dau. of Richard
Higby of Fly Creek, about 1867. Engaged in shipping
business with his father at Sheboygan; attends the
Presbyterian church.

458 3 George Nelson Lyman, b. at Cortlandville, N. Y., Nov. 16,
1817; m. to Elizabeth Sarah McKnight, of Truxton,
N. Y., Sept. 16, 1837. Resided a number of years after
marriage at Sheboygan Falls; now resides at Ripon, Wis.,
engaged in general speculation, and has been very successful in business. The family attend the Baptist church
of which Mrs. Lyman is a member.

Ch. 9th Gen. : 1 Ceylon Emery. 2 Hattie Frances. 3
Alice Elizabeth, and George Nelson, Jr., all reside with
their parents except Alice who d. some years since about
1858.

463 4 Franklin Coleman, b. in Cortlandville, Sept. 11, 1820; d.
at Cortlandville, Oct. 26, 1826, aged 6 years and 6 months.

464 5 Henry Franklin, b. at Cortlandville, N. Y., May 3, 1830;
m. Sarah North, daughter of Stephen North, of Fly Creek,
Jan. 20, 1853; after marriage resided at Cortlandville,
engaged in studies preparatory for the ministry, d. Nov.
3, 1856, aged 26 years and 6 months. Mr. and Mrs. Lyman
are both members of the Presbyterian church at Cortlandville.

450 DOLLY ANN FRANCES LYMAN[8], b. at Worthington, Mass., Oct. 26, 1810; m. July 17, 1833, Ceylon North, of Fly Creek, N. Y.   *Oswego, N. Y.*

Children, Ninth Generation:

470 1 Charles Gilbert, b. Aug .9, 1835, at Fly Creek ,N. Y.; m. Martha Ann Young, daughter of Andrew Young, of Fly Creek, March 25, 1855, had have five children; dry goods salesman.

    Ch. 10th Gen.: 1 Dolly Ann Frances. 2 Mary Amelia. 3 Cora Martha. 4, 5 Twins, boys, Charles Andrew and William Irving. The daughters are all dead, the sons living, aged seven years and six months. Mrs. North is a member of the Congregational church in Oswego.

471 2 Frances Amelia, b. at Fly Creek, N. Y., July 28, 1837; member of the Congregational church in Oswego; d. 1870.

472 3 Ceylon Henry North, b. Oct. 18, 1842, at Fly Creek, N .Y., m. Oct. 18, 1863, at Ripon, Wis., Sarah Emma Brown, dau. of Avery Brown, of Ripon.

    Ch. 10th Gen.: 1 Alice Adelia and Clara Belle. They now reside at Green Bay, Wis., and are members of the Presbyterian church at that place. Ceylon Henry is in grocery business at Green Bay, firm name, Crandall & North.

473 4 Albert and Asahel, twin boys, b. at Fly Creek, May 10, 1845; d. May 11, 1845.

474 5 George Lyman North, b. at Fly Creek, Dec. 23, 1846, resides at Oswego, N. Y., in commission business with his father, firm, C. North & Son,

The whole number of the descendants of Timothy Lyman is 161; all who have attained adult age are nearly without exception, communicants in the church of Christ, and they who have died in early life have manifested a Christian faith and hope. Eight have been graduates of college, of whom six have engaged in the ministry, and two have died in course of preparation for that office. One is a minister in the Methodist church.

3 EUNICE LYMAN[7], 2d dau. of Dea. *Elias[6]*, m. May 27, 1776, Lemuel Pomeroy, oldest son of Lemuel of Southampton, who d. Nov. 25, 1788, aged 39.   *Southampton, Mass.*

Children, Eighth Generation:

481 1 Eunice, b. March 30, 1777; d. May 23, 1777.

482 2 Lemuel, b. Aug. 18, 1778 : d. in Pittsfield, Aug., 1849.

483 3 Gamaliel, b. Feb. 15, 1780; d. May 12, 1856, in Southampton, aged 76.

484 4 Eunice, b. May 11, 1782; d. April 20, 1808, unmarried.

485 5 Theodore, b. March 14, 1785; d. about 1860.

486 6 Harriet, b. May 23, 1787; d. Oct. 17, 1824; m. William
    Atwater of Westfield, Mass., had 7 children, of whom the
    youngest John, M.D., lives in Westfield.

482 LEMUEL POMEROY[7], m. Hart Lester, woolen manufacturer; for many years received also large contracts from U. S.
government for manufacture of guns, the only private
armory in the country, d. Aug., 1849, a man of great
energy, executive ability and business capacity, by which
he acquired a large estate.   *Pittsfield, Mass.*

Children, Eighth Generation :
488 1 Lemuel, m. Aurelia Holliston, lived in Pittsfield; d. about
       1855, leaving 3 children.
           Ch. 9th. Gen.; 1 Lemuel. 2 Mary. 3 William.
492 2 Olivia, m. Prof. Chester Dewey.
           Ch. 9th Gen.: 1 Chester. 2 Sarah. 3 Elizabeth. 4
       Charles.
496 3 Elizabeth, m. Prof. Isaac Jackson, Union Coll.
           Ch. 9th Gen.: 1 William. 2 Gertrude. 3 Julia. 4
       George. 5 Elizabeth.
501 4 Parthenia, m. Henry A. Brewster, Washington, D. C.
           Ch. 9th Gen.: 1 Pomeroy. 2 Eunice. 3 Robert.
502   Eunice, m. Dr. Day of Syracus.
           Ch. 9th Gen.: 1 Edward. 2 Ellen. 3 George. 2d hus-
       band, Geo. T. M. Davis, N. Y.
503 6 Harriet, m. Collins Cheesebro.
           Ch. 9th Gen.: 1 Dewey. 2 Collins. 3 Fanny.
504 7 Emily, m. A. S. Dodge.
           Ch. 9th Gen.: 1 George. 2 Mary O. 3 Theodore.
       4 Pomeroy, she d. at Washington, 1867.
506 8 Theodore.
           Ch. 9th Gen.: 1 Fanny. 2 Silas. 3 Margaret. 4
       Mary. 5 Theodore.
509 9 Robert, m. Mary Jenkins.
           Ch. 9th Gen.: 1 Mary. 2 Agnes. 3 Maria C. 4
       Jessie. 5 Belle. 6 Catharine.

483 GAMALIEL POMEROY[7], lived in Southampton and had
eight children.   *Southampton, Mass.*
Children, Eighth Generation :
529 1 Eunice m. Daniel Chapman, resides in N. Y., no children.
530 2 Betsey, m. Daniel Kingsley of Northampton, Mass.
           Ch. 9th Gen.: 1 George, Freeport, Ill. 2 Wm. S.,
       Northampton. 3 Mary T.
534 3 Mary, m. Wm. Dickinson, Northampton, no children.
535 4 Jonathan, Minneapolis, Minnesota; three children.
536 5 Henrietta, deceased.

537 6 Harriet, deceased.
538 7 Jane, Southampton.
539 8 Charles, has three children.

485 Theodore Pomeroy[8], a physician in Utica, N. Y.; d. about 1860; 8 children, of whom several have children, names and number unknown.

5 Elias Lyman[6], 3d son of Dea. *Elias[5]*, b. in Southampton, June 27, 1752; m. Eunice Sheldon, d. May 26, 1804—farmer.   *Southampton, Mass.*
   Children, Seventh Generation:
551 1 Joseph, b. July 26, 1777; d. June 10, 1849.
552 2 Eunice, b. Dec. 25, 1778; d. June 23, 1859.
553 3 Simeon, b. April 15, 1781; d. July 12, 1841.
554 4 Noah, b. April 17, 1783; d. Dec. 16, 1803.
555 5 Luther, b. July 21, 1786; d. May 31, 1832.
559 6 Hannah, b. May 1, 1788.
557 7 Anna, b. Aug. 18, 1794; d. 1795.
559 8 Elias, d. in infancy.
560 9 Anna, b. May 18, 1796.

551 Joseph Lyman[7], b. July 26, 1777; d. June 10, 1849, m. June 13, 1810, Submit Clark, of Southampton, b. Jan. 30, 1774; d. Sept. 23, 1832.   *Southampton, Mass.*
   Child, Eighth Generation:
560*1 Joseph, b. June 9, 1811; m. Oct. 23, 1845, Maria Spencer, of E. Hartford — no children — carpenter and joiner.

552 Eunice Lyman[7], b. Dec. 25, 1778; d. June 23, 1859, m. Aug. or Sept. 1797, Phineas Strong, miller and dealer in grain.   *Southampton, Mass.*
   Children, Eighth Generation:
561 1 Elizabeth S., b. Oct. 5, 1798.
562 2 Pamelia, b. July 21, 1800; m. Rev. Sumner G. Clapp.
563 3 Eunice L., Feb. 17, 1803.
564 4 Phinehas, Jr., b. May 6, 1805.
565 5 Noah L., b. June 21, 1807.
566 6 Mary, b. July 10, 1809.
567 7 Horace E., b. November 9, 1811; d. Jan. 22, 1836.
568 8 Alexander Hanson, b. Feb. 17, 1814; d. Sept. 15, 1840.
569 9 Francis A., b. Feb. 15, 1818.

567 Horace E. Lyman[8], m. March 5, 1832, Sybella B. Clapp of Southampton, moved to Brunson, Ohio, where he d. farmer.   *Brunson, O.*

Children, Ninth Generation.

570 1 Henry R., b. Jan. 13, 1833; m. July, 1858, Addah H. Forbes.
571 2 Horace E., b. Feb. 2, 1834; d. March 11, 1834.

561 ELIZABETH S. LYMAN[8], m. July 8, 1827, Oliver Clark, of Southampton, who. d. Dec. 7, 1855 — seller of goods.   *Springfield, Ohio.*

Children, Ninth Generation :

572 1 Mary E., b. Oct. 13, 1828; d. June 25, 1844.
573 2 Charles E., b. July 25, 1830.
574 3 Caroline A., b. March 1, 1832.
575 4 Sarah L., b. Jan. 15, 1834; d. April 23, 1846.
576 5 John G., b. Feb. 1, 1836.
577 6 Lewis S., b. Nov. 7, 1837, in Massachusetts.
578 7 Emily H., b. Sept. 26, 1839.
579 8 Oliver S.   ⎱ Twins;   b. Nov. 13, 1841; Cynthia L., d.
580 9 Cynthia L. ⎰   Dec. 10, 1845.
582 10 Hiram Franklin, b. March 7, 1845.

573 CHARLES E. CLARK[9], m. May 7, 1855, Mary E. Christie, of Springfield, Ohio.   *Dayton, Ohio.*

Children, Tenth Generation

583 1 Fanny S., b. March 7, 1856.
584 2 Oliver L., b. July 9, 1862.

576 JOHN G. CLARK[8], m. Jan. 5, 1865, Mary E. Ward, of Springfield, Ohio; one daughter Kitty, b. March 14, 1866.

577 EMILY H. CLARK[8], m. May 8, 1862, Charles C. Petts, of Springfield, Ohio. He afterwards removed to Boston where he d. Sept. 24, 1866.

563 EUNICE L. STRONG[8], never m. but she has been a very useful help and friend among the sick and afflicted, and matron among the freedmen, of Washington.

565 NOAH L. STRONG[8], m. Sept. 28, 1837, Elizabeth Fowler, of Westfield.

Children, Ninth Generation :

585 1 Josephine E., b. Aug. 23, 1838; unmarried; spent two years after the close of the war in instructing the freedmen and children at the south.
586 2 Sarah L., b. June 11, 1842; m. Sept. 3, 1862, Edwin Emerson Kingsley, of Boston, merchant. A son, Frederick S., b. June 5, 1865.

564 PHINEHAS STRONG[8], m. Oct. 1, 1829, Fanny Pomeroy, of Southampton — a farmer.   *Onondaga Valley, N. Y.*

Children, Ninth Generation .

587 1 Charles A., b. May 3, 1831, unmarried — a fruit grower. Onondaga Valley, N. Y.

588 2 An infant daughter, b. March 18, 1832 ; d. April 1, 1832.

589 3 Edwin A., b. Jan. 3, 1834, resides in Grand Rapids, Mich. Teacher of high school, and superintendent of city school, m. Aug. 8, 1861, Hattie J. Pomeroy.
> *Ch. 10th Gen. :* 1 Lilly M., b. April 5, 1863. 2 Fanny P., b. March 10, 1866.

590 4 Horace E., b. Aug. 5, 1836, harness and trunk maker, Manhattan, Kansas; m. Dec. 6, 1866, Nellie B. Norton.
> *Ch. 10th Gen. :* 1 Frank B., b. Nov. 15, 1868.

591 5 James B. T., b. Oct. 7, 1838 ; d. Aug. 27, 1842.

566 MARY S. STRONG[8], m. Aug. 25, 1840, Thomas Hall, the minister of Dalton.

Child, Ninth Generation :

592 1 One daughter, Mary, b. May 6, 1842, in Dalton ; m. March 8, 1865, Henry W. Bosworth, a lawyer of Springfield, Mass.
> *Ch. 10th Gen. :* 1 One son Henry, b. March 16, 1868.

568 ALEXANDER H. STRONG[8], m. 1838, Priscilla G. Redd, of Vicksburg, Miss. He d. Sept. 15, 1840, at Narogdoshee, Texas; his widow, Priscilla, m. a German, by the name of Vogh, who shot her dead, July 25, 1854, at Vicksburg.

Children, Ninth Generation .

594 1 Alexander Hanson, b. Nov. 25, 1839, resides in Vicksburg.

595 2 Elizabeth D., b. May 22, 1841 ; m. Sept. 31, 1862, George Knapp, of Boston.
> *Ch. 10th Gen. :* 1 Clara, b. in Iowa, Sept. 28, 1859.
> 2 Jessie, b. in Cass, Iowa, Sept. 28, 1868 ; d. Jan. 28, 1869.

553 SIMEON LYMAN[7], son of *Elias[6]*, m. Dec. 3, 1801, Anna Clapp, of Southampton.

Children, Eighth Generation :

598 1 Lysander, b. Jan. 6, 1802 ; d. June 3, 1803.

599 2 Lysander, b. July 3, 1803 ; d. June, 1809.

600 3 Noah, b. July 22, 1805 ; d. Nov. 20, 1825.

601 4 Charles, b. June 27, 1807.

602 5 Lewis, b. Nov. 1, 1809 ; d. Dec. 26, 1844.

604 6 Elias, b. March 17, 1812 ; d. Dec. 13, 1852.

605 7 Benjamin, b. June 20, 1820 ; m. Mary Pomeroy, of Westfield ; one son, Herbert.

606 8 Juliann, b. June 16, 1825.

539 CHARLES LYMAN[8], m. Sophia Page of York.
Children, Ninth Generation .
607 1 Charles, b. March 12, 1839.
608 2 Anna, b. Aug. 29, 1842; m. June 10, 1858, John Woodruff, no children.
609 3 Morris W., b. Feb. 14, 1852.

559 HANNAH LYMAN[7], 2d dau. of *Elias*[6], m. Nov. 15, 1815, Theodore Sheldon of New Marlboro; a farmer.
Children, Eighth Generation:
609*1 Joseph P., b. Oct. 13, 1816.
610 2 Corinthia E., b. June 30, 1818.
611 3 Seth,   } twins, b. May 27, 1821.
612 4 Sarah Strong, }

610 CORINTHIA E. SHELDON[8], m. Oct. 4, 1846, Cephas Clary, of Deerfield.
Children, Ninth Generation:
613 1 Sarah Sheldon, b. Sept. 19, 1847; m. Oct. 22, 1868, Edward P. Clapp, of Deerfield.
614 2 Mary L., b. Oct. 2, 1850; d. June, 1852.
615 3 Martha, b. Dec. 21, 1852; d. Feb. 27, 1868.
616 4 Ella Almira, b. Feb. 19, 1855; d. Feb. 8, 1856.
617 5 Elihu Theodore, b. March 29, 1857; d. Oct. 3, 1859.

611 SETH LYMAN[8], m. Oct. 6, 1851, Phebe Ann Woodruff, of Vermont.
Children, Ninth Generation:
618 1 An infant son, b. and d. June 14, 1854.
619 2 Sarah Addah, b. June 26, 1859.
620 3 Emma Woodruff, b. May 16, 1861.
621 4 Hattie, b. March 7, 1864.

609 JOSEPH P. SHELDON[8], m. Nov. 13, 1845, Armenia Woodruff.
Children, Ninth Generation:
622 1 Charles H., b. July 12, 1847; d. Sept. 8, 1848.
623 2 An infant, b. July 22, 1848; d. July 25, 1848.
624 3 Edward William, b. March 28, 1852; d. July 11, 1852.
625 4 Henry Theodore, b. Aug. 1, 1854.

612 SARAH STRONG[8], m. Oct. 14, 1846, Pomeroy Sheldon, of Mt. Morris, N. J. ; and d. May 19, 1858.
Children, Ninth Generation
627 1 Cora E., b. Dec. 6, 1849.
628 2 Owen Theodore, b. Dec. 25, 1851.
629 3 Sarah Ann, b. June 11, 1855.
630 4 Joseph P., b. Dec. 22, 1857; d. April 24, 1863.

557 Anna Lyman[7], 3d and youngest dau. of *Elias*[6], m.
Dec. 14, 1849, Nathan Sheldon.   *New Marlboro.*

Children, Eighth Generation:

631 1 Pamelia A., b. Nov. 26, 1824.
632 2 Cordelia A., b. July 5, 1827.   3 Liberty L., b. May 9, 1830;
    d. March 1, 1833.   4 Gilbert L., b. Oct. 15, 1833; m.
    July 27, 1868, Jennie Fuller, of Egremont, Mass   5
    Harriet A., b. Feb. 4, 1837; m. F. H. Sanford, April 6,
    1858; d. Oct. 11, 1862.
       Ch. 9th Gen.: 1 Mary L., b. March 30, 1861. 1
    Anna P., b. May 19, 1862; d. March 15, 18....

631 Pamelia A. Sheldon[8], m. John Hollister of New
Marlboro.   *Rockford, Ill.*

Children, Ninth Generation:

637 1 Minerva C., b. Oct. 29, 1848.
638 2 George L., b. Jan. 1, 1851.
639 3 Ella, b. April 24, 1853; d. May 16, 1853.
641 4 John A., b. Jan. 23, 1855.
642 5 Hattie A., b. June 29, 1859.
643 6 Fanny E., b. Sept. 22, 1861.

7 Joel Lyman[6], fifth son of *Elias*[5], *Moses*[4], *Moses*[3], *John*[2],
Richard[1], b. Sept. 20, 1764, in Southampton, d. July 6,
1840, on the place where he was born, and cultivated a
farm; m. Dec. 29, 1791, Achsah Parsons, of Northampton,
who d. Aug. 29, 1856, aged 93 years. *Southampton, Mass.*

Children, Seventh Generation

643* 1 Moses, b. Oct. 26, 1792.
644   2 Aaron, b. Feb. 11, 1794.
645   3 Joel, b. March 7, 1796; d. May 4, 1863.
646   4 Elias, b. Feb. 15, 1798.
647   5 Asa, b. Feb. 10, 1800; d. Jan. 13, 1814.
648   6 Achsah, b March 22, 1803; d. Jan. 18, 1854.
649   7 Theodore, b. July 31, 1804.
650   8 Isaac, b. Oct. 22, 1806; d. Aug. 12, 1862.
651   9 Maria, b. Nov. 19, 1808.
652 10 Lucy, b. March 16, 1811.
653 11 Asa P., b. June 21, 1815; d. Dec. 9, 1821.

643 Moses Lyman[7], *Joel*[6], *Elias*[5], *Moses*[4], *Moses*[3], *John*[2],
Richard[1], b. Oct. 26, 1792; m. Oct. 22, 1817, Clarissa Clapp,
of Southampton, who d.   2d wife Sophronia L. Bell, who
d.   3d wife Elizabeth Smith, of Chester.   *Chester, Mass.*

Children, Eighth Generation:

654 1 Moses Dwight, b. July 28, 1818; d. in South America, May
    21, 1849.

655 2 William, b. June 16, 1820; m. June 14, 1855, in Kansas City, Sarah F. Baxter of Southampton, d. at Kansas City, Sept. 2, 1858.
Ch. 9th Gen.: Willie Wright, b. Sept. 18, 1858.

657 3 Clarissa Jane, b. April 23, 1822; m. May 20, 1847, Jonathan McElvain of Middlefield, Mass., d. March 22, 1851.

658 4 David Brainerd, b. Sept. 14, 1825; m. Sept. 10, 1857, Relief Reeder, lives in Chester.
Ch. 9th Gen.: 1 William Alva, b. Jan. 31, 1859. 2 Mary A., b. Nov. 18, 1860. 3 Ella Jane, b. Feb. 25, 1863. 4 Alice Eliza, Jan. 20, 1865. 5 Dwight M., b. Dec. 30, 1866.

665 5 Mary Ann, b. March 23, 1823; d. at Chester, June 3, 1852.

666 6 Achsah Parsons, b. May 24, 1830, Hatfield, Mass.

667 7 Elias C., b. March 30, 1833; m. July 3, 1865, Susan B. Stevens, of Chester, Northampton

668 8 By 2d marriage, Nancy Hoisington, b. Nov. 28, 1837; d. at Chester, Jan. 12, 1859.

669 9 Amelia Wright, Aug. 12, 1844; m. 1871, L. Gleason, of Hinsdale, Mass.

644 AARON LYMAN[7], m. Sept. 25, 1822, Harriet P. Baker of Mesopotamia, Ohio, who d. Sept. 25, 1846, when he again m. Feb. 9, 1848, Sophenia Otis of Cleveland, a farmer.
Children, Eighth Generation:
670 1 Franklin P., b. Aug. 16, 1825; m. Oct. 27, 1846, Tirzah Ann Warner of Mesopotamia.

671 2 Elizabeth H., b. March 16, 1827; d. July 17, 1842.

672 3 A son, b. April 25, 1829; d. same day.

673 4 William W., b. May 10, 1830; m. May 26, 1853, Sylvia A. Woodford of Mesopotamia.

674 5 Harriet N., b. March 13, 1832.

675 6 Ellen A., b. May 19, 1837; m. Jan 11, 1851, Virnum Strowbridge, who d. March 29, 1857. She afterwards m. June 20, 1865, George Lyman Gordon, of Youngstown, Ohio.

670 FRANKLIN P. LYMAN,[8] b. Aug. 16, 1825; m. Oct. 27, 1846.
Child, Ninth Generation:
676 1 Julia C., b. Nov. 9, 1847; m. Feb. 13, 1866, Charles Silliman.

673 WILLIAM W. LYMAN,[8] b. May 10, 1830, m. May 26, 1853. *Youngstown, Ohio.*
Children, Ninth Generation:
677 1 Virnum W., b. March 8, 1858.

678 2 Bertha, b. June 27, 1859.

680 3 Franklin L., b. May 17, 1865.

681 4 Hattie L., b. Dec. 10, 1866.

645 JOEL LYMAN[7], m. June 11, 1844, Sarah L. Moore, of W. Springfield. One daughter, Sarah, b. July 16, 1847.

646 ELIAS LYMAN[7], son of *Joel*[7], m. Jan. 11, 1838, Hannah Coggswell, of New Bloomfield, Ohio.

Children, Eighth Generation:

682 1 Charles P., b. Dec. 26, 1838; m. Oct. 7, 1867.
683 2 Ednah M., b. April 14, 1840.
684 3 Howard F., b. Nov. 30, 1841; m. Emira F. Fenn, d. April 4, 1866, Swede Point, Iowa.
685 4 Zuinglius P., b. Aug. 28, 1843; Chicago, Ill.
686 5 Albert T., b. March 18, 1845; Swede Point, Iowa.
687 6 Lucy Ann, b. Sept. 9, 1846; Mesopotamia, Ohio.
688 7 Celie A., b. June 13, 1848; d. March 7, 1866.
689 8 Francis E., b. Jan. 1, 1851; d. Aug. 11, 1857.
690 9 Hannah P., b. March 9, 1854; Mesopotamia.

683 EDNAH M. LYMAN[8], m. May 9, 1866, Dwight L. Wilbor, of Boonborough, Iowa.

Children, Ninth Generation:

691 1 Curton D , b. May 10, 1867.
692 2 Lottie W., b. Oct. 26, 1868.

648 ACHSAH LYMAN[7], m. Jan. 5, 1825, Dotus Strong of Southampton.

Child, Eighth Generation.

693 1 One daughter Caroline M., b. April 12, 1829, who m. Oct. 29, 1856, George A. Moore, of Southampton.
     Ch. 9th Gen : 1 Georgiana Boon, b. March 24, 1862, Achsah Lyman's daughter after 2d marriage, is Ellen, b. Aug. 14, 1841.

649 THEODORE LYMAN[7], m. Laura Griswold, of Norwich, Mass.

Children, Eighth Generation

696 1 Austin Elias, b. Sept. 4, 1829.
697 2 A son, b. Dec. 10, 1831; d. Dec. 31, 1831.
698 3 Laura C., b. Dec. 8, 1832. His wife having d. Dec. 23, 1832, Theodore again m. May 1, 1833, Eleanor Strong. Children by second m.,
699 4 Theodore C., b. Dec. 21, 1835; d. March 1, 1735. } Twins.
700 5 Edwin J., b. Dec. 21, 1835; d. Sept. 16, 1860. }
701 6 Harriet M., b. March 27, 1838.
702 7 Theodore S., b. Aug. 21, 1842; d. Nov. 5, 1861.

696 AUSTIN E. LYMAN[8], m. April 10, 1861, Sarah D. Rudolph— a dentist.   *Warren, Ohio.*

Child, Ninth Generation :

703 1 One son, John K., b. June 25, 1864.

698 LAURA C. LYMAN[8], m. March 25, 1858, Walter S.
Austin.

Children, Ninth Generation :

704 1 Flora.   705 2 Edson.

650 ISAAC LYMAN[7], m. Nov. 23, 1837, Jane P. Watts, of
Worthington.   *Southampton.*

Children, Eighth Generation .

706 1 Edgar P., b. July 23, 1832, supposed to be in Easthampton.
707 2 Isaac W., b. Oct. 1, 1841 ; d. March 7, 1866.
708 3 Lucy J., b. Sept. 14, 1844.
709 4 Alonzo A., b. Oct. 22, 1845 ; d. in the army in Georgia,
        Sept. 18, 1865.
710 5 Elizabeth A., b. Sept. 23, 1848.
711 6 An infant, b. April 26, 1851 ; Isaac M. m. Nov. 17, 1852,
        Janett Watts, his 2d wife.
712 7 Elias L., b. Nov. 23, 1853.
713 8 Homer C., b. Jan. 21, 1861.

706 EDGAR P. LYMAN[8], m. April 7, 1864, Mary L. Burleigh.

Children, Ninth Generation :

714 1 Nellie J., b. Aug. 2, 1865.
715 2 Lola, b. Oct. 23, 1868.

707 ISAAC W. LYMAN[8], m. July 1, 1862, Cerinthia A.
Bates, of Southampton.

Children, Ninth Generation .

716 1 George J., b. Sept. 19, 1865.

651 MARIA LYMAN[8], m. Jan. 16, 1845, Seth Porter of Norwich, a tanner and farmer.   *Norwich, Mass.*

Child, Ninth Generation :

717 1 Lucy M., b. June 25, 1849 ; m. Israel Morton, of Hatfield,
        Mass., a farmer, no children.

12 PHEBE LYMAN[5], sister of Dea. *Elias[7],* was b. Aug. 20,
1717 ; d. Jan. 5, 1804, aged 84, a sensible, resolute woman,
m. Nov. 5, 1736, Caleb Strong of Northampton, who was
b. March 21, 1810 ; and d. Feb. 13, 1776.

Children, Sixth Generation :

718 1 Caleb, b. Sept. 15, 1737 ; d. Jan. 11, 1738.
719 2 Phebe, b. Dec. 22, 1738 ; d. Jan. 15, 1816 ; m. Nov. 4,
        1766, Benjamin Bellows.
721 3 Esther, b. Feb. 12, 1741 ; m. Dec. 2, 1760, Samuel Hunt ;
        d. Nov. 20, 1806.

42

723   4 Mehitable, b. Feb. 16, 1743; m. Jan. 5, 1764, Caleb Ly-
         man ; she d. Feb. 28, 1800.
724   5 Caleb, the governor, b. Jan. 9, 1745; d. Nov. 7, 1819.
725   6 Eleanor, b. Jan. 17, 1747; m. May 28, 1771, Asahel Clark.
726   7 Martha, b. March 20, 1749; m. Sept. 14, 1773, Ebenezer
         Mosely, of Westfield.
727   8 Dorothy, b. April 19, 1751; d. Feb. 5, 1752.
728   9 Asahel, b. June 9, 1753; d. Feb. 4, 1759.
729   10 Isaac, b. Sept. 3, 1756; d. June 4, 1757.
730   11 Dorothy, b. Dec. 5, 1758; m. June 8, 1780, Samuel
         Hinckley, of Northampton, d. Aug. 25, 1802.
731   12 Achsah, b. Nov. 17, 1762; d. Sept. 29, 1770.

Both Caleb Strong and Phebe his wife were distinguished for
original strength of mind, sound judgment and exemplary Christian
deportment.   They were the parents of twelve children, one of whom
was Gov. Caleb Strong, one of the most distinguished Christian
statesmen of Massachusetts.   He was U. S. Senator in the First
Congress, 1788–94, 1794–1800.   He became eminent in the legal
profession; and equally distinguished for his moral worth and stern
integrity.   He was deservedly honored with the respect of his citizens throughout the state of which he received the highest evidence
in his appointment as governor of the commonwealth.   On his election
as governor of the state although party spirit ran high, not a vote was
cast against him in seven or eight towns of which Northampton was
the centre.   To the same office he was repeatedly elected.

As early as 1772 he was a professing Christian, and acted plainly
under the sense of religious obligation, and sought the praise of
God rather than that of men.   He was a pillar in the church
at Northampton, and for many years president of the Hampshire Co.
Missionary Society and of the Hampshire Bible Society.   In the
latter years of his life he was much given to the study of the
scriptures and of theological works.   Time grew less and eternity
ever more in his thoughts.   In private life he was affable and attractive.   He had those magnetic qualities of character, which, with
his integrity, simplicity and dignity, drew all eyes and hearts to him.
The Lymans and the Strongs, beginning at Northampton their career
together in America, have frequently intermarried.   Their mutual relations from these intermarriages are fully developed in the history
of the Strong Family, by the Rev. B. W. Dwight, from which the above
statements have been chiefly taken.

III. DESCENDANTS OF MOSES³ THROUGH THE REV.
ISAAC⁵.

14 REV. ISAAC LYMAN⁵, *Moses⁴, Moses³, John², Richard¹*,
1724–1810, b. in Northampton, Feb. 25, 1725, graduated
at Yale College, 1747, settled over parish in York, Maine,

1749; m. Ruth Plummer, of Gloucester, Mass., April 24, 1750; d. in York, Me., March 12, 1810, aged 86. Ruth Plummer, his wife, was b. July 22, 1730; d. Jan. 20, 1824, aged 86. *York, Me.*

Children, Sixth Generation.

731*1 Theodosia, b. Feb. 28, 1751; m. a Bragdon.
732 2 Theodore, b. Jan. 8, 1755; m. 1st Sarah Emerson, 2d Lydia Williams.
733 3 Olive, b. March 17, 1755; m. a Plummer.
734 4 Lucy, b. Feb. 18, 1758; m. a Keating.
735 5 Timothy, b. Aug. 7, 1760; d., unmarried, 1748.
736 6 Ruth, b. Jan. 22, 1763.
737 7 Mary, b. Oct. 11, 1765; m. Rev.-Dr. Buckminster no children.
738 8 Elizabeth, b. Feb. 8, 1768; m. a Gilman.
739 9 Sarah, b. Dec. 21, 1772; m. a Keating.

Nothing is known of any of his children except Theodore, who is still remembered in Boston as a man of great force and marked traits of character, of sterling worth, and generous impulses. He was one of the set of men who made the name of a "merchant of Boston" respected throughout the world.

Theodore was the only married son of Rev. Isaac L., therefore his descendants are the only ones of the male line from this branch. There were descendants in the collateral branches of *Bragdon, Plummer, Keating, Gilman, Keating.* Dr. Buckminster had no children.

The following is extracted from the funeral sermon of the Rev. Dr. Hemmingway of Wells, Me.:

His talents appeared to be rather solid than shining, qualifying him rather for usefulness in his particular calling, than to figure in the eye of the world. With a sound, sagacious judgment, his mind was well furnished with valuable and useful knowledge; particularly he understood the sacred doctrines and duties of the Christian religion, of which he was a public teacher. Prudence in the conduct of life was an eminent and acknowledged part of his character, as was also great integrity and probity. In him the wisdom of the serpent was joined with the innocence of the dove. His integrity and uprightness preserved him. He appeared always to maintain a mild, placid, and kind temper, happy to himself and those with him, and a conversation becoming the gospel. None appeared more universally loved and respected. Those who were most acquainted with him had the highest esteem for him. He was not a bigot. His religion was orthodoxy and charity united. As a public teacher the apparent aim and tendency of his discourses was not to show himself, but to promote true godliness and righteousness. He was an amiable example of the graces and virtues of the Christian temper and life. For many years he was wholly taken off, yet was useful to the last by his exemplary patience, and resignation to the will of God. The inscription upon the marble placed over the grave of Mr. Lyman is this:

In memory of the Rev. Isaac Lyman, the social, venerable and pious pastor of the 1st church in York, for more than sixty years. Was born at N. Hampton, Mass., Feb. 25, 1724, graduated at Yale College, 1747. Ordained Dec. 20, 1749, and d. March 12, 1810. aged 86 years.

649 THEODORE LYMAN⁶, m. in Kennebunk, Me., Sarah Emerson, Nov. 21, 1776, by whom he had four children. Removed to Boston, and married Jan. 24, 1786, Lydia Williams of Marlboro, Mass., by whom he had five children. Died at his country seat at Waltham, Mass., May 24, 1839. He was an eminent merchant in the north-west fur trade, the coast and China trade, and a man of strongly marked character.   *Waltham, Mass.*

     Children, Seventh Generation:

741 1 Waldo, d. young.
742 2 Sarah, d. young.
743 3 Olive, m. Henry Paine.
744 4 Sarah, d. young.
     Children by 2d wife, Lydia Williams.
745 1 George Williams, b. Dec. 4, 1786; m. 1st, May 31, 1810 ; 2d, May 3, 1827.
747 2 Theodore, b. Feb. 17, 1792 ; m. May 15, 1821; d. July 18, 1849 ; a man of mark, whose name is a part of the history of Boston, and of the public charities of Massachusetts.
748 3 Mary, b. Oct. 9, 1802
749 4 Charles, m. April 4, 1827.
750 5 William, d. young.

743 OLIVE LYMAN⁷, m. Henry Paine.
     Children, Eighth Generation:
749 1 Lucy, m. Russel Sturgis.

745 GEORGE WILLIAMS LYMAN⁷, m. Elizabeth Gray, dau. of Harrison Gray Otis, of Boston, b. May 21 ,1791; d. Dec. 20, 1824.   *Waltham, Mass.*
     Children, Eighth Generation:
750* 1 George Theodore, b. April 25, 1811 ; d. Oct. 11, 1819.
751 2 Arthur Wellesley, b. March 28, 1813 ; d. Feb. 24, 1826.
752 3 An infant, b. May 8, 1815 ; d. May 8, 1815.
753 4 Elizabeth Otis, b. July 29, 1817 ; m. April, 1844 ; d. June, 1847.
754 5 Mary Ellen, b. Sept. 8, 1819 ; m. June 18, 1841.
755 6 George Theodore 2d, b. Dec. 23, 1821 ; m. April 17, 1845.

By 2d wife, Ann Pratt, dau. of William Pratt of Boston b. May 9, 1798.

756   7 William Pratt, b. April 8, 1828; m. April 5, 1828; d. April 16, 1864.

757   8 Arthur Theodore, b. Dec. 8, 1832; m. April 5, 1858

758   9 Sarah Pratt, b. Feb. 5, 1835; m. April 23, 1861.

759   10 Lydia Williams, b. April 29, 1839; m. April 24, 1862.

George Williams Lyman, eldest son of Theodore by his marriage with Lydia Williams. The 4 children of his 1st marrriage, with Sarah Emerson, leaving no issue or dying young, is still living in Boston — he was b. in Kennebunk, Me. Dec. 4, 1786 — graduated at Harvard College. Joined his father in the N. W. coast and China trade — but afterwards turned his attention to the cotton manufacture, and was prominent among the men whose course of action laid the foundation of the city of Lowell. He still retains his vigor and interest in affairs, and resides upon the country estate of his father, Theodore, in Waltham, Mass. He has also taken an active interest in agriculture and has been for many years an active member of the Massachusetts Society for the Promotion of Agriculture.   *Walthvm, Mass.*

753 Elizabeth Otis[8], m. Francis Boott.   *Lowell, Mass.*

Child, Ninth Generation :

760   1 Elizabeth, b. April 13, 1846.

754 Mary Ellen Williams[8], m. James Amory Appleton.

Child, Ninth Generation :

761   1 George Lyman.

755 George Theodore Lyman[8], m. Sally Otis, dau. of James W. Otis, N. Y., b. Oct. 4, 1825.   *Bellport, L. I.*

Children, Ninth Generation .

762   1 George Gray, b. Aug. 28, 1846.

763   2 James Otis, b. Oct. 7, 1847.

764   3 Francis Marion, b. March 9, 1849 ; d. July 25, 1868.

765   4 Charles, b. April 27, 1850.

766   5 Alice, b. Jan. 14, 1852.

767   6 Elizabeth Gray, b. Jan. 17, 1858.

756 William Pratt Williams[8], m. Abby M. C. Humphreys, of Providence, R. I.   *Boston, Mass.*

Children, Ninth Generation :

768   1 Mary, b. Nov. 9, 1855 ; d. Feb. 9, 1864.

769   2 Olivia, b. Nov. 27, 1858 ; d. Jan. 16, 1864.

770   3 William Pratt, b. March 24, 1860.

757 ARTHUR THEODORE WILLIAMS[8], m. Ella, daughter of John A. Lowell, of Boston.　　　　　*Boston, Mass.*

Children, Ninth Generation :

771 1 Julia, b. Jan. 30, 1859.
772 2 Arthur, b. Aug. 31, 1861.
773 3 Herbert, b. May 24, 1864.
774 4 Ella, b. Feb. 26, 1866.
775 5 Susan Lowell, b. Feb. 8, 1869

758 SARAH PRATT WILLIAMS[8], m. Philip H. Sears.
　　　　　Boston, Mass.

Children, Ninth Generation :

776 1 Annie Lyman, b. March 10, 1862.
777 2 Mary Pratt, b. Aug. 21, 1864.
778 3 Richard, b. July 19, 1867.

759 LYDIA WILLIAMS[8], m. Robert Treat Paine, of Boston.

Children, Ninth Generation ·

779 1 Edith, b. April 6, 1863.
780 2 Fanny, b. Jan. 13, 1865.
781 3 Robert Treat, b. Aug. 9, 1866.

747 THEODORE LYMAN[7], m. Mary E. Henderson of New York d. Aug. 5, 1836.　　　　　*Brookline, Mass.*

Children, Eighth Generation :

782 1 Julia, b. Feb. 10, 1822 ; d. Feb. 15, 1835.
783 2 Henderson, b. Jan. 21, 1823 ; d. June 8, 1824.
784 3 Mary Henderson, b. April 30, 1825 ; d. Dec. 31, 1839.
785 4 Cora, b. Dec. 25, 1828 ; m. June 10, 1848.
786 5 Theodore, b. Aug. 23, 1833 ; m. Nov. 28, 1851

Theodore Lyman, a munificent benefactor of reformatory education in Massachusetts, was born in Boston on the 20th day of February, 1792, the son of a successful merchant, and therefore in circumstances favorable for the formation and development of a manly character, under the influence of practical views, and liberal instruction. He was educated at Phillips Academy, and Harvard College, and was graduated at the latter institution in 1810.

In 1812 he went abroad, and traveled in Europe for about four years, a part of the time in company with Hon. Edward Everett, visiting all the great centres of interest, including Greece, Egypt, and Palestine.. He was in Paris when the allied armies entered that city, and of the stirring incidents of that period he has given an account in a volume entitled *Three Weeks in Paris.* The fruits of his foreign travels and suggested studies, were subsequently embodied in an octavo volume on *Italy*, and two volumes on the *Diplomacy of the United States with Foreign Nations*, both of which were favorably received by the public.

In 1821, Mr. Lyman married Miss Mary E. Henderson of New York—a lady of rare personal attractions and mental accomplishments, who blessed his home by the birth of three daughters and a son. In that home for thirteen years, he found all the comforts which a sweet accord of temper, books, the converse of highly cultivated friends, and abundant means of doing good can command.

In 1833, he had the sorrow of losing his oldest daughter, just as she was arriving at a most interesting period of life, and developing the powers which had been wisely cultivated by careful training. In 1835, he was called to endure the still heavier loss of the mother of that child, who for fourteen years had been the object of a devotion rarely equaled, who had shared all his cares and interests, and had repaid his affection with all the sympathy it could not fail to call forth. Principally to gratify her taste, he had purchased, in the previous year, the estate in Waltham, which formerly belonged to Gov. Gore, and had already improved and embellished it with remarkable taste and judgment. This great sorrow, however, rendered it impossible for him to continue where every flower and tree was a memento of his loss, and he removed to the place in Brookline, which he renovated with the same taste and skill he had shown at Waltham, and which have rendered the house and grounds remarkable among the many beautiful residences in the vicinity of Boston. In the year following the loss of his wife, his second daughter became so ill as to render a change of climate desirable, and he took her to Cuba, with the hope of restoring her to her accustomed strength. It proved in vain, however, and his own health was so much affected by his repeated afflictions, that he was obliged to remain at the south on his own account for several months.

In the summer of 1848 he thought it advisable to go again to Europe, principally for the benefit of the health of his son. He remained abroad a year, and was in Frankfort, and in Paris, during some of the most exciting moments of that revolutionary period. The voyage home was a rough one, and proved a severe trial of the remaining strength of his constitution, and he reached his home in a state of great exhaustion. He remained in a feeble but nearly stationary condition for eight or ten days; and complaining one afternoon of a sudden pain, he desired to be removed from the sofa to the bed. In a short time he became apparently insensible, and expired on the eighteenth of July, 1849. Thus ended, in its maturity and strength, the life of one who was in several respects a remarkable and memorable man, of warm affections, of cultivated taste and sagacity, of delightful manners and incomparable temper, conscientious in the performance of all the duties and amenities of life, and thoughtful of those whose only claim on him was the want of opportunities which he had enjoyed. The recollection of his fine person and his dignified, polished and amiable manners, can survive only in the memory of his friends; but the remembrance of his virtues, his benevolence, his exactness, his kindness to all about him, will continue through many generations in the institution to which he so largely contributed, and which is an honorable memorial at once to him and to the community of which he was a part. Besides large donations during his life, he left by will, $10,000 to the Farm School; $10,000 to the Massachusetts Horticultural Society; and $50,000 to the State Reform School. Total for the Reform School, $72,500.

785 Cora Lyman[8], m. June 10, 1848, G. Howland Shaw, of Boston.

Children, Ninth Generation:

787 1 Amy, b. Oct. 15, 1850.
788 2 Frank, b. Nov. 17, 1854.
789 3 Henry R., b. April 25, 1859.

786 Col. Theodore Lyman[8], son of the eminent philanthropist, b. at Waltham, Mass., Aug. 23, 1833, graduated at Harvard College, 1855, with Agassiz, and graduated *scientiæ baccalaurius*, 1858 ; m. Nov. 28, 1866, Elizabeth, dau. of George R. Russell.   *Brookline, Mass.*

Child, Ninth Generation:

790 1 Cora, b. March 9, 1862.

Went to Europe, March, 1861, where he traveled and pursued his studies ; his dau. Cora, b. at Florence, Italy, March 9, 1862. Returned to the U. S., June, 1863, commissioned Lieut. Col., Aug., 1863, and by special permission of the secretary of war, appointed volunteer aide-de-camp, on the staff of Major Gen. Meade, commanding army of the Potomac. Was present in all subsequent movements, including those on Mine Run and Centreville (1863), and the great battles of the Wilderness, Spottsylvania, Cold Harbor, &c. &c. He served during the whole investment of Petersburg, and in the route and pursuit of Lee's army. He was one of the few officers who were allowed to ride through the rebel lines after the surrender at Appomattox Court House ; where he saw Lee, Longstreet, Gordon, etc. etc. Since the war he has lived at Brookline, Mass., as before, and has continued to interest himself more or less in science, and has also given some attention to the reformation of juvenile offenders, in which his father was so much engrossed. Col. Lyman has made valuable contributions to natural science, in the current and occasional literature of the day, among which are a report on the fisheries in Massachusetts, on fish culture and on forces.

748 Mary Lyman[7], m. Hon. Samuel M. Eliot, for many years a prominent, respected and active citizen of Boston. His name is connected with many public works of the city of which he was mayor for some years.   *Boston, Mass.*

Children, Eighth Generation: •

791 1 Mary, m. C. E. Guild, of Boston.
792 2 Elizabeth, m. H. Bullard.

793 ₃ Charles William, m. Ellen Peabody.
794 ₄ Catharine Atkins.
795 ₅ Frances Anne, m. Rev. H. W. Foote.

791 MARY ELIOT⁸, m. Charles E. Guild.   *Boston, Mass.*

Children, Ninth Generation:

796 ɪ Robert.   799 ₄ Charles.
797 ₂ Henry.   800 ₅ Catharine.
798 ₃ Eleanor.

792 ELIZABETH ELIOT⁸ m. Stephen Bullard. *Boston, Mass.*

Children Ninth Generation.

801 ɪ Mary Lyman.   803 ₃ Ellen L.
802 ₂ John E.   804 ₄ Theodore Lyman.

793 CHARLES W. ELIOT⁸, m. Ellen Peabody.
Boston, Mass.

Children, Ninth Generation:

805 ɪ Charles.   807 ₃ Samuel.
806 ₂ Frank.   808 ₄ Robert P.

795 FRANCES ANNE ELIOT⁸, m. Rev. H. W Foote.
Boston, Mass.

Children, Ninth Generation:

809 ɪ Mary, b. Nov. 4, 1864.

749 CHARLES LYMAN⁷, youngest son of *Theodore⁶* and Lydia Williams, m. Susan, dau. of Dr. John Ware of Boston, the distinguished metaphysician, by whom he had three children : Charles, Charles Frederick, Florence. He resides the greater part of the year at Newport, R. I., though still keeping up his connection with Boston.   *Boston, Mass.*

Children, Eighth Generation

810 ɪ Florence, b. Nov. 9, 1837.
811 ₂ Charles Frederick, b. Oct. 21, 1833; m. Annie, dau. of Patrick Grant of Boston, a child b. Aug. 1868.

It is worthy of notice that these marriages above mentioned *are with families of distinguished note in Boston:* Otis, Pratt, Sears, Paine, Russell, Shaw, Peabody, Boott, Appleton, Warren, Lowell, etc., and that the descendants 80 in number, with two exceptions, all live in Boston or the immediate vicinity.

Intermarriages : *Men*—Emerson, Williams, Otis, Pratt, Henderson, Warren, Humphreys, Lowell, Russell, Peabody, Grant. *Women*—Paine, Eliot, Sturgis, Boott, Appleton, Arnold, Sears, Shaw, Guild, Bullard, Foote.

Lineal Descent.

Richard Lyman[1], bapt. Oct. 30, 1580; d. 1640.　Came to New England in 1631.

John Lyman[2], b. in England, 1623; d. Aug. 20, 1690.

Moses Lyman[3], b. Feb. 20, 1662; d. 1701.

Moses Lyman[4], b. 1689; d. March 24, 1762.

Isaac Lyman[5], b. Feb. 25, 1725; d. March 12, 1810.

Theodore Lyman[6], b. Jan. 8, 1753; d. May 24, 1839.

Theodore Lyman[7], b. Feb. 19, 1792; d. July 18. 1849.

Theodore Lyman[8], b. Aug. 23, 1833, still living.

These first seven generations lived to an average of 66½ years.　They averaged 8 children each, and only one was married twice.

IV. DESCENDANTS OF MOSES[3], THROUGH SIMEON[5].

Simeon Lyman[5], 5th son of Capt. *Moses[4], Moses[3], John[2], Richard[1]*, 1725–1800, b. 1725, in Northampton, Mass., settled in Salisbury, Conn., and joined the church in that place in 1740, by letter from the church in Northampton.　He m. Abigail Beebe of Canaan, Ct., and both d. in Salisbury, in the year 1800, at an advanced age.　　*Salisbury, Conn.*

Children, Sixth Generation:

813　1 Noah, b. May 10, 1758; d. June 3, 1831.

814　2 Simeon, b. Jan. 17, 1754.

815　3 Elizabeth, bapt. in 1760; made a profession of religion; d. Jan. 23, 1813.

816　4 John, b. March 11, 1760; d. July 27, 1840, in Jericho, Vt.

817　5 Olivia, m. Nathaniel Tremain, of Pittsfield, Mass.; trom this branch of the family comes the Hon. Lyman Tremain, of Albany, N. Y., and the Tremains.

820　6 Chloe, m. a Wright, of Northampton, Mass.; two children, Fanny and Roxana; one is still living in Northampton.

823　7 Isaac, d. a young man, aged 14 years.

824　8 David, b. Aug. 20, 1768.

813 Noah Lyman[6], the first son of *Simeon* of Salisbury, Conn., was b. according to the record of the family March 10, 1753.　Hopa Bunn his wife, was b. March 13, 1765. They were m. May 12, 1784., In Feb., 1790, they removed to Jericho, Vt., with his brother John.　Hopa B. L., d. May 12, 1813, aged 48.　Noah, m. March 30, 1816, 2d wife, Urania Knowles.　He lived and d. June 3, 1831, on his farm in Jericho, aged 73.　He was remarka-

ble for his great stature, weighing more than 300℔s., requiring eight bearers to convey his body to the grave.

Jericho, Vt.

Children, Seventh Generation :

825 1 Stephen, b. Jan. 30, 1785; m. Dec. 24, 1817, Erminia Knowles, still living in Jericho Centre, Vt.
826 2 Caleb, b. Feb. 15, 1788; d. Aug. 29, 1809, aged 21 years.
827 3 Hopa, b. Jan. 30, 1791.
828 4 Noah, jr., b. March 27, 1793, lives in Jericho Centre, Vt.
829 5 Harvey, b. June 30, 1795. } Residence in the western states
830 6 Elisha, b. Feb. 4, 1798. } not known.
831 7 Ely, b. Aug. 18, 1800; d. Nov. 2, 1850, aged 50.
832 8 Chloe, b. Oct. 4, 1803; m. Sept. 28, 1859, Eliphalet Tomlinson. Six children are still living, but their marriages are not given. Only two grandsons bear the name of Lyman. With the exception of the children of Hopa who m. Asher Hall, there are but seven grandchildren.

814 SIMEON⁶, m. Dec. 7, 1780, Joannah Palmer, b. Jan. 23, 1753, and settled in Sharon, Conn., as a farmer, where he d. several years since. *Sharon, Conn.*

Children, Seventh Generation .

833 1 Hannah, b. Aug. 29, 1781; m. Samuel Elmore, Sharon.
834 2 Isaac, b. July 6, 1783.
835 3 Betsey, b. July 17, 1785; m. Abraham Weed, Sharon, one son Hiram, a man of remarkable business talents and a devoted Christian.
836 4 Timothy, b. Aug. 7, 1787; d. Aug. 12, 1787.
837 5 Barnis, b. July 30, 1788; m. a Curtis—Westmoreland, N. Y.
838 6 Anna, b. Feb. 22, 1791.
839 7 Simeon, b. Oct. 15, 1793; d. Aug 15, 1868.
840 8 Amanda, b. March 12, 1798; m. Alanson Hamlin, Sharon; he m. April 6, 1808, Mary Warner.

839 SIMEON LYMAN⁸, m. Betsey Strong, a lady of culture and refinement. He resided, a farmer, in Westmoreland, Oneida Co., where he d. Aug. 15, 1868. His 2d wife was Amanda C. King, of Sharon, Ct. They have one child, Charles S., b. Sept. 10, 1845, the lone representative of this branch of the family bearing the name of Lyman.

Westmoreland, N. Y.

834 ISAAC LYMAN⁷, lives a farmer, in Sharon, Ct., and d. Jan. 28, 1858.

Children, Eighth Generation :

841 1 Mary Ann, b. July 27, 1809; m. April 6, 1842, Martin Decker; d. May 12, 1847.

842 2 Harriet E., b. July 14, 1812; m. Oct. 12, 1831, Edgar G.
Reed, of Salisbury, now resident in Sharon, Conn.

843 3 Lucy Ann, b. Nov. 27, 1813 ; m. June, 1840, Martin Decker.
d. July 26, 1841.

844 4 Laura, b. May 28, 1815 ; m. May 3, 1843, Levi Bartram.

845 5 Betsey, b. April 5, 1818 ; d. Aug. 18, 1820.

846 6 Simeon T., b. Aug. 26, 1819; d. Aug. 22, 1823.

847 7 Sarah, b. June 26, 1824; m. Jan. 15, 1845, Charles Twitchell,
of Oxford, Conn., now resident in Bridgport. All but
Harriet and Sarah have d. leaving no issue.

816 JOHN LYMAN⁶, 3d son of *Simeon⁵*, of Salisbury, Conn.,
1760–1840; m. Huldah Brinsmade, of Stratford, Conn.,
who d. Jan. 1, 1833, aged 69 ; united with the Congregational church, in Jericho, Vt., Dec. 11, 1808, his wife had
joined in 1799. Their children, with one exception, are
members of the same church.   *Jericho, Vt.*

Children, Seventh Generation :

848 1 Betsey Elizabeth, b. Aug. 28, 1787 ; m. March 20, 1808,
Gideon Olds, of Norwich, Vt.; d. Aug. 2, 1830.
Ch. 8th Gen.: 1 Franklin L., b. Feb. 16, 1810. 2
Emeline Amelia, b. Dec. 12, 1812. 3 Albert Eben, b.
March 16, 1815. 4 Erastus William, b. April 16, 1817.
5 Laura Ann, b. March 6, 1819 ; d. Oct. 2, 1821, aged 2.
6 Olivia, b. Feb. 23 ; d. Aug. 19, 1866. 7 Lucretia, b.
July 11, 1824. 8 Amarilla, b. Oct, 4, 1826. 9 Milton,
b. Feb. 17, 1828 ; d. Aug. 21, 1855. 10 Rollin G., b.
April 11, 1830.

859 2 Laura, b. Nov. 10, 1789 ; m. Richardson.

860 3 Daniel, b. Dec. 6, 1791. He, and his son Charles H., are
farmers in Jericho Centre.

861 4 Simeon, b. Aug. 3, 1793 ; d. at Lafayette, Indiana. Simeon
was a clothier formerly. His sons are: 1 Baldwin. 2 Edwin. 3 Albers. 4 Charles.

866 5 Huldah, b. Aug. 5, 1795.

867 6 John, jr., b. April 2, 1798, known as Judge Lyman, tanner
and shoemaker with a small farm, has been town clerk
and treasurer some twenty-five years, and has held the
office of judge in the county court.

868 7 Erastus, b. March 2, 1801, was a clothier in Sheldon, Vt.,
now a farmer in Iowa.

John Lyman⁶, was a man like most of the connection, " very much
set in his ways." When once he had decided that a measure was
right, or had deliberately formed an opinion on any subject, it became a changeless sentiment, from which he seldom or never
swerved. He emigrated to Jericho, Vt., soon after the Revolutionary
war, among the first settlers in the state. He was well adapted to
enjoy pioneer life as a mighty hunter and an accurate marksman.

In the winter season he would leave his home in the morning and return late at night, occasioning by his long absence deep anxiety to his wife and children ; but, not unfrequently, on the following day he would bring in with his team, as the fruit of his hunting excursion, two or three deer, a wolf or a bear, or both. Even in old age, when leaning on his staff, he retained the skillful use of his gun.

Perhaps his characteristic as a successful hunter, together with his personal appearance, erect in stature, of dark complexion, with small black eyes, gave rise to the impression that he possessed Indian blood. On one occasion on taking lodgings at the public inn, he was invited by the deacon of the church to his house as the Indian preacher who was to be their supply on the sabbath, a mistake which his native humor and love of adventure keenly enjoyed. Although retiring and reticent in character, he was remarkably social with his friends. He was a man of deep thought and sound judgment, an earnest Christian and a constant attendant on the worship of God. Living three miles from church, he was always in the house of God with his family upon the sabbath, and a punctual attendant upon the meetings of the church during the week. It was his highest joy to witness the return of his children to God and welcome their admission to the church. As a bold and fearless soldier and sure marksman he served faithfully his country in the war of the Revolution ; and, in the last years of his life, received a pension which he delighted to distribute to his children and grandchildren on their visits to him.

859 LAURA LYMAN[7], dau. of Capt. *John* Lyman of Jericho, Vt., m. Sept. 33, 1807, William P. Richardson.

Jericho, Vt.

Children, Eighth Generation :

869   1 Betsey, b. July 8, 1808 ; m. Dec. 17, 1829, Russell French, of Jericho, Vt. ; d. April 9, 1830.

870   2 Nathan R., b. Jan. 20, 1810 ; m. May 21, 1837, Emily Home. Jericho, Vt.

871   3 Emily, b. Jan. 8, 1812 ; m 1834, Rev. James Hillhouse, a Presbyterian clergyman, in Newbern, Alabama, d. there, April 4, 1835, an example of Christian submission and triumph in death, worthy of record, as showing, "how blest the righteous when he dies." Calmly she resigned her infant babe, with her last adieu saying : "My dear husband ; a final farewell, I thank my blessed Saviour for a full assurance that I shall immediately be with Him in Paradise ; come Lord Jesus, come quickly." Newbern, Ala.

872   4 Hannah W., b. May 31, 1814 ; m. Nov. 4, 1840, A. G. K. Truair ; d. Aug. 31, 1849, at Norwich, Chenango Co., N. Y. Mr. T., now editor of the *Syracuse Journal*, N. Y. These four were b. at Westford, when Mr. R., removed to Jericho.

873   5 and 6 John Lyman and Wm. P., b. Sept. 1 5,1816.   John L.,
          m. June 30, 1847, Catharine Hermans, Scranton, Pa.—
          Waverly, Luzerne Co., Pa.
875   7 Martin P., b. June 2, 1818; m. May 12, 1842, Ann
          Beecher of Cambridge, Vt.— Brookfield, Vt.
876   8 William P., b. March 8, 1820; m. in 1842, Elmira Wilder,
          Cambridge, Vt., where he d. 1843.
877   9 Caroline, b. Jan. 21, 1822; m. May 23, 1848, Edward
          Converse, resides at Butternuts, Oswego Co., N. Y.
878   10 Minerva, b. April 4, 1824; d. March 31, 1839, aged 14.
879   11 Laura E. b. Nov. 10, 1826; d. March 24, 1839, aged 12.
880   12 Joseph L., b. April 17, 1828; d. March 28, 1839, aged 11.

These three d. at Cambridge, Vt., in one week of scarlet fever;
one year previous to their death they became interested in the subject of religion and all d. in the triumph of faith.

881   13 Burton, b. Dec., 1830; d. Nov. 1844, aged 13 years 11 mos.
882   14 Simeon R., b. March, 1832; m. April 16, 1850, Charlotte
          Dickinson, Lexington, Minnesota.

The parents of this numerous family have lived for several years
with their only surviving daughter Mrs. Conners, Butternuts, N. J.
Mrs Richardson d. Feb. 28, 1869. She was the daughter of Capt.
John Lyman, who emigrated from Salisbury, Conn., to Chittenden
county soon after the Revolutionary war. Her parents carried to
that then new country the religion of the Puritans, rearing their
numerous family in the faith of the gospel. Laura was the second
daughter, and very early in life was the subject of deep religious
impressions. She could not recollect when she did not love the
Saviour, and so thought it wrong to tell her pastor she did not
when she felt love toward God and his people, and loved to pray.
She was much troubled, however, because she knew not just the
time of her conversion. Thus, sometimes hoping and sometimes
doubting, she passed her early life.

Marrying quite young, and removing to Westford, Vt., she made
a public profession, uniting with the Congregational church, under
the care of Rev. Simeon Parmelee. Again removing to Jericho and
finding herself now in the midst of a powerful revival, she sought
of the Lord an assurance that she was indeed his. After a protracted agony of spirit, the assurance was given her. Her joy was
unbounded; doubts and fears all removed. Thus commenced anew
her ardent devotion to God. Ever after she gave her testimony in
the weekly meetings for Christ. Often she had precious seasons of
prayer with her children. Once when the father and other members of the family were at church she poured out her soul in the little
prayer meeting, and to her great joy had good evidence that three
of those dear children were then converted. About one year after,
those same dear children d. leaving most comforting evidence that
they were not dead, but " gone home to Heaven," in the submissive
and expressive language of their mother.

At the funeral of the third, the following lines, by Mrs. R.'s request, were sung :

> How can I sink with such a prop
> As my eternal God,
> Who bears the earth's huge pillars up,
> And spreads the heavens abroad.

She had faith in a covenant-keeping God, always finding great comfort in dedicating her children to God by baptism.

Daily now she seemed to be growing in grace. Fifteen years before her death she was raised again by a rich spiritual experience, to a higher, purer state of heavenly enjoyment, often saying that her last days were being her best ; that her peace was like a river. In all her conversation the love of God was the absorbing topic. Only a few days before her death she conversed most cheerfully and clearly of her coming decease, and the ground of her hope. She was reminded of the high opinion every where entertained of her Christian character, and then asked if it was not this — her holy life—that now so much comforted her ? " Oh ! " she said, in great surprise, " I am nothing ; my whole comfort is in my Jesus, who shed his precious blood for me."

She seems daily to have contemplated death with triumph, as being the gate to endless life. Finally, with the going down of the sabbath sun, she gently sank to rest, without a struggle. Among other requests was this, that her friends should not mourn but rejoice, when they should hear of her decease.

The husband still lives, waiting in the beauty of holiness, to rejoin her in the skies.—*Selected Obituary.*

860 Daniel Lyman[7], son of *John*[6], a farmer in Jericho ; m. 1st, Dec. 11, 1815, Olivia Lee, b. March 8, 1795 ; d. Feb. 23, 1818 ; m. 2d, Jan. 12, 1819, Harriet Hawley.

Jericho, Vt.

Children, Eighth Generation :

883 1 A dau. b. and d. Oct. 16, 1816.

884 2 George Lee, b. Feb. 23, 1818. He became a physician of superior talents and learning; residence in Jericho, where he d. Jan. 4, 1863, aged about 45 years.

885 3 Charles Hawley, b. May 8, 1820.

886 4 Olivia, b. Oct. 30, 1827.

884 Dr. George Lee Lyman[8], m. Aug. 15, 1844, Mabel A. Field, of Jericho, who d. Oct. 3, 1845, he m. 2d wife, Mary C. Boynton, of Hinesburg, Aug. 27, 1846, who d. Sept. 7, 1858, aged 36. *Jericho, Vt.*

Children, Ninth Generation :

887 1 George Field, b. in Hinesburg, Sept. 9, 1845 ; d. Jan. 18, 1846.

888 2 Auria Mary, b. Dec. 15, 1847 ; d. July 29, 1848.

889 ₃ Ella Maria, b. May 25, 1849, in Clarence, Canada East; m. Sept. 8, 1869.

885 CHARLES HAWLEY LYMAN⁶, m. Nov. 27, 1845, Eliza A. Blackman — a farmer *Jericho, Vt.*

886 OLIVIA LYMAN⁸, m. Nov. 25, 1852, Henry A. Burt, a lawyer, now resident in Swanton, of distinction in his profession. *Swanton, Vt.*

Children, Ninth Generation:
890 ₁ Henry A., b. Sept. 15, 1853.
891 ₂ Mary H., b. July 4, 1855.
892 ₃ Ellen C. b. Dec. 2, 1862.

861 SIMEON LYMAN⁸, 3d son of *John of Jericho.*

Children, Ninth Generation:

893 ₁ Laura Ann.   896 ₄ Edwin.
894 ₂ Olivia.   897 ₅ Albert.
895 ₃ Baldwin.   898 ₆ Charles.

These reside in Indiana; Laura A. m. Snyder of Fayette, Ind.; Edwin resides in the same city.

867 JOHN LYMAN,⁷ son of *Judge John,* m. Oct. 29, 1822, Mary Field. *Jericho, Vt.*

Children, Eighth Generation:
899 ₁ Homer, b. June 16, 1813, d. March 22, 1829.
900 ₂ Rollin, b. May 27, 1827; d. Dec. 28, 1829.
901 ₃ Seymour, b. Nov. 20, 1828; m. Feb. 15, 1854, Mary L. Turner, b. in Rutland, May 15, 1832, d. at Jericho, Vt., Aug. 10, 1862; m. 2d wife at Boston, Mass., May 1, 1868, Lucy B. Bowles. Mr. L. delivered a poem at the union of the Lyman family on Mt. Tom, Aug. 9, 1869, and another at their reunion, Aug. 30, 1871, Chicago, Ill.

Ch. 9th Gen.: ₁ Frederic Lyman, b. March 7, 1870.
903 ₄ Mary, b. Sept. 12, 1831.
904 ₅ Moses Parnell, b. Aug. 6, 1837; d. Sept. 15, 1838.
905 ₆ Myron Winslow, b. Aug. 6, 1838; m. Dec. 1, 1868, Annett Ferris, of Lawrenceville, N. Y.,— Chicago, Ill.

868 ERASTUS LYMAN⁷, youngest son of *John⁴*, from Salisbury, Conn., m. Jan. 25, 1825, Sarah C. White. Resided in Sheldon, Vt., many years. Removed to West Liberty, Muscatine Co., Iowa., m. March 8, 1868, his 2d wife widow Gibson. *West Liberty, Ia.*

Children, Eighth Generation:
906 ₁ Charlotte, b. Sept. 29, 1826; m. March 5, 1850, Charles Keith.

907 2 Philo Clark W., b. Oct. 8, 1828; m. June 5, 1858, Mary O. Gibbs.
908 3 Samuel W., b. June 25, 1831; m. Sept. 15, 1859, Caroline A. Phipp
909 4 Sarah Wooster, b. July 10, 1833; m. Aug. 14, 1853, George H. Atherton.
910 5 Edgar, b. Nov. 6, 1835; m. Aug., 1866, Lydia Gibson.
911 6 Homer, b. Sept. 9, 1837; m. July 7, 1857, Anna Stedman.
912 7 Mary T., b. Oct. 28, 1839.
913 8 Anna Elizabeth, b. Sept. 30, 1842.
914 9 Frances A. b. July 26, 1845; m. Nov. 12, 1867, Henry C. Kidder.
915 10 Andalusia Hamilton, b. Dec. 11, 1846.

817 OLIVIA LYMAN[6], dau. of *Simeon*[5], of Salisbury, Conn., m. Dec. 7. 1780, Nathaniel Tremain, of Pittsfield, Mass.

Children, Seventh Generation :

916 1 Isaac.
917 2 Levi.
918 3 William.
919 4 Olive.
920 5 Nathaniel.
921 6 Calvin.
922 7 Chloe.
923 8 Calvin, 2d.
924 9 Myron.
925 10 John.
926 11 Milton.
927 12 Eliza.
928 13 Milo.
929 14 Laura.
930 15 Milo, 2d.

These all are in their graves but Laura, Mrs. L. T. Goodrich, of Westfield, Mass.

929 LAURA TREMAIN[7], dau. of *Olivia*[6] and Nathaniel Tremain, m. L. T. Goodrich.   *Westfield, Mass.*

Children, Seventh Generation .

931 1 Lyman Porter, at Pittsfield, Sept. 22, 1825; d. Oct. 17, 1828.
932 2 Lyman Butler, b. Nov. 11, 1829; d. Oct. 16, 1855.
933 3 John Calvin, b. Dec. 11, 1831.
934 4 Eliza Tremain, b. March 22, 1833.
935 5 Edward Milton, b. Oct. 30, 1836.
936 6 Olive Augusta, b. Jan. 28, 1839.
937 7 Pluma, b. May 4, 1241.
938 8 Caroline Aletta, b. July 22, 1843.
939 9 Charles Tremain, b. April 4, 1846.
940 10 Laura Parthenia, b. March 29, 1849; d. March 12, 1865.

917 LEVI TREMAIN[6], the son of *Nathaniel* and Olivia Tremain, who was the dau. of Simeon Lyman of Salisbury, d. at Durham, Greene county, leaving the following descendants.   *Salisbury, N. Y.*

44

Children, Seventh Generation.

941 1 William, of Binghamton. Major Frank Tremain, his son, entered the army, as a private, but by his bravery and excellent conduct rose to the rank of major and was instantly killed by a bullet received in his forehead at the moment when, at the head of a storming party, he was about to enter a captured fort in Virginia.

942 2 Israel P. Tremain, of Monticello, N. Y.

943 3 Edwin R. Tremain, of New York. His two sons, Henry E. Tremain, and Walter Tremain, entered the army as privates, at the commencement of the Rebellion. Walter fell a victim to disease contracted in the camp. Henry E., went through the war, and rose to the rank of brigadier general.

946 4 Lyman Tremain, of Albany. His eldest son, Frederick Lyman Tremain, went from Hobart College, into the army, and rose to the rank of lieutenant colonel, of the 10th New York Cavalry. Having passed through twenty-five battles and skirmishes, and achieved a brilliant record, he was killed by a rebel sharpshooter, while leading his regiment at Hatcher's Run, Virginia, in Feb., 1865.

948 5 Pluma St. John, wife of Frederick St John, of Monticello, N. Y.

946 The Hon. LYMAN TREMAIN[8], a distinguished lawyer and statesman, has held the following public offices: supervisor, district attorney, county judge, attorney general of the state, and speaker of the assembly. He was the candidate for lieut. gov. on the ticket with Gen. Wadsworth for governor.
Albany, N. Y.

Children, Ninth Generation:

945 1 Frederick, killed in the late war.

950 2 Grenville.

951 3 Helen Elizabeth.

952 4 Lyman, Jr., deceased.

Col. Frederick Tremain. The brief and brilliant career of this youthful warrior, which for heroic daring in action, coolness, consummate skill and generalship has seldom been surpassed, deserves a further record than time and space will now allow. Parental affection has fondly and eloquently said.

To the pen of history belongs the noble task of recording the military operations in which he had the honor to participate during the ever memorable campaign of 1864. And yet, when we consider the bloody and obstinate nature of the battles that were fought—the glorious and unconquerable resolution which was displayed in conducting the movements of the Union armies—the immense loss of human life—the masterly combinations of those armies—the vast extent of country which constituted the field of their display—the number of those brilliant raids performed by the cavalry alone, through the heart of an enemy's country, each one constituting an interesting history of itself—the toil, the sacrifices, the fatigue, sufferings and perils to which the heroic soldiers in those armies were continually subjected, and to which, with unflinching fortitude and cheerfulness, they submitted—when we consider too, the innumerable deeds of personal bravery, performed both by officers and men—the holy patriotic purposes by which the great body of those armies was prompted—the unselfish willingness they manifested to sacrifice their lives for the preservation of the honor, the integrity, and the unity of their country—and, finally, the glorious and successful results of all these operations, we may well doubt whether history will ever contain more than an outline skeleton of them all.

He participated in no less than twenty-five battles and skirmishes in ten months, rose high in rank and achieved at the age of 21 years a reputation for military qualifications and talents which were the admiration of all and might well be the envy of renowned veterans. The scene of his splended achievements was the famous battles of the Wilderness and in connection with them the ever memorable raids of Gen. Sheridan in which he acted a conspicuous and brilliant part until struck down by the deadly aim of a rebel sharpshooter.

Col. Tremain went to the field in the fall of 1862, as Adjutant of the Seventh Volunteer Artillery. Not relishing the monotony and inactivity of garrison life — to which duty the regiment was assigned — he sought and obtained a transfer, and was detailed to staff service in the field, with Gen. Gregg, in the cavalry corps of Gen. Sheridan. And there he found an abundant opportunity for the display of his high soldierly qualities. He was foremost in every battle in which that corps engaged, and which has rendered it and its heroic leaders famous in the annals of the war. He was in that ever memorable ride from the Rapidan to the James, during which a score of battles were fought, millions of the enemy's property destroyed, the outer fortifications of Richmond entered, and prodigies of valor displayed by every member of the heroic band. On the James, he joined in most of the cavalry reconnoissances and raids which have passed into history as among the most dramatic of the war, and fell while engaged in driving back the rebel force which attempted to check the resistless progress of our troops.

Col. Tremain was a young man to be admired and loved. He combined, with a noble presence, winning manners and attractive social qualities. As a soldier, he was prompt and fearless. He was a brave rider, and coveted nothing so much as perilous adventure. He early attracted the attention of his superior officers by his manly bearing and gallant deeds, and earned his several promotions by his heroic achievements.

Educated, young and chivalrous, he speedily won the confidence of his superiors, and promotion soon followed the development of the soldierly accomplishments which distinguished him in the many battles in which he participated. No better evidence of his merits as a soldier need be cited than the fact that he earned the rank of lieut. colonel, at the early age of twenty-one. The history of this war, participated in by so many of the youth of the country, and offering unprecedented opportunities for promotion, affords but few instances of one so young attaining this distinction.

Four cousins, differing but little in age, entered the service at about the same time, all bright and promising young men, prompted by the highest sentiments of patrioti-m and duty. Of these, three lost their lives in the service of their country. Their names are: Lieutenant Walter Tremain, Lieutenant-Colonel Frederick L. Tremain, and Major Frank Tremain.

824 DAVID LYMAN[6], was b. Aug. 20, 1768, and d. Sept. 7, 1848, aged 80 years. He m. Flavia Collins of Long Meadow, Mass., May 20, 1791. He was by occupation a farmer, and lived and d. upon the old family homestead, respected and honored by the entire community.

Salisbury, Ct.

Children, Seventh Generation :

954 1 Sarah, b. April 7, 1793; d. in great peace, May 4, 1831, aged 38, unmarried.

955 2 Samuel, b. Aug. 18, 1794.

956 3 Victoria, b. July 29, 1796; m. Nov. 25, 1841, to A. Humphrey, M.D., of Salisbury. Ct.

967 4 Levi, b. July 22, 1798; lawyer in Penn Yan, N. Y.; removed to Illinois; d. Aug. 6, 1848.

968 5 Abigail, b. Nov. 24, 1800; m. Deacon A. Warner, of Bolton, Ct.; had one son, Rev. Lyman Warner, home missionary in Iowa; she d. June 7, 1828, aged 28, in full hope of a glorious immortality.

970 6 Calvin, b. May 17, 1803; d. Jan. 12, 1864, aged 60 years.

The conversion of David Lyman[6], forms one of the interesting incidents of his life, which occurred when he was near fifty years of age, under the faithful labors of the Rev. A. Nettleton, and is narrated in the following abstract of a letter to his brother :

Salisbury, 1815.

God in his infinite mercy has been pleased to bring my feet from the pit of miry clay, and established them on the rock, Christ Jesus, and I ought to bless his holy name for it. He has been pleased to bless, as we have reason to hope, four of our children. The work began about three months ago, and has been progressing rapidly ever since. Scarce a day falls but more or less. are brought from darkness to light. There are now more than 120 who indulge hope, children from 12 years old, to the man of 70, are subjects of the work.

I will give you a short account of my experience. I have been in an awfully stupid state of mind. I had tried deism and atheism, but was not satisfied and finally thought that morality was the best religion, and that God would do me justice and not punish me much. The Bible I put little or no confidence in. When the awakening first began, I thought little of the work of Divine grace until two of my daughters expressed a hope in redeeming grace. That awakened me to a sense of my condition as a sinner, and I continued in this frame of mind for three or four weeks, until I was brought to pray that God would be merciful to me a sinner. I had *faith* to believe that if I went to the throne of grace, I should not perish, therefore, I drew up the resolution to go, and if I perished, to perish there.

About this time, Calvin, aged 12 years, was brought out wonderfully clear. He began to tell me how I had lived and the awful situation I was in. I was sensible of it before he began, but it came with such force, and such anxiety that he appeared to have for me, that it cut me down. I trembled like Felix, and said "God be merciful to me a sinner." I continued most of the night crying for mercy, and have reason to hope that God pardoned my sins that night. Oh how precious are God's promises to me. The Bible is now my study, and I delight in its perusal. Every thing appears new. I have but just begun to live, and I pray " God that I may live the remainder of my days in his service."

He remained faithful to the close of life. The blessed results of that revival remain to the present day, and well illustrates the revivals of that age.

970 CALVIN LYMAN[7], b. May 16, 1803; d. Jan. 12, 1864, aged 60 years, in Brockport, N. Y.; m. Mary Robbins, of Hartford, Conn. He was converted at the early age of 12 years, but soon relapsed into a state of indifference, and remained so until his last sickness, when he was fully restored to the divine favor, and his son George C., writes that he d. happy, perfectly resigned to the will of heaven, assured of eternal life hereafter.   *Rockport, N. Y.*

Children, Eighth Generation :

971   1 Emily E, b. May 10, 1839 ; married ; no record.
972   2 George C., b. Nov. 29, 1841.
973   3 Mary J., b. Oct. 25, 1846.
974   4 Sarah S., b. Feb. 26, 1850.
975   5 Eliza, b. May 11, 1805 ; d. in Christian hope, Nov. 14, 1831, aged 26.
976   6 Chloe, b. March 10, 1808; m. D. T. Chadwick, of Alfred, N. Y.
          Ch. 9th Gen.: 1 George.   2 Adeline, m. H. G. West, of Alfred, N. Y.; she d. Feb. 26. 1859.
979   8 Maria, b. June 7, 1811 ; d. March 6, 1827, aged 16.
980   9 John, b. April 9, 1814 ; settled in Cleveland, Ohio ; resides in New York city ; has two sons.
          Ch. 9th Gen.: 1 Charles.   2 Frank.

983 10 Charles, b. Sept. 29, 1816; settled in Elyria, Ohio, as a
          farmer; enlisted in an Ohio regiment, in 1861; d. in
          1862, in Virginia. He was true to the flag and a de-
          cided follower of the Lord Jesus Christ. His end was
          triumphant.
               Ch. 8th Gen.: 1 Mary. 2 Lary. 3 Alonzo. 4 Moses.
988 12 David, b. Aug. 23, 1819. Studied law and was admitted
          to practice at the bar in Litchfield, Ct., Oct., 1841, and
          left the profession for the ministry, in 1845; m. Mary
          E. Bramble, of Norfolk, Ct., July 21, 1846. She was b.
          Aug. 9, 1825, and d. Feb. 17, 1872, in full hope of a
          glorious immortality. Springfield, Mass.
               Ch. 8th Gen.: 1 David Franklin, b. Nov. 18, 1848;
          and d. Feb. 15, 1854.

955 SAMUEL LYMAN[7], a farmer, *Rose, Wayne Co., N. Y.*
          Children, Eighth Generation:
990 1 Caroline, b. May 7, 1817; d. Feb. 27, 1869.
991 2 John, b. April 28, 1819, farmer in Rose.
992 3 Mary, b. May 16, 1821.
993 4 Charles, b. Feb. 7, 1824. } Twins.
994 5 David, b. Feb. 7, 1824.   }
995 6 Larius H., b. April 15, 1828, teacher in Benton, Ark.
996 7 Frederic, b. July 21, 1830, publisher in Pine Bluff, Ark.
997 8 Flavia E., May 31, 1833; d. Nov. 9, 1856.
998 9 Samuel, b. June 16, 1836, farmer, Wolcott, N. Y.

991 JOHN LYMAN[8], b. May 16, 1821.
          Children, Ninth Generation:
999 1 Caroline C., b. June 8, 1851.
1000 2 Charles F., b. Dec. 9, 1852.
1001 3 David M., b. Sept. 3, 1854.
1002 4 Dorcas E., b. March 16, 1857.
1003 5 John B., b. April 27, 1859.
1004 6 Samuel H., b. July 19, 1861.

998 SAMUEL LYMAN[8], b. June 16, 1836.   *Wolcott, N. Y.*
          Children, Ninth Generation:
1005 1 George Franklin, b. Dec. 16, 1861.
1006 2 Anna E., b. June 21, 1863.

996 FREDERIC LYMAN[8], 4th son of *Samuel[7]*, of Rose,
N. Y., m. Jan. 19, 1860, Lettie M. Mallory, settled a
farmer in McHenry Co., Ill., enlisted in the 95th Regt. of
Infantry, early in the rebellion, and served through the
war; now editor of the *Republican*, Pine Bluff, Arkansas.
                                        Dewitt, Ark.
          Children, Ninth Generation:
1007 1 Charles Lewis, b. Dec. 9, 1860; d. March 16, 1861.

1008 2 Minnie Clementina, b. Feb. 10, 1862.

1009 3 Freddie Clark, b. Oct. 5, 1866 ; d. Feb. 18, 1868. Mrs. L. d. Jan. 5, 1869.

The following chapters on pioneer life written by Samuel Lyman, son of David Lyman, who left Salisbury, Connecticut, in 1817, and settled in Rose, N. Y. are a quaint and amusing illustration of the spirit of the man and of the age :

THE THIRD BOOK OF MACCABEES.

CHAPTER I.

1. Now there dwelt in one of the eastern provinces an aged man, a man of renown, of the lineage of Simeon, and there were born unto him twelve children, six sons and six daughters, and they were comely in stature, and beautiful to look upon, and they were brought up under the law of Moses and the Saybrook platform, and they swerved not from the precepts of their Father but observed the ordinances of the law blameless.

2. And when his eldest son had grown to man's estate, he took to wife one of the daughters of the land, and when children were born unto him, he said, behold the land is too straight for us, and it was told him of a goodly land, lying west of the great mountains a province, flowing with milk and honey.

3. And he communed with his wife and said, thou seest the straits to which we shall be driven, behold the land is too straight for us, let us arise and seek a habitation beyond the great river, for ourselves and little ones, where there is room for our flocks and our herds, lest we come to poverty.

4. And the saying pleased her, and she said, thou hast well spoken. Now do as thou hast said, that we may find sustenance for ourselves and little ones.

5. And he gathered together his substance and took his wife and little one, with seventy shekels of silver, and bade his kindred farewell and departed.

6. And he journeyed westward over the great mountains of the province, and on the third day he arrived at the great river of the country, and he passed over it, and behold a level country opened before him.

7. And he pursued his journey for the space of seventeen days, and on the eighteenth he lifted up his eyes and said, we are drawing near our journey's end, and now behold, I have a kinsman living in this country, let us therefore seek him out and lodge with him, peradventure he may succor and befriend us, seeing we are strangers in the land.

8. And he inquired of the inhabitants of the land, saying, know ye such and such a man living near ? and they answered, yea, we know him, and he dwelleth with us in the Valley of Roses.

9. And he hastened and drew near the place and alighted, and presented himself before the man, and when he had saluted him he said : I am a stranger from a far country, and I come to seek a residence in this land. And the man said — Whose son art thou ?

And he said, I am the son of thy sister, whom she bare unto my father.

10. And the man said, Come in, thou blessed of the Lord, and tarry with us. And he ran and drew water and provided provender for his oxen and he sat meat before them, and they did eat and were satisfied.

11. And he said, now tell us of thy father and mother, and all thy kindred and of their welfare. And he told him all and kept nothing from him, and of the mighty men of renown in his country. And the man rejoiced exceedingly.

12. And he said, behold the land is before thee, choose thee out a place which liketh thee best.. If thou likest it not on the left, then turn thou to the right, for the place is large and the whole land is before thee.

13. And on the morrow he journeyed northward, and eastward a little way, and behold a level plain like the plains of Amram opened before him, and the trees thereof were sturdy as the oaks of Bashan, tall and stately as the cedars of Lebanon and their tops reached up toward heaven, and he lifted up his eyes, and looked northward and eastward, and he said, this suiteth me.

14. And he conferred with the magnates of the land, and said unto them, what must I give thee for the land running thus far northward, and eastward, and southward? and they said, thou shalt have it for 750 pieces of silver.

15. And he unloosed the mouth of his sack, and weighed out to them a part of the price, even 40 pieces, and he called witnesses, and it was sealed unto him, and his children after him forever.

16. And he set up his Ebenezer, and pitched his tent, and he called the name of the place Peth, which name it also bears unto this day. And the man Sambo was twenty and three years old, when he first entered into Peth.

CHAPTER II.

1. And it came to pass on the twenty-first day of the second month, that he removed from the Valley of Roses to his own house. And it was winter. And the boar-frost lay on the face of the country, to the depth of forty and eight inches. And he drew forth his axe of steel and swung it with vigor against the trees of the forest, and they fell prostrate before him.

2. And he clave the trees asunder, and drew the wood to his house and kindled great fires on his hearth, which ceased not to burn, night and day, till the frost ceased from the earth.

3. And at the end of forty and five days, the south wind began to blow, and the frost dissolved, and all the low places and pools of the country were filled with water. And the waters subsided, and the man said: I will go forth to my labors.

4. And the forest resounded with the blows of his axe, and the trees came tumbling with a mighty crash to the earth and he cut them asunder, and rolled them in piles, one upon the other, and set them on fire, and they were consumed.

5. And he prepared the ground and sowed it with wheat and corn and legumens, and the earth yielded her increase, some thirty, some sixty and some a hundred fold. And the man rejoiced greatly in the work of his hands.

6. And he spake to his wife and said, after a few more years of toil, and when this wilderness shall be subdued before us, we shall then have a goodly heritage, where our flocks and herds can feed in green pastures and lie down beside the still waters, for the land is fruitful and level as the garden of Eden and will produce all manner of fruits in their season, equal to the clusters of Eshcol.

7. And he rose with the lark, buoyant with, as it were, the strength of an unicorn, and he built stalls for his oxen, and outhouses for the products of the land, and he got him herds of cattle.

8. And when the season was far spent, and the products of the land had been gathered in, the inhabitants of the land said to him, our children are growing up in ignorance without schools. Come thou and teach them for ninety days, and we will give thee for thy hire, thirty-six pieces of silver.

9. And his wife said, go my husband, for the oil is clean gone in the cruise, and the meal runs low in the barrel, and there are but two pieces of silver left in the sack; go, therefore, that we may replenish our stores.

10. And he consented, and went. And when the ninety days had expired, he said, now pay me my hire, and he took the thirty-six pieces of silver, and brought them to his wife, saying: put them in the sack, and buy such things as are needed for our sustenance; till our own fields yield us a full supply.

11. And an angel appeared to him in a dream by night, and said: I have watched thy outgoings and thy incomings, these many days since thou hast been a sojourner in this wilderness, and how thou hast walked before me in thy integrity, and now I will reveal to thee things that must shortly come to pass.

12. And now evil genii are let loose in the land, and they are now going to and fro in the land and walking up and down in it, and they will pour out the vials of their wrath on the fountains of water, and all the pools shall become green, and the miasma shall overflow the country.

13. And sickness will follow, and death on his pale horse will traverse thy streets, and lamentation and woe shall be heard in thy gates, and thou canst not escape, for thou must pass through the mill, down through the hopper, between the upper and the nether mill stones and pass out through the cogwheel. But like my servant Job, stick thou to thine integrity, and like him thou shalt come off more than conqueror,

14. And thy captivity shall be turned, and thou shalt be greatly blessed in thy basket and in thy store, and thy seed shall be greatly multiplied and they shall inherit the land, and thou shalt live to a good old age, and thou shalt yet behold thy children's children in

45

troops gamboling in the streets of Peth; and he awoke and behold it was a dream.　And he told it to his wife and she marveled greatly.

CHAPTER III.

1. And about the beginning of barley harvest when the sun shineth in his strength, he assayed to go to the field as at other times, and he thrust in his sickle and it fell from his hand, for his hand shook like the aspen leaf, and he hastened to his house and said, kindle a fire and wrap me in blankets that I may get heat, for the icy hand of death is upon me.　And a mighty fever followed, and he said, bring me a drop of water to cool my tongue, for the marrow of my bones is on fire.

2. And sore disease was upon him, and he gat no rest.　Chilled with ague by day and scorched by fever at night, as days and weeks rolled on they brought him no relief.

3. And, in anguish of spirit, he cried, O, that I had remained on my own native hills, there to inhale the health-giving breezes wafted from their everlasting heights! O, that I could drink of the sweet, sparkling waters that gush from their thousand fountains, and that I could now bathe my feverish brow and aching limbs, in the soft, foaming waters as they dance in their onward course from the top of Riga, instead of these sluggish waters, which breed malaria, pestilence and death!

4. And while he was yet speaking, behold a messenger came running, and said: A mighty tempest hath shaken the forest, and the trees thereof have fallen upon thy cattle and left thee none remaining. And his wife and little ones were also smitten with the ague.

5. And the voice of mirth was hushed in the streets, and the weeks of Sundays commenced. And few went to their fields, for sore disease was upon them.　And the crops went back to the earth, for none could be found to harvest them.　And the man bowed his head to the blast, and said, My cup is filled to the brim and runneth over. And he covered him with sack-cloth and ashes.

6. And he spake not again for the space of two days.　Then he opened his mouth and said, Thy billows go over my soul and I sink in deep waters.　Let that day be darkened, let it not be counted among the days of the year in which it was said, the man first set foot into Peth.　And the man wept sore, for anguish was upon him.

7. And death on his pale horse traveled his rounds.　And many were borne to their long homes.　And a wayfaring man as he journeyed called in, and when he saw their affliction he said, be of good cheer, and fear not, I will cast out this shaking devil, that he torment you no more and ye shall be well, if so be I can find a certain herb which grows in the country; and he went on his way, and the man went with him a little way and he said, behold here it is, and he pulled up the herb and gave it to the man and said, steep it in water and drink of it, and ye shall be well.　And he brought it to his wife and she steeped it and drank of the water, and was cured. The man also drank of it, but was not cured.

8. And the man said, behold the woman is cured, howbeit he could not cast it out of the man also. And it was said, this kind goeth not out by a decoction of roots and herbs. And the man shook on, and in dreamy mazes he would revisit his fatherland and ramble over the old wonted lots and eat of the luscious fruit of the old trees of the fruit-yard or drink of their generous juices fresh from the press; but only to awake to disappointment as when a hungry man dreameth.

9. And when months of suffering had passed away, the man began to amend and his strength returned as his disease grew less, and he said, the bitterness of death is past, I am fast getting through the mill, except perchance the cogwheels. And he thanked God and took courage.

10. And he gained in strength daily, the chilling blasts of winter were over, and the ague gone, the genial sun of spring returned to bless the earth and awaken to new life the vegetable kingdom, and the man felt its genial influence, was invigorated, and went forth anew rejoicing to his labors, and he toiled on and the wilderness receded before him.

<h3 style="text-align:center">CHAPTER IV.</h3>

1. Now it came to pass at the end of twelve years, as he sat musing on the events af the past, that he greatly desired to visit once more the land of his nativity, and know of the welfare of his kindred.

2. And he said to his wife, go to, I pray thee, let me go and visit my kindred in the Eastern Province, and know of a surety of their health and of their welfare.

3. And she said, go and the Lord prosper thee on thy journey thither. Go and visit thy father and mother, for they are old and well stricken in years; go, therefore, and see them before they die.

4. And he arose, and put on change of raiment, and girded on his sandals, and took his staff in his hand, and kissed them and said, be of good cheer till I return in peace at the end of the full moon, and he departed.

5. And he journeyed onward, till he came to the great thoroughfare of the country, and he took shipping thereon, and sped on the way four days and nights, and he arrived at the great river, and passed over it.

6. And on the fifth day, he lifted up his eyes and behold, the great mountains which divide the provinces were before him, and he passed over them and drew near to the home of his father and his mother, and all his kindred.

7. And when he came in sight of his own native hills his emotions were unutterable, and he sat down on the ground and gazed with delight and wonder upon the mighty Taghanic over whose rugged cliffs in his younger days be bounded, like the young roe in the chase, after the foxes and the conies.

8. And he said, up, I may not thus tarry,—get thee down to thy father's house and know of their welfare; and he hastened and entered

into the house and saluted them, and he seemed unto them as a wayfaring man and they knew him not.

9. And he communed with them of their flocks and of their herds, and he said, I would see the master of the house if peradventure I may buy of him; and they said, he is in the field ploughing and as he assayed to go to the field he smiled; and his mother fixed her eyes upon him and she leaped from her seat and caught hold of the skirts of his garment and held him fast.

10. And she said, tell me, is this our son who has been gone from us these many years? tell me. And he dissembled no longer, and he said, yea, my mother, it is indeed he who has been gone so long, thy very son Sambo.

11. And she rejoiced and said, blessed be the God of thy fathers that he hath preserved thee alive and sent thee back in safety, that we may see thy face once more before we die. And she rejoiced as though she had seen the face of an angel.

12. And they brought forth the fatted calf and made a feast of fat things, butter, and honey and wine on the lees well refined. And they did eat and drink and were merry.

13. And when the end of the full moon drew near, he said, go to I pray thee; let me now return to my home and see how it fares with my wife and little ones. And they said, if now it must be so, bring thy sack for we may not send thee empty away.

14. And they brought forth their treasures, new and old, rich apparel and changes of raiment, and put them in the sack, and his father brought a lordly present, even 40 shekels of silver, and blessed him and said, the God of thy fathers bless and protect thee on thy journey, and may thy posterity inherit the land and make them as the stars of Heaven in multitude, and he bade them farewell and went on his way rejoicing.

15. And on the fifth day at the going down of the sun he drew near his own house, and his wife and little ones espied him afar off and they ran and fell on his neck and kissed him; and he unloosed the sack, and when they saw the treasures he had brought them they were filled with exceeding great joy.

16. And he again applied himself to his labor with renewed vigor, and blessings attended him in his outgoings and incomings, insomuch that sons were born unto him by couplets. And he named them after his younger brethren, and the lads grew and prospered greatly.

17. And he waxed strong in power, and his substance increased, and he gat him horses and chariots, and he rode upon the high places of Peth. He washed his steps in butter and the rock poured him out rivers of oil, and he sat as a prince among his people.

18. And he had six sons and three daughters, and among all the daughters of Peth there was none to vie with the daughters of Sambo.

19. And his sons were comely in person and walked in the steps of their father; and, like Recab, the son of Jonadab, drank no wine

or strong drink, and they became mighty in building up the name and the house of their father.

20. And they took them wives, of such as they chose among the daughters of the land, and got them possessions on the right hand and on the left, and children were born unto them, and the heavens were filled with their mirth.

21. And as Sambo sat at the gate at the entering in of the city, he said: Mine horn is exalted, for unto me is given a numerous progeny to build up my house and perpetuate my name in the archives of Peth forever.

V. DESCENDANTS OF MOSES[3] THROUGH SETH[5].

17 SETH LYMAN[5], sixth son of Capt. *Moses.* Of Seth[5], little appears to be known; no date is given of his birth, marriage, or death. Nothing is know of his wife. After the sale of his property in Northampton, and at an advanced age, he moved to Norwich, Mass., where he died. He is supposed to have been born about 1732. He is said to have had eight children.   *Norwich, Mass.*

Children, Sixth Generation :

1 1 Seth, b. Sept. 12, 1755.
2 2 Giles, b. Nov. 21, 1757.
3 3 Solomon, b. Feb. 14, 1760.
4 4 Theodosia, b. Feb. 24, 1762; m. Nov. 21, 1782, Israel Barnard.
5 5 Catharine, the names of the other children are unknown.

According to Mr. Judd one or two were living in 1842. Seth had the old homestead in Northampton, including Shop Row, managed badly, and was obliged to sell his property to pay his debts.

2 GILES LYMAN[6], m. at some time previous to 1771, Phebe ......, and soon after the birth of their first child removed to Norwich, Mass.   *Norwich, Mass.*

Children, Seventh Generation :

6 1 Luther, b. at Northampton, Jan. 19, 1781.
7 2 Theodore, b. in Norwich, Jan. 31, 1783.

6 LUTHER LYMAN[7]. In the records of Norwich, are entered the intentions of marriage between Luther Lyman, of Norwich, and Rebecca Warner, of Chesterfield, Mass., March 5, 1802. The issue of this marriage, so far as we have ascertained, was seven.   *Genesee, N. Y.*

Children, Eighth Generation :

8 1 Levi.
9 2 Laura.
10 3 Phebe.
11 4 Seth.
12 5 Dwight.
13 6 Samuel Warner.
14 7 Luther.

9 LAURA LYMAN[8], dau. of Luther Lyman, m. Paddock, of Oswego, N. Y. There is a George W. Lyman, in business in Oswego, N. Y., supposed to be the son of Luther; no further record. 　　　　　　　　　　　　　*Oswego, N. Y.*

VI. DESCENDANTS OF MOSES[3], THROUGH JOB[5], M.D.

18 JOB LYMAN[5], b. in Northampton, Mass., Sept. 22, 1735 ; d. in York, Me., March 29, 1791. Graduated at Yale College, 1756; settled in York, Maine—physician. Abigail Lyman, b. in York, Maine, June 25, 1745 ; d. Jan. 24, 1808, dau. of the Hon. Jeremiah Moulton, wife of Job Lyman, mother of eleven children, viz : 　　　　　*York, Me.*

Children, Sixth Generation :

1　1 Hannah, b. May 22, 1763.
2　2 Abigail, b. Feb. 24, 1765.
3　3 William, b. June 14, 1767.
4　4 Moses, b. April 16, 1769.
5　5 Mindwell, b. May 26, 1771.
6　6 Theda, b. Oct. 4, 1773.
7　7 Isaac, b. Oct. 29, 1775.
8　8 Theodosia, b. Oct. 5, 1777.
9　9 Narcissa, b. June 2, 1780.
10　10 Augusta, b. Sept. 30, 1787.
11　11 Lavinia, b. June 5, 1789.

The epitaphs of Job and Abigail Lyman, in York, Me., are as follows

JOB LYMAN, M.D.,
Obt.
March 29. 1791,
Aged 54.
" Eminent as a physician, beloved and respected
as a father and friend."
ABIGAIL LYMAN,
Widow of
JOB LYMAN, M.D.
And daughter of the Hon. Jeremiah Moulton,
Obt. Jan. 22, 1808,
aged 62.
Every virtue which could adorn the wife,
mother, and friend, was concentrated
in this most excellent woman.

1 HANNAH LYMAN[6], m. Thomas Wallingford, Esq., of Somersworth, N. H. They had two children, Lyman and George. 　　　　　　　　　　　　　*Somersworth, N. H.*

2 ABIGAIL LYMAN[6], m. Edward Emerson, of York. They had six children—Clarissa, m. Edward Wiggiu, Esq., of Boston, and after his death, Judge Williamson, of Bangor. Augustus. Miranda, who married Edward Kating, Esq., of Portland. Charles O., who m. Harriet Phillips, of Portland; and Andrew L., first mayor of the city of Portland, who m. Mary Clapp, of that city. *York, Me.*

3 WILLIAM LYMAN[6], a physician, settled in York, Me., and m. Hannah Sewall. They had two children : William, who died young ; and Navissa, who m. Robert Eben Carpenter, of York, Me. *York, Me.*

4 MOSES LYMAN[6], settled in York, Me., m. Mary Layiant. They had one child, a son. who d. young. *York, Me.*

5 MINDWELL LYMAN[6], m. Peter O. Alden, Esq., of Brunswick, Maine. No children. *Brunswick, Me.*

6 THEDA LYMAN[6], m..........Smith, Esq. of South Berwick, Maine. They had one child, Miranda, who m. Valentine, and they had one child. *South Berwick, Mass.*

7 ISAAC LYMAN[6], counselor at law, m. Lucretia Pickering of Portsmouth, N. H., chief justice of the Supreme Court in New Hampshire. They had ten children:
Portsmouth, N. H.

Children, Seventh Generation:

12   1 John Pickering, m. Mary Rantaul Peabody. They have three children, viz : John Pickering, a grad. of Harvard Coll., in class of 1868; Mary Rantaul, and Theodore.

13   2 Abby Frances, m. Joseph G. Lize, merchant. They had five children : Albert Fleetwood, Francis Parker, Abby Lyman, George Lyman, Horace Fleetwood.

14   3 Lucretia Ann.

15   4 George Sheofe, d. young.

16   5 Susan Pickering, m. William Haben, jr., and after his death m. Rufus Kittridge, M.D., of Portsmouth, N. H. Had one child, Nathan Parker Haben.

17   6 Hannah Walker, m. Samuel P. Long, artist.

18   7 Charles Augustus, m. Elizabeth Redwood Hollingsworth of Philadelphia. They have four children. Thomas Hollingwood, Emilie Redwood, Charles, Fannie.

23   8 Frances Pickering, d. young.

24   9 Isaac, unmarried, d. abroad.

25   10 Nathan Parker, merchant, Philadelphia.

8 THEODOSIA[6], m. John Bonell, Esq., of York, and had two children: Charles Colburn, and Abbie. *York, Me.*

9 NARCISSA[6], who m. Samuel Leent, merchant in York, Me. They had four children, Elizabeth, who m. Jeremiah McIntire, Esq., of York. Samuel, who m. Hannah Smith of York. Horace, graduate of Bowdoin College, and d. the same year. Narcissa d. at the age of 16. *York, Me.*

10 AUGUSTA[6], who m. Joshua Johnson, Esq. of York. They had three children, one only living, Lobenia Ellen, who m. Henry Robinson. *York, Me.*

Children, Seventh Generation:

34 ı Annie Huntington.   35 2 Nettie Lyman.

11 LAVINIA[6], youngest child d. unmarried.

The descendants of Job. Lyman, M. D., now living in York, are · Elizabeth McIntire and her son, Jerie McIntire, F. P. Emerson, m. Miranda Brooks, daughter of Jeremiah Brooks of York, Abbie C. Emerson, who m. Jerie McIntire, Esq. of York, A. L. Emerson, who m. Fannie L. Phillips, of York, Charles Colburn Bonell, who m. Martha Odlin of Exeter. They have nine children.

There are six great grandchildren, or children of the 8th generation, descendants of Job Lyman, M.D.

ALBERT FLEETWOOD LIZE, m. Edith Ware, dau. of Dr. John Ware. They had four children: Helen Ware, Lyman, Robert Ware, Gertrude.

ABBY LYMAN LIZE[7], m. *Charles* H. Burbank, surgeon U. S. N. They have one child: Edith.

GEORGE LYMAN LIZE[4], m. *Louisa* Rosenbury of Bavaria. They have one child: Theodora Fleetwood.

PART VIII.

Descendants of Benjamin.[3]

I. DESCENDANTS OF BENJAMIN[3], THROUGH JOSEPH[4].

LIEUT. BENJAMIN LYMAN[3], 4th son of Ensign *John*[2] and grandson of *Richard*[1], b. in Northampton, Aug. 10, 1674; m. Oct. 27, 1698, Thankful Pomeroy, dau. of Deacon Medad Pomeroy, and granddaughter to Eltweld Pomeroy, who came from Devonshire, England, in 1630, lived at Dorchester, and Windsor, Ct., and d. in Northampton, in 1673. Benjamin, d. Oct. 14, 1723, in the 50th year of his age, leaving ten children. He was an enterprising, thriving man, and his estate free from debt was appraised at £1,147. At the time of his death he owned five hundred acres of land in the Bedford tract near Granville. He also traded some, and his shop goods were appraised at £198. He was an extensive farmer and fatted cattle in the stall. He owned a negro slave named Nancy, who was appraised at £40. In the division of his estate, his sons Joseph and Caleb had the homestead. Joseph had the lot which had been in possession of his father and grandfather, and descended in his family to his widow Thankful, who m. 2d Ensign Nathaniel Lewis, of Farmington, Ct. ...... 4, 1726. She, however, returned to Northampton, in her old age, and d. there, Sept. 18, 1773, in her 95th year.   *Northampton, Mass.*

Children, Fourth Generation

1   1 Joseph, b. Aug. 22, 1699; m. Abigail Lewis of Farmington, Ct., d. 1764.
2   2 Benjamin, b. Dec. 19, 1701; d. in infancy.
3   3 Benjamin, b. Jan. 4, 1703; settled in Easthampton.
4   4 Aaron, b. April 1, 1705; settled in Belchertown.
5   5 Eunice, b. May, 1707; d. June, 1720.
6   6 Hannah, b. July 14, 1709; m. Nathaniel Dwight of Belchertown, d. 1794.
7   7 Caleb, b. Aug. 8, 1711, lived in Boston with his Uncle Caleb. He was never married.
8   8 Susannah, b. July 18, 1713; m. Mr. Baxter of Boston.
9   9 William, b. Dec. 12, 1715.
10 10 Daniel, b. April 18, 1718, graduated at Yale College in 1745. He was a judge in New Haven.

46

11 11 Elihu, b. July 10, 1720, graduated at Yale College in 1745.
He was an officer in the French war and never married.
12 12 Medad, b. March 20, 1722, kept a tavern in New Haven.

2 Joseph Lyman⁴, *Benjamin³, John², Richard¹,* 1699–1763,
b. 1699; m. Abigail Lewis of Farmington, Ct., who was
b. in 1701. He remained in Northampton where he d.
March 30, 1763, thirteen years before the death of his wife
on whose tombstone are inscribed these words:

> The grave is that home of man
> Where dwells the multitude. *Northampton, Mass.*

Children, Fifth Generation ·

14 1 Eunice, b. May 30, 1728; m. Capt. Lewis Clark of Northampton.
15 2 Mercy, b. Sept. 7, 1729 ; m. Hon. Joseph Hawley, the patriot
of the Revolution, who first uttered the sentiment, "We
must fight," afterwards quoted by Patrick Henry.
16 3 Joseph, b. May 4, 1731.
17 4 Eleanor, b. May 18, 1732; d. in infancy.
18 5 Elisha, b. June 22, 1734.
19 6 Eleanor, b. Sept. 24, 1737; m. Capt. Oliver Lyman, of Vt.
Ch. 6th Gen. 1 Erastus, b. Feb. 9, 1761, who m. Abigail Bracket. 2 Mary, b., 1765; m. Lynde Lord, of
Litchfield, Ct., Jan. 30, 1786. 3 Joseph, b. Oct. 22,
1767.

20 Maj. Erastus Lyman⁶, b. 1761 ; m. Abigail Bracket.
They had one dau. Abigail Bracket, who was m. at Northampton, April 30, 1821, to Wm. Greene, a lineal descendant
of Gen. Nathaniel Greene, of Revolutionary fame. He has
been in business in Cincinnati where he acquired a large
fortune, and where he was distinguished for his efforts in
connection with common school education. On the death
of his wife, a woman of rare gifts and of most elevated
character, July 18, 1862, he removed to East Greenwich,
R. I., and has since occupied his ancestral estate. He was
elected lieutenant governor of the state, in 1866, in the
gubernatorial term of Gov. Burnside, and held the office two
years. He is now m. a second time and has retired from
public life. *East Greenwich, R. I.*

Children, Seventh Generation :

23 1 Catharine Ray, b. Nov. 20, 1824.
24 2 Anne Jean, b. April 20, 1827 ; d. July 31, 1831.

By 2d wife, Rachel Hutchins of Northampton.
25 3 Sally, m. Dana, a broker in Cincinnati.
26 4 Harriet, d. unmarried about 1840.

27 5 Martha, b.— unmarried. Spends her winters in Cambridge, Mass., and her summers at Nahant.
28 6 Charlotte, m. Rev. Wm. Silobee, formerly pastor of the Unitarian church in Northampton, but now of Trenton, N. Y. She d. about 1850, leaving a son who graduated at Harvard in 1869, and is now studying medicine in Boston, and a dau. resides with her father in Trenton.

23 CATHARINE RAY LYMAN[7], m. Frederic R——n, M.D., of Cincinnati, O., Feb. 1, 1855, and d. May 22, 1864.

Cincinnati, O.

Children, Eighth Generation :

29 1 Wm. Greene, b. June 12, 1854.
30 2 Anne Lyman, b. Jan. 17, 1856.
31 3 Fritz, June 14, 1857.
32 4 Harry, b. July 16, 1858.
33 5 Catharine, b. Jan. 23, 1860.
34 6 Emil, b. Nov. 28, 1861, d. May, 1864.

22 JOSEPH LYMAN[6], 3d of the name, b. Oct. 22, 1767, graduated from Yale College in 1783, was admitted to the bar in Jan., 1787, practiced seven years in Westfield, Mass., which town he represented in the legislature. He returned to Northampton his native town, and was appointed clerk of the courts of Hampshire county in 1798, a position which he held till 1810, when he was appointed judge of the common pleas and of probate. The court of common pleas was broken up in 1811, and Hampshire county was divided. In 1816 he was appointed sheriff of Hampshire Co. which position he held till 1845, two years before his death which occurred Dec. 11, 1847.

It is related as quite remarkable, that in sixty years connection with the courts as attorney, clerk, judge, or sheriff, he never sued any one in any other than an official capacity nor was he ever sued by any one. It is said that he had little choice between losing a debt and suing for its recovery. He was president of the old Hampshire Bank during the whole of its existence from 1812 to 1835.

He m. first, Elizabeth Fowler, daughter of Hon. Samuel Fowler of Westfield, Jan. 10, 1792. She was b. Feb. 1, 1772; and d. July 16, 1808.

Children, Seventh Generation :

37 1 Elizabeth, b. Oct. 16, 1792.
38 2 Edmund Dwight, b. Nov. 20, 1795; d., 1834.
39 3 Frances Fowler, b. Aug. 31, 1797; d. Jan. 11, 1809.
40 4 Samuel Fowler, b. May 3, 1799.

41   5 Mary, b. March 27, 1802; d., 1834.
42   6 Jane, b. April 22, 1804.

Married 2d, Oct. 11, 1811, to Anne Jean, dau. of the Hon. E. H. Robbins, of Milton, Mass. She was b. July, 1789, and d. May 24, 1867, a woman of remarkable beauty of person, force of character and goodness of heart. The children of this second marriage were:

43   7 Joseph, b Aug. 17, 1812; m. Susan Bulfinch, of Boston.
44   8 Anne Jean, b. July 7, 1815; d. autumn of 1835.
45   9 Edward Hutchinson Robbins, b. Feb. 10, 1819.
46 10 Susan Inches, b. April 7, 1823; m. J. Peter Lesley, member of the National Academy of Science, and has two daughters, Mary and Margaret White.
49 11 Catharine Robbins, b. Jan. 12, 1825; m. Warren Delano, of N. Y., and has had eleven children.

43 Joseph Lyman was gifted with personal and mental endowments of the highest order. He was a noble example of a refined, cultivated gentleman and scholar. With a heart tender as that of a child, delicate, gentle and sensitive as that of a woman, he was a man of heroic fortitude, dauntless energy and perseverance in the pursuits of life. From the study of law he passed to that civil engineering mining and metallurgy, and bent all his varied attainments and energies for some time to the early development of the deposits of anthracite coal and beds of iron in Pennsylvania. The construction of rail roads, as a means of national wealth, also strongly enlisted his attention, while the condition of the poor the ignorant and the oppressed employed his active sympathies and wakeful benevolence. The emancipation of the slave, the enfranchisement, the education and improvement of all classes of his fellow men was the study and the labor of his life. Every form of human misery be comprehended in his wide wish of benevolence. "There was not a groan from the oppressed in the world's wide realm, that did not reach his ear and melt his heart. There was not a hand lifted for freedom in Europe or America that he did see and bless."

And yet he comprehended in his reading and study the wide range of literature, science and politics, though half his term through life stretched helplessly on his bed the subject of acute, excruciating pain. Worn down with these sufferings, he yielded up his noble, exemplary life, Aug. 13, 1871, at Jamaica Plain, Mass., leaving a wife and daughters whose reord has not been received.

37 Elizabeth Lyman[7], m. Samuel Henshaw of Boston.

Boston, Mass.

Children, Eighth Generation:

61 1 Samuel, d. unmarried.
62 2 Joseph, m. Jane Bradlee, and has three children.
63 3 John, unmarried.
64 4 Anne Brooks, unmarried.
65 5 Frank, m. Laura Nourse, and has two children.

49 Catharine R. Lyman[7], dau. of Hon. *Joseph*[6] b. Northampton, Jan. 12, 1825 ; m. Nov. 1, 1843, Warren Delano, who was b. in Fair Haven, Bristol Co., Mass., July 13, 1809. The ancestor of Mr. D., was one of the second company of pilgrim emigrants in 1621, in the Fortune, a ship of 55 tons. *China.*

Children, Eighth Generation:
70 1 Susan, b. in China, Oct. 13, 1844 ; d. June 29, 1846.
71 2 Louise, b. in China, June 4, 1845; d. May 26, 1869.
72 3 Deborah, b. Aug. 29, 1847 ; m. Wm. H. Forbes.
73 4 Annie, b. Jan. 8, 1849.
74 5 Warren, b. Sept. 20, 1850 ; d. Oct. 10, 1851.
75 6 Warren, b. July, 1852.
76 7 Sarah, b. Sept., 1854.
77 8 Phillippe, b. Feb. 3, 1857.
78 9 Catharine, b. May 24, 1860.
79 10 Frederick, b. Sept. 10, 1863, in China.
80 11 Laura, b. Dec. 23, 1864, in China.

40 Judge Samuel F. Lyman[7], b. May 3, 1799, graduated from Harvard College in 1818, studied law at Worthington, Mass., Litchfield, Ct., and at Northampton, and practiced law till 1830. He was appointed register of probate in 1827, an appointment which he held till 1855, when he was removed by Gov. Gardner for political reasons. In 1858, he was appointed judge of probate and insolvency, which post he still occupies. He was m. May 27, 1824, to Almira Smith of Hatfield. *Northampton, Mass.*

Children, Eighth Generation:
81 1 Elizabeth, b. April 10, 1828.
82 2 James Fowler, b. Aug. 28, 1830.
83 3 Harriet Willard, b. April 3, 1834.
84 4 Benjamin Smith, b. Dec. 11, 1835.
85 5 Mary, b. Aug. 10, 1837.

82 James Fowler Lyman[8], son of Judge *Samuel*[7], and F. Lyman, b. Aug. 28, 1830. graduated at Harvard College in 1850, studied law at the Harvard Law School, and is now engaged in life insurance. *Newark, N. J.*

84 Benjamin Smith Lyman[8], son of *Judge Samuel*[7], b. Dec. 11, 1835, graduated from Harvard College in 1855, studied geology, mining and kindred branches two years in Paris, and one year in Freiburg, Germany; was some time a mining engineer in Philadelphia, and was in the service of the British government in Hindustan, exploring

the mineral resources of the country in search of mineral oil or petroleum.

41 MARY LYMAN[7], daughter of Judge *Joseph[6]*, b. March 27, 1802 ; m. Thomas Jones, of Enfield.   She d. in 1834.
Enfield, Mass.
Children, Eighth Generation :
86 1 Thomas, Havana, Ill.
87 2 Joseph Lyman, Lecompton, Kan.
88 3 William Greene, Knoxville, Ill.

42 JANE LYMAN[7], dau. of Judge *Joseph[6]*, b. April 22, 1804; m. Stephen Brewer, Northampton, d. March, 1859 ; Mr. Brewer was drowned in the Connecticut river, in 1842.   *Northampton, Mass.*
Children, Eighth Generation ·
89 1 Hannah Elizabeth.
90 2 Frances.
91 3 Jane Lyman, d. in Dec., 1860.

45 EDWARD HUTCHINSON ROBBINS LYMAN[7], son of Hon. *Joseph[8]* and Anne Robbins, was b. Feb. 19, 1819; m. Sarah Elizabeth Lowe, dau. of Seth Lowe, Brooklyn, L. I., and was b. Aug. 16, 1822.   They were m. at Brooklyn, Aug. 26, 1846.   *Brooklyn, N. Y.*
Children, Eighth Generation :
92 1 Edward Robbins, b. Jan. 20, 1848; d. Aug. 14, 1849.
93 2 Anne Jean, b. June 12, 1850.
94 3 Joseph, b. Oct. 11, 1851.
95 4 Frank, b. Dec. 20, 1852.
Sarah Elizabeth Lyman d. April 27, 1863, and Mr. Lyman m. at Brooklyn, Aug. 1, 1865, Catharine Amelia Treadway, who was b. Aug. 11, 1823, and daughter of the late Alfred Treadway, M.D., of Harts Village, N. Y.

18 ELISHA LYMAN[5], son of *Joseph[4]*, and grandson of *Benjamin[3]*, the ancestor of this branch, was b. June 22, 1734, m. Abigail Janes; d. Aug. 13, 1798.   *Northampton, Mass.*
Children, Sixth Generation :
96 1 Elisha, b. April 25, 1765, d. early.
97 2 Micah Jones, b. Oct. 17, 1767, at Northampton.
98 3 Elisha, b. Jan. 26, 1770, Champlain, N. Y.
99 4 Lewis, b. June 8, 1772 ; m. Mary Parrot Paine, b. at Troy, Aug. 9, 1815.   He d. March 20, 1852, leaving no children.
101 5 Theodore, b. Nov. 3, 1784.

102 6 Henry, b. July 23, 1788; d. Sept. 20, 1809, at Burlington,
Vt., though a resident of Montreal, unmarried.
103 7 Lydia, b. Jan. 7, 1775; m. Samuel Hedge; d. in Montreal,
in 185...
104 8 Susannah, b. Feb. 10, 1780; m. Roswell Corse, resides in
Montreal; d. in 1852, leaving two daughters, viz :
Ch. 7th Gen.: 1 Susan, m. Dr. Arthur Fisher. 2
Mary, m. Henry Lyman, son of Elisha of the 6th Gen.,
all of Montreal.
107 9 Abigail, b. Dec. 30, 1782; d. Oct. 25, 1806.

97 MICAH JONES LYMAN⁶, son of *Elisha⁵* and Abigail
Lyman, was b. at Northampton, Oct. 17, 1767, m. Jan. 19,
1794, to Elizabeth, dau. of Benjamin and Elizabeth Sheldon
of Northampton. He was a graduate of Yale College in
1785; studied medicine with Dr. Ebenezer Hunt of Northampton, one of the most celebrated physicians of his time;
commenced the practice of medicine in Bennington, Vt.,
1790; removed to Montreal in 1810, and was engaged in
the drug business till the beginning of the war with Great
Britain in 1812, when he went to Troy, N. Y., and con-
tinned there in the same business till 1842. He continued
to reside there until Nov., 1850, when he removed to his
son's residence in Bennington, where he d. Dec. 20, 1851.
His wife d. Feb. 3, 1834. *Troy, N. Y.*

Children, Seventh Generation :
108 1 Charles, b. Oct. 17, 1794.
109 2 George, b. June 19, 1796.
110 3 Mary Sheldon, b. at Bennington, May 19, 1799; d. at Montreal, June 9, 1812.
111 4 Benjamin Sheldon, b. March 6, 1801.
112 5 James, b. at Bennington, Feb. 18, 1803; d. Dec. 3, 1811,
at Montreal.

108 CHARLES LYMAN⁷, *Micah Jones⁶, Elisha⁵, Elisha⁴, Benjamin³, John², Richard¹,* 1794–1848, was b. Oct. 17, 1794,
resided in Troy, N. Y., m. Elizabeth H., dau. of William
and Sarah Sheldon, of Clinton, Oneida Co., N. Y. He d.
at Troy, N. Y., Oct. 18, 1848, leaving no children. Mrs.
Lyman afterwards became the wife of the Rev. E. W.
Hooker, D.D., and d. at Fair Haven, Ct., Sept. 4, 1856.
Troy, N. Y.

109 GEORGE LYMAN⁷, b. at Bennington, Vt. June 19, 1796;
removed to Montreal, thence to Troy, N. Y., in 1812; member of Middlebury College from 1812 to 1815 ; m. Oct. 16,

1820, at Troy, Jane Bloom, daughter of Sylvester Bloom, of Dutchess Co., N. Y.; she d. April 25, 1822, aged 23 years. He m. 2d, March 23, 1824, Catharine Tichenor, widow of Moses D. Robinson, and niece and adopted daughter of the Hon. Isaac Tichenor, at Bennington, Vt. She was b. at Newark, N. J., May 6, 1793. *Bennington, Vt.*

Children, Eighth Generation:

113 1 Isaac Tichenor, b. Jan. 16, 1825; d. July 31, 1826.
114 2 Mary Elizabeth, b. Jan. 27, 1827.
115 3 Catharine Jane, b. March 1, 1829.
116 4 Micah Jones, b. April 2, 1831.
117 5 Elizabeth Sheldon, b. June 5, 1833.

The family removed to Bennington, Vt., in 1838, where Mrs. Lyman d. Jan. 4, 1856, and Mr. Lyman was m. at South Orange, N. J., Aug. 27, 1857, to Phebe Ann, dau. of David and Huldah Beach, who was b. Aug. 15, 1819. Mr. Lyman still resides at Bennington.

114 MARY ELIZABETH LYMAN[8], m. George O. Harrington at Bennington, Vt., June 8, 1847; graduated at Yale College in 1845; was civil engineer for some years; entered the commissary department of U. S. Volunteer Corps in 1863, with the rank of capt., but rose during his term of service, to that of col. He was stationed at Columbus, Ohio. When the state board of charities was constituted, he was appointed president thereof. One of the annual reports which he has made in this capacity was spoken of as a very able and interesting document. *Columbus, O.*

Children, Ninth Generation:

118 1 James Lyman, b. June 2, 1848, at Bennington.
119 2 Mary Lucina, b. Feb. 2, 1850, at Troy; d. May 12, 1854.
120 3 Charles Tichenor, b. May 26, 1851; d. Dec. 31, 1851.
121 4 William Gilbert, b. Oct. 3, 1854, at Bennington.
122 5 George Lyman, b. March 29, 1857, at Bennington.
123 6 Frank White, b. June 15, 1861; d. Oct. 3, 1861.
124 7 Laura Stark, b. Dec. 23, 1863, at Columbus, O.
124*8 Catharine Beach, b. March 11, 1867, at Columbus.

115 CATHARINE JANE LYMAN[8], m. Ezra W. Boughton, of Troy, N. Y., June 21, 1853. *Troy, N. Y.*

Children, Ninth Generation:

125 1 Edward Hooker, b. June 30, 1855.
126 2 Esther Anne Dana, b. April 17, 1857.
127 3 Thomas Blatchford, b. Sept. 4, 1859.
128 4 George Lyman, b. Dec. 1, 1862.
129 5 Ezra Palmer, b. May 9, 1866.

116 MICAH JONES LYMAN[8], b. April 2, 1831, graduated at Williams College in 1852. Studied medicine, settled at Geneseo, Ill. Here he was m. Jan. 10, 1858, to Mrs. Eliza J. Stewart, dau. of P. S. and Eliza Ward who was b. at Bergen, N. Y., June 2, 1831. *Montreal, C. E.*

Children, Ninth Generation:

130 1 Ward Tichenor, b. Nov. 10, 1858.
131 2 Libbie Lucina, b. Nov. 5, 1862.
132 3 Charles Perry, b. Dec. 4, 1864; d. Oct. 6, 1865.

117 ELIZABETH SHELDON LYMAN[7], b. June 5, 1833; m. Oct. 5, 1853, Theodore Lyman of Montreal, son of Theodore of Northampton who was a brother of Dr. Micah J. Lyman. The names of the children will be found in the paragraph below relating to their father. *Montreal, C. E.*

111 BENJAMIN SHELDON LYMAN[7], son of Dr. Micah, Jr., b. March 6, 1801, has resided successively at Utica, Cleveland, Troy and Brooklyn, and has for the past five years been connected with the consulate of the United States at Foo Chow, China. He m. Mary H. Wait of Clinton, N. Y. April 8, 1834, who was b. Feb. 25, 1807.
Foo Chow, China.

Children, Eighth Generation:

133 1 Elizabeth Sheldon, b. Jan. 23, 1835, Cleveland, O.
134 2 Charles, b. Nov. 11, 1836; d. Sept. 1, 1837.
135 3 A son, b. Aug. 29, 1837; d. same day.
136 4 Mary Sophia, b. April 13, 1840, at Troy.
137 5 Charles Wait, b. March 5, 1845, d. Jan. 27, 1846.
138 6 Benjamin Fisher, b. Dec. 1, 1849, at Brooklyn.

136 MARY SOPHIA LYMAN[8], dau. of *Benjamin* Sheldon Lyman and Mary L., b. April 13, 1840; m. at Brooklyn, Oct. 15, 1856, Lester S. Hubbard, a druggist of Brooklyn, N. Y., who was b. Aug., 1832, at Hartford, Ct.
Brooklyn, N. Y.

Children, Ninth Generation:

139 1 Mary Louise, b. Sept. 15, 1857; d Sept. 23, 1858.
140 2 Charles Lester, b. Jan. 9, 1859.
141 3 Frank, b. Sept. 21, 1862; d. Sept. 23, 1862.

133 ELIZABETH SHELDON LYMAN[8], dau. of *Benjamin* Sheldon Lyman and Mary L., b. Jan. 23, 1835; m. James B. Hubbard, Oct. 22, 1856. He d. Jan. 20, 1860.

Children, Ninth Generation:

142 1 William Lay, b. July 9, 1857.
143 2 James Edwin, b. May 31, 1859.

47

98 DEA. ELISHA LYMAN⁶, son of *Elisha⁵*, *Joseph⁴*, *Benjamin³*, *John²*, *Richard¹*, was b. at Northampton, Mass., Jan. 26, 1770. He inherited from his father the old family homestead, but on the death of the latter, he exchanged with his brother Theodore, and left Northampton. Jan. 10, 1793, he m. Hannah Stiles, of Windsor, Ct., granddaughter of Pres. Stiles, of Yale College. Mr. Lyman followed farming; settled first, in Conway, Mass., whence he removed to Derby, Vt., and afterwards to Montreal, where he resided from 1815 to 1828. From there he removed to Sunderland, Mass., and afterwards to Champlain, N. Y., where he d. Feb. 21, 1844. He was esteemed by all who knew him as a man of sterling integrity, strictly conscientious and religious. His first wife d. at Derby, Vt., Feb. 25, 1814. His second wife, Thankful Hunt, d. at Champlain, N. Y., Feb. 23, 1837. His third wife, Sarah Beaumont, also d. at Champlain, N. Y. *Champlain, N. Y.*

Children, Seventh Generation :

144   1 William, b. April 9, 1794 ; d. Sept. 7, 1857, at Champlain.
145   2 Asahel Stiles, b. May 27, 1796 ; d. June 3, 1796, at Conway, Mass.
146   3 Horace, d. April 11, 1798, in Derby, Vt.
147   4 Hannah, b. Sept. 20, 1799 ; now in London, Eng.
148   5 Fanny, b. Jan. 8, 1802, in Derby.
149   6 Elisha Stiles, b. Feb. 13, 1804; d. unmarried March 12 1852, druggist, city of Ottawa, Ill.
150   7 Edwin, b. May 3, 1806 ; d. of cholera at Montreal, Sept. 22, 1832 ; dau. Charlotte, m. Lewis Delano, Vt., had three children.
152   8 Lewis, b. Aug. 3, 1808 ; d. in N. J.
153   9 Benjamin, b. June 11, 1810.
154   10 Henry, b. Oct. 4, 1813, grad. at McGill College, Montreal, and Cambridge, Eng. ; admitted to the practice of law in the province of Quebec ; lieut. in the military service, for some time in Montreal, superintendent of West ward in city council, deacon in Congregational church, partner in the firm of Lymans, Clare & Co.

144 WILLIAM LYMAN⁷, son of *Elisha⁶* and Hannah, was b. at Conway, Mass., April 9th, 1794. Went to Montreal, Canada, in 1807. During the war of 1812, he returned to his father's home in Derby, Vt. Going back to Montreal in 1819, he began business as a druggist. Some years after this date, two younger brothers, Benjamin and Henry, having become partners, the firm was styled, William Lyman & Co. Under this name an increasing business was carried on, wholesale and retail, including the manu-

facture, on a larger scale, of drugs and other materials of the trade until 1855, when Wm. Lyman retired from the business. His death took place at his summer residence called Cold Spring Farm near Champlain, New York, on the 7th of Sept. 1857. His remains were afterwards removed to Mount Royal Cemetery, Montreal. Mr. Lyman carried on his business with success for nearly forty years, and left a competence to his family. He m. Mary Bancroft, April 30, 1820. She was b. Dec. 17, 1792, and d. March 2, 1824. After her death he m. Almira Caroline Fish, Oct. 2, 1826. She was b. March 27, 1799, and d. July 17, 1834. Aug. 31, 1836, he m. Caroline Williams, who was b. April 14, 1809, and d. Dec. 31, 1865. *Montreal, C. E.*

Children, Eighth Generation :

155   1 William L., Jr., b. March 2, 1821 ; d. Aug. 19, 1822.
156   2 William Bancroft, b. Dec. 7, 1822; d. March 28, 1823.
157   3 John, b. Aug. 11. 1828 ; d. Sept. 4, 1828.
158   4 Almira Caroline, b. Sept. 12, 1829 ; d. July 10, 1831.
159   5 Almira Caroline, b. April 9, 1832 ; d. Aug. 9, 1857 ; m. E. Lyman, Esq., merchant, Montreal.
160   6 Caroline, b. June 24, 1834 ; d. March 5, 1837.
161   7 Emma, b. April 3, 1838 ; d. Feb. 23, 1863.
162   8 William, Jr., b. Nov. 29, 1839 ; d. 1869, aged 30 years.
163   9 Elisha Stiles, b. Aug. 15, 1841 ; graduated at Yale College ; lawyer in Quebec ; studied theology ; merchant, in hardware house of Lyman & McNabb, Montreal.
164   10 Edwin, b. July 28, 1843 ; d. Sept. 1, 1843.
165   11 Louisa, b. Dec. 1844, in England; resides with her uncle and aunt, Mr. and Mrs. Henry Lyman, Montreal.

146 HORACE LYMAN[7], son of Dea. *Elisha*[6], b. April 11, 1798 ; lives in Granby, province of Quebec ; a retired merchant, postmaster, justice of the peace, and commissioner for trial of cases ; commanded a company in Granby for some time. *Granby, Prov. of Quebec.*

Child, Eighth Generation :
166   1 William Harvey, b. 1831 ; d. 1847 ; two adopted daughters.

147 HANNAH LYMAN[7], dau. of Dea *Elisha*[6], b. Sept. 20, 1799 ; m. John Easton Mills.
    3 *Clifton Villa, Putney, near London, England,*
    Children, Eighth Generation :
168   1 Four sons, d. young, of scarlet fever ; the oldest, John Easton Mills, d. at the age of 17 years.
169   2 Four daughters, Alice, m. Rev. George Redpath, of London— 2 children, d. at Glastenbury, England, Dec., 1869.

172 3 Hannah J., m. N. S. Whitney, merchant at Montreal, 8 or
9 children.
181 4 Ada, m. John J. Redpath, brother of Rev. George, England.
182 5 Mary Elizabeth, not m.

148 FANNY LYMAN[7], dau. of Dea. *Elisha*[6], b. Jan. 8, 1802;
m. Cephas Mills, Jan. 1, 1823. After his death she m.
Jacob Brouse, Dec. 18, 1850, and d. at Matilda, C. W.,
July 8, 1866.   *Matilda, C. W*
        Children, Eighth Generation
183 1 Elisha, b. Sept. 29, 1823; m. March 6, 1854, to Almira
Caroline, dau. of Wm. Lyman.
        Ch. 9th Gen.: 1 Alice Louisa, b. Aug. 8, 1856.
185 2 Frances, b. March 23, 1826; m. April 12, 1853, Edward
Chaflin; d. Sept. 11, 1854.
186 3 Mary, b. Sept. 28, 1830; m. July 19, 1852, Allan Turner.
187 4 Cephas, b. Oct. 10, 1832; m. Sept. 11, 1855, Nancy Brouse.
188 5 Cyrus Mason, b. May 29, 1836; m. July 14, 1864, Fanny Corse.
189 6 Emma Beers, b. Feb. 4, 1839; d. Feb., 1856.
190 7 Annie, b. July 30, 1841; m. June 23, 1864, Edward Chaflin.
191 8 Alice Louise, b. Aug. 8, 1856.

152 LEWIS LYMAN[7], son of Dea. *Elisha*[6], b. Aug. 3, 1808;
d. in Newark, New Jersey, May 27, 1860, educated at the
Caledonia Grammar School, Vt., developed remarkable
business talents, engaged in several schemes of business,
finally fell into irregular habits, and d. unmarried.

153 BENJAMIN LYMAN[7], son of Dea. *Elisha*[6] and Hannah, b.
June 11, 1810; removed with his father to Montreal. In
early life he, together with his brother Henry, were partners
with their brother William in a large wholesale and retail
drug business, in which business he still continues. He m.
Delia Almira Wills, of Waterbury, Vt., April 21, 1834;
capt. in active service six months; elder in the Presbyterian church, magistrate in the district of Montreal, and
partner in the firm of Lymans, Clare & Co.   *Montreal.*
        Children, Eighth Generation:
192 1 Benjamin Henry, b. March 22, 1835.
193 2 Frances, b. June 28, 1836.
194 3 Lewis, b. July 5, 1838; d. Oct. 13, 1842, at Montreal.
195 4 Delia Wills, b. Feb. 14, 1840; d. May 28, 1841.
196 5 George Mills, ⎱ Twins, b. Nov. 22, 1831; d. May 28, 1842.
197 6 Edwin Wills, ⎰
198 7 Lewis Tichenor, b. Oct. 19, 1843; d. Aug. 13, 1847, at
Champlain.
199 8 Hannah Stiles, ⎱ Twins, b. Nov. 5, 1845.
200 9 James,   ⎰ d. Nov. 5, 1845.

201 10 Anna Louisa, b. July 3, 1847 ; d. April 28, 1848.
202 11 Charles, b. April 3, 1849 ; senior in Yale Coll., 1870.
203 12 Frank Milton, b. Feb. 3, 1851 ; d. Aug. 2, 1869.
204 13 Cynthia, July 3, 1853 ; d. July 21, 1853.

192 Benjamin Henry Lyman[8], son of *Benjamin[7]*, b. March 22, 1835 ; m. Jan. 27, 1862, Ellen Elizabeth Brader.
Montreal.

Child, Ninth Generation:

205 1 Gen. Asher, b. Oct. 30, 1862. He is a druggist in business in Montreal. He has one son.
Ch. 10th Gen.: 1 Arthur, b. Oct. 23, 1863, at Montreal.

193 Frances Lyman[8], dau. of *Benjamin*, b. June 28, 1836; m. Geo. Turner Beard, of Toronto, Canada, April 21, 1859.
Toronto, C. W

Children, Ninth Generation :

206 1 Mary Elizabeth, b. May 9, 1860.
207 2 Alice Louise, b. July 29, 1861.
208 3 Edith Delia, b. Dec. 21, 1862.
209 4 Frances Ida, b. March 5, 1865.
210 5 An infant son. Still b. March 21, 1866.
211 6 Benjamin, b. March 27, 1868.
212 7 Florence Milton, b. June 11, 1869 ; d. Aug. 20, 1869.

154 Henry Lyman[7], son of Dea. *Elisha[6]*, b. at Derby, Vt. Oct. 4, 1813; m. Aug. 24, 1841, Mary Corse, dau. of Roswell Corse, of Northfield, Mass. and Susan Lyman, who was b. at Northampton, Feb. 10, 1780, a dau. of Elisha and sister of Dr. Micah J., Elisha, Lewis and Henry Lyman.

Children, Eighth Generation:

213 1 Henry Roswell, b. June 23, 1842 ; d. Jan. 19, 1843.
214 2 Frederick Stiles, b. Jan. 6, 1844 ; graduated at St. John's College, Cambridge, England.
215 3 Arthur Ellis, b. March 31, 1846 ; d. July 28, 1847.
216 4 Susan Alice, b. March 31, 1848; d. June 20, 1853.
217 4 Roswell Corse, b. June 26, 1850.
218 6 Henry Herbert, b. Dec. 21, 1854.
219 7 Albert Clarence, b. Oct. 19, 1856.
220 8 Walter Ernest, b. Nov. 3, 1861.

101 Theodore Lyman[6], son of *Elisha[5]* and Abigail, *Joseph[4]*, *Benjamin[3]*, 1784–1833, b. Nov. 3, 1784; m. Susan Willard Whitney, Oct. 9, 1806. He remained in his native town where he occupied the old homestead. In 1828, he sold the old family mansion, giving the first deed of it which had ever been made. In 1829, he moved to Am-

herst, and d. Aug. 13, 1833. His widow afterwards moved to Montreal, where she d. June 18, 1855, aged 67 years. *Amherst, Mass.*

Children, Seventh Generation :

221 1 Abigail Jones, b. June 16, 1807.
222 2 A son, b. Jan. 2, 1809 ; d. Jan. 11, 1809.
223 3 Henry, b. Nov. 23, 1809 ; d. June 28, 1834, in the island of Sumatra.
224 4 Edward Bellows, b. May 26, 1811 ; d. Sept. 25, 1854.
225 5 James B., b. Jan. 5, 1813.
226 6 Stephen Jones, b. Oct. 6, 1814 ; d. Oct. 8, 1814.
227 7 Hannah Willard, b. Jan. 29, 1816. Late lady principal of Vassar College.
228 8 Theodore, b. March 27, 1818.
229 9 Stephen Jones, b. Nov. 15, 1819 ; went to Canada in 1834, He now resides in Montreal and holds her majesty's commission as Lt. Col. of Artillery.
230 10 Susan Whitney, b. May 29, 1821.
231 11 Lewis, b. Nov. 4, 1822 ; d. April 29, 1823.
232 12 Mary Jane, b. 14, 1824 ; resides in Montreal.
233 13 Helen, b. Dec. 25, 1825 ; d. at Montreal, April 10, 1852.

OBITUARY.— Hannah Willard Lyman, daughter of the late Theodore Lyman, was born in " old Northampton " in 1816. Here amid these peaceful retreats, stately elms and lovely landscapes, the first years of her childhood were spent. Subsequently she removed with her family to Amherst, and after the distressing death of her elder brother, Henry Lyman, one of the missionary martyrs of Sumatra, she entered upon a course of preparative study at Ipswich Female Seminary, which was designed to fit her for the distinguished work which divine providence intended her to do. Miss Lyman commenced to teach at Gorham Academy, Maine, and she subsequently taught in Mrs. Gray's Seminary for Ladies in Petersburg, Virginia ; but her more important work was carried on in the city of Montreal ; surrounded by her nearest relatives, she commenced a select class for young ladies which speedily grew into a seminary of a very superior order.

For twenty-two years, though often oppressed with anxiety, by sorrow, by failing health, and most of all by the deep sense of her own insufficiency, she faithfully persevered in her work."

" Such earnest teaching could hardly fail to bear fruit ; and she, who sowed often in tears, and under a discouraging sense of failure, was often blessed by a rich reaping time even on earth, very many of her beloved ' children,' as she was wont affectionately to call them, gave her the delight of seeing them joined to the Lord, and walking in the truth." Her reputation as a successful and inspiring teacher had been so wide-spread that she had received frequent invitations to take the superintendence of large public educational institutions, which she had uniformly declined. In 1865, however, she received an urgent request to become first lady principal of a newly organized female college on a very large scale — Vassar College, Poughkeepsie, ani nstitution founded on a munificent bequest, with aims and resources greater than perhaps any other such institution in the world.

She would at once have dismissed the application, shrinking from the responsibility, but for the suggestion contained in the letter, " whether in this field the Master may not have work for you to do." She went, and it is needless to add that she carried her principles with her to the stately halls of Vassar where they had indeed wider scope, and greater development. " It was no easy task to which she was called, but to that task she brought no ordinary qualifications. Her natural gifts, amounting almost to a genius for her profession, had been enriched by an education of no ordinary range. Her early training in a college town of New England, her extensive acquaintance with teachers, professors and Christian ministers, her familiarity with many interesting questions which have of late been agitated respecting the education of woman, and her life-long experience in the actual management of the young, all made her counsel invaluable in the moulding of the great enterprise to which she had been called." She was genial but dignified, devout without austerity, cheerful without levity, and while very firm in all matters of principle and conscience, she was catholic and tolerant in respect of the religious convictions of others. There was nothing sickly or sentimental in the type of her piety, she hated *affectation and cant*. Her clear, incisive intellect enabled her with almost unerring certainty, to penetrate such disguises, and to distinguish between the meretricious and the true.

Miss Lyman was nowhere more at home than in the *sick room*, and beside the couch of suffering. Delicate in health herself, she was nevertheless always ready when the sick and the sorrowful needed her help.

When dangerous infection had driven others away, there she might have been found with her calm and gentle ministry, fearless of contagion. Her spirit was of a heroic sort, kindred indeed to that which animated her lamented brother at Sumatra, and that of a Florence Nightingale in the fever hospitals of Scutari. " *I was sick and ye visited me.*

I have said that Miss Lyman's character was well balanced, but it is fitting that I should add that her *almsgiving in proportion to her means and resources* were *munificent*, at the same time ostentation in giving was carefully avoided.

The amount of assistance, however, which she gave to *ministers* and *missionaries*, and their families, and to the indigent of Christ's flock would, if fully known, astonish her most intimate friends.

Who can estimate the value to the world of such a life? By what powers of arithmetic can its blessed results be computed? " *And I heard a voice from Heaven say, Blessed are the dead who die in the Lord ; yea, saith the Spirit, that they may rest from their labors, and their works do follow them.*"

Her struggle with death was long and painful. For three weeks she might truly be said to be dying; and "dying," said she, "is very hard work." She had no fears, no shrinking; she longed to depart. Her desire and prayer was that the end might come; and, as we looked upon her sufferings, we could not but join in her prayer. On Tuesday Feb. 21, 1871, the prayer was heard and answered. The gate at which she had so long been knocking opened, and she entered into rest.

"Wonderful was the change which passed upon the face as we stood, and watched the expression of weariness and pain passing away, and the features settling to a perfect repose."

> "Weep not for her! She is an angel now,
> And treads the sapphire floors of paradise,
> All darkness wiped from her refulgent brow,
> Sin, sorrow, suffering banished from her eyes,
> Victorious over death, to her appear
> The vista'd joys of Heaven's eternal year,
>   Weep not for her." — *Moir.*

221 ABIGAIL JONES LYMAN[7], dau. of *Theodore*[6], m. Joseph Savage, May 18, 1829, of Montreal, at Amherst, Mass. Mr. Savage, d. Feb. 6, 1859, at Montreal.

Children, Eighth Generation:

234 1 Frances Ann, b. Feb. 27, 1830; d. Sept., 1855.
235 2 Emily, b. Nov. 11, 1831; d. Jan. 4, 1851.
236 3 Susanna Whitney, b. Sept. 21, 1833; d. Jan. 25, 1855.
237 4 Joseph, Jr., b. March 4, 1836; d. May 25, 1838.
238 5 Joseph, Jr., b. May 2, 1838; m. Mary Workman, of Montreal.
239 6 Albert Buckley, b. March 1, 1840; m. Sarah Adams, Oct. 5, 1865, of Stockbridge, Mass.
240 7 Mary Pomeroy, b. June 20, 1842; d. Feb. 10, 1851.
241 8 Frederick Bolton, b. April 30, 1844.

223 HENRY LYMAN[7], son of *Theodore*[6], m. Eliza Pond, May 16, 1832. They went as missionaries of the A. B. C. F. M. He was massacred by the "Battas" with his companion Samuel C. Munson, June 28, 1834. His widow m. Rev. Charles Wiley, D. D. Mr. Lyman was a graduate of Amherst College of the class of 1829, of which class three others were foreign missionaries: Rev. Justin Perkins, D.D., Rev. Elias Riggs, D.D., and Rev. Benjamin W. Parker.

224 EDWARD BELLOWS LYMAN[7], son of *Theodore*[6], m. Mary Ann Oxenham, of Mobile, Ala., Dec. 20, 1835; d. at New York, Sept. 22, 1854; his wife d. in Nov., 1865.

Children, Eighth Generation.

242 1 Elizabeth Oxenham, b. Sept. 17, 1836; d. June 27, 1837.

243 2 Susan Kennedy, b. Feb. 29, 1839; m. Robert Ferguson, of Mobile, Ala., in 1863.
244 3 Cornelia, b. Sept. 28, 1840; d. July 13, 1854.
245 4 Isabella, d.
246 5 Elizabeth Oxenham, b. Aug. 17, 1846; d. Sept 18, 1847.
247 6 Edward Bellows, b. March 8, 1849.
248 7 Henry O., b. July 2, 1851.

225 JAMES B. LYMAN[7], son of *Theodore*[6], m. Frances Pomeroy Dickenson, of Northampton, Sept. 17, 1838.
Toledo, Ohio.

Children, Eighth Generation:
249 1 Mary Dickenson, b. July 19, 1840, at St. Louis; m. Albert E. Scott, Oct. 20, 1868, at Toledo, Ohio.
250 2 Henry Munson, b. March 18, 1843, at St. Louis; d. Sept. 4, 1843.
251 3 Wylys Pomeroy, b. Dec. 3, 1845, at Northampton; d. Sept. 14, 1846.

228 THEODORE LYMAN[7], b. March 27, 1818, moved to Mon treal, in 1833, and now holds her majesty's commission as Lt. Col. and Assist. Qr. Master Gen. He m. Elizabeth Sheldon Lyman, dau. of George and Catharine T. Lyman, Oct. 5, 1853, Bennington, Vt. *Montreal.*

Children, Eighth Generation:
252 1 Katherine Tichenor, b. Oct. 29, 1854.
253 2 Susannah Willard Savage, b. Nov. 6, 1855.
254 3 Henry Lyman, b. July 13, 1857.
255 4 Elizabeth Mary, b. Aug. 21, 1858.
256 5 Theodore Pomeroy, b. Jan. 8, 1860.
257 6 Anna Bisset, b. Dec. 5, 1861; d. Aug. 16, 1863.
258 7 Grace, b. Feb. 24, 1864.
259 8 Julia Eleanor, b. July 10, 1866.
260 9 George, b. Nov. 24, 1868.

230 SUSAN WHITNEY LYMAN[7], m. Alexander Frederick Sabine, at Montreal, May 17, 1842. She d. at Philadel phia, Nov. 24, 1867.

Children, Eighth Generation:
261 1 Theodore Clement, b. May 29, 1843.
262 2 Bertha Wenham, b. Dec. 15, 1844.
263 3 Alice Helen, b. Dec. 30, 1846.
264 4 Herbert Willard, b. Feb. 3, 1848; d. July 21, 1848.
265 5 Edward Ernest Black, b. March 17, 1849; d. July 14, 1849.
266 6 Frank Gerrard, b. May 30, 1850.
267 7 Alexander Frederick, jr., b. July 3, 1852; d. July 5, 1852.
268 8 Wilmer Harris, b. Aug. 4, 1854; d. May 1, 1855.

269 9 Anna Lyman, b. Aug. 24, 1858.
270 10 Fredenia Victoria, b. Jan., 1864.
271 11 ...., ..., b. Jan. 14, 1866; d. Jan. 20, 1866.

II. DESCENDANTS OF BENJAMIN,[3] THROUGH BEN-
JAMIN.[4]

4 BENJAMIN LYMAN[4], *Benjamin[3]*, *John[2]*, *Richard[1]*, 1703–
1762, b. in Northampton, Jan. 2, 1703; m. Mary Mosely of
Glastenbury, Ct., probably in the early part of the year
1726. She was b. in Westfield, Mass., in 1707. He lived
in Northampton nearly twenty years. In 1745 or soon
after, he removed with his family to Bartlett Mills on the
Manhan river, a district then in Northampton, but afterwards with other settlements set off and denominated Easthampton. On the 28th of May, 1745, the town deeded to
Benjamin Lyman and Stephen Wright, who was his
neighbor and had removed with him from Northampton,
for and in consideration of the sum of sixteen hundred
and twenty-five pounds in bills of public credit, old tenor,
" a tract of land known as ' School Meadow,' the same
being land sequestered by the town ' for the schools,' " about
eight acres of the Manhan meadow above the falls on the
river and the public road across the same. At that time
no place of worship had been erected in Easthampton.
He therefore retained his connection with the church in
Northampton where he was one of the early and constant
supporters of Rev. Jonathan Edwards, D.D., being one of
the nineteen who voted to retain him as pastor of the church
at the time of the opposition to him. He died May 1,
1762, aged 59. Mrs. L. died Aug. 17, 1782, in her 75th
year.

Children, Fifth Generation ·

1 1 Benjamin, b. Aug. 1, 1727; known as Deacon Benjamin.
2 2 Mary, b. Feb. 22, 1730; m. Oliver Pomeroy, of Northampton.
3 3 Thankful, b. March 30, 1731; m. Daniel Williams.
4 4 Lemuel, b. 1732; d. Feb. 14, 1732.
5 5 Lemuel, b. Aug. 17, 1735.
6 6 David, b. Dec. 14, 1737.
7 7 Solomon, b. Jan. 21, 1741; d. Jan. 27, 1746.
8 8 Esther, b. June, 1748; d. 1749.
9 9 Martha, b. 1750; m. Oliver Wright, Nov. 8, 1770.

The town record of Northampton gives the birth of Aaron, son of
Benjamin and Mary Lyman, Aug. 1, 1727. It has been said that
Benjamin was b. in that year. No Aaron grew up in the family,
and no such person is mentioned in the record of the deaths, though

the death of Lemuel and Solomon is recorded. It is hence inferred that Benjamin was at first called Aaron, and the name changed.

1 DEA. BENJAMIN LYMAN[5], b. Aug. 1, 1727 ; m. Hannah Jones, of Springfield, Mass. *Easthampton, Mass.*

Children, Sixth Generation.

10 1 Benjamin, bapt. July 27, 1759.
11 2 Mary, bapt. June 20, 1761 ; m. David Chapman.
12 3 Solomon, bapt. June 12, 1763.
13 4 Ruth, bapt. Dec. 29, 1765 ; m. Ebenezer White of South Hadley.
14 5 Dolly, bapt. May 24, 1767 ; m. Solomon Woolcott of West Springfield.
15 6 Hannah, m. Eli Clapp of Southampton.
16 7 Mercy, b. Oct. 11, 1772 ; m. Josiah Snow of S. Hadley.

In the town records of Northampton there is recorded the birth of Hannah, a dau. of Benjamin Lyman, jr., and Hannah, b. Aug. 27, 1756. It could probably refer to no other than Dea. Benjamin, and it is probable that he had a child of that name who d. in infancy.

Dea. Benjamin Lyman built a house on the plain, where his grandson, Rev. Solomon Lyman, now deceased, lived. He was very active and influential in the formation of the church and district or town. To him was directed the warrant, to call together the citizens to the first meeting of the district after its organization. Robert Breck, Esq., who was empowered by act of the general court to issue his warrant to some prominent citizen, was chosen moderator of the first meeting. Mr. Lyman was chosen moderator of the second meeting, and he occupied that position many times thereafter. In church matters, he was also a leader. Before the settlement of a pastor, it was needful that there be a moderator, who could legally call meetings of the church, an office to which he was appointed. At one of the earliest business meetings of the church, he was chosen deacon, which office he accepted, and performed its duties till his death in June, ·1798· He was a man of ardent piety, a faithful servant of Christ. His wife was Hannah Jones of Springfield. They had children, the dates of whose baptisms are given in the church records of Southampton, Rev. Jonathan Judd, pastor, which church they joined July 29, 1759, and attended until the organization of one in Easthampton.

10 BENJAMIN LYMAN[6], son of Dea. *Benjamin*[5], b. in 1759 ; m. Mary, dau. of Elijah Wright of Easthampton, in 1783 He was a farmer living in his native town Easthampton, where his grandson Ansel B. now lives. He served in the Revolutionary war, and stood guard over Major André at the time of his execution. He d. April 30, 1823.

Children, Seventh Generation :

17 1 Jeremiah, b. April 14, 1786.
18 2 Mary, b. 1788.

19 3 Benjamin, b. 1791; d. Jan. 8, 1807.
20 4 Eunice, b. Feb. 7, 1794.
21 5 Clarissa, b. Sept. 12, 1796; m. Nov. 23, 1820, Daniel Currier, of Ackley, Iowa.
22 6 Ansel Wright, b. 1798; d. Oct. 20, 1802.
23 7 Theodorus, b. 1800; d. Oct. 19, 1801.
24 8 Dorus, b. May 15, 1802.
25 9 Louisa, b. Feb. 7, 1807; d. March 28, 1823.

17 JEREMIAH LYMAN[7], son of *Benjamin*[6], b. April 14,
1786; m. Orpah Burt, dau. of Martin Burt of Southampton, Dec. 3, 1817. He resided in Easthampton, occupying
his father's place. He d. May 29, 1844. Mrs. Orpah B.
Lyman d. April 5, 1867, aged 76. *Easthampton, Mass.*

Children, Eighth Generation:
26 1 Theresa, b. Feb. 7, 1821; m. Rev. Addison Lyman, of Easthampton, Mass.
27 2 Henry Martyn, b. Jan. 28, 1823; d. Nov. 18, 1828.
28 3 Louisa, b. Dec. 30, 1824; m. James O. Waite, of Hatfield.
29 4 Ansel Burt, b. Oct. 21, 1826.
30 5 Henry Martyn, b. Sept. 13, 1828.
31 6 Adelle Semantha, b. Oct. 25, 1831; resides with Ansel B.
32 7 Jeremiah Munson, b. Feb. 13, 1835; d. April 27, 1835.

28 LOUISA LYMAN[8], dau. of *Jeremiah*[7], b. Dec. 30, 1824;
m. James O. Waite, of Hatfield, May 13, 1851.

Children, Ninth Generatoin:
33 1 Justin Lyman, b. June 28, 1852.
34 1 Clara Theresa, b. Aug. 2, 1854; d. June 6, 1860.
35 3 Frederick Henry, b. July 26, 1856; d. June 24, 1860.
36 4 Emma Adelle, b. Sept. 26, 1858. } Twins.
37 5 Mary Louisa, b. Sept. 26, 1858. }
38 6 Ellen Augusta, b. May 20, 1861.

29 DEA. ANSEL B. LYMAN[8], son of *Jeremiah*[7], was b.
Oct. 21, 1826; occupies his father's farm, the same containing some part of the "School Meadow," so called,
which the town of Northampton deeded to Benjamin
Lyman, ancestor of the Easthampton branch of the Lyman
family. He was chosen deacon of the Payson church soon
after its organization. He m. Clara Sophia Nash, daughter
of John B. Nash, of Granby, Mass., Dec. 27, 1860.
Easthampton, Mass.

Children, Ninth Generation:
39 1 Carrie, b. Jan. 3, 1862; d. Feb. 16, 1862.
40 2 John Nash, b. March 13, 1863.
41 3 Rose Clarissa, b. July 31, 1869.

30 HENRY MARTYN LYMAN[8], son of *Jeremiah*[7], b. Sept. 13, 1828; m. Martha C. Pomeroy of Southampton, who was b. Nov. 3, 1833. He removed to Minnesota in 1853, drove into the unbroken wilderness alone 25 miles, there halted, set up a few boards against his wagon which he had brought with him, and called that home. He was the first man to plough in the territory on the west side of the Mississippi river. *Chanhassan, Minn.*

Children, Ninth Generation :

42 1 Ansel Pomeroy, b. Oct. 31, 1857.
43 2 George Henry, b. Sept. 19, 1859 ; d. March 5, 1863.
44 3 Grace Adelle, b. May 17, 1862 ; d. March 4, 1863.
45 4 Albert Henry, b. May 17, 1864.
46 5 Ada, b. June 1, 1868; d. Aug. 10, 1868.

18 MARY LYMAN[7], dau. of *Benjamin*[6], b. 1788; m. Samuel Douglass of Meriden, Ct., Dec. 25, 1814. They afterwards moved to Omri, Winnebago Co., Wis., where they d. Her death occurred Sept. 25, 1853. He d. in Jan. 23, 1853. *Omri, Wis.*

Children, Eighth Generation :

47 1 Mary Maria, b. Oct. 8, 1815 ; m. Warren S. Bradley, May 1, 1842. She d. Feb. 7, 1845.
48 2 Samuel, b. Oct. 3, 1817; m. Mary A. Ives, May 1, 1842. She d. Sept. 29, 1843.
49 3 Louisa Jane, b. Oct. 29, 1821 ; m. Andrew J. Dickenson, Sept. 28, 1851.
50 4 Benjamin Lewis, b. June 1, 1824; d. Oct. 19, 1826.
51 5 Julia Ann, b. Oct. 2, 1827 ; m. Alvah Merriam, Jan. 18, 1846, who lives at Algonia, Iowa.
52 6 Emmeline, b. Sept. 18, 1830 ; m. Erastus R. Hough, Sept. 17, 1848.

20 EUNICE LYMAN[7], dau. of *Benjamin*[6], b. Feb. 7, 1794, m. Charles Van Sands of Stafford, Ct., July 4, 1819. They removed to Newton, N. J., where Mr. Van Sands d. Oct. 6, 1859. Shortly after her husband's death, Mrs. Van Sands removed to Middletown, Ct., where she now resides with one of her children. *Middletown, Ct.*

Children, Eighth Generation :

53 1 Charles Lymau, b. in Easthampton, March 29, 1821.
54 2 Horace, b. in Newton, N. J., March 7, 1823.
55 3 Mary Louise, b. in Newton, N. J., Jan. 12, 1828.
56 4 Lucius Julius, b. in Newton, N. J., Feb. 4, 1834; m. Lydia A. Clark, Sept. 17, 1857.
57 5 Berlinda Eunice, b. at Newton, N. J., Feb. 24, 1841; m. Wm. Howard, Feb. 11, 1862, and d. Dec. 6, 1869.

58 6 Caroline Amanda.
59 7 Charles Edward.
60 8 Lucy Emma.

61 9 Mary Almeda.
62 10 Horace Irving.
63 11 Lucius Oscar.

Of these eleven children only five survive.

53 Charles Lyman Van Sands[8], b. in Easthampton, Mass.,
March 29, 1821 ; m. Caroline Hayes, of N. Y., Jan. 1......
Branford, Ct.

Children, Ninth Generation :

64 1 Caroline Amanda.
65 2 Charles Edward.
66 3 Lucy Emma.

67 4 Mary Almeda.
68 5 Horace Irving.
69 6 Lucius Oscar.

54 Horace Van Sands, b. in Newton, N. J., March 7, 1823 ;
m. Sarah S. Hubbard, of Middletown, Ct., May 22, 1855,
and lives in that place at the present time.   He has three
children.   *Middletown, Ct.,*

Children, Ninth Generation :

70 1 Sarah.
71 2 Grace.

72 3 Horace, Jr.

55 Mary Louise Van Sands[8], b. in Newton, N. J., Jan. 12,
1828 ; m. William Davie, of Halifax, New Brunswick,
Aug. 16, 1846.   *Chicago, Ill.*

Children, Ninth Generation :

73 1 Mary Ellen.
74 2 William Edwin.

75 3 Winnie Emma.

21 Clarissa Lyman[7], dau. of *Benjamin[6]*, of Easthampton,
Mass., m. Daniel Currier, Nov. 23, 1820, and now lives at
Ackley, Iowa.   Since their marriage they have lived suc-
cessively at Breckville, Ohio, Marion, Ill., and Ackley,
Harding Co., Iowa.   *Ackley, Ia.*

Children, Eighth Generation :

76 1 Hiram, b. Aug. 27, 1821, at Easthampton.
77 2 Daniel W.
78 3 Mary.
79 4 Theodore Benjamin.

76 Hiram Lyman Currier[8] b. at Easthampton, Mass.,
Aug. 27, 1821 ; m. at Richfield, Ohio, Jan. 12, 1843, to
Julia Olmstead. He now resides in Oregon, Ill., carpenter,
and machinist. His children are ·   *Oregon, Ill.*

Children, Ninth Generation.

80 1 Samuel Lorenzo, b. Jan. 30, 1844. Served 4 months in the
        74th Ill. Regt., and two years in 46th Ill. Regt. Being
        injured in the service is now on the pension list.

81 2 Hiram Leroy, b. May 12, 1845, served in the 140th Ill.
Regt., during the period of its service.

82 3 Laura Clarissa, b. June 21, 1849; d. April 12, 1852.

83 4 Delano L., b. Feb. 27, 1851, engineer.

84 5 Marissa Adelle, b. Jan. 12, 1854.

85 6 Edwin Elmore, b. Nov. 30, 1856.

86 7 Wm. Emerson, b. Nov. 12, 1858.

87 8 Mary Alice, b. Jan. 8, 1860.

88 9 Ellen Eliza, b. July 7, 1862.

77 DANIEL W. CURRIER[8], resides at Ackley, Ohio, has one daughter.

78 MARY CURRIER[8], m. a Chaney, resides at Rockford, Ill., has three sons and two daughters.

79 THEODORE BENJAMIN CURRIER[8], resides in Shelby Co., Missouri, and has two sons and two daughters.

24 DORUS LYMAN[7], son of *Benjamin*[6], b. May 15, 1812, moved to Brecksville, Ohio, where he m. Mary Oakes, dau. of Carey Oakes, of Massachusetts. *Oberlin, Ohio.*

Children, Eighth Generation :

99 1 Ansel Wright, b. May 6, 1836.

100 2 Mary, d. in infancy.

101 3 Edmund, b. Dec. 29, 1859.

102 4 Louisa, b. Nov. 7, 1841.

103 5 Julia, b. Oct. 11, 1843.

104 6 Benjamin, b. Sept. 3, 1852.

99 ANSEL W. LYMAN[8], son of *Dorus*[7], m. Arrie, dau. of James, Benfer of Philadelphia, Pa., where he at present reisdes and occupies the position of inspector of customs, no children. *Philadelphia, Pa.*

101 EDMUND LYMAN[8], son of *Dorus*[7], m. Emily, dau. of James Winn, April 17, 1861, farmer. *Oberlin, Ohio.*

Children, Ninth Generation :

105 1 James Harrison, b. March 15, 1862.

106 2 Edmund Russell, b. Oct. 8, 1863.

107 3 Abner Winn, b. Jan. 15, 1867.

102 LOUISA LYMAN[8], dau. of *Dorus*[7], m. John McCarren of Canada, Jan. 6, 1859, a dealer in lumber. *Saginaw, Mich.*

Children, Ninth Generation :

108 1 William Anderson, d. April 24, 1861.

109 2 Charles Edward, b. Sept. 3, 1862; d. Feb. 12, 1864.

110 3 Mary Jane, b. April 28, 1868.

11 Mary Lyman[6], dau. of Dea. *Benjamin*[5], bp. June 20, 1761; m. David Chapman.   *Easthampton, Mass.*
Children, Seventh Generation:
111 1 David, lived and d. in Hatfield.
112 2 George, settled in Shelburne Falls.
113 3 Charles, lived in Southampton.
114 4 Sophia, m. John Clapp, of Easthampton. Her children were ·
      Sophia, Maurice, John Merrick, Eliakim and Amos B.,
      all of whom, excepting Eliakim, now live in Easthampton.
115 5 Mary, b. July 20, 1788; 2d wife of Obadiah Janes. Her
      son Oliver Ellsworth Janes, now resides in Princeton, Ill.
116 6 Martha, never married.
117 7 Dorcas, m. Barnes of Southampton, now wife of Milton
      Adams, of Worthington.

12 Dea. Solomon Lyman[6], son of Dea. *Benjamin*[5], settled in Easthampton on his father's place. He married Lois, daughter of Jonathan Janes, Sen. In 1807, he was chosen deacon, in which capacity he served eighteen years. In 1796, Dea. Solomon Lyman was married a second time to Martha Willard Park, widow of Asher Park, of Norwich. He died Oct. 14, 1848, aged 85. His wife died Oct. 12, 1850.   *Easthampton, Mass.*
Children, Seventh Generation:
118 1 Theodosia, died in infancy.
119 2 Theodosia, wife of Julius Edwards, of Northampton.
120 3 Lois, m. 1st Senaah Parsons; 2d Philip Clark.
122 4 Susan, b. Nov. 13, 1790; m. Elihu Lyman, of Easthampton.
123 5 Solomon, b. Jan. 11, 1795.
124 6 Mercy, March 31, 1796; died unmarried.

118 Theodosia Lyman[7], dau. of Dea. *Solomon*[6], m. Julius Edwards, of Northampton.   *Northampton, Mass.*
Children, Eighth Generation:
128 1 Theodore.
129 2 Lyman.   130 3 Richard.
131 4 Elvira, m. Giles T. Montague, of Granby.
132 5 Harriet, m. Isaac Bates, of Farmington, Ct.
133 6 Lucy, m. Ceylon Moody, of Granby.

120 Lois Lyman[7], dau. of Dea. *Solomon*[6], m. 1st Senaah Parsons, in 1811 and had one child, L. Watson Parsons, who now lives in Easthampton. Her 2d husband was Philip Clark, of Easthampton.   *Easthampton, Mass.*
Children, Eighth Generation:
134 1 Lawrence.   136 3 Gilbert A.
135 2 Uriel.   137 4 Melancey.

138 ₅ Martha, m. J. Emerson, son of Dea. Sylvester Lyman. Uriel and Gilbert A., live in Easthampton.

123 SOLOMON LYMAN[7], son of Deacon *Solomon[6]*, b. Jan. 11, 1795, received his education at Yale College in the class of 1822. In this class were Rev. Sumner G. Clapp, and Luther Wright, both deceased, both connected with the Lymans on their mother's side. He worked on a farm till he was twenty-one years of age, teaching school three winters, and then, in 1816, went to Phillips Academy, Andover; continued there two years; joined his class in 1819. After graduating, studied theology two years in New York city, with Drs. Spring, Cox and Baldwin, and was then licensed to preach; spent three years in preaching in Pittstown, N. Y., and was there ordained by the Presbytery of Troy. In 1826 was m. to Mary Curtis, of New York, daughter of Reuben and Silence Curtis, of Danbury, Conn.; was pastor of the Congregational church of Keeseville, N. Y., about eight years, commencing his labors there in 1828, and for the same number of years 1835–43, was pastor of the Congregational church in Poultney, Vt. His aged parents greatly needing his assistance, he then removed to Easthampton; preached for seven years at West Farms, a village about four miles distant from Easthampton Centre, continued to preach more or less until he was past seventy years of age. He had three children, sons, one d. at the age of 4 years; another lives near his parents, and another is living with them. There are three grandchildren, all daughters, the eldest about eight years of age.

Easthampton, Mass.

Children, Eighth Generation .

139 ₁ Edward, b. March 27, 1828.
140 ₂ Alpheus Janes, b. Oct. 7, 1829.
141 ₃ Reuben, b. Jan. 31, 1833; d. in 1837.

140 ALPHEUS J. LYMAN[8], son of Rev. *Solomon[7]* b. Oct. 6, 1827; m. Olive C. Geer, of Hartford, Conn., June, 1859; he is now a merchant. *Easthampton, Mass.*

Children, Ninth Generation :

143 ₁ Mary Elizabeth, b. June 23, 1862.
144 ₂ Harriet Geer, b. Feb. 18, 1864.
145 ₃ Fanny Pease, b. Dec. 23, 1866.

13 RUTH LYMAN[6], 2d dau. of Dea. *Benjamin[5]*, b. Dec. 9, bapt. Dec. 29, 1765; m. Ebenezer White of South Hadley,

Sept. 26, 1793, who d. March 29, 1829.   She d. March 11,
1839.   *Ludlow, Mass.*
         Children, Seventh Generation
145*₁ Ezra, b. Aug., 1794; m. Mary Wright, Chester, Vt.
146 ₂ Benjamin Lyman, b. April 16, 1796; m. Nov. 19, 1815,
       Anna Granger of Worthington, Mass., 8 children,
       Flanders, N. J.
147 ₃ Martha, b. Nov. 5, 1797; d. Oct. 17, 1803.
148 ₄ Ruth, b. Sept. 15, 1799.
149 ₅ Christian, b. July 24, 1801.
150 ₆ Hannah, b. July 17, 1803.
151 ₇ Ralph, b. Aug. 20, 1805; m. March 31, 1828, Ruth Lyon,
       7 children; 2d wife Julia Bliss of Ludlow, Mass.
152 8 Martha, b. Oct. 23, 1807.
153 ₉ Ebenezer, b. Dec. 13, 1810 or '11; m. 1st, Louisa Wright of
       Ludlow, Mass. 4 children; 2d, Emily Crouch, 3 children;
       Princeton, Ill.

14 DOLLY LYMAN⁶, dau. of Dea. *Benjamin⁵*, of Easthampton, bp. May 54, 1767; m. Solomon Woolcutt, of West
Springfield in 1791. They removed to Windham, N. Y.,
where they died. They had quite a family of children,
but we have not ascertained their names. *Windham, N. Y.*

15 HANNAH LYMAN⁶, 4th dau. of Dea. *Benjamin⁵*, m. Eli
Clapp of Southampton.   *Southampton, Mass.*
         Children, Seventh Generation :
154 ₁ Reuben, entered Yale College in.........; took a very high
       stand in his class and seemed full of promise. During
       his college course he was called away by death and a
       very fine monument was erected to his memory in the
       New Haven cemetery, by his classmates.
155 ₂ Rev. Erastus, grad. in Williams College and settled in the
       gospel ministry at Montgomery, Mass., and elsewhere; d.
       in Easthampton, Mass., in 1869.
156 ₃ Benjamin.
157 ₄ Eunice, d. in Easthampton.
158 ₅ Hannah, m. Russell Pomeroy.
159 ₆ Roxanna, m. Mr. Ripley.

16 MERCY LYMAN⁶, 5th dau. of Dea. *Benjamin⁵*, bapt. Oct.
11, 1772; m. Josiah Snow of South Hadley, in 1796.
                                        South Hadley, Mass.
         Children, Seventh Generation :
160 ₁ Spencer, lived in South Hadley.
161 ₂ Josiah, lived in South Hadley.
162 ₃ Azuba, m. Ripley.

163 4 Mercy, m. Brainard.
164 5 Elizabeth, m. Alfred E. Lyman, of Williamsburg, Mass.
The record seems imperfect; these last two m. Preston and White.

5 LEMUEL LYMAN[5], son of *Benjamin[4]*, who first settled in Easthampton, b. Aug. 17, 1735; moved with his father to Easthampton, at the age of ten. In 1755, at the age of twenty, in company with his neighbor, Lieut. Eliakim Wright, he joined the expedition then forming under command of Sir William Johnson against Crown point. A battle occurred at the south end of Lake George, Sept. 8, 1755, in which a portion of the troops were engaged, these being in command of Col. Ephraim Williams, the founder of Williams College, who was slain. Mr. Lyman was in this battle, and received a wound while in the act of firing at an Indian. The bullet passed across three of his fingers and struck his breast, passing through a leather vest, pierced his shirt three times on account of a fold in it, passed through his bullet pouch and half buried itself in his body. This pouch is still preserved in one of the numerous families of his descendants. Soon after this, he, with others, was sent with a drove of cattle for the northern army. It was supposed, that, in this expedition, by the privations and exposures which he endured, he laid the foundation for the rheumatism, a disease, which in later years rendered him, to some extent, unable to perform manual labor. He was a member of the board of selectmen for seven years, and one of the leaders in the establishment of a church, and the erection of a house of worship. He was a man of great physical strength, and was quick to perceive the best method of action in a moment of danger. He had a very retentive memory, great presence of mind, and native energy of character. He m. Lydia Clark, dau. of Eliakim Clark, of Easthampton, who was b. Sept., 1741. He d. July 16, 1810, aged 74. *Easthampton, Mass.*

Children, Sixth Generation :

165 1 Lydia, b. Jan. 6, 1765 ; m. Ebenezer K. Rust, Southampton.
166 2 Lemuel, b. Dec. 1, 1766.
167 3 Justus, b. Dec. 1, 1768.
168 4 Ahira, b. Dec. 20, 1770.
169 5 Sylvester, b. May 17, 1773.
170 6 Daniel, b. Sept. 3, 1777.
171 7 Esther, b. Oct. 19, 1779 ; m. Obadiah Janes of Easthampton.
172 8 Elihu, b. July 15, 1784.

165 Lydia Lyman[6], dau. of *Lemuel[5]*, b. Jan. 6, 1765; m. Ebenezer K. Rust of Southampton. She d. in Southampton, Sept. 27, 1800. *Southampton. Mass.*

Children, Seventh Generation.

173 1 Diana.
174 2 Bradley.
175 3 Norman.

176 4 Dennis.
177 5 Julietta.
178 6 Rosetta.

166 Capt. Lemuel Lyman[6], son of *Lemuel[5]*, b. Dec. 1, 1766; m. Olive Lyman, of Norwich, in Jan., 1795. She was b. Dec. 26, 1766. His trade was that of carpenter and joiner, although he owned and lived on a farm. About the year 1800, he superintended the removal of a dam across the Connecticut river at South Hadley Canal, which stood about two miles above the present dam, and set the water back into the meadows, occasioning much sickness. In answer to a petition on the subject, the legislature ordered its removal. He d. Jan. 10, 1854. Mrs. Oliver Lyman, d. Oct. 27, 1849. *Norwich, Ct.*

Children, Seventh Generation:

203 1 Dwight, b. Oct. 30, 1795.
204 2 Theodosia, m. Augusta Clapp.
205 3 Theodore, b. Feb. 5, 1800.
206 4 Dennis, b. April 19, 1802.
207 5 Lemuel.　　　　　　208 6 Miranda.

203 Dwight Lyman[7], son of *Capt. Lemuel[6]*, b. Oct. 30, 1795; m. Helena Janes, dau. of Enos Janes, of Easthampton, Dec. 26, 1823. He settled on the farm owned by his father where he still resides. *Easthampton, Mass.*

Children, Eighth Generation:

209 1 Mirauda, born Oct. 27, 1824; m. Sheldon W. Clark of Easthampton, Dec. 23, 1852, and died Aug. 9, 1865. She had two children.
　　　Ch. 9th Gen.: 1 Lewis Lyman, b. June 11, 1855. 2. Arthur Russell, b. Feb. 27, 1859; d. Nov. 13, 1860.
212 2 Lemuel Dwight, b. Jan. 1, 1827.
213 3 Lewis Dwight, b. Feb. 21, 1830; d. March 25, 1837.
214 4 Francis Dwight, b Aug. 26, 1833.
215 5 Jane Amelia Dwight, b. July 6, 1839.

204 Theodosia Lyman[7], dau. of Capt. *Lemuel[6]*, m. Augustus Clapp, then of Norwich, but now of Easthampton, in Oct. 1, 1826. Mr. Clapp on his removal to Easthampton, settled in the district known by the Indian name Nashawannuck, on the farm which was occupied by John Webb, who was the first settler of Easthampton. *Easthampton, Mass.*

Children, Eighth Generation

216 1 Harriet, b. April 2, 1830 ; m. Lewis S. Clark, of Easthampton.
217 2 Elvira, b. Feb. 5, 1832 ; d. Nov. 15, 1848.
218 3 Henry Augustus, b. Aug. 15, 1834.
219 4 Theodore, b. Sept. 5, 1836 ; d. May 21, 1840.

205 THEODORE LYMAN[7], son of Capt. *Lemuel[6]*, b. Feb. 5,
1800 ; m. Judith Clapp, dau. of Isaac Clapp, of Easthamp
ton, Dec. 2, 1824. He settled on a farm near where the
Williston Mills now stand. He recently removed to
Northampton, where he now resides. Mrs. Judith C. Lyman, d. Feb. 24, 1863, aged 59. *Northampton, Mass.*

Children, Eighth Generation :

220 1 Harriet, b. Dec. 11, 1825.
221 2 Anna Maria, b. May 31, 1829 ; m. Junius Poullain, of
Greensboro, Ga., Oct. 3, 1855.
   Ch. 9th Gen. : 1 Ann Maria, b. Nov. 4, 1856. 2
   Clara Celeste, b. March 19, 1858 ; d. March 28, 1862.
   3 Harriet Byron, b. June 28, 1860, Mr. Poullain, d.
   .May 19, 1862.
224 3 Frances Eliza, b. June 15, 1832 ; d. Feb. 5, 1837.
225 4 Judith Kirkland, b. Nov. 2, 1835; m. Charles H. Hilliard,
Aug. 19 1863.
226 5 Sarah Clapp, b. Oct. 12, 1838.

206 DENNIS LYMAN[7], son of Capt. *Lemuel[6]*, b. April 19,
1802; m. Eliza Clapp, dau. of Phinehas Clapp of Southampton, Nov. 29, 1832. He built a house in Easthampton,
just north of the bridge across the Manhan river and has
since worked at his trade as shoemaker. Mrs. Eliza C.,
d. June 19, 1859, in her 55th year. *Easthampton, Mass.*

Children, Eighth Generation :

227 1 Orlando, b. Dec. 10, 1833 ; d. Feb. 5, 1837.
228 2 Dennis Clapp, b. March 10, 1836.
229 3 Eliza Ann, b. Aug. 4, 1838; m. Charles Kinney, of Cummington, April 5, 1865.
230 4 Salmon Henry, b. Sept. 1, 1840 ; d. Aug. 26, 1862.
231 5 Olive Lucretia, b. Dec. 21, 1844.

228 DENNIS C. LYMAN[8], son of *Dennis[7]*, b. March 10,
1836; m. Harriet N. Ellis, dau. of John Ellis of Cummington, who was b. March 13, 1835, in Northampton, having
one child. *Northampton, Mass.*

Child, Ninth Generation :

232 1 Eudora J., b. March 9, 1862.

230 SALMON H. LYMAN[8], son of *Dennis[7]*, one of the first of the Easthampton soldiers to volunteer, was the first to fall. In the first summer of the war, when the soldiers were rallying to the standard, he went to New York, joined the regiment known as the Anderson Zouaves, was home once on a furlough, spent one winter in camp, started out with McClellan on his Peninsular campaign, and fought at the battle of Williamsburg; soon after which he was taken sick, and removed to New York, where he died. His remains were brought to his home, where they were buried with military honors, on the 18th of September, 1862.

167 JUSTUS LYMAN[6], son of *Lemuel[5]*, b. Dec. 1, 1768; m. March 8, 1798. Nancy Carey, dau. of Capt. Phineas Carey, Northampton. He owned and lived upon a farm in the North District of his native town. He was a man of influence in the affairs of the town which he served in the capacity of selectman eleven years. He d. Dec. 4, 1846. His wife d. May 21, 1848. *Easthampton, Mass.*

Children, Seventh Generation ·

233 1 George, b. Feb. 24, 1799.
234 2 Charles, b. Feb. 25, 1804.
235 3 Elisha Waldo, Aug. 9, 1809.

233 GEORGE LYMAN[7], son of *Justus[6]*, b. Feb. 14, 1799; m. Roann Frary, dau. of Isaac Frary, Nov. 21, 1829, and lived on his father's place till his death, Nov. 19, 1844. His widow m. Mr. Warner of Deerfield. *Easthampton, Mass.*

Children, Eighth Generation:

236 1 Albert, b. Dec. 15, 1830; d. Oct. 30, 1831.
237 2 Albert, b. Sept. 10, 1832; d. in Kansas, Oct. 15, 1860.
238 3 Henry, b. Sept. 5, 1834; m. Mary A., dau. of Wm. Bradwell, Jan. 20, 1858. Joined 52d Mass. Reg. in 1862, and d. at Baton Rouge, La., 1863.

234 CHARLES LYMAN[7], son of *Justus[6]*, b. April 25, 1804; m. Harriet Foote, dau. of John Foote, of Johnstown, N. Y. She, on her mother's side, was a descendant of the Knickerbockers of the Mohawk valley. Not many years after his marriage he left his family, and went to New Orleans, La., where he is supposed to have d. as he was never heard from after reaching that place. Mrs. Lyman, d. at the house of her dau. in Johnstown, N. Y., in April, 1867. *Johnstown, N. Y.*

Children, Eighth Generation.

239 ·1 Charles H.
240 2 John, d. in infancy at Johnstown, N. Y.
241 3 Nancy C.

239 CHARLES H. LYMAN[8], son of *Charles[7]*. He learned the printing business at Johnstown, N. Y., and worked in nearly all the cities of the large eastern and middle states before his marriage, Oct. 19, 1854, to Elizabeth H. Phelps, dau. of Lewis Phelps 2d, of Northampton, Mass. In 1864, he bought the printing office in Holyoke, Mass., and became editor and proprietor of the *Holyoke Transcript.*
Holyoke, Mass.

Children, Ninth Generation :

242 1 Willie Lester.   244 3 Hattie Elizabeth.
243 2 Frank Lewis.

241 NANCY C. LYMAN[8], m. William Argersinger, of Johnstown, N. Y., a flourishing merchant of that town. She has two children.

Children, Ninth Generation :

245 1 Lyman.
246 2 Rosamond.

235 E. WALDO LYMAN[8], son of *Justus[7]*, b. Aug. 9, 1809; m. Laura Alexander, daughter of Thaddeus Alexander, and settled on his father's farm in Easthampton, Mass., where he still lives.   *Easthampton, Mass.*

Children, Ninth Generation :

247 1 Justus, b. Feb. 24, 1835.
248 2 Mary S., b. March 1, 1837.
249 3 Thaddeus A., b. Nov. 12, 1838.
250 4 Elisha C., b. May 16, 1841.
251 5 Solon, b. Oct. 2, 1843.
252 6 Charles, b. June 21, 1846; d. Aug. 8, 1847.
253 7 George, b. Aug. 19, 1848.

247 CAPT. JUSTUS LYMAN[8], son of *E. Waldo[7]*, b. Feb.·24, 1835, joined Co. A, 27th Mass. Reg., in the fall of 1861. He participated in the capture of Roanoke island and Newbern, N.C., was in the defence of Washington during the unsuccessful siege of it by the rebels. In the spring of 1864, he was engaged with his regiment in its advance up the James under command of Gen. Butler. After several days of fighting on the rail road between Richmond and Petersburg, Va., he with many others of the regiment fell into the hands of the enemy at Drury's Bluff on the

16th of May.   He was confined two weeks in Libby
prison and then taken successively to Macon, Charleston,
Columbia, S. C. and Charlotte, N. C., where he was exchanged after an imprisonment of more than nine months.
He retained his connection with the army until the close
of the war, before which time he had received a captain's
commission.

He was m. to Lois P. Alexander, dau. of Philip Alexander of Easthampton, Feb. 13, 1864, and now lives in
Grafton, Vt.   *Grafton, Vt.*

Children, Ninth Generation:

254 1 Frank Ernest, b. Sept. 15, 1866.
255 2 Mary Daisy, b. July 4, 1869.

249 THADDEUS LYMAN[8], son of *E. Waldo*[7] b. Nov.
12, 1838; m. Lucy Kidder, dau. of Timothy Kidder, b.
July 11, 1868.   He joined Co. A, 27th Mass. Reg., with
his brother, but was discharged before active service on
account of sickness.

250 ELISHA C. LYMAN[8] son of *E. Waldo*[7], b. May 16, 1841,
joined Co. A, 27th Mass. Reg., in the summer of 1862.
He was not long spared to serve his country, but the
patriotic devotion was the same, and the sacrifice as costly,
as if he had been spared to meet the enemy many times
on the field of battle.   He died at Newbern, N. C., Dec.
26, 1866.

251 SOLON LYMAN[8] son of *E. Waldo*, b. Oct. 2, 1843; m.
Mattie P., dau. of Horace Mathews of Easthampton, April
16, 1866.   He lives on the farm with his father, and has
one child,   *Easthampton, Mass.*

Child, Ninth Generation:

256 1 Laura Rosamond, b. March 22, 1867.

168 AHIRA LYMAN[6], son of *Lemuel*[5], b. Dec. 20, 1770; m.
Sally Pomeroy, dau. of Lemuel Pomeroy of Southampton,
Jan. 15, 1809, who d. May 10, 1813.   He located himself
on the plain, west of the centre of Easthampton.   He was
a very active and prosperous business man, both as a
farmer and mechanic.   His death occurred Nov. 1, 1836,
in consequence of a severe wound in his foot, made by an
axe, while alone and at considerable distance from home
engaged in chopping wood.   He was able to reach home
though with considerable loss of blood, and for a number

of days there seemed to be a reasonable prospect of his recovery. His case, however, at length took an unfavorable turn, and he d. about three weeks after the injury.

Easthampton, Mass.

Children, Seventh Generation:

257 1 Roland, b. March 2, 1802.
258 2 Lemuel Pynchon, b. Sept. 27, 1804, Lowell, Mass.
259 3 Ahira, b. Oct. 13, 1807.
260 4 Quartus Pomeroy, b. Dec. 28, 1809.   Mrs. Sarah P. Lyman
        d., and Mr. L. m. 2d, Lydia Baldwin, of Westfield, Mass.,
        Sept. 22, 1814, who d. Feb. 1, 1833.
261 5 William, b. Jan. 9, 1818 ; m. Cordelia Hannum, of Easthamp-
        ton, Mass.   He d. Oct. 16, 1840, about a year after his
        marriage.
262 6 Jabez Baldwin, b. April 18, 1819.
    Mrs. Lydia B. Lyman, d. and Mr. Lyman, m. 3d, Mrs. Hannah
Judd Lyman, widow of Elihu Lyman, of Westhampton.   She d.
Feb. 16, 1865.

257 ROLAND LYMAN[7], son of *Ahira*[6], b. March 2, 1802; m. Dec. 30, 1831, Mary Howland, b. Aug. 11, 1805, dau. of John Howland, of Providence, R. I., being the sixth in the lineal descent from John Howland, the Puritan, who arrived in the Mayflower in Plymouth, in 1620.   Mr. Lyman removed to Lowell, Mass., where he became established in business as a watchmaker and jeweler.   Here he continued nearly forty years and longer with one exception, than any business man in Lowell.

Mr. Lyman was present at the reunion of the Lymans on Mt. Tom. Aug. 30, and d. Nov. 15, 1871.   When in ill health he was carried to the polls at an election, but the excitement resulted in a fainting fit, from which he never fully recovered.   He d. of congestion of the lungs.   He was an earnest and devout Christian, greatly respected for his strict integrity and sound judgment.   His word in matters of fact was often referred to in questions of law relating to points of evidence.   *Lowell, Mass.*

Children, Eighth Generation:

263 1 Elizabeth Russell, b. March 23, 1835 ; d. Aug. 29, 1835.
264 2 John Howland, b. May 17, 1836 ; d. Nov. 23, 1841.
265 3 Alfred Pynchon. b. March 31, 1841; m. Ida M. Nichols,
        May 14, 1867.
            Ch. 9th Gen.: 1 John Alfred, b. in 1868.   2 Roland,
        b. April, 1869 ; d. Dec., 1869.

258 LEMUEL PYNCHON LYMAN[7], son of *Ahira*[6], b. Sept. 27, 1804 ; m. Esther Phelps, dau. of Capt. John Phelps, of

Easthampton, Nov. 21, 1827. He built a house at the foot of " Meeting House Hill," Easthampton. For many years he owned the saw-mill on the Manhan near his residence, and carried on his lumber business, as extensive probably, as that of any man in the county. He also owned a share of the grist-mill opposite his saw-mill, standing where one has now stood little short of two hundred years. The first mill was erected by Samuel Bartlett, to whom in 1676–7 Northampton gave liberty " to set up a corn-mill upon Manhan river below the cartway on the falls of the river." Mr. L. P. Lyman d. Aug. 7, 1865. His death was hastened, by if not entirely, the result of an injury received on his head by the falling of a stick of timber at the raising of a house.

Easthampton, Mass.

. *Children, Eighth Generation :*

267 1 Sarah Pomeroy, b. Nov. 23, 1831 ; m. Frederick A. Shaw of Easthampton, April 23, 1862 ; d. Sept. 15, 1867.
268 2 Hannah Phelps, b. March 12, 1836 ; m. Dwight S. Jepson of Easthampton, Jan. 1, 1861.
269 3 Lewis Pynchon, b. Sept. 6, 1840 ; d. March 23, 1843.
270 4 Mary Esther, b. Feb. 1, 1847 ; m. Edwin E. Wakefield of Northampton.

Mrs. Esther P. Lyman, d. Dec. 15, 1854, and Mr. Lyman m. Naomi Phelps, dau. of Capt. John Phelps, April 23, 1856, Mrs. Naomi P. Lyman, d. Jan. 20, 1860, and Mr. Lyman m. Mary McIntire of Northampton, April 24, 1866, and d. Sept. 3, 1869. She still lives in Easthampton.

259 AHIRA LYMAN[7], JR., b. Oct. 13, 1807; m. Frances Burt, daughter of Gaius Burt, of Northampton, May 28, 1831, who d. May 18, 1839. He settled on the Park Hill, just over the Northampton line, though his church connections have always been in Easthampton. Mrs. Frances A. Lyman d. May 18, 1839 ; Mr. Lyman m. 2d, Theresa Lyman, daughter of Elihu Lyman, of Westhampton, Feb. 6, 1840. *Easthampton, Mass.*

Children, Eighth Generation :

272 1 Henry, b. July 31, 1832.
273 2 Gaius Burt, b. Aug, 25, 1834 ; d. Oct. 2, 1835.
274 3 Gaius Burt, b. July 19, 1836.
275 4 Frances Burt, b. Dec. 8, 1840 ; m. William P. Derby.
276 5 Arthur Judd, b. July 30, 1842; d. Jan. 18, 1864.
277 6 Albert Ahira, b. Dec. 27, 1845.
278 7 Richard, b. Sept. 8, 1847.
279 8 Robert Worthington, b. March 27, 1850.
280 9 William, b. May 22, 1854.

272 HENRY LYMAN[8], son of *Ahira[7]*, Jr., b. July 31, 1832; m. Jane A. Parsons, dau. of Ralph Parsons of Holyoke, Dec. 23, 1858. In the summer of 1832 he joined Co. A, 27th Mass. Regt. During his connection with the regiment it was stationed in Newbern, N. C. He was in the service a little more than one year when he sickened and d. His chaplain, Rev. C. L. Woodworth, bore testimony to his fidelity as a soldier and a Christian, saying that he was one of those upon whom he most relied for assistance in promoting the spiritual welfare of the men.
Easthampton, Mass.

Children, Ninth Generation :
280*1 Frederick Wilbur, b. April 28, 1860.
281 2 Edith M., b. Feb. 1, 1862.

274 G. BURT LYMAN[8], son of *Ahira[7]*, b. July 19, 1836; m. Eliza Manghem.　　　　　　　*Northampton, Mass.*

Children, Ninth Generation :
282 1 Francis Burt.
283 2 Edward Sheldon, d. in infancy.
284 3 Edward, ⎱ twins, b. July 12, 1860.
285 4 Arabella, ⎰

275 FRANCES B. LYMAN[8], dau. of *Ahira[7]*, m. Wm. P. Derby, May 4, 1865, and now resides in Northampton. He superintends the tape manufactory of Williston & Arms in that town.　　　　　　*Northampton, Mass.*

Children, Ninth Generation .
286 1 Stella, Oct. 1, 1866 ; d. March 29, 1870.
287 2 Mary Theresa, b. Dec. 19, 1867.
288 3 Fannie.

277 ALBERT A. LYMAN[8], son of *Ahira[7]*, b. Dec. 27, 1845, enlisted in Co. K, 52d Mass. Regiment, in Sept., 1862, and served under Gen. Banks, in the campaign resulting in the capture of Port Hudson, La, and the opening up of the Mississippi, July 8, 1863.

260 QUARTUS P. LYMAN[7], son of *Ahira[6]*, b. Dec. 28, 1809 ; m. in Granby, Ct., Tryphena Wright, dau. of John Wright, of Easthampton, Nov. 7, 1832. Mrs. Tryphena W. Lyman, d. Feb. 9, 1851. Mr. Lyman, m. Emelia Smith, of Granby, Mass., June 26, 1851　　　　　*Easthampton, Mass.*

Children, Eighth Generation :
289 1 A dau., b. Feb. 26, 1834.

290 2 John Wright, b. Nov. 9, 1836; m. Mary Lucy Mathews,
    dau. of Horace A. Mathews, of Easthampton, Jan. 17,
    1861, Williamsburgh.
          Ch. 9th Gen.: 1 Carrie, b. July 17, 1862.

262 Jabez Baldwin Lyman[7], son of *Ahira[6]*, graduated at
Amherst College in 1841, resided in Germany some years,
where he was a student in one of the universities. He
was afterwards principal of a Female Seminary in Abbe-
ville, S. C. He was for a time established as an oculist in
Chicago, but for several years has been engaged in the
practice of surgery in Rockford, Ill. He m. Lucy DuPay,
Sept. 5, 1860.   *Rockford, Ill.*
         Children, Eighth Generation :
291 1 Wm. Henry, b. Dec. 1861; d. Sept., 1863.
292 2 Charles Baldwin, b. Sept., 1863.
293 3 Mary, b. Feb., 1868.
294 4 Two children died under six months of age.

169 Dea. Sylvester Lyman[6], *Samuel[5]*, *Benjamin[4]*, *Benjamin[3]*, *John[2]*, *Richard[1]*, 1773–1835, b. May 17, 1773; m.
Naomi Janes, dau. of Capt. Noah Janes, Nov. 6, 1800.
She was b. Aug. 1, 1778. He lived on the place purchased
by Benjamin Lyman on his removal from Northampton,
owning and working the farm. He was chosen deacon of
the church in Easthampton in 1813, and continued in the
office twenty years. Mrs. Naomi Lyman d. Sept. 13, 1818.
and Mr. Lyman m. Betsey Rumrill, May 12, 1819, who
still survives. Dea. Sylvester d. May 31, 1835.
         Children, Seventh Generation :
295 1 A son, b. Sept. 15, 1801 ; d. Sept. 29, 1801.
296 2 A son, b. Sept. 10, 1802 ; d. Feb. 11, 1803.
297 3 Samuel Mosely, Dec. 23, 1803.
298 4 Ursula, b. May 13, 1806 ; m. Ithamar Clark.
299 5 Naomi Lyman, b. Aug. 26, 1808 ; m. Nov. 23, 1843, Warren
       Montague, of Sunderland, farmer, and had a son Warren,
       b. June 8, 1845, d. Oct. 8, 1845, she d. Aug. 10, 1869.
300 6 Sylvester Strong, b. 1813.
301 7 Melissa, b. Feb. 4, 1816 ; d. Feb. 10, 1816.
302 8 Joseph Emerson, b. April 2, 1817.
303 9 Elizabeth, b. May 25, 1820 ; m. Edward L. Snow.
304 10 Tirzah, b. Nov. 24, 1821 ; m. Eli S. Hoadly.
305 11 Edwin Bliss, b. June 4, 1825.

297 Samuel Mosely Lyman[7], son of Dea. *Sylvester[6]*, b.
Dec. 23, 1803; m. Harriet Avery, dau. of Worcester
Avery of Easthampton, Nov. 26, 1829, and settled on the

plain west of the village of Easthampton, where he now
resides. *Easthampton, Mass.*
Children, Eighth Generation :
306 1 Samuel Mosely, b. June 7, 1831.
307 2 Harriet Ann, b. Jan. 10, 1833 ; m. J. Edward Janes.
308 3 Edward Payson, b. April 23, 1839 ; m. Harriet Augusta
Randall, then of Springfield, but before of New York.
309 4 Sarah Maria, b. May 25, 1841.
310 5 Jennette Elizabeth, b. Aug. 5, 1846.

306 SAMUEL MOSELY LYMAN[8], jr., b. June 7, 1831; m.
Marian E. Rust of Chester, Ohio, June 3, 1856, and resides on his father's farm. *Easthampton, Mass.*
Children, Ninth Generation :
311 1 Irving Wright, b. April 27, 1860.
312 2 George Clifford, b. June 18, 1868.

307 HARRIET ANN LYMAN[8], dau. of *S. Mosely*[7], m. J.
Edward Janes, Nov. 30, 1854. *Easthampton, Mass.*
Children, Ninth Generation :
313 1 Bertha Anna, b. July 2, 1858.
314 2 Edward Lyman, b. Dec. 9, 1860.
315 3 Arthur Lyman, b. May 9, 1864.
316 4 Anna Maria, b. Aug. 10, 1866.

298 URSULA LYMAN[7], dau. of Dea. *Sylvester*[6], b. May 13,
1806; m. Dea. Ithamar Clark, Jan. 18, 1826; of Easthampton; d. Sept. 14, 1835. *Easthampton, Mass.*
Children, Eighth Generation :
317 1 Rev. Edson Lyman Clark, b. April 1, 1827, graduated at
Yale College in 1853, studied theology at Union Theological Seminary, 1858, preached a year at Woolcotville,
Ct., then was ordained and installed pastor of the Congregational church in Dalton, Mass., Nov. 30, 1859,
where he remained till 1867. He is now preaching in
Branford, Ct.
318 2 Emma Amelia, b. Nov. 10, 1829.
319 3 Oliver Strong, b. Nov. 11, 1831; d Jan. 24, 1838.
320 4 Sylvester, b. Sept. 29, 1833; d. May 19, 1856.
321 5 An infant, b. Sept. 7, 1835.
By 2d wife Louisa Ferry, whom he m. March 17, 1836.
322 6 Sereno, b. Nov. 30, 1836.
323 7 Oliver A., b. Nov. 8, 1841, was a member of Co. A, 27th
Mass. Regt., which he joined in the summer of 1862.
He was a faithful soldier and an earnest Christian, always
forward in endeavors for the spiritual welfare of his companions, and also of the freedmen among whom he was
thrown during one winter in Norfolk, Va., he being a

superintendent of an evening school established for their benefit. He was captured with many of his comrades at Drury's Bluff, Va., May 16, 1864, and after a brief stay in Libby Prison he was taken to Andersonville, Ga., where he d. June 27, 1864.

300 Sylvester Strong Lyman[7], sixth child of Dea. *Sylvester*[6], is a portrait painter. He m. in Brooklyn, N. Y., Lucinda Gaylord, of South Hadley, Mass., May 29, 1844; d. Sept. 29, 1870.   *Hartford, Ct.*
  Children, Eighth Generation:
324 1 Ellen Philomela, b. Oct. 31, 1847.
325 2 Helen Lucinda, b. June 14, 1849.
326 3 Frederick Sylvester, b. May 31, 1855.

302 Joseph E. Lyman[8], farmer, m. Oct. 14, 1842, Martha Clark, d. Jan. 11, 1848, m. 2d in the winter of 1848–9, Clarissa Daniel, of Sing Sing, N. Y.
  Children, Ninth Generation:
327 1 Clara J., b. March 4, 1853 ; d. Aug. 29, 1863.
328 2 Hattie Hyatt, b. Aug. 16, 1856.

304 Tirzah Lyman[7], daughter of *Sylvester*[6], b. Nov. 24, 1821, at Easthampton, Hampshire county, Mass., m. Jan. 9, 1850, Eli Smith Hoadly, b. in Worcester, Mass., Aug. 23, 1826. The mother of Tirzah Lyman, Betsey Rumrill, b Nov. 15, 1787, at Long Meadow, Hampden Co., Mass., dau. of Ebenezer R.

E. S. Hoadly has a music store in Springfield, was several years teacher of music in the Williston Seminary, Easthampton, Mass., is the author, in connection with William Mason, of New York, of two musical works, *Method for the Piano*, and *System for Beginners in the Art of Playing upon the Piano Forte."* The method was published by Mason Bros., New York, 1867; the system, by O. Ditson, & Co., Boston, Mass.
  Child, Eighth Generation:
329 1 Perry Lyman Hoadly, b. at Easthampton, April 9, 1859.

305 Edwin Bliss Lyman[7], son of Dea. *Sylvester*[6], was b. in Easthampton, Mass., June 4, 1825; m. Oct. 4, 1855; in Brooklyn, N. Y., to Frances Elizabeth Ann Rice.
                                              Brooklyn, N. Y.
  Children, Eighth Generation:
330 1 Sylvester Hoadly, b. June 29, 1856.
331 2 Emma Elizabeth, b. Sept. 15, 185–.
332 3 Joseph Emerson, July 21, 1864.

170 LIEUT. DANIEL LYMAN[6], son of *Lemuel*[5], *Benjamin*[4], *Benjamin*[3], *John*[2], *Richard*[1], 1771–1853, b. Sept. 3, 1777; m. Sally Clapp, dau. of Benjamin Clapp, Dec. 30, 1806. He lived on Park Hill, where his son, Lauren D., now lives. He was a man of more than ordinary religious feeling, a devoted friend and warm supporter of the institutions of religion, and a pillar in the prayer meetings of the church and neighborhood. He d. Sept. 23, 1853. Mrs. Sally C. Lyman was b. Nov. 15, 1780, and d. Jan. 9, 1844.

Easthampton, Mass.

Children, Seventh Generation:

333 1 Daniel Franklin, b. Aug. 28, 1809.
334 2 Josiah, b. Oct. 9, 1811.
335 3 Addison, b. Dec. 3, 1813.
336 4 Horace, b. Nov. 16, 1815.
337 5 Sarah Boynton, b. Feb. 24, 1818; d. Nov. 24, 1844.
338 6 Lauren Dwight, b. June 20, 1820.
339 7 James Harvey, b. Nov. 13, 1822.

Daniel Lyman, m. 2d wife, Mrs. Mary Taylor Searl, widow of Eggleston Searl, of Southampton. She now resides in Westfield, with her son, Myron E. Searl.

333 DANIEL F. LYMAN[7], of Easthampton, son of *Daniel*[6], b. Aug. 28, 1809; m. Eunice S. Ferry, b. June 16, 1813, dau. of Asa Ferry, of Easthampton, Dec. 24, 1840. Mrs. Eunice S. F. Lyman, d. Sept. 27, 1846, and he m. Almena Smith, dau. of Rufus Smith, of Worthington, Oct. 7, 1847. She was b. Oct. 3, 1810. Mr. Lyman built a house on a part of his father's farm where he resided till his death, Sept. 19, 1868.   *Easthampton, Mass.*

Children, Eighth Generation:

340 1 Rev. Payson Williston, b. Feb. 28, 1842.
341 2 Daniel Watson, b. Nov. 2, 1843, killed at Port Hudson, La.,
        June 14, 1863.
342 3 Alfred Ferry, b. Sept. 27, 1846; d. Oct. 3, 1868. Concern-
        ing him it was said: His death has cast a gloom over the
        community in which he moved and all feel that another
        working Christian has gone.
343 4 Horace Smith, b. Oct. 21, 1848.
344 5 Eunice Almena, b. Oct. 4, 1850.
345 6 Amelia Sophia, b. Nov. 21, 1853; d. May 30, 1869.

It was said of Daniel F. Lyman by one who knew him well and knew whereof he spoke: — Modest and retiring in his manners; he never sought to make himself prominent by seeking office, but was content to serve his generation by striving to do his duty as a citizen and a Christian in the sphere in which he was placed. Springing from a Puritan ancestry, he possessed in a large measure, the virtues which mark the genuine Puritan character, and it may truly be said of him that no man in town was more thoroughly respected, nor one whose integrity was more unquestioned. He had been for many years a member of the first church, and was regarded as one of its pillars. The Bible says, " A good name is rather to be chosen than great riches," and Mr. Lyman has certainly left that as an inheritance for his children.

Daniel W. Lyman, son of Daniel F. Lyman, was a member of Co. K, 52d regiment, in which he was one of the first to enlist. Not from any fondness for the adventures and perils of war, nor from any momentary impulse, but from a deliberate conviction that to him the voice of country was the voice of God, was he led to offer himself, a sacrifice if need be, for his country's salvation. Upon a Christian young man not absolutely forbidden by some higher call of duty, he felt that the claims of country then were paramount. Influenced by such considerations, it is not too much to say, that in the darkest hour, his purpose never wavered, nor did a regret for his course find place in his heart. To his faithful performance of the duties of a Christian soldier, many have borne ample testimony. His cordial, unwavering trust in God, in times of darkness and danger, though probably doubted by none, is best known to those who knew him intimately. To many whom he never saw, he was known by his letters from the regiment, which were published in the *Hampshire Gazette*.

Sabbath morning, June 14, 1863, an attack on Fort Hudson was ordered, and, though deprecating the selection of that day for the assault, he went forward without faltering. His regiment being engaged as skirmishers, he, with a few of his comrades, gained a position in a ravine somewhat in advance of the main line, and while here, very early in the engagement, a ball from a rebel sharpshooter struck him in his head, killing him instantly. Capt. Bissell wrote to me thus in relation to him : " Gentle hands placed him in his grave, and covered the earth over him near the spot where he fell, although obliged to wait till after dark, and to be exposed to a storm of rebel bullets. This tender tribute of affection is his monument, and, although his dust may not make the violets of his native hills, it will not be amiss, on the morning of the resurrection, that his body should arise from the spot, where the latest duties of his life were so faithfully concluded."

In the town of Easthampton, nine of the name of Lyman enlisted in the service of their country to subdue the rebellion, four of whom died of disease or fell in battle in the rebel states.

340 PAYSON W. LYMAN[8], son of *Daniel F.*[7], of Easthampton, b. Feb. 28, 1842, graduated from Amherst College in the class of 1867, and from Union Theological Seminary New York, in 1870. He is the author of a history of Easthampton, Mass., published in 1866. He is now pas-

tor of the Congregational church in Belchertown, Mass., ordained May 10, 1871.

334 REV. JOSIAH LYMAN[7], son of *Daniel[6]*, b. Oct. 9, 1811, graduated from Williams College, in 1836, took charge of an English and classical school, in Canaan, N. Y., for two years, taught afterwards for a short time at Ithaca, N. Y., and then at Easthampton, Mass. He studied theology at Auburn, and was licensed to preach in the fall of 1843. Following this, he taught school in Bristol, Ct. Here the blessing of God upon his efforts for the spiritual benefit of his pupils, was such as to lead him to decide to make teaching the business of his life. This profession he followed as principal of an Academy, at Williston, Vt. and Lenox, Mass., till he was compelled in consequence of ill health, to relinquish sedentary pursuits. For many years his business has been that of telescope manufacturer and civil engineer. A reflecting telescope of his manufacture, is admitted to be the best, as it is the largest of its kind ever made in this country. He has also invented and manufactured an instrument called the protracting trigonometer, a very superior drafting instrument. May 22, 1844, he m. Mary Bingham, dau, of Reuben Bingham, of Cornwall, Vt., and granddaughter of Dea. Jeremiah Bingham of the same place. *Lenox, Mass.*

Children, Eighth Generation :

346 1 Rev. Albert Josiah, b. Dec. 24, 1845; studied theology one year at the Cong. Theol. Sem., Chicago, and graduated from Union Theol. Sem. New York, in 1868. He is now settled over the 1st Congregational church in Milford, Ct. June 1, 1870, he m. Ella Stevens, dau. of P. Stevens, Esq., Brooklyn, N. Y.

347 2 Sarah Bingham, b. Jan. 17, 1848.

335 REV. ADDISON LYMAN[7], son of *Daniel[6]*, b. Dec. 3, 1813; graduated at Williams College in 1839; was principal of Cambridge Washington Academy, Cambridge, N. Y., for two years; graduated from Auburn Theological Seminary in 1844; preached four months in Torringford, Ct.; m. Theresa Lyman, daughter of Jeremiah Lyman, of Easthampton, Sept. 9, 1845, who d. Jan. 23, 1847, two weeks after the death of her infant child. Leaving Torringford, Rev. Mr. Lyman went to Geneseo, Ill., where he preached two years, and was seven years principal of Geneseo Seminary. Leaving Geneseo, he became and has continued for

51

fourteen years pastor of the Congregational church in Sheffield, Ill. Oct. 5, 1856, he organized a church at Buda, Ill.,
where he preached four years, in connection with his
charge at Sheffield. Dec. 4, 1847, he m. Mrs. Catharjne
A. Pitkin, of New York, and widow of Rev. Frederic H.
Pitkin, East Hartford, Ct. Her daughter, Emily H. Pitkin, has been adopted as his own since their marriage.
He is now pastor of the Congregational church in Kellogg,
Jasper Co., Iowa.

Children, Eighth Generation:

348 1 Elbert Porter, b. Dec. 14, 1848.
349 2 Theresa Maria, b. April 8, 1851.
350 3 John Frederic, b. Jan. 12, 1845.
351 4 Mary Lyon, b. Dec. 25, 1855.
352 5 Henry Martyn, b. Aug. 13, 1858.
353 6 Addison Franklin, b. Jan. 28, 1861.
354 7 Catharine Elizabeth, b. March 14, 1863.
355 8 Anna Louisa, b. Oct. 26, 1866.

336 REV. HORACE LYMAN[7], son of *Daniel[6]*, b. Nov. 16
1815, graduated at Williams College in 1839. Studied
theology at Auburn and at Andover, attended a course of
medical lectures at Castleton, Vt., where he m. Mary
Dennison, Oct., 1848, dau. of William Dennison. He was
ordained an evangelist and went to Oregon under the
auspices of the American Home Missionary Society about
the time of the California gold excitement. The journey
thither at that time, as may be supposed, was far more of
an undertaking then, than now. Mr. and Mrs. ·Lyman
went by way of Cape Horn, and were nearly or quite half
a year in making the passage from New York to San
Francisco. They remained some months in California, at
San Jose and then went to Portland, Oregon, where he was
largely instrumental in the establishment of a Congregational church there as also at Dallas, where he resided
some years after leaving Portland. He is now professor
of mathematics in Pacific University, at Forest Grove,
Oregon, a university whose primary object is to raise up
men \o supply the need of ministerial labor on the Pacific
Coast. During a year's respite from the labors of his professorship he was in the government employ in the Custom
house at Astoria, the *entrepot* of the upper Pacific Coast.
He is now discharging the duties of the professorship.

Forest Grove, Oregon.

Children, Eighth Generation:

356 1 Sarah Iola, b. Aug., 1850. 358 3 Horace Sumner.
357 2 William Dennison. 359 4 Mary.

338. LAUREN D. LYMAN[7], son of *Daniel[6]*, b. June 20, 1820 ; m. Charlotte R. Stearns, dau. of Dea. Theodore Stearns, of Southampton, Nov. 29, 1844. He settled in Easthampton, on his father's place, where he still resides. In 1870, he was chosen deacon of the First Congregational church.

Easthampton, Mass.

Children, Eighth Generation :

360 1 Addison Dwight, b. Sept. 22, 1850 ; d. June 17, 1853.
361 2 Theodore Stearns, b. Aug. 15, 1852; d. June 17, 1863.
362 3 Mary Charlotte, b. Oct. 4, 1854.
363 4 Sarah Elizabeth, b. Sept. 23, 1856.
364 5 Henry Lauren, b. March 30, 1859.
365 6 Addison Timothy, b. Jan. 3, 1861 ; d. Feb. 2, 1861. Mrs.
        Charlotte R. S. Lyman, d. Feb. 6, 1861 ; Mr. Lyman m. 2d
        Mary E. Stearns, dau. of Dea. Theodore Stearns, of South-
        hampton, April 2, 1861.

339 JAMES H. LYMAN[7], son of *Daniel[6]*, b. Nov. 13, 1822 ; m. Achsah Clapp, dau. of Levi Clapp of Easthampton, April 12, 1852.   *Easthampton, Mass.*

. *Child, Eighth Generation :*

366 1 Austin James, b. Jan. 21, 1855.

172 ELIHU LYMAN[6], son of *Lemuel[5]*, b. July 15, 1784, entered Williams College, and continued a member till the junior year, when he was compelled to leave in couse- quence of weakness of the eyes. He has lived since in New Lebanon, N. Y., and in Williamsburg, Mass., but spent the greater portion of the active part of his life in his native town where he d. Sept. 15, 1867. He m. Susanna Lyman, dau. of Dea. Solomon Lyman, June 28, 1808, who d. July 2, 1853, in her 63d year.   *Easthampton, Mass.*

Children, Seventh Generation :

366*1 Alfred Evander, b. Jan. 14, 1810.
367 2 Lydia Eliza, b. Oct. 1, 1812 ; m. John G. Mallory ; d. Dec.
        27, 1850.
368 3 William Janes, b. Oct. 14, 1814.
369 4 Mary Ann, b. March 31, 1817 ; m. William Leonard of
        Middlefield.
370 5 Susan Cornelia, b. Dec. 25, 1820 ; m. Elisha H. Rice of Wil-
        liamsburg, d. Dec. 8, 1853.
371 6 Nancy Esther, b. Oct. 11, 1821 ; m. Thaddeus K. Wright.
372 7 Martha Willard, b. Oct. 22, 1826 ; d. Nov. 27, 1846.
373 8 Ann Jane, b. April 5, 1828 ; d. July 31, 1846.
374 9 Solomon Curtis, b. Sept. 1, 1837 ; d. March 22, 1857.

366* Alfred E. Lyman[7], son of *Elihu*[6], b. Jan. 14, 1810, m. Octavia Smith, dau. of James Smith of Northampton. She d. June 28, 1843 ; m. 2d, Elizabeth Snow. dau. of Josiah Snow of South Hadley, Dec., 1843.

Northampton, Mass.

Children, Eighth Generation :

375 1 Susan Augusta, m. W. W. Rice, M.D., then of Williamsburg, now of Great Barrington, Mass , one child.

Ch. 9th Gen. : Willie, d. at the age of eight.

376 2 Annie Cornelia, m. John Gibson of New Marlboro, Mass., one child :

Ch. 9th Gen. : Annie Louisa.

377 3 Evander Smith, d. June 24, 1851.

378 4 Helen Octavia, b. Dec., 1844.

379 5 William Arthur, b. Sept., 1846.

368 William J. Lyman[7], son of *Elihu*[6], b. Oct. 14, 1814 ; m. Sarah A. Washburn, of Springfield, Nov. 1, 1838, and settled in his native town where for many years he carried on the business of wagon making but for several years past he has been employed as patent right dealer and has received several patents for inventions of his own.

Children, Eighth Generation .

380 1 Charles Homer, b. March 20, 1844 ; d. Aug. 17, 1844.

381 2 Sarah G., b. Dec. 20, 1846.

382 3 Dwight Monroe, b. May 1, 1850.

383 4 Lucy Arabelle, b. March 20, 1854.

369 Mary Ann Lyman[7], dau. of *Elihu*[6], b. March 31, 1817 ; m. William Leonard, of Middlefield, in 1839. He d. in Oct., 1846. His wife resides at present, in New York city, occupying a position in the deaf and dumb asylum on Washington Heights. *New York City.*

Children, Eighth Generation :

384 1 Ellen E., m. Lawrence B. Valk.

Ch. 9th Gen.: 1 Arthur. 2 Lawrence. 3 Franklin. 4 Rudolph. Besides these two, Eugene and Lewis, d. in infancy.

385 2 Mary J., m. Hugh H. St Aldenhein, of Scotland.

370 Susan Cornelia Lyman[7], dau. of *Elihu*[6], b. Dec. 25, 1820 ; m. Elisha H. Rice, of Williamsburg, who afterward removed to Easthampton. Mrs. Rice d. in Easthampton, Dec. 8, 1853. *Easthampton, Mass.*

Children, Eighth Generation :

386 1 Albert Monroe, d. in infancy.

387 2 Luann Cornelia, Feb. 5, 1845.

388 3 Arthur Monroe, Oct. 4, 1847.
389 4 Lewis Hubbard, Dec. 8, 1853.

371 NANCY LYMAN[7], dau. of *Elihu[6]*, b. Oct. 11, 1821;
m. Thaddeus K. Wright, of Westhampton, Sept. 11, 1838.
He was b. Dec. 19, 1839; d. Dec. 20, 1861.
Northampton, Mass.

Children, Eighth Generation:
390 1 Frances Henry, b. Dec. 19, 1839; d. Feb. 19, 1862, aged
     23, a soldier in the 37th Mass. Regt.
391 2 Harriet Dewey, b. Feb. 4, 1844; m. Henry Nicholas, April
     20, 1865.
392 3 Charles, b. Jan. 7, 1847.
393 4 William King, b. March 5, 1849.
394 5 Mary Jane, b. July 14, 1854.

171 ESTHER LYMAN[6], dau. of *Lemuel[5]*, b. Oct. 19, 1779,
m. Obediah Janes, Nov. 29, 1799; d. Sept. 28, 1813.

Children, Seventh Generation.
395 1 Theodore, b. Aug. 13, 1800; book binder, resides in Boston.
396 2 Obadiah Lyman, b. Dec. 30, 1801, settled in Hadley.
397 3 Francis, b. May 18, 1803.
398 4 Esther, b. Dec. 4, 1804; m. Coleman Clark, of Easthampton,
     now of Ohio.
399 5 Justus Lyman, b. Sept. 1808.
400 6 Alexander Hamilton, b. Jan. 6, 1810; resides in Princeton,
     Ill.
401 7 Oliver Ellsworth, b. Nov. 1, 1811; d. Aug. 15, 1814.
402 8 Lydia, b. Jan. 19, 1813.

Rev. Francis Janes graduated at Williams College, in 1830;
studied theology at Auburn, N. Y., and labored in several different
places in Central New York. He was last at Colchester, where he
d. Jan. 20, 1855.

In speaking of him, the *Independent* said: " In every church
where he has labored, God has blessed his instrumentality with precious revivals, and as the fruits of these revivals, about 300 have
been gathered into the churches under his care. He was noted for
his ardent piety, implicit faith, and a heart full of Christian sympathy and knowledge. He was a man full of faith and the Holy
Spirit. During his whole ministry he lost not a Sabbath or a day
from sickness." He left three sons, all of whom have graduated or
are to graduate at Hamilton College, and the oldest of whom, Rev.
Leigh Richmond Janes, has been a very successful pastor at Shorts-
ville, N. Y., for several years.

399 REV. JUSTUS L. JANES[8], b. Sept., 1808; graduated
at Amherst College in 1835. He studied theology;
was ordained pastor of the First Presbyterian church in

Guilford, N. Y., where he labored sixteen years. He is now pastor of the Presbyterian church in Chester, Ohio, where he has been thirteen years. He has two children.

Chester, O.

Children, Ninth Generation :

403 1 John Ely, graduated at Western Reserve College, and is now principal of Shaw Academy, Columbus, O.

404 2 Amelia Louise, graduated at Lake Erie Female Seminary, at Painesville, O.; married; is now a teacher in Washington, O.

6 CAPT. DAVID LYMAN[5], one of the three sons of *Benjamin[4]*, who moved from Northampton to Easthampton, with his family, was b. Dec. 14, 1737; m. Sarah Wright, April 12. 1763, and settled on the plain west of the village of Easthampton, where S. Mosely Lyman now lives. He d. Jan. 10, 1822. Mrs. Sarah W. Lyman, d. Dec. 23, 1817, aged 78.

Children, Sixth Generation :

405 1 A dau., b. July 27, 1764.

406 2 A son, b. June 5, 1765.

407 3 A son, b. Dec. 2, 1766.

408 4 David, b. March 9, 1768; d. in in infancy.

409 5 Sarah, b. May 6, 1769; m. Eli Brown, in 1790; m. O. Ocran Clapp, 1796.

410 6 Eunice, b. Nov. 4, 1772; m. Job Strong.

411 7 A son, b. April 19, 1775.

412 8 Rachel, b. June 11, 1776; m. Sylvester Knight.

413 9 Fidelia, b. March 22, 1780; m. Solomon Pomeroy.

It appears from records that Sarah was baptized May 14, 1769. Eunice, Nov. 8, 1772. Rachel, June 23, 1776. Fidelia, May 21. By comparison of these two series of dates, an illustration will be seen of the former custom of baptizing children within a few days of birth.

409 SARAH LYMAN[6], dau. of Capt. *David[5]*, b. May 6, 1769, m. Eli Brown. Their intention of m. was published according to law, and a certificate given April 7, 1790; m. April 21.

Children, Seventh Generation :

414 1 David Lyman, b. Oct. 18, 1790.

415 2 Laura, b. Aug. 21, 1792. Eli Brown, d. and Mrs. Sarah L. Brown, m. Ocran Clapp, of Easthampton, July 6, 1796. The children of this m. were.

416 3 Lucy, m. Milton Loyd, of Blandford.

417 4 Lorenzo.

418 5 Algernon, unmarried,— Dahlonega, Wapello Co., Iowa.

419 6 Florilla, d. in Easthampton, unmarried.

420 7 Climena.

691 DAVID LYMAN BROWN[7], son of *Eli*[6] and Sarah Lyman b. Oct. 18, 1790 ; m. Violet Searle, of Westfield, Mass.

Children, Eighth Generation :

421 1 Louisa, m. Charles Athians, of Westfield, one son Charles.
422 2 Elvira, m. John Bagg, of West Springfield.
 Ch. 9th Gen.: 1 Elvira, m. George F. Wright, of Agawam, one son Geòrge. 2 Helen M., m. Joseph A. Wiggs, of Springfield. She m. again, Solomon F. Griggs, of West Springfield. *Ch. 10th Gen.:* (1) Lillie M. (2) John. She m. a third time, Austin Gillett, of Granby, Ct.
427 3 Laura, m. Francis D. Loomis, of New Haven.
 Ch. 9th Gen. : 1 William, m. Anna Merrifield. *Ch. 10th Gen :* (1) Henry. (2) Eldora.
430 4 David Ashmun.
431 5 Frances, m. George Bowe, of Agawam.
 Ch. 9th Gen. : 1 Edward Lyman. 2 David. 3 Adelle.
434 6 Rosalia.
By 2d wife.
435 7 Ellen J., m. Henry Jones, of Indianapolis, Ind.
436 8 Louisa, m. Edward F. Morris, of Munson, Mass.
437 9 Adelle, m. Flavel Sheldon, of Southampton, one child Alice.
438 10 Frostine.
439 11 Edward, d. in infancy.

695 LAURA BROWN[7], dau. of *Eli* and *Sarah Lyman*[6], b. April 21, 1792 ; m. Anson K. Clark, Dec. 20, 1815.
West Springfield Mass.

Children, Eighth Generation :

440 1 Edson, b. May 21, 1817 ; d. June 1, 1825.
441 2 Harriet, b. Aug. 14, 1819 ; m. Harrison Bennett, of Williamsburg, May 20, 1846, Waterbury, Ct.
 Ch. 9th Gen.: 1 Herbert E. 2 Frank W. 3 Clarence, d. in early life.
445 3 Lewis Foster, b. July 3, 1822 ; d. Feb. 21, 1823.
446 4 Mary Ann, b. Feb. 27, 1824 ; m. O. F. Penny, Springfield, Mass.
447 5 Edson, b. April 1, 1826.
448 6 Henry Augustus, b. Nov. 21, 1828 ; d. Aug. 21, 1830.
449 7 Julia W., b. May 25, 1831.
450 8 Horace Lyman, b. Oct. 2, 1837, resides in Easthampton, is bookkeeper for the National Button Co.

696 LUCY CLAPP[7], dau. of *Ocran*[6] and Sarah Lyman Brown[5] Clapp, b. 1798 ; m. Milton Loyd, of Blandford, Feb. 23, 1825, and d. Sept. 28, 1855.

Children, Eighth Generation :

451 1 Homer, b. Dec. 24, 1825 ; m. Sarah Clapp, dau. of Justin
      Clapp, of Westhampton, June 12, 1850.
452 2 Sarah Ann, b. Aug. 23, 1828 ; d. Aug. 13, 1855.

451 HOMER LOYD[8], m. Sarah Clapp, dau. of Justin
Clapp, of Westhampton, June 12, 1850. *Easthampton, Mass.*

Children, Ninth Generation :

454 1 Lucy Ellerslie, b. July 21, 1851.
455 2 Willet Homer, b. Jan. 21, 1853.
456 3 Alice Lucena, b. May 13, 1855.
457 4 George Clapp, b. March 23, 1857.
458 5 Rosella Parker, b. March 12, 1859.
459 6 Emily Lawrence, b. Dec. 12, 1861.
460 7 Herbert Pomeroy, b. Jan. 4, 1864.
461 8 Edward, b. Nov. 8, 1865; d. the same month.
462 9 Lewis Lincoln, b. Oct. 12, 1866.

417 LORENZO CLAPP[7], son of *Ocran*[6] and Sarah Lyman
Brown Clapp, m. Mrs. Sophronia Clapp, widow Lucius
Clapp, of Easthampton, and daughter of Justin Clark, of
Southampton, May 13, 1841. He moved to Deer Ridge,
Lewis Co., Mo., where he d. Dec., 1861. *Deer Ridge, Mo.*

Children, Eighth Generation :

463 1 Lucius Lorenzo, b. Aug. 9, 1842.
464 2 Justin Ocran.
465 3 Martha Sereno, d. at the age of five years.

410 EUNICE LYMAN[6], dau. of Capt. *David*[5], b. Nov. 4,
1772; m. Job Strong, of Easthampton, in 1794.

Children, Seventh Generation :

466 1 Alfred Lyman, now occupies his father's place in Easthamp-
      ton. He has been somewhat widely known as the author
      of a system of penmanship and as a writing teacher. In
      this branch he has for many years been instructor in Wil-
      liston Seminary, Easthampton, Mass.
467 2 Martha, d. in early life.
468 3 Fanny, m. Leonard Ainsworth, of Stockbridge.
469 4 David, settled in Stockbridge, Vt,, afterwards removed to
      Chicago, and then to Joliet, Ill., where he d. He was
      the father of Gen. George C. Strong, who was killed in
      the late war at Fort Wagner.

Much of Gen. Strong's early life was spent in Easthampton, Mass.,
with his uncle to whose care he was consigned by his father on his
death bed. He graduated at Williston Seminary and at West Point,
in 1857, standing third in his class. He was stationed at Selma,
Ala., and then had command of Watervliet Arsenal, in Troy. He
was successively on the staff of Gen. McDowell, Gen. McClellan, and

was chief of staff and acting chief of ordnance to Gen. Butler, in Louisiana. On Gen. Butler's recall from New Orleans he was promoted to brigadier general for his gallantry, courage and efficiency. He had the command of one of the brigades under Gen. Gilmore in the expedition against Charleston, and led the attack on Morris Island. Here he was placed in charge of the troops and given charge of the column which was to assault Fort Wagner. In this attack he received his death wound while leading and inspiriting his men who almost worshiped him for his daring, his kindness of heart and his strict though impartial discipline. He d. July 30, 1863.

412 RACHEL LYMAN[6], dau. of Capt. *David[5]*, b. Jan. 11, 1776; m. Sylvester Knight then of Norwich, as is shown by the record of the declaration of intention of marriage which was made June 10, 1808. They were m. July 13, 1808. He however afterwards removed to Easthampton, and occupied the place of his father-in-law, where he d. Nov. 22, 1858. His wife d. Oct. 31, 1866.

Easthampton, Mass.

Children, Seventh Generation :

470 1 Alice Luce, b. in Norwich, June 23, 1809; m. Dr. Jared Bement of Ashfield, April, 17, 1839. Dr. Bement d. Oct. 11, 1839, and she m. Isaac K. Clapp of Easthampton, Nov. 25, 1842.

471 2 Lathrop Elderkin, b. in Northampton, Jan. 14, 1812; m. Harriet Strong of Northampton, Nov. 22, 1839.
Ch. 8th Gen.: 1 William Sylvester, b. June 8, 1852; d. May 19, 1861. 2 Isaac Lathrop, b. Jan. 1, 1845; d. March 25, 1863. 3 Esbon Pringle, b. July 9, 1848; d. aged 9 months.

475 3 Rachel Mosely, b. in Easthampton, July 25, 1814.

476 4 Horatio Gates, b. March 24, 1817.

477 5 Sarah Wright, b. Nov. 20, 1819; m. Chester Crafts, Sept. 22, 1840; d. Oct. 9, 1841. One child.
Ch. 8th Gen.: 1 Sarah Elizabeth Crafts, b. July 7, 1841; d. Dec. 22, 1852.

476 HON. HORATIO G. KNIGHT[7], son of *Sylvester[6]* and Rachel Lyman Knight, b. March 24, 1817; m. Mary A. Huntoon, of New York, Sept. 28, 1841, and settled in Easthampton, where he now resides, and is one of the leading manufacturers of the town. On the establishment of the button works of Hon. Samuel Williston in Easthampton, Mr. Knight, who had been before clerk and salesman for Mr. Williston, became a partner. Since then, the button works have been carried on by the firm of Williston,

Knight & Co., until the recent organization of the National Button Co., in which the same persons are stockholders. Mr. Knight is also largely interested in the Nashawannuck and Glendale Companies, and next to Mr. Williston has been most prominent in the manufacturing operations of the place.

He has also been very prominent in the public affairs of the town, which he has twice represented in the lower house of the legislature. He also occupied a seat in the Senate during two sessions, and was a member of the Republican National Convention at Chicago, by which Abraham Lincoln was first placed before the people as a candidate for the presidency. He was a member of the Executive Council of the state of Mass., in the administration of Gov. Bullock, to which position he was elected under circumstances very complimentary to himself. He also filled the same office in the first term of Gov. Claflin. In the early part of the war Mr. Knight was very active in procuring volunteers, paying bounties to Easthampton men who enlisted in the 27th Regiment, and subsequently to those who enlisted in the 31st Regiment, amounting in the aggregate to several thousand dollars.

Easthampton, Mass.

Children, Eighth Generation :

479 1 Alice, b. Aug. 20, 1844 ; m. Rev. Henry Hopkins, son of President Hopkins, of Williams College; d. in 1868.
480 2 Horatio Williston, b. Aug. 8, 1846.
481 3 Lucy, b. Feb. 6, 1848.
482 4 Charles H., b Nov. 22, 1849.
483 5 Russell Wright, b. Nov. 27, 1851; d. Aug. 24, 1854.
484 6 Frederick Allen, b. Aug. 6, 1854 ; d. April 15, 1857.
485 7 Mary, b. April 7, 1857.

413 Fidelia Lyman[6], daughter of Capt. *David*[4], b. March 22, 1780; m. Solomon Pomeroy, of Easthampton, Mass.

Child, Seventh Generation ·

486 1 Emeline, m. Alfred L. Strong, of Easthampton.

III. DESCENDANTS OF BENJAMIN[3], THROUGH AARON[4].

5 Dea. Aaron Lyman[4], *Benjamin*[3], *John*[2], *Richard*[1], 1705–1788; b. April 1, 1705, moved to Cold Springs, Belchertown, in 1728, being one of the earliest settlers of that town and long kept a public house there. He was chosen deacon of the church at its first organization. He m.

Eunice Dwight, dau. of Rev. Josiah Dwight, of Woodstock, Conn., Dec. 12, 1733, O. S. She d. March 28, 1760, and he m. widow Joanna Holton, of Northfield. He d. June 12, 1780, according to another record 1788.

Children, Fifth Generation.

1   1 Susanna, b. Nov. 16, 1734; m. Mr. Kent, of Suffield, Conn.
      Ch. 6th Gen.: 1 Susanna. 2 Gamaliel. 3 Henry.
5   2 Josiah, b. March 9, 1736.
6   3 Anna, b. July 28, 1737; m. Capt. Granger of Suffield.
      Ch. 6th Gen.: (1) Fanny, who m. Stephen Barnard
      and d. 1851. (2) Amelia. (3) Nancy unmarried.
10 4 Aaron, b. March 20, 1740; d. Feb. 23, 1758.
11 5 Elihu, b. Dec. 25, 1741; d. Sept. 12, 1823; m. King of Westfield.
12 6 Eunice, b. May 29, 1744; m. Jonathan Arms of Deerfield.
13 7 Mary, b. Nov. 12, 1745; m. Capt. Elisha Hunt.
14 8 Dorothy, b. June 17, 1747; d. Aug. 16, 1789.
15 9 Caleb, b. Aug. 7, 1750.
16 10 Dolly, b. Oct. 4, 1756; d. Sept. 14, 1787.

5 MAJ. JOSIAH LYMAN[5], son of *Aaron*[4], b. March 9, 1736; is said to have been the first white child b. in Belchertown. He was baptized at Northampton, by President Edwards; m. Jan. 9, 1759, Sarah Worthington, of Colchester, Ct., who was b. 1734, d. Feb. 19, 1799, aged 65; m. 2d, Mrs. Stone. He removed to Goshen late in life, and died there Nov. 18, 1822, in the 87th year of his age. He was deacon of the church in Goshen, Mass.   *Goshen, Mass.*

Children, Sixth Generation:

17 1 Aaron, b. Oct. 1, 1760; m. Electa Graves, d. Aug. 14, 1845, in Clermont, N. H.
18 2 Sophia, b. Jan. 1, 1763; m. Amasa Smith, of Belchertown, in 1787.
19 3 Giles, b. May 2, 1765.
20 4 Dea. Jonathan, b. March 20, 1767.
21 5 Augustus, b. May 26, 1769; m. his cousin Eunice, dau. of Jonathan Arms.

17 AARON LYMAN[6], *Josiah*[5] *Aaron*[4], *Benjamin*[3], *John*[2], *Richard*[1], 1760–1845, son of Major *Josiah*, settled in Charlemont, where he was for many years deacon of the church. He was a very noble and earnest Christian man. He lived to an advanced age. At a late period in his life he tried to lay aside the office of deacon, but the church would not accept of his resignation. They said to him, "Your day is not done." "Well," said he, "I always want to have the chores done up Saturday night before the day is done."

At one time he was thought to be near his death, but was restored almost miraculously. He seemed to regret the restoration, and said he did not see why he was spared. Shortly after, a revival occurred in the town, and often the young converts would gather about him to hear him converse about the interests of the soul, and to receive Christian counsel. His neighbors and friends told him they could see why he was spared. He was a man quite given to anecdote and illustration. He m. Electa Graves, Jan. 9, 1788. She was b. Jan. 11, 1769, and d. Aug. 14, 1848.

Children, Seventh Generation.

22 1 Josiah, b. Dec. 12, 1788; m. Zeruiah A. Loop, May 26, 1819, d. March 11, 1848; no children; his wife still living.

23 2 Eunice, b Oct. 21, 1790 ; d. Nov. 25, 1826.

24 3 Sophia, b. Oct. 27, 1792; d. April 16, 1811.

25 4 Almira, b. Sept. 30, 1794; d. May 4, 1828.

26 5 Susanna, b. Sept. 15, 1796; m. Thomas Carter, March 6, 1827, d. Sept. 20, 1869.

Ch. 8th Gen.: Aaron, b. Nov. 14, 1829.

28 6 Emily, b. Oct. 14, 1798; d. April 19, 1822.

29 7 Margaret, b. Nov. 22, 1800; m. Josiah Ballard, Aug. 19, 1827.

Ch. 8th Gen.: 1 Charles Henry, b. Jan. 1, 1832. 2 Frederic Lyman, b. Oct. 1, 1837.

32 8 Abigail, b. Feb. 25, 1803; m. April 3, 1822, Gurdon Swan, of Shenango Co., N. Y.

Ch. 8th Gen.: 1 Electa, b. Dec. 31, 1832. 2 Angeline, b. July 10, 1834. 3 Margareta P., b. no date.

36 9 Electa, b. March 28, 1805; m. Oct. 25, 1831, James M. Claghorn, Erie, N. Y.; still living.

Ch. 8th Gen.: 1 Josiah Lyman, b. Dec. 2, 1832. 2 James Augustus, b. May 13, 1835. 3 Ellen Elmina, b. Sept. 15, 1837.

40 10 Myron, b. May 5, 1807; d. Oct. 5, 1808.

41 11 Frederic Augustus, b. June 25, 1809; d. July 8, 1809.

42 12 Lyndon Graves, b. June 14, 1810.

43 13 Augustus La Barron, b. June 20, 1813; d. March 8, 1815.

42 LYNDON G. LYMAN[7], only surviving son of Dea. *Aaron*[6] of Charlemont, Mass., a dentist in Newark, N. J. He m. Mary W. Chester, July 28, 1844. She was b. May 12, 1815, and d. Oct. 16, 1847. He m. Jane Robb, Jan. 12, 1859. She was b. July 23, 1821. He d. Sept. 4, 1871.

Children, Eighth Generation :

44 1 Emma Castner, b. Dec. 8, 1845.

45 2 Mary Castner, b. Oct. 5, 1847.

46 3 Elizabeth Ballard, b. April 12, 1854.
47 4 Anna Nichols, b. Oct. 17, 1855 ; d. Sept. 20, 1856.
48 5 William Lyndon, b. April 21, 1858.
49 6 Jennie Robb, b. Feb. 26, 1860.
50 7 Julia Simonton, b. Jan. 12, 1866; d. Dec. 26, 1868.

45 Mary Castner Lyman[8], m. Dec. 26, 1866, and has one son Lyman M., b. Aug. 25, 1868.

19 Giles Lyman[6], son of Maj. *Josiah[5]*, of Goshen, was b. May 2, 1765 ; m. Mary Hubbard, dau. of Nehemiah Hubbard, of Middletown, Ct., b. Aug. 20, 1768. They were m. Nov. 11, 1795. Mrs. L., was " a lady of great refinement, intelligence and piety." The family lived in Shelburne, Mass., from 1809 to 1833, afterwards in Fowlersville, a village in the town of York, Livingston Co., N. Y., where Mr. Lyman, d. May 4, 1848. *Fowlersville, N. Y.*

Children, Seventh Generation :

52 1 Mary, b. July 30, 1796 ; d. July 31, 1796.
53 2 Lucy, b, Aug. 1, 1797 ; m. in 1846, to Ebenezer G. Hubbard, of Middletown, Ct. She d. Aug. 31, 1866, leaving no children. Her husband, d. Feb. 19, 1868.
54 3 Maria Augusta, b. Nov. 11, 1798 ; d. Sept. 4, 1801.
55 4 Elihu Hubbard, b. Aug. 19, 1800.
56 5 Giles, b. March 16, 1802.
57 6 Frederick, b. June 30, 1804 ; d. Aug. 28, 1808.
58 7 Henry, b. March 30, 1806 ; d. Aug. 12, 1806.
59 8 Mary, Nov. 17, 1809 ; d. March, 1850.
60 9 Sophia Augusta, b. Dec. 25, 1811.

55 Elihu Hubbard Lyman[7], son of *Giles[5]* and Mary, m. Martha Collins, of Fowlersville, N. Y.

Lyons, Iowa Co., Mich.

Children, Eighth Generation :

61 1 William Collins.   62 2 Frank Hubbard.

56 Giles Lyman[7], son of *Giles[6]* and Mary was b. March 16, 1802, graduated from Amherst College, in 1827, and from Andover Theological Seminary, in 1831, was ordained pastor of the Congregational church in Jaffery, N. H., Jan. 11, 1832, after a successful pastorate of five years was dismissed on account of impaired health, May 10, 1837, and from Dec., 1840 to 1868 labored in connection with the Congregational church in Marlborough, N. H., resigning the charge of this church also on account of feeble health. He was m. to Louisa Whitney, dau. of Phinehas Whitney, of Winchendon, Mass., Dec. 14, 1835. They have no children.

60 SOPHIA AUGUSTA LYMAN[7], dau. of *Giles*[6] and Mary, b. Dec. 25, 1811; m. William Fullerton, M.D., of Chilicothe, O., May 15, 1834.   *Chilicothe, O.*

Children, Eighth Generation :

63 1 Lyman, b. April 1, 1835; graduated at Marietta College, studied law at Cambridge, Mass. Residence, Kansas city, Mo., where he is engaged in the practice of law.
64 2 Humphrey, b. Aug. 29, 1836; d. Dec. 23, 1863.
65 3 William, b. June 19, 1838; d. Aug. 9, 1838.
66 4 Mary Hubbard, b. Sept. 16, 1839; d. Feb. 5, 1840.
67 5 Martha Catharine, b. Dec. 28, 1840; d. May 29, 1842.
68 6 Sophia, b. Dec. 18, 1843; d. March 11, 1868.
69 7 Margaret, b. Nov. 11, 1845.
70 8 William Dixon, b. Nov. 25, 1847, Rose Co., O., where he is engaged in farming.
71 9 Frank, b. Sept. 27, 1850.
72 10 Lucy Hubbard, b. April 14, 1853.

20 DEA. JONATHAN LYMAN[6], son of Maj. *Josiah*[5], b. 1767; m. Electa Bardwell, of Goshen, Mass. He settled in Goshen, where he was chosen deacon of the Congregational church. He removed to Granby, Mass., in advanced life where he died Sept. 27, 1846. He had a second wife Lydia Town, of Granby, who is still living. Dea. Lyman had no children of his own, but adopted one named Charles, who married and lived in Greenfield for a time. He died in middle life leaving no children.   *Granby, Mass.*

21 AUGUSTUS LYMAN[6], son of Maj. *Josiah*, b. May 26, 1769, m. Eunice Arms, dau. of Jonathan Arms of Deerfield, Nov. 6, 1795. She was b. 1776, and d. in Deerfield, Mass. where the family resided April 14, 1859. Mr. Lyman d. Oct. 14, 1829.   *Deerfield, Mass.*

Children, Seventh Generation .

73 1 Harriet, b. Nov. 18, 1796.
74 2 Miriam Arms, b. April 8, 1798.
75 3 Frederick Augustus, b. May 21, 1801.
76 4 Dolly Ann, b. Sept. 6, 1803.
77 5 Sarah Worthington, b. April 8, 1807.
78 6 Amelia, b. July 9, 1811.

74 MIRIAM ARMS LYMAN[7], dau. of *Augustus*[6] and Eunice, commonly called Mary, April 8, 1798; m. Jonathan Winship, of Brighton, Mass., Jan. 20, 1824.

Ch. 8th Gen. : 1 Francis Lyman, b. Jan. 25, 1828. 2 Amelia Miriam, b. Dec. 14, 1830. 3 John Perkins · Cushing, b. May 16, 1826. 4 Joseph Putnam Bradley, b. July 23, 1839.

76 DOLLY ANN LYMAN[7], dau. of *Augustus*[6] and Eunice, b. Sept. 6, 1803; m. Joseph Anderson, of Shelburne, Mass., May, 1830. Mr. Anderson is a graduate of Williams College. He now resides in Shelburne, where he is engaged in farming, being somewhat noted as a breeder of choice cattle.

Children, Eighth Generation:
83 1 Mary.   84 2 Joseph.

77 SARAH WORTHINGTON LYMAN[7], dau. of *Augustus*[6] and Eunice, b. April 8, 1807; m. Francis Winship, of Brighton, Mass., who d. March 9, 1850.

Children, Eighth Generation:
85 1 Franklin, b. April 5, 1835; d. Oct., 1867.
86 2 Herman, b. Nov. 6, 1841.
87 3 George, b. Feb., 1843.

11 MAJOR ELIHU LYMAN[5], *Aaron*[4], *Benjamin*[3], *John*[2], *Richard*[1], 1741–1823, son of *Aaron*, and Eunice Lyman, b. in Belchertown, Mass., Dec. 25, 1741. He lived in Northfield, Mass., and afterwards in Greenfield, in the same state. He m. in 1770, Esther King, of Westfield, Mass., aud 1781, he m., the second time, Sarah Stebbins, of Deerfield, Mass. He d. Sept. 12, 1823, aged 82. He was a captain in the expedition under Benedict Arnold, for the invasion òf Canada. In that toilsome, suffering march through the wilds of Maine, the hardships the troops endured in the forms of hunger, fatigue and cold, were almost beyond expression. There were sailors among them who became so ungovernable that Major Lyman was deputed to take them back to Boston, which he finally succeeded in doing, although many times in the homeward march his life from them was in great peril. But when, on one occasion, there was every indication of mutiny. his decision and courteous manners towards them completely subdued them. He remained in the army sometime after, and did good service in many important posts.
Greenfield, Mass.

Children, Sixth Generation:
88 1 Sarah, b. Sept. 12, 1771, in Northfield, Mass.; m. Ephraim Wells, son of Joel and Abigail Wells, of Greenfield, Mass., in 1816; d. March 30, 1860, no children.
89 2 Elihu, b. at Northfield, Mass., Sept. 25, 1782; d. at Boston, Mass., Feb. 11, 1826, aged 43. He was graduated from Dartmouth Coll., in 1803; read law with Ebenezer Fòot, of Troy, N. Y., and Richard English Newcomb, of

Greenfield, Mass.; began practice in Greenfield in 1807; removed to Greenwich, Mass., in 1810; returned to Greenfield, and was high sheriff of Franklin Co., from 1811 to 1815, when his law office was reopened at Greenwich. He was a state senator, and d. when the legislature was in session, greatly lamented as a gentleman of high standing as well as of fine personal appearance and courtly manners. He m. Mary, dau. of Robert Field, of Greenwich, and relict of Joshua N. Upham, Esq.

Ch. 7th Gen.: 1 Eliza Jones, who d. June 9, 1830. 2 Mary Field. 3 Catharine Dwight. 4 Anne Jean. 5 Elihu, who d. early. 6 Charlotte Augusta. 7 An infant son.

90 3 Joseph Stebbins.

91 4 Henry.   92 5 Theodore Dwight.

93 ANNE JEAN LYMAN[7], dau. of *Elihu* and Mary Field[6], m. Prof. Charles Short, son of Charles and Rebecca Short of Salem, Mass., Oct. 9, 1849.

Children, Eighth Generation :

97 1 Charles Lancaster.   99 3 Edward Lyman.
98 2 Mary.   100 4 Henry Alford.

90 JOSEPH STEBBINS LYMAN[6], b. at Northfield, Mass., Feb. 14, 1785; grad. at Dartmouth, in 1806; d. at Cooperstown, N. Y., March 21, 1821, aged 36, unmarried. He read law and settled in practice at Cooperstown, was deservedly popular, and represented his district in congress, from 1819 to 1821.

91 HENRY LYMAN[6], b. at Northfield, Mass., June 30, 1787; d. March 13, 1811, aged 23, unmarried.

92 THEODORE DWIGHT LYMAN[6], b. in 1790; d. March 18, 1845, aged 55. He m. Rebecca Butler Bull, dau. of Thomas and Ruth Butler Bull, of Hartford, Ct., Dec. 30, 1817; m. the second time, Julia D. Dwight, dau. of Jonathan Dwight, of Belchertown, Mass., Oct. 11, 1827.

Children, Seventh Generation :

105 1 Abby Hall, b. April 5, 1819; d. at Ann Arbor, Michigan, in 1824, d. aged five years.
106 2 Jonathan Dwight, b. Aug. 16, 1828; d. April 7, 1832.
107 3 Abby Eliza, b. Aug. 30, 1830; d. Aug. 29, 1845.
108 4 Emily Dwight, b. Oct. 7, 1834; d, 1854. Both were daughters of rare personal attractions and promise.
109 5 A son, b. Oct. 20, 1836; d. in infancy.

12 EUNICE LYMAN⁵, dau. of *Aaron⁴*, of Belchertown, b. May 29, 1744; m. Jonathan Arms, of Deerfield, and d. May 3, 1832. She was a very superior woman of sterling natural abilities and personal endowments, and yet her opportunities for education extended through one week only at school.

Children, Sixth Generation.

110 1 Eunice, b. 1775; Augustus Lyman.
111 2 Pliny, b. 1778; m. Thankful Dickinson, 1810.
112 3 Dorothy, b. and d. 1779.
113 4 George, b. 1781; d. 1819.
114 5 Dorothy, b. 1783.
115 6 Josiah Lyman, 1788; d. 1828.

13 MARY LYMAN⁵, dau. of *Aaron⁴*, of Belchertown, b. 1745; m. Elisha Hunt of Northfield, d. 1819.

Children, Sixth Generation:

116 1 Samuel.
117 2 Polly.
118 3 Ellsworth.
119 4 Patty.
120 5 Elisha.
121 6 Frederick.
122 7 Jonathan.
123 8 Sarah.

15 CALEB LYMAN⁵, son of *Aaron⁴*, of Belchertown, b., 1750; m. Catharine Swan, of Worcester, Mass., Oct. 25, 1774. She was b., 1753; d. Aug. 22, 1809. He d. Aug. 17, 1822, m. 2d wife April 4, 1716, Tirzah Philena Field, dau. of Abner Field of Northampton, b. April 6, 1781—a hatter by trade, but unable to labor at this business by reason of lameness. He obtained the office of deputy sheriff, which he sustained in Franklin and Hampshire counties more than 30 years, at the same time conducting his business by journeymen and apprentices.

Children, Sixth Generation:

124 1 William Swan, b. Sept. 5, 1775; d. Feb. 26, 1801.
125 2 Charles, b. May 4, 1778; d. unmarried, April 1, 1814, in New London, a portrait painter.
126 3 Josiah Dwight, b. Feb. 27, 1780; m. Whitney —a hatter, d. in 1869.
127 4 Francis Dwight, b. Oct. 6, 1782; d. Dec. 27, 1784.
128 5 Francis, b. Feb. 15, 1786, lived in Alabama, now in Northfield, unmarried.
129 6 Caleb, b. Oct. 14, 1787; d. unmarried Aug. 26, 1823, in South Carolina. Both he and Frances were clerks in mercantile business.
130 7 Daniel, b. May 23, 1790.
131 8 Myra, b. Feb. 23, 1793; m. Alexander.

132 9 Catharine S., b. March 19, 1797.
·133 10 Edwin, b. July 30, 1800, printer, d. in New Orleans, Jan. 29, 1841. Northfield, Mass.

126 JOSIAH DWIGHT LYMAN[6], m. Feb. 1, 1808, Betsey Whiting of Northfield, b. Aug. 12, 1784. Mr. Lyman was appointed about 1810, capt. of a company of state artillery and afterwards was promoted to the rank of colonel.

Northfield, Mass.

Children, Seventh Generation:
135 1 William Swan, b. Feb. 27, 1805.
136 2 Caleb, b. Feb. 11, 1807 ; d. 1854, unmarried — hatter, and lived with his parents till he died.
137 3 Elizabeth, b. May 9, 1809.
138 4 Josiah Dwight, b. July 16, 1811 ; d. Sept. 24, 1857.
139 5 Catharine Frances.
140 6 Augustus, b. Sept. 26, 1818.
141 7 Jabez Whiting.
142 8 Ann Whiting.

135 WILLIAM SWAN LYMAN[7], hatter, m. 1799, Fanny Pomeroy, dau. of Dr. Medad Pomeroy, of Warwick, Mass., b. Jan. 7. 1780; d. Aug. 23, 1813.

Child, Eighth Generation.
143 1 William Swan, b. June 29, 1800, merchant in N. Orleans, d. of yellow fever, 1840.

137 ELIZABETH LYMAN[7], m. Cullen Sawtelle, of Norridgewock, Maine, Aug. 24, 1830, attorney, now in New York city, residence in the country, formerly a representative of his district in Maine, two terms in congress.

Children, Eighth Generation
144 1 Henrietta Lovell, b. May 30, 1832.
145 2 Charles Greene, b. May 10, 1834, a graduate of West Point, and after passing through the late war, has been appointed brigadier general, stationed in N. Y.
146 3 Catharine Lyman, b. May 23, 1842.

139 CATHARINE F. LYMAN[7], m. May 20, 1851, Dr. Cyrus Lee Hunter. Dr. H. is a retired physician, a gentleman of taste and culture, devoted to the studies of natural science and an elder in the Presbyterian church. After a happy union of nearly 14 years, Mrs. Hunter d. after a short illness in the firm hope of a blessed immortality. *Southern States.*

Child, Eighth Generation:
147 1 Cyrus Lee Hunter, b. Sept. 22, 1852.

141 JABEZ WHITING LYMAN[7], b. Feb. 17, 1821, merchant, New York City, m. Mary Ainsworth Parker, of Boston Nov. 17, 1845, and d. Nov. 19, 1862.

Child, Eighth Generation:
148 1 Charles Parker, b. Sept. 1, 1846.

142 ANN WHITING LYMAN[7], b. Oct. 12, 1823; m. Francis Jewett Parker, merchant of Boston, b, March 3, 1825, and m. April 28, 1846. Member of Boston common council 1856; a land commissioner 57, 58 and 59; member of Massachusetts senate 1858. Appointed major Nov., 1861, and assigned to duty in command of 1st Battalion, Mass., Vol. Inft., then in garrison at Fort Warren, Boston Harbor. Appointed lieut. colonel, and assigned to command of same battalion then designated 32d Mass. Infantry, May 23d, 1862, and hastily ordered to Washington, then menaced by Gen. T. J. Jackson, after his success against Maj. Gen. Bank's forces. The 32d Mass., was the first to reach Washington and was encamped in the district until June 30th, when it was ordered in haste to Fort Monroe, and thence to report to Gen. McClellan, whose army Col. Parker joined on the day succeeding the first battle of Malvern, and the regiment remained attached to the army of the Potomac, until the close of the war.

Lt. Col. Parker was appointed colonel July, 1862, and resigned January 1863' having before that time served through the campaign under Gen. Pope in Virginia, the Antietam campaign and battles, battles of Shepardstown and Leetown and the campaign under McClellan and Burnside which terminated in the first battle of Fredericksburg, Dec. 13, 1863. In 1864 Col. Parker was appointed aid de camp on the staff of Maj. General Franklin, but the war closed before Gen. Franklin's wound permitted him to take command in the field.

Children, Eighth Generation:
149 1 Francis Vose, b. March 13, 1847.
150 2 Clara Virginia, b. March 7, 1850.
151 3 Cullen Sawtelle, b. Aug. 1857; d. Feb. 16, 1860.
152 4 Elizabeth Lyman, b. Oct. 11, 1861.

131 MYRA LYMAN[6], dau. of *Caleb*[5], m. Dec. 11, 1816, Major Elisha Alexander — farmer. *Northfield, Mass.*

Children, Seventh Generation:
153 1 Catharine Swan, b. Feb. 26, 1818.
154 2 Francis Lyman, b. May 29, 1821.

155 3 Edward, b. March 30, 1823; d. Sept. 17, 1865, merchant,
New York City.
156 4 Josiah, b. June 6, 1825.
157 5 Wm. Dwight, b. Feb. 11, 1827, farmer on the same farm,
first settled by his grandfather, with a prospect of hand-
ing it down to the next generation unimpaired.
158 6 Emily Cordelia, b. June 18, 1829; d. Sept. 25, 1836.
159 7 Joseph, b. Jan. 28, 1831; d. Dec. 15, 1831.

153 CATHARINE SWAN ALEXANDER[7], m. Nov. 13, 1839,
Dea. Moses Field of Northfield, b. May 11, 1808; d.
March 27, 1868. *Northfield, Mass.*

Children, Eighth Generation

160 1 Lucius, b. Aug. 15, 1840.
161 2 Mira A., b., May 15, 1843; d. Dec. 27, 1845.
162 3 Francis E., b. Feb. 23, 1845.
163 4 Catharine Swan, b. June 15, 1847.
164 5 Christiana C., b. Feb. 12, 1853.
165 6 Josiah Alexander, b. Oct. 21, 1860.

160 LUCIUS FIELD[8], m. Aug. 14, 1862, Sophia Harrington of Weston, Mass., merchant. *Clinton, Mass.*

Child, Ninth Generation :

166 1 Mary Althea, b. May 28, 1866.

154 FRANCIS L. ALEXANDER[7], m. Jan. 1, 1846, Mary
Ann Walker, of St. Charles, Ill.—merchant.
St. Charles, Ill.

156 JOSIAH[7], m. Sept. 13, 1848, Lucy C. Valentine, of
Northboro, Mass.—merchant in Boston. *Clinton, Mass.*

Children, Eighth Generation :

166* 1 Emily, b. in Northfield, April 21, 1850.
167 2 Fanny E., b. in Clinton, May 26, 1852; d. Aug. 19, 1854.
168 3 Edward L., b. Sept. 5, 1854.
169 4 Carrie C., b. June 1, 1857.
170 5 William Valentine, b. Oct. 18, 1859.
171 6 Charles E., b. March 21, 1861.
172 7 Josiah F., b. April 2, 1862.
173 8 Mira L., b. April 18, 1863; d. Sept. 19, 1863.

157 WILLIAM D.[7], m. Feb. 10, 1864, Elizabeth H.
Severance, of Northfield. *Northfield, Mass.*

Children, Eighth Generation :

174 1 Mira E., b. Nov. 22, 1864.
175 2 Lucy Valentine, b. April 9, 1866.
176 3 Nelson Dwight, b. Jan. 13, 1868.

6 HANNAH LYMAN[4], dau. of *Benjamin[3]*, and sister of
Dea. Aaron of Belchertown, m. Nathaniel Dwight of
that place, son of Nathaniel of Northampton. Dea. Aaron
m. Eunice Dwight, sister of Nathaniel. Both were among
the first settlers of the place in 1731; Nathaniel d. 1784'
aged 72; his wife d. in 1792, aged 84; Dea. Aaron d. in 1780,
aged 76.

Children, Fifth Generation:

This record is given as copied from their family Bible illustrative
of the character of the man and the spirit of the times.

1st. Is a record of his marriage. He says: 1735, I appeared before a
small assembly at the house of Joseph Lyman, and there promised
to love, honor and cherish and live with my dear wife as the law of
God and man directs in a marriage covenant, and I pray the God of
love and peace to enable me to keep that covenant, and be found
blameless. Then follows an account of births and deaths in their
family, copied from the original manuscript. 1 Elijah, 1st son, b.
Nov. 30, 1735; d. Jan. 19th, 1736, aged 7 weeks. 2 Elihu, b.
March 31st, 1737. 3 Justus, b. Jan. 13, 1739, and then he says:
Praised be God for his goodness in giving us two living children —
and perfect — and I pray God to grant that they may live in His
sight, and also give His servant and handmaid hearts to bring
them up for Him. 4 Eunice. 5 Jonathan, with no dates of birth.
6 Susanna, b. Oct. 20, 1766. 7 and 8 Elijah and Josiah without
dates. 9 Pliny, Aug. 11, 1753, being the first year after new style
began. Then, he says: "We have now eight living children, which
we desire to give *wholly* to God the giver, and pray for direction to
bring them up for Him, or return them to Him in death, according
to his will.

March 22, 1760, my eldest son, Elihu, departed this life, being
near 23 years of age. There is quite an extensive account of this
young man, and so of the others.

Jonathan died Sept. 7th, 1766, in the 23d year of his age; he
had made great proficiency in learning, was a student in Yale College, had entered upon his fourth and last year.

Josiah died March 19th, 1767, in the 17th year of his age.

Pliny died of consumption, March 15th, 1783.

Capt. Nathaniel Dwight, died of pleurisy, March 30, 1784, aged
72. Dr. David Parsons, of Amherst, preached a sermon at his
funeral from Rev. xiv, 13.

Mrs. Hannah Dwight, wife of Nathaniel Dwight, died Dec. 25,
1793, in the 84th year of her age. Rev. Justus Forward preached
a sermon at her funeral from Rev. xiv, 13. Her record is, that she
lived a godly life, beloved and respected, waiting and longing for
her departure.

IV. DESCENDANTS OF BENJAMIN³, THROUGH WILLIAM⁴

Capt. William Lyman⁴, son of *Benjamin³, John², Richard¹*, b. Dec. 12, 1715; m. Jemima Sheldon, and settled in Northampton, where he died March 13, 1774. On his tombstone in the cemetery at Northampton, is this inscription

> The wise and the just, the pious and the brave,
> Live in their death and flourish in the grave.

Mrs. Lyman b. in Northampton, Nov., 1721; d. Feb. 16, 1785.

1733, a guardian is appointed to William and Daniel Lyman, sons of Lieut. Benjamin Lyman, of Northampton, minors over fourteen. Will of Capt. William Lyman dated March 4, 1774, and proved the following month. His sons were William; Cornelius, Levi and Samuel; daughters, Rachel, Jemima and Submit. His widow Jemima—formerly Jemima Sheldon — b. April, 1785, leaving a will, and making her son William and Joseph Lyman her executors.

Children, Fifth Generation:

1 1 Rachel, b. Nov. 22, m. Rev. Noah Atwater of Westfield.
     Ch. 6th Gen.: 1 William, b. Jan. 7, 1780; grad. Yale, 1807. Two children no record.
2 2 William, b. Dec. 7, 1755; known as Gen. William Lyman.
3 3 Cornelius, b. Jan. 7, 1758; Capt. U. S. A., was in what was called John Allen's army; d. at Presque Isle, now Erie, Pa.; m. Sarah Mason of Boston, one son who d. unm.
4 4 Asahel, b. Feb. 8, 1760; d. in infancy.
5 5 Jemina, b. Feb. 5, 1761; m. Samuel Fowler, had seven children. She d. Feb. 28, 1826.
6 6 Levi, b. Jan. 30, 1763, registrar of deeds in Northampton, Mass., March 7, 1830.
7 7 Capt. Samuel, b. Jan. 12, 1765; m. Mary, only child of Gen. Joseph Warren, of Boston, who lost his life in the battle of Bunker Hill. He settled in Greenfield where he d. April 29, 1802; but was buried in Northampton. He had no children. His widow m. the late Judge Newcomb, of Greenfield, by whom she had one son who is still living.
8 8 Submit, b. Dec. 9, 1767; d. Jan. 9, 1797, unmarried. Killed by the falling of a tree on her way to Northampton. She was much beloved because of the grace with which she was enabled to *submit* to the personal deformity of a hare lip, which appears to have given to her originally her name.

2 GEN. WILLIAM LYMAN⁵, son of *William⁴*, b. Dec. 7, 1775, graduated at Yale College, in 1776, and soon after entered the army of the Revolution and served through the war. He was afterwards elected to congress, and he and Gen. Jackson were the only two men who voted against the resolutions of congress on the retirement of Gen. Washington from the presidency and public life. On Mr. Jefferson's accession to the presidency he was sent abroad as consul to London, where he d. Sept. 2, 1811, aged 54. He m. Jerusha.........who d. at Northampton, June 11, 1803, aged 44 years. He was buried in Gloucester Cathedral, in England.

Children, Sixth Generation :

9 1 William, m. a dau. of Kirke Boott of Lowell, Mass., and lived near Boston, d. without children.

10 2 Jerusha, the oldest dau. and executrix of Gen. William, m. Bishop Kemper of Wisconsin, deceased.

11 3 Martha, m. John Cox, of Philadelphia.
  Ch. 7th Gen.: 1 James S. Cox, Orange, N. J. 2 Mrs. Thomas Biddle, of Philadelphia. 3 Mrs. Henderson, residing in Europe.

12 4 Helen, b. in Northampton, Sept. 1, 1795; m. Samuel Cox, of Philadelphia. One child, the Rev. Samuel Cox, of Newton, Long Island. These four are the only descendants of Gen. Lyman in the third generation.

13 5 Ann, m. Rev. Samuel Sitgreaves, Jr., of Easton, Penn., who d. at Georgetown, Md. Mrs S. d. in Philadelphia, no children.

14 6 Frances, d. in Europe, unmarried.

The daus. of Gen. Lyman, after his decease, established and taught a flourishing school in Philadelphia previous to their marriage.

5 JEMIMA LYMAN⁵, b. Feb. 5, 1761; m. Samuel Fowler.

Children, Sixth Generation :

15 1 Hon. James, resides in Westfield, Mass., which town he represented in the assembly a number of years; was state senator six years, and was one of the governor's council two years. He grad. at Yale College, 1807; studied law, but has followed agricultural pursuits. He m. 1st, Lucy L., dau. of Maj. Thomas James Douglas, Feb. 9, 1820; she was b. Aug. 16, 1791, and d. July 16, 1840; he m. 2d, Charlotte, dau. of Capt. Silas Whitney, of Stockbridge, Oct. 6, 1841; she was b. Sept. 8, 1804.

16 2 Francis, b. June 20, 1791; d. in a fit, Sept. 3, 1798, at Northampton.

17 3 Wm. Henry, b. Nov. 19, 1794; d. Feb. 17, 1820.

18 4 Frances, b. Sept. 19, 1797 ; m. Nov. 10, 1824, Col. Henry W.
Dwight, of Stockbridge. He was member of congress
for many years from Berkshire district. He d. Feb. 21,
1845, leaving two sons.

Ch. 7th Gen. : 1 Henry W., b. Sept. 23, 1825. 2
James F., b. Jan. 30, 1830 ; grad. Williams College,
1849 ; studied law and now practising in New York city.
3 Frances, b. July 14, 1827 ; d. March 28, 1828.

21 5 Mitty Lyman, b. July 11, 1799 ; d. June 30, 1815, at Dorchester, Mass.

22 6 Catharine, b. Jan. 3, 1802 ; d. Aug. 31, 1803.

23 7 Samuel, b. Sept. 18, 1803 ; d. May 31, 1804.

6 LEVI LYMAN⁵, *William⁴*, *Benjamin³*, *John²*, *Richard¹*,
1763 – 1829, m. Sept. 1, 1789, Lucretia Kingsley ; was for
many years cashier of Hampshire Co. Bank, and held many
other offices in town and county. He was chairman of
the Northampton board of selectmen, chairman of the
county commissioners, and registrar of deeds for the county
Hampshire. He held the office of registrar of deeds from
1796 to 1811, and from 1821 to his decease. The duties of
the various offices to which he was elected or appointed
nnder the state and general governments were discharged
with fidelity, and to the acceptance of his fellow citizens —
" Died in Northampton, on sabbath morning, March 7,
1830, Levi Lyman, Esq., aged 67. He was ' a man of
infinite humor, great suavity of manners, and much given
to anecdote and facetious remarks. ' "

Children, Sixth Generation :

24 1 Robert, b. 5th of April, 1790, Lieut. U. S. Army, d. 10th
Oct., 1820.

25 2 William Richard, afterwards William C., 10th March, 1792 ;
d. near New Orleans.

26 3 Charles, d. in Georgia, aged 25.

27 4 Clarissa, d. 10th June, 1794 ; m. 30th Oct., 1821, William
Richards, missionary to the Sandwich Islands, and after
20 years he returned and d. in N. Haven, 1861.

28 5 Lucretia, b. 1st September, 1795 ; d. 31st March, 1807.

29 6 Elizabeth, m. 19th Aug., 1799 ; George A. Clark, of Northampton, d. 1852.

30 7 John, b. 31st July, 1801 ; d. 14th Oct., 1802.

10 HON. JAMES LYMAN⁶, m. 1st, Lucy L., dau. of Maj.
Thomas James Douglas ; m. 2d Charlotte, dau. of Silas
Whitney. Children all by first wife :

Children, Seventh Generation :

31 1 Samuel, b. Nov. 16, 1820; m. May 24, 1848, Sarah Maria
Jones, dau. of Samuel Jones, Esq., of Stockbridge. He
graduated at Yale College, 1839, and settled at Westfield.
Ch. 8th Gen.: 1 James, b. May 8, 1849. 2 Samuel,
b. June 26, 1851. 3 Gilbert, b. May 1, 1854. Frances,
b. Oct. 5, 1856.

34 2 Frances, b. July 23, 1822 ; d. Oct. 20, 1833. She was a
very interesting and promising child, and a memoir of
her was published at the time of her death.

35 3 James, b. July 16, 1824 ; d. Aug. 11, 1825.

36 4 James, b. Feb. 5, 1826; d. Aug. 5, 1827.

37 5 James, b. March 31, 1828 ; d. at Cambridge, Sept. 19, 1847,
a member of the senior class of Harvard College.

38 6 Lucy, b. Feb. 18, 1830 ; m. Edward B. Gillett, Esq., Nov. 1,
1848.
Ch. 8th Gen.: 1 Edward B., b. Feb. 6, 1850 ; d. Nov.
15, 1850. 2 Frederic Huntington, b. Oct. 16, 1851.
3 Edward Bates, b. July 24, 1853. 4 Lucy Douglas, b.
Nov. 20, 1856.

27 CLARISSA LYMAN, m. Rev. William Richards.

Children, Seventh Generation :

42 1 William Lyman, b. 1823 ; d. 1851.

43 2 Charles Stewart, b. 1825 ; d. 1838.

44 3 James Austin, b. 1827 ; d. 1858.

45 4 Harriet K., b. 1829 ; no other record given.

46 5 Levi Lyman, b. 1830 ; no other record given.

47 6 Elizabeth Lyman, b. 1832; d. 1855.

48 7 Helen Clarissa, b. 1834 ; d. 1860.

49 8 Julia Maria, b. 1836.

V. DESCENDANTS OF BENJAMIN³, THROUGH DANIEL⁴.

10 DANIEL LYMAN⁴, son of *Benjamin³*, graduated at Yale
College, 1745, was steward of the college from 1747 to 1752;
m. 1748, Sarah Whitney, of New Haven, issue, two daughters, the first d. when about one month old, the other d.
with its mother, Aug. 1, 1751. June, 1752, m. 2d wife,
Sarah Miles, eldest dau. of Capt. Samuel Miles, of New
Haven. M. 3d wife Eleanor Fairchild Benedict, in 1768,
who d. March 23, 1825, aged 95. He was chosen deacon
of the 1st church 1754, resigned 1758; in April of the same
year chosen deacon of the White Haven church ; by union
with the Fair Haven church in 1796, became the North
church in N. H. In this office he remained until his death

54

Oct. 16, 1788.   He was a lawyer, a magistrate, representative and member of the city council, greatly esteemed for many excellences of character.   His tombstone stands in the Sanford lot in the old cemetery, in N. H.

Children, Fifth Generation :

1 1 Daniel, b. July 13, 1753.
2 2 Roswell, b. July 9, 1755.
3 3 Sarah, b. Dec. 11, 1757 ; m. Peter Colt ; d. Aug. 22 or 25, 1844.
4 4 Elihu, b. Aug. 24, 1760 ; m. Dec. 26, 1789, Polly Forbes, dau. of Capt. Elijah Forbes, of New Haven.
      Ch. 6th Gen.: 1. Mary, b. Oct. 22, 1790.   2 James Rice, b. March 14, 1794.

5 MARY LYMAN⁶, b. Oct. 22, 1790 ; m. Jan. 29, 1812, Henry Sanford, of New Haven, one of the wealthiest and most respectable citizens of that city, for many years president of the New Haven Bank.   She m. 2d, James Rice, b. March 14, 1794.   Lost at sea in the U. S. Sloop Wasp in the year 1814, was a midshipman with Farragut on the Essex in her engagement with British frigate, Phebe and sloop of war, Cherub, 1813–14.

7 1 James, b. Dec. 17, 1812 ; m. Sept. 8, 1859, Lucy Sistaire.
8 2 William E., b. Nov. 9, 1816, in N. H. ; m. Dec. 11, 1837, Margaret L. Orange.
9 3 Mary, b. Feb. 23, 1817 ; m. John Orton.
10 4 Catharine S., b. Nov. 11, 1818 ; m. Sept. 12, 1840, George Bliss, firm of Morton, Bliss, & Co., N. Y.
11 5 Alfred, b. Oct. 10, 1820, lost at sea in the brig Belvidere, 1836.
12 6 Henry, b. Sept. 20, 1824 ; d. Oct. 21, 1846.
13 7 Charles F., b. March 22, 1827 ; m. Aug. 24, 1853.
14 8 Emily, b. April 23, 1830 ; m. Jan. 6, 1858, James F. Armstrong, commander in U. S. Navy.

8 WILLIAM E. LYMAN⁷, m. Dec. 11, 1818, Margaret L. Orange.

Children, Eighth Generation :

16 1 Catharine G.
17 2 George B , Lieut. Col., by brevet, distinguished as the only field officer who has conducted a successful Indian campaign.
18 3 Charlotte T., m. Morris W. Seymour, Conn.
19 4 James H.
20 5 Emily A.   23   8 Margaret L.
21 6 Helen McG.   24   9 Susan C.
22 7 Frederic C.   25 10 William C.

77 CATHARINE LYMAN[7], m. June 30, 1863, Charles H. Woodruff, of N. Y.

Children, Ninth Generation :
26 1 An infant, d. at the day of its birth.
27 2 Lewis B.   28 3 Frederic Sanford.

11 ELIHU LYMAN[4], son of *Benjamin*[3], graduated at Yale College, 1745, classmate with his brother Daniel, taught school in Oyster Bay, L. I., in 1747, studied law, partner with his brother Daniel in his law office in New Haven, until the old French war, in the battle of Lake George, Sept., 1755, said to have been commissary of Conn. troops at the time of his death, in 1758 ; left neither wife nor child, probably was never married.

VII. DESCENDANTS OF BENJAMIN[3], THROUGH MEDAD[4].

12 MEDAD LYMAN[4], ninth son of *Benjamin*[3]; resided in New Haven, and kept a public house or tavern, marriage unknown.

Children, Fifth Generation :
1 1 Mary, d. about 1775, unmarried.
2 2 Esther, d. unmarried, about the same time as her sister Mary.
3 3 Martha, b. 175 7; m. Joseph Whiting, of New Haven, who d. Feb. 3, 1794, aged 34. She d. Feb. 4, 1829, aged 72.

3 MARTHA LYMAN[5], m. Joseph Whiting.   *New Haven.*

Children, Sixth Generation :
4 1 John, died in infancy.
5 2 Grace Caroline, b. 1785 ; m. Jan. 6 or 10, 1806, Jared Bradley ; d. 1824.
     Ch. 7th Gen.: 1 Jared, d. young. 2 Harriet, m. George Robinson, Hartford. 3 Caroline, m. Nathan Smith, N. Y. 4 Abraham. 5 Martha, m. J. C. H.
6 3 Arabella, b. April 17, 1789; d. in Penn., Feb., 1867 ; m. Wm. Mix, New Haven about 1819.
     Ch. 7th Gen.: 1 Caroline, d. single. 2 Harriet, m. Wm. Thompson, of Philadelphia, brother of Rev. J. P. Thompson, D.D.,
11 4 Harriet, d. 1805, aged 16.
12 5 Martha, b. Jan. 25, 1792, still living in N. H., m. 1815, Henry C. Flagg, had several children, many of whose descendants are still living.
13 6 George J., b. Oct. 22, 1793, still living in N. H., m. Mary A. Barnes, Dec. 10, 1817 ; son Wm. Joseph—Ansonia Conn.

LYMAN FAMILIES.

LINEAGE NOT ASCERTAINED.

Levi Lyman.

This family first comes into notice in Litchfield Co., Conn., and seem to be related to the Lymans in New Hartford; lived at one time in Bridgeport; Levi the father apparently of this Levi above mentioned, " came into Dutchess Co., N. Y., about 1765, from New Milford, Conn." He was named after his father. He had a numerous family.

Levi, one of these children, left home when a youth, after the death of his father, and became the architect of his own fortune. He acquired a good education; first a farmer, then overseer of a woolen factory; he d. Feb. 22, 1845; and Sarah Cornwall, his wife, d. Aug. 20, 1841, both devoutly religious people. *Stanfordville, Dutchess Co., N. Y.*

1 AMY LYMAN, a woman of superior character, m. Samuel Scott, a master carpenter, removed to Akron, Ohio, to Du Quoin, Ill., then to St. Joseph, Mo., and d. March 6, 1854. Their children were:

1 Drusilla, b. in Stanfordville; m. 1843, John Sheewood, Ohio.
2 Lyman S., b. in Winsted, Conn., went to California, and in the war of the rebellion was Capt. of Co. D, California Volunteers.
3 William Wallace, in Perryville, Mo., 1851, unmarried.
4 George M., b. in Ohio, his last address was Magnolia, Iowa.
5 Julia, m. and settled in Nebraska.

4 Wagar W., the 4th child of Levi, b. in Stanfordville, June 12, 1812; m. Dec. 11, 1832, Ada Shattuck, of Winsted, Conn.; both faithful, consistent members of the Methodist church. *Du Quoin, Perry Co., Ill.*
 Children :
1 Adah Elizabeth, b. in New Hartford, Conn., May 11, 1834; m. Feb. 22, 1852, Isaac James Hosteller, of Penn., and when in St. Louis on business, in 1855, mysteriously disappeared; she m. 2d, Charles Biggar Merchant, R. R. agent.
 Children :
 1 Alice, b. in Chester, Ill., June 14, 1853.
 2 Wagar S., b. March 6, 1855; adopted by his grandfather.
 3 Charles Hanford, b. Feb. 11, 1861.
 5 Willard Stuart, b. Sept. 12, 1866.

2. Jane Ann, 2d child of Wagar, b. in New Hartford, Feb. 6, 1836;
   m. May 7, 1850, Albert S. Palmer, adopted in infancy after
   the death of his mother by his grandmother in Poughkeepsie,
   N. Y., and at the age of 18, entered into the U. S. naval service
   as engineer. His subsequent course is given as illustrative of
   the eventful and adventurous career of many a young American.

   The greater part of the first year was spent on board the
United States steamer Fulton under command of Com. M. C.
Perry, afterwards famous as commander of the United States
expedition to Japan.

   Was transferred from the Fulton to the steamer Missouri.
This vessel, which had been singularly unfortunate from the
beginning, was sent on her first cruise in 1843, with Caleb
Cushing, United States minister to China, on board, and was
bound for Alexandria in Egypt, but burnt at Gibraltar on her
way out, twenty-four hours after anchoring at the latter place.
Nothing was saved from the vessel.

   He returned to the United States on a sailing merchantman.
Was afterwards sent to the S. Union then in the Gulf of Mexico.
On his way home was in a gale nineteen days off Cape Hatteras;
the vessel was nearly disabled and came near being lost.

   After getting her back to the Washington Navy Yard, he
was put in charge of her, which office he retained for eight
or ten months, when he was ordered to the Water Witch, and
soon afterwards was sent on the S. Princeton to the Gulf of
Mexico at Vicksburg during the Mexican war and remained
nearly a year, in or near the harbor of Vera Cruz, and until
the taking of the Castle of San Juan d'Ulloa by the United
States forces, when the Princeton was ordered to Philadelphia
with dispatches.

   He was soon afterwards transferred to the steamer Michigan
on the lakes, where he remained nearly a year, when he went
to Chester, Ill., on furlough, and soon afterwards resigned his
commission in the navy, remaining in Chester, until the year
1867, when he removed to Du Quoin where he still resides.

   He was in Chester, first dry-goods merchant, then Capt. and
part owner of a steam ferry boat on the Mississippi river, and last,
furniture merchant, which business he still conducts.

   He has always been upright and honorable in all his business and social relations, a good husband, and a kind father;
respected by all who knew him.

   Children.

1 Albert Wagar Lyman, b. in Chester, June 1, 1854, has been
   a very dutiful son, and is industriously working out his
   own future. Is a watch maker.

2 Julian Somers, b. in Chester Dec., 20, 1862.

2 Henry Ernest, b. in Chester, May 27, 1865.

4 Richmond Shattuck, b. in Du Quoin, Feb. 14, 1868.

5 Don Churchill, b. in Du Quoin, Aug. 9, 1870.

Moses Lyman.

One Moses Lyman of Connecticut, by supposition was in service in the Revolutionary war, an officer according to tradition; had three daughters: 1 Lucy, 2 Nicy, 3 Phebe.

1 Lucy, who m. Daniel Wightman; is about seventy years of age, residing in Cortland Co. N. Y.

2 Nicy Lyman, m. Barnet Wood, in Clinton, Oneida Co., N. Y. She d. many years since without issue.

3 Phebe Lyman, m. a Benjamin, and lived at one time in Herkimer Co., N. Y., a very superior woman of engaging manners and character, and a devout Christian. She had a son, Mason Wood Benjamin, b. May 3, 1837, in Norway, Herkimer Co., N. Y., now a lawyer, in Little Rock, Ark., where he m. Sept. 29, 1869, Sue E. Reddell, b. Sept. 19, 1842, in Irvin, Estell Co., Kentucky. Has been a member of the state legislature, and solicitor general for the state; served in the rebel army in the late war, first as a private and then on staff duty as assistant adjutant general. His mother died when he was about eight years old. He has lost his lineal connection with the Lyman family through his mother Phebe and grandfather Moses Lyman. Information is earnestly solicited.

Enoch William Lyman.

Enoch William Lyman, was b. in Buffalo, N. Y., Sept. 3, 1798. His father was a ship carpenter and was killed by accident when his son was 4 years old. The name and parentage of the father are unknown, The son was received into the family of Mr. Sewell, of Poughkeepsie, N. Y., with whom he lived until he was 18 years old. He appears then to have lived in Eastern Mass., and R. I., and m. Sophia A. Norris, b. in Providence, R. I., Aug. 26,

1802, who d. in Middleboro, Mass., May 13, 1858. He d. at the same place Feb. 23, 1867, a R. R. contractor. Their children were :

1. William, b. Aug. 24, 1827 ; d. April 8, 1831.
2. Sarah Elizabeth, b. June 10, 1831 ; m. May 1, 1853, William H. Derby, of Watertown, d. May 22, 1856, at Middleboro. He d. at N. Y. Aug. 5, 1856.
3. Maria Louisa, b. Aug. 24, 1835 ; m. Nov. 5, 1855, at Marion, Mass., J. G. Campbell, carpenter. Brighton, Mass.
4. William Henry, b. Dec. 8, 1836, enlisted in the 16th Mass. Regiment, July 21, 1861, discharged July 6, 1865 ; m. Aug. 9, 1870, Dorcas Harvey. Brighton, Mass.
5. Edward, b. Nov. 9, 1840, enlisted with his brother in the 16th Mass. Regiment, July 21, 1861, d. in service, in Acquia Creek Hospital, Virginia, June 6, 1863, buried at Newton, Mass.

Elijah Lyman.

From the record of Coventry Conn. " ELIJAH LYMAN and Patty Chamberlain, m. Nov. 20, 1766. Elijah Lyman, Jr., son of Elijah and Patty his wife b. Nov. 14, 1767." Elijah Lyman resides in Pomfret, Vt. Their children were :

1. Asenath, b. Dec., 1796 ; m. Moses Rankin, of Morristown, Vt.
2. Sylvanus, b. June 10, 1799; m. Minerva Hawkins; he has one son Eugene O., b. in 1845, lives in Pomfret, Vt., and is postmaster.
3. Cynthia, b. July 4, 1801, in Wheelock, N. H. unmarried.
4. Laura, b. July 12, 1803, in Barnston, Canada, unmarried, resides in Stow, Vermont, is a tailoress.
5. Erastus, b. Sept. 12, 1807, in Barnston, Canada, m. Dolly Corey, and has no children.
6. Harriet, b. July 31, 1810; m. Enos W. Cady, Iowa ; has 6 children.
7. Oren, b. Aug. 28, 1813, in Pomfret, Vt. ; m. Margaret Crellar. Morristown, Vt., no children.
8. George, b. Aug. 26, 1817 ; m. Mary Talbot; he has 6 daughters, and resides in Cambridge, Vt., a farmer.

Luke Lyman.

The following from GEN. LUKE LYMAN, was not received in time to be inserted in its proper place, p. 299, No. 817 :

"My regiment, the 27th Mass., was a part of the 'Burnside Expedition' which went to North Carolina. It took an active part in the capture of Roanoke island, and Newbern, N. C., and afterwards in the battles of Kingston, Whitehall, Goldsboro and Gum Swamp, all in North Carolina (two battles at the latter place), and was one of only two regiments which were besieged and surrounded at Washington, N. C., for 18 days, without any communication with our friends outside. At all these above named places, I was present and acting as Lieut Col., or in the command of the regiment, the Col. being absent."

APPENDIX.

By particular request the opening and closing addresses of the Hon.
Lyman Tremain, president at the late reunion of the Lymans, with
that on the characteristics of the family is subjoined.

OPENING ADDRESS.

Fellow cousins, and other relations of the Lyman Family:

I beg you to accept my thanks for the honor you have conferred
upon me, by selecting me to act as your presiding officer, upon this
interesting occasion. The compliment is the more appreciated,
because there are many others present, more deserving of this distinction, who bear the Lyman surname, while my nearest ancestral
relation, with that name, was my paternal grandmother who was a
full blooded Lyman, my own double Christian name, David Lyman,
having been bestowed on me by my parents, in honor of my father's
uncle, who resided in Salisbury, Connecticut, and was the son of
Simeon Lyman.

Washington Irving gives expression to the following sentiment,
in one of his beautiful essays for the *Sketch Book*, wherein he de-
scribes Westminster Abbey : " There was a noble way, in former
times, of saying things simply, and yet saying them proudly ; and
I do not know an epitaph that breathes a loftier consciousness of
family worth and honorable lineage than one which affirms, of a
noble house, that ' all the brothers were brave, and all the sisters
virtuous.' " If this broad and comprehensive eulogium, dictated as
we may reasonably infer, by a surviving member of the family of the
deceased, escaped criticism from an observer so acute, and a gentleman so cultivated and correct in his tastes, so delicate in his
sense of propriety, and so elevated and honorable in his views, as
the world renowned American author, Washington Irving, surely,
we have no occasion to withhold the expression of our honest sentiments, concerning the Lyman family, by any morbid apprehensions
that we shall seem to be unduly influenced by pride, vanity, or
egotism.

While it may be freely conceded, that there is no personal merit,
whatever, in the accident of our being born members of a family,
which has ever maintained an honorable position in the country, the
fact, nevertheless, is one which may, naturally, and properly, excite
in our breasts, emotions of lively exultation, and profound gratitude.

55

Nor is the consciousness of such a relationship calculated, in any degree, as we think, to produce feelings of satisfaction, on our part, with the reputation which others have achieved, and thus to relieve us from the duty of maintaining and increasing the good name of the family. On the contrary, its natural tendency would be to impress upon every sound and well-balanced mind, the necessity of upholding the family honor, and to stimulate its members, to prove, by their life and conduct, that they are not degenerate or unworthy descendants of such ancestors.

Love of family, and a feeling of pride in the distinction which has been acquired by those who are related to us, and in whose veins flows the blood of our common ancestor, are sentiments, which naturally result from that family relation, that was ordained by the Almighty. They are creditable to our common humanity, and are well calculated to exert a salutary influence, in moulding our principles of action, and in controlling our destinies. They are virtues which belong to the same family, with love of country.

As patriotism is one of the most ennobling passions which can influence the action of a citizen, so the emotions of which I speak, when properly guided and directed, lead to the performance of the noblest aims, and highest duties. Napoleon Bonaparte inspired his troops, in Egypt, with intense enthusiasm, by the famous apothegm : " Forty ages look down upon you, from the height of yonder pyramids." He was accustomed to excite his soldiers to the performance of extraordinary feats of bravery and heroism, by appeals to the former achievements which they. or the army to which they belonged, had accomplished ; such as, " You belong to the Army of Italy," or, on beholding the cloudless sun, in the morning of the battle of Moscow, he exclaims " It is the sun of Austerlitz."

To me, however, it would seem as if no influences or appeals could be more powerful for good, than those unseen, and silent, but resistless forces that flow from family traditions, and from virtue possessed, and noble deeds performed, by one's own ancestors, for many generations. Let me give you, for example, a case, which, I trow, is not altogether suppositious, so far, at least, as it assumes to give the past record of the family.

Suppose that the Lyman family had been ever known and honored as a family loyal to its country, under all circumstances ; that during the war of the Revolution, it was steadfast in its devotion to the cause of the colonies ; that in all subsequent contests, and trials, its voice and influence had been uniformly exerted in the same direction ; that during the late great conflict, it had freely poured forth its means, and the blood and lives of its members had been freely offered, for the preservation of our nation, and our free institutions.

Suppose, also, that in the present or future history of our country, other troubles and wars should arise and a member of this same family should be surrounded by influences and circumstances hostile to his country ; that he should even feel and acknowledge the errors of administration, and then suppose that he should be insidiously approached by the foes of his country, and invited to join in some movements looking to the overthrow of his government: I think, in such an hour, I can see him rising, in the dignity of his manhood casting the tempter behind him, and exclaiming indignantly: " I belong to the family of Lymans: a family which has never, yet. given birth to a traitor to his country; I know well the consequence of the position I am about to take. It may lead to the rupture of my life-long associations, social and political; it may result in the sacrifice of my property, and the loss of valued friendships, aye, it may even lead to my imprisonment and death, but I can not, and I will not, be the first to bring the foul reproach of treason upon the honored name of my family. Before one disloyal sentiment can be uttered, or one treasonal act be performed by me, may my right arm wither and perish, and my tongue cleave, forever, to the roof of my mouth.

Influences similar to those which we assume, as the result of family patriotism, naturally flow from all other virtues. If the women of the family have hitherto sustained, by their influence and example, their husbands, brothers, fathers, and sons, in their patriotic efforts; if, in other days, they were known as women of piety, attending faithfully to the ways of their household, and performing acts of charity and benevolence, while creating no sensation, by eccentricities of dress or demeanor, on the platform, or in the public streets, we may expect that their descendants of the same sex, under all changes of name and circumstances, will prove, that they have profited by the examples and teachings of their patriotic and Christian mothers.

We accept, with joy, the accomplished facts in our family history. We acknowledge, gratefully, the historical truths, that among the members of that family who have been gathered to their fathers, and others who still survive, are many honored names of those who have acquired enviable distinction in the council chamber, and upon the field of battle; who have become eminent in the learned professions, as divines, lawyers, and physicians; who have risen about the common level of humanity, in the pursuit of literature and science, agriculture, and the mechanic arts.

We feel that the renown and honors, thus acquired, are the common inheritance of all who belong to the family. We take pride in acknowledging these achievements, and we hope and trust that the present and future members of the family, taking up the Lyman standard, will proudly carry it forward to more decisive and brilliant successes, in the future battle of life.

In monarchical governments, the subject who has become preeminent by reason of heroic actions, rare merits, or long service, is sometimes raised to distinction by a patent of nobility, conferred upon him by the king, who is deemed the fountain of all honors and distinction. As these patents descend to the *heirs* of the first taken, according to the terms therein expressed, it soon comes to pass, that they cease to be evidence of merit in their present owner, and prove only, that his ancestor was made a baron, a viscount, an earl, a marquis, or a duke.

Such aristocratic distinctions were justly regarded by the framers of our government, as hostile to the spirit of equality and personal dignity, which lies at the foundation of free republican institutions. In endeavoring, therefore, to perpetuate the memory of those who have deserved favorable recognition for their service to the state, we are acting in strict conformity with the spirit of our national constitution, which by a double prohibition, denies to the United States, and to the state, the power to grant any titles of nobility. We believe that the true and genuine nobleman, is he, who, by noble deeds, and virtuous conduct, has been accorded a place among the real nobles of the land, by the voice of the American people.

We have come together, to-day, from widely separated localities, to revisit the New England homes of the Lyman family. We would make, and renew our acquaintance, with those in whose veins flows the blood of the Lymans. We would cultivate, and strengthen, the bonds of our relationship; we desire to honor and cherish the memory of our ancestors. We have gathered here, in obedience to that law of natural affection, which prompted the ancients to revere the burial places of their dead, before they had learned to perpetuate their virtues, in poetry or by the sculptured monument.

Two hundred and forty years have elapsed, since Richard Lyman, the common ancestor of all the Lymans in this country, emigrated from the parish of High Ongar, near London, England, to America. He sailed from Bristol, in the ship Lion, in company with the wife and oldest son of John Winthrop, the governor of Massachusetts, and sixty other passengers, and on the 4th of November, 1631, they landed at Boston. Their safe arrival was announced by the firing of cannon, and on the 11th of November, a public thanksgiving was held in Boston, in honor of the event.

Four years later, he left Charlestown, Massachusetts, with Sarah his wife and his children, accompanied by a colony of about sixty persons, and driving with them one hundred and sixty head of cattle, for the purpose of establishing settlements in Connecticut. Their journey lay through a trackless wilderness, and was attended with great perils, difficulties, and trials, during which, they subsisted mainly, upon the milk of their cows, and after fourteen days travel, they had made the distance of about one hundred miles. He was one of the first settlers, and original proprietors of Hartford. It is supposed that he, and his wife, became members of the first church, in Hartford, of which the renowned Rev. Thomas Hooker was pastor. He died in August, 1640, and his name was inscribed upon a stone column, in the rear of the centre church, in Hartford.

The sons of Richard Lyman were among the first settlers of Northampton, and from this central point, his descendants have gone forth to every part of our country. After this long interval, we, who are present here to-day have assembled on Mount Tom, in

Northampton, upon the soil of the noble old commonwealth of Massachusetts, the cradle of American liberty, to honor the name and memory of Richard Lyman, and to kindle anew, that love of pure religion, and civil liberty, which impelled him to leave his native land, and to seek a home amid the forests of New England.

How mighty and marvellous are the physical, moral, and political changes that have been wrought in the condition of our country, since he first entered the valley of the Connecticut! These can only be briefly sketched, on this occasion. Eleven years before he landed at Boston, the Pilgrims had planted their footsteps upon the rock at Plymouth, and laid. broad and deep, the foundations of free religious worship, and republican liberty. Two years before, King Charles the first had granted the charter incorporating "The Governor and Company of the Massachusetts Bay, in New England." One year before, John Winthrop had been chosen governor of Massachusetts, and had emigrated to the colony, leaving his wife in England, to follow him when her health would allow.

When Richard Lyman immigrated to Connecticut, the surrounding country was thickly covered with the aboriginal inhabitants; the Pequods alone numbering seven hundred warriors. They had evinced a hostile spirit, and several years before, had murdered the crew of a small vessel, in the Connecticut river.

Bancroft, in his *History of the United States*, thus speaks of the emigration by the party to which Lyman was attached: "Never before had the forests of America witnessed such a scene. But the journey was begun too late in the season: the winter was so unusually early, and severe, that provisions could not arrive by way of the river; imperfect shelter had been provided, cattle perished in great numbers; and the men suffered such privations that many of them, in the depth of winter, abandoned their newly chosen homes, and waded through the snows to the seaboard.

"Yet, in the opening of the next year, a government was organized and civil order established; and the budding of the trees and the springing of the grass were signals for a greater emigration to the Connecticut."

From such inauspicious beginnings, must we date the establishment of the Lyman family in America. God smiled upon the enterprise, and who shall set limits to its wonderful results?

These feeble colonists have become a mighty nation. Where stood those primeval forests, now stand populous cities, flourishing towns and villages, and smiling farms and farmhouses, while the journey that then required fourteen days for its accomplishment is now made by the iron horse, several times, every day.

The descendants of that brave old immigrant may be numbered by thousands.* On the printed circular announcing this meeting,

---

*About 7,300 of these descendants are now recorded in this Genealogy. Before this work is finished, we hope to give the number living at the present time.

I find the names of a committee, composed of Lymans, residing in England, in Canada, and in twenty-three states and territories of the Union. Who can estimate the vast amount and extent of influence for good in favor of morality, Christianity, the church, and civil and religious liberty, which, during all these two hundred and forty years, have been sent forth from the descendants of Richard Lyman, to bless the country?

We may learn from this brief retrospective review, that, with the blessing of Almighty God resting upon it, the smallest rivulet may become the mighty river. We perceive also, what means and influences may be set in motion, by one earnest, devoted, faithful man.

With hearts overflowing with gratitude, let us improve the lessons of this hour. Deeply impressed with a sense of our individual obligations and responsibilities, let us carry away with us, from Mount Tom, a fixed resolution to bring no discredit, by any act of ours, upon the good name of the Lymans, and, with God's help, to do what we can, to promote the welfare of our beloved country, and the happiness of mankind.

Address on the Characteristics of the Lymans, by Rev. Lyman Coleman, D.D.

The love of kindred and country is common to man of whatever character, condition, or climate; whether savage or civilized, in the frozen regions of the north, or on the parched desert, he clings with fond affection to his native land and kindred tribe. Before our ancestral home in this beautiful valley was enlightened by learning, or blessed with religion, it was moistened by the tears of the savage, as he wandered from the graves of his fathers, and the forests and friends of his youth.

> Breathes there the man with soul so dead,
> Who *never* to himself hath said
> This is my own, my native land!
> Whose heart hath ne'er within him burned,
> As home his footsteps he hath turned,
> From wandering on a foreign strand?
>   *   *   *   *   *   *
> Land of my sires! what mortal hand
> Can *e'er* untie the filial band,
> That knits me to thy rugged strand.

With filial reference and affection we come back to the home of our fathers. With patriotic pride we come to this good land which they loved so well. In obedience to the noblest instincts of our nature we gladly come to this reunion, this greeting of surviving friends. We come to talk of our noble ancestry, of their stern trials and their toils in preparing the goodly heritage which they have transmitted to us. We come to speak of their piety, their patriotism, and deeds of daring in defense of their homes, and the freedom of their country. With heart and mind crowded with reflections on the present and memories of the past, we engage in these duties, conversing now, with the living, and now, communing with the dead.

Many of us, as we turn away from this place, will visit the scenes of our childhood, to hear and to tell the story of our childish companions. But the visages of these, if they yet survive, we shall find so marred that in their frosty brow, furrowed cheek, and trembling limbs we shall scarce discern the lingering lineaments of their youth. Our most familiar friends will be our native hills, their woods and streams, and sequestered glens, the village church and the church-yard, "where the rude forefathers of the hamlet sleep." Conversing with these we shall visit the hamlet, the house, and the home of our forefathers. We shall live over with them the life they lived in their rude simplicity. We shall sit by their frugal board, and talk of their tireless toil and self-denial; their firm and faithful training of ourselves, mixed " with admonition due," by which they led us up to a vigorous, virtuous manhood. In sad, yet pleasing illusion conversing thus with the old folks at home, we naturally fall back into days bygone and live over again our childhood and our youth.

> Dear lovely bow'rs of innocence and ease,
> Seats of my youth when ev'ry sport could please :
> How often have I loiter'd o'er th' green,
> Where humble happiness endear'd each scene !
> How often have I paused on ev'ry charm,
> The sheltered cot, the cultivated farm :
> The never-failing brook, the busy mill,
> The decent church that top't the neighb'ring hill.

At home thus in our native village, charmed with the endearing memories of the old folks themselves, we can best appreciate their varied virtues, and characteristics which we here commemorate.

The physical features of our ancestors and some genealogical statistics respecting them may claim a passing notice.

Nothing is known of the personal appearance of Richard our common ancestor, but the early generations of his descendants appear to have been a tall, stalwart race, well developed in large proportions, with strong, trusty hands capable of carving their way through life. The largest of the family on record brought down the scales far above 300lbs., requiring eight bearers to convey his body to the grave. The tallest of the family was *six feet* and *four inches* in height; many have been six feet and upwards. Some have been men of gigantic powers who might have stood against Ajax himself for agility and strength, and wrestled even with Hercules for his club.

> Their limbs were cast in manly mould,
> For hardy sports, or contest bold.

For longevity, the Lymans have not been particularly distinguished, though many have passed beyond four-score years, some of whom are present with us to-day. Of more than 7,000, not one has attained to 100 years. One, however, a lineal descendant from the family, has passed that extreme limit of human life. This venerable lady, Mrs. Robinson of Lebanon, Conn., died Sept. 1st, 1871, aged *one hundred and two years, one month, and twenty days*. Her mother was a Lyman, the youngest daughter of Lieut. Jonathan of Lebanon. This daughter, Ann, married a Tiffany of Norwich Landing, where Mrs. (Tiffany) Robinson was born July 11, 1769, the only survivor of the *sixth* generation. She remembered many events of the war of the Revolution, especially those which occurred in Lebanon. As the governor of the state then resided there, and was the only legal colonial governor; and as the council of safety of which the governor was chairman, which was to act when the legislature was not in session, sat there more than nine hundred days during these seven years of the war, Lebanon had some claim to be substantially the capital of the state, and was a centre of intelligence and of important events. She remembered the fact that the larger part of a legion of French cavalry was stationed there in 1780, and recalled the namesa nd appearance of the officers. Thus she connected us directly with that remote and now historical period, and enabled us vividly to conceive of its events.

Her funeral was very numerously attended at the brick church, Sunday morning; many being present from other parts of the town and from surrounding towns; a testimony to the interest with which she was regarded.

Of the Lymans proper the venerable mother of the speaker is foremost on the record for longevity. After a married life with her only husband of almost 66 years, and surviving him 10 years, she rested from her labors at the age of 95 wanting a few weeks, having been a housekeeper more than 70 years, and a communicant in the church nearly the same length of time.

The most prolific *branch* of the family is that of Richard, the oldest of the six grandsons of Richard.[1] He settled at Lebanon, Conn., and from that wonderful hive his descendants have swarmed out over all the land; *two thousand seven hundred and thirty-four* of this fraternity are recorded in this book, about twice the number of the posterity of any other grandson of Richard. The most prolific family in our connection is that of Dea. Stephen Lyman of Chester in this state, father of our venerable friend, here present, Dea. Samuel Lyman of Southampton, who himself has given the record of 337 of his father's descendants all having sprung into life from one within the range of 100 years. At the same rate of increase, what an army one hundred years hence from this one family! But the earliest generations, in all their hardships and poverty, have been the most prolific. The ratio of increase has steadily decreased as successive generations have increased in wealth and luxury. The largest issue from one marriage is fifteen. The total number of descendants of Richard the ancestor of all the Lyman Family cannot be estimated even by probable conjecture. The record of 7,000 has been collected. Many who have been addressed have neglected, and some have peremptorily refused to give any record of their families or those of their ancestors. The descendants of the daughters bearing other names cannot be estimated with any accuracy, but the sum total who, in 250 years, have sprung from the original immigrant, including the living and the dead, may be not far from 15,000 more or less.

Could that venerable patriarch, disheartened by all his losses and sufferings, wandering, " sick and melancholy," in the wilderness in search of a solitary home, who only by " God's mercy obtained some little reviving before he died" — could he have beheld in vision this great and glad assembly of his children, how would his sorrowing soul have expanded with wonder, gratitude and joy! Well that distant vision may be to him now a present, a blest reality. Perhaps from his orb on high he has, not only a full vision of this scene, rejoicing with us in gladness of the day, but beholding the great assembly of all his children who, both on earth and in heaven, but one communion make — strikes his harp to the loudest, sweetest notes of praise to God for all his goodness and grace to himself and his family.

The adventurous, enterprising spirit of the Lymans, should be noted as a prominent characteristic.

In every enterprise for the settlement of the country and development of its resources they have been pioneers. After the settlement of the other Hamptons, east, west and south, Durham, Goshen, Salisbury, and ·Lebanon, Conn., became early centres of emigration to the Green Mountains, in Massachusetts, and Vermont, to New Hampshire, and the Canadas. Age after age they have had a quick, attentive ear to the rallying cry, Westward, ho! and have been among the first to start in full pursuit of that ever receding, expanding, undiscovered country, THE FAR WEST. Within the memory even of some of us, the far west was just beyond Albany, the German Flats on the Mohawk, the Johnstown purchase, including Utica, and Oneida county. Within the lifetime of the speaker, the whole city of Utica was purchased for twelve cents an acre and regarded as a poor speculation at that. The original contractor, ridiculed by his neighbors for wasting his money on lands distant, inaccessible and useless as the mountains in the moon, gave up his bargain in despair. Next, the region of Black river became the far west, then the Genesee country and Holland purchase became the land of invitation, then New Connecticut in Ohio, and Pennsylvania, and finally the whole state of Ohio, then the great north-west territory and its subdivisions, Michigan, Illinois, Iowa, Minnesota, and the territories beyond. Into all these regions the Lymans have pressed foremost to possess the land, and in them all they or their descendants are still found. They have traversed the broad plains beyond the Mississippi, explored the remotest parks and recesses of the Rocky mountains, scaled their tremendous heights, and spread themselves out over the western slopes of the mountains to the Pacific coast where every river and stream rolls down its golden sands. Indeed it may be questioned whether there is a state or territory of the Union which has not been marked by the footprints of the Lymans, always excepting Alaska, that God-forsaken land, swathed in perpetual mist, drenched with rain, or encased in thick-ribbed ice and snow.

The hardships, self-denials and sufferings of their pioneer and frontier life is another characteristic of the family.

Cold New England winters passed in rude shanties with crevices open to the wintry winds wide enough for the hand to be thrust through the walls into the open air, the garments on going to rest laid by in a compact roll to protect them from the snow that filtered in by night, the bed in the morning covered with a counterpane of driven snow which melted as it fell upon the face of the sleepers without disturbing their slumbers; these are the familiar nursery tales of frontier life, often told in the ears of the speaker as the training in which his own infancy was nursed.

Long journeys of six weeks with an ox team, in a covered sled, the palace car by day and the sleeping car by night, running through a trackless wilderness only passable in winter when swamps and sloughs and streams are bridged over by the enginery of the severest cold; these were the luxuries of pioneer travel in the new settlements. One goes alone into the forest eighteen miles from the nearest neighbor, driving a young beef creature which is to give up its life for the support of the adventurous pioneer; the meat is salted in a trough cut out of a tree felled for the purpose; the hide, spread on the roof of his cabin, is soon stolen by the wolves; and the cabin itself, on returning from his day work, the solitary backwoodsman finds occupied by an Indian who instantly levels his rifle to his breast, but the savage is overpowered before he has time to fire, and, divested of his rifle, is sent peaceably away. Six months the brave pioneer labors alone in the solitude and perils of the wilderness, and thus begins the settlement of one of the rich, flourishing towns of Ohio.

Another goes two days' journey into the wilderness, returning from time to time for provisions which he bears on his shoulder, camping by night on the cold earth with the canopy of heaven for the curtains of his bed chamber. This veteran still lives, the patriarch of a numerous progeny and a flourishing settlement in Pennsylvania, delighting to tell the story of his frontier life, facetiously recognizing the kindness of the landlord who charged him nothing either for entertainment or lodgings. One dies of consumption contracted by similar exposures and hardships. Another kindles a fire at night by the side of a rock from which a mass, loosened by the heat, falls upon the sleeper whose slumbers will only be broken by the trump of God awaking the dead to life. Another goes with his ox team twenty-four miles into the forest, sleeps under his cart until he builds a log cabin and begins a flourishing settlement in Minnesota.

But time would fail to tell of the endless hardships, the heroic daring and dangers of pioneer life, the horrors of the war whoop, tomahawk and scalping knife; of the labors of the field prosecuted with rifle at hand; women and children hurrying, horror stricken, into stockades for protection; guns stacked in the church preliminary to the worship of God on the sabbath, and all the barbarities of savage warfare. More of this in the Genealogy.

Among the *mental* characteristics of the family may be enumerated a highly nervous, mercurial temperament.

This has often arisen to such intensity as to disturb the due balance of the mind, sinking sometimes to a morbid depression of spirits and again rising to an unnatural exhilaration, not unfrequently ending in insanity, sometimes in raving madness. So frequent and far-spread has been this mental bias in different branches of our brotherhood, that we must accept a tendency to insanity as a characteristic of the Lyman family. But this, be it remembered, is the infirmity of high intellectual powers: men of the finest intellect are oftenest insane. It requires a man of mind and spirit, of ardent impulsive temperament, and highly wrought mental powers to be the subject of insanity. Such a fever is never stirred in the veins of a man of sluggish, torpid mould, whose mind is dull as night and dark as Erebus; you can not, perhaps, expect much of such a man, but of one thing be assured, he will never go crazy.

But the temperament which we contemplate, in its normal action inspires great buoyancy of spirits, irrepressible elasticity under adversity, and dauntless energy and enterprise in the pursuits of life. In domestic and social life it manifests itself in habitual cheerfulness mingled with a quiet humor, facetiousness and pleasantry which relishes a jest, a joke, a ready retort and repartee, with a dash sometimes of eccentricity, for which the Lymans are somewhat famous.

The inventive faculty of the Lymans claims a passing notice.

We cannot, perhaps, ascribe to them the highest order of inventive genius, the profoundest insight into the laws of nature and the mechanical powers, which calls into play new combinations of machinery, or undeveloped natural laws that open unknown avenues of industry and undeveloped sources of national wealth, making the inventor the benefactor of the world. But we may ascribe to them many useful inventions and labor saving machines, from the wringer in the wash tub to the reaper in the field, the threshing machine, the steam engine and the telescope. Many of these inventions are of curious workmanship, requiring the most skillful manipulation and combination of mechanical powers. Not a few have been highly remunerative, and amply repaid the time and skill of the fortunate inventor. Others evince surprising ingenuity and skill. How wonderful the skill that can accurately record the weight of each car in the train of a lightning express as it sweeps by like some heavenly body wandering from its course in the heavens!

Next in the enumeration may be specified great fixedness of character and firmness of principle as a characteristic trait of the Lymans.

Slow they may be in coming to a conclusion, tenacious of their established modes of thought and " very much set in their way." How often has this very expression been given as the characteristic of some patriarch of our family. Sometimes this fixedness may become a dogged obstinacy, and ripen into a character thoroughly untractable and detestable, — none more detestable than a willful man perversely conscientious in a bad cause. Reason with him and he only becomes more unreasonable. Ply him with arguments, press upon him your views of duty and you only confirm him in his own. You can do nothing with him, but let him alone; handle him as you would a porcupine, leave off before you begin. You may perhaps find in the family some of this character, but even this is an infirmity that leans to virtue's side. Rightly directed, such decision of character is the noblest characteristic of a great and good man.

Enter into the history of the patriarchal representatives of the family and you will find that in the political, religious and sensational tumults of church and society, they have stood firm as the rock on the beach upon which the billows harmlessly beat and break. Amid all the commotions of society such an one stands fixed and immovable as yonder holyoke resting in settled tranquillity on its own immovable base.

Our family are worthy of an honorable memorial, for their patriotic public spirit.

In the early, forming periods of our new settlements, many an one has been the pillar of the church and society, the life and soul of the settlement, foremost in organizing the government of the town or county, establishing the regular administration of justice, and the ordinances of religion; foremost in opening roads, and lines of public travel; in erecting the school house, the church, the court house, the academy, the college. They have been strict observers of the sabbath, steady attendants upon public worship, and liberal supporters of every patriotic enterprise, the friend of the friendless, the father of the fatherless, the counselor of the poor, the stay and support of the community.

The family have an honorable military and patriotic record.

In every war of our country, they have bravely borne their part. In the Indian and French wars, in the war of the Revolution, of 1812, and the Rebellion, they have left the field, the shop, the counting room, the bar, the pulpit, at their country's call to the battle field in her defense. ever ready to rally round her flag, whether in the heat of battle or in the forlorn hope storming the stronghold of the foe. From the town of Lebanon, Conn., containing only about 2,000 inhabitants, more than 500 were, at one time, in the ranks of the Revolutionary army.

Lieut. John commanded the first expedition against the Indians from Northampton, in the famous Falls fight, above Deerfield. Gen. Phineas Lyman of Durham, Conn., was for a time commander in chief of the American forces. By his generalship and bravery at the battle of Lake George, though holding a subordinate office, he gained a decisive victory over the French forces, taking their commander, Baron Dieskau, a prisoner of war. He possessed military talents of the highest order, second only to our own great Washington.

Gen. Daniel Lyman, colonel in the continental army, lawyer, judge, and chief justice, assisted at the capture of Ticonderoga, Crown point and St. John's and was president of the Society of Cincinnati. Col. Moses Lyman of Goshen, Conn., was detailed to watch the movements of Burgoyne on the night before the battle, and was the first to report his change of position which opened the way for the battle and the surrender of Burgoyne. For these important services Col. Lyman was commissioned as a special messenger to bear to Gen. Washington the tidings of the victory. He was also commander of the guard over Major Andrè; and on the night previous to his execution, Benjamin Lyman of Easthampton, Mass., stood guard over that gallant, distinguished and unfortunate captive. Another was an aid to Gen. Putnam in the battle of Bunker bill; so efficient and daring that Putnam said, that with a thousand of such men he would drive every red coat out of the land. Major Lyman of Vergennes, Vt., at the battle of Plattsburgh bravely fought with heroic endurance at the risk of his life. Every grade of office in military life, from corporal to commander-in-chief, has at some time been occupied by one or more of the Lyman family.

Great numbers crowded the ranks of the noble army of volunteers for the suppresion of the late rebellion. Four brothers from one family, all married men, with young wives and children dependent on them for their daily bread, went into the fight, braved every hardship, every danger of long campaigns and bloody battle-fields, and all returned unharmed to the embrace of their families. Nine from East Hampton, Mass., enlisted in their country's service and four of them, on rebel soil, gave up their lives in her defense.

Not a few in this assembly gave their gallant sons at their country's call. The first-born of our honored chairman, a youth of lofty talents, rarest culture and highest promise passed bravely through twenty-five battles, arose high in rank and then, laden with honors, gave up his young life on the field of battle in defense of the flag and freedom of his country.

The ladies were, if possible, more daring, more devoted than the men. One rode alone twelve miles on horseback in a dark rainy night through a rebel country, past the enemy's lines to convey important intelligence to the loyal army. Another saved the life of her loyal father by throwing her sacred person between him and the weapon of the rebel assassin aimed at his breast in her own parlor.

Nor must we forget the little drummer boy who at the age of thirteen, before he was able himself to bear arms, joined the army that, by the tap of his drum, he might summon others of stronger arm and firmer foot to the deadly combat. The brave boy quailed not at the shock of contending ranks, but everywhere when needful was heard, rising above the din of battle, his rat-tat-too rallying the lines to march on to their " gory bed, or to victory." All honor to the noble mother who gave the child to her country at this tender age. All honor to the brave boy who firmly stood where the bravest might well have quailed.

But the crowning excellence of this family is and ever has been their purity of morals and high Christian character.

In these virtues all and each of the six branches of the family have been distinguished. No exemption is claimed for them from the depravity and sin which infest the race. Instances of irreligion and impiety and immorality there may have been. But of the thousands whose record has been collected, none has been convicted of high crimes and misdemeanors; none has suffered the extreme penalties of the law; not one is known to have been a defiant, scoffing unbeliever; one only, so far as the record goes, has filled a drunkard's grave. Other inebriates there may have been ; we have not been careful to search into the secret history of individuals or of families, nor would we if we could expose each less pleasing feature of their characters. If any have done evil let it not live after them in the memory of surviving friends, nor be chronicled in history. But we may speak of the *virtues* of our forefathers, their high conscientiousness, their firmness of principle, their devout and humble piety, and their steadfast adherence to the faith of their fathers. None better understood the chief end of man. They learned it early in the catechetical instructions of the patriarchal fireside when Sunday schools were unknown. None have more faithfully sought or more fervently prayed for grace so to live as to " glorify God and enjoy Him forever." Few, very few, have ever swerved from the faith of their fathers to other Christian denominations ; fewer still have denied that faith, or received another gospel which yet is no gospel. One is a Roman Catholic priest, one has been a Mormon, one of the twelve apostles of that sect whom he has now abandoned, and a few of his connections are still enrolled among the Latter Day Saints of Salt Lake City.

But whole households, generation after generation, have without an exception professed the faith, the hopes, the personal piety of their ancestors. Many families, already passed beyond the flood, are safely gathered there we doubt not, an unbroken household in heaven. And many a lingering remnant of death-divided families awaits .only the summons to go and complete again the circle of his own family in that far off sinless land to which they have been received before him.

But this visit with the old folks at home will be incomplete and unsatisfactory unless we go " to meeting" with them on Sunday. The good man goes on horseback, with his good wife on pillion behind him, a child, or grand-child in one arm while the other holds her securely in her seat behind her husband. The boys and girls are trudging silently along barefoot with shoes and stockings in hand to keep them neat and clean and free from useless wear until the old square meeting house, with horse block hard by coming into view, stiff, stately and cold on the green, becomes the signal for completing with stockings and shoes their Sunday suits. Within the church there are the old square pews compactly arranged like cattle pens at a fair, with high backs, and seats hung on hinges for the people conveniently to lean on the railing during the prayer of half an hour or an hour's length ; then at the conclusion the startling rattle of seats falling down awakes the profoundest slumbers into which any in the prayer have fallen, bending over the railings of the pews. These pews have been duly " dignified " by a committee appointed for the purpose, and the families carefully assorted and seated according to their " ages, state and parentage." The young folks according to their sex are assigned to the opposite galleries, and the old bachelors and unmarried maidens, — well they are seated under the stairs leading to the galleries, or, as a kind of small change, they fill every vacant gap about the house. There is the old pulpit and the winding staircase leading up to its towering height. The deacons are in their seats below and the man of God, perched high above, with the huge sounding board overhead to reflect the preacher's voice, as he, for an hour or more, through fifteen or twenty heads and as many inferences, screams out to his hearers down below, many of whom, in spite of their " smelling bottles," dill and caraway seeds have fallen fast asleep, under the dead monotony of his dull discourse.

The service ended, a short intermission follows, spent in *the sabbath houses* built for this purpose on the common. Here the family take their Sunday dinner, which has been carefully brought in one side of the saddlebags, balanced on the other by milk in a wooden bottle ; the remainder of the intermission is occupied with the discussion of the sermon and the reading aloud of some of the children until the services of the afternoon begin.

But we are admonished that the hour has come when we must break this charming illusion in which, communing with former generations, we have again lived over our childhood and renewed departed joys — departed never to return. Farewell, departed scenes ! Native village and sacred homes, farewell ! Venerable ancestors ! Kindred dear passed unto the skies, farewell! a long farewell !

Swiftly, oh, how swiftly, the generations of men are swept away on the ceaseless tide of time. They rise, like the waves of the ocean, roll awhile on its tumultuous waters, alternately gilded by the sunbeam and darkened by the storm, then sink and mingle with their original element undistinguished, unheeded. Time, in its ceaseless course, has swept away seven generations of our family, and we of the eighth, standing now on the verge of dark eternity, shall sink soon in the devouring depths of that dread ocean that lies outspread before us. As a collective assembly we shall never meet again. Other generations may gather here as we do now when we are gathered with the dead. But though a man die, yet shall he live again. And you, ye sons of sainted sires in heaven, here on this goodly mountain, now in glad communion met for *one brief day* — may you all — without exception — all — meet again on Mount Zion above, in a reunion infinitely more perfect, more joyous, to be prolonged and yet prolonged through blest eternity's long day.

Closing Address by the Chairman.

The hour of eleven having arrived, on the morning of the second day, the moderator, the Hon. Lyman Tremain, arose and addressed the meeting as follows :

My friends, I am admonished by the hand on yonder clock, that the hour has arrived when I am obliged to separate from you, and take the cars for my home. But before I leave you, I desire to express my acknowledgments and thanks to those thoughtful members of the family by whom the idea of calling this meeting of the Lyman family was conceived and has been carried into execution.

It was a happy thought, and notwithstanding the inauspicious weather which we had yesterday in the grove, I am sure that in the future, we shall forget that, and that the occasion will be remembered with gratitude and satisfaction by all who have had the good fortune to participate in its pleasures and privileges.

We have, some of us, been enabled, for the first time, to visit the beautiful locality where we assembled yesterday, to behold the delightful scenery in the valley of the Connecticut, which surrounds it, to renew old acquaintances, and to form new ones with those who are related to us by the ties of a common kindred ; we have, also, learned from the Rev. Dr. Coleman's excellent address, many interesting and valuable facts, concerning the characteristics and history of the family, of which we might, otherwise, have remained uninformed. I speak, I am sure, the sentiments of all present when I add that we never can be too grateful to the Doctor, for his willingness to continue the work of publishing the book containing the history of the family, notwithstanding the great affliction under which he is suffering, from the recent death of his wife and child, in which he has our most profound sympathy.

And now the time has come, when we are called upon to separate and return to our respective homes. perhaps, many of us, never more to meet again, on earth. But we shall carry away with us, renewed regard for our New England homes, for our New England ancestry, and for those great truths which had their American origin, in this section of our country.

In many respects, this family gathering and others of a similar character, serve to symbolize or typify the nation to which we belong, which is only an aggregation of numerous families. Many, and perhaps most of those who have gathered here, to-day, had their birth place, and have their present residence, outside of the boundaries of New England. Their social associations, their pecuniary interests, their local attachments, and all those natural and honorable feelings of state pride which are connected with the land of our birth place, unite us with other and perhaps distant states. Indeed, our union with New England, rests mainly upon that sentiment, wholly incapable of definition or analysis, which draws us with its silken and mysterious, but powerful bonds, to the home of our ancestors. And yet, I know that no unjust censures could be uttered in our presence against New England, nor any blow be aimed at her welfare, prosperity and happiness, that would not occasion emotions of grief, and be regarded by us all almost as a personal injury. (Much applause). And in such sentiments, everywhere prevailing, throughout our country, lies, I think, one of the secret sources of our national union, and its strength, cohesion and perpetuity.

We all remember, that at the commencement of our late civil war, there were those, among us, who claimed that it was the restless, meddling spirit of interference, in the affairs of others, which characterized the New Englander, that had caused the war, and the sovereign remedy recommended by these wise-acres for existing evils, was the formation of a new union with " New England left out in the cold." These shallow and superficial quacks were mainly those who sympathized with the rebellion. They wholly failed to comprehend the true nature, or the gigantic magnitude of the great contest, and it was not long, before the prompt, the patriotic, and the noble efforts made by New England to preserve our common country, silenced these senseless clamors.

It has been related of a prominent Ohio politician, who had, thoughtlessly, repeated the outcry against New England, that when he came to look around him, and consider the elements of which the community was composed, and when he came to take out from among the people those who were born in New England, or were the descendants of New Englanders, those who had married New England wives, or the children of New England parents, and, also, those who had been instructed by New England school masters, or school mistresses, he found that those who were left would not amount to much, and so he concluded to say no more about " leaving New England out in the cold." (Laughter and applause).

Indeed should that day ever come when a new union should be formed that did not embrace the territory of New England, the object sought to be accomplished, by her foes, would be only partially effected. It would still be necessary to annihilate those great political doctrines of liberty and equality which have been disseminated, throughout the length and breadth of the land, by the influence, the teachings, and the example of New England. You must then change the entire structure of your government, and undermine the great bulwarks of popular rights, which lie at the very foundation of our republican institutions.

When you shall have succeeded in destroying the system of local self-government by town meetings, which is the child of New

England; when you shall have destroyed free schools, free churches, freedom of speech, and a free press; when you have subverted that inherent love of fair play, and of political and religious liberty that constitute the essential elements in the character of our people, then and not till then, will New England be really left out in the cold.

These great changes once wrought, and our boasted free institution would be like the play of Hamlet, with Hamlet's part omitted : the shell without the oyster, the body, without the soul.

True you might, then, have peace and order, but it would be the peace of the grave, the order that prevailed at Warsaw. Indifference on the part of the people as to public and political affairs, would take the place of that eternal vigilance which, we are taught, is the price of liberty.

True, we might, under the new order of things, allow the few to govern the many, and thus be relieved from a world of responsibility and care. We might sleep on, while corruption was destroying the very vitals of the nation. We might hear the pleasant signals of our sentinels declaring that all is well, at the moment when scheming and ambitious men were plotting the destruction of our liberties, or corruption, ignorance and vice had already fired the train which they had prepared, while the flames were ready to burst forth and destroy the government of our fathers.

True, we might, no longer, be disturbed by the strong and stimulating breezes that sometimes blow over the country, from the hills and mountains of New England, but these, I think, are far better than the nauseous odors that indicate incipient decay, and approaching dissolution.

For myself, I would not substitute that robust, and, if you please, rough spirit of New England equality, that declares one man to be as good as another, for the rule of the best king or queen that ever sat upon a throne. Give me that searching and restless spirit of investigation which is the attribute of an enlightened popular liberty, although it transgresses, at times, the ordinary rules of courtesy, rather than the popular indifference, bigotry, superstition and intolerance which, for so many years, have impeded the progress of human rights and Christian civilization.

The day has gone by, I trust forever, when we shall again hear the shameful proposal mooted to leave any part of our beloved country out in the cold. The union and every part of it has been cemented by the best blood of the American people.

Let us, then, not be ashamed of our New England origin or our New England ancestors. The soil that we find throughout that little cluster of commonwealths, which we call New England, may not be as rich as the prairie lands of the great northwest, or the fertile valley of the Mississippi, but it was in that soil that the seeds of liberty were planted on this continent, and there the roots have penetrated deep into the earth. Nor need we be disturbed by the ridicule which is sometimes uttered against the puritans of New England.

What if they do say, that those old fellows were accustomed to whip their beer barrels because the beer would work on Sundays. Better do that we answer, than to spend Sunday in guzzling down villainous bad whisky that will " kill at forty rods," that leads to rioting and drunkenness, and causes broken bones, bruised heads and bloody noses. (Laughter and applause).

Permit me, in conclusion, to say that the best advice I can give to the youth of the Lyman family is, that they may display, in their future career, those same sterling qualities of courage, patience, endurance and heroic devotion to the principles of civil and religious freedom, which were so honorably exemplified by their ancestors, in the early history of New England.

INDEX.

Betsey E.,
  m. Smith, 70
  m. Trumbull, 71
Betsey K., 145
Betsey W.,
  m. Stewart, 256
Beulah, 51
  Janes, 220
Birney G., 165
Blanche I., 167
Bloomfield M., 284
  Lynn, Pa., 305
Braza, 84
Brenton M., 73
Brewster O., 96
Burrill, 147
  Lymansville, 149
Burke, 62
  Buffalo, N. Y., 61
Burke W., 62
Burnham, 324, 332
  Ohio, 332
Burton, 65
Byron A., 296

Calah,
  Northampton, Mass.,
  50
Caleb, 142, 199, 202, 208,
  244, 246, 360, 369,
  441, 447, 448
  Boston, Mass., 391
  Hadley, Mass., 246
  Lorraine, N. Y., 256
  N. Y., 142
  Weston, Mass., 40, 42
Caleb, Dea., 40
Caleb, Jr., 244
Caleb N., 257
Caleb S., 256, 257, 329
  Adams, N. Y., 257
Calista M., 115
Calvin, 157, 230, 239
  Michigan, 154
  Rockport, N. Y., 378,
  379
  Westfield, N. Y., 162
  West Turin, 76
  Winchester, N. H., 238
Calvin W., 279
Cara, 109
Cardelia,
  Curtiss, 68
Carleton, M.D., 62
Caroline, 142, 288, 306,
  380, 401
  m. Bidwell, 61
  m. Brackett, 59, 60
Caroline A., 185
  m. Reynolds, 185

Caroline B., 176, 185
Caroline C., 380
Caroline D., 65
Caroline E., 145
Caroline L., 289
  m. Breed, 187
Caroline M., 185
Carrie, 84, 410, 426
Carrie E., 95
Carrie F., 347
Carrie L., 257
Cassandana, 329
Cassius S., 338
Catharine, 52, 56, 126,
  199, 202, 387
  m. Benton, 204
  m. Brown, 279
  m. Cook, 226
Catharine A., 236
Catharine B., 300
Catharine D., 446
Catharine E., 302, 325,
  432
  m. Bates, 326
Catharine F., 407
  m. Hunter, 448
Catharine J.,
  m. Boughton, 398
Catharine M., 182
Catharine R., 392, 393
  m. Delano, 394, 395
Catharine S., 447
Cecilia, 288
  m. Williston, 265
Celeste, 84
Celestia E, 149
Celia A., 358
Celia E., 298
Ceylon E., 343, 349
Chancey, 85
Charity, 228
  m. Griffin, 332
Charles, 65, 130, 136,
  144, 146, 147, 152,
  153, 157, 193, 261,
  272, 285, 287, 354,
  355, 363, 367, 370,
  374, 379, 380, 389,
  399, 403, 420, 441,
  444, 447, 454
  Boston, Ms., 362, 367
  Northampton, Mass.,
  277
  Petaluma, Cal., 226
  Royal Oak, Mich., 77
  Troy, N. Y., 397
  Washington, D C., 287
Charles A., 59, 65, 79,
  82, 117, 135, 145,
  233, 296, 389

Charles B., 67, 337, 426
  Southampton, Mass.,
  338
Charles C., 213, 329, 331
Charles D., 138, 297
Charles, Dea., 189
Charles E., 99, 117, 215,
  290, 298
  Iowa, 152
Charles F., 139, 193, 294,
  305, 367, 380
  Granby, Mass., 239
Charles G., 101
  Brimfield, Mass., 59,
  60
Charles H., 65, 81, 138,
  183, 209, 269, 282,
  289, 295, 306, 370,
  434
  Holyoke, Mass., 421
  Jericho, Vt., 373, 374
  Minnesota, 306
Charles H. P.,
  Chicago, Ill., 289
Charles K., 107
Charles L., 230, 380
Charles M.,
  Rutland, Vt., 161
Charles M. W., 293
Charles N., 97
Charles P., 67, 141, 185,
  302, 309, 338, 358,
  399, 449
  Jacksonville, Ill., 185
Charles R., 97, 211, 213,
  219, 235, 318
  Albany, N. Y., 218
  Elmira, N. Y., 219
Charles S., 156, 283, 369
Charles T., 98
Charles W., 68, 134, 185,
  235, 293, 347, 399
  Chicago, Ill., 334
  Northfield, Minn., 68
  Shelby, O., 287
Charlie, 237, 332, 339
Charlina, 81
Charlotte, 52, 54, 81
  m. Burt, 148
Charlotte A.,
  m. Carpenter, 272
  m. Clark, 251
  m. Delano, 400
  m. Keith, 374
  m. Silobee, 393
  m. Wells, 147
Charlotte A., 85, 139,
  446
Charlotte M., 79
Charlotte S., 81

Newman R., 275
  Chester, O., 298
Nicy,
  m. Wood, 460
Noah, 48, 198, 200, 201,
  204, 210, 308, 322,
  324, 328, 331, 352,
  354
  Columbia, N. H., 328
  Jericho, Vt., 368
  Northampton, Mass.,
  48, 50, 51, 55
Noah, Jr., 200, 369
Noah R., 206
Noble, 305
Norman, 129
  Bolton, Conn., 189
  Warren, Ct., 139
Norman S.. 141
Normand, 260, 284, 306
  Hartford, Conn., 284
Normand, Jr.,
  Hartford, Conn., 305

Olive, 329, 418
  m. Germain, 143
  m. Paine, 362
  m. Plummer, 361
Olive L., 419
Olive P., 95
Oliver, 200, 206, 245,
  269, 292
  Charlotte, Vt., 251
  Genoa, O., 291
  New Jersey, 251
  Northampton, Ms., 52
Oliver, Capt., 392
Oliver E., 103, 112
Oliver G., 270
Oliver W., 79
  Newark, N. Y., 79
Olivia, 363, 374
  m. Tremain, 368, 375
  m. Burt, 373, 374
Ora H., 119
Ora S., 208
Orange, 143
  Norwich, Vt., 144
Orange, Rev., 129, 136
Oren,
  Morristown, Vt., 461
Orin, 162
Orison, 123
Orlando, 419
Orpha, 100
Orpha J., 99
Orra Almira,
  m. Bolles, 261
Orren, 99
Orrie, 236

Orril H.,
  m. Willis, 145
Orrilla,
  m. Burt, 149
Orville B., 106
  Hartford, Ct., 107
Orville P., 84
Oscar, 84
Oscar C., 122
Oscar S., 300
Oshea G., 256
  Raymond, Minn., 257
Osman A., 275
Othella, 157
Otis,
  Springfield, Mich.,
  147
  Lenawee Co., Mich.,
  152
Otis J. P., 148
Otis W., 332
Otto B., 119
Ozias, 77
  Coventry, Ct., 58
  Dover, Vt., 58

Pamelia, 91
  m. Wood, 142
Parnee, 162
  m. Huson, 163
Parthenia,
  m. Lamfear, 162
Pattie F., 332
Patty, 260
Payson, Rev. Williston,
  429, 430
Penuniah,
  m. Elwell, 278
Penelope,
  m. Mattoon, 222
Percy, 306
Peres C.,
  Eugene, Kansas, 302
Perez C., 280
Persis, 52, 58, 246
Persis,
  m. Smead, 222
Persis W., 221
Peter,
  Northampton, Mass.,
  50
Peter S.,
  Buffalo, N. Y., 61, 62
Phebe, 51, 52, 54, 246,
  387
  m. Benjamin, 460
  m. Clark, 256
  m. Ellsworth, 310
  m. Garrison, 283
  m. Strong, 308, 359

Phebe D.,
  m. Tileston, 330
Philander P., 292
Philip, 81
  Chicago, Ill., 292
Phillis, 32, 33, 36, 37
  m. Hills, 36, 37
Philo C. W., 375
Philomela T.,
  m. Fisher, 278
Philomelia, 122
  m. Martin, 124
Philomelia E., 122
Philota,
  m. Bliss, 83
Phineas, 51, 58, 199,
  201, 203, 204, 205,
  210, 212, 225, 243,
  244, 247
  Menominee, Wis., 237
  Northampton, Ms., 247
  Winchester, N. H., 229
Phineas, Gen., 198, 200,
  204
Phineas H., 237
Phinehas, 48, 201
  Northampton, Ms., 48
Pliny, 303
Pliny O., 279
Pliny S., 279
P. Maranda,
  m. Eaton, 281
Polly, 88, 184, 200, 204,
  225
  m. Bennet, 255
  m. Bliss, 230
  m. Dunwell, 208
  m. Hoyl, 154
  m. Robinson, 210
  m. Smith, 144
Polly A.,
  m. Taggart, 148
Porter G., 136
Portus, 142
Prentis, 259
  Meshoppen, Pa., 284
Prentis H., 303
Preserved, 50
  m. Ellison, 44
Princess,
  m. Root, 225
Prudence, 151, 291
  m. Boyington, 149
  m. McCrea, 70
Prudentia A., 329

Quartus, 223
Quartus P., 423
  Easthampton, Mass.,
  425

INDEX OF ALL OTHERS THAN LYMAN.

Made in the USA
Middletown, DE
18 June 2023

32803747R00305